T0214802

Lecture Notes in Computer Science   12466

More information about this subseries at http://www.springer.com/series/7409

Tran Khanh Dang · Josef Küng ·
Makoto Takizawa · Tai M. Chung (Eds.)

Future Data and Security Engineering

7th International Conference, FDSE 2020
Quy Nhon, Vietnam, November 25–27, 2020
Proceedings

Editors
Tran Khanh Dang (iD)
Ho Chi Minh City University of Technology
Ho Chi Minh City, Vietnam

Josef Küng
Johannes Kepler University of Linz
Linz, Austria

Makoto Takizawa
Hosei University
Tokyo, Japan

Tai M. Chung
Sungkyunkwan University
Suwon, Korea (Republic of)

ISSN 0302-9743   ISSN 1611-3349   (electronic)
Lecture Notes in Computer Science
ISBN 978-3-030-63923-5   ISBN 978-3-030-63924-2   (eBook)
https://doi.org/10.1007/978-3-030-63924-2

LNCS Sublibrary: SL3 – Information Systems and Applications, incl. Internet/Web, and HCI

This Springer imprint is published by the registered company Springer Nature Switzerland AG
The registered company address is: Gewerbestrasse 11, 6330 Cham, Switzerland

Preface

In LNCS 12466 and CCIS 1306 volumes we present the accepted contributions for the 7th International Conference on Future Data and Security Engineering (FDSE 2020). The conference took place during November 25–27, 2020, in an entirely virtual mode (Quy Nhon University, Binh Dinh Province, Vietnam). The proceedings of FDSE are published in the LNCS series by Springer. Besides DBLP and other major indexing systems, the FDSE proceedings have also been indexed by Scopus and listed in Conference Proceeding Citation Index (CPCI) of Thomson Reuters.

The annual FDSE conference is a premier forum designed for researchers, scientists, and practitioners interested in state-of-the-art and state-of-the-practice activities in data, information, knowledge, and security engineering to explore cutting-edge ideas, to present and exchange their research results and advanced data-intensive applications, as well as to discuss emerging issues on data, information, knowledge, and security engineering. At the annual FDSE, the researchers and practitioners are not only able to share research solutions to problems of today's data and security engineering themes, but are also able to identify new issues and directions for future related research and development work.

The two-round call for papers resulted in the submission of 161 papers. A rigorous peer-review process was applied to all of them. This resulted in 24 accepted papers (acceptance rate: 14.9%) and 2 keynote speeches for LNCS 12466, and 37 accepted papers (including 8 short papers, acceptance rate: 23%) for CCIS 1306, which were presented online at the conference. Every paper was reviewed by at least three members of the International Program Committee, who were carefully chosen based on their knowledge and competence. This careful process resulted in the high quality of the contributions published in these two volumes. The accepted papers were grouped into the following sessions:

- Advances in Big Data Query Processing and Optimization (LNCS)
- Advanced Studies in Machine Learning for Security (LNCS)
- Big Data Analytics and Distributed Systems (LNCS and CCIS)
- Blockchain and Applications (LNCS)
- Security Issues in Big Data (LNCS)
- Data Analytics and Healthcare Systems (CCIS)
- Machine Learning based Big Data Processing (CCIS)
- Security and Privacy Engineering (CCIS)
- Industry 4.0 and Smart City: Data Analytics and Security (LNCS and CCIS)
- Emerging Data Management Systems and Applications (LNCS and CCIS)

In addition to the papers selected by the Program Committee, five internationally recognized scholars delivered keynote speeches:

- Prof. Johann Eder, Alpen-Adria-Universität Klagenfurt, Austria
- Prof. Dirk Draheim, Tallinn University of Technology, Estonia

- Prof. Tai M. Chung, Sungkyunkwan University, South Korea
- Prof. Sun Jun, Singapore Management University, Singapore
- Prof. Jian Yang, Macquarie University, Australia

The success of FDSE 2020 was the result of the efforts of many people, to whom we would like to express our gratitude. First, we would like to thank all authors who submitted papers to FDSE 2020, especially the invited speakers for the keynotes. We would also like to thank the members of the committees and external reviewers for their timely reviewing and lively participation in the subsequent discussion in order to select such high-quality papers published in these two volumes. Last but not least, we thank Prof. Do Ngoc My and the Organizing Committee members from Quy Nhon University, for their great hospitality and support of FDSE 2020.

November 2020

Tran Khanh Dang
Josef Küng
Makoto Takizawa
Tai M. Chung

Organization

Honorary Chair

Do Ngoc My   Quy Nhon University, Vietnam

Program Committee Chairs

Tran Khanh Dang	Ho Chi Minh City University of Technology, Vietnam
Josef Küng	Johannes Kepler University Linz, Austria
Makoto Takizawa	Hosei University, Japan
Tai M. Chung	Sungkyunkwan University, South Korea

Steering Committee

Dirk Draheim	Tallinn University of Technology, Estonia
Dinh Nho Hao	Institute of Mathematics, Vietnam Academy of Science and Technology, Vietnam
Dieter Kranzlmüller	Ludwig Maximilian University of Munich, Germany
Fabio Massacci	University of Trento, Italy
Erich Neuhold	University of Vienna, Austria
Silvio Ranise	Fondazione Bruno Kessler, Italy
A Min Tjoa	Technical University of Vienna, Austria
Fukuda Kensuke	National Institute of Informatics, Japan

Local Organizing Committee

Do Ngoc My (Co-chair)	Quy Nhon University, Vietnam
Tran Khanh Dang (Chair)	Ho Chi Minh City University of Technology, Vietnam
La Hue Anh	Ho Chi Minh City University of Technology, Vietnam
Josef Küng	Johannes Kepler University Linz, Austria
Nguyen Tien Trung	Quy Nhon University, Vietnam
Tran Tri Dang	RMIT University, Vietnam
Nguyen Le Hoang	Ho Chi Minh City University of Technology, Vietnam
Ta Manh Huy	Ho Chi Minh City University of Technology, Vietnam

Publicity Chairs

Tran Minh Quang	Ho Chi Minh City University of Technology, Vietnam
Nguyen Quoc Viet Hung	Griffith University, Australia
Le Hong Trang	Ho Chi Minh City University of Technology, Vietnam
Nam Ngo-Chan	University of Trento, Italy

Program Committee

Artur Andrzejak	Heidelberg University, Germany
Pham The Bao	Saigon University, Vietnam
Hyunseung Choo	Sungkyunkwan University, South Korea
H. K. Dai	Oklahoma State University, USA
Vitalian Danciu	Ludwig Maximilian University of Munich, Germany
Nguyen Tuan Dang	Saigon University, Vietnam
Tran Tri Dang	RMIT University, Vietnam
Thanh-Nghi Do	Can Tho University, Vietnam
Nguyen Van Doan	Japan Advanced Institute of Science and Technology, Japan
Johann Eder	Alpen-Adria-Universität Klagenfurt, Austria
Jungho Eom	Daejeon University, South Korea
Michael Felderer	University of Innsbruck, Austria
Fukuda Kensuke	National Institute of Informatics, Japan
Alban Gabillon	University of French Polynesia, France
Verena Geist	Software Competence Center Hagenberg, Austria
Osvaldo Gervasi	University of Perugia, Italy
Manuel Clavel	Viatnamese-German University, Vietnam
Raju Halder	Indian Institute of Technology Patna, India
Nguyen Huu Hoa	Can Tho University, Vietnam
Tran Van Hoai	Ho Chi Minh City University of Technology, Vietnam
Phan Duy Hung	FPT University Hanoi, Vietnam
Nguyen Viet Hung	University of Trento, Italy
Trung-Hieu Huynh	Industrial University of Ho Chi Minh City, Vietnam
Kien Huynh	Stony Brook University, USA
Kha-Tu Huynh	International University - VNU-HCM, Vietnam
Tomohiko Igasaki	Kumamoto University, Japan
Koichiro Ishibashi	The University of Electro-Communications, Japan
Eiji Kamioka	Shibaura Institute of Technology, Japan
M. Tahar Kechadi	University College Dublin, Ireland
Andrea Ko	Corvinus University of Budapest, Hungary
Duc-Anh Le	Center for Open Data in the Humanities, Tokyo, Japan
Lam-Son Le	Ho Chi Minh City University of Technology, Vietnam
Nhien-An Le-Khac	University College Dublin, Ireland
Truong Thi Dieu Linh	Hanoi University of Science and Technology, Vietnam
Cao Van Loi	Le Quy Don Technical University, Vietnam
Hoang Duc Minh	National Physical Laboratory, UK
Nguyen Thai-Nghe	Can Tho University, Vietnam
Nam Ngo-Chan	University of Trento, Italy
Thanh Binh Nguyen	Ho Chi Minh City University of Technology, Vietnam
Binh Thanh Nguyen	International Institute for Applied Systems Analysis, Austria
Anh-Tuan Nguyen	Ho Chi Minh City University of Foreign Languages and Information Technology, Vietnam

Benjamin Nguyen	Institut National des Sciences Appliqués Centre Val de Loire, France
An Khuong Nguyen	Ho Chi Minh City University of Technology, Vietnam
Khoa Nguyen	CSIRO, Australia
Vu Thanh Nguyen	Van Hien University, Vietnam
Truong Toan Nguyen	Curtin University, Australia
Luong The Nhan	Amadeus IT Group, France
Alex Norta	Tallinn University of Technology, Estonia
Duu-Sheng Ong	Multimedia University, Malaysia
Eric Pardede	La Trobe University, Australia
Cong Duc Pham	University of Pau, France
Vinh Pham	Sungkyunkwan University, South Korea
Nhat Hai Phan	New Jersey Institute of Technology, USA
Thanh An Phan	Institute of Mathematics, Vietnam Academy of Science and Technology, Vietnam
Phu H. Phung	University of Dayton, USA
Nguyen Van Sinh	International University - VNU-HCM, Vietnam
Erik Sonnleitner	Johannes Kepler University Linz, Austria
Huynh Quyet Thang	Hanoi University of Science and Technology, Vietnam
Nguyen Hoang Thuan	RMIT University, Vietnam
Michel Toulouse	Hanoi University of Science and Technology, Vietnam
Thien Khai Tran	Ho Chi Minh City University of Foreign Languages and Information Technology, Vietnam
Ha-Manh Tran	Hong Bang International University, Vietnam
Le Hong Trang	Ho Chi Minh City University of Technology, Vietnam
Tran Minh Triet	HCMC University of Natural Sciences, Vietnam
Takeshi Tsuchiya	Tokyo University of Science, Japan
Le Pham Tuyen	Kyunghee University, South Korea
Hoang Huu Viet	Vinh University, Vietnam
Edgar Weippl	SBA Research, Austria
Wolfram Woess	Johannes Kepler University Linz, Austria
Honguk Woo	Sungkyunkwan University, South Korea
Sadok Ben Yahia	Tallinn University of Technology, Estonia
Szabó Zoltán	Corvinus University of Budapest, Hungary

Additional Reviewers

Thu Le Thi Bao	National Institute of Informatics, Japan
Tran Manh Hung	Sungkyunkwan University, South Korea
Le Thi Kim Tuyen	Heidelberg University, Germany
Trung Ha	University of Information Technology, Vietnam
Dan Ho Duc	Ho Chi Minh City University of Technology, Vietnam
Hieu Le	Ho Chi Minh City University of Technology, Vietnam
Pham Nguyen Hoang Nam	Industrial University of Ho Chi Minh City, Vietnam
Manh-Tuan Nguyen	COFICO Company, Vietnam
Trung-Viet Nguyen	Can Tho University of Technology, Vietnam

Thai-Minh Truong	Ho Chi Minh City University of Technology, Vietnam
Chau D. M. Pham	Zalo, Vietnam
Tan Ha Mai	Ho Chi Minh City University of Technology, Vietnam
Pham Thi Vuong	Saigon University, Vietnam

Contents

Advanced Studies in Machine Learning for Security

Emerging Data Management Systems and Applications

Invited Keynotes

Blockchain Technology: Intrinsic Technological and Socio-Economic Barriers
FDSE'2020 Keynote

Ahto Buldas[1], Dirk Draheim[2(✉)], Takehiko Nagumo[3,4], and Anton Vedeshin[5]

[1] Centre for Digital Forensics and Cyber Security,
Tallinn University of Technology, Tallinn, Estonia
`ahto.buldas@taltech.ee`

[2] Information Systems Group, Tallinn University of Technology, Tallinn, Estonia
`dirk.draheim@taltech.ee`

[3] Graduate School of Management, Kyoto University, Kyoto, Japan
`takehiko.nagumo.4s@kyoto-u.ac.jp`

[4] Mitsubishi UFJ Research and Consulting, Tokyo, Japan
`takehiko.nagumo@murc.jp`

[5] 3D Control Systems Ltd., San Francisco, USA
`anton@3dprinteros.com`

Abstract. Since the introduction of Bitcoin in 2009 and its immense resonance in media, we have seen a plethora of envisioned blockchain solutions. Usually, such blockchain solutions claim to be disruptive. Often, such disruptiveness takes the form of a proclaimed blockchain revolution. In this paper, we want to look at blockchain technology from a neutral, analytical perspective. Our aim is to understand technological and socio-economic barriers to blockchain solutions that are intrinsic in the blockchain technology stack itself. We look into the permissionless blockchain as well as the permissioned blockchain. We start with a characterization of cryptocurrency as one-tiered uncollateralized M1 money. We proceed with defining essential modes of business communications (message authentication, signature, registered letter, contract, order etc.) and how they are digitized classically. We review potential blockchain solutions for these modes of communications, including socio-economic considerations. At the technical level, we discuss scalability issues and potential denial-of-service attacks. On the other hand, we also look into four successful blockchain solutions and explain their design. Now: what is the blockchain revolution and how realistic is it? Will it shake up of our institutions? Or, vice versa: does it have to rely on a re-design of our institutions instead? Can we design useful blockchain solutions independent of fundamental institutional re-design? It is such questions which have motivated us to compile this paper and we hope that we are able to bring some light to them.

Keywords: Blockchain · Distributed ledger · Monetary system · Transaction cost economics · New institutional economics

© Springer Nature Switzerland AG 2020
T. K. Dang et al. (Eds.): FDSE 2020, LNCS 12466, pp. 3–27, 2020.
https://doi.org/10.1007/978-3-030-63924-2_1

1   Introduction

Triggered by the quick, unexampled spread of the cryptocurrency Bitcoin [1] since its introduction in 2009 and its immense resonance in media, we have seen, in the last decade, a plethora of envisioned blockchain solutions. Often, such envisioned blockchain solutions claim to be *disruptive*. Such blockchain disruptiveness is often fundamental, i.e., it takes the form of (or is embedded into an overall) proclaimed *blockchain revolution*, i.e., goes beyond the total transformation (and take-over) of an existing business model or even business (sub-)domain, as is the target of the usual start-up (with Booking, Uber, Airbnb as prominent examples). The proclaimed blockchain revolution targets the shake-up of whole vertical and horizontal markets, today's monetary system, the institutional design of the state including the judiciary system, i.e., whole societies and political systems. But how realistic is such a blockchain revolution? Is it the blockchain revolution that enacts a shake-up of the institutions around us; or does the blockchain revolution need to rely on a hypothetical re-design of the institutional design instead? How critical is the blockchain revolution when it comes to the design of concrete blockchain technologies, let them be permissionless or permissioned? It is such questions which have motivated us to compile the recent paper and we hope that we can bring some light to them, at least to create some awareness for them.

In service of these questions, we contribute the following, mutually dependent discussions:

- We characterize cryptocurrency as one-tiered uncollateralized M1 money.
- We define essential modes of business communications (message authentication, signature, registered letter, contract, order etc.) and how they are digitized classically. We review potential blockchain solutions for these modes of communications, including socio-economic considerations.
- At the technical level, we discuss scalability issues and potential denial-of-service attacks.
- We look into four successful blockchain solutions and explain their design:
  - Guardtime: A tamper-proof timestamping service.
  - 3DPrinterOS: An automated manufacturing software ecosystem.
  - Agrello: an electronic identity and digital signature solution.
  - Thinnect: a sensors-as-a-service marketplace.

We proceed as follows. In Sect. 2, we summarize essential preliminaries and some theoretical background. We discuss related work throughout the paper and highlight some selected, important literature in Sect. 3. In Sect. 4, we characterize Bitcoin – and cryptocurrency in general – as an uncollateralized, one-tier M1 money. In Sect. 5, we explain modes of business communications and their possible blockchain realization. In Sect. 6 we discuss intrinsic technological barriers of permissionless blockchain technology. In Sect. 7, we discuss a series of successfull blockchain-based solutions. We finish the paper with a conclusion in Sect. 8.

2   Preliminaries and Theoretical Background

2.1   The Bitcoin Vision

The Bitcoin vision was published in 2008 as a white paper by the anonymous author (or author collective) Satoshi Nakamoto [1]. The aim was to create a peer-to-peer payment system that works free from third party intervention in which payments were instant and irreversible. "Ordinary" bank money was not considered suitable for free electronic commerce as banks may (in principle) delay and revert payments and – for security reasons – require too much sensitive personal information from their clients. The Bitcoin system can be described as a fully automated financial transaction provider – the rules of which are public and cannot be broken due to the principal design of the system. Payment orders are automatically processed in accordance with these rules and are added to an append-only public ledger that can be verified by everybody.

The syntax and semantics of the ledger (as a data structure) are supposed to guarantee its verifiable uniqueness – a successful verification of the ledger must be unique, i.e., so that alternative versions of the ledger cannot exist. In Bitcoin, this is supposed to be guaranteed via the *proof-of-work* consensus protocol. Note that verifiable uniqueness of the ledger means that it is not important at all how and by whom the ledger was created. Only the data of the ledger itself is important for verification. Automation assumes data processing, which certainly needs a machine. Now, it is possible to identify Bitcoin with the machine that is needed to run its data processing, and, henceforth, we can therefore talk about the *Bitcoin machine*. In the Bitcoin vision, such a Bitcoin machine has to be flawless and unstoppable. Destroying the machine would stop the payments. This necessarily leads us to the following considerations:

(i) *What is the Bitcoin machine and which organisation runs it?* By assumption, such a machine cannot be under control of any organisation as such an organisation would be able to stop the machine. Therefore, the Bitcoin machine is a network of servers that are run on voluntary basis. All network nodes (servers) maintain the exact same copy of the Bitcoin ledger.

(ii) *But what guarantees that there are sufficiently many volunteers that run a server?* For that, Bitcoin has an incentive mechanism. Each volunteer who wins a round in the infinitely repeating proof-of-work consensus race is paid with a certain amount of Bitcoin currency (a fixed *(coinbase) reward*, plus variable *transaction fees*). Volunteers are economically motivated as far as the Bitcoin "currency" presents some *economical value* to them.

(iii) *But what is the economical value of the Bitcoin "currency"?* Bitcoin has an economic value *if* it is accepted as payment in exchange of goods or services (in marketplaces) or currency (in financial markets).

Given (i) above, we have that Bitcoin is a technical machine, given (ii–iii), we have that Bitcoin can be characterized as a *"social machine"*.

Table 1. Economics of institutions; compiled from Williamson 1998 [2].

Level	Purpose	Frequency
L1 (social theory) *Embeddedness*: informal institutions, customs, traditions, norms, religion	Often noncalculative; spontaneous	100–1000 years
L2 (economics of property rights) *Institutional Environment*: formal rules of the game – esp. property (polity, judiciary, bureaucracy)	Get the institutional environment right. 1st-order economizing	10–100 years
L3 (transaction cost economics) *Governance*: play of the game – esp. contract (aligning governance structures with transactions)	Get the governance structure right. 2nd-order economizing	1–10 years
L4 (Neo-classical economics/agency theory): resource allocation and employment (prices and quantities, incentive alignment)	Get the marginal conditions right. 3rd-order economizing	Continuous

2.2 New Institutional Economics

We have chosen Williamson's *new institutional economics* [2] as a theoretical reference framework to strengthen (to provide anchors for) many of our arguments throughout the paper. In Table 1, we have compiled the "four levels of social analysis" of new institutional economics (from Fig. 1 in [2]), L1 trough L4, which continuously evolve, at different pace and with different volatility; where they all influence each other (back and forth, even across several levels) in this evolvement. Level L1 is about culture at the societal level; level L2 is about laws, regulations and government; level L3 is about organizational governance in so far it concerns inter-organizational transactions; whereas level L4 is the most fine-grained level of individual actors. It makes sense to study large, complex socio-technical systems with the help of such an institutional analysis framework, compare with Koppenjan and Groenewegen [3]. We are interested in two kinds of questions, i.e., in how far emerging technologies impact institutional design at the different levels of analysis, on the one hand, and (vice versa) in how far changes to institutional design are prerequisites (or at least enablers) for the successful introduction of emerging technologies. Here, not only the amount but, in particular, the level of impact makes a difference in the degree of *disruptiveness* of a technology.

3 Related Work

The multi-author volume [4] (edited by Malcolm Campbell-Verduyn) provides an interdisciplinary assessment of Bitcoin and cryptocurrency from several perspectives of social sciences as well as technology studies. In [5], Arvind Narayanan and Jeremy Clark review a series of seminal papers and contributions in cryptography that are related to Bitcoin technology. This way, the paper also increases the understanding of the building blocks of blockchain technology.

With [6], Jan Mendling et al. provide a mature analysis of the potential of blockchain technology for business process management (BPM) (and the challenges thereof). The authors elaborate a thorough understanding of the utilization of blockchain technology in terms of the established BPM lifecycle and beyond, i.e., in terms of established BPM capability areas. They conclude with identifying seven future research directions that are relevant to the adoption of blockchain technology for (and its impact on) BPM.

In [7], Rikken, Janssen and Kwee have compiled a catalogue of governance challenges of blockchain technology, in particular decentralized autonomous organizations. In [8], Janssen et al. have developed a conceptual framework for the analysis of blockchain technology adoption (as reference point for both practitioners and researchers in the field). Furthermore, they characterize the key challenges that come with each of several factors (institutional/market/technical) and indicate that the factors depend on each other in mutual, complex relationships. In [9], Nitin Upadhyay compiles a framework for adoption of blockchain technology based on a systematic literature review. The paper concludes with a compilation of open research questions in the categories of management, impact and application. With [10], Shermin Voshmgir provides a comprehensive treatment of the past, present and future of the blockchain vision.

With [11], Andreas M. Antonopoulos provides a comprehensive description of the Bitcoin implementation. After an explanation of Bitcoin basics, he explains, in detail, the data structures and algorithms of the Bitcoin implementation. Several further, auxiliary topics such as scripting, security and example blockchain applications are treated as well.

4 Bitcoin as an Uncollateralized, One-Tier M1 Money

Governments do not print money out of thin air, simply by fiat; instead, they are steering the money supply via a set of complex measures in a tiered, collateralized monetary system – in these endeavors they are supported by resp. team together with independent, legally trusted, accountable institutions. Today's monetary system is tiered. It relies on the interplay of a central bank with commercial banks in guaranteeing the money supply needed for the functioning of a country's economy. Different countries might have different monetary systems, not only with respect to their concrete steering parameters, but also with respect to their design; however, the basic mechanism of money supply is always the same. The crucial point is in the distinction between central bank money and commercial bank money. Only a small fraction of money exists as physical currency (cash/coin), actually, less than 10% of the money is cash/coin. Most of the money exists as pure deposit in banks. Money creation is a permanent process. Money is created and destroyed continuously by the commercial banks via their credit function. Whenever a credit is granted, new money is created. Whenever a credit is payed back, money is destroyed. This means, that it is the commercial bank that creates money out-of-nothing (not the government); however, only within in the narrow boundaries of regulated mechanisms, mainly: collaterals and capital adequacy ratios.

The tiers in today's monetary systems are called M0, M1, M2 and M3. The exact definitions of which kind of money is included in which tier varies from country to country (also, their might be further tier names such as MB and MZM in the US system), however, this should not concern us too much here, as there are strong similarities between the systems. Roughly, it can be said that M0 money consists of commercial bank deposits plus cash deposits at commercial banks, M1 money consists of demand deposits (book money that can be instantly accessed by the owner for financial transactions) at commercial banks plus circulating cash (in wallets and cash registers), whereas M2–M3 contains saving, time deposits, large-time deposits and others. So, it is fair to say that M0 is the central bank money, M1 is the money that is used in *purchasing* (buyer/seller financial transactions), and M2–M3 is about all kinds of other money. For us, this rough (imprecise) categorization is enough to characterize Bitcoin (and any kind of cryptocurrency that follows the Bitcoin paradigm) as M1 money: it can be used in purchasing (in so far and as long as it is accepted in payments in exchange for goods or services, compare with Sect. 2.1).

We characterize Bitcoin as a *one-tiered, uncollateralized money*. Bitcoin lacks a crucial function of today's regulated monetary systems: the *credit function*. In today's monetary systems the credit function is bound *sine-qua-non* to the creation of collateralized money. And this is the crucial insight: as everyone is used to talk about collaterals of a loan, it is important to see that it is the *issued* money that is collateralized – collateralized money. In the same vein, Bitcoin is an uncollateralized money. Money creation (money issuance) in the Bitcoin system is a side-effect of the proof-of-work consensus mechanism (as incentive for the so-called mining efforts). But via mining, no collateral is bound to the created (mined) Bitcoin. Therefore, Bitcoins are *purely speculative* assets.

5 Modes of Business Communications

From a purely observational perspective, economy manifests in interactions between actors. Economy can be considered as a the entirety of these interactions. Looking at an economy merely as a huge play of interactions would not equip us with any better understanding of it. Here is, where theory building needs to start, eventually, to come up with hypotheses on structures and laws governing the interactions. The transactions of transaction cost economics are interactions. But they are also composed of many smaller interactions. Business interactions show in business communications. When it is said that a certain (emerging) IT technology would lower transaction costs, this can mean several things – depending on which *institutional level* is primarily affected.

It could mean that the technology is disruptive in a *revolutionary* manner (the "blockchain revolution" is something that is heard often) at Williamson institutional level L2 – compare with Table 1. Its emergence would allow for opening *protected* rooms in the society/economy in which players do not need to adhere to the established "formal rules of the game – esp. property (polity, judiciary, bureaucracy)" [2]. Opening such protected (private) rooms is in the tradition of *cypherpunks* (see "A Cypherpunk's Manifesto" by Eric Hughes [12]) and it is fair to count leading figures of the blockchain community to the cypherpunk scene, e.g., Hal Finney (inventor of RPoW (reusable proof-of-work; receiver of the first Bitcoin transaction).

Then, in these opened rooms, new forms of organizations and co-operations would become possible at level L3 ("get the governance structure right" [2]) that would drastically decrease or even eliminate transaction costs (a recent example in that vein is the Ethereum *decentralized autonomous organization* (DAO) [13]). We call such arguments L2/L3-level arguments. We learned form transaction cost economics why people might form organizations at all: to separate transactions into external and internal transactions with the purpose of *economizing*. Now, L2/L3-level arguments (on reducing transactions costs) seem to have an opposite direction: decreasing transaction costs by *deconstruction* of established forms of companies hand-in-hand with deconstructing the established institutional stack.

The other strand of argumentation is more straightforward. It is about increasing the *efficiency* and *effectiveness* of business communications, directly, by the exploitation of best available tools. If established forms of communications are simply replaced, the changes are just about "getting marginal conditions right" [2], i.e., happen at level L4, compare with Table 1. Sometimes, business processes need to be re-engineered on behalf of the introduction of new IT technology. Actually, technology is a major driver in the *business process re-engineering* of Hammer and Champy [14]. Then, there are not only cost-savings with respect to the business communications themselves, but indirect cost-savings due to the improvement of business processes. Business process re-engineering can amount to deep organizational and cultural changes of the organization [15] and, therefore, can also show impact at level L3, but still in the framework of the institutional environment set by level L2. Therefore, we call these kinds of arguments L3/L4-level arguments.

In this section, we conduct the discussion *bottom-up*: we identify essential business communications and analyze how and why they are realized with standard IT technology approaches, see Table 2 for an overview. We call these essential business communications *modes of business communications* or just *modes of communications* for short. The aim is, that (on the basis of such an analysis) it becomes easier to assess the potential of blockchain technology. The idea is to bring the arguments about established and emerging IT solutions that are around into a more systematic and coherent form. The modes of communication are: message authentication, digital record, digital signature, digital registered letter, digital contract, digital order, and smart contract. We will walk through all of them step-by-step, but first we need to explain the importance of the concept of *trust* for business communications.

Table 2. Modes of (trusted) digital business communications together with addressed problems and classical trust and enforcement anchors.

	Mode of communication	Addressed problem
i	Message Authentication	forgery-proof message
ii	Digital Document	*sender-proofs-sender* timestamp
iii	Digital Signature	*sender*-non-repudiation
iv	Digital Registered Letter	*receiver*-non-repudiation
v	Digital Contract	*sender/receiver*-non-repudiation
vi	Digital Order	repeatable *sender/receiver*-non-repudiation
vii	Smart Contract	*automatic* contract enforcement
	Mode of communication	Classical trust/enforcement anchors
i	Message Authentication	trustworthy public key exchange
ii	Digital Document	trusted TSA (timestamping authority)
iii	Digital Signature	trusted CA (certification authority); (trusted TSA)
iv	Digital Registered Letter	trusted VAN (value-added network) provider; framework contract (VAN with receiver)
v	Digital Contract	trusted VAN provider; framework contract (VAN with all parties)
vi-a	Digital Order (symmetric)	trusted VAN provider; message-related framework contract (VAN with all parties); business-related framework contract between all parties (justiciable business rules)
vi-b	Digital Order (asymmetric)	(trusted or (at least) trustworthy CA); business-related framework contract between dominating consumer and dominated supplier; supplier portal at consumer site (via certified IT service provider)
vii	Smart Contract	– xxx –

Trust is essential in business communications, but we need a deeper understanding of the difference between just *trustworthy* and *trusted* parties, in order to understand, how the issue of trust actually shapes business communication solutions. If parties trust each other *unconditionally*, we usually would say that they consider each other as *trustworthy*. Scenarios of unconditional trust ("gentlemen agreements" [3]) can be considered as non-standard scenarios in the professional business world. Rather, parties would like to co-operate with each other, even if they do not trust each other unconditionally. Actually, when it comes to *auditability*, a party must show that it does not simply trusts other parties unconditionally! Here is, where the concept of *trusted party* emerges. The concept of trusted party makes sense only with respect to the judiciary system. A party is trusted, if other parties have "enough reason" to *believe* that the party's witness statements would be *believed* in court cases (dealing with disputes involving business communications). The level of formality of what is considered as "enough reason to believe" can greatly vary. For example, it might be formalized by requiring certain certificates on the (technical) maturity of the trusted party, such as would be required by auditors. At a very formal level, we would say that a party is a *legally trusted party*, if it has been directly granted the status of an officially trusted party by respective legal regulations, or (indirectly) granted by a state authority in accordance with respective legal regulations. A standard example for such legally trusted parties are the certification authorities of national eID (electronic identification) solutions [16–18].

Less precise, but in the same vein, we can talk about a trusted IT solution, if it allows for reliable/stable/replicable argumentation in court cases involving business communications that are supported by the solution. Digital business communication solutions are large-scale solutions that consist of a technical design and an institutional design, compare with Koppenjan and Groenewegen 2005 [3]. We call the components (trusted parties; auxiliary technical/non-technical assets) of a trusted solution also *trust anchors*.

Business parties turn to court to enforce their interests (in case of dispute). The judiciary serves as enforcement system. The judiciary system might not be the only possible enforcement system. Interests can be enforced by dominating (powerful) players in asymmetric business relationships. Similarly, the *risk of damaged reputation* can serve as (trustworthy) self-regulating enforcement mechanism in some business sub communities. Such business communities are often (relatively) small, at least, they show a low degree of anonymity; often they show also an asymmetric distribution of powers among their players. Both of the described scenarios are independent of the judiciary, instead, they rely on informal rules at level L3. Now, the envisioned business models (products, platform etc.) based on smart contracts usually heavily rely on the idea of establishing an enforcement system independent of the judiciary. In general, IT solutions for business communications can be considered as composed of enforcement anchors. Trust anchors are a special, ubiquitous kind of enforcement anchors. (Enforcement anchors are relevant to an existing enforcement system. The enforcement system of trust anchors is the judiciary.) Table 2 shows the different modes of communication together with the business communication problems that they address, on the one hand, and the classical trust resp. enforcement anchors of their stereotypical IT solutions, on the other hand. Message authentication (i) is a basic mode of communication that is independent of the existence of a judiciary. The vision of smart contracts (vii) targets the independence of the judiciary and so do the usual smart contract business models (products, platforms etc.), although, smart contracts could also be useful in emerging (classically) trusted solutions. Solutions for the modes of communication (ii) through (vi) are usually always designed against the background of the judiciary; although, some solutions might not be (perfectly) designed with respect to it and/or not oriented towards it – we will discuss an example of such also with solution (vi-b).

Message authentication (i) is a basic mode of communication that addresses the problem of forgery-proof message. The business parties unconditionally trust each other, but they have the problem that some intruder might tamper a sent message, or might sent a message claiming to be one of the parties. The problem can be solved simply by trustworthy public key exchange so that, henceforth, a sender can authenticate a message with its private key. We could call the authentication of the message a digital signature, but it is not. The authentication of the message serves only the protection against a forgery attack and is (not yet) feasible to proof that a sender has sent a message, exactly, because of the lack of a trust anchor that will be part of *digital signature* solutions (iii). The simplest form of trustworthy public key exchange is to meet in the real world. Also, they could be send via any other channel that is already considered sufficiently trustworthy (e.g., snail mail).

Several definitions of electronic documents exist, each coming with different intentions: from the domain of libraries (ISO 2709, MARC, Dublin Core etc.) over technical exchange formats (ODF, PDF etc.) to enterprise computing (ISO 10244, Moreq etc.). In this paper, we use *digital document* (ii) as the name of a communication mode. The purpose of a digital document is to add a timestamp to it, so that a party can proof that it created/possessed a *record of information* at a certain point in time. A standard use case of this is about saving *intellectual property rights*. A timestamp is a trusted piece of information about such point in time. To stay in the picture of communication modes, we call the addressed problem *sender-proofs-sender* timestamp, because it is about one party (sender) that wants to timestamp a information record (message). This becomes clear, when we look into the standard solution for this problem. In the standard solution, the interested party sends an information record to a *trusted timestamping authority* (TSA). This TSA adds a timepoint information to is, authenticates the resulting document with its private key and sends it back to the interested party. Actually, the TSA has *digitally signed* (iii) the information record, just, the addressed problem is slightly different: the senders themselves want to proof that they have sent messages, not a third party receiver. An alternative solution (Guardtime) that exploits a publication mechanism is described in Sect. 7.1.

Digital signatures (iii) address the problem of *sender*-non-repudiation as follows. The receiver of a message wants to proof that the message has been sent by the sender, often in combination with proving the timepoint of when the message has been sent. Use cases emerge whenever the sender has confirmed/approved something (e.g., a business certificate) or has committed to something (e.g., an order, compare with (vi) below). The standard solution works as follows. The senders sign the messages with their private keys. The role of the trusted CA is to confirm and to witness that a public key belongs to a sender. The sender and the trusted CA together generate the private/public key pair of the sender. Henceforth, the senders uses their private keys to sign documents. A receiver can request a *public key certificate* (public key of the sender plus sufficient identity information about the sender; signed by the trusted CA with its private key) from the trusted CA (technically, typically via OCSP (Online Certificate Status

Protocol)). So far, with this confirmation, a scalable solution for message authentication (i) has been achieved. Requesting a public key certificate is a means of scalable, trustworthy public exchange. But with the trusted CA even more has been achieved. The trusted CA (or the issued public key certificate on its behalf) can serve as witness at court; and this way, *sender*-non-repudiation is achieved. Often, a digitally signed document also needs to contain a timestamp. But the timepoint of signature can be added by the sender before signing, there is no need for a trusted TSA, because the addressed problem is *sender*-non-repudiation. It is the receiver who wants to prove that s/he has received a message at a certain time; if s/he receives a message with a wrong timepoint s/he can just ignore it as if not sent (getting a document with the correct timepoint is a different issue; however, it makes no difference whether the receiver aims to get that for the first time or after s/he has received a message with a wrong timepoint). Practically, we see that digital signature solutions also include a trusted TSA, and typically the trusted CA would (at the same time) take the role of the trusted TSA. This is so, because digital signatures usually appear in solutions for the more complex business communications *digital contract* (v) and *digital order* (vi) that we will discuss in due course.

The digital registered letter (iv) addresses the problem that a sender would like to proof that the receiver has received a message at a certain timepoint (in snail mail it is the resp. postal services organization that serves as witness: registered letter). We call the problem *receiver*-non-repudiation. The problem of *receiver*-non-repudiation is dual to the problem of *sender*-non-repudiation. It is often overlooked, that it is important to distinguish cleanly between *receiver*- and *sender*-non-repudiation. Actually, the problem of *receiver*-non-repudiation is much harder to solve than the problem of *sender*-non-repudiation. It is not a sufficient solution that the sender proofs that s/he has sent a message (as in *sender-proofs-sender*-timestamping (ii) above) – even if s/he can proof that, this does not proof that the message actually arrived at the receiver. The receiver could always deny that s/he has received it, if the message is simply sent via an ordinary open network. The *ad-hoc* idea to require a signed acknowledgment message from the receiver makes no sense: the problem is exactly about the receiver claiming that s/he has not received the message (so s/he just would not send the acknowledgement message as promised). A solution to this problem can be provided by the concept of *value added network* (VAN) that has been used in typical EDI (electronic data interchange) [19] solutions in the 1990s. In the VAN-based solution, the sender does not send a message directly to the receiver, instead, s/he sends it to the trusted VAN provider with the receiver as addressee. The VAN provider stores the message in a persistent message queue (i.e., technically, the VAN is a MOM (message-oriented middleware)) where it waits for being picked from the receiver. This means, that the message delivery to the receiver is switched from *push* to *pull*. Now, in case of dispute, the VAN provider can witness that the receiver has *either* picked the message (at a certain timepoint) *or* did not try to pick it from the queue. In both cases, the receiver cannot simply claim any more that s/he has not received the message, which provides *receiver*-non-repudiation. It is the responsibility of the receivers to pick their messages from the VAN. Such responsibility can be formalized in a framework contract, in which the receiver commits to pick messages regularly. Here, it needs to be the interest of the receiver to commit to such responsibility. The interest exists, because the receiver is interested to get engaged in certain business communications (and therefore transactions), i.e., contracts (v) and orders (vi) below. No trusted CA is needed in this solution. The trusted VAN can identify both the sender and the receiver by their *user credentials*. Sender *"send"* messages to the VAN provider by logging in into the provider's systems (of course, as part of a secured API call) with their user credentials, same with the receivers when they pick their messages. Therefore, the VAN provider exactly knows, who and when has sent/received which messages via the VAN.

We define the digital contract (v) as the communication mode, in which both parties agreed on and committed to the content of a (timestamped) information record, so that the addressed problem is both *sender-* and *receiver*-non-repudiation in sending and signing the contract back and forth. A solution can be designed, e.g., again with a VAN as for *receiver*-non-repudiation; this time, all parties need to be obliged to pick their messages from the VAN provider.

The *digital order* (vi) is the essential communication mode in B2B e-commerce. A digital order is a *contract* between an *consumer* (sender) and a *supplier* (receiver). The contract is considered accepted by *both* parties, if it has been sent by the sender and has been received by the receiver. Both parties need to commit to that mode; therefore, it needs a business-related framework contract that also regulates further justiciable business rules with respect to the orders (how much will the consumer order at least per month? how much can the supplier deliver at most per month? how fast will products be delivered? etc.). If the business-related framework contract is not a digital contract, a solution for digital orders just needs a solution for digital registered letters (iv) as a basis. Otherwise, it needs a solution for digital contracts (v) as a basis. In practice, digital orders are more complex and contain also messages send to the consumer (e.g., order acknowledgement, compare with resp. EDI standards) that need to be provable. Therefore, digital orders usually need a digital contract solution as their basis anyhow, compare with (vi-a) in Table 2.

In practice, other solutions for *digital orders* (vi) exist. (In practice, even in mission-critical supply chains, orders are often just sent by email with little to no systematic measures for resilience – the confidence in the enforceability is accordingly low.) Today's supply chains often show asymmetric business relationships, i.e., business relationships with a dominating (powerful) consumer and a dependent (much smaller) supplier. In such scenarios, we can see solutions (vi-b) as follows. Again, there is a business-related framework contract, however, this time the suppliers commits to pick orders directly from a server (as part of a supplier portal) at the customer site (e.g. via Web service, REST service etc.). A sufficiently trustworthy CA, as well as a certified IT service provider who runs the supplier portal, can part of the solution. The objective of such solutions is to streamline and advance the consumers procurement processes (supplier "enablement") and not, in first place, the legally solid proof of messages – as other enforcement mechanisms (concerning dependency/reputation of the supplier) gain more importance.

Smart contracts (vii) address the problem of *automatic* contract enforcement, i.e., they aim at providing a contract enforcement system as part of their solution. Smart contracts (vii) are fundamentally different from the other modes of communication (i) through (vi); and there exists no classical solution for them. Rather, smart contracts can be identified with today's canonical solution that is provided for the problem that they address. The smart contract solution consists of

- a (typically permissionless) distributed ledger (blockchain for short)
- a cryptocurrency (realized by the blockchain)
- a formal contract language that is rich enough to express *self*-enforceable (*smart*) contracts (in the boundaries of the solution) in terms of
  - information in the ledger
  - accessible information outside the ledger (*basic* real-world embeddedness)
  - accessible (steerable) assets outside the ledger such as locks, signals, machines, i.e., all kinds of IoT (Internet-of-Things) devices (real-world embeddedness)
- Smart contracts that are written in the contract language and stored in the ledger

A prominent smart contract implementation is the distributed ledger platform Ethereum with the cryptocurrency Ether and the contract language Solidity. Now, how can a smart contract solution help in implementing the essential business communication modes that we have identified in Table 2? We discuss this for the communication mode *digital order* (vi) as it is the most encompassing one and can be considered the essence of a stereotypical ICO aiming at *disrupting* the "way business is done" in a certain business domain or in general. More concrete, we review the enforcement anchors in (vi-a) to conduct the discussion.

First, we want to discuss a potential solution that is "maximally" disruptive, i.e., aims at enabling business independent of the established judiciary and currency, and independent of any dominating player. The goal has to be that neither a trusted CA nor a trusted VAN is needed. Consequentially, the message-related contracts (VAN with all parties) will also become obsolete in the solution. Now, both business-related framework contracts and orders are stored as *smart contracts* in the blockchain. Now, the problem of *sender/receiver*-non-repudiation that is addressed by the *digital order* (vi) is simply not an issue any more. The messages are recorded – tamper-proof – in the ledger. The information in the ledger can be used in contract enforcement. A question could be, whether the ledger information would be accepted by the judiciary. We will turn to that later, but for now, it is not a question at all: we have said that the solution is about getting independent of the judiciary and establishes its own enforcement system.

What happens if a contract is not fulfilled? It is the solution itself that reacts, according to what has been specified in the smart contract. Types of reactions can be about *enforcing* well-behavior, *punishing* misbehavior (penalty) or *compensating* misbehavior (escrow). All cases of potential misbehavior need to be understood and appropriate reactions have to be programmed. For example, the product of an order could delivered with an IoT lock (that is accessible from the contract language). The lock is only unlocked, after the payment has been made. All of this can be programmed before the smart contract is signed. But what happens if the product (that has been unlocked) is not working? The idea is that then the payment for the product is *automatically* paid back. But how can the ledger decide that the product is not working according to its specification? Can we program an automatic surveillance of the product (via sensors) that decides that? Rather not. The parties can decide beforehand about a neutral *arbitrator*, whom they both trust and who is asked (automatically) to decide in that case by reviewing the product in the real world. Does this still adhere to the initial vision of fully automatic self-enforceable contracts? Is it not too complicated, is it not even impossible to understand all potential eventualities and to design and program appropriate reactions to them? Each transaction could be secured with an escrow. Escrow mechanisms are well-known from established business communications. But only a small fraction of business transactions is actually secured by escrows in today's business world (rather, penalties are fixed in contracts – to be enforced by the judiciary). Securing each and every order in B2B is simply not possible, because for this, the needed financial *liquidity* would be way beyond what could be considered reasonable – we would like to talk about *escrow-superheaviness* in case of such an approach.

To overcome the questions posed in the previous paragraph, a middle position is possible that aligns a smart contract solution with the established judiciary and official currency. Here, the underlying ledger would be permissioned. In the extreme case, in which the ledger is provisioned by a single player, the solution does not differ a lot from a classical VAN-based solution. It still could be argued that a chosen smart contract platform is (with its specific features) particularly appropriate for the indicated domain of digital orders and/or that is favorable for other reasons (scalable, resilient, manageable, contemporary, future-proof etc.). Conceptually, stepping from a single provider to a group of providers does not change a lot. It could be argued that the resilience and/or the "trustworthiness" of such a permissioned solution is particularly high. However, also the opposite can always be claimed, in particular, because there exist (to our best knowledge) yet no documented approaches to make distributed ledger technologies auditable (to be assessed positively in operational risk management audits). Similarly, a solution can only be as trusted as it is *believed to be believed* in court cases (see the discussion earlier in this section) and again, from our current perspective, we claim that there is still a severe lack of proven experience/approaches/standards that would provide a sufficient level of *trustability* for distributed ledger technologies.

6   Intrinsic Technological Barriers

In this section, we investigate blockchain technology that follows the original blockchain paradigm, i.e., proof-of-work [1]. The findings are also relevant in discussions of alternative blockchain paradigms (following other consensus mechanisms), as they reveal fundamental *requirements* for (permissionless) blockchain-based solutions. There are several, mutual dependent technical barriers intrinsic in blockchain technology, i.e., protocol-related *denial-of-service* (DoS) attacks (both from the *user* and from the *operator*), protocol-related *scalability* (both with respect to *usage* and with respect to *operation*) and the possibility of *double-spending*. We say that the potential DoS attacks are protocol-related (and therefore intrinsic), because they arise from the design of blockchain technology itself, i.e., they are not just DoS attacks that threaten every IT system that operates in an open network. The same is for protocol-related *scalability*, where the potential of *double-spending* is specific to blockchain technology anyhow.

If the block size of a blockchain technology is not limited, trivial DoS attacks are possible (for the user, if transaction costs are achievable; for the operator always). Limiting the block size leads to limited scalability. We define:

$$
\begin{array}{ll}
N & \text{maximal (limit) number of transactions per block} \\
N' & \text{average number of requested transactions per block} \\
T & \text{average time needed for mining a bock} \\
N/T & \text{available performance of the blockchain} \\
N'/T & \text{requested performance of the blockchain} \\
N'/N & \text{load of the blockchain} \\
N'/N > 1 & \text{overload of the blockchain} \\
\tau & \text{threshold value of } N'/N \text{ rendering the blockchain impractical} \\
\tau' & \text{threshold value of } N'/N \text{ collapsing the blockchain}
\end{array}
\tag{1}
$$

The available performance of the blockchain N/T in (1) is neither a peak performance nor a maximal performance measure. As T itself, N/T is an average measure and makes sense only when considering a sufficiently large time period (sufficiently large number of (mined) blocks). The same is with the measures N'/T, N'/N etc. The requested performance of the blockchain N'/T comes from transactions *requesting* to be added to the blockchain. Whenever N'/T is larger then N/T, we talk about an *overload* of the blockchain ($N'/N > 1$), characterized by the existence of waiting/dangling transactions. An overload of the blockchain is not a problem *per se*, it becomes a problem, when the requested performance is way larger than the available performance ($N'/T \gg N/T$). The threshold τ marks the value of N'/N, from which the blockchain is *perceived* as impractical. It is not possible to determine the value of τ theoretically, only *empirically*, i.e., it is a value determined by the users of the blockchain. The threshold τ' marks the value of N'/N that would lead to a collapse of the blockchain, meaning, that the value of its cryptocurrency assets massively diminishes (e.g.., by users starting to withdraw their cryptocurrency assets on a massive scale). Obviously, we have that $\tau' \geqslant \tau > 1$. Typically, we are interested in τ, when analysing scalability, whereas we are interested in τ' rather when analysing potential DoS attacks. More precisely, let us assume that N' is composed of transactions n and n' (i.e., $N' = n + n'$) as follows:

n average number of requested non-incidental transactions per block

n' average number of requested incidental transactions per block   (2)

Now, we could say that both τ and τ' are analyzed as scalability issues if we assume that $n' \approx 0$, whereas we would analyse them in service of understanding potential DoS attacks if we assume that $n' \gg n$. A typical countermeasure against incidental/critical overload $N'/N \gg 1$ can be seen in the introduction of a lower bound (so-called *dust limit*) for the amount transferred by a single transaction – at least against *ad-hoc* occurrences/attempts. Another protection against incidental/critical overload can be provided by transaction fees, as a side-effect of their development, and only in so far as they have been developed. In both cases (dust limits and transaction fees) there exists the question of the *sweet spot* between protection against overload and enablement of microtransactions. Too high transaction costs contradict microtransactions. Note, that the enablement of microtransactions was among the main objectives of the original Bitcoin vision [1].

An operator (or group of operators who conspire) with sufficient mining power can attack the blockchain. Actually, more precisely, each operator can always (try to) attack the blockchain, but s/he needs sufficient mining power to be successful with it. A well-known kind of attack is the so called *double spending* attack [1]. Here, the attacker replaces a previously done transaction by an updated one (here, the replaced/deleted transaction was spent for a good/service that has been delivered to the attacker in the mean time). The essence of the double-spend attack is that the attacker changes the blockchain history permanently; the fact that this might be done in service of double-spending is just an instance of that more general scheme. We would like to speak of an *overwrite attack* instead. If an attacker is successful with an overwrite attack, the attacker can overwrite not just one certain transaction in the first block of the recent changed history (double-spend) but all transactions in all blocks in the recent history. For instance, if the attacker creates blocks that consist only of (void/dummy) transactions, this would amount to a severe DoS attack. The described attack is more than a plain denial-of-service attack. It has some negative impact in terms of availability, but its actual damage is in the level of *business confusion* that arises from all the reverted/lost transactions. We assert that, in case of Bitcoin, it is rather unlikely that an *overwrite* attack is tried in purpose of a *double-spend* attack – given the expensiveness of an overwrite attack (given the current overall mining power currently spent in Bitcoin) as opposed to realistic amounts in business transactions. If an overwrite attack occurs, we would rather assume that it has been done in purpose of a DoS attack (the lost transaction fees can be considered marginal as compared to the costs of the needed mining efforts in such case).

An overwrite attack is expensive. The more mining power, the faster it will succeed (in the sense of: expected time in case that it succeeds). To show that, we develop a statistical model of overwrite attacks as follows. We model the mining of blocks in the main blockchain and the attacker's blockchain as two **i.i.d.** sequence of random variables X (main blockchain) and Y (attacker blockchain) that are also *mutually independent w.r.t. each other*, i.e.:

$$X = (X_i : \Omega \longrightarrow \mathbb{R})_{i \in \mathbb{N}} \tag{3}$$

$$Y = (Y_i : \Omega \longrightarrow \mathbb{R})_{i \in \mathbb{N}} \tag{4}$$

We have that Ω is the set of all possible *evolvements* of the blockchain (with respective probability space $(\Omega, \Sigma, \mathsf{P})$ as usual) after the attempt to attack has started. The attempt to attack starts at timepoint 0. Assume that we name the blocks in the main chain and the attacker chain as follows:

$$\cdots x_{-3} x_{-2} x_{-1} \ x_0 \ x_1 x_2 x_3 \cdots \tag{5}$$

$$\cdots x_{-3} x_{-2} x_{-1} \quad y_1 \ y_2 \ y_3 \cdots \tag{6}$$

The attack starts with mining x_1 and y_1. The target of the attacker is to overwrite x_0. Therefore, y_1 in the attacker block points to the block before x_0, i.e., x_{-1}. This way, y_1 "overwrites" x_0.

Now, a random variable X_i models the time that has been needed to *mine and distribute* the *i-th* block x_i of the main chain (more precise: the *i-th* block after the start of the attack). Now, we make a typical simplification (in service of coming up with a model): we assume that the mining effort in the mining/distribution is so dominant that we can neglect the time needed for distribution of blocks through the network. This assumption greatly simplifies the scenario and our model. It immediately implies that we do not need to model the differences between the timepoints at which a block arrives at different nodes of the blockchain network – we can simply assume that a block arrives at (is distributed to) all nodes at the same time point. Now, the random variable $X^n = X_1 + \cdots + X_n$ models the *timepoint* at which (or: overall elapsed time until) the *n-th* block of the main chain x_n has been mined. Similarly, a random variable Y_i models the time that has been needed to mine the *i-th* block of the attacker chain y_i and so forth.

Note that X and Y are both **i.i.d.** individually. Furthermore, they are mutually independent w.r.t. each other. In general, they are not identically distributed as compared to each other. In the special case that the owner of the main blockchain and the attacker have the same computational power, we have that X and Y are also identically distributed as compared to each other. In all other cases, they are not. If the computational power of the attacker is weaker (stronger) than the computational power of the main blockchain owner, the *mean* of Y is larger (smaller) than the mean of X, as then, *on average*, the attacker needs more (less) time to mine a block than X.

At each point in time, the blockchain protocol decides for the longest chain in our model. (At each point in time, the blockchain protocol decides for the strongest chain. We assume that the attacker and the main chain proceed with the same difficulty in our model. Note, that a chain of equal length that is formed later does not replace the main chain.) The attacker chain needs to pace up with one additional block, i.e., the block x_0 which is omitted from the attacker chain, compare with (6). Therefore, the probability that the attacker succeeds with an *overwrite* has the following value:

$$P\left(\exists n \in \mathbb{N} . Y^{n+1} < X^n\right) \tag{7}$$

In order to specify the average time needed to succeed with an overwrite, we first define the random variable H of *first overwrite success times* as follows:

$$H : \Omega \longrightarrow \mathbb{R} \cup \infty \tag{8}$$
$$H(\omega) = \min\left\{n \mid Y^{n+1}(\omega) < X^n(\omega)\right\} \tag{9}$$

Now, we can specify the *average time needed to succeed with an overwrite* as a conditional expected value as follows:

$$\mathsf{E}\left(H \mid \exists n \in \mathbb{N} . Y^{n+1} < X^n\right) \tag{10}$$

Whenever $\mathsf{P}\left(\exists n \in \mathbb{N} . Y^{n+1} < X^n\right) = 1$, we have that $H : \Omega \longrightarrow \mathbb{R}$ and, therefore, the *average time needed to succeed with a an overwrite* is obtained by $\mathsf{E}(H)$. Given a fixed X, we see that (10) decreases, whenever $\mathsf{E}(Y)$ decreases. $\mathsf{E}(Y)$ decreases, whenever the mining power of the attacker increases.

The value of (10) depends on the kind of distribution of block mining times X (and Y). A natural assumption is that X is distributed approximately *geometrically* as follows. Mining is about repeatedly choosing a value (by random, or by incrementation) as a nonce in the block – until the block's hash meets a specified difficulty target. Now, we need to make two assumptions. First ("unit time"), we assume that the time needed to compute a block's hash is always the same. Second ("memorylessness"), we need to assume that the probability that a block's hash meets the specified difficulty target is equal for each chosen value (which we can, approximately, if the set of values from which we draw nonces is sufficiently large). Based on theses assumption, we would have that X shows a *geometric* distribution ("number of tosses till success").

7   Working Blockchain Solutions

7.1   A Tamper-Proof Timestamping Service

Document timestamping solutions that implement *sender-proofs-sender* timestamping (communication mode (ii) in Table 2) are mission-critical in many organizational contexts. Organizations want to have tamper-proof and provable document logs not only in the communications with other organizations; they also want to be safe against failure (accidental or intentional) of their own members/employees. Equally, the state wants to be confident with the operations of its authorities and, again, the authorities want to be confident with the operations of their employees. Since 2007, Guardtime offers a document time stamping solution as a service, i.e., the so called KSI blockchain (keyless signature infrastructure blockchain). In the Estonian e-government ecosystem, the solution is successfully used to secure the healthcare registry, the property registry, the succession registry, the digital court system and the state gazette [20].

The KSI blockchain achieves a practical implementation of an idea that goes back to Stornetta et al. in 1993 [21], i.e., it stores timestamped document hashes in a Merkle tree [22] and publishes the root hash of the tree *periodically* (e.g., once a month) in a newspaper (e.g., in the Financial Times, among others, in case of the Guardtime solution). The idea is straightforward and effective: the published root hash serves as a *real-world trust anchor*. However, to turn this idea into a robust solution that is highly performant and at the same time highly available is a challenge, and this is exactly what is achieved by the KSI blockchain [23,24] as follows. Time is divided into rounds (e.g., one second). Hashes of all documents signed during a round are aggregated into a per-round hash tree. The root hashes of the per-round trees are collected into a perpetual hash tree, the so-called *hash calendar*. It is the root hash of this hash calendar that then is published periodically to newspaper(s). Now, the Merkle tree is distributed and replicated to make the solution resilient, i.e., the nodes are deployed on several distributed servers. The servers are operated by the KSI blockchain service provider, with a mix of *owned* servers at the premises of the KSI blockchain service provider and servers of trusted *third-party* compute service providers, to make the solution even more resilient.

7.2   An Automated Manufacturing Software Ecosystem

There is a global trend and paradigm shift in manufacturing towards *personal manufacturing* [25]. In this new paradigm, people and organizations would not buy a ready-made product [26]. Instead, they would obtain raw material and produce products using their own (or locally accessible) automated manufacturing (AM) machinery. People and companies have access to a lot of different types of automated manufacturing (AM) machinery such as 3D printers, CNC mills, laser jets, and robotics to manufacture products locally, at the point and time of need. The impressively fast adoption of these technologies strongly indicates that this novel approach to manufacturing can become a key enabler for the real-time economy of the future [27]. Already now, software platforms such as 3DPrinterOS [27–29] and ZAP [30] are available, which cover the whole personal manufacturing workflow from the initial idea to the physical object using real-time command-and-control of AM machinery to manufacture production-grade functional parts. An Important problem is how to ensure information integrity and consistency through all the stages of AM; i.e., an intentional or accidental corruption or loss of information can happen, which can affect the final quality and reliability of product parts and the final product. In this section, we further explain the 3DPrinterOS platform. The platform realizes a mechanism to securely deliver content to 3D printers from the cloud. The first generation of the solution [31] has been introduced in 2015. Today, the 3DPrinterOS cloud has more than 123.000 users who have generated over five million CAD designs and machine codes and have produced more than 1.500.000 physical parts on 40.000 3D printers in 100 countries; these values double every six months [32]. The technology is licensed to Bosch, Kodak, and other popular desktop 3D printer manufacturers. Currently, the solution is completely reworked [28] and extended to any type of manufacturing machine or complex IoT device with command, control, and telemetry.

In the sequel, we describe how permissioned blockchain technology is used at 3DPrinterOS to ensure the integrity of several critical manufacturing parameters of product parts and end products. We use Hyperledger Fabric [33] as a microtransaction ledger solution for the 3DPrinterOS software ecosystem [27]. The software ecosystem can be understood as a kind of broker: its purpose is to enable several organizations to bring value to end users. A platform orchestrator sets up, configures and runs multiple ordering service nodes on different infrastructure providers such as AWS, Azure, GCE, this way forming a private blockchain network. The orchestrator of the ecosystem is a network initiator in terms of Hyperledger Fabric and has administrative rights over the network. Both the nodes and administrators of orchestrator access the network through the usage of X.509 certificates issued by the orchestrator's certificate authority. Certificates issued by this certification authority are also used for signing the transactions to be accepted into the ledger.

Other players (vendors, end users, external actors) of the ecosystem [27] are added to the network via creation of consortia; then establishing channels for storing information in corresponding ledgers. The participating players establish certificate authorities to grant their employees and their technology (IT systems, machines etc.) access to the ecosystem through individual channel configurations. Certificates issued by the organizations' certificate authorities are used to sign all transactions. Chain code is stored in smart contracts. The applications of participating organizations can access corresponding channels as well as the software ecosystem's application platform. This way, all participating users and assets such as 3D printers, CNC mills, material batches can be identified; and therefore, it becomes easy to track responsibilities even on a large scale. This increases the transparency of the processes, e.g., in case of part malfunctioning, it is easy to track the participants and the involved processes. Established channels are private to participants (thus only participating parties have access). The blockchain keeps all information in the ledgers. Ledger data is updated using smart contracts. Smart contracts are executed only if they are confirmed by all channel participants using a voting-based consensus mechanism. All information in the ledger is tamper-proof, and all information is entered only if digitally signed by a responsible organization. All of these issues would be hard to solve without permissioned blockchain technology.

7.3   An Electronic Identity and Digital Signature Solution

There are just a few countries in the world who offer convenient, fully integrated electronic identity (eID) and digital signature solutions [17] to their citizens. The majority of e-signature services worldwide [34] still use "flinstone" techniques for signing documents such as drawing a signature on the screen, or uploading a picture with signature. There are many barriers to implement contemporary eID and digital signature solutions in many countries in the world including EU in a secure, user-friendly, and scalable manner and – as a consequence – to have them adopted by the citizens [16,18,35,36]. As indicated by several studies [37–39], eIDs and digital signatures are used mostly by major enterprises, whereas their usage by SMEs (small/medium enterprises) and ordinary citizens is marginal – due to the lack of a broad range of e-government services and a low usability of the systems. This marginal use of eIDs and digital signatures is mostly in online payments; and only a fraction is in contract signing [34,37]. With the advent of blockchain technology, easier and more secure solutions potentially became possible, which would allow for a seamless user experience and would show (at the same time) a high scalability.

An example of such a solution is Agrello ID [40] – a blockchain-based solution for eID and digital signature. The solution is based on elliptic curve key threshold encryption [41], where one part of the key is kept inside a smart device such as a smartphone, and the other part is stored in the cloud. When these key pairs are combined, they are capable of providing a fully functioning digital signature behaving in accordance with the eIDAS regulation [42]. Each physical object in the world is matched with a digital twin in an instance of the Ethereum [43] blockchain. A person's digital identity is a smart contract in the blockchain; also, objects such as cars or apartments have digital twins in the form of chaincodes (smart contracts). Each participant of the private network has a right to publish information about the identities of such objects. More specifically, the identity of a person is confirmed by a *know your customer* (KYC) provider [44]. Each confirmation and validation is done by executing chaincode on the digital identity smart contract, which activated the digital identity. By using their private keys, the owners of digital identities can perform operations such as signing service or sales contracts.

We analyzed numerous CA software products and found that none of them is scalable enough for our purposes: country-wide authentications and digital signatures with millions of citizens performing many thousands of operations per day. Also, the used solution should be future-proof. We found that solutions based on permissioned blockchains have these capabilities, as they are already tested in the field, e.g., Ethereum [43].

7.4 A Sensors-as-a-Service Marketplace

Permissioned blockchains can enable completely new business models. In particular, they have the potential to allow for calculating and accounting microtransactions more precisely. Still, today's microtransactions are often quite costly to maintain and audit. Blockchain technology has the potential to make this easier. An example is Thinnect, a SolaaS (Solution as a Service) platform that allows to use a comprehensive hardware utilization and monitoring solution (including cloud-based connectivity dashboards for hardware such as temperature sensors or CO_2 sensors) using a pay-per-reading business model. Often, high quality hardware is expensive and value can be created for the end customers only by utilizing a full-fledged solution; therefore, businesses who need to make specific parameter measurements (food logistics, smart cities etc.) need to invest a considerable amount of money to acquire hardware and to keep networks of sensors up and running reliably – outsourcing is not a solution here, as it is equally expensive or even more expensive.

A way out of this is yielded by a SolaaS model where companies only pay for the value they get - they *pay per measurement* and are not involved at any stages of hardware purchasing, delivery or deployment. Hardware is subsidized by the hardware manufacturer or a third party willing to invest and get interest. Each party is paid trough micro-payments for each measurement. Solutions based on classical database products and traditional ways of calculating and auditing the ledgers can take a lot of time and money, because separate databases at different locations (at participants' premises) can create a lot of trouble in synchronization and finding out truth in auditing processes. Blockchains have the potential to make all of this much easier due to their consensus mechanisms, uniquely identifiable and digitally signed transactions, as well as the fact that they continuously check balances by their design. Thinnect uses Hyperledger Fabric [33] blockchain as a micro-transaction ledger solution to keep track of the sensors readings batches, nonpayments from actual users of hardware to Thinnect, and micro-payments to hardware manufacturers and investors subsidizing the cost of hardware. To summarize, blockchain technologies have the potential to bring many advantages to micropayments and nanopayments as needed in solutions such as Thinnect [45].

8   Conclusion

With this paper we wanted to contribute to a more informed discussion of the potential of blockchain technology. We wanted to look at blockchain technology from a neutral, analytical perspective. Our aim was to understand technological and socio-economic barriers to envisioned blockchain technology solutions that are intrinsic in the blockchain technology stack itself. We looked into the *permissionless blockchain* and the *permissioned blockchain*, where the *permissionless blockchain* gained our major interest – at least in this paper (we have designed successfull permissioned blockchain solutions with large customer bases ourselves, we have glimpsed over them shortly in this paper, in service of the big picture that we addressed). The permissionless blockchain came first, i.e., it is the blockchain *per se*. Permissioned blockchain solutions have a higher *capability-to-perform*, at the same time they have less fundamental disruptive potential; still their corresponding initiatives gain (from a marketing perspective) from the perceived immense (seemingly boundless) disruptiveness of the permissionless blockchain.

References

1. Nakamoto, S.: Bitcoin: A Peer-to-Peer Electronic Cash System (2008). https:// bitcoin.org/bitcoin.pdf
2. Williamson, O.: Transaction cost economics: how it works; where it is headed. De Econ. **146**, 23–58 (1998)
3. Koppenjan, J., Groenewegen, J.: Institutional design for complex technological systems. Int. J. Technol. Policy Manag. **5**(3), 240–257 (2005)
4. Campbell-Verduyn, M. (ed.): Bitcoin and Beyond: Cryptocurrencies. Blockchains and Global Governance. Routledge, Abingdon (2017)
5. Narayanan, A., Clark, J.: Bitcoin's academic pedigree. Commun. ACM **60**(12), 36–45 (2017)
6. Mendling, J., Weber, I., van der Aalst, W., et al.: Blockchains for business process management - challenges and opportunities. ACM Trans. Manag. Inf. Syst. **9**(1), 1–16 (2018)
7. Rikken, O., Janssen, M., Kwee, Z.: Governance challenges of blockchain and decentralized autonomous organizations. Inf. Polity **24**(4), 397–417 (2019)
8. Janssen, M., Weerakkody, V., Ismagilova, E., Sivarajah, U., Irani, Z.: A framework for analysing blockchain technology adoption: integrating institutional, market and technical factors. Int. J. Inf. Manag. **50**, 302–309 (2020)
9. Upadhyay, N.: Demystifying blockchain: a critical analysis of challenges, applications and opportunities. Int. J. Inf. Manag. **54**, 1–26 (2020)
10. Voshmgir, S.: Token Economy - How the Web3 reinvents the Internet, 2nd edn. BlockchainHub Berlin, Berlin (2020)
11. Antonopoulos, A.M.: Mastering Bitcoin: Programming the Open Blockchain. O'Reilly, Sebastopol (2017)
12. Hughes, E.: A cypherpunk's manifesto. In: Schneier, B., Banisar, D. (eds.) The Electronic Privacy Papers: Documents on the Battle for Privacy in the Age of Surveillance, pp. 285–287. Wiley, Hoboken (1997)
13. DuPont, Q.: Experiments in algorithmic governance: a history and ethnography of "The DAO," a failed decentralized autonomous organization. In: Campbell-Verduyn, M. (ed.) Bitcoin and Beyond: Cryptocurrencies, Blockchains and Global Governance, pp. 1–18. Routledge (2017)
14. Hammer, M., Champy, J.: Reengineering the Corporation. HarperCollins, New York (1993)
15. Schein, E.H.: Organizational Culture and Leadership. Wiley, Hoboken (2016)
16. Lips, S., Aas, K., Pappel, I., Draheim, D.: Designing an effective long-term identity management strategy for a mature e-state. In: Kő, A., Francesconi, E., Anderst-Kotsis, G., Tjoa, A.M., Khalil, I. (eds.) EGOVIS 2019. LNCS, vol. 11709, pp. 221–234. Springer, Cham (2019). https://doi.org/10.1007/978-3-030-27523-5_16
17. Pappel, I., Pappel, I., Tepandi, J., Draheim, D.: Systematic digital signing in Estonian e-government processes - influencing factors, technologies, change management. Trans. Large Scale Data Knowl. Cent. Syst. **16** (2017)
18. Tsap, V., Pappel, I., Draheim, D.: Key success factors in introducing national e-identification systems. In: Dang, T.K., Wagner, R., Küng, J., Thoai, N., Takizawa, M., Neuhold, E.J. (eds.) FDSE 2017. LNCS, vol. 10646, pp. 455–471. Springer, Cham (2017). https://doi.org/10.1007/978-3-319-70004-5_33
19. Emmelhainz, M.A.: EDI: A Total Management Guide. Van Nostrand Reinhold, New York (1993)

20. Martinson, P.: Estonia – The Digital Republic Secured by Blockchain. Pricewater-houseCoopers, London (2019)
21. Bayer, D., Haber, S., Stornetta, W.S.: Improving the efficiency and reliability of digital time-stamping. In: Capocelli, R., De Santis, A., Vaccaro, U. (eds.) Sequences II, pp. 329–334. Springer, New York (1993). https://doi.org/10.1007/978-1-4613-9323-8_24
22. Merkle, R.: Protocols for public key cryptosystems. In: Proceedings of the 1st IEEE Symposium on Security and Privacy, S&P 1980, p. 122 (1980)
23. Buldas, A., Saarepera, M.: Document verification with distributed calendar infrastructure. US Patent Application Publication No.: US 2013/0276058 A1 (2013)
24. Buldas, A., Kroonmaa, A., Laanoja, R.: Keyless signatures' infrastructure: how to build global distributed hash-trees. In: Riis Nielson, H., Gollmann, D. (eds.) NordSec 2013. LNCS, vol. 8208, pp. 313–320. Springer, Heidelberg (2013). https://doi.org/10.1007/978-3-642-41488-6_21
25. Mota, C.: The rise of personal fabrication. In: Proceedings of the the the 8th ACM Conference on Creativity and Cognition, C&C 2011, pp. 279–288. ACM (2011)
26. Tao, F., Cheng, Y., Zhang, L., Nee, A.Y.C.: Advanced manufacturing systems: socialization characteristics and trends. J. Intell. Manuf. **28**(5), 1079–1094 (2015). https://doi.org/10.1007/s10845-015-1042-8
27. Vedeshin, A., Dogru, J.M.U., Liiv, I., Draheim, D., Ben Yahia, S.: A digital ecosystem for personal manufacturing: an architecture for a cloud-based distributed manufacturing operating system. In: Proceedings of the 11th International Conference on Management of Digital EcoSystems, MEDES 2019, pp. 224–228. ACM (2019)
28. Vedeshin, A., Dogru, J.M., Liiv, I., Ben Yahia, S., Draheim, D.: A secure data infrastructure for personal manufacturing based on a novel key-less, byte-less encryption method. IEEE Access **8**, 40039–40056 (2019)
29. Vedeshin, A., Dogru, J.M.U., Liiv, I., Yahia, S.B., Draheim, D.: Smart cyber-physical system for pattern recognition of illegal 3D designs in 3D printing. In: Hamlich, M., Bellatreche, L., Mondal, A., Ordonez, C. (eds.) SADASC 2020. CCIS, vol. 1207, pp. 74–85. Springer, Cham (2020). https://doi.org/10.1007/978-3-030-45183-7_6
30. Brian Heater: Zap brings the manufacturing process to the cloud (2016). https://techcrunch.com/2016/09/12/zap/
31. Isbjörnssund, K., Vedeshin, A.: Secure streaming method in a numerically controlled manufacturing system, and a secure numerically controlled manufacturing system. U.S. Patent 2014111587 A3, 3 December 2015
32. 3D Control Systems Inc.: 3DPrinterOS cloud world statistics (2020). https://cloud.3dprinteros.com/dashboard/#/world-statistics
33. Androulaki, E., Barger, A., Bortnikov, V., et al.: Hyperledger fabric: a distributed operating system for permissioned blockchains. In: Proceedings of the 13th European Conference on Computer Systems, EuroSys 2018, pp. 1–15. ACM (2018)
34. FinancesOnline: 47 Essential e-Signature Statistics: 2020 Market Share Analysis & Data (2020). https://financesonline.com/25-essential-e-signature-statistics-analysis-of-trends-data-and-market-share/
35. Everis: Study on the Use of Electronic Identification (eID) for the European Citizens' Initiative. Final Assessment Report. Everis, European Commission (2017)
36. Tsap, V., Pappel, I., Draheim, D.: Factors affecting e-ID public acceptance: a literature review. In: Kő, A., Francesconi, E., Anderst-Kotsis, G., Tjoa, A.M., Khalil, I. (eds.) EGOVIS 2019. LNCS, vol. 11709, pp. 176–188. Springer, Cham (2019). https://doi.org/10.1007/978-3-030-27523-5_13

37. Cavallini, S., Bisogni, F., Gallozzi, D., Cozza, C., Aglietti, C.: Study on the supply-side of EU e-signature market: Final Study Report. Fondazione FORMIT, European Commission, Directorate-General Information Society and Media of the European Commission (2012)
38. Alzahrani, L., Al-Karaghouli, W., Weerakkody, V.: Analysing the critical factors influencing trust in e-government adoption from citizens' perspective: a systematic review and a conceptual framework. Int. Bus. Rev. **26**(1), 164–175 (2017)
39. Carter, L., Liu, D.: Technology humanness, trust and e-government adoption. In: Proceedings of the 18th Australasian Conference on Information Systems, ACIS 2018. Association for Information Systems (2018)
40. Agrello: Agrello ID - Identity based digital signatures (2020). https://www.agrello.id
41. Liu, Yu., Liu, T.: A novel threshold signature scheme based on elliptic curve with designated verifier. In: Sun, X., Pan, Z., Bertino, E. (eds.) ICAIS 2019. LNCS, vol. 11635, pp. 332–342. Springer, Cham (2019). https://doi.org/10.1007/978-3-030-24268-8_31
42. The EU Parliament and the Council of the Eurpean Comission: Regulation (EU) No 910/2014 of the European Parliament and of the Council of 23 July 2014 on electronic identification and trust services for electronic transactions in the internal market and repealing Directive 1999/93/EC. Official Journal of the European Union L 257/73 (2014)
43. Wood, G., et al.: Ethereum: a secure decentralised generalised transaction ledger. Ethereum Proj. Yellow Pap. **151**, 1–32 (2014)
44. Veriff: Veriff - identity verification done in seconds (2020). https://www.veriff.com. Accessed 05 Sept 2020
45. Thinnect: Thinnect - IoT Edge of Network Service Provider (2020). https://www.thinnect.com

Data Quality for Medical Data Lakelands

Johann Eder$^{(\boxtimes)}$ and Vladimir A. Shekhovtsov

Alpen-Adria-Universität Klagenfurt, Universitätsstraße 65-67,
9020 Klagenfurt am Wörthersee, Austria
{johann.eder,volodymyr.shekhovtsov}@aau.at

Abstract. Medical research requires biological material and data. Medical studies based on data with unknown or questionable quality are useless or even dangerous, as evidenced by recent examples of withdrawn studies. Medical data sets consist of highly sensitive personal data, which has to be protected carefully and is only available for research after approval of ethics committees. These data sets, therefore, cannot be stored in central data warehouses or even in a common data lake but remain in a multitude of data lakes, which we call Data Lakelands. An example for such a Medical Data Lakelands are the collections of samples and their annotations in the European federation of biobanks (BBMRI-ERIC). We discuss the quality dimensions for data sets for medical research and the requirements for providers of data sets in terms of both quality of meta-data and meta-data of data quality documentation with the aim to support researchers to effectively and efficiently identify suitable data sets for medical studies.

Keywords: Biobank · Meta-data · Data quality · Data lake

1 Introduction

Data lakes are architectures for the storage of data for further use [11,19,37]. What were the major reasons for the development of the data lake concepts, which arouse with the advent of *Big Data*? Organizations were not able to keep up with the ever increasing possibilities for collecting and storing data and to integrate all these data in structured data repositories. Data Warehouses [12,44] require that data, which should be stored in a data warehouse or a data mart, is structured, cleaned, harmonized and integrated, before it is entered into the data warehouse - usually through a carefully designed process of extracting data from the sources, transforming the data into the structure and formats defined in the data warehouse, and loading the data into the data warehouse in defined intervals (ETL process).

Data lakes, in contrast to data warehouses, do not require that the collected data is integrated and pre-processed and harmonized, when it is included in the

This work has been supported by the Austrian Bundesministerium für Bildung, Wissenschaft und Forschung within the project BBMRI.AT (GZ 10.470/0010-V/3c/2018).

T. K. Dang et al. (Eds.): FDSE 2020, LNCS 12466, pp. 28–43, 2020.
https://doi.org/10.1007/978-3-030-63924-2_2

data repository. In contrast, the transformation and integration of data sets is only performed, when it is needed for a specific purpose, in particular, when performing big data analytics (statistics, data mining, machine learning). Until such a usage, the data usually remains in its initial form and format.

Of course, data lakes cannot be mere storages of unrelated data sets remaining in their original formats, as this would leave the data unsuitable for the intended usage (called data swamps or data dumps [6,14]). Storage architectures to effectively store data sets, catalog the data sets to make them available, when needed, is subject of ongoing research efforts [33]. Most of the approaches follow the principle to characterize data sets with metadata such that the data sets can be found and used, when they are needed for exploitation [37].

Most of these approaches, however, assume that both the data sets and their schemas are available to support the search for useful data sets. In this paper, we will focus on situations, where data and schemas are not easily available. Such situations are common in the field of medical research, where lots of different data sets are collected by various stakeholders. Novel and unforeseeable research questions trigger innovative analytical processing of available data and require adequate support for finding relevant data sets and prepare them for the requested processing methods. This profile matches the characteristics of data lake architectures to very high degree. However, the legal and operational constraints for the highly relevant but also highly sensitive data sets imply that they are only available through a complex elaborated process [9,23].

Medical data is usually produced and collected in institutions for providing health care (e.g. hospitals, clinics), and public and private institutions for medical research (e.g. research institutes, pharmacological companies, medical universities). Each of these institutions or even subunits (e.g. clinical departments) of these institutions might organize the data in its own data lake. Access to the content of other data lakes is complex and time consuming. Nevertheless, the combination and joint, integrated processing of these data is indispensable for progress in biomedical research and thus for the development of future drugs and therapies. Central storage of such data in anonymized form [40] is no viable alternative, as it suffers from the problem of information loss leaving the data typically useless for scientific studies.

We call such a distributed system a *Data Lakelands*, i.e. a collection of data lakes with commonalities in the scope, purpose, or methods of data collections, which ought to be used together for analytical processing, but which are not directly accessible by the involved or interested parties.

Which are the requirements for a data lakeland architecture to support its intended purpose? We propose a generic architecture based on the exchange of ontological meta data and of meta data quality characteristics to support the identification of data sets which are potentially useful for specified processing needs. And we show with the example of data sets associated with biobanks and biorepositories [31,39,47], how such a data lakeland can be organized, emphasizing the need of meta data quality assessment to support how researchers are able to identify useful data sets for testing their hypotheses.

2   Biobanks and Medical Data Sets

2.1   Biobanks and Biobank Networks

Medical research requires biological material and data to perform medical studies, to launch hypothesises generating projects and to test hypothesis about diseases, therapies, and drugs.

Biobanks are infrastructures for medical research collecting and storing biological material such as tissue, blood, cell cultures, or body fluids together with data describing these materials. Biobanks are interdisciplinary research platform that providing material and data for (medical) research projects [4,8,15,17].

For a particular research project data from different biobanks might be necessary for various reasons. The European research infrastructure BBMRI-ERIC (Biobanking and Biomolecular Resources Research Infrastructure - European Research Infrastructure Consortium) [8,17,18,24,30,45,46] provides an infrastructure to connect the different biobanks in Europe and provide researchers with means to efficiently and effectively search for suitable material and data needed for their studies. BBMRI.AT is the Austrian national node of BBMRI-ERIC connecting Austrian biobanks and link hem with the European infrastructure.

While biobanks traditionally were mainly concerned with the harvesting, processing, conservation and storing of the biological materials, the importance of data associated with these biological materials is gaining importance and attention. The annotation of the biological samples with quality-controlled data about the donors considerably increases the usefulness of biological material collected in biobanks. Data in biobanks can come from various sources: from data derived in medical studies, from health care provisioning, or from data gathered together with the material. The data is very heterogeneous in every aspect possible. A rather recent development allows individuals to donate date for medical research. These data may range from personal health records with measurements from various health care providers to data which is not collected by health care providers but by a variety of different devices like fitness bracelets or smart watches [16,35,38].

The data is derived from different sources and different processes, it is collected and stored for supporting different purposes and by different stakeholders. The data might even be contained in different information systems and storage architectures for various reasons - securing the privacy of donors is one of the most noble reasons for the distributed architecture and organization. Therefore, data is only integrated for an acceptable and approved purpose. Hence the situation of the data sets maintained in a biobank can be characterized as a data lake, i.e. for a certain research project usually these data has to be identified, collected, harmonized and prepared to make it useful for pursuing a research project. The requirements of the research projects are hugely varying and by their very nature these requirements cannot be known, when the data for the biobank is collected.

Data in biobanks is extremely sensitive as it represents health status and bodily characteristics of donors. Therefore, maintaining the privacy of data and sophisticated processes and protocols to ascertain strict confidentiality and pedantically controlling that material and data is only used for consented and approved purposes. As a consequence, storing biobank data in central repositories easily accessible by many researchers is out of question.

As each biobank data collection can be seen as a data lake, we view this infrastructure landscape as a *Data Lakeland*, an area with a high number of data lakes which are connected by some (communication) channels. And the number of these lakes is huge - the BBMRI-ERIC directory already lists more than 650 biobanks with almost 2500 collections (www.bbmri-eric.eu).

An important question for biobanks and biobank federation infrastructures is how researcher can find collections, which might have appropriate data sets and materials for a given research project. In particular, which information biobanks should and are able to provide for making such a search efficient and effective.

2.2   Data in Biobanks

We classify data in biobanks along several dimensions: data types, ontologies, data source, etc.

Medical data comprises a wealth of different types of data: classical records with numeric data (e.g. lab measures), alphanumeric data, data in natural language texts (e.g. discharge letter, pathology findings), images (e.g. MRT scans), to specific data formats (e.g. gene expression profile), etc.

In medicine also many different ontologies and taxonomies are used for the same type of data (e.g. ICD or SNOMED for diagnostic codes).

Typical problems related to medical data in biobanks include the following:

- Completeness and quality: required parts of medical documentation may not be available any more, or donors don't remember or deliver wrong information (e.g. childhood diseases, prior medication).
- Transformation: unreadability of handwritten documents, transformation errors when transcribing data from documents; furthermore the diversity of formats and technologies regarding health care data, makes it very difficult to provide unified transformation, mapping, and search interfaces,
- Interpretation: problems to give meaning to data, as it probably relates to undocumented or unknown proprietary semantics, which requires input of the original author to translate and interpret it; even worse, the semantics of data produced by one data provider may evolve over time leading to heterogeneity between and within data sources.
- Distribution and technical heterogeneity: the required information is usually stored in the databases of hospitals and other health service providers, thus it is distributed over multiple organizational units, each running different systems with diverse technologies and different interface technologies.
- Access: BBMRI.at-associated biobanks reported that they have often only very marginal information about the donors and their medical history mainly because of organizational and legal reasons but also because of technical barriers.

– Laws and regulations: and last, but definitely not least, access to and use of health-related personal data is regarded extremely sensitive and therefore very restricted, often prohibited, heavily regulated by laws and regulations, as well as corporate ethical rules and guidelines.

All these problems indicate that adequate data quality management for medical data sets is a quite difficult and complex undertaking, nevertheless, it is absolutely essential - not only for treating patients but also for medical research.

2.3   Data Heterogeneity

Medical data coming from different sources (various health care providers, questionnaires, labs, clinical studies, life style gadgets, public registries, etc.) show all different types of heterogeneity. The following types of heterogeneities are frequently observed:

– Different data semantics
– Different data encoding
– Use of different ontologies (e.g. disease codes)
– Different units (e.g. kg vs. lbm)
– Different methods of measurement (fast vs. thorough test)
– Different data naming (attribute names)
– Different schemas
– Different language used
– Different database technologies (e.g. relational, XML)
– Different data quality
– Differences due to evolution of ontologies, standards, measurement methods, etc.

Although there are long running efforts to harmonize medical data, and many standard data formats, ontologies and taxonomies were developed, the area is still haunted by these heterogeneities.

2.4   Biobanks as Data Brokers

The biobanks frequently serve as *data brokers*. They do not produce the data, they might not even store the data associated with their biological material collections. The associated data might reside in departmental databases, general hospital information systems, or external data repositories, like registries of health records, or data of social security insurances.

Biobanks are also not users of the data. The data is needed by researchers in research organizations. Thus biobanks serve as mediators or brokers matching the information needs of researchers with the data availability of the data producers and data providers.

Data in biobanks can come from the following sources:

1. *The data produced by the biobank.* This contains mainly data about handling and storage of biological materials, standard operating procedures applied (e.g. ischemia time, storage temperature, etc.)
2. *The data produced for the biobank.* This includes in particular data about material collected in cohort studies for population based biobanks, where data about donors is collected together with the biological material (e.g. Vaccination history).
3. *The data produced by scientific studies.* Such data is added to the biobank because the materials used in these studies are stored there. An example of such data is the donor data collected by means of disease-based collection from ontology, when the typical approach is to have such data collected in the clinical departments and not by the biobanking unit.
4. *The data produced by routine healthcare.* The most important category of this data is the data from Electronic Health Records (EHRs). An example is the information from the patient health record such as height, weight, or anamnesis: the whole health record is typically not produced by the biobank but is used there.
5. *The data from linked collections.* Such data comes from any data collections containing the data produced elsewhere but used in the biobank (e.g. by linking to such collections from the materials in the biobank).
6. *Data collected from donors* this might range from general electronic health records to questionnaires of life-style properties.

As we will discuss below, biobank operators cannot be responsible for the quality of all these data from external sources, but will be responsible for a proper documentation of the data quality of these sources.

3 Obtaining Data for Research Projects

A typical process for a researcher to obtain material and data sets for a research project or a clinical study contains the following steps (simplified) [9]. The researcher specifies the data requirements. These include search attributes describing the conditions the cases, which the researcher intends to study, have to fulfill (e.g. data about patients over 50 years of age, body mass index above 30, blood group "A+", who tested positive for Covid-19). In addition these requirements also specify, which (other) data has to be available in the data set and in which quality (e.g. prior diseases, lab data, lifestyle information).

With this profile a researcher then searches for biobanks, resp. collections in biobanks, which likely have the required data. As mentioned before, the researcher cannot access the data directly. So currently, such request are mostly communicated to a number of biobanks through person-to-person communication channels (letters, emails, phone calls) or through tools provided by BBMRI-ERIC (biobank directory, sample/locator, sample/data negotiator) or other biobank providers. When a suitable collection is found, the researcher formulates a project, which states in detail for which purpose the data and material is requested, why the data is necessary and the expected outcome of the project. The proposal is then submitted to an ethics committee. The data is only accessible to a researcher after the project is approved by an ethics committee.

The difficulty in this process is that a researcher might not just query a database and run a series of queries to search for promising data sources. The biobank can only offer meta-data describing the data for such a search. The biobank directory of BBMRI-ERIC or of BBMRI.AT are tools to help researchers to identify potentially useful collections and biobanks in a rather course grained way. To improve the situation is the aim of the following considerations.

The crucial question is: which kind of meta-data can a biobank provide for facilitating the search for relevant data sets without risking to exhibit personal data of the donors? Another question is: how can such meta-data be published in a harmonized way in face of the heterogeneities outlined above?

4   Generic Architectures for Data Lakelands

It is generally acknowledged that data lakes require an adequate provision and management of metadata to avoid data swamps [33]. We consider that these metadata has to contain mainly two types of information:

- Content
- Data Quality

Due to the heterogeneity of the data sets in the different data lakes and the differences in meta-data representation, the contents of a data set is best represented by concepts or sets of concepts of a reference ontology. Thus we propose that each data lakeland declares a reference ontology. Then in each data lakes the available data sets provides meta-data characterizing their content by referring to concepts of this reference ontology. Each data lake offers then possibilities to search for data sets specifying a set of concepts of the reference ontology. The meta data can also be exchanged between data lakes and search infrastructures for the whole data lakeland can be established. The level of support and the specificity of both queries and results then depends on the level of details provided by the reference ontology.

It is not necessary that in the whole data lakeland only one reference ontology is used. If there are several reference ontology, then there is a need for providing mappings between the different ontologies [20].

As ontologies might evolve over time (e.g. the different versions of the ICD ontology for encoding diagnosis), such ontologies frequently require a temporal representation and mappings between different ontology versions to support search over evolving data collections or data collected in different periods [10].

Besides the content of data sets, the search requires information about the quality of the data in the data sets. Typical data quality criteria (e.g. reliability,

precision, completeness, accuracy) are discussed below. For assessing the usefulness of a data set, the data lake management has to provide information about
the data quality management and the data quality representation for the data
sets. We call this information the meta data quality.

A particular challenge of the data quality management is the definition of
data quality. The usual definition of data quality as *fitness for use* [43] is problematic, as the use of the collected data is not yet known. The usage of the
meta data, nevertheless, is known in advance: supporting search for appropriate data sets. Therefore, the meta data quality is of major importance for the
organization of data lakes.

5   Data Lakeland Architecture for Biobanks

As we discussed above, the situation of biobanks and networks of biobanks can
be seen as a data lakeland architecture. Therefore, we discuss here, how the
infrastructure for searching such a data lakeland for useful data sets can be
established, in particular, which reference ontologies can be used and how the
management of data and metadata quality can be organized. In particular, we
discuss, which information biobanks can publish to support researchers, when
they search for appropriate cases.

Essentially we base the considerations on the following principle conceptual
model of a biobank: A biobank stores biological material (e.g. piece of tissue
from a biopsy, blood, saliva, etc.) where each storage item is called a sample.
Samples collected together according to some criteria are called a collection (e.g.
a collection of colon cancer tissue).

Direct access to the data is not possible as outlined above. Publishing metadata in form of schemas faces the difficulty that the schemas are very heterogeneous. Even if XML-Schema is used as a uniform schema language too many differences between different biobank data collections remain and therefore searching through a single point of service would be quite difficult. In addition, the
schema contains the data model, but does not contain sufficient information
about the content.

We therefore argue, that biobanks should publish the content of their collection in form of concepts of a shared reference ontology. In this way, the information is centered on the contents of a data set rather than on the particular
representation.

For medical data sets, the LOINC (Logical Observation Identifiers Names
and Codes) [2] provides a suitable basis for representing the contents of a data
collection. LOINC is a standard for clinical nomenclature, which provides a
code system for identifying laboratory and clinical observations and test results.
Examples of such information could be the vital signs, the blood hemoglobin
etc.

The goal of creating such a set of codes is to facilitate exchange of information
for clinical and research purposes, in particular, between heterogeneous software
solutions. It also allows to store information from heterogeneous sources for

later use in a unified way. To support this goal, the LOINC codes can be used to substitute for the observation and test information in documents, software applications, or messages.

The level of detail for a LOINC allows to completely cover the observations from reports made by clinical laboratories and other institutions. LOINC codes and the relevant information are stored in centralized way and can be queried online. New LOINCs are created for new types of observations and tests which are not compatible with any existing LOINCs; they are added to the existing body of codes after approval.

The LOINCs can represent the individual tests and measurements (variables) and their collections (explicitly enumerated or arbitrary).

The information coded by LOINC is structured as containing five or six main parts [1]: the name of the measured component or analyte (e.g., glucose, propranolol), the property which was observed as a result of a test or observation (e.g., substance concentration, mass, volume), the time aspect of the measurement, e.g., is it periodical (over time) or singular (momentary), the type of a system or sample (e.g., urine, serum), the scale of measurement (e.g. qualitative or quantitative), and, where relevant, the method of the measurement (e.g., radioimmunoassay, immune blot)

The above information can be coded as:

1. a unique LOINC code, which identifies the related set of information;
2. a full name which includes the abbreviated information on all parts of the LOINC definition;
3. a friendly name which is a short description of LOINC information in natural language.

Figure 1 shows the place of LOINCs in a conceptual schema for the biobank collection and its data attributes.

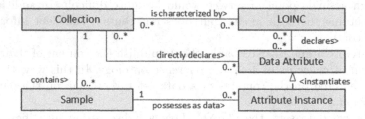

Fig. 1. A fragment of the collection conceptual schema related to data completeness

On this schema, the collection can be characterized by a set of LOINCs defining the content metadata. Every LOINC can contain the declarations of the data attributes, such as the set of names of the allowed data collection methods.

6 Data Quality

6.1 Data Quality Definition and Issues

The working definition of data quality used for this paper is as follows: *Data quality serves as a measure of how well the data represents facts of the real world.* As discussed above the usual definition of data quality as the degree to which the data meets the expectations of data consumers based on their intended use of the data is problematic, as this use is not known for scientific databases in advance. We have to focus, therefore, on the intrinsic data quality characteristics. Meta data quality on the other hand as the representation of the data quality High-quality meta data meets consumer expectations and truthfully represents the content and quality of data collections to a greater degree than low-quality data. For the meta data quality this means that the meta data can be used by researchers to search for appropriate data sets.

To elaborate on this definition, it is necessary to agree on a set of data quality characteristics, which help in achieving proper understanding of data quality, reflecting its different aspects specific for a medical domain [32]. Such characteristics can be supplemented with quality metrics, which allow for their quantification by means of a measurement process resulting in the specific quality values. The characteristics can be combined to obtain the integrated data quality.

The data quality values can be also interpreted as metadata as they contain the information describing the data [36], such as precision, validity period etc.

Data quality characteristics can be categorized

1. based on the meta-level of the data elements being characterized – as either *data item quality characteristics* assessing the quality of the data item level [5], i.e. both the data originated in the biobank, and the external data, or *metadata quality characteristics* [7, 42] assessing the quality of the metadata level;
2. based on the origin of the data being characterized [42], as either *intrinsic data quality metrics and characteristics* assessed by relying only on the existing biobank data, and *relative metrics and characteristics* assessed by relying on subjective judgements or external data;
3. based on the aggregation level of the data being characterized, as *single item, sample,* and *collection metrics and characteristics*.

6.2 Data Quality Characteristics for Data Items, Samples, and Collections

We define first the data quality criteria for the level of data items, resp. measurements, i.e. for the instantiation of an attribute. Then we aggregate these characteristics for the level of a sample and the level of a collection. We use the term combination for the aggregation of data quality measures, as different formulas have been proposed and can be used to aggregate the individual data quality measures deriving data quality measures for aggregates for different purposes. Discussing the different aggregation methods is beyond the scope of this paper.

Data completeness [5] reflects the need in collecting all required data. Sufficient completeness (contributing to high quality) usually means that all such data is present. For biobank data, insufficient completeness is detected when some data attributes are missing because they were either not recorded due to unavailability, or simply not transmitted. In particular, in data derived from health care, typically only those data are determined, which are necessary and useful for an diagnosis, treatment, or therapy.

On the level of a data item (measurement, attribute instance), completeness refers to whether a data item is available or not. For complex data items (e.g. fever chart, a time series, etc.) completeness means to which degree all elements of a data item are recorded.

Completeness on sample level relies on distinguishing between declared and possessed data attributes. Attributes can be declared as part of LOINCs characterizing the collection, making them valid for all collections characterized by a specific LOINC, or directly in the description of a collection, making them valid only for this collection. The samples in a collection instantiate the declared data attributes by possessing their values. Failing to do so means that the data is less complete.

Following this, sample completeness is the degree of available attribute instantiation for a sample, resp. the combination of all completeness measures on data item level for instantiating of declared attributes.

On the collection level we can define completeness for each declared attribute. For simple attributes it is usually defined as the fraction of non-missing values. In general, completeness for an attribute in a collection is the combination of the completeness values of the attribute in all samples.

Data accuracy [34] reflects the need to represent the real world truthfully. Low accuracy means that the data is vague and not precise enough, or plainly incorrect (not corresponding to reality). High quality data is accurate. We distinguish between *syntactic accuracy metrics*, which measure the degree of correspondence between the data items and the syntactic constraints related to a given domain e.g. the ratio of valid calendar dates in the birthday attribute, and *method-based accuracy metrics* which reflect the accuracy of the diagnostic methods used for collecting the data.

As an example of the method-based accuracy, the data for a tentative diagnosis will be less accurate, if this diagnosis is made through a rapid test rather than a thorough test, because the rapid tests are typically designed to have a minimum fraction of false negatives, even at the expense of higher rates of false positives. Usually thorough tests aim at minimizing both false negatives and positives. Method-based metrics are based on the metrics for method accuracy e.g. their sensitivity, specificity, or likelihood ratio [27]. Such metrics are connected to samples and collections by making the collection methods declared in their LOINCs or descriptions, and instantiated for the sample attributes. Then the collection metrics are aggregated over samples e.g. as the average degree of method sensitivity.

Data reliability characterizes the underlying measured concept. For the medical data related to a concept (such as e.g. the depressive mood), reliability [13] can be defined as a degree to which a question triggering the collection of this data, represents a reliable measure of that concept. Another possible definition derives reliability of the data from the reliability of its source [29] i.e. to its provenance. For example, the reliability of the data about the cause of death is much higher in a coroner's inquest, if it was provided by a trained pathologist after an autopsy, than if it was given by a general practitioner. Another example, the reliability of immunity against measles is higher after a titer assessment, than if patients remember childhood diseases.

Low reliability means that the data cannot be trusted, so its quality is low. Method-based data reliability reflects the reliability of the diagnostic methods [22] e.g. calculated as their test-retest coefficients or split-half measures; it is connected to samples and collections e.g. as the sample-based average test-retest coefficient for a collection.

Data consistency reflects the need for non-conflicting data. For the medical data sufficient consistency [3] (contributing to high quality) means that there is no contradiction in the data as the real-world states reflected by data items are not in conflict. It is measured as a reverse degree of variability with respect to the data collection method used within a sample or collection.

Consistency on the collection level (sometimes also called uniformity) mainly informs whether the data items were derived with the same methods, with the intention that data derived with different methods might not be easily comparable. Consider for example the different tests and test procedures for a COVID-19 infection with their different properties, sensitivities and selectivities. We define data as more consistent, if it was collected by smaller number of methods, or most of the items were collected by a small number of methods.

Data timeliness reflects the need for the data to represent actual real-world states [25]. We define data timeliness as the reverse distance of time between creating the sample and creating its data attributes. Good quality data is current and is collected in timely manner (shortly after observation). An example of low data timeliness is asserted when measuring BMI or blood pressure is not done when a blood sample is collected but taken from an earlier hospitalization: such situations are usually unacceptable.

Data precision is defined as the degree of rule resolution (e.g. the number of used categories) for the values of categorical attributes [26], and the number of significant digits - for the values of numeric data attributes. For example, having just three categories for blood pressure is obviously not very precise and contributes to quality negatively. Other examples of precision are the scale for the ischemia time (which can be specified in hours, minutes, or seconds) or the precision of blood pressure measurement equipment.

Data provenance [41] reflects the degree of linking between the data sources and collection methods on the one side, and the data values on the other side. It can be calculated as a completeness with respect to a collection method or source. For low-provenance data (contributing to low quality), it is not possible or difficult to understand, where the data comes from or how it was collected, or by whom. For an example, for the data item "Covid-19 test positive" it is important to know with which method this test result was derived. Knowing the provenance typically improves also the understanding of the measures for reliability and accuracy.

6.3   Meta Data Quality Characteristics

The description of data quality is meta-data of the data sets, i.e. it describes certain properties of the data. Now these data quality characteristics is data as well, and as such it has data quality characteristics. For an example, it might be helpful to know, whether the accuracy of the documentation of data provenance for the data items is high or low, i.e. to which degree we can trust the provenance characteristics. Therefore, we now elaborate on metadata quality characteristics [7,28,42].

Metadata accuracy [7,42] reflects the need for the metadata values to correspond to its domain i.e. it is defined as syntactic accuracy. An example of the domain constraint served well by such metric, is the non-negativity constraint for the data accuracy value domain. In more general, metadata accuracy signifies the level of meeting the requirements of data quality management and assessment.

Metadata completeness [7,21,28] reflects the need of supplementing all data items with the corresponding quality metadata. We define it as a degree of completeness with respect to the metadata connected to the data values. It can be calculated for a specific sample as a degree of presence of metadata values for its attributes, or for a collection - as an average of all metadata completeness values for its samples. It can be also based on a subset of attributes for a given collection, reflecting the degree of presence of the metadata values connected to these attributes for all the samples in this collection.

Metadata timeliness [7] reflects the need for the metadata to reflect the real state of the data items. It can be defined as a the reverse distance of time between creating the data attribute value and creating its supplementing meta-data values. An example of low metadata timeliness is the case when collecting the information about the diagnostic method used to collect the disease data is done in two years after collecting the data item: this is usually unacceptable as the method information can become forgotten in a course of time.

When biobanks act as data brokers, they are not primarily responsible for the data quality of the offered data sets. However, it is their primary responsibility to asses and describe the data quality management, documentation and assessment, and thus to provide a high degree of meta data quality. Only with reliable descriptions of the data quality research may assess whether data can be used for their intended studies and whether these data sets can be processed in combination with other data sets.

7   Conclusions

Proper documentation of data sets associated with the material stored in biobanks in form of metadata describing inadequate ways the contents and the data quality of the data sets increase the usefulness of data collections for medical research. The goal is to make medical studies more efficient and effective. In particular, the time and cost for obtaining appropriate data sets can be reduced when researchers are able to quicker identify such data sets for the medical studies and avoid effort for chasing to obtain data sets which then turn out to be not useful. Also the identification of appropriate data sets reduces the time and cost for performing medical studies when the data sets already provide the necessary data rather than they have be produced from the collected material. Management of meta data and data quality thus contribute to improving medical research.

References

1. LOINC Users' Guide, version 2.68. loinc.org (2020)
2. loinc.org: Logical Observation Identifiers Names and Codes (2020). https://loinc. org. Accessed Sept 2020
3. Almeida, J., Santos, M., Polónia, D., Rocha, N.P.: Analysis of the data consistency of medical imaging information systems: an exploratory study. Procedia Comput. Sci. **164**, 508–515 (2019)
4. Asslaber, M., et al.: The genome Austria tissue bank (GATIB). Pathology **74**, 251–258 (2007)
5. Batini, C., Scannapieco, M.: Data and information quality: dimensions, principles and techniques (2016)
6. Brackenbury, W., et al.: Draining the data swamp: a similarity-based approach. In: Proceedings of the Workshop on Human-In-the-Loop Data Analytics, pp. 1–7 (2018)
7. Bruce, T.R., Hillmann, D.I.: The continuum of metadata quality: defining, expressing, exploiting. In: Metadata in Practice, ALA editions (2004)
8. Eder, J., Dabringer, C., Schicho, M., Stark, K.: Information systems for federated biobanks. In: Hameurlain, A., Küng, J., Wagner, R. (eds.) Transactions on Large-Scale Data- and Knowledge-Centered Systems I. LNCS, vol. 5740, pp. 156–190. Springer, Heidelberg (2009). https://doi.org/10.1007/978-3-642-03722-1_7
9. Eder, J., Gottweis, H., Zatloukal, K.: IT solutions for privacy protection in biobanking. Public Health Genomics **15**, 254–262 (2012)
10. Eder, J., Koncilia, C.: Modelling changes in ontologies. In: Meersman, R., Tari, Z., Corsaro, A. (eds.) OTM 2004. LNCS, vol. 3292, pp. 662–673. Springer, Heidelberg (2004). https://doi.org/10.1007/978-3-540-30470-8_77
11. Giebler, C., Gröger, C., Hoos, E., Schwarz, H., Mitschang, B.: Leveraging the data lake: current state and challenges. In: Ordonez, C., Song, I.-Y., Anderst-Kotsis, G., Tjoa, A.M., Khalil, I. (eds.) DaWaK 2019. LNCS, vol. 11708, pp. 179–188. Springer, Cham (2019). https://doi.org/10.1007/978-3-030-27520-4_13
12. Golfarelli, M., Rizzi, S.: From star schemas to big data: 20+ years of data warehouse research. In: Flesca, S., Greco, S., Masciari, E., Saccà, D. (eds.) A Comprehensive Guide Through the Italian Database Research Over the Last 25 Years. SBD, vol. 31, pp. 93–107. Springer, Cham (2018). https://doi.org/10.1007/978-3-319-61893-7_6
13. Greiver, M., Barnsley, J., Glazier, R.H., Harvey, B.J., Moineddin, R.: Measuring data reliability for preventive services in electronic medical records. BMC Health Serv. Res. **12**(1), 116 (2012)

14. Hai, R., Geisler, S., Quix, C.: Constance: an intelligent data lake system. In: Proceedings of the 2016 International Conference on Management of Data, pp. 2097–2100 (2016)

15. Hainaut, P., Vaught, J., Zatloukal, K., Pasterk, M.: Biobanking of Human Biospecimens: Principles and Practice. Springer, New York (2017). https://doi.org/10.1007/978-3-319-55120-3

16. Henriksen, A., et al.: Using fitness trackers and smartwatches to measure physical activity in research: analysis of consumer wrist-worn wearables. J. Med. Internet Res. **20**(3), e110 (2018)

17. Hofer-Picout, P., et al.: Conception and implementation of an Austrian biobank directory integration framework. Biopreservation Biobanking **15**(4), 332–340 (2017)

18. Holub, P., Swertz, M., Reihs, R., van Enckevort, D., Müller, H., Litton, J.-E.: BBMRI-ERIC directory: 515 biobanks with over 60 million biological samples. Biopreservation biobanking **14**(6), 559–562 (2016)

19. Inmon, B.: Data lake architecture: designing the data lake and avoiding the garbage dump. Technics publications (2016)

20. Kalfoglou, Y., Schorlemmer, M.: Ontology mapping: the state of the art. Knowl. Eng. Rev. **18**(1), 1–31 (2003)

21. Király, P., Büchler, M.: Measuring completeness as metadata quality metric in Europeana. In: 2018 IEEE International Conference on Big Data (Big Data), pp. 2711–2720. IEEE (2018)

22. Kyriacou, D.N.: Reliability and validity of diagnostic tests. Acad. Emerg. Med. **8**(4), 404–405 (2001)

23. Lemke, A.A., Wolf, W.A., Hebert-Beirne, J., Smith, M.E.: Public and biobank participant attitudes toward genetic research participation and data sharing. Public Health Genomics **13**(6), 368–377 (2010)

24. Litton, J.-E.: BBMRI-ERIC. Bioreservation Biobanking **16**(3) (2018)

25. Lorence, D.: Measuring disparities in information capture timeliness across healthcare settings: effects on data quality. J. Med. Syst. **27**(5), 425–433 (2003)

26. Lozano, L.M., García-Cueto, E., Muñiz, J.: Effect of the number of response categories on the reliability and validity of rating scales. Methodology **4**(2), 73–79 (2008)

27. Mandrekar, J.N.: Simple statistical measures for diagnostic accuracy assessment. J. Thorac. Oncol. **5**(6), 763–764 (2010)

28. Margaritopoulos, M., Margaritopoulos, T., Mavridis, I., Manitsaris, A.: Quantifying and measuring metadata completeness. J. Am. Soc. Inf. Sci. Technol. **63**(4), 724–737 (2012)

29. Mavrogiorgou, A., Kiourtis, A., Kyriazis, D.: Delivering reliability of data sources in IoT healthcare ecosystems. In: 2019 25th Conference of Open Innovations Association (FRUCT), pp. 211–219. IEEE (2019)

30. Merino-Martinez, R., et al.: Toward global biobank integration by implementation of the minimum information about biobank data sharing (MIABIS 2.0 Core). Biopreservation Biobanking **14**(4), 298–306 (2016)

31. Müller, H., Dagher, G., Loibner, M., Stumptner, C., Kungl, P., Zatloukal, K.: Biobanks for life sciences and personalized medicine: importance of standardization, biosafety, biosecurity, and data management. Curr. Opin. Biotechnol. **65**, 45–51 (2020)

32. Nahm, M.: Data quality in clinical research. In: Richesson, R., Andrews, J. (eds.) Clinical Research Informatics. Health Informatics, pp. 175–201. Springer, London (2012). https://doi.org/10.1007/978-1-84882-448-5_10

33. Nargesian, F., Zhu, E., Miller, R.J., Pu, K.Q., Arocena, P.C.: Data lake management: challenges and opportunities. Proc. VLDB Endow. **12**(12), 1986–1989 (2019)

34. Olson, J.E.: Data Quality: The Accuracy Dimension. Morgan Kaufmann, Burlington (2003)

35. Pichler, H., Eder, J.: Supporting the donation of health records to biobanks for medical research. In: Holzinger, A., Goebel, R., Mengel, M., Müller, H. (eds.) Artificial Intelligence and Machine Learning for Digital Pathology. LNCS (LNAI), vol. 12090, pp. 38–55. Springer, Cham (2020). https://doi.org/10.1007/978-3-030-50402-1_3

36. Radulovic, F., Mihindukulasooriya, N., García-Castro, R., Gómez-Pérez, A.: A comprehensive quality model for Linked Data. Semantic Web, Preprint (2017)

37. Sawadogo, P., Darmont, J.: On data lake architectures and metadata management. J. Intell. Inf. Syst., 1–24 (2020). https://doi.org/10.1007/s10844-020-00608-7

38. Skatova, A., Ng, E., Goulding, J.: Data donation: sharing personal data for public good. Application of Digital Innovation. N-Lab, London, England (2014)

39. Spjuth, O., et al.: Harmonising and linking biomedical and clinical data across disparate data archives to enable integrative cross-biobank research. Eur. J. Hum. Genet. **24**(4), 521–528 (2016)

40. Stark, K., Eder, J., Zatloukal, K.: Priority-based k-anonymity accomplished by weighted generalisation structures. In: Tjoa, A.M., Trujillo, J. (eds.) DaWaK 2006. LNCS, vol. 4081, pp. 394–404. Springer, Heidelberg (2006). https://doi.org/10.1007/11823728_38

41. Stark, K., Koncilia, C., Schulte, J., Schikuta, E., Eder, J.: Incorporating data provenance in a medical CSCW system. In: Bringas, P.G., Hameurlain, A., Quirchmayr, G. (eds.) DEXA 2010. LNCS, vol. 6261, pp. 315–322. Springer, Heidelberg (2010). https://doi.org/10.1007/978-3-642-15364-8_26

42. Stvilia, B., Gasser, L., Twidale, M.B., Shreeves, S.L., Cole, T.W.: Metadata quality for federated collections. In: Proceedings of the Ninth International Conference on Information Quality (ICIQ-04), pp. 111–125 (2004)

43. Tayi, G.K., Ballou, D.P.: Examining data quality. Commun. ACM **41**(2), 54–57 (1998)

44. Vaisman, A., Zimányi, E.: Data Warehouse Systems. Springer, Heidelberg (2014). https://doi.org/10.1007/978-3-642-54655-6

45. van Ommen, G.-J.B., et al.: BBMRI-ERIC as a resource for pharmaceutical and life science industries: the development of biobank-based expert Centres. Eur. J. Hum. Genet. **23**(7), 893–900 (2015)

46. Vuorio, E.: Networking biobanks throughout Europe: the development of BBMRI-ERIC. In: Hainaut, P., Vaught, J., Zatloukal, K., Pasterk, M. (eds.) Biobanking of Human Biospecimens, pp. 137–153. Springer, Cham (2017). https://doi.org/10.1007/978-3-319-55120-3_8

47. Zatloukal, K., Hainaut, P.: Human tissue biobanks as instruments for drug discovery and development: impact on personalized medicine. Biomark. Med. **4**(6), 895–903 (2010)

Security Issues in Big Data

Authorization Policy Extension for Graph Databases

Aya Mohamed[1,2(✉)], Dagmar Auer[1,2(✉)], Daniel Hofer[1,2], and Josef Küng[1,2]

[1] Institute for Application-oriented Knowledge Processing (FAW), Linz, Austria
[2] LIT Secure and Correct Systems Lab, Linz Institute of Technology (LIT),
Johannes Kepler University (JKU) Linz, Linz, Austria
{aya.mohamed,dagmar.auer,daniel.hofer,josef.kueng}@jku.at

Abstract. The high increase in the use of graph databases also
for business- and privacy-critical applications demands for a sophisticated, flexible, fine-grained authorization and access control approach.
Attribute-based access control (ABAC) supports a fine-grained definition
of authorization rules and policies. Attributes can be associated with the
subject, the requested resource and action, but also the environment.
Thus, this is a promising starting point. However, specific characteristics of graph-structured data such as attributes on vertices and edges
along a path to the resource, are not yet considered. The well-established
eXtensible Access Control Markup Language (XACML), which defines
a declarative language for fine-grained, attribute-based authorization
policies, is the basis for our proposed approach - XACML for Graph-
structured data (XACML4G). The additional path-specific constraints,
described in graph patterns, demand for specialized processing of the
rules and policies as well as adapted enforcement and decision making in
the access control process. To demonstrate XACML4G and its enforcement process, we present a scenario from the university domain. Due to
the project's environment, the prototype is built with the multi-model
database ArangoDB. The results are promising and further studies concerning performance and use in practice are planned.

Keywords: Authorization policy · Access control · ABAC · XACML ·
Graph database · ArangoDB

1 Introduction

The amount of data in IT systems is still growing exponentially. Besides the
amount, the value of data is increasing as well [21]. Enterprises, public services,
public and private organizations as well as individuals are highly interested not
to risk this value – more than that lost-, or stolen data could be used for harmful
and damaging actions. Consequently, data must be protected and access to data
must be controlled. This control has to be as close as possible to the data itself,
with no bypassing options.

© Springer Nature Switzerland AG 2020
T. K. Dang et al. (Eds.): FDSE 2020, LNCS 12466, pp. 47–66, 2020.
https://doi.org/10.1007/978-3-030-63924-2_3

More and more data is stored in graph databases today. Because of their natural and direct support of connected data objects, e.g., in social networks, identity and access management, recommendation systems, master data management, and the increasing expectations in knowledge graphs, graph databases are considered to have the potential to replace the existing relational market by 2030[1].

As graph databases are continuously entering business- and privacy-critical application domains, flexible, fine-grained authorization and access control are increasingly necessary. For now, established graph database systems such as *Neo4j*[2] or multi-model database systems such as *Microsoft Azure Cosmos DB*[3] and *ArangoDB*[4] provide role-based access control (RBAC), which is not sufficient for our demands with respect to applying fine-grained constraints on vertices and edges.

By now, authorization policies and access control mechanisms that support graph characteristics such as patterns on access paths are still missing. Therefore, access control in graph databases needs to be enhanced.

This work provides a solution for access control in graph databases from the policy specification to the enforcement of the proposed authorization policy language in graph databases. The overall process is demonstrated in a proof of concept prototype. Specifically, the contributions of our work are the following:

1. The *eXtensible Access Control Markup Language for Graph-structured data (XACML4G)*, a policy language based on the XACML structure (described in the JSON format) for expressing authorization policies for graph-structured data. XACML4G allows to describe patterns in terms of constraints on vertices and edges.
2. An initial implementation for enforcing XACML4G in the data layer.
3. A proof of concept prototype in the university domain, i.e., professors, students and courses.

The rest of the paper is structured as follows. Section 2 provides details concerning access control models, especially attribute-based access control and the well-established policy language XACML. They are the basis for the authorization and access control approach for graph databases developed within our research presented in Sect. 3. The proposed policy definition language, XACML4G, and the enforcement process are demonstrated by a proof of concept prototype in the university domain in Sect. 4. The paper concludes with a summary and an outlook on future work in Sect. 5.

---

[1] https://www.forbes.com/sites/cognitiveworld/2019/07/18/graph-databases-go-mainstream/#79c0f5d5179d.

[2] https://neo4j.com/docs/operations-manual/current/authentication-authorization/access-control/index.html.

[3] https://docs.microsoft.com/en-us/azure/cosmos-db/role-based-access-control.

[4] https://www.arangodb.com/docs/stable/oasis/access-control.html.

2 Related Work

The focus of our work is on highly flexible, fine-grained authorization policies for graph-structured data and their enforcement in a graph database. As authorization policies are an established means to allow for flexibility and separation of concerns, policies are one of the driving forces for including the following approaches into this discussion. An authorization policy defines the regulations, which define whether a requested access can be granted or not. Policies are applied in the access decision making during the enforcement process.

Regarding graph databases, we do not go into details here. For the basic concept it is sufficient to consider that a graph is a set of vertices which can be related in pairs to each other by edges. Both of them, vertices and edges are distinct entities with attributes. When traversing a graph, a certain path is paced [14].

In the following, we concentrate on potentially suitable access control models such as attribute-based access control (ABAC) and relation-based access control (RelBAC) before discussing the eXtensible Access Control Markup Language (XACML) that provides a policy definition language, along with the architecture and processing model for handling access requests.

2.1 Access Control Models

Due to the focus on graph-structured data, the flexible ABAC model and the RelBAC model, which specializes in relationships, are studied in more detail.

Attribute-Based Access Control (ABAC). The attribute-based access control model (ABAC) is a flexible access control model, based on arbitrary attributes of the subject (i.e., the user) and the requested resource, but also on action attributes and environmental conditions (e.g., time, device, location). It allows for fine-grained definition of access rights as rules. Access is granted or denied by evaluating the attributes against these authorization rules. No relationship between subject and resource is needed. The rules are typically defined in policies. Thus, ABAC is also often characterized as policy-based. Defining and managing the policies independently from the application. i.e., externalizing authorization, makes it much easier to coordinate access rights with dynamically evolving IT systems and authorization scenarios [18,20].

Even though ABAC is more complex than many other access control models, it is considered to be the most robust, scalable and flexible one in practice. Compared with the widely spread role-based access control model (RBAC), it not only avoids a huge number of difficult to manage roles, but especially problems due to overlapping roles with contradicting access right definitions. For example, with RBAC students who are also teaching assistants and are allowed to edit student's grades, such RBAC students cannot be denied to edit their own grades. With ABAC such ownership scenarios can be easily defined [7].

With ABAC relationships between the subjects, the resource, actions and the environment can be flexibly defined. Therefore, ABAC is very well suited for the flexible, fine-grained definition of access rights required in this project. However, it does not support patterns on the path from the subject to the resource, which is relevant for the access decision for some of our authorization scenarios (see Sect. 4).

Relation-Based Access Control (RelBAC). To deal with access rights in social networks, which can be naturally described by graph-structured data, the relation-based access control model (RelBAC) has been developed [15,16]. The focus is on interpersonal relationships between users, where permissions are modeled as relations between subject and object classes. However, RelBAC does not consider fine-grained access rights unlike ABAC.

Cheng et al. published a policy language in 2014 that integrates ABAC with RelBAC. Regular expressions are used to describe relations and their characteristics (e.g., depth and trust value) as an enhancement to their user-to-user relationship-based access control model (UURAC) [12] and subsequently user-to-resource and resource-to-resource relationships [11].

As conditions on the attributes of the entities are not considered with these models, we will concentrate on the very flexible ABAC model in the further.

2.2   eXtensible Access Control Markup Language (XACML)

While XACML stands for eXtensible Access Control Markup Language, it is not only a language, but also an architecture and processing model of how to evaluate access requests. XACML is an established OASIS[5] standard for nearly 20 years and widely used for ABAC. XACML has a strong and active community that continuously works on enhancements since the first version was approved in 2003.

Policy Language. It defines an XML-based declarative access control policy language with focus on fine-grained, attribute-based access control policies. It is hierarchically structured (see Fig. 1) with three main levels: policy set, policy and rule [1,18]:

- **Rule**: is the basic building block. Each rule holds a target, an effect, and one or more conditions. All rule elements are optional except for the rule effect. The effect determines whether access to an object is granted or denied.
- **Policy**: contains one to multiple rules which are combined according to the defined rule-combining algorithm.
- **Policy Set**: is a collection of policies and policy sets (i.e., a recursive structure). The policies and policy sets are combined according to the defined policy-combining algorithm.

---

[5] Organization for the Advancement of Structured Information Standards, www.oasis-open.org.

The target specifies the component's subject (who), action (what), and resource (which) by giving attributes and literals to compare with. The definition of the target is optional with all three components. It is a kind of filter to specify the relevant target. If the target is not defined in the rule, the one of the surrounding policy will be used, the same is true for the policy and the policy set. Defining no target at all, indicates that the rule is relevant for all access requests.

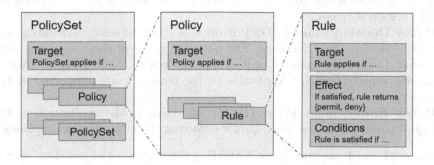

Fig. 1. XACML policy structure [6]

Since policies within the same policy set and rules inside a policy can return different decisions, the overall result is determined by combining the single decisions with a combining algorithm [4]. The following list provides some basic combining algorithms which are mostly implemented on policy level (rule-combining) as well as on policy set level (policy-combining) [9]:

- **Permit/Deny overrides:** with *permit overrides* the decision is permit if any of the rules or policies returns permit. The same is true for *deny overrides*, the safest combining algorithms.
- **First applicable:** the first decision taken is the overall decision
- **Only one applicable:** is only valid for combining policies and policy sets, but not for rules. A valid output is only achieved if exactly one of the children either returns the decision *Permit* or *Deny*.
- **Ordered permit/deny overrides:** like the Permit/Deny overrides algorithm, but takes the order of rules, policies, and policy sets into account.
- **Permit unless deny/Deny unless permit:** guarantees that either *Permit* or *Deny* is returned. *Not Applicable* and *Indeterminate* are not considered.

Authorization requirements are specified in authorization policies using the policy definition language of XACML. These XACML policies are used with the XACML architecture to determine the result of the access control request. This allows for a high level of flexibility as they are not implemented within the source code.

Architecture. The XACML architecture (see Fig. 2) consists of several functional components, so-called points [17,18]:

- **Policy Administration Point (PAP)**: its role is to create, modify, and distribute policies.
- **Policy Retrieval Point (PRP)**: it represents the point where XACML authorization policies are stored.
- **Policy Information Point (PIP)**: it is an intermediate point between the data source, to which attribute requests are sent, and the PDP, to which the information is passed.
- **Policy Decision Point (PDP)**: it decides about access by evaluating and issuing authorization decisions. The outcome is one of these four decisions: Permit, Deny, Indeterminate (if it cannot be decided, e.g., in case of error or missing values), and Not Applicable (if the request is not supported by the policy).
- **Policy Enforcement Point (PEP)**: employed in the application as the logical point, which is responsible for enforcing the authorization decisions.

An established way to enforce XACML polices with relational databases is query rewriting. Query rewriting extends the user query with information from the authorization policy. This approach is used for example with the Virtual Private Database (VPD) mechanism introduced by Oracle [10] and the Truman model [22]. Besides the inconsistencies between user expectations and system output (e.g., unexpected incorrect query results instead of rejected user request) also decidability issues [8] pose practical problems.

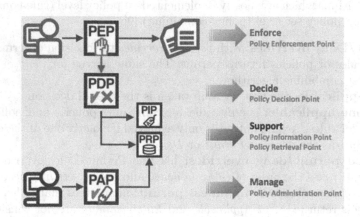

Fig. 2. XACML architecture [3]

This architecture supports separation of concerns, so that authorization policies are managed independently of their application in access control.

For now no applications of XACML for graph-structured data have been reported. Some research is available on using graph databases to manage XACML policies using policy graphs [5,13,19], but not for graph-structured data sources. The well-established XACML policy description language and its architecture are still a promising viable starting point for our approach. Therefore, XACML is the basis for the proposed extensions to be discussed in the next section.

3   XACML4G

The proposed idea presented in this paper is to extend authorization policies so that they can support graph-specific access control as well. The standard BPMN 2.0[6] diagram visualized by Fig. 3 is representing the architecture of our framework. XACML architecture has been used as a reference basis. Policy processing in this methodology is independent of the user access requests and database queries. Very often policy enforcement approaches are based on implementing an intermediate layer between the user and the database at the application level where the policy preprocessing takes place and the user query is rewritten to embed the access rights requirements. In our solution the system works in the database layer for better performance and security. The upcoming subsections will address each of the modules in detail beginning with a motivation and definition of the problem.

3.1   Policy Languages Limitations

Most of the current policy languages are limited to describing subjects, objects, and access rights. Relations between entities could be represented using joining conditions by mapping primary and foreign keys of the tables in relational databases. However, when it comes to specifying policies for graph databases, it will be necessary to formulate conditions on edges and vertices that are neither subject nor resource vertices. They belong to the path between them. An example of such a policy to be applied to a graph data model is given below to demonstrate how the policy components are extracted and the relation between them is described. Thus, policy languages need to be extended to detect paths with certain patterns. Since XACML is the most commonly used language for specifying fine-grained security policies, the policy format in this work is an extension for XACML structure. For easier formulation and parsing, it is implemented in JSON instead of XML. Our approach overcomes the limitations of XACML to adapt with graph-structured data by adding an extra feature to specify the patterns, how subject and object vertices are related to each other, and conditions on the attributes of the vertices as well as edges along the path.

---

[6] https://www.omg.org/spec/BPMN/2.0/PDF
http://www.bpmb.de/images/BPMN2_0_Poster_EN.pdf.

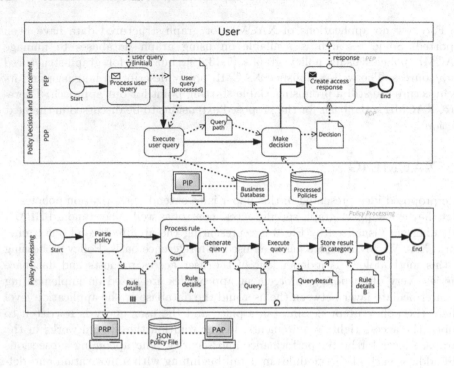

Fig. 3. Policy enforcement process

> *Example 1.* "Professors are allowed to read data of
> students enrolled in their courses"

- **Subject:** professor
- **Object:** student
- **Action:** read
- **Additional constraints that could not be mapped in XACML:** their
  courses, where a pattern like "professor → course → student" is needed to
  indicate that the professor and student entities are connected through a vertex
  of type course. Otherwise, undesired output could result because there could
  be various paths, with respect to length or content, between the given subject
  and resource. Thus, there is a significant demand for adding path patterns in
  policies for graph-structured data.

3.2   Extended Policy Format

Based on the current limitations to express policies for graph databases, the
JSON formatted authorization policy definition language XACML4G is introduced. This novel policy format extends the state of the art security policies in a
way such that the JSON file consists of a list of policies structured like XACML
with an extra feature for specifying graph requirements such as conditions on the
vertices along with the in-between relations. This pattern property is inspired by

the syntax of Cypher[7] for matching patterns of nodes and relationships in the graph. Note that being well familiar with the graph model and its architecture is a requirement for policy writing. Listing 1 depicts the template used for defining the authorization policies in this work to be enforced in any graph database. Each policy is composed of policy ID, rule combining algorithm, and rules list. Rules are the fundamental elements defined with a design similar to XACML rules implementing the concept of *effect, target,* and *condition* as explained in the rule components list:

- **Rule ID:** unique identifier for each rule.
- **Target:** action type, subject and resource vertices are specified along with their conditions.
- **Pattern (optional):** to specify nodes, their connections, and characteristics on the attributes level. If no pattern is specified, the result is the shortest path between the subject and object vertices. Long or unknown patterns can be split and joined in the condition.
- **Condition (optional):** to join vertices/edges upon certain attributes.
- **Effect:** represents the rule decision whether to grant access to the resource through the returned paths satisfying the described patterns or not.

```
{
   "policy-combining-algorithm":"first-applicable,permit/deny-
        override,etc",
   "policy":[
   {
     "id":"policy_id",
     "rule-combining-algorithm":"first-applicable,
        permit/deny-override,etc",
     "rule":[
     {
       "id":"rule_id",
       "target":{
       "subject":"entity.attribute op value",
       "resource":"entity.attribute op value",
       "action":"read/write"
       },
       "pattern":"(var1:entity{key:value})
                     -[]->
                     (var2:entity{key:value})",
       "condition":"var1.attribute op var2.attribute",
       "effect":"permit/deny"
     }]
   }]
}
```

Listing 1. Policy in JSON format

3.3   Policy Processing

After establishing the authorization policies and converting them from the text to JSON format in the previous step, the procedure of policy processing is carried out in three stages: policy parsing, query generation and execution as well as

---

[7] Cypher is the declarative query language used to work with graphs in Neo4j (https://neo4j.com/docs/cypher-manual/current/introduction/).

classification. These components along with the decision maker belong to the PDP. Firstly, the list of policies has to be parsed to get the parameters and filter conditions (Rule details A in Fig. 3) which will serve as input to the database query which is dynamically generated to get the paths with the designated patterns. The query execution component communicates with the database for retrieving further attributes related to subject, action, resource and environment of the request. Listing 2 shows an example of the query template in AQL (see Sect. 4.1) with variables representing the inputs extracted from the policy file and the statements that correspond to the selected database query language syntax are generated accordingly.

```
FOR x in ${subjectCollection}
${subjectQueryFilter}
FOR v, e, p IN ${depth}..${depth}
ANY x GRAPH ${graphName}
${graphQueryFilters}
RETURN p.vertices[*]._key
```

Listing 2. AQL Query Template

The variable *subjectCollection* is equivalent to entity in the policy. *subjectQueryFilter* represents the subject conditions. *depth* is the length of each path in the pattern such that it is calculated from the count of the edges representing the number of hops. Finally, *graphQueryFilters* is a variable consisting of several AQL filter statements generated from the rule pattern conditions for each vertex/edge in the path including the resource vertex.

Meanwhile extracting the query requirements, the parser also saves the name of the combining algorithms that will be used to resolve conflicts not only between rules of the same policy, but also on the policies level. For each policy, the rule combining algorithm is obtained from the policy file and both are represented as key-value pair. The same is true for the policy combining algorithm, but in this case *"general"* is the key. All of the policies are identified by their id and stored as subset of the object as illustrated below.

```
{
    "general":"policy-combining-algorithm",
    "policyID":"rule-combining-algorithm"
}
```

Based on the rule effect (Rule details B in Fig. 3), the paths resulting from the query execution module are assigned to one of the categories, either permit or deny. In this process, the output paths satisfying the specified description in the policy are saved in a way that will also help in the next step, decision-making, as stated in the data structure below. This JSON snippet is composed of the categories as keys and the value is a list of other objects where each of them has a key consisting of a concatenated string of an integer index along with the ID of the policy and rule to which the value, an array of the resulting paths, is associated. Each path is a list of vertices. The role of the variable index in the access decision procedure will be explained in the upcoming subsection.

```
{
    "permit":[{"index:policyID.ruleID":[path,..]}],
    "deny":[{"index:policyID.ruleID":[path,..]}]
}
```

3.4   Decision-Making

This is the last phase in the enforcement process where the final decision is taken for the response to the user requesting access. For each access control request, the query path from the principal to the requested resource, i.e. query result, is checked against the categorized output of the policy patterns. The decision is according to Table 1. For instance, if the query result exists in the permit category and not in the denied one, this means that access to the resource is granted using this path according to the predetermined policies. Hence, the access decision response, in this case, will be *Permit*.

Table 1. Access decision for categories permutations

Access decision	Category	
	Permit	Deny
Permit	✓	✗
Deny	✗	✓
Not Applicable[a]	✗	✗
Indeterminate[b]	✓	✓

[a]Nothing is specified in the policy to decide the access and the PEP will handle this situation.
[b]Conflict between rules of the same or different policies. Rule/ Policy combining algorithm (see Sect. 2.2) resolves the conflicts to determine the final decision.

The entire decision-making process is summarized in Fig. 4. The procedure starts with one start event, but has several end events to reflect the different possible decision-making situations: without any conflict, with conflicts resolved within the policies and no overall conflict resolution and finally the end point which requires full conflict resolution, i.e. within the policies but also by integrating all policies. The upcoming subsection discusses the conflict resolution on both levels in details.

As per Fig. 5, the output from checking the user query path against the prespecified policies is converted from the format that is returned and examined in the decision making process to a structure where the policies are the keys instead of the categories. This conversion is crucial to differentiate between the levels of conflict, whether between rules within one policy, or rules across several policies, and also might result in automatic conflict resolution at one of these

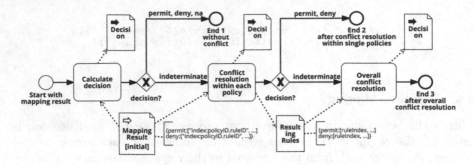

Fig. 4. Decision-making process

levels. Before this conversion the format was a collection of categories with a list of some compound variables indicating the rule and the policy containing this input, the query path, combined together with an index representing the rule order. This compound variable is used earlier in the result of the *Permit/Deny Classifier* as a key in the categorized list of collections (*index:policyID.ruleID*). Then, it becomes a collection of policies having rule indices as the value.

Starting from this intermediate result, the duplicate elimination stage takes place before the conflict resolution. For each policy, duplicates are handled per category by selecting the rule with the minimum index regardless of the combining algorithm. This is to guarantee that the right access permission will be returned in case of having a *first-applicable* as a combining algorithm for rule and/or policy.

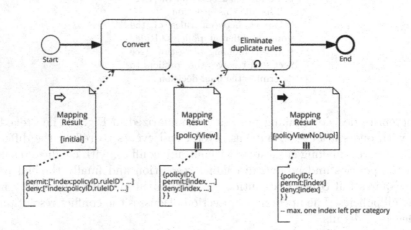

Fig. 5. Subprocess: convert and eliminate duplicates

Until now, the JSON-formatted authorization policies are parsed to retrieve the subject, resource, action and environment conditions which are then passed to the query generator module. Upon retrieving the results which are basically paths satisfying the described patterns in the policy, they are classified and stored to end up the policy processing phase. The decision maker component in this subsection eventually takes part by checking the output of a user query against the existing paths causing conflicts if the respective rules have different effects. Thus, the next step is executed in the case of having an *Indeterminate* decision after the conversion and duplicate elimination subprocess trying to reach a determined access decision by applying the rule and policy combining algorithms.

3.5 Conflict Resolution

In this context a conflict occurs when the criteria of more than one rule having different effects are satisfied. For achieving a determined decision, the conflicts, regardless of their level, have to be resolved using the combining algorithm. Although the resolution method is the same for any conflict level, the conflict for each level is investigated and resolved individually according to the outcome of the check point, i.e. decision.

The conflict is resolved after the completion of the post-decision-making subprocess, which is responsible for converting the output of decision-making and eliminating duplicated rules having identical effects within the same policy (if any), in two steps as exemplified in Fig. 5 starting with the rules within policies followed by rules across different policies if a conflict still exists. The conflict resolution function input parameters are the combining algorithm along with a group of collections having the category and the winning rule index after eliminating duplicates as key and value respectively. The combining algorithm is retrieved from the previously stored data structure using either the policy identifier, or *general* as a key depending on the level of conflict. Conflicts are resolved by returning *permit* in case of *permit-overrides*, or *deny-unless-permit* and *deny* for the opposite combining algorithms, i.e. *deny-overrides* and *permit-unless-deny*. For the *first-applicable* combining algorithm, the decision of the minimum rule index will be returned. Otherwise, the default access decision, *indeterminate*, will be returned.

In accordance with the first conflict resolution attempt, the winning rule index is saved in the category of the returned decision and an intermediate decision is made according to the strategy discussed in Sect. 3.4. Based on this decision, it may be needed to repeat the process of the conflict resolution, but on the level of rules across policies.

4 Demonstration Case

To demonstrate the applicability of the proposed extension for the authorization policy language and how constraints on paths of graph-structured data are expressed and enforced in a graph database, this section presents a case study.

A policy for a scenario is formulated and applied starting with an overview of the chosen graph database and the framework used in the implementation followed by a description of the selected scenario along with a proper visualization for our database model. Finally, the results for each step from representing the policy in terms of rule(s) having a target, conditions on vertices as well as edges, and an effect till obtaining the access decision are exemplified.

4.1 ArangoDB and Foxx Microservices

ArangoDB is the selected database management system for the prototype discussed in this paper because of several reasons. It will fit the storing requirements for any application since it supports more than one data model. Moreover, it has an application framework named Foxx that is directly communicating with the database. Finally, dealing with graphs in AQL, ArangoDB's query language, is not straight forward like in Neo4j, the leading GraphDB according to DB-Engines Ranking of Graph DBMS in July 2020[8]. Thus, if some concept proves to be doable with ArangoDB, it will be feasible for other graph databases.

ArangoDB is a non-relational open source multi-model database management system written in C++. This system supports documents, key/value, and graphs. These schema-free No-SQL models have one database core and one declarative query language for retrieving and modifying data. Its query language is called AQL and has some extra functionality to enable complex graph traversals. However, it does not support data definition operations including creating and dropping databases, collections, and indexes.

Foxx services are embedded inside ArangoDB that can be run as an application directly within the database with native access to in-memory data and hence, network overhead is avoided. Furthermore, it makes ArangoDB extensible because custom HTTP endpoints are added to ArangoDB's REST API using pure structured JavaScript. Actually, this tool is optimal in case of using queries frequently. Moreover, the synchronicity of ArangoDB APIs is maintained because the JavaScript code is running inside the database [2].

4.2 Model and Scenario

A university scenario is chosen for demonstrating and testing the proposed approach. The database is composed of *professors* teaching *courses* that are attended by *students* who are graded for their course(s). The graph constructed for this use case is illustrated in Fig. 6. The model is composed of one entity named *dataObjects* with an attribute called *typeCode* to differentiate between the data groups.

4.3 Results

Recalling the policy example defined for this scenario earlier in Sect. 3.1, it can now be expressed using the new format. The text and the corresponding policy

---

[8] https://db-engines.com/en/ranking/graph+dbms

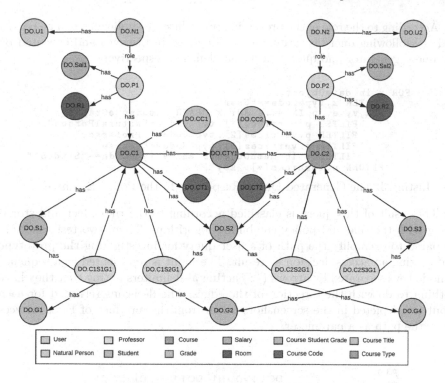

Fig. 6. Uni scenario database model

syntax in JSON are demonstrated in the below example bearing in mind that conditions not only could be added on vertices but also on edges.

Example 2. "Professors are allowed to view students in their courses"

```
{
  "policy-combining-algorithm":"first-applicable",
  "policy":[
  {
    "id":"user_to_students",
    "rule-combining-algorithm":"permit-overrides",
    "rule":[
    {
      "id":"allow_professors_students_theirCourses",
      "target":{
        "subject":"dataObjects.typeCode=='User'",
        "resource":"dataObjects.typeCode=='Student'",
        "action":"read"
      },
      "pattern":["(subject)<-[]-(dataObjects{typeCode:'
        NaturalPerson'})-[]->(dataObjects{typeCode:
        'Professor'})<-[]-(dataObjects{typeCode:'Course'
        })-[]->(resource)"],
      "effect":"permit"
    }]
  }]
}
```

According to the role of the processing procedure, the policy file will be parsed and the following query is formulated as depicted in Listing 3 and executed by the query generator and query execution elements respectively.

```
FOR x in dataObjects
    FILTER x.typeCode=="User"
    FOR v, e, p IN 4..4 ANY x GRAPH 'InstanceGraph'
        FILTER p.vertices[1].typeCode=="NaturalPerson"
        FILTER p.vertices[2].typeCode=="Professor"
        FILTER p.vertices[3].typeCode=="Course"
        FILTER v in dataObjects and v.typeCode=="Student"
    RETURN p.vertices[*]._key
```

Listing 3: The Generated Query Respective to the Policy Example

The result of this query is classified according to the rule effect and stored along with the rule and policy combining algorithms. Then, two test cases are prepared to exemplify the path of a user query for investigating the prototype and getting an access decision as result. The input is represented as a sequence of node keys separated by arrows (->) acting as delimiters noting that they have nothing to do with the direction of the edges. The decisions returned for each input are depicted in the screenshots taken from the interface of Foxx services given the path as a parameter.

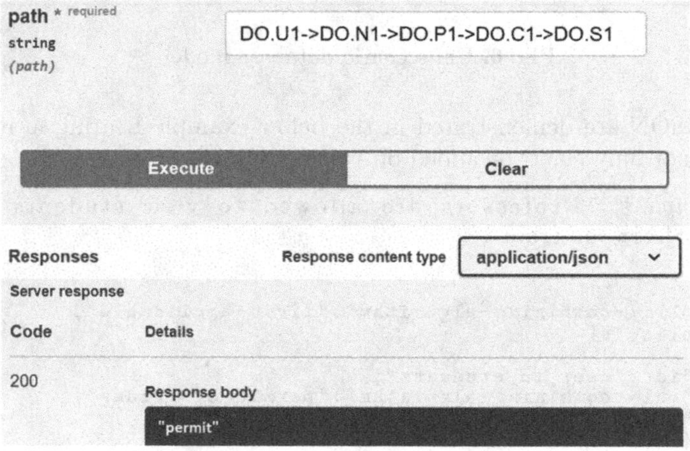

Fig. 7. Test case 1 result: permit

Case 1. DO.U1→DO.N1→DO.P1→DO.C1→DO.S1

Since *"S1"* is one of the students attending the course *"C1"* that is lectured by user *"U1"* who has a role of professor *"P1"*, the access should be allowed (see Fig. 7) for any user query returning this path because of the *Permit* rule effect. A *Deny* decision would have been returned for the same path if stated in the rule effect of the policy. On the contrary, if the legitimate users are trying to access a resource in a non-recognized pattern, the response will be *Not Applicable (NA)*. Thus, the authorization of principal, resource, and pattern is mandatory for obtaining access.

Case 2. DO.U2→DO.N2→DO.P2→DO.C2→DO.S1

According to the data model in Fig. 6, there is no such path. However, any other path will return the same *NA* decision as per the output in Fig. 8 even if there is a valid connection. This is because the policy defined for this scenario does not support this input.

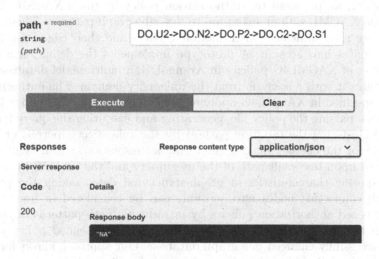

Fig. 8. Test case 2 result. NA

To sum up, this initial implementation demonstrates the feasibility of the proposed concept. Fine-grained attribute-based policies can be enforced as shown be the results of testing the prototype for the above two cases as well as for other complex ones. Due to the current size of the test dataset, no reliable statements regarding the performance of the policy enforcement can be provided. Hence, more testing is necessary, especially with more complex application scenarios and much more data. Furthermore, the following additional requirements for the policy description have been identified when working on the test cases:

- Reuse of graph patterns (iterative or recursive). The main challenge is to determine the depth of recursive calls or iterations in advance, as this is needed for generating the respective query.
- Syntax for optional sub-patterns directly within the rule or by reusing an additional rule via double curly brackets, e.g., {{*subpath/ruleID*}}.
- Inconsistent direction of edges along the path (inbound and outbound): handling different directions on a path is supported by Neo4j, but complicated to handle for each hop in ArangoDB.

– Extend subject, resource, and condition in policies to have more than one statement joined with and/or. Applying this on the condition will give a privilege to our language as this is not possible in XACML. A possible syntax for this notion could be exemplified via the following example:

```
"subject":{"or":["dataObjects._key=='DO.U1'","dataObjects.
    _key=='DO.U2'"]}
```

5   Conclusion

In this paper, we proposed the authorization policy language XACML4G that is based on XACML with an extension to describe graph patterns. These graph patterns are used to define constraints on vertices and their edges also taking their attributes into account. A prototype implements the definition and the enforcement of XACML4G policies in ArangoDB, a multi-model database, and demonstrates it with a scenario from the university domain. The authorization policy is specified in XACML4G applying the JSON format. The policy is processed (incl. parsing the policy file, generating and executing the query for each rule, and clustering the resulting path(s) by the rule effect - permit or deny) to prepare for the decision making (incl. conflict resolution) which finally takes place based upon the result path of the user query and the processed policy.

The specific characteristics of graph-structured data, taking the path in the graph connecting nodes into account, can be considered in fine-grained, attribute-based authorization policies by introducing path patterns in the policy. With the demonstration case, we show that this extended policy format can be successfully enforced in a graph database. Our approach allows for more sophisticated attribute-based authorization policies than role-based access control, which is the choice in existing graph database tools (e.g., Neo4j[9]). Very specific authorization scenarios as presented in the demonstration before, e.g., a professor can only read their student's data, or typical ownership requirements (e.g., every student can read their own data) can be easily implemented.

The results of the demonstration cases show that the approach is promising. The application of XACML4G in graph databases is feasible for demonstration scenarios. Still more research is needed to test this approach on a larger scale with more complex policies, data models and data sets. Furthermore, additional requirements concerning the policy definition have been identified when working on the demonstration case such as the reuse of graph patterns, allowing for optional patterns, inconsistent direction of edges along a path and more complex path patterns including several conditions. Thus, in future work we will concentrate on performance testing as well as the requirements concerning the advanced features for the policy description language and the resulting policy enforcement.

---

[9] https://neo4j.com/blog/role-based-access-control-neo4j-enterprise/,
https://neo4j.com/docs/operations-manual/current/authentication-authorization/
access-control/.

Acknowledgement. The research reported in this paper has been partly supported by the LIT Secure and Correct Systems Lab funded by the State of Upper Austria and by the Austrian Ministry for Transport, Innovation and Technology, the Federal Ministry of Science, Research and Economy, and the Province of Upper Austria in the frame of the COMET center SCCH.

References

1. A Brief Introduction to XACML. https://www.oasis-open.org/committees/download.php/2713/Brief_Introduction_to_XACML.html. Accessed July 2020
2. Foxx Microservices. https://www.arangodb.com/docs/stable/foxx.html. Accessed July 2020
3. Scaling XACML architecture deployment. https://www.axiomatics.com/blog/scaling-xacml-architecture-deployment/. Accessed July 2020
4. eXtensible Access Control Markup Language (XACML) Version 3.0 - OASIS Standard, 22 January 2013. http://docs.oasis-open.org/xacml/3.0/xacml-3.0-core-spec-os-en.html. Accessed July 2020
5. Ahmadi, H., Small, D.: Graph model implementation of attribute-based access control policies. arXiv preprint arXiv:1909.09904 (2019)
6. Anderson, A.: Extensible access control markup language (XACML). Technology report (2003)
7. Axiomatics: What is attribute-based access control? White Paper (2016). https://ma.axiomatics.com/acton/ct/10529/s-02c9-1707/Bct/l-0586/l-0586:3307/ct7_0/1?sid=TV2%3AmFBxh9FWI
8. Bertino, E., Sandhu, R.: Database security-concepts, approaches, and challenges. IEEE Trans. Dependable Secur. Comput. **2**(1), 2–19 (2005)
9. Brossard, D.: Understanding XACML Combining Algorithms, 15 June 2014. https://www.axiomatics.com/blog/understanding-xacml-combining-algorithms/. Accessed July 2020
10. Browder, K., Davidson, M.A.: The virtual private database in oracle9ir2. Oracle Technical White Paper, Oracle Corporation **500**, 280 (2002)
11. Cheng, Y., Park, J., Sandhu, R.: Relationship-based access control for online social networks: beyond user-to-user relationships. In: 2012 International Conference on Privacy, Security, Risk and Trust and 2012 International Conference on Social Computing, pp. 646–655. IEEE (2012)
12. Cheng, Y., Park, J., Sandhu, R.: A user-to-user relationship-based access control model for online social networks. In: Cuppens-Boulahia, N., Cuppens, F., Garcia-Alfaro, J. (eds.) DBSec 2012. LNCS, vol. 7371, pp. 8–24. Springer, Heidelberg (2012). https://doi.org/10.1007/978-3-642-31540-4_2
13. Diez, F.P., Vasu, A.C., Touceda, D.S., Cámara, J.M.S.: Modeling XACML security policies using graph databases. IT Prof. **19**(6), 52–57 (2017)
14. Fletcher, G., Hidders, J., Larriba-Pey, J.L.: Graph Data Management - Fundamental Issues and Recent Developments. Springer, Cham (2018). https://doi.org/10.1007/978-3-319-96193-4. ISBN 978-3-319-96192-7
15. Fong, P.W.: Relationship-based access control: protection model and policy language. In: Proceedings of the First ACM Conference on Data and Application Security and Privacy, pp. 191–202 (2011)
16. Giunchiglia, F., Zhang, R., Crispo, B.: RelBAC: relation based access control. In: 2008 Fourth International Conference on Semantics, Knowledge and Grid, pp. 3–11. IEEE (2008)

17. Hu, V.C., et al.: Guide to attribute based access control (ABAC) definition and considerations. NIST Special Publication **800**(162) (2019). https://doi.org/10.6028/NIST.SP.800-162
18. Hu, V.C., Ferraiolo, D.F., Chandramouli, R., Kuhn, D.R.: Attribute-Based Access Control. Artech House, Norwood (2018)
19. Jin, Y., Kaja, K.: XACML implementation based on graph database. In: Proceedings of 34th International Conference on Computers and Their Applications, vol. 58, pp. 65–74 (2019)
20. Mohan, A.: Design and implementation of an attribute-based authorization management system. Ph.D. thesis, Georgia Institute of Technology (2011)
21. Reinsel, D., Gantz, J., Rydning, J.: Data age 2025: the digitization of the world - from edge to core (2018). https://www.seagate.com/files/www-content/our-story/trends/files/idc-seagate-dataage-whitepaper.pdf
22. Rizvi, S., Mendelzon, A., Sudarshan, S., Roy, P.: Extending query rewriting techniques for fine-grained access control. In: Proceedings of the 2004 ACM SIGMOD international conference on Management of data, pp. 551–562 (2004)

A Model-Driven Approach for Enforcing Fine-Grained Access Control for SQL Queries

Phước Bảo Hoàng Nguyễn[(✉)] and Manuel Clavel

Vietnamese-German University, Thu Dau Mot City, Vietnam
ngpbhoang1406@gmail.com, manuel.clavel@vgu.edu.vn

Abstract. In this paper we propose a novel, model-driven approach for enforcing fine-grained access control (FGAC) policies when executing SQL queries. More concretely, we define a function SecQuery() that, given a FGAC policy $\mathcal{S}$ and a SQL select-statement q, generates a SQL stored-procedure, such that: if a user is authorized, according to $\mathcal{S}$, to execute q, then calling this stored-procedure returns the same result that executing q; otherwise, if a user is not authorized, according to $\mathcal{S}$, to execute q, then calling this stored-procedure signals an error. We have implemented our approach in an open-source project, called SQL Security Injector (SQLSI).

1 Introduction

Model-Driven Security (MDS) [1,2] is a specialization of model-driven engineering for developing secure systems. In MDS, designers specify system models along with their security requirements, and use tools to generate security-related artifacts, such as access control infrastructures. SecureUML [8] is 'de facto' modeling language used in MDS for specifying *fine-grained access control policies* (FGAC). These are policies that depend not only on static information, namely the assignments of users and permissions to roles, but also on dynamic information, namely the satisfaction of *authorization constraints* by the current state of the system. The Structure Query Language (SQL) [15] is a special-purpose programming language designed for managing data in relational database management systems (RDBMS). Its scope includes data insert, query, update and delete, and schema creation and modification. None of the major commercial RDBMS currently supports FGAC policies in a "native" way.

In [12] we have proposed a model-based characterization of FGAC *authorization* for SQL queries. In our proposal, FGAC-policies are modeled using a "dialect" of SecureUML. The challenge we address now is how to effectively *enforce* FGAC policies when executing SQL queries. Our solution consists of defining a function SecQuery() that, given a SecureUML model $\mathcal{S}$ and a SQL select-statement q, generates a SQL stored-procedure, such that: if a user is authorized, according to $\mathcal{S}$, to execute q, then calling this stored-procedure

© Springer Nature Switzerland AG 2020
T. K. Dang et al. (Eds.): FDSE 2020, LNCS 12466, pp. 67–86, 2020.
https://doi.org/10.1007/978-3-030-63924-2_4

returns the same result that executing q; otherwise, if a user is not authorized, according to $\mathcal{S}$, to execute q, then calling this stored-procedure signals an error. Informally, we can say that the stored-procedure generated by SecQuery() is the *secure* version of the query q with respect to the FGAC policy $\mathcal{S}$, or that the stored-procedure generated by SecQuery() *secures* the query q with respect to the FGAC policy $\mathcal{S}$.

Organization. The rest of the paper is organized as follows. In Sect. 2 we motivate with examples some of the problems we aim to address when securing SQL queries. Then, in Sect. 3 we introduce our modeling language for specifying FGAC policies. This section, along with the technical definitions related to it in Appendixes A and B, includes background material, which is needed for the rest of the paper. Next, in Sect. 4 we propose our novel model-driven approach for enforcing FGAC policies for SQL queries, and in Section 5 we present SQLSI, a Java application that implements our solution. These two sections, along with the technical definition related to them in Appendix C, contain the main contributions of our paper. Finally, in Sects. 6 and Sect. 7, we discuss related and future work. Notice that, for the sake of readability, we have moved all technical definitions to the appendix.

2 Motivation

Informally, enforcing an FGAC policy when executing a SQL query means guaranteeing that the execution of the query does not leak confidential information. Interestingly, this implies much more than simply checking that the final result satisfies the applicable FGAC policy, since a clever attacker can devise a query such that the simple fact that a final result is obtained reveals already some additional information, which maybe confidential. To illustrate this problem, we introduce a simple example of information leakage resulting from allowing users to execute "unsecured" queries.

Let us consider a simple database `UniversityDB` containing three tables: `Lecturer`, for representing lecturers; `Student`, for representing students; and `Enrollment`, for representing the links between the students and their lecturers. The tables `Lecturer` and `Student` have the columns `Lecturer_id` and `Student_id` as their respective primary keys. The table `Enrollment` has two columns, namely, `lecturers` and `students`, which are foreign keys, associated respectively to `Lecturer_id` and `Student_id`. Finally, both tables `Lecturer` and `Student` have columns `name` and `email`.

Consider now the select-statements in Figs. 1, 2 and 3. For the sake of this example, suppose that, for a given scenario, the three of them return the same final result, namely, a non-empty string, representing an email, which is not confidential. On a closer examination, however, we can realize that, for each of these select-statements, the final result is revealing *additional* information, which may in turn be confidential. In particular,

- Query#1 reveals that the resulting email belongs to Huong.
- Query#2 reveals not only that the resulting email belongs to Huong, but also that Thanh is enrolled in a course that Huong is teaching.
- Query#3 reveals that the email belongs to Huong, and that Huong and Manuel are "colleagues", in the sense that there some students who have both Huong and Manuel as their lecturers.

```
mysql> SELECT email FROM Lecturer WHERE Lecturer_id = 'Huong';
```

Fig. 1. Example. Query#1.

```
mysql> SELECT DISTINCT email FROM Lecturer
-> JOIN (SELECT * FROM Enrollment
->        WHERE students = 'Thanh' AND lecturers = 'Huong' ) AS TEMP
-> ON TEMP.lecturers = Lecturer_id;
```

Fig. 2. Example. Query#2.

```
mysql> SELECT DISTINCT email FROM Lecturer
-> JOIN (SELECT e1.lecturers as lecturers
->        FROM (SELECT * FROM Enrollment WHERE lecturers = 'Huong' ) AS e1
->        JOIN (SELECT * FROM Enrollment WHERE lecturers = 'Manuel' ) AS e2
->        ON e1.students = e2.students ) AS TEMP
-> ON TEMP.lecturers = Lecturer_id;
```

Fig. 3. Example. Query#3.

As the above example shows, in order to enforce an FGAC policy when executing a SQL query, it is not enough to simply check that displaying the final result is policy-compliance. On the contrary, we claim that *any* information that is *used* to reach this final result (in particular, information involved in subqueries, where-clauses, and on-clauses) should be also checked for policy-compliance. In this way, for example, if a user is not authorized to know whether Huong is Thanh's lecturer or not, then, when attempting to execute Query#2, he/she should receive an authorization-error, even when he/she may be authorized to access Huong's email. Similarly, if a user is not authorized to know whether Huong and Manuel are "colleagues" or not, then, when executing Query#3, he/she should receive an authorization-error, even when he/she may be authorized to access lecturers' emails.

3   Modeling Fine-Grained Access Control Policies

Our approach for enforcing FGAC policies for SQL queries is *model-driven*. This means, first of all, that policies are specified using *models*, and, secondly, that the corresponding policy-enforcement artifacts are *generated* from these models. Next, we introduce the language SecureUML for modeling FGAC policies. In the next section, we will introduce the policy-enforcement artifacts that can be generated from SecureUML models for executing *securely* SQL queries.

SecureUML [8] is a modeling language for specifying FGAC policies. It is an extension of Role-Based Access Control (RBAC) [6]. As it is well-known, in RBAC permissions are assigned to roles, and roles are assigned to users. However, in SecureUML one can model access control decisions that depend on two kinds of information: namely, static information, i.e., the assignments of users and permissions to roles; and dynamic information, i.e., the satisfaction of *authorization constraints* by the current state of the system.

SecureUML leaves open the nature of the protected *resources*,—i.e., whether these resources are data, business objects, processes, controller states, etc.—and, consequently, the nature of the corresponding controlled *actions*. These are to be declared in a so-called SecureUML dialect. In particular, in our approach, the data that is protected is modelled using *classes* and *associations*,—as in standard UML class diagrams—, while the actions that are controlled are *read*-actions on class attributes and association-ends. Authorization constraints are specified in SecureUML models using OCL expressions. Concretely, in our approach, we consider authorization constraints whose satisfaction depend on information related to: (i) the user who is attempting to perform the read-action; (ii) the object whose attribute is attempted to be read; and, (iii) the objects between which a link is attempted to be read. By convention, we denote (i) by the keyword `caller`; we denote (ii) by the keyword `self`; and we denote (iii) by using as keywords the corresponding association-ends.

In Appendix A we give the formal definition of SecureUML models, as well as of their underlying data models. We also give there a short description of the OCL language. To end this section, we introduce some examples of SecureUML models that will be used throughout the rest of this paper. The interested reader can find in [12] a more thorough discussion about the *meaning* of SecureUML models, i.e., about the actions that they authorize, making use of the same examples presented below.

Let us consider a simple data model `University` that contains two classes, `Student` and `Lecturer`, and one association `Enrollment` between both of them. Both classes, `Student` and `Lecturer`, have attributes `name` and `email`. The class `Student` represents the students of the university, with their names and emails. The class `Lecturer` represents the lecturers of the university, with their names and emails. The association `Enrollment` represents the links between the students (denoted by `students`) and their lecturers (denoted by `lecturers`). In the rest of the paper, we will consider the following two scenarios of `University`. First, let us consider a scenario `VGU#1` containing five students: `An`, `Chau`, `Hoang`, `Thanh`, and `Nam`, with the expected names and emails (`name@vgu.edu.vn`).

The scenario VGU#1 also contains three lecturers: Huong, Manuel, Hieu, again with the expected names and emails. Moreover, VGU#1 contains Enrollment-links between the lecturer Manuel and the students An, Chau, and Hoang, and also between the lecturer Huong and the students Chau and Thanh. Secondly, consider a scenario VGU#2 that is exactly as VGU#1 except that includes two additional Enrollment-links: one between the lecturer Hieu and the student Thanh, and the other link between the lecturer Hieu and the student Nam.

Consider now the following three SecureUML models, specifying three different FGAC policies, for the data modelled by University. First, the SecureUML model SecVGU#A consisting of only one role Lecturer, which is the role to be assigned to lecturers, and two authorization constraints:

- *Any lecturer can know its students.* Referring to the action of reading a link of the association Enrollment, this constraint can be formalized in OCL as follow:

  caller = lecturers.

- *Any lecturer can know his/her own email, as well as the emails of his/her students.* Referring to the action of reading the attribute email of an object of the class Lecturer, this constraint can be formalized in OCL as follow:

  (caller = self) or (caller.students->includes(self)).

Secondly, consider the SecureUML model SecVGU#B, which is exactly as SecVGU#A except that it includes the following additional authorization constraint:

- *Any lecturer can know its colleagues' emails, where two lecturers are colleagues if there is at least one student enrolled with both of them.* Referring to the action of reading the attribute email of object of the class Lecturer, this constraint can be formalized in OCL as follow:

  caller.students ->exists(s|s.lecturers->includes(self)).

Thirdly, consider the SecureUML model SecVGU#C, which is as SecVGU#B except that includes the following additional authorization constraint:

- *Any lecturer can know the lecturers of his/her own students.* Referring to the action of reading a link of the association Enrollment, this constraint can be formalized in OCL as follow:

  caller.students->includes(students).

4   Enforcing FGAC Policies for SQL Queries

Given a user u, an FGAC policy S—modelled in SecureUML—, and a SQL query q, we have formally defined in [12] the *conditions* that need to be satisfied for u to be authorized to execute q according to S. Here we present our solution for *enforcing* these conditions when executing queries in SQL. In a nutshell, we define a function SecQuery() that, given a FGAC policy S and a SQL query q, it generates a SQL stored-procedure, which takes two arguments, *caller* and *role*, representing, respectively, the user attempting to execute q and his/her role. This stored-procedure creates a list of *temporary tables*, corresponding to the different conditions that need to be satisfied for *caller*, using *role*, to be authorized to execute q, according to S. If all temporary tables can be successfully created, then the stored-procedure generated by SecQuery() will execute q; if any of the temporary tables cannot be created, then an error will be signalled. The reason for using *temporary tables* instead of *subqueries* is to prevent the SQL optimize for "skipping" (by rewriting the subqueries) some of the conditions that SecQuery() introduces to guarantee that a query is executed *securely*.

A subtle, but important point in our definition of SecQuery() has to do with our way of handling read-access authorization for tables representing *associations*. The definition of SecQuery() assumes that the policies' underlying data models are implemented in SQL following a specific *mapping*, which we define in Appendix B. According to this mapping, tables representing associations only contain the rows corresponding to the *links that exist between objects*. To illustrate the problem of handling read-access authorization for tables representing *associations*, consider the select-statement Query#4 in Fig. 4. According to the policy SecVGU#C, for the scenario VGU#1, Huong is not authorized to execute this query, since she is not authorized to know the students of Hieu (unless they happen to be her own students, which is not the case in this scenario). However, a naive implementation of read-access authorization for table representing associations may give Huong authorization for executing this query, and leaking as a result that Hieu has no students in this scenario. In particular, consider an implementation that may only perform authorization checks on the rows contained in the tables representing associations. Since in this scenario there are no links between Hieu and students, if we follow this naive implementation, there will be no rows on which to check for read-access authorization. Hence, Huong will be authorized to know that Hieu has no students in this scenario, and, logically, to conclude that neither An nor Nam, for example, are students of Hieu in this scenario, Our definition of SecQuery() avoids this problem by performing the authorization checks not only on the rows contained in the tables representing associations, which, as mentioned before, represent links that *exist* between objects, but also on the rows contained in the *complements* of these tables, i.e., on the rows representing that *do not exist* links between objects. In particular, in the definition of SecQuery(), when handling read-access authorization for tables representing associations, we consider the Cartesian product of the two tables/classes involved in the association, checking read-access authorization for *all* the rows in this Cartesian product. In fact, if we follow our implementation of read-access authorization for tables representing associations, Huong will not be authorized to execute Query#4 for this scenario, according to the policy SecVGU#C, because she is not authorized to know that An, Nam, and Hoang *are not* students of Hieu in this scenario. On the other hand, as expected, Hieu is authorized to execute Query#4 for this scenario, according to the policy SecVGU#C, because he is authorized to know if any student is or not *his* student.

```
mysql> SELECT COUNT(students) FROM Enrollment WHERE lecturers = 'Hieu';
```

Fig. 4. Example. Query#4.

In AppendixC we formally defined the SQL create-statements generated by SecQuery(). As expected, our definition proceeds recursively. It assumes that the FGAC policy's authorization constraints have been correctly implemented in SQL. In order to follow the definition of SecQuery() in the appendix, we informally introduce below the conditions that need to be satisfied for a user to be authorized to execute a SQL query according to a FGAC policy. As mentioned before, we have formally defined these conditions in [12]. Notice that, in particular, any data *used* when executing a query (in particular, data used by subqueries, where-clauses, and on-clauses) is checked for policy-compliance, and not only the data that appears in the final result.

Authorization Conditions for Executing SQL Queries

Case q = SELECT *selitems* FROM c WHERE *exp*. To execute q, the following conditions must be satisfied:

- The user is authorized to access the information required to evaluate the where-clause *exp*.
- The user is authorized to access the information referred to by *selitems*, but only for the objects/rows that satisfy the where-clause *exp*.

Case q = SELECT *selitems* FROM *as* WHERE *exp*. To execute q, the following conditions must be satisfied:

- The user is authorized to access the information referred to by both association-ends, but only for the rows contained in the Cartesian product between the classes involved in the association that satisfy the where-clause *exp*.

Case q = SELECT *selitems* FROM *subselect* WHERE *exp*. To execute q, the following conditions must be satisfied:

- The user is authorized to execute the subquery *subselect*.

Case q = SELECT *selitems* FROM c JOIN *as* ON *exp* WHERE *exp'*. To execute q, the following conditions must be satisfied:

- The user is authorized to access the information referred to by both association-ends.
- The user is authorized to access the information required to evaluate the on-clause *exp*.
- The user is authorized to access the information required to evaluate the where-clause *exp′*, but only for the objects/rows and links/rows that satisfy the on-clause *exp*.
- The user is authorized to access the information referred to by *selitems*, but only for the objects/rows and links/rows that satisfy the on-clause *exp* and the where-clause *exp′*.

Case q = SELECT *selitems* FROM c JOIN *subselect* ON *exp* WHERE *exp′*. To execute q, the following conditions must be satisfied:

- The user is authorized to execute the subquery *subselect*.
- The user is authorized to access the information required to evaluate the on-clause *exp*.
- The user is authorized to access the information required to evaluate the where-clause *exp′*; but only for the objects/rows and links/rows that satisfy the on-clause *exp*.
- The user is authorized to access the information referred to by *selitems*, but only for the objects/rows and links/rows that satisfy the on-clause *exp* and the where-clause *exp′*.

Case q = SELECT *selitems* FROM *as* JOIN *subselect* ON *exp* WHERE *exp′*. We must consider three cases:

First, the case when ase_l appears in *exp*, but ase_r does not appear in *exp*. Let *col* be the column in *subselect* that ase_l is related to in *exp*. To execute q, the following conditions must be satisfied:

- The users is authorized to execute the subquery *subselect*.
- The user is authorized to access the information referred to by both association-ends, but only for the rows contained in the Cartesian product between the classes involved in the association that satisfy the where-clause *exp*.

Secondly, the case when ase_r appears in *exp*, but ase_l does not appear in *exp*. This case is resolved analogously to the previous case. Thirdly, the case when both ase_r and ase_l appear in *exp*. To execute q, the following conditions must be satisfied:

- The users is authorized to execute the subquery *subselect*.
- The user is authorized to access the information referred to by both association-ends.

Case q = SELECT *selitems* FROM $subselect_1$ JOIN $subselect_2$ ON *exp* WHERE *exp′*. To execute q, the following conditions must be satisfied:

- The users is authorized to execute the subqueries $subselect_1$ and $subselect_2$.

Examples (Policy-Compliance)

We end this section with some non-trivial examples involving the queries Query#1, Query#2, and Query#3, the policies SecVGU#A, SecVGU#B, and SecVGU#C, and the scenarios VGU#1 and VGU#2. Concretely, in Fig. 1 we show the result of lecturers Manuel, Huong and Hieu calling the stored-procedure generated by SecQuery() for each of the aforementioned queries, policies, and scenarios. Notice in particular that:

– Manuel is not authorized to execute Query#2 for any of the scenarios VGU#1 and VGU#2, according to the policy SecVGU#C. This is to be expected, since Thanh is not a student of Manuel in any of these scenarios, and, therefore, Manuel is not authorized to know that Thanh is a student of Huong.
– Hieu is not authorized to execute Query#2 for the scenario VGU#1, according to the policy SecVGU#C. This is to be expected, since Thanh is not a student of Hieu in this scenario, and, therefore, Hieu is not authorized to know that Thanh is a student of Huong. However, in the scenario VGU#2, Thanh is in fact a student of Hieu, and, therefore, Hieu is authorized to know that Thanh is also a student of Huong, according to the policy SecVGU#C.
– Huong is not authorized to execute Query#3 for any of the scenarios VGU#1 and VGU#2, according to the policies SecVGU#C. This is to be expected, since for each of these scenarios there is at least one student who is a student of Manuel but he/she is not a student of Huong, and therefore, Huong is not authorized to know that he/she is in fact a student of Manuel, according to the policy SecVGU#C.

Table 1. Results of calling stored-procedures generated by SecQuery() for different queries and policies, with different users and scenarios.

caller	query	SecVGU#A		SecVGU#B		SecVGU#C	
		VGU#1	VGU#2	VGU#1	VGU#2	VGU#1	VGU#2
Manuel	Query#1	✗	✗	✓	✓	✓	✓
Huong		✓	✓	✓	✓	✓	✓
Hieu		✗	✗	✗	✓	✗	✓
Manuel	Query#2	✗	✗	✗	✗	✗	✗
Huong		✓	✓	✓	✓	✓	✓
Hieu		✗	✗	✗	✗	✗	✓
Manuel	Query#3	✗	✗	✗	✗	✗	✗
Huong		✗	✗	✗	✗	✗	✗
Hieu		✗	✗	✗	✗	✗	✗

5   The SQLSI Application

The SQL Security Injector (SQLSI) is a Java application implementing our solution for enforcing FGAC policies when executing SQL queries. In a nutshell, SQLSI takes two inputs, namely, an FGAC policy and a SQL query, and returns the corresponding stored-procedure generated by SecQuery(). SQLSI is an open-source project, available at:

https://github.com/SE-at-VGU/SQLSI.

SQLSI is also available as a web application at:

http://researcher-paper.ap-southeast-1.elasticbeanstalk.com/sqlsi/.

Currently, our web application enforces a fix FGAC policy, namely, SecVGU#C, and also automatically assigns the role Lecturer to the lecturers. On the other hand, it allows the visitor to input arbitrary SQL queries (within the class of queries supported by SecQuery()), to change the scenarios (by adding/removing objects and/or links), and to select the actual *caller* (i.e., the lecturer) of the query execution.

6   Related Work

Based on our model-based characterization of FGAC authorization for SQL queries [12], we have proposed here a novel *model-driven* approach for *enforcing* FGAC policies when executing SQL queries. A key feature of this approach is that it *does not modify* the underlying database, except for adding the stored-procedures that configure our FGAC-enforcement mechanism. This is in clear contrast with the solutions currently offered by the major commercial RDBMS. which recommend—like in the case of MySQL or MariaDB [10]—to manually create appropriate *views*, and to modify the queries so as to referencing these views, or request—like Oracle [3], PostgreSQL [14], and IBM [4]—to use other non-standard, proprietary enforcement mechanisms. As we have argued in [12], the solutions currently offered by the major RDBMS are far from ideal: in fact, they are time-consuming, error-prone, and scale poorly.

The second key feature of our model-driven approach is that FGAC policies and SQL queries are kept *independent* of each other, except for the fact that they refer to the same underlying data model. This means, in particular, that FGAC policies can be specified without knowing which SQL queries will be executed, and vice versa. This is in clear contrast with the solution recently proposed in [9] where the FGAC policies must be (re-)written depending on the SQL queries that are executed. Nevertheless, our model-driven approach certainly shares with [9], as well as with other previous approaches like [7], the idea of enforcing FGAC-policies by *rewriting* the SQL queries, instead of by modifying the underlying databases or by using non-standard, proprietary RDBMS features.

The third key-feature of our model-driven approach is that the enforcement mechanism can be *automatically generated* from the FGAC-policies, by using available mappings from OCL to SQL—for example [11]—in order to implement the authorization constraints appearing in the FGAC policies. In practice, however, our experiments show that, for the sake of execution-time performance, manually implementing in SQL the authorization constraints appearing in the FGAC policies is to be preferred over using the implementations generated by the available mappings from OCL to SQL.

7   Conclusions and Future Work

In this paper we have proposed a novel, *model-driven* approach for *enforcing* fine-grained access control (FGAC) policies when executing SQL queries. It is characteristic of FGAC policies that access control decisions depend on dynamic information: namely, whether the current state of the system satisfies some *authorization constraints*. In our approach, FGAC policies are modelled using the SecureUML language [8], in which authorization constraints are specified using the Object Constraint Language (OCL) [13].

In a nutshell, to enforce FGAC policies when executing SQL queries we define a function SecQuery() that, given a policy S and a select-statement q, generates a SQL stored-procedure, such that: if a user is authorized, according to S, to execute q, then calling this stored-procedure will return the same result that executing q; otherwise, if a user is not authorized, according to S, to execute q, then calling the stored-procedure will signal an error. To illustrate our approach we have provided a number of non-trivial examples, involving different FGAC policies, queries, and scenarios, We have also implemented our approach in a Java application, called SQLSI. This application is available as a web application for the interested reader to conveniently experiment with our approach.

We recognize that there is still work to be done. Firstly, we need to formally prove the *correctness* of the function SecQuery(), with respect to our model-based characterization of FGAC authorization for SQL queries [12]. This proof will certainly involve the formal semantics of both OCL and SQL, since authorization constraints are specified in OCL and SecQuery() generates SQL stored-procedures. Secondly, we need to evaluate the *efficiency* of our approach, from the point of view of the execution-time performance of the queries generated by SecQuery(), and how it compares with other approaches. Thirdly, we need to extend our definition of SecQuery() to cover as much as possible of the SQL language, including, in particular, left/right-joins and group-by clauses. Last but not least, we want to provide a more abstract characterization of our approach, including a formal definition of our *attacker* model. In this context, we will discuss more formally how our approach relates to the traditional distinction between Truman and Non-Truman models for secure database access (our approach clearly leaning towards the latter).

A   Data Models, Object Models, and Security Models

In this section we first define our notion of *data models* and *object models*. Data models specify the *resources* to be *protected*. Object models (also called

scenarios) are instances of data models. Next, we briefly introduce the Object
Constraint Language (OCL) [13], which is a language for specifying queries and
constraints on models. Then, we define our notion of *security models*. Security
models specify fine-grained access control policies for executing *actions* on protected resources. The actions that we consider here are *read*-actions on data
specified in data models. Finally, we formalize the semantics of our security
models by defining a predicate Auth() that declares when a user, using a specific role, is authorized to execute a read-action upon an object in a scenario.

Definition 1. *Let T be a set of predefined types. A* data model $\mathcal{D}$ *is a tuple*
$\langle C, AT, AS \rangle$, *where:*

- C *is a set of* classes *c.*
- AT *is a set of* attributes *at, $at = \langle ati, c, t \rangle$, where ati is the attribute's
  identifier, c is the class of the attribute, and t is the type of the values of the
  attribute, with $t \in T$ or $t \in C$.*
- AS *is a set of* associations *as, $as = \langle asi, ase_l, c_l, ase_r, c_r \rangle$, where asi is the
  association's identifier, ase_l and ase_r are the association's ends, and c_l and
  c_r are the classes of the objects at the corresponding association's ends.*

Definition 2. *Let $\mathcal{D} = \langle C, AT, AS \rangle$ be a data model. An* object model $\mathcal{O}$ *of $\mathcal{D}$
(also called an* instance *of $\mathcal{D}$) is a tuple $\langle OC, OAT, OAS \rangle$ where:*

- OC *is set of objects o, $o = \langle oi, c \rangle$, where oi is the object's identifier and c is
  the class of the object, where $c \in C$.*
- OAT *is a set of* attribute values *atv, $atv = \langle \langle ati, c, t \rangle, \langle oi, c \rangle, vl \rangle$, where
  $\langle ati, c, t \rangle \in AT$, $\langle oi, c \rangle \in OC$, and vl is a value of the type t. The attribute
  value atv denotes the value vl of the attribute $\langle ati, c, t \rangle$ of the object $\langle oi, c \rangle$.*
- OAS *is a set of* association links *asl, $asl = \langle \langle asi, ase_l, c_l, ase_r, c_r \rangle, \langle oi_l, c_l \rangle,
  \langle oi_r, c_r \rangle \rangle$, where $\langle asi, ase_l, c_l, ase_r, c_r \rangle \in AS$, $\langle oi_l, c_l \rangle \in OC$, and $\langle oi_r, c_r \rangle \in
  OC$. The association link asl denotes that there is a link of the association
  $\langle asi, ase_l, c_l, ase_r, c_r \rangle$ between the objects $\langle oi_l, c_l \rangle$ and $\langle oi_r, c_r \rangle$, where the later
  stands at the end ase_r and the former stands at the end ase_l.*

Without loss of generality, we assume that every object has a unique identifier.

Object Constraint Language (OCL). OCL [13] is a language for specifying constraints and queries using a textual notation. Every OCL expression is written
in the context of a model (called the contextual model). OCL is strongly typed.
Expressions either have a primitive type, a class type, a tuple type, or a collection type. OCL provides standard operators on primitive types, tuples, and
collections. For example, the operator `includes` checks whether an element is
inside a collection. OCL also provides a dot-operator to access the value of an
attribute of an object, or the collect the objects linked with an object at the end
of an association. For example, suppose that the contextual model includes a
class c with an attribute at and an association-end ase. Then, if o is an object of
the class c, the expression $o.at$ refers to the value of the attribute at of the object

o, and $o.ase$ refers to the objects linked to the object o at the association-end ase. OCL provides operators to iterate over collections, such as `forAll`, `exists`, `select`, `reject`, and `collect`. Collections can be sets, bags, ordered sets and sequences, and can be parameterized by any type, including other collection types. Finally, to represent *undefinedness*, OCL provides two constants, namely, `null` and `invalid`. Intuitively, `null` represents an unknown or undefined value, whereas `invalid` represents an error or an exception.

Notation. Let $\mathcal{D}$ be a data model. We denote by $\mathrm{Exp}(\mathcal{D})$ the set of OCL expressions whose contextual model is $\mathcal{D}$. Now, let $\mathcal{O}$ be an instance of $\mathcal{D}$, and let e be an OCL expression in $\mathrm{Exp}(\mathcal{D})$. Then, we denote by $\mathrm{Eval}(\mathcal{O}, e)$ the result of evaluating e in $\mathcal{O}$ according to the semantics of OCL.

Definition 3. *Let $\mathcal{D}$ be a data model $\mathcal{D} = \langle C, AT, AS \rangle$. Then, we denote by $\mathrm{Act}(\mathcal{D})$ the following set of read-actions:*

- *For every attribute $at \in AT$, $\mathrm{read}(at) \in \mathrm{Act}(\mathcal{D})$.*
- *For every association $as \in AS$, $\mathrm{read}(as) \in \mathrm{Act}(\mathcal{D})$.*

Definition 4. *Let $\mathcal{D} = \langle C, AT, AS \rangle$ be a data model. Let $\mathcal{O} = \langle OC, OAT, OAS \rangle$ be an instance of $\mathcal{D}$. Then, we denote by $\mathrm{Act}(\mathcal{O})$ the following set of instance read-actions:*

- *For every attribute $at = \langle ati, c, t \rangle$, $at \in AT$, and every object $o = \langle oi, c \rangle$, $o \in OC$, the action $\mathrm{read}(at, o)$ of reading the value of the attribute at in o.*
- *For every association $as = \langle asi, ase_1, c_1, ase_r, c_r \rangle$, $as \in AS$, and every pair of objects $o_1 = \langle oi_1, c_1 \rangle$, $o_r = \langle oi_r, c_r \rangle$, such that $o_1, o_r \in OC$, the action $\mathrm{read}(as, o_1, o_r)$ of reading if there is a link of the association as between o_l and o_r.*

Definition 5. *Let $\mathcal{D}$ be a data model. Then, a security model $\mathcal{S}$ for $\mathcal{D}$ is a tuple $\mathcal{S} = (R, \mathrm{auth})$, where R is a set of roles, and $\mathrm{auth} : R \times \mathrm{Act}(\mathrm{D}) \longrightarrow \mathrm{Exp}(\mathcal{D})$ is a function that assigns to each role $r \in R$ and each action $a \in \mathrm{Act}(\mathcal{D})$ an authorization constraint $e \in \mathrm{Exp}(\mathcal{D})$.*

Definition 6. *Let $\mathcal{D}$ be a data model. Let $\mathcal{S} = \langle R, \mathrm{auth} \rangle$ be a security model for $\mathcal{D}$. Let r be a role in R. Let $\mathcal{O} = \langle OC, OAT, OAS \rangle$ be an object model of $\mathcal{D}$. Let u be an object in OC. Then, we define the predicate Auth as follows:*

- *For any action $\mathrm{read}(at, o) \in \mathrm{Act}(\mathcal{O})$,*

$$\mathrm{Auth}(\mathcal{S}, \mathcal{O}, u, r, \mathrm{read}(at, o))$$
$$\Longleftrightarrow \mathrm{Eval}(\mathcal{O}, \mathrm{auth}(r, \mathrm{read}(at)))[\texttt{self} \mapsto o; \texttt{caller} \mapsto u]).$$

- *For any action $\mathrm{read}(as, o_1, o_r) \in \mathrm{Act}(\mathcal{O})$,*

$$\mathrm{Auth}(\mathcal{S}, \mathcal{O}, u, r, \mathrm{read}(as, o_1, o_r))$$
$$\Longleftrightarrow \mathrm{Eval}(\mathcal{O}, \mathrm{auth}(r, \mathrm{read}(as)))[as_1 \mapsto o_1; as_r \mapsto o_r; \texttt{caller} \mapsto u].$$

B   Mapping Data and Object Models to Databases

In this section we define the specific *mapping* from data models (and object models) to SQL that we use in our solution for enforcing FGAC policies when executing SQL queries. Notice that other mappings from data models to SQL are also possible [5]. As expected, if a different mapping from data models to SQL is chosen, then our enforcement of FGAC policies for SQL queries should be changed accordingly.

Definition 7. *Let* $\mathcal{D} = \langle C, AT, AS \rangle$ *be a data model. Our mapping of* $\mathcal{D}$ *to SQL, denoted by* $\overline{\mathcal{D}}$, *is defined as follows:*

– *For every* $c \in C$,

CREATE TABLE c (c_id varchar PRIMARY KEY);

– *For every attribute* $at \in AT$, $at = \langle ati, c, t \rangle$,

ALTER TABLE c ADD COLUMN ati SqlType(t);

where:
  – *if* $t =$ Integer, *then* SqlType(t) = int.
  – *if* $t =$ String, *then* SqlType(t) = varchar.
  – *if* $t \in C$, *then* SqlType(t) = varchar.
Moreover, if $t \in C$, *then*

ALTER TABLE c ADD FOREIGN KEY fk_c_ati(ati) REFERENCES t(t_id);

– *For every association* $as \in AS$, $as = \langle asi, ase_l, c_l, ase_r, c_r \rangle \in AS$,

CREATE TABLE asi (
    ase_l varchar NOT NULL,
    ase_r varchar NOT NULL,
    FOREIGN KEY fk_c_l_ase_l(ase_l) REFERENCES c_l(c_l_id),
    FOREIGN KEY fk_c_r_ase_r(ase_r) REFERENCES c_r(c_r_id));

Moreover,

ALTER TABLE asi ADD UNIQUE unique_link(ase_l, ase_r);

Definition 8. *Let* $\mathcal{D} = \langle C, AT, AS \rangle$ *be a data model. Let* $\mathcal{O} = \langle OC, OAT, OAS \rangle$ *be an object model of* $\mathcal{D}$. *Our mapping of* $\mathcal{O}$ *to SQL, denoted by* $\overline{\mathcal{O}}$, *is defined as follows:*

– *For every object* $o \in OC$, $o = \langle oi, c \rangle$,

INSERT INTO c(c_id) VALUES (oi);

– *For every attribute value* $atv \in OAT$, $atv = \langle\langle ati, c, t \rangle, \langle oi, c \rangle, vl \rangle$,

UPDATE c SET ati = vl WHERE c_id = oi;

– *For every association link* $asl \in OAS$, $asl = \langle\langle asi, ase_l, c_l, ase_r, c_r \rangle, \langle oi_l, c_l \rangle, \langle oi_r, c_r \rangle\rangle$,

INSERT INTO asi(ase_l, ase_r) VALUES (oi_l, oi_r);

C   Secure SQL Queries

In this section we define the key component in our model-driven solution for enforcing FGAC policies when executing SQL queries. In particular, we define a function SecQuery() such that, given a FGAC policy $\mathcal{S}$ and a SQL select-statement q, it generates a SQL stored-procedure satisfying the following: if a user is authorized, according to $\mathcal{S}$, to execute q, then calling this stored-procedure returns the same result that executing q; otherwise, if a user is not authorized, according to $\mathcal{S}$, to execute q, then calling this stored-procedure signals an error. By convention, we denote by $\ulcorner$SecQuery$(\mathcal{S}, q)\urcorner$ the name of the stored-procedure generated by SecQuery, for a FGAC policy $\mathcal{S}$ and a query q.

The function SecQuery() uses a number of auxiliary functions to generate the *body* of the aforementioned stored-procedure: namely, AuthFunc(), AuthFuncRole(), SecExp(), and SecExpList(). Both AuthFunc() and AuthFuncRole() generate SQL functions, which we denote using the same convention as for the SQL stored-procedures generated by the function SecQuery(). As expected, before we introduce the definition of SecQuery(), we provide the definition of the aforementioned auxiliary functions. However, we leave "open" the concrete implementation in SQL of the authorization constraints specified in a given FGAC policy. More precisely, given an authorization constraint *auth* in OCL, we assume that there exists a function map() that generates the corresponding query map($auth$) in SQL. We also assume that this function returns a table with a column res containing the result of executing map($auth$). Our mapping OCL2PSQL [11] can certainly be used as such function map(). However, our current experiments suggest that, for non-trivial authorization constraints, manually-written implementations significantly outperforms those automatically generated by OCL2PSQL, when checking FGAC authorization in large databases.

Definition 9. *Let* $\mathcal{D} = \langle C, AT, AS \rangle$ *be a data model. Let* $\mathcal{S} = (R, \text{auth})$ *be a security model for* $\mathcal{D}$. *Let* r *be a role in* R. *Let* $at = \langle ati, c, t \rangle$ *be an attribute in* AT. *Then,* AuthFuncRole$(\mathcal{S}, at, r)$ *generates the following SQL function:*

```
CREATE FUNCTION ⌜AuthFuncRole(at, r)⌝ ( self varchar(250),
  caller varchar(250))
RETURNS INT DETERMINISTIC
BEGIN
  DECLARE result INT DEFAULT 0;
  SELECT res INTO result FROM map(auth(r, read(at))) AS TEMP;
  RETURN result;
END
```

Similarly, let $as = \langle asi, ase_\text{l}, c_\text{l}, ase_\text{r}, c_\text{r} \rangle \in AS$, *be an association in* AS. *Then,* AuthFuncRole$(\mathcal{S}, as, r)$ *generates the following SQL function:*

```
CREATE FUNCTION ⌜AuthFuncRole(as, r)⌝ ( left varchar(250),
  right varchar(250), caller varchar(250))
RETURNS INT DETERMINISTIC
```

```
BEGIN
  DECLARE result INT DEFAULT 0;
  SELECT res INTO result FROM map(auth(r, read(as))) AS TEMP;
  RETURN result;
END
```

Definition 10. *Let* $\mathcal{D} = \langle C, AT, AS \rangle$ *be a data model. Let* $\mathcal{S} = (R, \mathrm{auth})$ *be a security model for* $\mathcal{D}$, *with* $R = \{r_1, r_2, \ldots, r_n\}$. *Let at be an attribute in* AT. *Then,* $\mathrm{AuthFunc}(\mathcal{S}, at)$ *generates the following SQL function:*

```
CREATE FUNCTION ⌈AuthFunc(at)⌉ ( self varchar(250),
  caller varchar(250), role varchar(250))
RETURNS INT DETERMINISTIC
BEGIN
  DECLARE result INT DEFAULT 0;
  IF (role = r₁)
    THEN RETURN ⌈AuthFuncRole(at, r₁)⌉(self, caller)
  ELSE IF (role = r₂)
    THEN RETURN ⌈AuthFuncRole(at, r₂)⌉(self, caller)
  ⋮
  ELSE IF (role = rₙ)
    THEN RETURN ⌈AuthFuncRole(at, rₙ)⌉(self, caller)
  ELSE RETURN 0
  END IF;
  ⋮
  END IF;
  END IF;
END
```

Similarly, let as be an association in AS. *Then* $\mathrm{AuthFunc}(\mathcal{S}, as)$ *generates the following SQL function:*

```
CREATE FUNCTION ⌈AuthFunc(as)⌉ ( left varchar(250),
  right varchar(250), caller varchar(250), role varchar(250))
RETURNS INT DETERMINISTIC
BEGIN
  DECLARE result INT DEFAULT 0;
  IF (role = r₁)
    THEN RETURN ⌈AuthFuncRole⌉(as, r₁) (left, right, caller)
  ELSE IF (role = r₂)
    THEN RETURN ⌈AuthFuncRole(as, r₂)⌉ (left, right, caller)
  ⋮
  ELSE IF (role = rₙ)
    THEN RETURN ⌈AuthFuncRole(as, rₙ)⌉ (left, right, caller)
  ELSE RETURN 0
  END IF;
```

$\vdots$

```
  END IF;
  END IF;
END
```

Definition 11. *Let* $\mathcal{D} = \langle C, AT, AS \rangle$ *be a data model. Let* $\mathcal{S} = (R, \mathrm{auth})$ *be a security model for* $\mathcal{D}$. *Let exp be a SQL expression in* $\overline{\mathcal{D}}$. *We denote by* $\mathrm{SecExp}(\mathcal{S}, exp)$ *the SQL expression in* $\overline{\mathcal{D}}$ *that results from replacing:*

- *each attribute* $at = \langle ati, c, t \rangle$ *in exp by the following case-expression*

```
  CASE ⌜AuthFunc(at)⌝ (c_id, caller, role)
    WHEN 1 THEN at
    ELSE throw_error() END as at.
```

- *each association-end* $ase_{[l|r]}$ *in exp, with* $ase_{[l|r]}$ *in as* $= \langle asi, ase_l, c_l, ase_r, c_r \rangle$, *by the following case-expression:*

```
  CASE ⌜AuthFunc(as)⌝ (asel, aser, caller, role)
    WHEN 1 THEN asel[l|r]
    ELSE throw_error() END as ase[l|r].
```

where the function `throw_error()` *is defined as followed:*

```
CREATE FUNCTION throw_error()
RETURNS INT DETERMINISTIC
BEGIN
  DECLARE result INT DEFAULT 0;
  SIGNAL SQLSTATE '45000'
  SET MESSAGE_TEXT = 'Unauthorized access';
  RETURN (0);
END
```

Definition 12. *Let* $\mathcal{D} = \langle C, AT, AS \rangle$ *be a data model. Let* $\mathcal{S} = (R, \mathrm{auth})$ *be a security model for* $\mathcal{D}$. *Let selitems* $= exp_1, \dots, exp_n$ *be a list of SQL expressions in* $\overline{\mathcal{D}}$. *We denote by* $\mathrm{SecExpList}(\mathcal{S}, selitems)$ *the following SQL expression list:* $\mathrm{SecExp}(\mathcal{S}, exp_1), \dots, \mathrm{SecExp}(\mathcal{S}, exp_n)$.

Notation. Let $\mathcal{D} = \langle C, AT, AS \rangle$ be a data model. Let $\mathcal{S} = (R, \mathrm{auth})$ be a security model for $\mathcal{D}$. Let *exp* be a SQL expression in $\overline{\mathcal{D}}$. We denote by $\mathrm{RepExp}(exp, as)$ the SQL expression in $\overline{\mathcal{D}}$ that results from replacing each association-end *ase* in *exp* by its corresponding class identifier.

Definition 13. *Let* $\mathcal{D} = \langle C, AT, AS \rangle$ *be a data model. Let* $\mathcal{S} = (R, \mathrm{auth})$ *be a security model for* $\mathcal{D}$. *Let q be a SQL query in* $\overline{\mathcal{D}}$. *Then,* $\mathrm{SecQuery}(\mathcal{S}, q)$ *generates the following stored-procedure:*

```
CREATE PROCEDURE ⌜SecQuery(𝒮, q)⌝ (
    caller varchar(250), role varchar(250))
BEGIN
DECLARE _rollback int DEFAULT 0;
DECLARE EXIT HANDLER FOR SQLEXCEPTION
BEGIN
```
  If an error is signalled, then set _rollback *to* 1 *and*
  return the error message.
```
  SET _rollback = 1;
  GET STACKED DIAGNOSTICS CONDITION 1
    @p1 = RETURNED_SQLSTATE, @p2 = MESSAGE_TEXT;
  SELECT @p1, @p2;
  ROLLBACK;
END;
START TRANSACTION;
```
    For each authorization condition *applicable to the original query,*
    create the corresponding temporary table.

    SecQueryAux(𝒮, q)

  If after creating all the temporary tables, no error has been signalled yet,
  i.e., _rollback *has still value* 0, *then execute the original query.*
```
IF _rollback = 0
  THEN q;
END IF;
END
```

Case q = SELECT *selitems* FROM c WHERE *exp*. Then, SecQueryAux() returns the following create-statements:

```
  CREATE TEMPORARY TABLE ⌜TempTable(q, exp)⌝ AS (
    SELECT * FROM c WHERE SecExp(𝒮, exp));
  CREATE TEMPORARY TABLE ⌜TempTable(q, selitems)⌝ AS (
    SELECT SecExpList(𝒮, selitems) FROM ⌜TempTable(q, exp)⌝);
```

Case q = SELECT *selitems* FROM *as* WHERE *exp*. Then, SecQueryAux() returns the following create-statements:

```
  CREATE TEMPORARY TABLE ⌜TempTable(q, exp)⌝ AS (
    SELECT cₗ_id as aseₗ, cᵣ_id as aseᵣ FROM cₗ, cᵣ WHERE RepExp(exp, as) );
  CREATE TEMPORARY TABLE ⌜TempTable(q, selitems)⌝ AS (
    SELECT SecExp(𝒮, aseₗ), SecExp(𝒮, aseᵣ) FROM ⌜TempTable(q, exp)⌝ );
```

Case q = SELECT *selitems* FROM *subselect* WHERE *exp*. Then, SecQueryAux() returns the following create-statements:

    SecQueryAux(𝒮, *subselect*)

Case q = SELECT *selitems* FROM c JOIN *as* ON *exp* WHERE *exp'*. Then, SecQueryAux() returns the following create-statements:

>SecQueryAux($\mathcal{S}$, SELECT ase_l, ase_r FROM as)
>CREATE TEMPORARY TABLE $\ulcorner$TempTable(q, exp)$\urcorner$ AS (
>SELECT * FROM c JOIN as ON SecExp($\mathcal{S}$, exp)) ;
>CREATE TEMPORARY TABLE $\ulcorner$TempTable(q, exp')$\urcorner$ AS (
>SELECT * FROM $\ulcorner$TempTable$\urcorner$(q, exp) WHERE SecExp($\mathcal{S}$, exp')) ;
>CREATE TEMPORARY TABLE $\ulcorner$TempTable(q, $selitems$)$\urcorner$ AS (
>SELECT SecExpList($\mathcal{S}$, $selitems$) FROM $\ulcorner$TempTable(q, exp')$\urcorner$) ;

Case q = SELECT *selitems* FROM c JOIN *subselect* ON *exp* WHERE *exp'*. Then, SecQuery($\mathcal{S}$, q) returns the following create-statements:

>SecQueryAux($\mathcal{S}$, *subselect*)
>CREATE TEMPORARY TABLE $\ulcorner$TempTable(q, exp)$\urcorner$ AS (
>SELECT * FROM c JOIN $subselect$ ON SecExp($\mathcal{S}$, exp)) ;
>CREATE TEMPORARY TABLE $\ulcorner$TempTable(q, exp')$\urcorner$ AS (
>SELECT * FROM $\ulcorner$TempTable(q, exp)$\urcorner$ WHERE SecExp($\mathcal{S}$, exp')) ;
>CREATE TEMPORARY TABLE $\ulcorner$TempTable(q, $selitems$)$\urcorner$ AS (
>SELECT SecExpList($\mathcal{S}$, $selitems$) FROM $\ulcorner$TempTable(q, exp')$\urcorner$) ;

Case q = SELECT *selitems* FROM *as* JOIN *subselect* ON *exp* WHERE *exp'*.
We must consider three cases. First, the case when ase_l appears in exp, but ase_r does not appear in exp. Let *col* be the column in *subselect* that ase_l is related to in exp. Then, SecQueryAux($\mathcal{S}$, q) returns the following create-statements:

>SecQueryAux($\mathcal{S}$, *subselect*)
>CREATE TEMPORARY TABLE $\ulcorner$TempTable(q, exp)$\urcorner$ AS (
>SELECT c_l_id as ase_l, col as ase_r FROM c_l, $subselect$
>ON RepExp(exp, as) WHERE RepExp(exp', as)) ;
>CREATE TEMPORARY TABLE $\ulcorner$TempTable(q, as)$\urcorner$ AS (
>SELECT SecExp($\mathcal{S}$, ase_l), SecExp($\mathcal{S}$, ase_r) FROM $\ulcorner$TempTable(q, exp)$\urcorner$) ;

Secondly, the case when ase_r appears in exp, but ase_l does not appear in exp. This case is resolved analogously to the previous case. Thirdly, the case when both ase_l and ase_r appear in exp. Then SecQueryAux($\mathcal{S}$, q) returns the following SQL create-statements:

>SecQueryAux($\mathcal{S}$, *subselect*)
>SecQueryAux($\mathcal{S}$, SELECT * FROM as)

Case q = SELECT *selitems* FROM $subselect_1$ JOIN $subselect_2$ ON *exp* WHERE *exp'*. Then, SecQuery($\mathcal{S}$, q) returns the following create-statements:

>SecQueryAux($\mathcal{S}$, $subselect_1$)
>SecQueryAux($\mathcal{S}$, $subselect_2$)

References

1. Basin, D.A., Clavel, M., Egea, M.: A decade of model-driven security. In: Breu, R., Crampton, J., Lobo, J.(eds.) Proceedings of the 16th ACM Symposium on Access Control Models and Technologies, SACMAT 2011, Innsbruck, Austria, 15–17 June 2011, pp. 1–10. ACM (2011)
2. Basin, D.A., Doser, J., Lodderstedt, T.: Model driven security: from UML models to access control infrastructures. ACM Trans. Softw. Eng. Methodol. **15**(1), 39–91 (2006)
3. Browder, K., Davidson, M.A.: The virtual private database in Oracle9iR2. Technical report, Oracle Corporation (2002). https://www.cgisecurity.com/-database/oracle/pdf/VPD9ir2twp.pdf
4. Row and column access control support in IBM DB2 for i. Technical report, International Business Machines Corporation (2014)
5. Demuth, B., Hussmann, H., Loecher, S.: OCL as a specification language for business rules in database applications. In: Gogolla, M., Kobryn, C. (eds.) UML 2001. LNCS, vol. 2185, pp. 104–117. Springer, Heidelberg (2001). https://doi.org/10.1007/3-540-45441-1_9
6. Ferraiolo, D.F., Sandhu, R., Gavrila, S., Kuhn, D.R., Chandramouli, R.: Proposed NIST standard for role-based access control. ACM Trans. Inf. Syst. Secur. **4**(3), 224–274 (2001)
7. LeFevre, K., Agrawal, R., Ercegovac, V., Ramakrishnan, R., Xu, Y., DeWitt, D.: Limiting disclosure in Hippocratic databases. In: Proceedings of the Thirtieth International Conference on Very Large Data Bases, VLDB 2004, vol. 30, pp. 108–119. VLDB Endowment (2004)
8. Lodderstedt, T., Basin, D., Doser, J.: SecureUML: a UML-based modeling language for model-driven security. In: Jézéquel, J.-M., Hussmann, H., Cook, S. (eds.) UML 2002. LNCS, vol. 2460, pp. 426–441. Springer, Heidelberg (2002). https://doi.org/10.1007/3-540-45800-X_33
9. Mehta, A. Elnikety, E., Harvey, K., Garg, D., Druschel, P.: Qapla: policy compliance for database-backed systems. In: Proceedings of the 26th USENIX Conference on Security Symposium, SEC 2017, pp. 1463–1479, USA. USENIX Association (2017)
10. Montee, G.: Row-level security in MariaDB 10: Protect your data (2015). https://mariadb.com/resources/blog/
11. Nguyen Phuoc Bao, H., Clavel, M.: OCL2PSQL: an OCL-to-SQL code-generator for model-driven engineering. In: Dang, T.K., Küng, J., Takizawa, M., Bui, S.H. (eds.) FDSE 2019. LNCS, vol. 11814, pp. 185–203. Springer, Cham (2019). https://doi.org/10.1007/978-3-030-35653-8_13
12. Nguyen Phuoc Bao, H., Clavel, M.: Model-based characterization of fine-grained access control authorization for SQL queries. J. Object Technol. **19**(3), 3:1–13 (2020). https://doi.org/10.5381/jot.2020.19.3.a15
13. Object Constraint Language specification version 2.4. Technical report, Object Management Group, February 2014. https://www.omg.org/spec/OCL/
14. PostgreSQL 12.2. Part II. SQL The Language. Chapter 5. Data Definition. 5.8. Row Security Policies. https://www.postgresql.org/docs/current/
15. ISO/IEC 9075-(1–10) Information technology - Database languages - SQL. Technical report, International Organization for Standardization (2011). http://www.iso.org/iso/

On Applying Graph Database Time Models for Security Log Analysis

Daniel Hofer[1,2]([✉]) [iD], Markus Jäger[3] [iD], Aya Mohamed[1,2], and Josef Küng[1,2]

[1] Institute for Application-Oriented Knowledge Processing (FAW),
Faculty of Engineering and Natural Sciences (TNF),
Johannes Kepler University (JKU) Linz, Linz, Austria
`{dhofer,aya.mohamed,jkueng}@faw.jku.at`
[2] LIT Secure and Correct Systems Lab, Linz Institute of Technology (LIT),
Johannes Kepler University (JKU) Linz, Linz, Austria
`{daniel.hofer,aya.mohamed,josef.kueng}@jku.at`
[3] Pro2Future GmbH, Altenberger Strasse 69, 4040 Linz, Austria
`markus.jaeger@pro2future.at`

Abstract. For aiding computer security experts in their work, log files are a crucial piece of information. Especially the time domain is of interest, since sometimes, timestamps are the only linking points between associated events caused by attackers, faulty systems or similar. With the idea of storing and analyzing log information in graph databases comes also the question, how to model the time aspect and in particular, how timestamps shall be stored and connected in a proper form.

This paper analyzes three different models in which time information extracted from log files can be represented in graph databases and how the data can be retrieved again in a form that is suitable for further analysis. The first model resembles data stored in a relational database, while the second one enhances this approach by applying graph database specific amendments while the last model makes almost full use of a graph database's capabilities. Hereby, the main focus points are laid on the queries for retrieving the data, their complexity, the expressiveness of the underlying data model and the suitability for usage in graph databases.

Keywords: Graph databases · Security · Logfile analysis · Time model representation

1 Introduction

When analyzing logging information, the time domain is most important since timestamps are usually the only means for finding corresponding log entries when data from different sources are combined. Therefore, it is crucial having a data model at hand which allows all sort of different queries and at the same time must not become too complex for performance and maintainability reasons. The overall question this paper tries to contribute to is, whether it is a good idea employing graph databases as a combined storage for all systems logs, ranging

© Springer Nature Switzerland AG 2020
T. K. Dang et al. (Eds.): FDSE 2020, LNCS 12466, pp. 87–107, 2020.
https://doi.org/10.1007/978-3-030-63924-2_5

from one single machine up to a whole enterprise network. Following a top-down approach for the design of such a data model, the part representing the temporal domain appears as a good starting point. This paper will outline the aspects the proposed models are checked against, the data used for testing and will then analyze three different data model designs for time information.

Each model's quality is measured by its expressiveness, the complexity of the queries from a human being's point of view and by the suitability for a graph database employing pattern matching for its queries. During the evaluation of these properties, the model must be capable of answering the following questions:

Q1: For a given event beginning, where is the corresponding ending?

Q2: Which IP addresses were connected at a given timestamp?

Q3: Which of two given log entries occurred earlier?

Q4: Which events occurred X time units before/after a given event?

As a testing platform, Neo4J [16] was chosen because it is a native graph database[1] and there exists an open source community version. Furthermore, an web application called *Neo4J Browser* [15] for developing queries exists which is also open source.

2   Related Work

To the best knowledge of the authors, there is no related work dealing with time modelling in graph databases in the specific context of this research. Nevertheless there are some scientific publications which can be used as anchor points for further literature research in this field.

Theodoulidis and Loucopoulos [21] introduce time modelling concepts in a conceptual schema. Patton [17] tries to model time-varying dependencies between random distributed variables in the context of currencies (exchange rates). Wiese and Omlin [22] give an approach for modelling time with LSTM recurrent neural networks in the context of security and safety applications in credit card transactions, fraud detection, and machine learning.

A more security related research field is presented by Schwenk [18], modelling time for authenticated key exchange protocols. Semertzidis and Pitoura [19] give a first insight into managing historical time queries by using structured data, represented in graph databases.

Recent literature was presented by Maduako and Wachowicz [12], who model places and events in a network with space-time varying graphs and by Chu et al. [5], who present a novel deep learning method for query task execution time prediction in graph databases.

---

[1] Native graph databases are characterized by implementing ad-hoc data structures and indexes for storing and querying graphs.

Using time spacial modelling methods in ontologies, Hobbs and Pan [10] describe an OWL-2 DL ontology of temporal concepts (OWL = Web Ontology Language), which was verified by Grüninger [9] in 2011.

Further, non scientific sources [8] and [3] propose variations of the model introduced in Sect. 4.3 but do not give any recommendations for which purpose their models should be used or how to query them.

More literature is found on the general use of graph databases for network security monitoring like proposed by Diederichsen, Choo and Le-Khac [7] or by Tao et al. [20] but without going into detail on the representation of the time domain.

3 Input Data

Testing data originate from a live and personal postfix server. A small example of the input data can be seen in Listing 1. Due to privacy reasons, the IP addresses displayed where replaced by ones from the *Private Address Space* defined in RFC 1918. All other values remained unchanged.

```
1  Apr 26 05:32:55 smtp postfix/smtps/smtpd[728399]: connect from
   ↪ unknown[10.8.21.42]
2  Apr 26 05:33:01 smtp postfix/smtps/smtpd[728399]: disconnect from
   ↪ unknown[10.8.21.42]
3  Apr 26 05:33:01 smtp postfix/smtps/smtpd[728399]: connect from
   ↪ unknown[10.8.21.42]
```

Listing 1: Example of log information used as test data. For privacy reasons, the public IP addresses were replaced by random private ones.

This type of test data was chosen, because it is comparable easy to read for a human being, all lines share a common format and most importantly, the log file contains events with an explicitly stated beginning and ending. For example a connection initiation is denoted by *connect from X* and it's termination *disconnect from X*. Between these two lines, the connection is alive.

In the analysis of the graph database models, the following information will be used:

- **Timestamp** (*Apr 26 05:32:55*): The main data of interest to model.
- **Process identifier** (*728399*): Since multiple remote systems can connect to postfix, multiple instances need to run. As a result, the system wide process identifier or PID is required for matching corresponding lines together.
- **The action executed** (*connect from/disconnect from*): Denoting the beginning and ending of each event or in the following the connection.
- **The remote IP address** (*10.8.21.42*): Denoting the remote client.

By default, the timestamps produced by postfix only have a granularity down to seconds. As a result, multiple lines can share the same timestamp, rendering their order is indistinguishable if only relying on this information. To compensate this problem, it is assumed that the relative order of one line compared to its neighbors is known during processing and therefore must be encoded in the data model.

4   Data Model

This work proposes three different data models for storing timestamp information in graph databases. The first one is basically a one-to-one copy originating from relational databases, storing the time information as properties in the nodes representing events or in this case, *connection* and *disconnection*. In the second model, the timestamp information is still kept inside one dedicated node for each entry, but the order of nodes is represented by directed edges between the timestamp nodes. For the third model, the hierarchical structure of a timestamp is exploited, basically building a tree like structure.

Most parts of the models are common for all three versions which are described here once for all with generic names. In order to make nodes of a model distinguishable from other models, the naming convention <*model prefix*>_ <*node type name*> is used. The *model prefix* consists of two letters losely derived from the model name. For the *property-based model* the prefix is *Pt*, for *timeline model Tl* is used and the *hierarchical model* is marked with *Hr*.

The core of all models are the *Event* nodes. Each of these nodes correspond to one *connect/disconnect* line in the processed log file. Since the remaining properties for each line are reused, they are modeled in dedicated nodes (except for the timestamps of course). Edges are usually directed from the *Event* node to the referenced/shared nodes. Remote IP addresses are represented by *Ip* nodes, connected to the event node by *ATTACKER_IP* edges. The local IP also uses the type of node, but is connected using *TARGET_IP* edges. The type of the event is stored by connecting *IS_TYPE* from the event node to *Type* nodes and to group events by process ids, *Process* nodes in conjunction with *HAS_PID* edges are used. Because a productive environment might be up for a long time, the process id is bound to be reused at some point in time. While this has to be taken into account in real world, the currently observed time frame is too short so that a PID rollover can be neglected for the observations in this paper [4,6].

An example for the common part of the data model based on the *property-based model* can be found in Fig. 1.

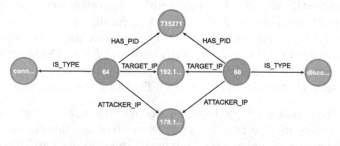

Fig. 1. Part of the graph structure common for all three versions of the data model.

4.1 Property-Based Model

For this very basic model, the complete timestamp information is solely one property contained in the *Pt_ Event* node. Neo4J offers support for this by providing several dedicated datatypes [13]. Apart from the timestamp itself, additional information is required due to the coarse granularity of whole seconds for the timestamp, the order for multiple events with the same timestamp is not distinguishable anymore. As a workaround, the property *order* is containing an increasing number starting at 1 denoting the position in the logfile for a group of events sharing the same timestamp. An example for an event node of the *property-based model* can be seen in Fig. 2.

Pt_Event   <id>: 64   order: 1   timestamp: 2020-04-27T05:57:27.000Z

Fig. 2. Example for an event node of the *property-based model*. The timestamp information is encoded as property inside the node using a dedicated datatype.

4.2 Timeline Model

In the *timeline model*, every log line from the input files receive a dedicated timestamp node. All these nodes are connected by *NEXT* edges pointing towards younger timestamps. Event nodes are then attached using *HAPPENED_AT* edges to the timeline nodes (see Fig. 3). As for the *property-based model*, again problems concerning event order on equal timestamps arise. For this model, the solution is to allow multiple timestamp-nodes per actual timestamp, maintaining order by *NEXT* edges.

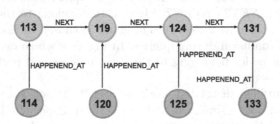

Fig. 3. Example for the *timeline model*. The upper row (green in the online version) of nodes contain timestamp information, the lower row (orange) represent events.

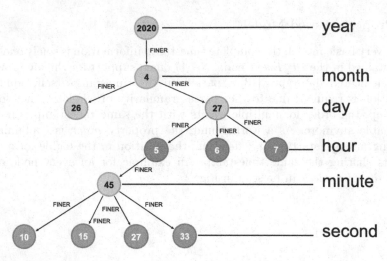

Fig. 4. Example for a part of a basic timestamp tree. The top node represents the year and the *FINER* edges lead to the nodes with smaller time granularity.

4.3 Hierarchical Model

A timestamp itself is some kind of hierarchical construct. Every year has a fixed amount of months which themselves have a certain number of days and so on. The *hierarchical model* tries to exploit this relationship by creating dedicated nodes for years down to a desired level. Every time unit is connected to the more granular one with *FINER* edges. For lateral movement, *NEXT* edges are used for connecting nodes in ascending order, if they share the same layer and parent node. Parts of the resulting structure are later referred to as *time tree*, although the year level does not share an existing common parent node. An example for a part of the resulting tree can be seen in Fig. 4.

The *Hr_Event* nodes are then attached to the nodes representing seconds using *HAPPENED_AT* edges. For the problem of equal timestamps, event nodes are connected with *NEXT_EVENT* edges, if they belong to the same process (again going from older to younger). The name is chosen differently to *NEXT* in order to avoid confusion during queries. In Fig. 5, a whole example is shown with several event nodes belonging to the same process and partly sharing the same *Hr_Second* node.

As already outlined in related work at Sect. 2, in non scientific literature [3,8] the same and a very similar model is described. Especially [3] contains the same structure for the timestamp part as proposed here, but also enhances it by adding *FIRST* and *LAST* edges directing from a time unit to the next finer one.

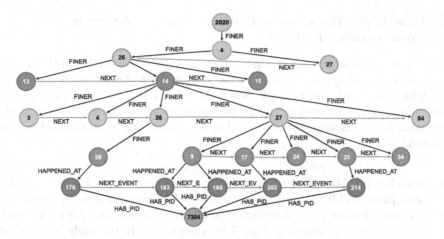

Fig. 5. A complete example of the hierarchical model with several event nodes. The dark green nodes represent log lines, the grey node at the bottom stands for a process and the remaining hierarchy expresses the timestamp as described in Fig. 4.

5   Evaluation

This part proposes queries for the questions formulated in Sect. 1 for each of the previously defined data models.

In order to make the queries more readable and generic, it is usually tried to split each of them in two parts. The first part is only responsible for fetching a specific event node by different means. Examples here are simply using the id of a node or specific values. In any case, this part of the query delivers the event nodes or other data a user might wish to operate on in a generic way so that the implementation details are easily exchanged according to a use-case. The second part does the actual work answering the user's question. It is specific for the data model and the contained data but should not require changes when working for different applications.

In some cases, it might be possible to write a shorter expression for a query, but with the intention to create more readable versions of the queries, the proposed versions have been chosen.

Under the assumption, that not only connect and disconnect events are present but also other types, it is always necessary to filter for the desired event node type. However, it is still assumed a single process can only handle a single remote connection at a time.

5.1 Question 1: For a Given Event Beginning, Where Is the Corresponding Ending?

For the first question, the beginning of an event is known, which is in the actual test data an incoming connection, and the user wants to know, when this event ends, which means for this example, when the remote machine disconnects. The *connect* event node is found by a hard coded *id*, which simulates that a specific connection is currently under investigation and the matching disconnect has to be found.

Property-Based Model. In Listing 2, the disconnect log entry is found by the shared process id between connection and disconnection log entry. Since the process cannot handle two connections simultaneously, filtering for nodes with the same process id as shown in Line 5 is enough, if only the node is returned which is from a time perspective point of view the closest one.

```
1  match (connect:Pt_Event) where id(connect) = 17 with connect
2  match
3  (connect:Pt_Event), (process:Pt_Process), (disconnect:Pt_Event),
4  (connect)-[:HAS_PID]->(process)<-[:HAS_PID]-(disconnect),
5  (disconnect)-[:IS_TYPE]->(:Pt_Type{name:'disconnect'})
6  where connect.timestamp <= disconnect.timestamp
7  return disconnect
8  order by disconnect.timestamp ASC, disconnect.order ASC limit 1
```

Listing 2: Finding the *disconnect* event node for a given *connect* in the *property-based model.*

Timeline Model. The query for the timeline model in Listing 3 is slightly more complicated. It works by exploiting the single timeline bringing all time nodes in one global order. Since the disconnect event must have occurred later, the search can make use of the directed edges (see Line 8). The shortest paths between the given start node and all satisfying *disconnect* nodes are queried there. By selecting the minimal one, the connection ending is found.

```
1  match (connect:Tl_Event) where id(connect) = 172 with connect
2  match
3  (connect)-[:HAPPENED_AT]->(connectTimestamp),
4  (disconnect)-[:HAPPENED_AT]->(disconnectTimestamp),
5  (disconnect:Tl_Event)-[:IS_TYPE]->(:Tl_Type{name:'disconnect'}),
6  (connect)-[:HAS_PID]->(t:Tl_Process)<-[:HAS_PID]-(disconnect),
7  p=shortestPath((connectTimestamp)-[:NEXT*1..]->(disconnectTimestamp))
8  with disconnect, length(p) as len order by len ASC limit 1
9  return disconnect
```

Listing 3: Finding the *disconnect* event node for a given *connect* in the *timeline based model.*

Hierarchical Model. For finding the disconnect log entry in the hierarchical model, there are basically two possible different approaches in the proposed data model.

The first is denoted in Listing 4. This query works by finding the shortest path in the *time tree* but unlike the previous query for the *timeline model*, it is not possible to indicate the direction since the search must also go up the hierarchy. To ensure that only events after the *connect* are returned, Line 8 is used which at the same time restricts to the right process.

```
1   match (connect:Hr_Event) where id(connect) = 121 with connect
2   match
3   (disconnect:Hr_Event), (ip:Hr_Ip), (connect:Hr_Event),
4   (disconnect)-[:ATTACKER_IP]->(ip)<-[:ATTACKER_IP]-(connect),
5   (connect)-[:HAPPENED_AT]->(con_sec:Hr_Second),
6   (disconnect)-[:HAPPENED_AT]->(dis_sec:Hr_Second),
7   (connect)-[:NEXT_EVENT*]->(disconnect),
8   (disconnect)-[:IS_TYPE]->(connectType:Hr_Type {name:
    ↪  'disconnect'}),
9   p=shortestPath((con_sec:Hr_Second)-[:FINER|NEXT*0..]-(dis_sec:Hr_Second))
10  return disconnect order by length(p) asc limit 1
```

Listing 4: Finding the *disconnect* event node for a given *connect* in the *hierarchical model* using the time information.

The second possibility is by exploiting the *NEXT_EVENT* edges which are basically local timelines comparable to the *timeline model*. As a result, it is possible to adapt the query from Listing 3 and create a slightly less complicated query not taking the detour over the *time tree*.

5.2   Question 2: Which IP Addresses Were Connected at a Given Timestamp?

For this question, it is required that the event type under investigation lives over a measurable timespan, which is the case for a connection bound by the *connect* and *disconnect* log entries and their associated event nodes. As input data, a point in time is given and as output, a list of ip addresses is expected which were connected at the specified point in time. In the following examples, the timestamp *2020-04-26 06:30:17 CEST* is used. Since *datetime* objects of Neo4J are timezone aware, a conversion to UTC might be required and is implicitly done if required [13]. It is also notable that the selected timestamp is not represented directly by any node because nothing happened at this timestamp in the input log file. As a result, it is not possible to directly use a node representing the desired timestamp for the subsequent queries.

Property-Based Model. The *property-based model* can work with the provided timestamp directly since the time information is, in any case, not stored in dedicated nodes. In Listing 5, the aim of the query, apart from the usual restrictions, is to create a temporary *datetime* object and compare all nodes in the database against it.

```
1   with datetime("2020-04-26T04:30:17.000Z") as timestamp
2   match
3   (connect:Pt_Event), (process:Pt_Process), (disconnect:Pt_Event),
4   (connect)-[:HAS_PID]->(process)<-[:HAS_PID]-(disconnect),
5   (connect)-[:IS_TYPE]->(:Pt_Type{name:'connect'}),
6   (disconnect)-[:IS_TYPE]->(:Pt_Type{name:'disconnect'})
7   where
8   datetime(connect.timestamp) <= timestamp and
9   datetime(disconnect.timestamp) >= timestamp and
10  (
11      datetime(connect.timestamp) < datetime(disconnect.timestamp)
12      or
13      datetime(connect.timestamp) = datetime(disconnect.timestamp)
    ↪   and
14      connect.order < disconnect.order
15  )
16  with disconnect
17  match (disconnect)-[:ATTACKER_IP]->(ip)
18  return distinct ip.ip as connected_ips
```

Listing 5: Finding the currently connected IP addresses for a specified point in time for the *property-based model*.

Timeline Model. Finding the connected IP addresses at a specific point in time in Listing 6 requires several steps. It works by first filtering all *connect* events before the given timestamp. For all resulting nodes, possible disconnection nodes are found and the shortest paths between them are calculated (multiple per connection node). In the next step, for each *connect* node, only the shortest path is retained. Based on this result, in the third step, all the *disconnect* nodes occurred before the desired timestamp are filtered out. The resulting nodes now have a connection before and a disconnection after the desired timestamp. Now the remaining task is fetching the remote IP addresses.

```
1  with datetime("2020-04-26T04:30:17.000Z") as timestamp
2  match
3  (connect:T1_Event)-[:HAPPENED_AT]->(connectTimestamp:T1_Timestamp),
4  (connect)-[:IS_TYPE]->(:T1_Type{name:'connect'}),
5  (disconnect:T1_Event)-[:HAPPENED_AT]->(disconnectTimestamp:T1_Timestamp),
6  (disconnect)-[:IS_TYPE]->(:T1_Type{name:'disconnect'}),
7  (connect)-[:HAS_PID]->(:T1_Process)<-[:HAS_PID]-(disconnect),
8  p=shortestPath((connectTimestamp)-[:NEXT*1..]->(disconnectTimestamp))
9  where
10 datetime(connectTimestamp.timestamp) <= timestamp
11 with timestamp, connect, p order by length(p) asc
12 with timestamp, connect, collect(p) as paths
13 with timestamp, connect, paths[0] as p
14 unwind nodes(p) as disconnectTimestamp
15 with timestamp, connect, disconnectTimestamp
16 match
17 (connect)-[:HAS_PID]->(:T1_Process)<-[:HAS_PID]-(disconnect),
18 (disconnect)-[:HAPPENED_AT]->(disconnectTimestamp),
19 (disconnect)-[:ATTACKER_IP]->(ip:T1_Ip)
20 where datetime(disconnectTimestamp.timestamp) >= timestamp
21 return ip.ip as connected_ips
```

Listing 6: Finding the currently connected IP addresses for a specified point in time for the *timeline model*.

Hierarchical Model. For finding the currently connected remote machines at a point in time in the hierarchical model, the approach from the *timeline model* is slightly adapted in Listing 7. Because this model does not support different timezones by default, the reference timestamp has to be adapted accordingly compared to the other models, which means adding two hours to convert UTC to CEST. Apart from this, the main difference is the way the time information is processed since the values for the *datetime* objects have to be extracted from the *time tree* first.

```
1   with datetime("2020-04-26T06:30:17.000Z") as timestamp
2   match
3   (year:Hr_Year)-[:FINER]->(month:Hr_Month)
4       -[:FINER]->(day:Hr_Day)
5       -[:FINER]->(hour:Hr_Hour)
6       -[:FINER]->(minute:Hr_Minute)
7       -[:FINER]->(second:Hr_Second),
8   (connect:Hr_Event)-[:HAPPENED_AT]->(second),
9   (connect)-[:IS_TYPE]->(:Hr_Type{name: 'connect'}),
10  (disconnect:Hr_Event)-[:IS_TYPE]->(:Hr_Type{name: 'disconnect'}),
11  p=shortestPath((connect)-[:NEXT_EVENT*1..]->(disconnect))
12  where
13  datetime({year: year.value, month: month.value, day: day.value,
    ↪   hour: hour.value, minute: minute.value, second:
    ↪   second.value})<=timestamp
14  with timestamp, connect, disconnect, p
15  with timestamp, connect, disconnect, p order by length(p) asc
16  with timestamp, connect, collect(p) as paths
17  with timestamp, connect, paths[0] as p
18  unwind nodes(p) as disconnect
19  with timestamp, connect, disconnect
20  match
21  (year:Hr_Year)-[:FINER]->(month:Hr_Month)
22      -[:FINER]->(day:Hr_Day)
23      -[:FINER]->(hour:Hr_Hour)
24      -[:FINER]->(minute:Hr_Minute)
25      -[:FINER]->(second:Hr_Second),
26  (connect)-[:HAS_PID]->(:Hr_Process)<-[:HAS_PID]-(disconnect),
27  (disconnect)-[:HAPPENED_AT]->(second),
28  (disconnect)-[:ATTACKER_IP]->(ip:Hr_Ip)
29  where
30  datetime({year: year.value, month: month.value, day: day.value,
    ↪   hour: hour.value, minute: minute.value, second:
    ↪   second.value})>=timestamp
31  return ip.ip as connected_ips
```

Listing 7: Finding the currently connected IP addresses for a specified point in time for the *hierarchical model*.

5.3   Question 3: Which of Two Given Log Entries Occurred Earlier?

For answering this question, two *Event* nodes are given by id and the query answers, which of the provided log entries occurred earlier. This time, the query solely uses the timestamp and ignores the precedence information. The query takes the first given node A as a reference and answers whether the second one B is less, equal or greater.

Property-Based Model. Finding the query for the actual question is as easy as Listing 8 which consists of selecting two nodes and then comparing their timestamp values.

```
1  match (a), (b) where id(a) = 168 and id(b) = 48
2  return
3      a.timestamp > b.timestamp as less,
4      a.timestamp = b.timestamp as equal,
5      a.timestamp < b.timestamp as greater
```

Listing 8: Answering which event occured before/after the other one in the *property-based model.*

Timeline Model. The query for the *timeline model* basically works like the previous one and is shown in Listing 9. Mainly, the time comparison is based on the existence of a directed *NEXT* path between the two nodes in question. For the case of value equality, an appropriate check is done. This leads to the unique property that the *equals* answer can be true in addition to *less* and *greater*.

```
1  match (a), (b) where id(a) = 51 and id(b) = 140 with a, b
2  match
3  (a)-[:HAPPENED_AT]->(aTimestamp:Tl_Timestamp),
4  (b)-[:HAPPENED_AT]->(bTimestamp:Tl_Timestamp)
5  return
6      exists((aTimestamp)<-[:NEXT*]-(bTimestamp)) as less,
7      datetime(aTimestamp.timestamp) =
   ↪  datetime(bTimestamp.timestamp) as equals,
8      exists((aTimestamp)-[:NEXT*]->(bTimestamp)) as greater
```

Listing 9: Answering which event occured before/after the other one in the *timeline model.*

Hierarchical Model. The answer for the precedence of event nodes in the *hierarchical model* is determined by the query in Listing 10.

Here, also a form of path existence check is used, but this time with *optional match.* The usage of *optional* allows the query to set the path variables to *null*, if no appropriate path is found. Like for the *timeline model*, the directions of *NEXT* edges are used, but to overcome the presence of the hierarchy of the *time tree*, the empty nodes, which are denoted by *()*, are required. Also, it has to be differentiated between the case where the shortest path is built using *NEXT* edges and a special case where only a common parent node is found.

```
1   match (a)-[:HAPPENED_AT]->(timestampA) where id(a) = 119 with *
2   match (b)-[:HAPPENED_AT]->(timestampB) where id(b) = 136 with *
3   optional match
4   p=((timestampA)<-[:FINER*0..]-()<-[:NEXT*]-()-[:FINER*0..]->(timestampB))
5   with *
6   optional match
7   q=((timestampA)<-[:FINER*0..]-()-[:NEXT*]->()-[:FINER*0..]->(timestampB))
8   with *
9   optional match
10  r=((timestampA)<-[:FINER*0..]-(commonA)<-[:FINER]-()-[:FINER]-
    ↪ >(commonB)-[:FINER*0..]->(timestampB))
11  return
12      p is not null or commonA.value > commonB.value as less,
13      timestampA = timestampB as equal,
14      q is not null or commonA.value < commonB.value as greater
```

Listing 10: Answering which event occured before/after the other one in the *hierarchical model*.

5.4   Question 4: Which Events Occurred X Time Units Before/After a Given Event?

When trying to find the root cause of an event, it may be of interest, which events occurred in a timeframe before or after a specific event. Accordingly, the id and timeframe of an event are given as input for this question (in this example, one hour ago). The expected results for the queries are all event nodes enclosed by the calculated timestamp on one side and the previously given event on the other side.

Property-Based Model. For answering the question in the property-based model, Listing 11 starts by querying an event node by id and extracting the timestamp. With this information, the second timestamp is calculated and then used for filtering all events in the database.

```
1  match (event:Pt_Event) where id(event) = 1267
2  with datetime(event.timestamp) as timestamp
3  with
4  datetime({year: timestamp.year, month: timestamp.month, day:
   ↪    timestamp.day, hour: timestamp.hour-1, minute:
   ↪    timestamp.minute, second: timestamp.second}) as
   ↪    lowerTimestamp,
5  timestamp as upperTimestamp
6  match (events:Pt_Event)
7  where
8  lowerTimestamp <= datetime(events.timestamp) and
9  datetime(events.timestamp) <= upperTimestamp
10 return events
```

Listing 11: Finding all events in a certain timeframe in the *property-based model*.

Timeline Model. The *timeline model* version is shown in Listing 12. Since it is unknown whether a *timestamp* node representing the second boundary exists, the timeline can only be exploited for one boundary and for the second, roughly the same approach as for the *property-based model* is applied.

```
1  match (event:Tl_Event)-[:HAPPENED_AT]->(timestamp:Tl_Timestamp)
2  where id(event)=1179
3  with timestamp, datetime(timestamp.timestamp) as timeVar
4  match
5  (earlierTimestamp:Tl_Timestamp)-[:NEXT*0..]->(timestamp),
6  (event:Tl_Event)-[:HAPPENED_AT]->(earlierTimestamp)
7  where
8  datetime(earlierTimestamp.timestamp) >=
   ↪    datetime({year:timeVar.year, month:timeVar.month,
   ↪    day:timeVar.day, hour:timeVar.hour-1, minute:timeVar.minute,
   ↪    second:timeVar.second})
9  return event
```

Listing 12: Finding all events in a certain timeframe in the *timeline model*.

Hierarchical Model. In the hierarchical model, we were not able to exploit the actual data structure at all. Instead, the solution in Listing 13 consists of an approach in which the data is read and converted from the hierarchical model and then processed like in the *property-based model*.

```
1   match (event:Hr_Event)-[:HAPPENED_AT]->
2       (second:Hr_Second)<-[:FINER]-
3       (minute:Hr_Minute)<-[:FINER]-
4       (hour:Hr_Hour)<-[:FINER]-
5       (day:Hr_Day)<-[:FINER]-
6       (month:Hr_Month)<-[:FINER]-
7       (year:Hr_Year)
8   where id(event) = 2150
9   with
10  datetime({year: year.value, month: month.value, day: day.value,
    ↪    hour: hour.value, minute: minute.value, second: second.value})
    ↪    as upperTimestamp,
11  datetime({year: year.value, month: month.value, day: day.value,
    ↪    hour: hour.value-1, minute: minute.value, second:
    ↪    second.value}) as lowerTimestamp
12  match
13      (event:Hr_Event)-[:HAPPENED_AT]->
14      (second:Hr_Second)<-[:FINER]-
15      (minute:Hr_Minute)<-[:FINER]-
16      (hour:Hr_Hour)<-[:FINER]-
17      (day:Hr_Day)<-[:FINER]-
18      (month:Hr_Month)<-[:FINER]-
19      (year:Hr_Year)
20  with lowerTimestamp, upperTimestamp, event,
21  datetime({year: year.value, month: month.value, day: day.value,
    ↪    hour: hour.value, minute: minute.value, second: second.value})
    ↪    as timestamp
22  where lowerTimestamp <= timestamp and timestamp <= upperTimestamp
23  return event
```

Listing 13: Finding all events in a certain timeframe in the *hierarchical model*.

6   Comparison of the Models

In the introduction, some criteria are mentioned upon which the three different models are compared against. The following only applies to the timestamp part of the models whereas the remaining information like *EventType* or *Process* is not of interest here.

Table 1 contains three dimensions for each model. *Expressiveness* covers, what kind of semantics can be encoded inside the model and to some extend, how this is done. More accurately this draws the line between implicit knowledge located outside the model and knowledge explicitly stored and displayed by the model. An Example: a user of the *Property-based Model* must know, how timestamps in the nodes can be accessed how they have to be sorted. In contrast, the *Timeline model* already covers this knowledge by explicitly providing directed edges between the nodes. With *complexity*, mainly the effort made by the user for writing the query is described. However, as can be concluded from [14], the *with* keyword divides the query into several logical parts, limiting the possibilities for the query optimizer. Therefore, a query with a lot of *with* statements is also costly to execute which also flows to some extend into the *complexity* measure. The row for *suitability* takes into account, that graph databases work by analyzing the structure of stored data and comments, whether such data is present in a usable form.

Performance measures have been conducted by selecting fixed events for each type of query for all three models and selecting their IDs so that the queries from Sect. 5 could be executed as proposed. The measurements where done by executing the query 1000 times as warm up allowing caches and optimizations to adapt and the execution times to converge, already with time measurement in place. Immediately following, the queries were executed 10000 times for the actual measurement. Finally, the arithmetic mean was used on the measurement executions, yielding the numbers shown in Table 2 and for better comparability visualized as bar chart in Fig. 6. The abbreviations used in Table 2, are the same as described in Fig. 5 and *Rl* is the relational database for reference. All numbers are given in milliseconds. The relational database for reference is an instance of MariaDB.

Table 1. Comparison of the different data models.

	Property-based model	Timeline model	Hierarchy model
Expressiveness	Low, simple property with dedicated datatype (only storage, no semantic information), supports timezones, property is not unique, needs additional property to resolve timestamp equality, user must know how to interpret stored data	Medium, simple property with dedicated datatype in dedicated node, supports timezones, node is not unique, semantic information: absolute temporal order given by directed edges	High, tree like structure with shared nodes, each node is unique, allows indication of timestamp precision, fine grained node fetching possible, no timezone support, relative temporal order of nodes of the same level and sub tree by directed edges, requires directed edge on timestamp equality
Complexity	Low, comparable complex as the equivalent query in a relational database	Medium, problem described in Sect. 7.1 forces usage of two different approaches for node access and matching	High, requires complex queries due to different levels when searching specific nodes
Suitability	Does not exploit graph database specific functionality	Basic usage of nodes and directed edges by constructing a global timeline	Extensive usage of nodes and edges, most information expressed by these elements

7   Findings

The following section contains some remarkable findings which arouse during the investigation of the three representations for timestamps.

7.1   How to Reference Arbitrary Timestamps

A major problem during the work with the three models was, how an arbitrary timestamp can be accessed. While this is not an issue for the *property-based model*, because every representation of a timestamp is only an instance of *date-time* with no further dedicated objects, a fully-fledged representation can be created instantly within the query without changing the database. This is not the case for the *timeline-* and *hierarchical model*. These two require at least one dedicated node per represented timestamp. As a result, it is not possible to use any arbitrary timestamp in a query because this timestamp may not exist in the database and would have to be created. Questions where this problem occurred are in Sect. 5.2 and 5.4.

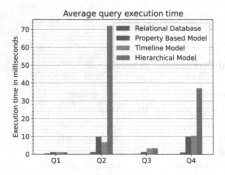

Fig. 6. Average execution time for each query in milliseconds.

Table 2. Absolute values of Fig. 6.

	Rl	Pt	Tl	Hr
Q1	0.50	1.16	1.16	1.15
Q2	1.19	9.82	6.72	71.89
Q3	0.24	1.22	7.22	3.41
Q4	1.03	10.00	10.42	37.01

7.2   Encoding the Order of Entries Is Mandatory

It is not sufficient to only rely on the timestamps saved to each log entry. For one log source, this problem might be omitted by adding precision to the timestamp, but in an environment producing large amounts of log lines, also this approach is not guaranteed to work. Latest when log entries from multiple machines need to be merged, precise timestamps require a sufficient synchronization between all involved clocks. According to [1], a clock synchronization in a LAN using Linux in it's default implementation came down to 8 to 10 μs and with their proposed implementation down to 2 μs, which might still not be accurate enough since thousand events in one second for a large enterprise are a very realistic number.

Without a sufficient encoding of log entry order, matching errors did occur. For example the question from Sect. 5.1 required precise information which events happened after itself. Otherwise, an disconnect before an instant reconnect can be recognized as the nearest event to the reconnect from a time perspective and be mistakenly paired together.

7.3   Complexity of Queries

Although this is not backed by metrics, the overall complexity of queries per question seem to differ whereas the *property-based model* being the model with the shortest queries, the *timeline model* being an intermediate one and the *hierarchical model* yields the most complex queries.

7.4   Expressiveness of the Models

The idea behind modeling timestamps in graph databases was in exploiting graph database specific characteristics for easier handling of the stored data. Due to the problem described in Sect. 7.1, with the current possibilities it is in some cases (especially Sect. 5.2 and Sect. 5.4) not possible to fully make use of graph database specific query techniques. Instead, the data need to be forced in a model which is already well used in relational databases.

Furthermore, one idea behind the *hierarchical model* was being able to represent different levels of precision by attaching event nodes accordingly which is also proposed in [3]. Attaching and matching event nodes on different levels might make the queries even more complicated but this needs further investigation.

8   Conclusion and Outlook

In this paper, three different models for representing timestamps in graph databases have been proposed. These models were then filled with test data originating from a live mail server and queries were developed retrieving certain predefined information out of the databases for each model. By comparing the resulting queries according to their complexity and by properties about the models themselves, they were compared against each other.

At the beginning, the *hierarchical model* seemed to be the most promising model because it heavily used of graph database specific structures and allowed indicating the precision of the data. Furthermore, variations of this model were proposed several times in non scientific sources [3,8]. In fact, it turned out that this model leads to very complex and inscrutable queries.

Another main finding was, that for making full use of a graph database's features, some queries require temporary structures which must not persist in the database. This was especially a problem of the *timeline model*, because if an arbitrary timestamp could be treated like an existing node, it would be easy to find all events located between two timestamp nodes. To circumvent this problem, an algorithm is required returning an equivalent node. As a fallback, the stored data is currently processed like it would be in a relational database.

The research results presented in this work will further be used in the authors ongoing research, e.g. applying the models and methods in the application in cyber physical systems (see Auer et al. [2]). Another applicable usage would be on earlier research of the authors, e.g. using the time-modelling on secure token-based communications for authentication and authorization servers (see Kubovy et al. [11]).

Acknowledgements. The research reported in this paper has been mostly supported by the LIT Secure and Correct Systems Lab.

Additionally this work has partially been supported by the FFG, Contract No. 854184: "Pro^{2}Future is funded within the Austrian COMET Program Competence Centers for Excellent Technologies under the auspices of the Austrian Federal Ministry of Transport, Innovation and Technology, the Austrian Federal Ministry for Digital and Economic Affairs and of the Provinces of Upper Austria and Styria. COMET is managed by the Austrian Research Promotion Agency FFG".

References

1. Aichhorn, A., Etzlinger, B., Mayrhofer, R., Springer, A.: Accurate clock synchronization for power systems protection devices over packet switched networks. Comput. Sci. Res. Dev. **32**(1–2), 147–158 (2017)
2. Auer, D., Jäger, M., Küng, J.: Linking trust to cyber-physical systems. In: Anderst-Kotsis, G., et al. (eds.) DEXA 2019. CCIS, vol. 1062, pp. 119–128. Springer, Cham (2019). https://doi.org/10.1007/978-3-030-27684-3_16
3. Bachman, M.: Graphaware neo4j timetree (2013). https://github.com/graphaware/neo4j-timetree
4. Chazelas, S.: PID reuse possibility in linux (2020). https://unix.stackexchange.com/a/414974
5. Chu, Z., Yu, J., Hamdulla, A.: A novel deep learning method for query task execution time prediction in graph database. Future Gener. Comput. Syst. **112**, 534–548 (2020)
6. cnicutar: Linux PID recycling (2020). https://stackoverflow.com/a/11323428/8428364
7. Diederichsen, L., Choo, K.-K.R., Le-Khac, N.-A.: A graph database-based approach to analyze network log files. In: Liu, J.K., Huang, X. (eds.) NSS 2019. LNCS, vol. 11928, pp. 53–73. Springer, Cham (2019). https://doi.org/10.1007/978-3-030-36938-5_4
8. GraphGrid, I.: Modeling time series data with neo4j (2015). https://www.graphgrid.com/modeling-time-series-data-with-neo4j/
9. Grüninger, M.: Verification of the OWL-time ontology. In: Aroyo, L., et al. (eds.) ISWC 2011. LNCS, vol. 7031, pp. 225–240. Springer, Heidelberg (2011). https://doi.org/10.1007/978-3-642-25073-6_15
10. Hobbs, J.R., Pan, F.: Time ontology in owl (2013). https://www.w3.org/TR/owl-time/
11. Kubovy, J., Huber, C., Jäger, M., Küng, J.: A secure token-based communication for authentication and authorization servers. In: Dang, T.K., Wagner, R., Küng, J., Thoai, N., Takizawa, M., Neuhold, E. (eds.) FDSE 2016. LNCS, vol. 10018, pp. 237–250. Springer, Cham (2016). https://doi.org/10.1007/978-3-319-48057-2_17

12. Maduako, I., Wachowicz, M.: A space-time varying graph for modelling places and events in a network. Int. J. Geogr. Inf. Sci. **33**(10), 1915–1935 (2019)
13. Neo4j, Inc.: 2.10. temporal (date/time) values (2020). https://neo4j.com/docs/cypher-manual/current/syntax/temporal/
14. Neo4j, Inc.: 7.5. shortest path planning (2020). https://neo4j.com/docs/cypher-manual/current/execution-plans/shortestpath-planning/
15. Neo4j, Inc.: Neo4j browser (2020). https://github.com/neo4j/neo4j-browser
16. Neo4j, Inc.: Neo4j graph platform (2020). https://neo4j.com/
17. Patton, A.J.: Modelling time-varying exchange rate dependence using the conditional copula. SSRN (2001)
18. Schwenk, J.: Modelling time for authenticated key exchange protocols. In: Kutyłowski, M., Vaidya, J. (eds.) ESORICS 2014. LNCS, vol. 8713, pp. 277–294. Springer, Cham (2014). https://doi.org/10.1007/978-3-319-11212-1_16
19. Semertzidis, K., Pitoura, E.: Time traveling in graphs using a graph database. In: EDBT/ICDT Workshops (2016)
20. Tao, X., Liu, Y., Zhao, F., Yang, C., Wang, Y.: Graph database-based network security situation awareness data storage method. EURASIP J. Wirel. Commun. Netw. **2018**(1), 294 (2018)
21. Theodoulidis, C.I., Loucopoulos, P.: The time dimension in conceptual modelling. Inf. Syst. **16**(3), 273–300 (1991)
22. Wiese, B., Omlin, C.: Credit card transactions, fraud detection, and machine learning: modelling time with LSTM recurrent neural networks. In: Bianchini, M., Maggini, M., Scarselli, F., Jain, L.C. (eds.) Innovations in Neural Information Paradigms and Applications. SCI, vol. 247, pp. 231–268. Springer, Berlin (2009). https://doi.org/10.1007/978-3-642-04003-0_10

Big Data Analytics and Distributed Systems

Integrating Web Services in Smart Devices Using Information Platform Based on Fog Computing Model

Takeshi Tsuchiya[1]([⊠]), Ryuichi Mochizuki[1], Hiroo Hirose[2], Tetsuyasu Yamada[1],
Norinobu Imamura[3], Naoki Yokouchi[3], Keiichi Koyanagi[4],
and Quang Tran Minh[5,6]

[1] Suwa University of Science, Chino, Japan
{tsuchiya,yamada}@rs.sus.ac.jp
[2] Suwa University of Science, Kitakyushu, Japan
hirose@rs.sus.ac.jp
[3] BIP Systems Inc., Tokyo, Japan
{imamura,yokouchi}@bip.co.jp
[4] Waseda University, Tokyo, Japan
keiichi.koyanagi@waseda.jp
[5] Faculty of Computer Science and Engineering, Ho Chi Minh City University
of Technology, 268 Ly Thuong Kiet, District 10, Ho Chi Minh City, Vietnam
[6] Vietnam National University Ho Chi Minh City, Linh Trung Ward,
Thu Duc District, Ho Chi Minh City, Vietnam
quangtran@hcmut.edu.vn

Abstract. In the present research, we propose an information platform
for integrating ordinary web services in smart devices. It is based on a
fog computing model that enables a fog node to mediate between web
services and smart devices. The proposed platform enables the use of
the same services and data regardless of the type of smart devices. As an
example of such a platform, we construct a ToDo management service
for teams collaborating via the Internet. The presented proposal outlines
the way of establishing communications between such a web service and
different kinds of smart speakers.

Keywords: Fog computing model · Smart speaker · Web Service

1 Introduction

At present, as a result of the advancement of the Internet of Things (IoT)
technologies improves, several kinds of devices called smart devices have been
developed that have both conventional functions and Internet connectivity. Such
devices have conventional functions and provide Internet connectivity. They are
aimed at improving the usability of conventional devices by adding new information services, as well as utilizing sensors and information from the Internet. The
emergence of various smart devices and services is expected in the future. However, most of the services available for smart devices are limited to the devices
provided by the same manufacturers or those sharing key components, such as

© Springer Nature Switzerland AG 2020
T. K. Dang et al. (Eds.): FDSE 2020, LNCS 12466, pp. 111–123, 2020.
https://doi.org/10.1007/978-3-030-63924-2_6

the same operating system. In other words, current services for smart devices usually do not enable connectivity with other services, for example, those used on PCs and smartphones. The usage of such services is limited to smart devices despite its convenience. A general strategy to resolve this problem is referred to as a business model for user enclosure. Amazon Alexa [1], Google home [2], and LINE Clova [3] compete in enabling these functions of their respective services, for example, such as smart speakers.

From the viewpoint of users, all smart speakers are designed to register speech upon triggering particular predefined keywords pronounced by users. Then, voice is converted to text using an individual cloud. A smart speaker recognizes a specific task based on the obtained textual information, such as providing weather information or the schedule of today. Generally, there is no large difference in services between two smart speakers, although they may differ in terms of quality. A service called skill is introduced to provide conformity to standards used in each smart speaker so that a service can be applicable to all smart speakers. In other words, although detailed protocols, data formats, and other details are different, it is considered that skills are executed with the similar data flow in smart speakers.

In the present paper, we propose a service integration platform for skill development to address differences in data formats, protocols, and environments of smart devices with similar data flows. As a specific target for development, a smart speaker is considered. The proposed platform enables users to connect to web services through various devices, including PC and smart phones, thereby overcoming the limitation of using a particular device only for a specific service. In this way, we aim to improve the development of smart device services and applications. In addition, in this paper, we clarify the differences between protocols for two different types of smart speakers and discuss features required in a service integration platform. To realize these features in the proposed platform, we utilize a fog computing model. Using this model allows connecting to the same web service through both PC and smart phones. As a result, heterogeneous smart speakers can collaborate on the application level. A discussion on the quality of skills of heterogeneous smart speakers is provided. Moreover, we investigate the linkage of existing web services with web application programming interfaces (APIs) within the proposed integration platform. The implementation of this paper shows that the web services that can be connected to smart devices are limited to those services that expose APIs such as REST.

2   Related Research and Approaches

IIn this section, we describe the related research works and introduce a novel approach constituting the main contribution of this study that is aimed to solve the research problem raised in the related publications.

2.1   Related Research

In recent years, fog computing has been proposed to improve the throughput of the cloud by distributing cloud functions to the edge nodes of the network.

Fog computing has been proposed to improve the throughput of cloud services by distributing cloud functions to the edge nodes of a network [4,5]. In this model, fog nodes at the edge of a network provide the functionality of a conventional cloud network (for example, data management and specific data processing functions).

A fog node works as a service gateway and a local server for users. It enables the transparent implementation of data processing in cloud networks and middleware. At present, load-balancing methods for cloud networks based on fog nodes are widely discussed. In this paper, we propose a method to ensure the privacy of the information managed in user groups, utilizing fog nodes as a private proxy function.

In the present research, we assume that fog nodes are allocated to each data unit, specifically, the information managed by user groups.

In [6], the aforementioned fog computing model was applied to personal data management. The speech data describing medical conditions that contained personal information was processed through speech analysis in a fog node. Then, only the text data corresponding to a diagnosis were sent to a cloud network. Fog nodes dynamically determined whether the information should have been sent to a cloud or not, and whether the privacy of information was protected appropriately. This method allowed protecting the user's privacy and at the same time, reducing the voice processing load in a cloud network.

In [7], the fog computing model was applied to a distributed IoT environment. It was found unfeasible to integrate all information in the case when sensors were distributed on a large scale, as it required large costs to aggregate all sensed information. Therefore, information was aggregated and processed in the vicinity of a sensor and then aggregated and sent to a server. Here, fog nodes we utilized as servers aggregating various sensed information in a local network. Moreover, a method to synchronize the information from multiple fog nodes in a cloud network was proposed [10,11].

In the present research, we focus on the processing of the textual information managed by a user group instead of the sensing information aggregated in a local server. To realize it, it is necessary to combine and synchronize the data from multiple fog nodes to apply a machine learning analysis. Therefore, it is required to introduce a new method to link information among fog nodes, as the function of a specific cloud network is insufficient.

2.2 Proposed Approach

The development environment on smart devices is more limited compared with those of conventional computers. Therefore, in this study, we adopt the fog computing model that implies deploying fog nodes in the proximity of a smart device [8,9]. A fog node behaves as a gateway and is aimed at connecting external web services to a smart devices, as shown in Fig. 1. Fog nodes provide necessary functions for web service clients that are unavailable in smart devices. For example, the use of APIs provided by web services and the registration of user login information can be realized on a smart device by interconnecting "skills"

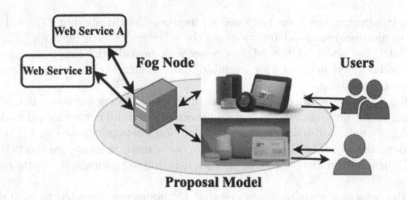

Fig. 1. Outline of proposal model

(applications) of nodes with a smart device in advance. As mentioned above, considering that there are several kinds of smart devices, it is required to connect standard web services using fog nodes. In this way, it is possible to share information with other smart devices. As a result, interconnection among different types of devices can be realized.

3   Development Environment of a Smart Device

In this section, we describe the development of smart speaker skills, which is equivalent to the development of ordinary applications. We consider Amazon Alexa and Google Home, the two most popular smart devices.

3.1   Skill Development in Amazon Alexa

Realizing a web service that links Amazon Alexa and an external web data source requires using Amazon Web Service (AWS) by Amazon in combination with a web server running an application. As shown in the upper part of Fig. 2, AWS employs Alexa to extract user intentions from voice information and utilizes Lambda to execute the program code based on the retrieved user intentions. This means that smart speaker applications (skills) are managed by Alexa and executed by AWS Lambda using the information acquired from user conversations. Utilizing https, it is possible to execute this procedure on an arbitrary web server outside an AWS network.

Alexa skills can be created by defining several types of intents in the Alexa developer console. To define an intent means to specify the relationship between a text message acquired based on pronounced words and a task to be processed. An intent can be considered as an intention of a speaker. Each intent may also correspond to a variable called a slot (for example, the weather today). In this case, a value of "2020-11" is inserted, corresponding to the date of "today".

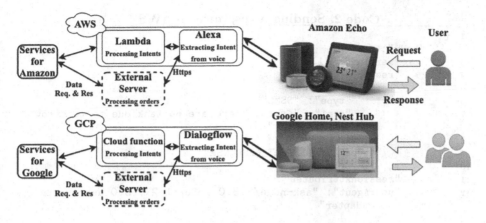

Fig. 2. Development environment of smart speakers

Then, the user's original skills are executed by extracting commands from the words pronounced by a user, and the corresponding processes based on the predefined intents are executed. The definition of an intent and its processing is described in JSON format, as shown in the upper part of Fig. 2. The information required to generate a response is also created in advance in JSON format (Code 1), and a processing result is inserted as a slot. All this information is communicated using http, facilitating the collaboration with external web services using representational state transfer (REST). The JSON code provided below is an example of setting up commands and responses to extract from user speech.

Code 1. Receiving an intent from AWS

```
1  {
2      "version": "1.0",
3      "request": {
4          "type": "IntentRequest",
5          "requestId": "amzn1.echo-api.request.3180b2f-2980-406b-8
                cb4-921073729ddd",
6          "timestamp": "2020-03-18100:57:221",
7          "locale": "ja-JP",
8          "intent": {
9              "name": "ShowTomorrowTaskIntent",
10             "confirmationStatus": "NONE",
11             "slots": {
12                 "dateslot": {
13                     "name": "dateslot",
14                     "value": "2020-03-19",
15                     "confirmationStatus": "NONE",
16                     "source": "USER"
17                 }
18             }
19         }
20     }
21 }
```

Code 2. Sending a response to AWS

```
1  {
2      "body": {
3          "version": "1.0",
4          "response": {
5              "outputSpeech": {
6                  "type": "SSML",
7                  "ssm1": "<speak>There are no task due to tomorrow
                        </speak>"
8              },
9              "type": "_DEFAULT_RESPONSE"
10         },
11         "sessionAttributes": {},
12         "userAgent": "ask-node/2.3.0 Node/v1 2 . 6.0 ask-express
                -adapter"
13     }
14 }
```

3.2   Skill Development in Google Home

Skill development in Google Home is illustrated at the lower part of Fig. 2. It is generally similar to that of Alexa but requires using the Google Cloud Platform (GCP) provided by Google. Here, the user's statements are transmitted to Dialogflow in GCP and are executed through a cloud function in a program execution environment. It is also possible to consider collaboration with external web services.

The development of skills is similar to the definition of intents in ADB mentioned above, describing the relationship between text information and the corresponding processes defined in Dialogflow. In this case, the date and other variables are defined as requirements. Then, a cloud function is executed based on these definitions. In the same manner as in the case AWS, https can be employed to enable execution on own web server outside a cloud, without running a cloud function. Thereafter, the data required to generate a response are acquired from an external service, and the relevant response text is defined by embedding this information in JSON. This procedure is represented by **Code 3 and 4**.

Code 3. Receiving an intent from GCP

```
1  {
2       "responseId": "7c5a13ad-5201-4add-bf35-4dd8c9b4390e-dd2bbea9
         ",
3       "queryResult": {
4          "queryText": "Let me know my task until tomorrow",
5          "parameters": {
6              "date": "2020-03-26712:00:00+09:00"
7          },
8          "allRequiredParamsPresent": true,
9          "outputContexts": [
10             {
11                 "name": "projects/sample-todoapp",
12                 "parameters": {
13                     "no-input": 0,
14                     "no-match": 0,
15                     "date": "2020-03-26712:00:00+09:00",
16                     "date.original": "Tomorrow"
17                 }
18             }
19         ],
20         "intent": {
21             "displayName": "showTaskIntent"
22         }
23      }
24  }
```

A service integrated platform is intended to receive user intents in textual format from each environment and executes them by itself instead of using a cloud. Accordingly, an integrated platform can be used as an interface for external services to acquire and control data, as shown in Fig. 3. A response from an application is received by such an integrated platform. Then, it is adapted to the requesting environment of a smart speaker and is sent to a user in a form of a final response.

To support multiple environments underlying different types of smart speakers, an integrated platform can identify a speaker using a unique ID, such as a device ID added in an intent and a response. In the near future, as multiple intents may be transmitted from the same smart device, employing a session ID for each intent will be also considered.

Code 4. Sending a response to GCP

```
1  {
2       "fullfillmentText": "There are no task due tomorrow.",
3       "outputContexts" : []
4  }
```

3.3 Features of the Proposed Service Integration Platform

Both of the aforementioned cases, Amazon Alexa and Google Home, are identical in terms of the upper levels of functionality: extracting parameters and a speaker intent (for example, date), executing programs based on extraction, and retrieving and vocalizing processing results. However, the details of a protocol and parameters that are actually coded, as well as an execution environment, are different. Therefore, it is necessary to convert them aiming to adapt to the proposed service integration platform. To convert an intent of a speaker into text, it is necessary to register an intent for each application separately.

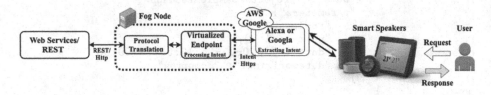

Fig. 3. Sequence of converting data in the proposed platform

4 Implementation

In this section, we evaluate the feasibility of the proposed approach named service integrated platform by constructing a web service and connecting smart speakers.

4.1 Converting the Data by the Proposed Service Integrated Platform

Data processing required to integrate smart speakers and external web applications is conducted on the proposed service integration platform using a fog node, as shown in Fig. 3. The smart speaker requests the executing the skill based on user intent, since fog node providing the integrated platform is virtualized as connecting web service in the view of smart speaker and then waits for a response. The received request is converted into a message according to the type of a smart speaker using the integrated platform, and the request is sent to a URL corresponding to an external web service. The response provided to a smart speaker is adapted based on that provided by a web application and then is sent to a user.

4.2 Target Web Service

In the present study, we developed a web application called the ToDo app to manage task deadlines. It was realized as a web application for both browser-based services and smart speakers. It had an update function to display a list of managed tasks, the status of tasks, and so on. The composition of this application is illustrated in Fig. 2.

The web application included the main application and a view function. Specifically, the main body of the application comprised a database to manage task information and an application for task management application. The view function included a graphic user interface (GUI) representing a user view and a REST-type API that served as an interface for a smart speaker. Table 1 describes the REST API realized in this application. REST provided URLs corresponding to each function of the application so that each URL could be used as an endpoint for transmission and reception. This allowed using web applications from an outside service.

Table 1. REST interface

Functions	URL
Get Information of Task	GET /api/c1/tasks
Insert Task	POST /api/v1/tasks/create
Update Task Info.	POST /api/v1/tasks/update/task ID
Get User Information	GET /api/v1/user/userID
Update User Info.	POST /api/v1/user/update/user ID

Fig. 4. Interface of web application

The tasks managed in a web application had entries, as described in Table 1. The interface provides for the retrieval of the following data via the API; task name, due date, creation, update, and summary. Figure 4 represents a screenshot of these tasks as displayed in a browser. The interface provided a simple structure and was easy to add or to modify.

The REST interface used for smart speakers was designed to separate a web server from a browser. This allowed providing combined services. It enabled a mapping between a web service and a user intent for each smart speaker and allowed addressing the differences between different devices.

4.3 Behaviors of the Proposed Service Integration Platform

The proposed service integration platform is designed to acquire resource information from REST or similar interfaces in endpoint web applications. It allows incorporating the differences between devices by mapping web service APIs to a user intent obtained from each smart speaker.

We applied the integrated platform to the aforementioned the ToDo apps in this paper. Table 2 shows the mapping between the features of the ToDo app and intents in the integrated platform as an example. All functions listed in Table 1 correspond to the features described in this table. The format of URL is "/fullfillment/intent name".

Table 2. Mapping to the web Apps interface

URL	Intent
/fullfillment/ShowTaskIntent	Show Task Intent
/fullfillment/ShowTomorrowTaskIntent	Show Tomorrow Task Intent
/fullfillment/NumSpecifiedIntent	Num Specified Intent
/fullfillment/TaskCheckIntent	Task Check Intent
Functions	Parameters
Confirmation recent tasks	None
Confirmation of deadline on tomorrow	Date
Confirmation of a specified number of previous tasks	Number
Confirmation of the specified task	Intent Name

A protocol corresponding to URLs of each smart speaker and each function of a web application was defined in JSON, as shown in **Code 5**. "In" shown in **Code 5.** means an intent based on user speech, and the values of variables, such as date, are included. The response content is passed to a smart speaker in a textual format, as shown in **Code 5**.

Code 5. Data format between integrated platform and web application

```
1  In
2  {
3      "Intent" : string,
4      "param" : {
5          "value" : string | number
6      }
7  }
8  Out
9  {
10     "speakText" : string
11 }
12 {
13     "appname" : "todoapp",
14 "
15     "fullfillments" : [
16         {
17             "name" : "Show Task Intent",
18             "locale" : "http://localhost/api/fullfillment/
                   showtaskintent",
19             "parameter" : [ ]
20         },
21         {
22             "name" : "Show Task By Date Intent",
23             "locale" : "http://localhost/api/fullfillment/
                   shottaskbydateintent",
24             "parameter" : ["date"]
25         }
26     ]
27 }
```

4.4 Mapping to Web Apps

The proposed service integrated platform is aimed to manage the mapping between an intent corresponding to each smart speaker and the functionality of a web app. To do this, the platform virtualizes the functions of a web application as "skills" (applications in smart speakers) for each smart speaker. Specifically, the integrated platform manages each function of a web application. Therefore, it is possible to represent skills transparently to web applications and receive responses. In this way, the integrated platform manages the mapping between intents received from users and the functions of a web application in JSON format, as shown in **Code 5**.

5 Issues and Summary

In the present paper, we introduced a method of interconnecting web services through a service integrated platform using a REST interface in the ToDo app. At present, applications for smart speakers are implemented independently for each type of device. The integrated platform proposed in this paper was aimed at enabling smart speaker manufacturers and users to connect to the same web application regardless of the type of a smart speaker manufacturer or a user. The use of the proposed platform revealed an expansion of the application of smart speakers by expanding the available services.

Namely, we considered smart devices including smart speakers. We noted that currently available applications (skills) did not store the user and account information on smart devices. Accordingly, it was not possible to provide the minimum functionality required to use web services, such as managing the devices utilized by a user and operating session information for each skill. In this way, smart speakers could not provide advanced services for users, such as optimization and personalization of the utilization of an application. To provide the same usability as that available for web users, we introduced a platform that could cover missing functionality. Similarly as the mapping between REST API and user intents described in this paper, it is possible to consider a method to manage users and session information at a fog node. At the same time, it is necessary to improve the usability of the proposed method by registering information on an integrated platform and facilitating the convenience of mapping between information an skills.

At present, smart speakers from Google and Amazon are mainly the devices with a screen display. It is expected that the functions of smart devices will be improved, and other similar smart devices developed by other companies will appear on the market in the future. Therefore, the provision of advanced skills while using video, sensors, and other technologies will be required. In this case, the same level of serviceability will be expected from service integration platforms. We will focus on these considerations to improve the functionality and expandability of the proposed integrated platform in the future.

References

1. Amazon Alexa. https://alexa.amazon.com/
2. Google Home. https://store.google.com/jp/product/google_home
3. LINE Colva. https://clova.line.me/
4. Bonomi, F., Milito, R., Natarajan, P., Zhu, J.: Fog computing: a platform for Internet of Things and analytics. In: Bessis, N., Dobre, C. (eds.) Big Data and Internet of Things: A Roadmap for Smart Environments. SCI, vol. 546, pp. 169–186. Springer, Cham (2014). https://doi.org/10.1007/978-3-319-05029-4_7
5. Alrawais, A., Alhothaily, A., Hu, C., Cheng, X.: Fog computing for the Internet of Things: security and privacy issues. IEEE Internet Comput. 21(2), 34–42 (2017)
6. Dubey, H., et al.: Handbook of Large-Scale Distributed Computing in Smart Healthcare, pp. 281–321 (2007)
7. Abuseta, Y.: A fog computing based architecture for IoT services and applications development. Int. J. Comput. Trends Technol. (IJCTT) 67(10) (2019)
8. Tsuchiya, T., et al.: Dynamic data management strategy on cloud network by fog computing model. In: Dang, T.K., Küng, J., Takizawa, M., Bui, S.H. (eds.) FDSE 2019. LNCS, vol. 11814, pp. 332–342. Springer, Cham (2019). https://doi.org/10.1007/978-3-030-35653-8_22

9. Tsuchiya, T., Mochizuki, R., Hirose, H., Yamada, T., Koyanagi, K., Minh Tran, Q.: Distributed data platform for machine learning using the fog computing model. SN Comput. Sci. **1**(3), 1–9 (2020). https://doi.org/10.1007/s42979-020-00171-6
10. Minh, Q.T., Huu, P.N., Tsuchiya, T., Toulouse, M.: Openness in fog computing for the Internet of Things. In: Dang, T.K., Küng, J., Takizawa, M., Bui, S.H. (eds.) FDSE 2019. LNCS, vol. 11814, pp. 343–357. Springer, Cham (2019). https://doi.org/10.1007/978-3-030-35653-8_23
11. Tran, Q.M., Nguyen, P.H., Tsuchiya, T., Toulouse, M.: Designed features for improving openness, scalability and programmability in the fog computing-based IoT systems. SN Comput. Sci. **1**(4), 1–12 (2020). https://doi.org/10.1007/s42979-020-00197-w

Adaptive Contiguous Scheduling for Data Aggregation in Multichannel Wireless Sensor Networks

Van-Vi Vo, Tien-Dung Nguyen, Duc-Tai Le, and Hyunseung Choo[✉]

Sungkyunkwan University, Suwon, South Korea
{vovanvi,ntdung,ldtai,choo}@skku.edu

Abstract. These days multichannel wireless sensor networks (MWSNs) have been concerned in data aggregation since the data aggregation delay is significantly reduced. However, in these environments we must consider not only timeslot collisions but also channels collisions. Along with that problem, the data collection rate and energy consumption of the networks are also important problems needed to be solved. In this paper, we propose a scheduling scheme named Adaptive Contiguous Scheduling for the data aggregation in MWSNs. This proposed scheme applies the parents changing approach and channels reused strategy to reduce the number of channels used to allocate nodes in the network leading to preserve the energy consumption. The experimental results show that our scheme reduces the amount of used channels up to 69.57% and 72%, as compared to state-of-the-art algorithms.

Keywords: Multichannel WSNs · Data aggregation · Parent changing

1 Introduction

A wireless sensor networks (WSN) consists of a large amount of sensor nodes deploying in such dangerous, unreachable area where human cannot reach to monitor the environments in disaster areas or collect information, detect events in military field, and so on. Recently multichannel wireless sensor networks (MWSNs) have been concerned in data aggregation to maximize data collection rate since more sensor nodes simultaneously transmit data to their parents. However, the single-channel wireless sensor networks (SWSNs) only consider timeslots collisions while doing nodes schedule, whereas NWSNs consider both channels and timeslot collisions separately because channels and timeslots are mutually resources.

The sensor nodes have limited energy resources and are non-rechargeable devices thus both energy preservation and network lifetime improvement for sensor nodes are primary problems in WSNs. The reduction of using channels to allocate sensor nodes in a network is one of the methods to reduce the energy consumption as well as improve the network lifetime. In [1–3], the authors use tree based multichannel allocation approach connects nodes between trees with no collisions. The approach leaves some channel conflicts then it is solved later by retransmitting the failed data. In [4], the authors

T. K. Dang et al. (Eds.): FDSE 2020, LNCS 12466, pp. 124–133, 2020.
https://doi.org/10.1007/978-3-030-63924-2_7

propose a cluster-based distributed data aggregation scheduling that can minimize the data aggregation delay and save the energy. They name their scheme as DMPMC, which divides the network into clusters and uses low transmissions power inside clusters, high transmission power between cluster heads. There is an approach that allocates different channels for neighbor nodes [5–7], this approach is known as interference-free approach. Data transmitting between nodes are channel interference-free, but it makes the number of channels used expressively increases.

In [8], the authors propose a scheme that allocate channels and assign timeslots to reduce channels and minimize data aggregation delay in the multichannel networks. Based on the received-based constraint graph (RCG) proposed in [9], the authors minimize the channel switching by allocating same channel to neighbors after calculating the size of subtrees, moreover they minimize the energy consumption by reducing the number of channels. The Largest Degree First scheme (LDF) in [9] also builds the RCG, then they allocate channels for nodes having highest degrees first. Adjacent nodes are allocated different channels, so [9] just focuses on avoiding channels collision.

In this paper, we address the problem of reducing the number of channels using to allocate sensor nodes in a network since used channels reduction leads to preserve the energy consumption. We present the scheme named Adaptive Contiguous Scheduling based on the RCG and subtrees grouping, we apply parents changing approach to maximize the number of descendent nodes in a subtree and we reuse the used channels in previous working periods so that the number of channels using to allocate the nodes in a network can be reduced.

The rest of this paper is organized as follows: In Sect. 2, we describe the network model and problem formulation. The scheduling scheme is described in detail in the Sect. 3 along with an illustrative example. Section 4 presents the simulation scenarios and results. Finally, we conclude the paper and discuss our future research directions in Sect. 5.

2 Preliminaries

We consider a WSN to be a graph $G(V, E)$ where V is the set of sensor nodes including a sink, and E is the set of edges. Each node in the network is considered as a single station, and each node uses an omnidirectional antenna. If two nodes in the network are in each other's transmission ranges, they are neighbors and can communicate to each other. We assume that a network is always connected, it means that any node in the network can find a way to connect and send its data to the sink. Each sensor node can only transmit or receive the data at a time, it means that a collision happens when the sensor node gets data from two or more neighbors at the same time. There are two types of collisions in wireless sensor networks as shown in the Fig. 1.

We assume that sensor nodes in a network are assigned active slots based on the scheduling scheme, and these active slots assignments for those sensor nodes are maintained throughout the data aggregation. This approach is called Dynamic Duty Cycle. In this approach, at a designated slot, a sensor node wakes up to get data from its neighbor, we call this is active slot, then the sensor node goes back to sleep mode.

We consider to group subtrees based on the number of timeslots in a working period. We assume that the time to transmit or receive data and aggregate it can fit into one timeslot. Nodes in a subtree are allocated in a same channel. When doing nodes schedule in a new working period, the channels used before can be reused to allocate to sensor nodes in higher layers. This strategy helps to reduce the number of allocated channels as well as number of channels switching so that the energy consumption of sensor nodes is also reduced.

In previous studies, after the aggregation tree is built, the nodes in tree are assigned their parents and children (for non-leaf nodes). After that they keep parent-children assignments for those nodes while doing nodes schedule until the scheduling completes. In this paper, we perform parent changing approach while scheduling. This approach is applied aiming to increase number of nodes in a subtree as well as reduce the total number of subtrees grouped so that the number of allocated channels is also reduced.

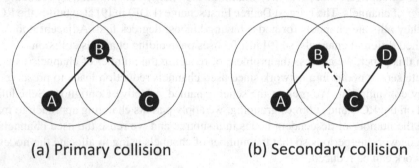

(a) Primary collision   (b) Secondary collision

Fig. 1. Two types of collisions: primary collision and secondary collision. (a) The primary collision happens at node B as it receives data from nodes A and C at the same time. (b) The secondary collision happens at node B as it received unexpected data from its neighbor - Node C

3   Scheduling Scheme

This paper focuses on the reducing number of channels when doing nodes schedule, so we will only present the scheduling scheme in detail. We firstly build the aggregation tree using Shortest Path Tree (SPT) algorithm, then we build the RCG same as [9] to prevent the secondary collision. Two nodes u and v in the communication graph are adjacent nodes in RCG when neighbors of u are from the descendent nodes of v. So that two adjacent nodes in the RCG should be allocated in different channels.

We describe our scheduling scheme in this section. The Table 1 lists the notations used throughout the paper.

3.1   Adaptive Contiguous Scheduling

The Algorithm 1 shows the procedures of nodes schedule of Adaptive Contiguous scheduling algorithm. Assume that we have done the aggregation tree construction T and the constraint graph G_c, given the number of timeslot in a working period, and the set of given channels (we can use unlimited number of channels). The output after running the

Table 1. Notations and explanation

Notation	Explanation
$G = (V, E)$	Communication graph G consists of V nodes and E edges
$T = (V, E_T)$	Aggregation tree T consists of V nodes and E_T edges
$G_c = (V_c, E_c)$	Constraint graph G_c consists of V_c non-leaf nodes and E_c conflict links
$u.tx\_channel$	Transmitting channel of node u
$u.rx\_channel$	Receiving channel of node u
$u.timeslot$	Timeslot of node u
$neighbors(u)$	Set of neighbor nodes of node u
$desc(u)$	Set of descendent nodes of node u

algorithm is that all nodes in the aggregation tree are allocated channels and assigned timeslots without any collisions happens.

Initially, all nodes in the tree have not assigned channels and timeslots yet, the number of scheduled nodes is empty, the set of channels needs to be avoided for the channels conflict is set empty (lines 1–4). We find the set S_L contains nodes having the number of descendent nodes is less than or equal to L, and set S_L^+ consists of nodes that have the number of descendent nodes is larger than L (These steps determine subtrees) (lines 6–8). Then we consider if there are existing nodes in S_L, the algorithm selects the nodes having highest number of descendent nodes, if the largest subtree has small number of descendent nodes, the parent changing approach is invoked to extend the length of the subtree closely to the length of timeslot in a working period. After that since the parent and as well as children nodes of the node applying parent changing approach has changed, we update the constraint graph G_c (lines 9–13).

After updating the subtree, the set I adopts channels that belong to adjacent nodes of the subtree root node. Then we start to assign the current working period of the root node and all its descendent nodes. The root node of the subtree is allocated a receiving channel by avoiding all channels in set I. The descendent nodes in the subtree are then assigned transmitting channel (same as receiving channel of root node) and timeslots in a bottom-up manner (lines 19–24).

Algorithm 1: Adaptive Contiguous Scheduling algorithm

Input: $T = (V, E_T)$, $G_c = (V_c, E_c)$, L, F

    $//L$: number of timeslots in a working period,

    $//F$: Set of given channels

Output: Channel and Timeslot assignment for every node u in V

1. $\forall u \in V$, $u.tx\_channel \leftarrow unallocated$, $u.rx\_channel \leftarrow unallocated$,
    $u.timeslot \leftarrow unassigned$ // Initialization

2. $SCH = \emptyset$

3.   **while** $|SCH|\ != = |V|$ **do**

4. $I = \emptyset$ // I is a set of channels for avoiding the channel conflicts

5. $//S_L$ is a set of nodes that the number of descendants is less than or equal to L

6. $S_L = \{ u \in V_c \text{ such that } |desc(u)| \leq L \}$

7. $//S_L^+$ is a set of nodes that the number of descendent nodes is larger than L

8. $S_L^+ = \{ u \in V_c \text{ such that } |desc(u)| > L \}$

9.   **if** $S_L\ !=\emptyset$ **then**

10.   Find node $x = \text{argmax}_{u \in S_L} |desc(u)|$

11.   **if** $|desc(x)| < L$ **then**

12.   Let x acquire more unscheduled nodes to maximize $|desc(x)|$ such
              that $|desc(x)| \leq L$ //Parent changing operation

13.   Update $G_c = (V_c, E_c)$

14.   **end if**

15.   **end if**

16.   **if** $S_L = \emptyset$ and $S_L^+\ !=\emptyset$ **then**

17.   Find node $x = \underset{u \in S_L^+}{\text{argmin}} |desc(u)|$

18.   **end if**

19. $I = \{v.tx\_channel | v \in neighbors(x) \text{ in } G_c\}$

20.   **if** $|desc(x)| \leq L$ **then**

21.   Assign working period to x and all descendent nodes

22. $x.rx\_channel = min(F \backslash I)$ // Assign channels to root node of subtree

23.   Assign channel and timeslots to all nodes in the subtree

24.   **end if**

25.   **if** $|desc(x)| > L$ **then**

26.   Break the subtree rooted at x into several subtrees such that all the subtrees
        have the number of descendent nodes less than or equal to L

27.   Assign same channel but different working periods to above subtrees by
        considering collisions with neighbor nodes

28.   Assign working periods, channel and timeslot to all nodes in the subtrees

29.   **end if**

30.   Add scheduled nodes to SCH

31.   Remove $desc(x)$ from T

32. **end while**

When all subtrees which have number of descendent nodes smaller or equal than L have been scheduled, there are cases that some subtrees have higher number of descendent nodes than L, we find the subtree having smallest number of descendent node and still larger than L (it means that we consider subtrees in lower layers first). The algorithm breaks the subtree into several subtrees such that all the subtrees have the number of descendent nodes less than or equal to L. As each small subtree is scheduled in one working period, so that these small subtrees are allocated a same channel (reused the channel in previous working periods) but different working periods. Then we assign working periods, transmitting channels and timeslot for descendent nodes in small subtrees (lines 25–29). The set of scheduled nodes SCH appends scheduled nodes, and the nodes which are already scheduled will be removed all descendent nodes from tree T (lines 30–31). The algorithm works in the same procedures until SCH includes all nodes of the considering network.

3.2 Example

To illustrate the proposed scheme, we present a sample network topology shown in the Fig. 2a. Node S is the sink node placed at the top of the network, the length of timeslots in a working period is $L = 4$. The aggregation tree is built based on hop distance to the sink, also known as shortest-path tree, given in Fig. 2b. At the working period 1, there are two subtrees are determined which are rooted at nodes A (the subtree has two descendent nodes) and B (the subtree has one descendent node) shown in the Fig. 2c. Since the length $L = 4$, and the descendent nodes of the subtrees are small, so we try to maximize the number of descendent nodes of the subtree by changing parent of neighbors. The node B is the child of node sink S and the neighbor of node A, we break the link connecting between node B and node S to connect between node B and node A. As displayed in Fig. 2d, node B adopts node A as its parent, the sink S becomes neighbor of node B. Up to now there is only one subtree rooted at node A has four descendent nodes, all nodes in this subtree are allocated a same channel f1, the timeslots are assigned to the links in the subtree in a bottom-up manner. There is no more subtree to schedule in the working period one, we consider the remaining nodes in the working period 2.

In the working period 2, there is one subtree left rooted at sink node S, we reuse the channel f1 to allocate to the nodes in this subtree, and the timeslots are one by one assigned to links as shown in Fig. 2e. So far, we have done the nodes schedule for nodes in the sample network, the Fig. 2f shows the final aggregation time, with two working periods we use one channel only and all four timeslots.

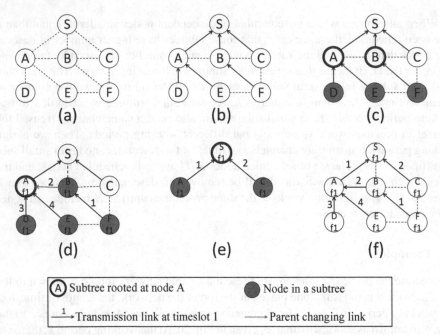

Fig. 2. Example. (a) Original graph, (b) Aggregation tree, (c) Subtrees determined, (d) Parent changing operation and nodes schedule, (e) Nodes schedule, (f) Final data aggregation time

4   Performance Evaluation

In this section, we evaluate the performance of channels reuse and parents changing methods applying to the nodes schedule algorithm to show how effective of the improvement on number of channels used through different network simulation scenarios.

All the simulations in this paper are programmed by using Python. We first build a well-known aggregation tree – SPT, then based on that we schedule nodes in the tree. We use same environment settings as in [8]. A sensor network consists of 100 sensor nodes randomly deployed including the sink node in a two-dimensional square area with the size $200 \times 200\,\text{m}^2$. We assume that the data in each node are already collected before sending it to its parent, and each node transmits its data to all neighbor at once as well as receives data from its neighbors at once if two more neighbors send data at a time. The transmission range is varying from 25 to 50 m, the length of timeslots in a working period is changed with values 4, 6, 8, 10.

We generate 100 random network topologies to do the simulation for each combination of the parameters, and then collect the average results.

We compare our scheme with the two existing schemes [8, 9] under different simulation settings. As a matter of convenience, we name the scheme in [8] as CTCS and the scheme in [9] is LDF.

By increasing the transmission range of a node, we conduct the simulation to measure how the dense networks impact on number of used channels. As the transmission range increases, it means the density of networks is higher, the interferences between nodes also increase. The Fig. 3 shows that our proposed scheme – Adaptive Contiguous scheduling required a smaller number of channels compared with the reference schemes – LDF and CTCS schemes. Like the reference schemes, when the transmission range increases, the number of channels used to allocate nodes in a network in adaptive contiguous scheduling scheme also increases because when the transmission range increases, the number of links in the RCG increases, the neighbors of each node in RCG become higher so that the possibility of using different channels for surrounding nodes increases. The reason that our proposed scheme presents better performance than LDF and CTCS is that we reuse channels at every new working period and apply parent changing approach.

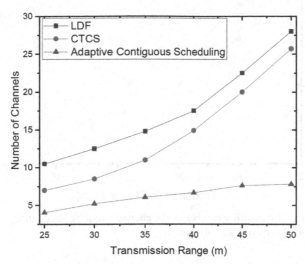

Fig. 3. Performance of the number of channels used according to the increasing of transmission range.

When applying the parent changing approach, the number of descendent nodes of each subtree is maximized to the length of timeslot in a working period, so that we utilize the number of timeslots used in each subtree and the number of the subtrees is reduced, then the number of assigned channels is also reduced. Compared with LDF and CTCS, the Adaptive Contiguous Scheduling scheme can improve the number of used channels at transmission range 25 m is 61.3% and 42%, respectively. When the transmission range increases up to 50 m, our proposed scheme shows 72% and 69.57% of channels reduction compared with LDF and CTCS. Our proposed scheme operates more efficient when the transmission range increases.

Figure 4 shows the impact of increasing the transmission range on number of used channels for each case of dynamic duty cycle. As the higher of the number of timeslots is, the lower of the duty is. The results show that when the duty is reduced, the number of channels using for allocating nodes is decreased because the smaller of the duty is, the higher of number of timeslots in a working period, so that more nodes are added to a subtree assigned a same channel with different timeslots, leading to the number of the subtrees is reduced. The Fig. 4 also presents that when the transmission range enlarges, the number of allocated channels enhances since the number of neighbor nodes extends when the transmission range increases so that adjacent nodes must be allocated in different channels.

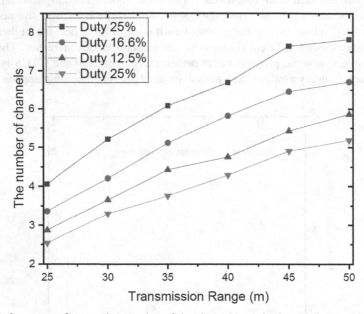

Fig. 4. Performance of measuring number of the channels required according to the increasing of transmission ranges for dynamic duty cycles.

5   Conclusion and Future Work

In this paper, we propose an approach that allocates channels and assigns timeslots to reduce used channels in MWSNs. The scheme first builds a constraint graph for non-leaf nodes to avoid secondary collisions when allocating channels for nodes in the network. Then the scheme groups subtrees rooted at the nodes in the constraint graph to allocate channels and assign timeslots in a bottom-up manner for descendent nodes. At that time, the scheme tries to maximize the number of descendent nodes of the subtrees by applying parent changing method. Also, when a new working period starts, the channels can be reused from previous working periods. Through the network simulation, the proposed scheme improves the number of used channels so that the sensor nodes can preserve the energy leading to the network lifetime is improved. As the current scheme is working on unlimited channels allocation, which is not practical in the real life, so we will study other works on data aggregation in limited number of channels in MWSNs in our future research.

Acknowledgement. This work was partly supported by Institute of Information & communications Technology Planning & Evaluation (IITP) grant funded by the MSIT (Ministry of Science and ICT), Korea, under the ICT Creative Consilience program (IITP-2020-2051-001) and grant funded under the GITRC support program (IITP-2020-2015-0-00742), and also supported by the National Research Foundation of Korea (NRF-2020R1A2C2008447).

References

1. Abdulaziz, M., Simon, R.: Multi-channel network coding in tree-based wireless sensor networks. In: 2015 International Conference on Computing, Networking and Communications (ICNC), Garden Grove, CA, pp. 924–930 (2015). https://doi.org/10.1109/iccnc.2015.7069470
2. Yigit, M., et al.: On the interdependency between multi-channel scheduling and tree-based routing for WSNs in smart grid environments. Comput. Networks **65**, 1–20 (2014)
3. Soua, R., Minet, P.: A survey on multichannel assignment protocols in Wireless Sensor Networks. In: 2011 IFIP Wireless Days (WD), Niagara Falls, ON, 2011, pp. 1–3. https://doi.org/10.1109/WD.2011.6098201
4. Ren, M., Li, J., Guo, L., Li, X., Fan, W.: Distributed data aggregation scheduling in multi-channel and multi-power wireless sensor networks. IEEE Access **5**, 27887–27896 (2017). https://doi.org/10.1109/ACCESS.2017.2734847
5. Wu, Y., et al.: Efficient multichannel communications in wireless sensor networks. ACM Trans. Sensor Networks (TOSN) **12**(1), 1–23 (2016)
6. Bagaa, M., et al.: Reliable multi-channel scheduling for timely dissemination of aggregated data in wireless sensor networks. J. Network Comput. Appl. **46**, 293–304 (2014)
7. Xing, G., et al.: Multi-channel interference measurement and modeling in low-power wireless networks. In: 2009 30th IEEE Real-Time Systems Symposium. IEEE (2009)
8. Yeoum, S., et al.: Channel and timeslot co-scheduling with minimal channel switching for data aggregation in MWSNs. Sensors (Basel, Switzerland) **17**(5), 1030 (2017). https://doi.org/10.3390/s17051030
9. Ghosh, A., Incel, Ö.D., Kumar, V.S.A., Krishnamachari, B.: Multichannel scheduling and spanning trees: throughput-delay tradeoff for fast data collection in sensor networks. IEEE/ACM Trans. Network. **19**(6), 1731–1744 (2011). https://doi.org/10.1109/TNET.2011.2146273

Relating Network-Diameter and Network-Minimum-Degree for Distributed Function Computation

H. K. Dai[1(✉)] and M. Toulouse[2]

[1] Computer Science Department, Oklahoma State University,
Stillwater, Oklahoma 74078, USA
dai@cs.okstate.edu
[2] School of Information and Communication Technology,
Hanoi University of Science and Technology, Hanoi, Vietnam
michel.toulouse@soict.hust.edu.vn

Abstract. Distributed computing network-systems are modeled as directed/undirected graphs with vertices representing compute elements and adjacency-edges capturing their uni- or bi-directional communication. To quantify an intuitive tradeoff between two graph-parameters: minimum vertex-degree and diameter of the underlying graph, we formulate an extremal problem with the two parameters: for all positive integers n and d, the extremal value $\nabla(n, d)$ denotes the least minimum vertex-degree among all connected order-n graphs with diameters of at most d. We prove matching upper and lower bounds on the extremal values of $\nabla(n, d)$ for various combinations of n- and d-values.

Keywords: Distributed function computation · Linear iterative schemes · Information dissemination · Finite convergence · Graph-parameter · Vertex-eccentricity

1 Preliminaries

Parallel and distributed computation algorithms, decentralized data-fusion architectures, and multi-agent systems are modeled as networks of interconnected vertices that compute common value(s) based on initial values or observations at the vertices. Key computation and communication requirements for these network/system paradigms include that their vertices perform local/internal computations and regularly communicate with each other via an underlying protocol. Fundamental limitations and capabilities of these algorithms and systems are studied in the literature with wide scopes of viable applications in computer science, communication, control and optimization, and distributed machine learning (see, for examples, [1,7,14,15], and [8]). Representative research areas and studies include: quantized consensus [9], collaborative distributed hypothesis testing [10], solitude verification [7], distributed machine learning over wireless

© Springer Nature Switzerland AG 2020
T. K. Dang et al. (Eds.): FDSE 2020, LNCS 12466, pp. 134–150, 2020.
https://doi.org/10.1007/978-3-030-63924-2_8

network [13], and fundamental iterative limits of distributed function computation [6,14,21].

While there is a wide spectrum of algorithms in the literature that solve distributed computation problems such as the above, there are also studies that deal with algorithmic and complexity issues constrained by underlying time-(in)variant network-topology, resource-limitations associated with vertices, time/space and communication tradeoffs, convergence criteria and requirements, etc. We present in the following sections a model of distributed computing systems and some previous related works.

1.1   Model of Distributed Computing Systems

Most graph-theoretic definitions in this article are given in [2]. We will abbreviate "directed graph" and "directed path" to digraph and dipath, respectively.

Our main result on an extremal problem is developed in a graph-theoretic framework. We introduce the topological model and algorithmics detailed in [14] for distributed function computation over directed network-topologies, and provide its abstraction components below; most notions and notations are applicable interchangeably to undirected network-topologies:

1. Network-topology: A distributed computing system is modeled as a digraph G with $V(G)$ and $E(G)$ denoting its sets of vertices and directed edges, respectively. Uni-directional communication on $V(G)$ is captured by the adjacency relation represented by $E(G)$: for all distinct vertices, $u, v \in V(G)$, $(u, v) \in E(G)$ if and only if vertex u can send information to vertex v (and v can receive information from u). Note that bi-directional communication between u and v is viewed as the co-existence of the two directed edge (u, v) and (v, u) in $E(G)$.

    Distributed computation over the network proceeds in a sequence of time-steps. At each time-step, all vertices update and/or exchange their values based on the underlying algorithm constrained by the network-topology, which is assumed to be time-invariant.

2. Resource capabilities in vertices: The digraph G of the network-topology is vertex-labeled such that messages are identified with senders and receivers. The vertices of $V(G)$ are assumed to have sufficient computational capabilities and local storage. Generally we assume that: (1) all communications/transmissions between vertices are reliable and in correct sequence, and (2) each vertex may, in the current time-step, receive the prior-step transmission(s) from its in-neighbor(s), update, and send transmission(s) to its out-neighbor(s) in accordance to the underlying algorithm.

    The domain of all initial/input and observed/output values of the vertices of G is assumed to be an algebraic field $\mathbb{F}$.

3. Linear iterative scheme (for algorithmic lower- and upper-bound results): For a vertex $v \in V(G)$, denote by $x_v[k] \in \mathbb{F}$ the vertex-value of v at time-step $k = 0, 1, \ldots$. A function with domain $\mathbb{F}^{|V(G)|}$ and codomain $\mathbb{F}$ is computed in accordance to a linear iterative scheme. Given initial vertex-values $x_v[0] \in \mathbb{F}$

for all vertices $v \in V(G)$ as arguments to the function, at each time-step $k = 0, 1, \ldots$, each vertex $v \in V(G)$ updates (and transmits) its vertex-value via a weighted linear combination of the prior-step vertex-values constrained by neighbor-structures: for all $v \in V(G)$ and $k = 0, 1, \ldots$,

$$x_v[k+1] = \sum_{u \in V(G)} w_{vu} x_u[k],$$

where the prescribed weights $w_{vu} \in \mathbb{F}$ for all $v, u \in V(G)$ that are subject to the adjacency-constraints $w_{vu} = 0$ (the zero-element of $\mathbb{F}$) if u is not adjacent to v (that is, $(u, v) \notin E(G)$); equivalently,

transpose of $(x_v[k+1] \mid v \in V(G)) = W \cdot$ transpose of $(x_v[k] \mid v \in V(G))$,

where the two vectors of vertex-values and W are indexed by a common discrete ordering of $V(G)$ with $W = [w_{vu}]_{(v,u) \in V(G) \times V(G)}$.

1.2   Related Work in Literature

Based on the framework and its variants for distributed function computation, researches and studies are focused on mathematical interplays among:

- time-(in)variance of network-topology
- granularity of time-step: discrete versus continuous
- choice of base field: special (real or complexes) versus arbitrary (finite or infinite)
- characterization of calculable functions
- convergence criteria and rates (finite, asymptotic, and/or probabilistic)
- adoption and algebraic properties of weight-matrix for linear interactive schemes: random weight-matrix, spectrum of eigenvalues, base field, etc.
- resilience and robustness of computation algorithmics for network-topology in the presence/absence of malicious vertices
- lower and upper bounds on (linear) iteration required for the convergence of calculable functions in terms of common graph-parameters of underlying network-graphs, and their induced extremal problems

Summarized results, research studies, and references are available in, for examples, [11, 12, 14–17, 19–22], and [18].

2   Recent Studies on Distributed Function Computation

The motivation for our present theoretical study on distributed function computation stems from the lower- and upper-bound results in [4,6], and [5]. These results relate common graph-parameters, such as order and size, maximum in-degree, vertex-eccentricity, and/or in-diameter, in the framework of digraphs. The research in this article complements these lower- and upper-bound studies in the context of (undirected) graphs, and addresses a tradeoff between minimum vertex-degree and diameter of connected graphs. We proceed to summarize in this section the main findings in our recent studies.

For a time-invariant topology with underlying digraph G and a vertex $u \in V(G)$, denote by $\deg_{G,in}(u)$ the in-degree of u in G, and by $\Gamma_{G,in}(u)$ the in-neighbor of u in G; hence $\Gamma^*_{G,in}(u)$ denotes the in-closure of u in G, that is,

$$\Gamma^*_{G,in}(u) = \cup_{\eta \geq 0} \Gamma^\eta_{G,in}(u)$$
$$= \{v \in V(G) \mid \text{ there exists a dipath in } G \text{ from } v \text{ to } u\}.$$

Consider all possible families of directed trees that are: (1) a vertex-decomposition of $\Gamma^*_{G,in}(u) - \{u\}$, and (2) rooted in (as subset of) $\Gamma_{G,in}(u)$. Denote by:

$$\alpha_{G,u} = \min\{\max\{\text{order}(T_i) \mid 1 \leq i \leq n\} \mid$$
$$\{T_i\}_{i=1}^n \text{ is a family of directed trees that are: (1) a vertex-}$$
$$\text{decomposition of } \Gamma^*_{G,in}(u) - \{u\}, \text{ and (2) rooted in (as}$$
$$\text{subset of) } \Gamma_{G,in}(u)\}.$$

Sundaram conjectures in [14] that $\alpha_{G,u}$ may also serve as a lower bound on the number of time-steps for a vertex $u \in V(G)$ to receive the initial vertex-values of all $v \in \Gamma^*_{G,in}(u)$ regardless of underlying protocol or algorithmics. Hence, linear iterative schemes are time-optimal in disseminating information over arbitrary time-invariant connected networks.

Toulouse and Minh [18] refute the conjecture via the notion of rank-step sequences for linear iterative schemes over a small-scale (explicit) connected network. We extend the explicit counter-example in [6] with a simple direct combinatorial argument in disproving the conjecture.

2.1 Revised Lower Bound for Distributed Function Computation and Information Dissemination

In order to complement the explicitly constructed counter-example to the lower-bound conjecture on the number of time-steps for distributed function computation and information dissemination with respect to a given vertex, we follow with a lower-bound study on the number of time-steps for a vertex $u \in V(G)$ to receive the initial vertex-values of all $v \in \Gamma^*_{G,in}(u)$ regardless of underlying protocol or algorithmics in a time-invariant network via the notion of vertex-eccentricity.

Consider an arbitrary vertex $u \in V(G)$, and assume a non-trivial $\Gamma^*_{G,in}(u)$ ($|\Gamma^*_{G,in}(u)| > 1$) hereinafter. We develop a lower bound on the number of time-steps required for the vertex u to receive the (initial) vertex-values of all vertices of $\Gamma^*_{G,in}(u)$ (regardless of underlying protocol, including linear iterative schemes).

For two vertices u and v of G, $\overrightarrow{d}_G(u,v)$ denotes the directed distance from u to v in G, that is,

$$\overrightarrow{d}_G(u,v) = \begin{cases} \text{length of a shortest dipath from } u \text{ to } v \text{ in } G & \text{if exists,} \\ \infty & \text{otherwise.} \end{cases}$$

For a vertex u of G, $e_{G,\text{in}}(u)$ denotes the in-eccentricity of u in G, which is the maximum directed distance from a vertex to u in G, that is,

$$e_{G,\text{in}}(u) = \max\{ \underbrace{\vec{d}_G(v, u)}_{\text{minimum length of a dipath from } v \text{ to } u \text{ in } G} \mid v \in V(G)\}.$$

Following the above-stated distributed computation framework as in [15] and for their conjecture, we develop in [4, 6] a lower-bound result based on the notion of eccentricity (instead of "order" or "size" as in the conjecture).

For every (linear or non-linear) iteration scheme, in which a vertex's value or information is transmitted to its out-neighbors via their incidence directed edges in unit time-step, requires at least $e_{G,\text{in}}(u)$ time-steps for vertex u to access values/information of all the vertices in $\Gamma^*_{G,\text{in}}(u)$. Thus, $e_{G,\text{in}}(u)$ serves as a lower bound on the number of time-steps required for function computation by vertex u via such iteration scheme.

In accordance with the distributed framework for our function computation, Theorem 1 gives a min-max formulation of $e_{G,\text{in}}(u)$ via in-eccentricities of root-vertices of directed forest decomposing $\Gamma^*_{G,\text{in}}(u) - \{u\}$.

Theorem 1 [4, 6]. *For a digraph G and a vertex $u \in V(G)$, $e_{G,\text{in}}(u)$, the maximum directed distance from a vertex to u in G, satisfies that:*

$$e_{G,\text{in}}(u) = 1 + \min\{\max\{\underbrace{e_{T_i,\text{in}}(\text{root}(T_i))}_{= \text{depth}(T_i)} \mid 1 \le i \le n\} \mid$$

$\{T_i\}_{i=1}^n$ is a family of directed trees that are:
(1) a vertex-decomposition of $\Gamma^*_{G,\text{in}}(u) - \{u\}$, and
(2) rooted in (as subset of) $\Gamma_{G,\text{in}}(u)\}$.

The min-max formulation of $e_{G,\text{in}}(u)$, which is developed above in Theorem 1 for lower-bounding the number of time-steps for function computation by vertex u in $\Gamma^*_{G,\text{in}}(u)$, motivates us to study lower bounds for (maximum) vertex-eccentricity in terms of common graph-parameters of the underlying digraph G: (1) maximum in-degree (in [4, 6]), and (2) order and size (in [6]).

2.2   Lower Bounds for Vertex-Eccentricity via Graph-Parameters: Maximum In-Degree, and Graph-Order and -Size

We give in Theorem 2 a lower bound on $e_{G,\text{in}}(u)$ from the knowledge of the maximum in-degree of G (vertex-spanned by $\Gamma^*_{G,\text{in}}(u)$), which yields a (possibly weaker) lower bound on the number of time-steps for vertex u to access values/information of all the vertices in $\Gamma^*_{G,\text{in}}(u)$.

Denote by $\Delta_{G,\text{in}}(u)$ (≥ 1) the maximum in-degree of the subdigraph of G vertex-spanned by $\Gamma^*_{G,\text{in}}(u)$.

Theorem 2 [4,6]. *For a digraph G and a vertex $u \in V(G)$,*

$$e_{G,\mathrm{in}}(u) \geq \begin{cases} |\Gamma^*_{G,\mathrm{in}}(u)| - 1 & \text{if } \Delta_{G,\mathrm{in}}(u) = 1, \\ \log_{\Delta_{G,\mathrm{in}}(u)}((\Delta_{G,\mathrm{in}}(u) - 1)|\Gamma^*_{G,\mathrm{in}}(u)| + 1) - 1 & \text{otherwise} \\ & (\Delta_{G,\mathrm{in}}(u) \geq 2). \end{cases}$$

We can obtain desired lower bounds in analogous fashion with similar graph-parameters such a regularity in-degree, and maximum and regularity degrees.

The in-diameter of a digraph G, denoted by $\mathrm{dia_{in}}(G)$, is the maximum in-eccentricity of all the vertices of G; that is,

$$\mathrm{dia_{in}}(G) = \max\{e_{G,\mathrm{in}}(u) \mid u \in V(G)\}$$
$$= \max\{\overrightarrow{d}_G(u,v) \mid u, v \in V(G)\}.$$

A digraph G is strongly connected if for every pair of vertices $u, v \in V(G)$, there exists a dipath from u to v (and vice-versa) in G.

For a strongly connected digraph, we study a lower bound on its in-diameter in terms of its order and size, and show the optimality of the diameter-bound with a family of explicitly constructed strongly connected digraphs.

Theorem 3 [5,6]. *For a strongly connected digraph G,*

$$|E(G)| \geq \begin{cases} |V(G)| & \text{if } \mathrm{dia_{in}}(G) = |V(G)| - 1, \\ |V(G)| - 1 + \frac{2(|V(G)|-1)}{\mathrm{dia_{in}}(G)} & \text{otherwise} \\ \text{equivalently, } \mathrm{dia_{in}}(G) \geq \frac{2(|V(G)|-1)}{|E(G)|-|V(G)|+1} & (\mathrm{dia_{in}}(G) \leq |V(G)| - 2). \end{cases}$$

We construct a family of strongly connected digraphs that achieve the optimality of the above-derived diameter-bound. For each positive integer γ, denote by C_γ a directed cycle of $\gamma + 1$ vertices, and for each positive integer k, define a strongly connected digraph $G_{k,\gamma}$ to be an amalgamation of k (mutually edge-disjoint) copies of C_γ: $C_{\gamma,1}, C_{\gamma,2}, \ldots, C_{\gamma,k}$ that share a common vertex z. Figure 1(a) show the topological structure of $G_{k,\gamma}$.

Corollary 4 [5,6]. *The family of strongly connected digraphs $G_{k,\gamma}$ for all positive integers k and γ is optimal for the relationship of the graph-parameters: order, size, and in-diameter established in Theorem 3—as illustrated with the annotated digraph $G_{k,\gamma}$ in Fig. 1(b).*

3 Extremal Problem with Diameter and Minimum Degree for Graphs

The lower-bound studies for digraphs motivate us to further examine possible tradeoffs in digraphs between in-diameter and minimum in-degree or out-degree. Note that, for a length-l dipath in a digraph, we may add $O(l^2)$ directed edges to the dipath without decreasing the in-distance from the initial to terminal vertices

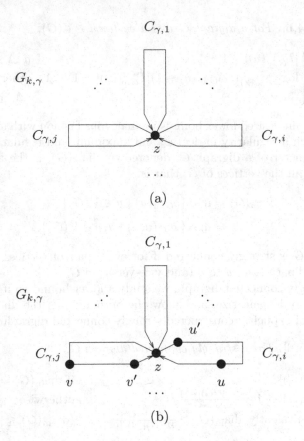

Fig. 1. For each positive integers k and γ: (a) the strongly connected digraph $G_{k,\gamma}$ is an amalgamation of k (mutually edge-disjoint) copies of a directed cycle of $\gamma + 1$ vertices: $C_{\gamma,1}, C_{\gamma,2}, \ldots, C_{\gamma,k}$ that share a common vertex; (b) when $\gamma \geq 2$ and $i, j \in \{1, 2, \ldots, k\}$ with $i \neq j$, (u', v') is a diametrical pair of vertices in $C_{\gamma,i}$ and $C_{\gamma,j}$, respectively, with $\overrightarrow{d}_{G_{k,\gamma}}(u', v') = 2\gamma$.

of the dipath. However, an intuitive tradeoff exists between the minimum degree and diameter of a connected (undirected) graph. We quantify such tradeoff via a formulation of an extremal problem with diameter and minimum degree for graphs as follows.

The definitions and notions/notations for digraphs introduced in the previous sections are adapted, hereinafter, to (undirected) graphs. For a graph G, denote by $\delta(G)$ the minimum degree of all vertices of G. For all positive integers n and d with $d \leq n - 1$, denote by:

$$\nabla(n, d) = \min\{ \text{ positive integer } \nabla \mid \text{ for all connected order-}n \text{ graphs } G,$$
$$\text{if } \delta(G) \geq \nabla \text{ then dia}(G) \leq d\}.$$

For extreme values of d, $\nabla(n, d)$ is readily known:

1. Case when $d = 1$: Note that the diameter of the underlying connected graph G is necessarily 1. Therefore, for each vertex $u \in V(G)$, the unit-diameter of G implies that there exists an edge between every other vertex of G and u, that is, $\deg_G(u) = n - 1$ (and $\delta(G) = n - 1$); so $\nabla(n, 1) = n - 1$.
2. Case when $d = n-1$: For every underlying connected graph G, the inequality: $\text{dia}(G) \leq d\ (= n - 1)$ is trivially satisfied; so $\nabla(n, n - 1) = 1$.

For all positive integers n and d with $2 \leq d \leq n - 2$, we obtain three exact formulas for $\nabla(n, d)$ according to the three possible values of $d \bmod 3$:

$$\nabla(n, d) = \begin{cases} \lfloor \frac{n}{(d+4)/3} \rfloor & \text{if } d \geq 2 \text{ and } d \bmod 3 = 2, \\ \lfloor \frac{n-1}{(d+3)/3} \rfloor & \text{if } d \geq 3 \text{ and } d \bmod 3 = 0, \\ \lfloor \frac{n-2}{(d+2)/3} \rfloor & \text{if } d \geq 4 \text{ and } d \bmod 3 = 1. \end{cases}$$

Note that we present the skeletons for proving the main results without lengthy details in the abstract. Complete results, proofs, and derivations of claims/theorems are provided in the full version of this article.

3.1   Determining $\nabla(n, d)$ When $d \geq 2$ and $d \bmod 3 = 2$

We show that, for all positive integers n and d with $2 \leq d \leq n-2$ and $d \bmod 3 = 2$,

$$\nabla(n, d) = \lfloor \frac{n}{(d + 4)/3} \rfloor,$$

by proving the two embedded inequalities in the following two theorems.

Theorem 5. *For all positive integers n and d with $2 \leq d \leq n-2$ and $d \bmod 3 = 2$,*

$$\nabla(n, d) \leq \lfloor \frac{n}{(d + 4)/3} \rfloor.$$

Proof. Suppose the contrary that $\nabla(n, d) > \lfloor \frac{n}{(d+4)/3} \rfloor$. According to the extremal definition of $\nabla(n, d)$, the inequality: $\nabla(n, d) > \lfloor \frac{n}{(d+4)/3} \rfloor$ is equivalent to the statement: there does not exist any positive integer $\nabla \in \{1, 2, \ldots, \lfloor \frac{n}{(d+4)/3} \rfloor\}$ such that for all connected order-n graphs G, if $\delta(G) \geq \nabla$ then $\text{dia}(G) \leq d$. In particular, when $\nabla = \lfloor \frac{n}{(d+4)/3} \rfloor$, there would exist a connected order-n graph G such that $\delta(G) \geq \nabla\ (= \lfloor \frac{n}{(d+4)/3} \rfloor)$ and $\text{dia}(G) > d$.

Suppose that such connected order-n graph G exists. We transform G to a connected order-n graph G' with $V(G') = V(G)$, $\delta(G') \geq \delta(G) \geq \lfloor \frac{n}{(d+4)/3} \rfloor$, and $\text{dia}(G') = d + 1$ in two steps described below—from which a contradiction can be deduced.

Step 1. Construction of a vertex-spanning breadth-first search tree of G:

Denote by $D = \text{dia}(G)$ ($> d$), and by $r \in V(G)$ a vertex with its eccentricity $e_G(r) = D$ (that is, r is a terminal vertex of a diametrical path of length D in G).

We augment the breadth-first search algorithm (see, for example, [3]) to: (1) build a breadth-first search tree of G rooted at a source-vertex that yields the distance between the source/root-vertex and each (reachable) vertex of G, and (2) decompose $V(G)$ into a level-partition: a disjoint family of levels, $\{L_i\}_{i=0}^{D}$, such that the i-th level L_i consists of all the vertices of G at distance of exactly i from the source/root-vertex. The augmented breadth-first search algorithm is presented in the pseudocode: BFS_Level.

Algorithm. BFS_Level (H, s)

Require: An input connected order-n graph H with a source-vertex $s \in V(H)$.
Ensure: Construct: (1) a vertex-spanning breadth-first search tree T of H rooted at the source-vertex s, and (2) a level-partition, $\{L_i\}_{i=0}^{e_H(s)}$, of $V(H)$ with respect to the source/root-vertex s with $e_H(s) = \text{depth}(T)$.
1: {Initialization.}
2: **for all** vertices $u \in V(H)$ **do**
3:    $Visit(u) := unvisited$;
4: **end for**
5: $T := \emptyset$ (empty tree);
6: $Visit(s) := visited$;
7: $L_0 := \{s\}$;
8:
9: {Construction of T with a level-partition of H: }
10: {i-th level L_i at distance of exactly i from the source/root-vertex.}
11: $i := 0$;
12: **while** $L_i \neq \emptyset$ **do**
13:    $L_{i+1} := \emptyset$;
14:
15:    **for all** vertices $u \in L_i$ **do**
16:       **for all** vertices $v \in \Gamma_H(u)$ **do**
17:          **if** $Visit(v) = unvisited$ **then**
18:             $Visit(v) := visited$;
19:             $E(T) := E(T) \cup \{\{u, v\}\}$;
20:             $L_{i+1} := L_{i+1} \cup \{v\}$;
21:          **end if**
22:       **end for**
23:    **end for**
24:
25:    $i := i + 1$;
26: **end while**

The algorithm BFS_Level, when implemented with a first-in first-out queue data structure, runs in $O(|V(H)| + |E(H)|)$ time.

We apply the algorithm BFS_Level to the connected order-n graph G and the source-root-vertex r to obtain a vertex-spanning breadth-first search tree T of G rooted at r that enjoys the following properties:

1. $V(T) = V(G)$, and $\text{depth}(T) = e_G(r) = D\ (> d)$,
2. For every $i \in \{0, 1, \ldots, D\}$,

$$L_i = \{u \in V(T)\,(= V(G)) \mid d_G(r, u) = i\},$$

   and $V(G)$ is decomposed into the level-partition $\{L_i\}_{i=0}^{D}$,
3. Every edge $\{u, v\} \in E(G)$ is in one of the following three types:
   (a) "tree-edge" (that is, $\{u, v\} \in E(T)$) bridging successive levels: $u \in L_i$ and $v \in L_{i+1}$ for some $i \in \{0, 1, \ldots, D-1\}$,
   (b) "(non-tree) forward/backward-edge" (that is, $\{u, v\} \in E(G) - E(T)$) bridging successive levels: $u \in L_i$ and $v \in L_j$ for some $i, j \in \{0, 1, \ldots, D\}$ with $|i - j| = 1$, or
   (c) "(non-tree) cross-edge" (that is, $\{u, v\} \in E(G) - E(T)$) with both vertices u and v in the same level: $u, v \in L_i$ for some $i \in \{1, 2, \ldots, D\}$.

Step 2. Transformation of G via the vertex-spanning breadth-first search tree T:

With respect to the level-partition of the vertex-spanning breadth-free search tree T of G as a basis, we augment the connected order-n graph G to a connected order-n graph G', via adding sufficient number of edges to merge successive distant-levels, $\{L_d, L_{d+1}, \ldots, L_D\}$, in the level-partition of G (if necessary), which satisfies the followings:

1. $V(G) = V(G')$ and $E(G) \subseteq E(G')$, and
2. a possibly coarser level-partition of $V(G')$, $\{K_i\}_{i=0}^{d+1}$, such that:
   (a) $K_0 = \{r\}$ and $|K_{d+1}| = 1$, and for every $i \in \{0, 1, \ldots, d+1\}$, K_i is a subgraph of G' with:

$$K_i = \{u \in V(G')\,(= V(G)) \mid d_{G'}(r, u) = i\}$$

   (which can be achieved by denoting $K_i = L_i$ for $i \in \{0, 1, \ldots, d-1\}$ and organizing the levels $\{L_d, L_{d+1}, \ldots, L_D\}$ into the levels K_d and K_{d+1}), and
   (b) $E(G')$ is partitioned into two sources of adjacency relations: either an adjacency relation within each level K_i for every $i \in \{0, 1, \ldots, d+1\}$, or an adjacency relation between successive levels: for every $i \in \{0, 1, \ldots, d\}$, the subgraph of G' vertex-induced by $K_i \cup K_{i+1}$ is a bipartite graph with bipartition (K_i, K_{i+1}), and
3. Inheritance of the minimum-degree constraint from G:

$$\delta(G') \geq \delta(G)\ (\geq \lfloor \tfrac{n}{(d+4)/3} \rfloor).$$

The topological and adjacency structures of the augmented connected order-n graph G' is illustrated in Fig. 2.

We now deduce a contradiction from the augmented connected order-n graph G', hence its predecessor G can not exist, that is, we must have $\nabla(n, d) \leq \lfloor \frac{n}{(d+4)/3} \rfloor$.

Consider the topological and adjacency structures of G': the cardinalities of the levels in the level-partition of G' and the lower-bound constraint of the minimum degree of G'. We examine the following two cases of d-value: $d = 2$, and $d > 2$ and $d \bmod 3 = 2$.

For the case when $d = 2$:

1. For the vertex (r) of K_0,

$$|K_1| = \deg_{G'}(r) \geq \delta(G') (\geq \lfloor \frac{n}{(d+4)/3} \rfloor = \lfloor \frac{n}{2} \rfloor),$$

2. For the vertex of $K_{d+1} (= K_3)$,

$$|K_2| \geq \text{ degree of the vertex in } K_3 \geq \delta(G').$$

The summation of the two inequalities above yields that:

$$|K_1| + |K_2| \geq 2\delta(G'),$$

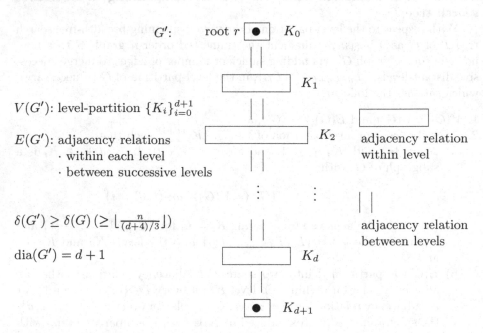

Fig. 2. The topological and adjacency structures of the connected order-n graph G' (transformed from a connected order-n graph G with $\delta(G) \geq \lfloor \frac{n}{(d+4)/3} \rfloor$ and $\mathrm{dia}(G) > d$—a counter-example graph from the supposition of $\nabla(n, d) > \lfloor \frac{n}{(d+4)/3} \rfloor$) with a vertex-spanning breadth-first search tree T rooted at vertex r.

that is:

$$n - 2 = |K_1| + |K_2| \geq 2\delta(G') \geq \lfloor \frac{n}{2} \rfloor > 2(\frac{n}{2} - 1) = n - 2,$$

which is a contradiction.

For the case when $d > 2$ and $d \bmod 3 = 2$ (hence $d \geq 5$):

1. For the vertex (r) of K_0,

$$|K_1| = \deg_{G'}(r) \geq \delta(G') (\geq \lfloor \frac{n}{(d+4)/3} \rfloor),$$

2. For each vertex of K_3,

$$|K_2| + (|K_3| - 1) + |K_4| \geq \text{ degree of the vertex in } K_3 \geq \delta(G'),$$

3. In general, for each vertex of K_i for $i = 3, 6, \ldots, d - 2$,

$$|K_{i-1}| + (|K_i| - 1) + |K_{i+1}| \geq \text{ degree of the vertex in } K_i \geq \delta(G'),$$

4. For the vertex of K_{d+1},

$$|K_d| \geq \text{ degree of the vertex in } K_{d+1} \geq \delta(G').$$

The summation of the inequalities in items 1, 3, and 4 yields that:

$$|K_1| + \sum_{i \in \{3,6,\ldots,d-2\}} (|K_{i-1}| + (|K_i| - 1) + |K_{i+1}|) + |K_d|$$

$$\geq (1 + \frac{d-2}{3} + 1)\delta(G'),$$

that is,

$$\sum_{k=1}^{d} |K_k| + \frac{d-2}{3}(-1) \geq (\frac{d-2}{3} + 2)\delta(G'),$$

which gives that:

$$n - 2 = \sum_{k=1}^{d} |K_k| \geq \frac{d+4}{3}\delta(G') + \frac{d-2}{3}$$

$$\geq \frac{d+4}{3} \lfloor \frac{n}{(d+4)/3} \rfloor + \frac{d-2}{3}$$

$$> \frac{d+4}{3} (\frac{n}{(d+4)/3} - 1) + \frac{d-2}{3}$$

$$= n - \frac{d+4}{3} + \frac{d-2}{3}$$

$$= n - 2,$$

which is a contradiction.

Thus, both cases ($d = 2$, and $d > 2$ and $d \bmod 3 = 2$) arrive at a contradiction, and we have $\nabla(n, d) \leq \lfloor \frac{n}{(d+4)/3} \rfloor$ as desired. ∎

Theorem 6. *For all positive integers n and d with $2 \leq d \leq n-2$ and $d \bmod 3 = 2$,*

$$\nabla(n, d) \geq \lfloor \frac{n}{(d+4)/3} \rfloor.$$

Proof. According to the extremal definition of $\nabla(n, d)$, the inequality: $\nabla(n, d) \geq \lfloor \frac{n}{(d+4)/3} \rfloor$ is equivalent to the statement: there does not exist any positive integer $\nabla \in \{1, 2, \ldots, \lfloor \frac{n}{(d+4)/3} \rfloor - 1\}$ such that for all connected order-n graphs, if $\delta(G) \geq \nabla$ then $\mathrm{dia}(G) \leq d$. In order to show that $\nabla(n, d) \geq \lfloor \frac{n}{(d+4)/3} \rfloor$, it suffices to prove that there exists a connected order-n graph G such that $\delta(G) \geq \lfloor \frac{n}{(d+4)/3} \rfloor - 1$ and $\mathrm{dia}(G) = d + 1$ ($> d$). We construct such graphs G with $\mathrm{dia}(G) = d + 1$ for the three cases of d-value: $d = 2$, $2 < d \leq n - 4$ and $d \bmod 3 = 2$, and $5 \leq d \in \{n - 3, n - 2\}$ and $d \bmod 3 = 2$.

The candidate graphs G have the analogous topological and adjacency structures as the connected order-n graph G', which is employed in the proof of Theorem 5 and illustrated in Fig. 2, with a level/clique-partition $\{K_i\}_{i=0}^{d+1}$ such that:

1. $K_0 = \{r\}$ and $|K_{d+1}| = 1$, and for every $i \in \{0, 1, \ldots, d+1\}$, K_i is a complete subgraph of G with:

$$K_i = \{u \in V(G) \mid d_G(r, u) = i\},$$

and
2. $E(G)$ is partitioned into two sources of adjacency relations: either a complete adjacency relation within each level/clique K_i for every $i \in \{0, 1, \ldots, d + 1\}$, or a complete adjacency relation between successive levels: for every $i \in \{0, 1, \ldots, d\}$, the subgraph of G vertex-induced by $K_i \cup K_{i+1}$ is a complete bipartite graph with bipartition (K_i, K_{i+1}).

For the case when $d = 2$:

Consider a level/clique-partition $\{K_i\}_{i=0}^{d+1}$ ($= \{K_0, K_1, K_2, K_3\}$) of the candidate graph G:

$$\begin{cases} |K_0| = |K_3| = 1, \\ \min\{|K_1|, |K_2|\} \geq \lfloor \frac{n}{(d+4)/3} \rfloor - 1 (= \lfloor \frac{n}{2} \rfloor - 1). \end{cases}$$

The feasibility of the level/clique-partition entails the following inequalities:

$$\begin{cases} \lfloor \frac{n}{2} \rfloor - 1 \geq 1 & \text{(non-emptiness of } K_1 \text{ and } K_2\text{)}, \\ |K_0| + |K_1| + |K_2| + |K_3| \leq |V(G)| \\ \qquad\qquad\qquad\quad = n & \text{(feasibility of level/clique-partition)}. \end{cases}$$

Note that the minimum-degree constraint of G: $\delta(G) \geq \lfloor \frac{n}{(d+4)/3} \rfloor - 1$ is trivially satisfied.

From the assumption, we have $d \leq n-2$ and $d = 2$, which yield that $\lfloor \frac{n}{2} \rfloor - 1 \geq 1$. We notice that the feasibility of the level/clique-partition: $|K_0| + |K_1| + |K_2| + |K_3| \leq n$ is satisfied by verifying the inequality: $1 + (\lfloor \frac{n}{2} \rfloor - 1) + (\lfloor \frac{n}{2} \rfloor - 1) + 1 \leq n$, that is, $2\lfloor \frac{n}{2} \rfloor \leq n$, which is trivially true.

For the case when $2 < d \leq n - 4$ and $d \bmod 3 = 2$:

Consider a level/clique-partition $\{K_i\}_{i=0}^{d+1}$ of the candidate graph G:

$$\begin{cases} |K_0| = |K_{d+1}| = 1, \\ \min\{|K_1|, |K_d|\} \geq \lfloor \frac{n}{(d+4)/3} \rfloor - 1, \\ \min\{|K_3|, |K_6|, \ldots, |K_{d-2}|\} \geq \lfloor \frac{n}{(d+4)/3} \rfloor - 2, \\ |K_2| = |K_4| = |K_5| = |K_7| = \cdots = |K_{d-6}| = |K_{d-4}| = |K_{d-3}| = |K_{d-1}| = 1. \end{cases}$$

The feasibility of the level/clique-partition entails the following inequalities:

$$\begin{cases} \lfloor \frac{n}{(d+4)/3} \rfloor - 1 \geq 1 & \text{(non-emptiness of } K_1 \text{ and } K_d), \\ \lfloor \frac{n}{(d+4)/3} \rfloor - 2 \geq 1 & \text{(non-emptiness of } K_3, K_6, \ldots, K_{d-2}), \\ |K_0| + |K_1| + \cdots + |K_{d+1}| \leq |V(G)| \\ \qquad\qquad = n & \text{(feasibility of level/clique-partition).} \end{cases}$$

Note that the minimum-degree constraint of G: $\delta(G) \geq \lfloor \frac{n}{(d+4)/3} \rfloor - 1$ is trivially satisfied.

From the assumption, we have $5 \leq d \leq n - 4$, which yields that $\frac{n}{3} \geq \lfloor \frac{n}{(d+4)/3} \rfloor \geq 3$, and $(\lfloor \frac{n}{(d+4)/3} \rfloor - 1 \geq) \lfloor \frac{n}{(d+4)/3} \rfloor - 2 \geq 1$. We notice that the feasibility of the level/clique-partition: $|K_0| + |K_1| + \cdots + |K_{d+1}| \leq n$ is satisfied by verifying the inequality:

$$2(1) + 2(\lfloor \frac{n}{(d+4)/3} \rfloor - 1) + \frac{d-2}{3}(\lfloor \frac{n}{(d+4)/3} \rfloor - 2) + ((d+2) - (2+2+\frac{d-2}{3}))(1)$$
$$\leq n,$$

that is, $\frac{d+4}{3}\lfloor \frac{n}{(d+4)/3} \rfloor \leq n$, which is implied by the inequality: $\frac{d+4}{3} \frac{n}{(d+4)/3} \leq n$, which is trivially true.

For the case when $5 \leq d \in \{n-3, n-2\}$ and $d \bmod 3 = 2$:

Consider a level/clique-partition $\{K_i\}_{i=0}^{d+1}$ of the candidate graph G:

$$\begin{cases} |K_0| = |K_{d+1}| = 1, \\ 1 \leq |K_1| \leq 2, \\ |K_2| = |K_3| = \cdots = |K_{d-1}| = |K_d| = 1. \end{cases}$$

Note that, from the assumption, we have:

$$3 > \frac{3n}{n+1} \geq \frac{n}{(d+4)/3} \geq \frac{3n}{n+2} \geq 2 \text{ (as } n \geq 4),$$

and $\lfloor \frac{n}{(d+4)/3} \rfloor = 2$; hence the minimum-degree constraint of G is satisfied: $\delta(G) = 1 \geq \lfloor \frac{n}{(d+4)/3} \rfloor - 1$.

Also, the feasibility of the level/clique-partition: $|K_0| + |K_1| + \cdots + |K_{d+1}| \leq |V(G)| = n$ is trivially satisfied.

Combining the three cases, we have shown the existence/construction of a connected order-n graph G with $\delta(G) \geq \lfloor \frac{n}{(d+4)/3} \rfloor - 1$ and dia$(G) = d + 1$, as desired. ∎

3.2 Determining $\nabla(n,d)$ When ($d \geq 3$ and $d \bmod 3 = 0$) or ($d \geq 4$ and $d \bmod 3 = 1$)

We state the exact formulas for $\nabla(n,d)$ in the two theorems below (without proofs) for the two cases of d-value: $d \geq 3$ and $d \bmod 3 = 0$, and $d \geq 4$ and $d \bmod 3 = 1$.

Theorem 7. *For all positive integers n and d with $3 \leq d \leq n-2$ and $d \bmod 3 = 0$,*

$$\nabla(n,d) = \lfloor \frac{n-1}{(d+3)/3} \rfloor.$$

Theorem 8. *For all positive integers n and d with $4 \leq d \leq n-2$ and $d \bmod 3 = 1$,*

$$\nabla(n,d) = \lfloor \frac{n-2}{(d+2)/3} \rfloor.$$

4   Conclusion

Distributed function computation has a wide spectrum of major applications in distributed systems. There is a natural need to understand and approximate, if possible, lower and upper bounds on the number of time-steps for some or all vertices to receive (initial) vertex-values of all vertices of the network-graph, regardless of the underlying protocol or algorithmics.

We address lower-bound and extremal studies on vertex-eccentricity and its maximum version, graph-diameter, in terms of common graph-parameters, such as graph-order, graph-size, and minimum vertex-degree, of the underlying (di)graph in a graph-theoretic framework.

In digraph-theoretic frameworks (for applications such as consensus and cooperation in network-systems), our recent work [5,6] includes the followings:

1. For a vertex of a digraph, we have shown that its vertex-eccentricity, in accordance with a min-max distributed framework, is the minimum of the maximum tree-depth of a directed forest among all possible directed forests that are vertex-decomposition of the in-neighbor closure and rooted in the in-neighbor of the vertex in the underlying digraph, and
2. For a strongly connected digraph, we have proved a lower bound on its in-diameter in terms of the graph-order and -size, and have demonstrated the optimality of the diameter-bound for a family of (explicitly constructed) strongly connected digraphs.

In graph-theoretic frameworks (for applications such as distributed network-algorithms and wireless networks) for our present study, we quantify an intuitive tradeoff between two graph-parameters: minimum vertex-degree and diameter of the underlying connected graph, via the formulation of an extremal problem with these two graph-parameters: for all positive integers n and d, the extremal value $\nabla(n, d)$ denotes the least minimum vertex-degree among all connected order-n graphs with diameters of at most d. We prove matching upper and lower bounds on the extremal values of $\nabla(n, d)$ for various combinations of n- and d-values.

A practical implication of our lower- and upper-bound results for distributed function computation is that the constraints imposed on the underlying (di)graph-parameters: order and size, minimum/maximum vertex-degree, and/or vertex-eccentricity/diameter, translate into (theoretical) parameter-bounds, which can optimize the performance of distributed network simulation/emulation software.

References

1. Ayaso, O., Shah, D., Dahleh, M.A.: Information theoretic bounds for distributed computation over networks of point-to-point channels. IEEE Trans. Inf. Theory **56**(12), 6020–6039 (2010)
2. Bondy, J.A., Murty, U.S.R.: Graph Theory. Graduate Texts in Mathematics, vol. 244. Springer London (2008)
3. Cormen, T.H., Leiserson, C.E., Rivest, R.L., Stein, C.: Introduction to Algorithms, 3rd edn. MIT Press, Cambridge (2009)
4. Dai, H.K., Toulouse, M.: Lower bound for function computation in distributed networks. In: Dang, T.K., Küng, J., Wagner, R., Thoai, N., Takizawa, M. (eds.) FDSE 2018. LNCS, vol. 11251, pp. 371–384. Springer, Cham (2018). https://doi.org/10.1007/978-3-030-03192-3_28
5. Dai, H.K., Toulouse, M.: Lower bound on network diameter for distributed function computation. In: Dang, T.K., Küng, J., Takizawa, M., Bui, S.H. (eds.) FDSE 2019. LNCS, vol. 11814, pp. 239–251. Springer, Cham (2019). https://doi.org/10.1007/978-3-030-35653-8_16
6. Dai, H.K., Toulouse, M.: Lower-bound study for function computation in distributed networks via vertex-eccentricity. Springer Nat. Comput. Sci. **1**(1), 10:1–10:14 (2019)
7. Fich, F.E., Ruppert, E.: Hundreds of impossibility results for distributed computing. Distrib. Comput. **16**(2–3), 121–163 (2003)
8. Hendrickx, J.M., Olshevsky, A., Tsitsiklis, J.N.: Distributed anonymous discrete function computation. IEEE Trans. Autom. Control **56**(10), 2276–2289 (2011)
9. Kashyap, A., Basar, T., Srikant, R.: Quantized consensus. Automatica **43**(7), 1192–1203 (2007)
10. Katz, G., Piantanida, P., Debbah, M.: Collaborative distributed hypothesis testing. Computing Research Repository, abs/1604.01292 (2016)
11. Kuhn, F., Moscibroda, T., Wattenhofer, R.: Local computation: lower and upper bounds. J. ACM **63**(2), 17:1–17:44 (2016)
12. Olshevsky, A., Tsitsiklis, J.N.: Convergence speed in distributed consensus and averaging. SIAM J. Control Optim. **48**(1), 33–55 (2009)

13. Raceala-Motoc, M., Limmer, S., Bjelakovic, I., Stanczak, S.: Distributed machine learning in the context of function computation over wireless networks. In: Matthews, M.B. (ed.) 52nd Asilomar Conference on Signals, Systems, and Computers, ACSSC 2018, Pacific Grove, CA, USA, 28–31 October 2018, pp. 291–297. IEEE (2018)
14. Sundaram, S.: Linear iterative strategies for information dissemination and processing in distributed systems. Ph.D. thesis, University of Illinois at Urbana-Champaign (2009)
15. Sundaram, S., Hadjicostis, C.N.: Distributed function calculation and consensus using linear iterative strategies. IEEE J. Sel. Areas Commun. **26**(4), 650–660 (2008)
16. Sundaram, S., Hadjicostis, C.N.: Distributed function calculation via linear iterative strategies in the presence of malicious agents. IEEE Trans. Autom. Control **56**(7), 1495–1508 (2011)
17. Toulouse, M., Minh, B.Q.: Applicability and resilience of a linear encoding scheme for computing consensus. In: Muñoz, V.M., Wills, G., Walters, R.J., Firouzi, F., Chang, V. (eds.) Proceedings of the Third International Conference on Internet of Things, Big Data and Security, IoTBDS 2018, Funchal, Madeira, Portugal, 19–21 March 2018, pp. 173–184. SciTePress (2018)
18. Toulouse, M., Minh, B.Q., Minh, Q.T.: Invariant properties and bounds on a finite time consensus algorithm. Trans. Large-Scale Data Knowl. Centered Syst. **41**, 32–58 (2019)
19. Wang, L., Xiao, F.: Finite-time consensus problems for networks of dynamic agents. IEEE Trans. Autom. Control **55**(4), 950–955 (2010)
20. Xiao, L., Boyd, S.P., Kim, S.-J.: Distributed average consensus with least-mean-square deviation. J. Parallel Distrib. Comput. **67**(1), 33–46 (2007)
21. Xu, A.: Information-theoretic limitations of distributed information processing. Ph.D. thesis, University of Illinois at Urbana-Champaign (2016)
22. Xu, A., Raginsky, M.: Information-theoretic lower bounds for distributed function computation. IEEE Trans. Inf. Theory **63**(4), 2314–2337 (2017)

Growing Self-Organizing Maps for Metagenomic Visualizations Supporting Disease Classification

Hai Thanh Nguyen[1]([✉]), Bang Anh Nguyen[1], My N. Nguyen[1,2],
Quoc-Dinh Truong[1], Linh Chi Nguyen[1], Thao Thuy Ngoc Banh[1],
and Phung Duong Linh[1]

[1] College of Information and Communication Technology,
Can Tho University, Can Tho, Vietnam
{nthai,nnmy,tqdinh}@cit.ctu.edu.vn, bang98.2016@gmail.com,
nchilinhith@gmail.com, bntthao1912@gmail.com, linhphung15999@gmail.com
[2] Kyoto Institute of Technology, Kyoto, Japan
d9821501@edu.kit.ac.jp

Abstract. Numerous medical models based on the personalized medicine approach have been investigated to provide more efficient treatments and improved health-care service. Metagenomic data - the genomic samples of microbial communities - appear to be one of the most valuable sources to test the hypotheses for these models. However, interpreting this source is hard due to its very high dimension. As a result, some visualization methods have been proposed to deal with metagenomic data. These methods are not only for representing the numerical data but also for leveraging deep learning algorithms on the generated images to improve the diagnosis. In this study, we present an approach that uses Growing Self-Organizing Maps to transform features of three species metagenomic datasets into images. Then, generated images are fetched into a Convolutional Neural Network to do disease prediction tasks. The proposed method produces promising performance compared to other visualization approaches.

Keywords: Growing Self-Organizing Maps · Medical models · Personalized medicine · Visualization · Convolutional Neural Network

1 Introduction

Precision medicine is a model that proposes medical treatments based on each person's condition such as genes, environment, and lifestyle. This practice is believed to give much better results because a particular therapy may not fit all patient conditions, the therapy should be shaped by a specific patient condition. The study on the biological context of an individual is helpful to detect agents that cause the disease, and the most popular agents are microbiomes.

© Springer Nature Switzerland AG 2020
T. K. Dang et al. (Eds.): FDSE 2020, LNCS 12466, pp. 151–166, 2020.
https://doi.org/10.1007/978-3-030-63924-2_9

Microbiomes are the microorganisms that live on and inside our bodies. Most microbes are useful, they help to regulate the immune system and nutrition synthesis process. Meanwhile, some microbes are pathogens. The majority of microbes reside in our gut, especially in the large intestine. Therefore, the analysis of gut microbiota to find the pathogen will contribute to the disease identification and treatment. However, there are three problems with this work. Firstly, most bacteria cannot be isolated in the laboratory in pure culture. Secondly, the difference in host-associated microbial communities. Lastly, focusing on a single 'headline pathogen' in clinical samples may be insufficient. As a result, the study on the mixture of gut microbiomes seems to be more suitable, and this approach is called metagenomics analysis.

Metagenomics is a research field focusing on discovering genomes from microorganisms collected from samples such as the human gut, without collection of pure cultures. A metagenomic sample contains information on its microbial taxonomic composition which can be a relative abundance of microbial taxonomic of seven taxonomic ranks consisting of domain, kingdom, phylum, class, order, family, genus, and species. Information from the relative abundance of bacteria in the human gut can help people to deeply understand diseases. However, because of the limited amount of data observed but complex disease diagnosis and prognosis, results of the links of individual microbes to a particular type of the disease are inconsistent. In fact, the number of considered features is higher than the number of samples and diseases are very diverse and complex.

Instead of working with data of numerous features as they are, we translate these features into visual pixels. By using this way of representation, data are seen in an easy-to-read format for human, and the insight on underlying patterns can be revealed. Besides, powerful algorithms dedicated for images can be used. However, there are still some challenges on the data visualization. The most essential problem is how to decide the representative intensity for a pixel. In addition, the arrangement strategy of pixels to form an image is also worth consideration.

In this work, we present a method that uses Growing Self-Oraganizing Maps (GSOM) as a visualization method combining deep learning techniques to support disease prediction tasks. Our study includes multi-contributions:

- We have investigated the spread scores ranging from 0.2 to 5.0 with different colormaps on three datasets related to Liver Cirrhosis, Colorectal Cancer and Inflammatory Bowel Disease. Starting at 4 nodes, the size of maps is increased and adjusted automatically during the learning.
- A comparison of rectangular and hexagonal topologies for GSOM is also considered to generate visualizations for metagenomic data. Additionally, we also evaluate the performance on various colormaps including gray and jet colormaps.
- The proposed method obtained results with pretty high accuracy compared to the one using SOM [1].

The remaining of this study is presented as follows. We introduce and describe some state-of-the-arts for metagenomics problem solutions in Sect. 2. Section 4 introduces the GSOM algorithm and explain its steps in detail. We present the metagenomic datasets and the visualization results using GSOM on them in Sect. 3 and 5, respectively. In Sect. 6, we do some investigations, comparisons, and explain the experimental results. Finally, we discuss and summarize our work in Sect. 7.

2 Related Work

The main method used in this study, i.e. GSOM, is a modification of Kohonen's Self-Organizing Map (SOM) [2]. SOM is an unsupervised neural network that transfers N-dimensional inputs into a two-dimensional array with fixed number of neurons. In other words, SOM represents the high dimensional data as a visual two-dimensional map, which helps to see whether the unlabelled input data has any pattern to it or not. The map updates itself at each iteration based on the distance of current input and all neurons, so it is called Self-Organizing Map.

There are numerous studies which use classic machine learning algorithms for solving metagenomic problems. Authors in [3] proposed a computational framework based on metagenomics for prediction tasks using quantitative microbiome profiles to avoid risks from shotgun metagenomic analysis of the human. They presented MetAML including algorithms such as SVM and Random Forests to learn from metagenomic datasets. MetAML revealed promising results on predicting Liver Cirrhosis, Colorectal Cancer, IBD, obesity, and T2D. In [4], the authors evaluated the feasibility of combining Metagenomics Quick Annotations based-on Subsystem Technology (MG-RAST) server and the NEON soil metagenomic sequencing dataset to illustrate the advantages of WGS compared to 16S amplicon sequencing. WGS brought a variety of microbial resolution, enhanced accuracy, and allowed the identification of more genera of bacteria, archaea, viruses, and Eukaryota, and putative functional genes that would have gone undetected using 16S amplicon sequencing. Authors [5] presented a method to solve the problem of metagenomic reads classification by improving the reference k-mers library with novel discriminative k-mers from the input sequencing reads. It was evaluated by the performance in different conditions against several other tools. The result is that the F-measure can be improved evenevent when close reference genomes are not available. The purpose of this study is to associate metagenomics and metabolomics in gut extracellular vesicles (EVs) of CRC with healthy subjects. Assessing microbial diversity was performed by Metagenomic profiling by sequencing 16S rDNA. The result proved that there is a significant alteration of bacterial phyla, particularly of Firmicutes and Proteobacteria in patients with colorectal cancer. Seven amino acids, four carboxylic acids, and four fatty acids; including short-chain to long-chain fatty acids, also altered in the disease group [6]. Authors [7] used metagenomic sequences to investigate the bacterial species composition in the tongue microbiome, as well as single-nucleotide variant profiles and gene in never and current smokers. The result showed that in current smokers, genes related to the lipopolysaccharide biosynthesis pathway in Veillonella dispar were present more frequently. They also found species-level tongue microbiome differed between never and current smokers, and 5 species from never and current smokers likely harbor different strains, as suggested by the difference in SNV frequency. M. J. PALLEN reviewed several recent promising proof-of-principle applications of metagenomics in virus discovery, analysis of outbreaks, and detection of pathogens in contemporary and historical samples. The future prospects for diagnostic metagenomics in the light of relentless improvements in sequencing technologies were also evaluated [8]. Authors [9] proposed a method to diagnose lung cancer that based on analyzing metagenomic on a gene present in a bacterium-derived extracellular vesicle. This method allows to predict the risk of the onset of lung cancer and a lung cancer risk group and delay the time of the onset or prevent the onset with suitable care. Authors [10] demonstrated the relation between Pangenomics and Metagenomics by leveraging metagenome-assembled genomes, to create a comprehensive representation of the genetic content of a taxonomic group in a particular environment. They presented the concept of the totality of genes belonging to a species identified in multiple metagenomic samplings of a particular habitat. Then, the importance was emphasized to show stringent quality assessment and validation to ensure the high quality of metagenomic deconvoluted genomes.

Techniques for metagenomic data processing based on deep learning algorithms are also proposed in numerous studies. Authors [1] presented Met2Img framework that has improved performance and visualizes biomedical signatures such as species, genus, order, family, class, and phylum. They arranged abundance/presence values into a square matrix sizing by the number of features. Moreover, supervised and unsupervised methods such as Linear Discriminant Analysis (LDA), Isomap, and t-Distributed Stochastic Neighbor (t-SNE) are used to reduce the dimensionality. Authors also proposed three binning methods for mapping abundance/presence values into images. Authors [11] introduced PopPhy-CNN, a framework for Convolutional Neural Network to predict Host Phenotype From Metagenomic Data via Phylogenetic Tree Embedded Architecture for Convolutional Neural Networks. The input is a 2D matrix representing the phylogenetic tree populated with the relative abundance of microbial taxa in a metagenomic sample. It can detect relationship of the taxonomic annotations on the tree and their quantitative characteristics in metagenomic data. Authors show its effect by comparing to other available methods using nine metagenomic datasets of moderate size for binary classification and the superior and robust performance of the model for multi-class classification. To solve difficulties such as inherent noise, complexity of the data, and high cost when collecting data samples, authors proposed to use a deep learning framework for constructing a data-driven simulation of microbiome data using a conditional generative adversarial network. This network can train two models against each other while leveraging side information learn from a given dataset to compute larger simulated datasets that are representative of the original dataset [12]. Authors [13] introduced PhyloPhlAn, a method using to scale large microbial genome characterization and phylogenetic analysis at multiple levels of resolution. Based on more than 230000 available sequences, it can classify genomes from isolate sequencing or metagenome-assembled genomes to species-level genome bins built. Besides, it reconstructs strain-level phylogenies based on the closest species using clade-specific maximally informative markers. Authors in [1] also attempted to deploy Self-organizing maps to visualize features.

3 Metagenomic Data for the Visualization Experiments

Three metagenomic datasets used in our experiment are derived from [3]. These datasets are respectively related to liver cirrhosis (Cirphy), colorectal cancer (Colphy), and inflammatory bowel disease (Ibdphy). The brief description of each one is described in Table 1. The dataset indicates the presence percentage of OTUs (Operational taxonomic units) in the human gut. The measurement was performed across stages of the same study, and across different studies. A single measurement is corresponding to a column. A column is featured by multiple rows, which denote different species of bacteria identified by the hierar-chical clustering (kingdom, phylum, class, order, family, genus, and species). By learning from these data, we aim to link species of the microbe with a specific disease.

Table 1. Experimental metagenomic datasets

Disease	Liver Cirrhosis	Colorectal Cancer	Inflammatory Bowel Disease
Dataset name	Cirphy	Colphy	Ibdphy
No. of features	542	503	443
No. of samples	232	121	110
Positive rate	0.51	0.40	0.32
Negative rate	0.49	0.60	0.77

4 Growing Self-Organizing Maps

With the emerging combination of computer science and biomedical science, many new achievements have been made. Once the genetic samples are digitized into data, modern machine learning algorithms can be applied to discover under-lying patterns. For these patterns, it is effective to present them in a visual way. In our study, GSOM algorithm is selected as a solution for visualization. With the appropriate value of the spread factor, this technique will generate a good map, which contributes to our disease prediction task.

GSOM is an unsupervised neural network that improved from SOM. In SOM, an input set of multidimensional data points is used to update weights to 2D nodes of the output map, which has a fixed size. In GSOM, data points update nodes' weights and also expand the size of the initial map until converged. The detail of the GSOM algorithm is as follows.

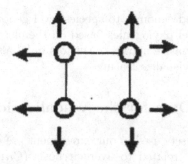

Fig. 1. Four initial nodes of GSOM used in [14]

- **Input**
  - Set of n data points, each data point is featured by a vector v of D-dimensional space.
  - Spread factor SF: controls the expansion of the map.
  - Learning rate LR.
- **Step 1. Initialization:**
  - Randomize values for weight vectors and initial size for the map, e.g. four nodes (Fig. 1).
  - Compute the growth threshold (GT) for the dataset using the formula GT = −D × ln(SF).
- **Step 2. Growing:**
  - Present input to the network.
  - Measure the distance to find the nearest weight vector with input vectors mapped to the current feature map. For interval data, the Euclidean distance is widely used. For binary data, Hamming distance is also a choice.
  - Modify the weight vector in the neighborhood (the neighborhood is a set of neurons around the winner). The weight of node j (w_j) is updated as follows.

$$w_j(k+1) = \begin{cases} w_j(k), & j \notin N_{k+1} \\ w_j(k) + LR(k)x \\ -(x_k - w_j(k)), & j \in N_{k+1} \end{cases}$$

  where the learning rate (LR) is a sequence of positive parameters converging to zero and N_{k+1} is the neighbourhood of the winning neuron.
  - Increase the error value of the winner (error value is the difference between the input vector and the weight vectors).
  - When the total error of a node is less than or equal to the growth threshold, grow nodes if it is a boundary node. Distribute weights to neighbors if i is a non-boundary node.
  - Initialize the new node weight vectors to match the neighboring node weights.

- Initialize the learning rate (LR) to its starting value.
- Repeat steps until all inputs have been presented and node growth is reduced to a minimum level.
- **Step 3. Smoothing:**
  - Decrease learning rate and fix a small starting neighborhood.
  - Identify the winner, update weights of the winner and neighbors in the same way as in step 2. The smoothing phase is stopped when the error values of nodes in the map become very small.

- **Output**
  - The result of GSOM that return coordinates.
  - Visualization for the images based on coordinate using gray or jet colormap.

5 GSOM for Metagenomic Data Visualization

The authors in [15] proposed a visualization method so-called "Fill-up" that maps 1D numerical features to a 2D square image. In this method, the filling of features to pixels of the square image is performed in a top-to-down then right-to-left manner. By making features pixelated with Fill-up, it usually presents better performance than other visualization approaches based on manifold learning, which suffers from overlapping issues.

In this study, we take into account GSOM to represent features onto images. This algorithm is commonly used in numerous applications to group samples with similar feature data into clusters. Samples belonging to the same group will be visualized by the same output node or a pixel. The intensity for a pixel is obtained by combining features value together, each feature has a transparent level (alpha) of 0.5. Beginning with 4 initialized nodes, GSOM will grow these nodes in various directions until the generated image stable. The output image of GSOM is represented in the form of a hexagonal grid or rectangular grid an example in Fig. 2. Each cell of this structure is a neuron that has a weight vector voted by its nearest samples. Between these two forms, the rectangular grid is preferred because it is symmetric, orthogonal, and used by the raster from Geographic Information Systems. Besides, to create a grid with a lower resolution, the combination of cells in this form is easier. However, it is undeniable that the hexagonal grid also has efficient coordinate systems and multi-resolution partitions. The nearest neighborhood in a hexagonal grid is simpler and less ambiguous than in a rectangular grid. Figure 3 and Fig. 4 illustrate the visualization of the Cirphy dataset using hexagonal and rectangular grid [16] of image size 48×48 and jet color map on the range of spread score from 0.2 to 3.0.

We deploy the GSOM algorithm to visualize features into images in this study. The features are clustered by GSOM method which generates coordinates of clusters which may contain many features exhibited in maps. These coordinates then are used to show features onto an image. Then, we use these synthetic images for the classification tasks with deep learning techniques. Because some features which belong to the same cluster are overlapped, we implement "transparency" technique which was attempted in [1].

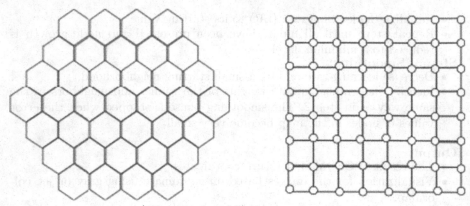

a) Hexagonal grid b) Rectangular grid

Fig. 2. Topologies of GSOM output image

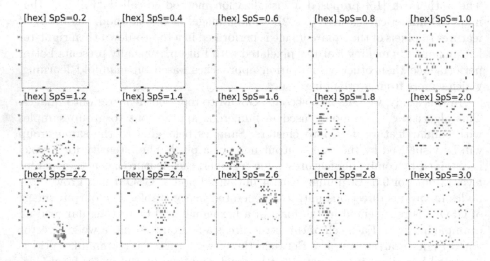

Fig. 3. Visualization result of Cirphy dataset using hexagonal grid of size 48 × 48 and jet colormap on a range of spread score (Sps) from 0.2 to 3.0

6   Experimental Results

This section presents the experiment outcome of GSOM on the Cirphy, Colphy, and Ibdphy datasets. We aim to investigate the appropriate value of the spread score with regard to different settings of grid topology, colormap, and final image size. Each result obtained from a specific setting is shown as a bar chart, which denotes the accuracy over various values of the spread score. At the end, the setting that gives the best performance examined by an average accuracy on 10 cross-validations for each dataset is reported.

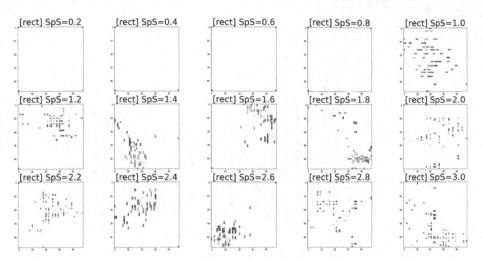

Fig. 4. Visualization result of the Cirphy dataset using rectangular grid of size 48 × 48 and jet color on a range of spread score (Sps) from 0.2 to 3.0

In respect of image size, we use the same size (48 × 48) as in [15] to determine which method gives better accuracy.

6.1 Hyperparameter Search

The experiments of hyperparameters search run on the Liver Cirrhosis dataset to investigate an appropriate set of hyperparameters for the latter experiments. Some hyperparameters such as spread factors, types of typologies, and colormaps are taken into account in this section.

Spread Scores Investigation. When data analysts study the feature maps to detect the clusters, in some cases, they want to observe the map of selected attributes according to their intention. Besides, a measure for controlling the spread of the map such that better clustering of the dataset can be achieved hierarchically as required by the data analyst and on the regions of interest is also indispensable. To realize this, a concept named "spread score" was created. At the beginning, the spread score is given a low value and it will be gradually increased until we get the map as expected. This score is independent of the number of features. It allows observers to compare the result of different datasets with a different number of features by mapping them with the same spread score. The system will use this value to calculate the growth threshold, which is considered as a threshold value for initiating node generation [14].

The experiment outcome on the Cirphy dataset using 48 × 48 hexagonal grid with jet colormap is shown in Fig. 5. The spread scores less than 1.0 do not catch good results. For the range greater than 1.0, the accuracy is high. The spread scores of 1.8 and 3.6 give very high accuracy compared to other values.

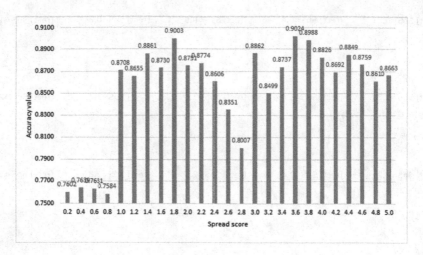

Fig. 5. Result of Cirphy dataset using jet color hexagonal grid of size 48 × 48 with the spread score from 0.2 to 5.0

Figure 6 shows the results of GSOM on the Cirphy dataset using the hexagonal grid, final image size of 48 × 48, and gray colormap. Each of them corresponds to a spread score in the range of 0.2 to 3.0. With the spread scores from 1.0 to 3.0, the accuracy varies considerably but always higher than 0.83. The best result can be found with the spread score of 3.0.

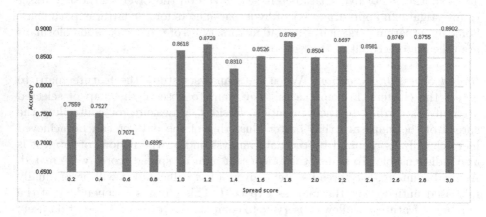

Fig. 6. Result of the Cirphy dataset using gray hexagonal grid of size 48 × 48

Figure 7 illustrates the results of GSOM on the Cirphy dataset using hexagonal grid of size 48 × 48 and jet color. Each result corresponds to a spread score in the range of 0.2 to 3.0. From the spread score of 1.0, the accuracy tends to increase slowly (from 0.8708) and reaches the highest value at 0.9003 with the spread score of 1.8. Next, it drops slightly for the spread scores from 2.0 to 2.8. Then, the accuracy goes up suddenly as the spread score changes from 2.8 to 3.0. This setting of GSOM gives the best result with a spread score of 1.8

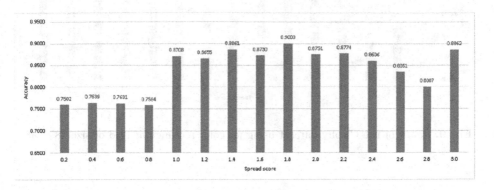

Fig. 7. Result of the Cirphy dataset using jet color hexagonal grid of size 48 × 48

Figure 8 indicates the results of GSOM on the Cirphy dataset using the rectangular grid of size 48 × 48 and gray color. Each of the results corresponds to a spread score in the range of 0.2 to 3.0. With the spread scores greater than 1.0, the accuracy changes moderately with the lowest value of 0.8401. The most suitable spread score for this setting is 2.0 Fig. 9 shows the experiment outcomes of GSOM on the Cirphy dataset using the rectangular grid of size 48 × 48 and gray color. Each of them corresponds to a spread score in the range from 0.2 to 3.0. For the spread scores from 1.0 to 3.0, the accuracy has slightly fluctuated with pretty high values (higher 0.85). With the spread score of 2.0, this setting achieves the best result.

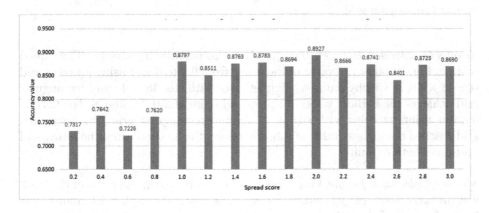

Fig. 8. Result of the Cirphy dataset using gray rectangular grid of size 48 × 48

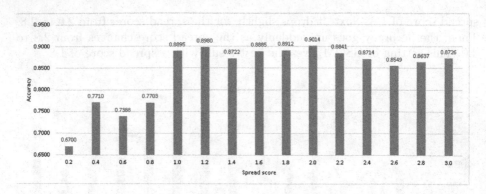

Fig. 9. Result of the Cirphy dataset using jet color rectangular grid of size 48 × 48

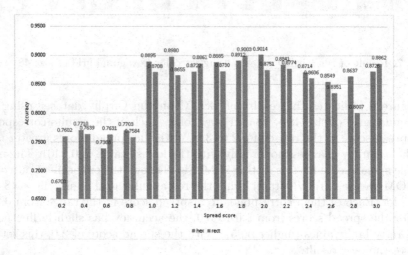

Fig. 10. Comparison Cirphy dataset using jet color with size 48 × 48 between hexagonal and rectangular grid

Results Comparison Between Hexagonal and Rectangular Typologies. The spread score in Fig. 10 takes the value of the range from 0.2 to 3 and using jet color and size 48 × 48. In Cirphy dataset using jet color with size 48 × 48 and rectangular grid achieves the highest value in the spread score of 2.0. Similar to the Cirphy dataset using jet color with size 48 × 48 and rectangular grid, the hexagonal grid reached the highest value at 1.8. Therefore, the method using the hexagonal grid gives better results.

Various Colormaps for the Visualizations. In this research, the focus of the work was on two colormaps: jet and gray color. The result shows that jet colormap is better for GSOM than the gray one.

In Fig. 11, the Cirphy dataset using the rectangular grid of size 48 × 48 with gray and jet color gives the best result at spread score 2.0. Figure 12 shows that using jet color often offers better results. The Cirphy dataset using the rectangular grid of size 48 × 48 with jet color gives the best result at spread score 1.8

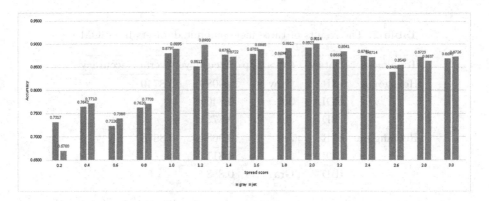

Fig. 11. Comparison of Cirphy dataset using rectangular grid of size 48 × 48 between gray and jet color

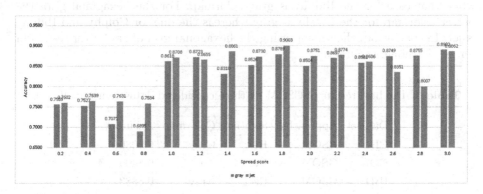

Fig. 12. Comparison of Cirphy dataset using hexagonal grid of size 48 × 48 between gray and jet color

The results shown from Figs. 6, 7, 8 and 9 give us some remarks as follows.

- Spread scores greater than 1.0 gives high accuracy (>80%). For the following remarks, we only focus on this score band.
- The setting using a rectangular grid of size 48 × 48 and jet colormap dominate others in terms of accuracy. The accuracy of this setting ranges between 0.8549 and 0.9014.
- For the hexagonal grid with an image size of 48 × 48, gray colormap gives the best result at the spread score of 3.0, whereas that case of jet colormap is 1.8. The rectangular grid with the image size of 48 × 48 achieves the best result at the spread score of 2.0 for whichever colormap.

6.2   Comparison with The-State-of-the-Art

In this section, the best setting (grid topology, colormap) for GSOM on three datasets and comparison with state of the art will be reported.

Table 2. The results of three metagenomic datasets in GSOM

Topology	Dataset	Colormap	Accuracy	Average accuracy
Hexagonal	CIR	Gray	0.9080	0.8740
	COL	Jet	0.8409	
	IBD	Jet	0.8731	
Rectangular	CIR	Jet	0.9034	0.8676
	COL	Jet	0.8112	
	IBD	Gray	0.8883	

Table 2 shows the best results for each grid topology of GSOM. For the rectangular grid, the Cirphy and Colphy give the best result with jet colormap while that case for the Ibdphy is gray colormap. For the hexagonal grid, the better colormap for the Cirphy is gray whereas the one for Colphy and Ibdphy is jet. In conclusion, the setting using the hexagonal grid offers better results in terms of average accuracy.

Table 3. The best results of GSOM on three considered datasets using all grids

Dataset	Approaches	Solution	Colormap	Accuracy
CIR	GSOM	Hex	Gray	0.9080
COL	GSOM	Hex	Jet	0.8409
IBD	GSOM	Rect	Gray	0.8883
Average				0.8790

The best result of GSOM using all grids and images of size 48 × 48 on three datasets (Cirphy, Colphy, and Ibdphy) is presented in Table 3. The Cirphy dataset achieves the highest result using the hexagonal grid and gray color maps, the Colphy dataset gets the best result with hexagonal grid and jet colormap, Ibdphy dataset gives the highest accuracy using the rectangular grid and gray colormap.

The experiment outcome on three datasets including Cirphy, Colphy, and Idbphy using visualizations based on GSOM and other methods is shown in Table 4. The two methods using GSOM achieve very high accuracy, just less than the Fill-up [15] (on the Cirphy dataset) and the "SOM using Semitransparent color" [1] (on the Colphy dataset). For the experimental results on the Ibdphy

Table 4. Performance comparison between state-of-the-art and our method with GSOM

Methods	Cirphy	Colphy	Ibdphy
SOM using semitransparent color [1]	0.888	0.852	0.848
Fill-up [15]	0.905	0.793	0.868
RF [3]	0.877	0.805	0.809
GSOM with hexagonal grid	0.9080	0.8409	0.8731
GSOM with rectangular grid	0.9034	0.8112	0.8883

dataset, those two methods are ranked first and second in terms of accuracy. In summary, the "GSOM with the hexagonal grid" obtains the highest average accuracy compared to other methods.

7 Conclusion

Growing Self-Organizing Map is deployed in this study and provides good visualizations for metagenomic data. Besides, these visualizations enable to enhance the prediction performance via using deep learning techniques for the image classification.

A vast number of main parameters for Growing Self-Organizing Map are also taken into account to compare the performance. We also investigated different typologies of Growing Self-Organizing maps and tests with a range of spread scores. As shown from the results, the performance depends on those parameters. A small value which is lower 1.0 gives poor visualization leading to a decrease in the performance.

We only run shallow architectures of the Convolutional Neural Network to perform the classification tasks. Further studies should investigate deeper architectures which can lead to higher performance in classification. Further work should investigate patterns in performance changes when using several hyperparameters such as colormaps and topologies.

Acknowledgements. This work is funded by Can Tho University under Grant number T2020-12.

References

1. Nguyen, T.H.: Metagenome-based disease classification with deep learning and visualizations based on self-organizing maps. In: Dang, T.K., Küng, J., Takizawa, M., Bui, S.H. (eds.) FDSE 2019. LNCS, vol. 11814, pp. 307–319. Springer, Cham (2019). https://doi.org/10.1007/978-3-030-35653-8_20
2. Kohonen, T.: Self-Organizing Maps. Springer Series in Information Sciences, vol. 30. Springer, Heidelberg (1997). https://doi.org/10.1007/978-3-642-97966-8

3. Pasolli, E., Truong, D.T., Malik, F., Waldron, L., Segata, N.: Machine learning meta-analysis of large metagenomic datasets: tools and biological insights. PLoS Comput. Biol. (2016). https://doi.org/10.1371/journal.pcbi.1004977
4. Brumfield, K.D., Huq, A., Colwell, R.R., Olds, J.L., Leddy, M.B.: Microbial resolution of whole genome shotgun and 16S amplicon metagenomic sequencing using publicly available NEON data. PLoS ONE (2020). https://doi.org/10.1371/journal.pone.0228899
5. Storato, D., Comin, M.: Improving metagenomic classification using discriminative k-mers from sequencing data. BioRxiv. The present server for biology (2020). https://doi.org/10.1101/2020.02.20.957308
6. Kim, D.J., et al.: Colorectal cancer diagnostic model utilizing metagenomic and metabolomic data of stool microbial extracellular vesicles. Sci. Rep. (2020). https://doi.org/10.1038/s41598-020-59529-8
7. Sato, N., et al.: Metagenomic analysis of bacterial species in tongue microbiome of current and never smokers. npj Biofilms Microbiomes (2020). https://doi.org/10.1038/s41522-020-0121-6
8. Pallen, M.J.: Diagnostic metagenomics: potential applications to bacterial, viral and parasitic infections. Parasitology (2014). https://doi.org/10.1017/S0031182014000134
9. Kim, Y.-K.: Method for diagnosing lung cancer via bacterial metagenomic analysis. Patentscope, US Patents, 05 July 2018. https://patents.google.com/patent/US20200157608A1/en.
10. Ma, B., France, M., Ravel, J.: Meta-pangenome: at the crossroad of pangenomics and metagenomics. In: Tettelin, H., Medini, D. (eds.) The Pangenome, pp. 205–218. Springer, Cham (2020). https://doi.org/10.1007/978-3-030-38281-0_9
11. Reiman, D., Metwally, A., Sun, J., Dai, Y.: PopPhy-CNN: a phylogenetic tree embedded architecture for convolutional neural networks to predict host phenotype from metagenomic data. IEEE J. Biomed. Health Inform. (2020). https://doi.org/10.1109/JBHI.2020.2993761
12. Reiman, D., Dai, Y.: Using conditional generative adversarial networks to boost the performance of machine learning in microbiome datasets. bioXiv: 2020.05.18.102814, May 2020. https://doi.org/10.1101/2020.05.18.102814
13. Asnicar, F., Thomas, A.M., Beghini, F., et al.: Precise phylogenetic analysis of microbial isolates and genomes from metagenomes using PhyloPhlAn 3.0. Nat. Commun. 11, 2500 (2020). https://doi.org/10.1038/s41467-020-16366-7
14. Alahakoon, D., Halgamuge, S.K., Srinivasan, B.: Dynamic self-organizing maps with controlled growth for knowledge discovery. IEEE Trans. Neural Networks (2000). https://doi.org/10.1109/72.846732
15. Nguyen, T.H., Prifti, E., Sokolovska, N., Zucker, J.D.: Disease prediction using synthetic image representations of metagenomic data and convolutional neural networks. In: The 13th IEEE-RIVF International Conference on Computing and Communication Technologies 2019, Da Nang, 20–22 March 2019, pp. 231–236 (2019). ISBN 978-1-5386-9313-1. IEEE Xplore
16. Birch, C.P., Oom, S.P., Beecham, J.A.: Rectangular and hexagonal grids used for observation, experiment and simulation in ecology (2007). https://doi.org/10.1016/j.ecolmodel.2007.03.041

Advances in Big Data Query Processing and Optimization

On Norm-Based Locality Measures of 2-Dimensional Discrete Hilbert Curves

H. K. Dai[1(✉)] and H. C. Su[2]

[1] Computer Science Department, Oklahoma State University,
Stillwater, Oklahoma 74078, USA
dai@cs.okstate.edu
[2] Department of Computer Science, Arkansas State University,
Jonesboro, Arkansas 72401, USA
suh@astate.edu

Abstract. A discrete space-filling curve provides a 1-dimensional indexing or traversal of a multi-dimensional grid space. Sample applications of space-filling curves include multi-dimensional indexing methods, data structures and algorithms, parallel computing, and image compression. Locality preservation reflects proximity between grid points, that is, close-by grid points are mapped to close-by indices or vice versa. The underlying locality measure for our studies, based on the p-normed metric d_p, is the maximum ratio of $d_p(v, u)^m$ to $d_p(\tilde{v}, \tilde{u})$ over all corresponding point-pairs (v, u) and $(\tilde{v}, \tilde{u})$ in the m-dimensional grid space and 1-dimensional index space, respectively. Our analytical results close the gaps between the current best lower and upper bounds with exact formulas for $p \in \{1, 2\}$, and extend to all reals $p \geq 2$, and our empirical results will shed some light on determining the exact formulas for the locality measure for all reals $p \in (1, 2)$.

Keywords: Index structures · Space-filling curves · Hilbert curves · z-order curves · Locality

1 Introduction

Discrete space-filling curves have a wide range of applications in databases, parallel computation, algorithms, in which linearization techniques of multi-dimensional arrays or computational grids are needed. Sample applications include heuristics for combinatorial algorithms and data structures: traveling salesperson algorithm [21] and nearest-neighbor finding [8], multi-dimensional space-filling indexing methods [3,7,12,15], image compression [16], dynamic unstructured mesh partitioning [14], and linearization and traversal of sensor networks [5,24]. For a comprehensive historical development of classical space-filling curves, see [22] and [4].

For a positive integer n, denote $[n] = \{1, 2, \ldots, n\}$. For a positive integer m, and m-dimensional (discrete) space-filling curve of length n^m is a bijective

© Springer Nature Switzerland AG 2020
T. K. Dang et al. (Eds.): FDSE 2020, LNCS 12466, pp. 169–184, 2020.
https://doi.org/10.1007/978-3-030-63924-2_10

mapping $C : [n^m] \rightarrow [n]^m$, which provides a linear indexing/traversal or total ordering of the grid points in $[n]^m$. For a positive integer k, an m-dimensional grid is of order k if it has side-length $n = 2^k$; a space-filling curve has order k if its codomain is a grid of order k. A mathematical construction of a sequence of multi-dimensional space-filling curves of successive orders usually follows a recursive framework on the dimensionality and order, with which a few classical families arise, such as Gray-coded curves, Hilbert curves, Peano curves, and z-order curves (see, for examples, [2] and [18]).

A mathematical formulation of discrete Hilbert curves based on generators and permutations (on a corner-labeling hypercube) in [2] shows that the descriptional complexity and structural analysis of multi-dimensional Hilbert curves can be reduced to a combinatorial analysis of their generators. One of the salient characteristics of space-filling curves is their "self-similarity". Denote by H_k^m and Z_k^m an m-dimensional Hilbert and z-order, respectively, space-filling curve of order k. Figure 1 illustrates the recursive geometric generations of H_k^m and Z_k^m for $m = 2$, and $k = 1, 2$, and $m = 3$, and $k = 1$.

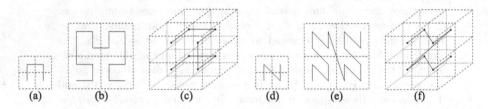

(a)   (b)   (c)   (d)   (e)   (f)

Fig. 1. Recursive self-similar generations of Hilbert and z-order curves of higher order (respectively, H_k^m and Z_k^m) by interconnecting symmetric subcurves, via reflection and/or rotation, of lower order (respectively, H_{k-1}^m and Z_{k-1}^m) along an order-1 subcurve (respectively, H_1^m and Z_1^m): (a) H_1^2; (b) H_2^2; (c) H_1^3; (d) Z_1^2; (e) Z_2^2; (f) Z_1^3.

We gauge the applicability of a family of space-filling curves based on: (1) their common structural characteristics that measure locality and clustering, (2) descriptional simplicity that facilitates their construction and combinatorial analysis in arbitrary dimensions, and (3) computational complexity in the grid space-index space transformation. Locality preservation measures proximity between the grid points of $[n]^m$, that is, close-by points in $[n]^m$ are mapped to close-by indices/numbers in $[n^m]$, or vice versa. Clustering performance evaluates the distribution of continuous runs of grid points (clusters) over identically shaped subspaces of $[n]^m$, which can be characterized by the average number of clusters and the average inter-cluster distance (in $[n^m]$) within a subspace.

2   Commonly Studied Locality Measures and Related Work

The locality preservation of space-filling curve families is crucial for the efficiency of their supported indexing schemes on computational grids, and data structures and algorithmic applications for combinatorial optimization; for examples, spatial correlation in multi-dimensional indexings, compression in image processing, and communication optimization in mesh-connected parallel computing. Rigorous analyses of locality depends on the availability of robust and practical measures: good bounds (lower and upper) on the locality measure translate into good bounds on the declustering (locality loss) in one space in the presence of locality in the other space.

A few locality measures have been proposed and analyzed for space-filling curves in the literature for their diverse applications. Denote by d and d_p the Euclidean metric and p-normed metric (rectilinear metric ($p = 1$) and maximum metric ($p = \infty$)), respectively. Let $\mathcal{C}$ denote a family of m-dimensional curves of successive orders.

For quantifying the proximity preservation of close-by points in the m-dimensional space $[n]^m$, Pérez, Kamata, and Kawaguchi [20] employ an average locality measure:

$$L_{\mathrm{PKK}}(C) = \sum_{i,j \in [n^m] | i < j} \frac{|i - j|}{d(C(i), C(j))} \text{ for } C \in \mathcal{C},$$

and provide a hierarchical construction for a 2-dimensional $\mathcal{C}$ with good but suboptimal locality with respect to this measure.

Mitchison and Durbin [17] use a more restrictive locality measure parameterized by q:

$$L_{\mathrm{MD},q}(C) = \sum_{i,j \in [n^m] | i < j \text{ and } d(C(i),C(j))=1} |i - j|^q \text{ for } C \in \mathcal{C}$$

to study optimal 2-dimensional mappings for $q \in [0, 1]$. For the case $q = 1$, the optimal mapping with respect to $L_{\mathrm{MD},1}$ is very different from that in [20]. For the case $q < 1$, they prove a lower bound for arbitrary 2-dimensional curve C:

$$L_{\mathrm{MD},q}(C) \geq \frac{1}{1 + 2q} n^{1+2q} + O(n^{2q}),$$

and provide an explicit construction for 2-dimensional $\mathcal{C}$ with good but suboptimal locality. They conjecture that the space-filling curves with optimal locality (with respect to $L_{\mathrm{MD},q}$ with $q < 1$) must exhibit a "fractal" character.

Dai and Su [10] consider a locality measure similar to $L_{\mathrm{MD},1}$ conditional on a 1-normed distance of δ between points in $[n]^m$:

$$L_\delta(C) = \sum_{i,j \in [n^m] | i < j \text{ and } d_1(C(i),C(j))=\delta} |i - j| \text{ for } C \in \mathcal{C}.$$

They derive exact formulas for L_δ for the Hilbert curve family $\{H_k^m \mid k = 1, 2, \ldots\}$ and z-order curve family $\{Z_k^m \mid k = 1, 2, \ldots\}$ for $m = 2$ and arbitrary δ that is an integral power of 2, and $m = 3$ and $\delta = 1$:

$$L_\delta(H_k^2) = \begin{cases} \frac{17}{2 \cdot 7} \cdot 2^{3k} - \frac{5}{2 \cdot 3} \cdot 2^{2k} - \frac{2^3}{3 \cdot 7} & \text{if } \delta = 1 \\ \frac{17}{2 \cdot 7} \cdot 2^{3k+2\log\delta} - \frac{2^3 \cdot 3 \cdot 5^2 \cdot 7(k - \log\delta) + 5 \cdot 7 \cdot 383}{2^4 \cdot 3^3 \cdot 5 \cdot 7} \cdot 2^{2k+3\log\delta} \\ \quad + \frac{2 \cdot 3 \cdot 5(k - \log\delta) - 1}{2^2 \cdot 3^3} \cdot 2^{2k+\log\delta} - \frac{2^2 \cdot 41}{3^3 \cdot 5 \cdot 7} \cdot 2^{5\log\delta} \\ \quad - \frac{2}{3^3} \cdot 2^{3\log\delta} - \frac{2}{3 \cdot 5} \cdot 2^{\log\delta} & \text{otherwise,} \end{cases}$$

$$L_\delta(Z_k^2) = \begin{cases} 2^{3k} - 2^k & \text{if } \delta = 1 \\ 2^{3k+2\log\delta} - (\frac{2}{3^2}(k - \log\delta) + \frac{1949}{2^5\cdot3^3\cdot7})2^{2k+3\log\delta} & \\ +(\frac{2}{3^2}(k - \log\delta) + \frac{7}{2^2\cdot3^3})2^{2k+\log\delta} + \frac{19}{2^2\cdot3\cdot7}\cdot2^{2k} - \frac{2^2}{7}\cdot2^{k+4\log\delta} & \\ -\frac{3}{7}\cdot2^{k+\log\delta} + \frac{2\cdot5}{3^3\cdot7}\cdot2^{5\log\delta} - \frac{2^2}{3^3}\cdot2^{3\log\delta} + \frac{2}{3\cdot7}\cdot2^{2\log\delta} & \text{otherwise,} \end{cases}$$

$$L_1(H_k^3) = \frac{67}{2\cdot31}\cdot2^{5k} - \frac{11}{2\cdot7}\cdot2^{3k} - \frac{2^6}{7\cdot31}, \text{ and}$$

$$L_1(Z_k^3) = 2^{5k} - 2^{2k}.$$

With respect to the locality measure L_δ and for sufficiently large k and $\delta \ll 2^k$, the z-order curve family performs better than the Hilbert curve family for $m = 2$ and over the δ-spectrum of integral powers of 2. When $\delta = 2^k$, the domination reverses. The superiority of the z-order curve family persists but declines for $m = 3$ with unit 1-normed distance for L_δ.

Xu and Tirthapura [25] consider a variant of the all-pairs locality measure L_δ via the notion of nearest-neighbor stretch of a single-source grid point—conditional on the unit 1-normed metric d_1; that is, for an m-dimensional space-filling curve C and a grid point v indexed by C, denote the nearest-neighbor of v in $[n]^m$, $N_1(v, C) = \{u \in [n]^m \mid d_1(u, v) = 1\}$, and:

$$\text{average nearest-neighbor stretch}(v, C) = \frac{\sum_{u \in N_1(v,C)} |C^{-1}(v) - C^{-1}(u)|}{|N_1(v, C)|}, \text{ and}$$

$$\text{maximum nearest-neighbor stretch}(v, C) = \max_{u \in N_1(v,C)} |C^{-1}(v) - C^{-1}(u)|.$$

The average-quantifications of these two nearest-neighbor stretches for C result in: average-average nearest-neighbor stretch $D^{\text{avg}}(C)$ and average-maximum nearest-neighbor stretch $D^{\text{max}}(C)$ for C. They obtain a lower bound for $D^{\text{avg}}(C)$ for arbitrary m-dimensional curve C with grid space $[n]^m$:

$$(D^{\text{max}}(C) \geq) \; D^{\text{avg}}(C) \geq \frac{2}{3m}(n^{m-1} - n^{-m-1}),$$

and show that, for an m-dimensional row-major space-filling curve S with grid space $[n]^m$,

$$D^{\text{avg}}(S) \sim \frac{1}{m}n^{m-1} \text{ and } D^{\text{max}}(S) = n^{m-1}.$$

Voorhies [23] defines a heuristic locality measure, tailored to computer graphics applications, and the corresponding empirical study indicates that the Hilbert space-filling curve family outperforms other curve families.

For measuring the proximity preservation of close-by points in the indexing space $[n^m]$, Gotsman and Lindenbaum [13] consider the following measures:

$$L_{\text{GL,min}}(C) = \min_{i,j\in[n^m]|i<j} \frac{d(C(i), C(j))^m}{|i - j|}, \text{ and}$$

$$L_{\text{GL,max}}(C) = \max_{i,j\in[n^m]|i<j} \frac{d(C(i), C(j))^m}{|i - j|}, \text{ for } C \in \mathcal{C}.$$

They show that for arbitrary m-dimensional curve C,

$$L_{\text{GL,min}}(C) = O(n^{1-m}), \text{ and}$$

$$L_{\text{GL,max}}(C) > (2^m - 1)(1 - \frac{1}{n})^m.$$

For the m-dimensional Hilbert curve family $\{H_k^m \mid k = 1, 2, \ldots\}$, they prove that:

$$L_{\text{GL,max}}(H_k^m) \leq 2^m (m+3)^{\frac{m}{2}}.$$

Alber and Niedermeier [1,2] generalize $L_{\text{GL,max}}$ to L_p by employing the p-normed metric d_p for real norm-parameter $p \geq 1$ in place of the Euclidean metric d, which is the locality measure studied in our work (and the preliminary versions in [10] and [11]).

We summarize below: (1) the representative lower- and upper-bound results and exact formulas for the locality measure L_p of the 2-dimensional Hilbert curve family H_k^2 for various norm-parameter p-values and grid-order k-values, and (2) the contribution of our studies:

1. For $p = 1$: Niedermeier, Reinhardt, and Sanders [19] give a lower bound for $L_1(H_k^2)$: for all $k \geq 1$,

$$L_1(H_k^2) \geq \frac{(3 \cdot 2^{k-1} - 2)^2}{4^{k-1}},$$

and Chochia, Cole, and Heywood [9] provide a matching upper bound for $L_1(H_k^2)$ for all $k \geq 2$. We state the exact formula for $L_1(H_k^2)$ for all $k \geq 2$ (presented, without proof, in the preliminary version in [10]).

2. For $p = 2$: Gotsman and Lindenbaum [13] derive a lower and upper bounds for $L_2(H_k^2)$: for all $k \geq 6$,

$$\frac{(2^{k-1} - 1)^2}{\frac{2}{3} \cdot 4^{k-2} + \frac{1}{3}} \leq L_2(H_k^2) \leq 6\frac{2}{3},$$

and Alber and Niedermeier [2] improves the upper bound for $L_2(H_k^2)$: for all $k \geq 1$,

$$L_2(H_k^2) \leq 6\frac{1}{2}.$$

We state that the lower bound above [13] is the exact formula for $L_2(H_k^2)$ (presented, without proof, in the preliminary version in [10]): for all $k \geq 5$,

$$L_2(H_k^2) = 6 \cdot \frac{2^{2k-3} - 2^{k-1} + 2^{-1}}{2^{2k-3} + 1}.$$

Bauman [6] obtains a matching lower and upper bounds for $L_2(H_k^2)$ for $k = \infty$:

$$L_2(H_\infty^2) = 6.$$

3. For $2 < p \leq \infty$: Due to the monotonicity of the underlying p-normed metric: for every grid-point pair (v, u), the p-normed metric $d_p(v, u)$ is strictly decreasing in $p \in [1, \infty)$, we provide the same exact formula for $L_p(H_k^2)$ as for the case when $p = 2$ (presented, without proof, in the preliminary version in [10]):

$$L_p(H_k^2) = 6 \cdot \frac{2^{2k-3} - 2^{k-1} + 2^{-1}}{2^{2k-3} + 1} \text{ for all reals } p \geq 2.$$

When $p = \infty$, Alber [1] and Alber and Niedermeier [2] establish a lower and upper bounds for $L_\infty(H_k^2)$, respectively:

$$6(1 - O(2^{-k})) \leq L_\infty(H_k^2) \leq 6\frac{2}{5}.$$

We present analytical and empirical studies on the locality measure L_p for the 2-dimensional Hilbert curve family over the entire spectrum of possible norm-parameter values. Our proofs of the exact formulas of $L_p(H_k^2)$ for $p \in \{1, 2\}$ follow a uniform approach: identifying all the representative grid-point pairs, which realize the $L_p(H_k^2)$-value, for each $p \in \{1, 2\}$. The analytical results close the gap between the current best lower and upper bounds with exact formulas for $p \in \{1, 2\}$, and extend to all reals $p \geq 2$.

While not addressing the candidate exact formulas for $L_p(H_k^2)$ for $p \in (1, 2)$ (partial result in [11]), we present an empirical study on $L_p(H_k^2)$ for all norm-parameters $p \in [1, 2]$, which complements the incomplete analytical study and shows that: (1) The analytical results are consistent with program verification over various norm-parameter p-values and sufficiently large grid-order k-values, (2) As p increases over the real unit interval $[1, 2]$, the locations of candidate representative grid-point pairs agree with the intuitive interpolation effect over the two delimiting p-values, and (3) Our empirical study will shed some light on determining the exact formulas for the locality measure for all reals $p \in (1, 2)$.

With diverse applications of the 2-dimensional Hilbert curve family H_k^2, a practical implication of our results on the locality measure $L_p(H_k^2)$ over all real norm-parameters $p \in \{1\} \cup [2, \infty)$ is that the exact formulas provide precise bounds on measuring the loss in data locality in the 1-dimensional index space, while spatial correlation exists in the 2-dimensional grid space, or vice versa.

Note that we present the skeletons for proving the main results without lengthy details in the abstract. Complete results, proofs, and derivations of claims/theorems are provided in the full version of this article.

3   Analytical Studies of $L_p(H_k^2)$ with $p \geq 1$

For 2-dimensional Hilbert curves, the recursive self-similar structural property decomposes H_k^2 into four identical H_{k-1}^2-subcurves via reflection and/or rotation, which are amalgamated together by an H_1^2-curve—inducing unique orientations of the four H_{k-1}^2-subcurves relative to that of the H_1^2-curve for only the case of a

2-dimensional H_k^2. Following the linear order along this H_1^2-curve, we denote the four H_{k-1}^2-subcurves (quadrants) as $Q_1(H_k^2)$, $Q_2(H_k^2)$, $Q_3(H_k^2)$, and $Q_4(H_k^2)$.

We extend the notations to identify all H_l^2-subcurves of a structured H_k^2 for all $l \in [k]$ inductively on the grid-order. Let $Q_i(H_k^2)$ denote the i-th H_{k-1}^2-subcurve (along the amalgamating H_1^2-curve) for all $i \in [2^2]$. Then for the i-th H_{l-1}^2-subcurve, $Q_i(H_l^2)$, of H_l^2, where $2 < l \leq k$ and $i \in [2^2]$, let $Q_j(Q_i(H_l^2))$ denote the j-th H_{l-2}^2-subcurve of $Q_i(H_l^2)$ for all $j \in [2^2]$. We write $Q_i^{q+1}(H_l^2)$ for $Q_i(Q_i^q(H_l^2))$ for all $l \in [k]$ and all positive integers $q < l$. The notation $Q_i^l(H_l^2)$ identifies the i-th grid point in the H_1^2-subcurve $Q_i^{l-1}(H_l^2)$.

For a 2-dimensional Hilbert curve H_k^2 indexing the grid $[2^k]^2$, with a canonical orientation shown in Fig. 2(a), denote by $\partial_1(H_k^2)$ and $\partial_2(H_k^2)$ the entry and the exit, respectively, grid points in $[2^k]^2$ (with respect to the canonical orientation). Figure 2 depicts the decomposition of H_k^2 and the ∂_1- and ∂_2-labels of four H_{k-1}^2-subcurves.

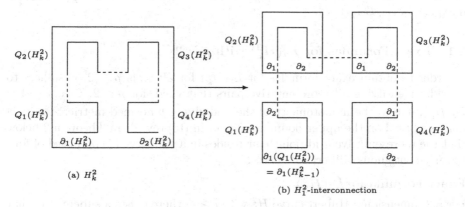

(a) H_k^2

(b) H_1^2-interconnection

Fig. 2. Generation of H_k^2 from a H_1^2-interconnection of four H_{k-1}^2-subcurves with their labeled entries and exits.

For a 2-dimensional Hilbert curve H_k^2 in a Cartesian x-y coordinate system, and for a grid point v indexed by H_k^2, we denote by $\mathrm{X}(v)$ and $\mathrm{Y}(v)$ the x- and y-coordinate of v, respectively, and by $(\mathrm{X}(v), \mathrm{Y}(v))$ the grid point v in the coordinate system. For an H_l^2-subcurve C of H_k^2, where $l \in [k]$, notice that its entry $\partial_1(C)$ and exit $\partial_2(C)$ differ in exactly one coordinate: x- or y-coordinate, say $z \in \{x, y\}$. We say that the subcurve C is z^+-oriented (respectively, z^--oriented) if the z-coordinate of $\partial_1(C)$ is less than (respectively, greater than) that of $\partial_2(C)$. Note that: (1) the x- and y-coordinates of $\partial_1(H_k^2)$ and $\partial_2(H_k^2)$ uniquely determine those of $\partial_1(H_l^2)$ and $\partial_2(H_l^2)$ for all $l \in [k]$, and (2) the two subcurves $Q_2(H_k^2)$ and $Q_3(H_k^2)$ inherit the orientation from their supercurve H_k^2.

For a space-filling curve C indexing an m-dimensional grid space, the notation "$v \in C$" refers to "the grid point v indexed by C", and $C^{-1}(v)$ gives the index of v in the 1-dimensional index space. The locality measure in our studies is, for all reals $p \geq 1$,

$$L_p(C) = \max_{\text{indices } i,j \in [n^m]} \frac{d_p(C(i), C(j))^m}{d_p(i,j)} \quad (= \max_{\text{indices } i,j \in [n^m]} \frac{d_p(C(i), C(j))^m}{|i-j|})$$

$$= \max_{v,u \in C} \frac{d_p(v,u)^m}{|C^{-1}(v) - C^{-1}(u)|}$$

(argument of the maximum: a representative for C with respect to L_p).

When $m = 2$, the following denotations represent the above locality measure with respect to a grid-point pair and a subcurve pair. We write $\mathcal{L}_{C,p}(v,u) = \frac{d_p(v,u)^2}{\delta_C(v,u)}$, where $\delta_C(v,u)$ denotes the index-difference $|C^{-1}(v) - C^{-1}(u)|$, and generalize the notations $L_p(C)$ and $\mathcal{L}_{C,p}$ for a subcurve C (of a 2-dimensional space-filling curve) in an obvious manner. For two subcurves C_1 and C_2 of a 2-dimensional space-filling curve C, denote $\mathcal{L}_{C,p}(C_1, C_2) = \max_{(v,u) \in C_1 \times C_2} \mathcal{L}_{C,p}(v,u)$.

3.1   Exact Formulas for $L_p(H_k^2)$ with $p \geq 2$

In order to obtain exact formulas for $L_p(H_k^2)$ for all reals $p \geq 2$, it suffices to consider identifying all representative pairs that yield, for $p = 2$, $\mathcal{L}_{H_k^2,2}(v,u) = L_2(H_k^2)$, due to the monotonicity of the underlying p-normed metric. A refined analysis based on the upper-bound argument in [13] reveals in Theorem 2 below that the representative grid-point pair resides in a subcurve C composed of four linearly-contiguous Hilbert subcurves.

Exact Formula for $L_2(H_k^2)$

For a 2-dimensional Hilbert curve H_l^2 with $l \geq 4$, there exists a subcurve C that is composed of four linearly-contiguous H_k^2-subcurves with $k = l - 3$. Figure 3 depicts the arrangement in a canonical Cartesian coordinate system. Denote the leftmost and rightmost (first and fourth in the traversal order) H_k^2-subcurves by $_1H_k^2$ (y^--oriented) and $_4H_k^2$ (y^+-oriented), respectively.

We assume the canonical coordinate system as shown in Fig. 3 such that the lower-left corner grid point of $_1H_k^2$ is the origin $(1,1)$ of the coordinate system. Theorem 1 asserts that the unique representative grid-point pair reside at the lower-left and lower-right corners of C.

Theorem 1. *For all positive integers $k \geq 1$, and all $(v,u) \in {}_1H_k^2 \times {}_4H_k^2 - Q_3^k({}_1H_k^2) \times Q_2^k({}_4H_k^2)$, there exist $v' \in Q_3^k({}_1H_k^2)$ and $u' \in Q_2^k({}_4H_k^2)$ such that $\mathcal{L}_{C,2}(v',u') = 6 \cdot \frac{2^{2k+3} - 2^{k+2} + 2^{-1}}{2^{2k+3} + 1}$.*

The grid-point pair at the lower-left and lower-right corners of C: $v' \in Q_3^k({}_1H_k^2)$ with coordinates $(1,1)$ and $u' \in Q_2^k({}_4H_k^2)$ with coordinates $(2^{k+2}, 1)$ maximizes the $\mathcal{L}_{C,2}$-value. Notice that $\delta_C(v',u') = 2(\sum_{i=0}^{k-1} 2^{2i} + 1 + 2 \cdot 2^{2k}) - 1$, hence, $\mathcal{L}_{C,2}(v',u') = \frac{d_2(v',u')^2}{\delta_C(v',u')} = 6 \cdot \frac{2^{2k+3} - 2^{k+2} + 2^{-1}}{2^{2k+3} + 1}$.

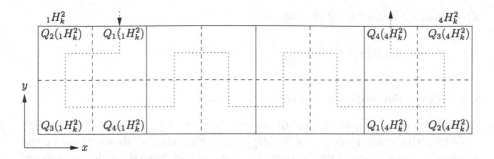

Fig. 3. Four linearly-contiguous H_k^2-subcurves in a canonical Cartesian coordinate system.

The current best bounds for the 2-dimensional Hilbert curve family with respect to L_2 (lower bound in [13] and upper bound in [2]) are:

$$6(1 - O(2^{-k})) \leq L_2(H_k^2) \leq 6\frac{1}{2}.$$

Following the argument in [13] with a refined analysis, together with the exact formula for $\mathcal{L}_{C,2}(Q_3(_1H_k^2), Q_2(_4H_k^2))$ $(= \mathcal{L}_{C,2}(Q_3^k(_1H_k^2), Q_2^k(_4H_k^2)))$ in Theorem 1, we close the gaps between the two bounds with an exact formula for $L_2(H_k^2)$.

Theorem 2. *For all positive integers $k \geq 5$,*

$$L_2(H_k^2) = 6 \cdot \frac{2^{2k-3} - 2^{k-1} + 2^{-1}}{2^{2k-3} + 1}.$$

For an x^+-oriented Hilbert curve H_k^2 with $\partial_1(H_k^2) = (1,1)$, where $k \geq 5$, the representative grid-point pair for H_k^2 with respect to L_2 reside at the lower-left corner (with coordinates $(2^{k-2} + 1, 2^{k-1} + 1)$) and the lower-right corner (with coordinates $(2^k - 2^{k-2}, 2^{k-1} + 1)$) of four linearly-contiguous largest subquadrants (H_{k-3}^2-subcurves).

Exact Formulas for $L_p(H_k^2)$ with $p > 2$

In order to study L_p for arbitrary real $p > 2$, we first investigate the monotonicity of the underlying p-normed metric.

Lemma 3. *For every positive real constant α, the function $f : (0, \infty) \to (1, \infty)$ defined by $f(p) = (1 + \alpha^p)^{\frac{1}{p}}$ is strictly decreasing over its domain.*

An immediate consequence of Lemma 3 is that for all grid points v and u, the p-normed metric $d_p(v, u)$ as a function of $p \in (0, \infty)$ is decreasing over its domain. Hence for a space-filling curve C, $\mathcal{L}_{C,p}(v, u) = \frac{d_p(v,u)^2}{\delta_C(v,u)}$ is decreasing in $p \in (0, \infty)$, as $\delta_C(v, u)$ is independent of p.

Theorem 4. *For all positive integers* $k \geq 5$,

$$L_p(H_k^2) = 6 \cdot \frac{2^{2k-3} - 2^{k-1} + 2^{-1}}{2^{2k-3} + 1} \quad \text{for all reals } p \geq 2.$$

3.2   Exact Formula for $L_p(H_k^2)$ with $p = 1$

We develop an argument similar to the one in Sect. 3.1 in establishing $L_2(H_k^2)$ to obtain the exact formula for $L_1(H_k^2)$. Adopting similar denotations in the proof of Theorem 2, consider the subpath-containment analysis with an arbitrary subcurve/subpath P of length l embedded in a 2-dimensional Hilbert curve. There exists a sufficiently large positive integer r such that $(2^{r-1})^2 < l \leq (2^r)^2$ and P is contained in two adjacent quadrants Q' and Q'' of size $(2^r)^2$ grid points each. Figure 4 provides the three possible arrangements of the two adjacent H_κ^2-subcurves where $\kappa \leq r$ (modulo symmetry).

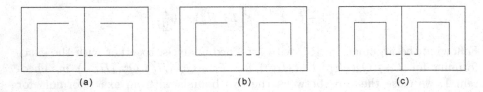

(a)   (b)   (c)

Fig. 4. The three possible adjacent H_κ^2-subcurves: (a) y^--oriented and y^+-oriented subcurves, (b) y^--oriented and x^+-oriented subcurves, (c) x^+-oriented and x^+-oriented subcurves.

We follow a case-analysis of subpath-containment of P in subquadrants of size $(2^{r-1})^2$ within $Q' \cup Q''$ with a uniform approach to identifying all representative grid-point pairs that realize the $L_1(H_k^2)$-values for $p \in \{1, 2\}$, and obtain the same matching lower and upper bounds for $L_1(H_k^2)$ in [19] and [9], respectively: for all $k \geq 2$,

$$L_1(H_k^2) = \frac{(3 \cdot 2^{k-1} - 2)^2}{4^{k-1}}.$$

Theorem 5. *For all positive integers* $k \geq 2$,

$$L_1(H_k^2) = 9 - 3 \cdot 2^{-k+3} + 2^{-2k+4}.$$

For an x^+-oriented Hilbert curve H_k^2 with $\partial_1(H_k^2) = (1, 1)$, where $k \geq 2$, the two representative grid-point pairs for H_k^2 with respect to L_1 reside at: (1) $Q_2^{k-1}(Q_1(H_k^2)) \times Q_2^k(H_k^2)$ with coordinates $((2^{k-1}, 1), (1, 2^k))$, and (2) their symmetry $Q_3^k(H_k^2) \times Q_3^{k-1}(Q_4(H_k^2))$ with coordinates $((2^k, 2^k), (2^{k-1} + 1, 1))$.

4   Empirical Study on $L_p(H_k^2)$ with $p \in [1,2]$

To complement the analytical results for $L_p(H_k^2)$ for all reals $p = 1$ and $p \geq 2$, we conduct an empirical study on $L_p(H_k^2)$ for all $k \in \{2, 3, \ldots, 16\}$ and a discrete spectrum of real values of $p \in [1,2]$. With respect to the canonical orientation of H_k^2 shown in Fig. 2(a), we cover the 2-dimensional order-k grid space $[2^k]^2$ of H_k^2 in Cartesian coordinates: 2^k columns (respectively, rows) indexed by x-coordinates (respectively, y-coordinates) $1, 2, \ldots, 2^k$. For every grid-order $k \in \{2, 3, \ldots, 16\}$ and real $p \in [1,2]$ with granularity of 0.01 (for $2 \leq k \leq 16$), we locate with computer programs all representative pairs of grid points for H_k^2 with respect to L_p. Figure 5(a) illustrates the three sources $\{A, B, C\}$ of candidate representative grid-point pairs for $k \geq 2$, which are elaborated below:

1. Source A identifies the grid-point pair $(v_A, u_A) = ((1, \frac{1}{4} \cdot 2^k + 1), (1, 2^k))$ and its symmetry-pair. The pair (v_A, u_A) serves as the representative grid-point pair "briefly"—for $k = 4$ and $1.83 \leq p \leq 2.00$.
2. Source B identifies the grid-point pair $(v_B, u_B) = ((2^{k-1}, 1), (1, 2^k))$ and its symmetry-pair. The pair (v_B, u_B) serves as the representative grid-point pair for every $k \in \{2, 3, \ldots, 16\}$ and all reals p of a (shrinking) prefix-interval $[1, \rho_k) \subseteq [1, 2]$—where, empirically, ρ_k decreases and stabilizes as k increases in $\{2, 3, \ldots, 12\}$ and in $\{13, 14, 15, 16\}$, respectively.
3. Source C identifies a sequence $(C_1, C_2, \ldots, C_{k-2})$ of grid-point pairs:

$$C_t = (v_{C_t}, u_{C_t}) = ((\frac{1}{4} \cdot 2^k + 1, 2^{k-1} + 1), (\frac{3}{4} \cdot 2^k, 2^{k-1} + 2^{k-2-t})),$$

for $t = 1, 2, \ldots, k - 2$, and their symmetry-pairs, with:

$$X(u_{C_{t+1}}) = X(u_{C_t}), \text{ and}$$

$$Y(u_{C_{t+1}}) - 2^{k-1} = \frac{Y(u_{C_t}) - 2^{k-1}}{2}$$

and eventually u_{C_t} converges to $u_{C_{k-2}}$.
Note that, for $t = 0$, the grid-point pair $C_0 = (v_{C_0}, u_{C_0}) = ((\frac{1}{4} \cdot 2^k + 1, 2^{k-1} + 1), (\frac{3}{4} \cdot 2^k, 2^{k-1} + 2^{k-2}))$ is not included in C since C_0 can not be a candidate representative grid-point pair (for any k and real $p \in [1, 2]$):

$$\mathcal{L}_{H_k^2, p}(v_B, u_B) = \frac{((2^{k-1} - 1)^p + (2^k - 1)^p)^{\frac{2}{p}}}{2^{2k-2}}$$

$$> \mathcal{L}_{H_k^2, p}(v_{C_0}, u_{C_0}) = \frac{((2^{k-1} - 1)^p + (2^{k-2} - 1)^p)^{\frac{2}{p}}}{\frac{1}{3} \cdot 2^{2k-3} + \frac{1}{3} \cdot 2^{2k-4}}.$$

Empirically, for all $k \in \{5, 6, \ldots, 16\}$ and all reals p in the (growing and stabilized) suffix-interval $(\rho_k, 2] \subseteq [1, 2]$, all the representative grid-point pairs form a subsequence C' of C composed of: (1) a prefix of C and (2) isolated grid-point pair(s) of C including $(v_{C_{k-2}}, u_{C_{k-2}})$. The suffix-interval $(\rho_k, 2]$ is partitioned into disjoint successive p-subintervals, each of which supports a grid-point pair in the subsequence C' as the representative grid-point pair for $L_p(H_k^2)$ (for all reals p of the subinterval). The length of C' (number of all representative grid-point pairs from the source C) should depend on k in general, and on the p-granularity in our empirical setting. Figure 5(b) depicts the sequence of candidate representative grid-point pairs from the source C.

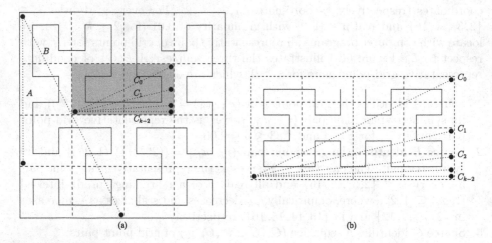

Fig. 5. Candidate representative grid-point pairs for H_k^2 with respect to L_p for $k \geq 2$: (a) three sources $\{A, B, C\}$ of candidate representative grid-point pairs; (b) detailed view of the source C.

Table 1 tabulates: (1) for selected grid-order k-values: $k \in \{14, 15, 16\}$, the partitioning p-subintervals of $[1, 2]$, and the corresponding representative grid-point pair and its source; and (2) $\mathcal{L}_{H_k^2, p}(v, u)$ $(= L_p(H_k^2))$ for a representative grid-point pair (v, u) in the three sources A, B, and C:

$$\mathcal{L}_{H_k^2, p}(v, u) = \begin{cases} \frac{(3 \cdot 2^{k-2} - 1)^2}{\frac{5}{3} \cdot 2^{2k-4} + \frac{1}{3}} & \text{if } (v, u) \text{ is in } A \\ \frac{((2^{k-1} - 1)^p + (2^k - 1)^p)^{\frac{2}{p}}}{2^{2k-2}} & \text{if } (v, u) \text{ is in } B \\ \frac{((2^{k-1} - 1)^p + (2^{k-2-t} - 1)^p)^{\frac{2}{p}}}{\frac{1}{3} \cdot 2^{2k-3} + \frac{1}{3} \cdot 2^{2k-4-2t}} & \text{if } (v, u) = (v_{C_t}, u_{C_t}) \text{ in } C, \\ & \text{where } t = 1, 2, \ldots, k - 2. \end{cases}$$

Figures 6(a) and (b) show the graphs, using the mathematical software Maple, of the locality measure $\mathcal{L}_{H_k^2, p}(v, u)$ for selected grid-order k-values: $k = 16$, and for all reals $p \in [1, 2]$ and all (v, u) in the two sources B and C. Our future work will involve determining, for each k, the dominant functions/measures over successive subintervals of $[1, 2]$, whose piece-wise combination yields the (overall) locality measure $L_p(H_k^2)$ for all reals $p \in [1, 2]$.

For selected grid-order k-values: $k \in \{4, 12, 16\}$, we elaborate below the empirical statistics that relate the p-subintervals partitioning $[1, 2]$ to their

Table 1. Representative grid-point pairs for H_k^2 with respect to L_p for $k \in \{14, 15, 16\}$ and $p \in [1.00, 2.00]$ with granularity of 0.01.

k	p	(x, y)-coordinates	Representative grid-point pair coordinates in terms of k	Source
14	[1.00, 1.30]	$((8192, 1), (1, 16384))$	$((2^{k-1}, 1), (1, 2^k))$	B
	[1.31, 1.58]	$((4097, 8193), (12288, 10240))$	$((\frac{1}{4} \cdot 2^k + 1, 2^{k-1} + 1), (\frac{3}{4} \cdot 2^k, 2^{k-1} + 2^{k-3}))$	C_1
	[1.59, 1.70]	$((4097, 8193), (12288, 9216))$	$((\frac{1}{4} \cdot 2^k + 1, 2^{k-1} + 1), (\frac{3}{4} \cdot 2^k, 2^{k-1} + 2^{k-4}))$	C_2
	[1.71, 1.77]	$((4097, 8193), (12288, 8704))$	$((\frac{1}{4} \cdot 2^k + 1, 2^{k-1} + 1), (\frac{3}{4} \cdot 2^k, 2^{k-1} + 2^{k-5}))$	C_3
	[1.78, 1.81]	$((4097, 8193), (12288, 8448))$	$((\frac{1}{4} \cdot 2^k + 1, 2^{k-1} + 1), (\frac{3}{4} \cdot 2^k, 2^{k-1} + 2^{k-6}))$	C_4
	[1.82, 1.84]	$((4097, 8193), (12288, 8320))$	$((\frac{1}{4} \cdot 2^k + 1, 2^{k-1} + 1), (\frac{3}{4} \cdot 2^k, 2^{k-1} + 2^{k-7}))$	C_5
	[1.85, 1.86]	$((4097, 8193), (12288, 8256))$	$((\frac{1}{4} \cdot 2^k + 1, 2^{k-1} + 1), (\frac{3}{4} \cdot 2^k, 2^{k-1} + 2^{k-8}))$	C_6
	[1.87, 1.87]	$((4097, 8193), (12288, 8224))$	$((\frac{1}{4} \cdot 2^k + 1, 2^{k-1} + 1), (\frac{3}{4} \cdot 2^k, 2^{k-1} + 2^{k-9}))$	C_7
	[1.88, 1.88]	$((4097, 8193), (12288, 8208))$	$((\frac{1}{4} \cdot 2^k + 1, 2^{k-1} + 1), (\frac{3}{4} \cdot 2^k, 2^{k-1} + 2^{k-10}))$	C_8
	[1.89, 2.00]	$((4097, 8193), (12288, 8193))$	$((\frac{1}{4} \cdot 2^k + 1, 2^{k-1} + 1), (\frac{3}{4} \cdot 2^k, 2^{k-1} + 1))$	C_{12}
15	[1.00, 1.30]	$((16384, 1), (1, 32768))$	$((2^{k-1}, 1), (1, 2^k))$	B
	[1.31, 1.58]	$((8193, 16385), (24576, 20480))$	$((\frac{1}{4} \cdot 2^k + 1, 2^{k-1} + 1), (\frac{3}{4} \cdot 2^k, 2^{k-1} + 2^{k-3}))$	C_1
	[1.59, 1.70]	$((8193, 16385), (24576, 18432))$	$((\frac{1}{4} \cdot 2^k + 1, 2^{k-1} + 1), (\frac{3}{4} \cdot 2^k, 2^{k-1} + 2^{k-4}))$	C_2
	[1.71, 1.77]	$((8193, 16385), (24576, 17408))$	$((\frac{1}{4} \cdot 2^k + 1, 2^{k-1} + 1), (\frac{3}{4} \cdot 2^k, 2^{k-1} + 2^{k-5}))$	C_3
	[1.78, 1.81]	$((8193, 16385), (24576, 16896))$	$((\frac{1}{4} \cdot 2^k + 1, 2^{k-1} + 1), (\frac{3}{4} \cdot 2^k, 2^{k-1} + 2^{k-6}))$	C_4
	[1.82, 1.84]	$((8193, 16385), (24576, 16640))$	$((\frac{1}{4} \cdot 2^k + 1, 2^{k-1} + 1), (\frac{3}{4} \cdot 2^k, 2^{k-1} + 2^{k-7}))$	C_5
	[1.85, 1.86]	$((8193, 16385), (24576, 16512))$	$((\frac{1}{4} \cdot 2^k + 1, 2^{k-1} + 1), (\frac{3}{4} \cdot 2^k, 2^{k-1} + 2^{k-8}))$	C_6
	[1.87, 1.87]	$((8193, 16385), (24576, 16448))$	$((\frac{1}{4} \cdot 2^k + 1, 2^{k-1} + 1), (\frac{3}{4} \cdot 2^k, 2^{k-1} + 2^{k-9}))$	C_7
	[1.88, 1.88]	$((8193, 16385), (24576, 16416))$	$((\frac{1}{4} \cdot 2^k + 1, 2^{k-1} + 1), (\frac{3}{4} \cdot 2^k, 2^{k-1} + 2^{k-10}))$	C_8
	[1.89, 1.89]	$((8193, 16385), (24576, 16400))$	$((\frac{1}{4} \cdot 2^k + 1, 2^{k-1} + 1), (\frac{3}{4} \cdot 2^k, 2^{k-1} + 2^{k-11}))$	C_9
	[1.90, 2.00]	$((8193, 16385), (24576, 16385))$	$((\frac{1}{4} \cdot 2^k + 1, 2^{k-1} + 1), (\frac{3}{4} \cdot 2^k, 2^{k-1} + 1))$	C_{13}
16	[1.00, 1.30]	$((32768, 1), (1, 65536))$	$((2^{k-1}, 1), (1, 2^k))$	B
	[1.31, 1.58]	$((16385, 32769), (49152, 40960))$	$((\frac{1}{4} \cdot 2^k + 1, 2^{k-1} + 1), (\frac{3}{4} \cdot 2^k, 2^{k-1} + 2^{k-3}))$	C_1
	[1.59, 1.70]	$((16385, 32769), (49152, 36864))$	$((\frac{1}{4} \cdot 2^k + 1, 2^{k-1} + 1), (\frac{3}{4} \cdot 2^k, 2^{k-1} + 2^{k-4}))$	C_2
	[1.71, 1.77]	$((16385, 32769), (49152, 34816))$	$((\frac{1}{4} \cdot 2^k + 1, 2^{k-1} + 1), (\frac{3}{4} \cdot 2^k, 2^{k-1} + 2^{k-5}))$	C_3
	[1.78, 1.81]	$((16385, 32769), (49152, 33792))$	$((\frac{1}{4} \cdot 2^k + 1, 2^{k-1} + 1), (\frac{3}{4} \cdot 2^k, 2^{k-1} + 2^{k-6}))$	C_4
	[1.82, 1.84]	$((16385, 32769), (49152, 33280))$	$((\frac{1}{4} \cdot 2^k + 1, 2^{k-1} + 1), (\frac{3}{4} \cdot 2^k, 2^{k-1} + 2^{k-7}))$	C_5
	[1.85, 1.86]	$((16385, 32769), (49152, 33024))$	$((\frac{1}{4} \cdot 2^k + 1, 2^{k-1} + 1), (\frac{3}{4} \cdot 2^k, 2^{k-1} + 2^{k-8}))$	C_6
	[1.87, 1.87]	$((16385, 32769), (49152, 32896))$	$((\frac{1}{4} \cdot 2^k + 1, 2^{k-1} + 1), (\frac{3}{4} \cdot 2^k, 2^{k-1} + 2^{k-9}))$	C_7
	[1.88, 1.89]	$((16385, 32769), (49152, 32832))$	$((\frac{1}{4} \cdot 2^k + 1, 2^{k-1} + 1), (\frac{3}{4} \cdot 2^k, 2^{k-1} + 2^{k-10}))$	C_8
	[1.90, 1.90]	$((16385, 32769), (49152, 32784))$	$((\frac{1}{4} \cdot 2^k + 1, 2^{k-1} + 1), (\frac{3}{4} \cdot 2^k, 2^{k-1} + 2^{k-12}))$	C_{10}
	[1.91, 2.00]	$((16385, 32769), (49152, 32769))$	$((\frac{1}{4} \cdot 2^k + 1, 2^{k-1} + 1), (\frac{3}{4} \cdot 2^k, 2^{k-1} + 1))$	C_{14}

dominant grid-point pairs—subject to the underlying p-granularity and numerical approximation:

1. For the extreme case of $k = 4$ with p-granularity of 0.01, two representative grid-point pairs emerge from the sources B and A over the partitioning subintervals $[1.00, 1.82]$ and $[1.83, 2.00]$, respectively.
2. For the case of $k = 12$ with p-granularity of 0.01, the representative grid-point pairs are from the sources B and C over the partitioning subintervals $[1.00, 1.31]$ and $[1.32, 2.00]$, respectively. Observe that the subsequence C' of all representative grid-point pairs (from the source $C = \{C_t \mid 1 \leq t \leq 10\}$) is the prefix $\{C_1, C_2, C_3, C_4, C_5, C_6\}$ of C with the isolated grid-point pair C_{10}.
3. For the case of $k = 16$ with p-granularity of 0.01, the representative grid-point pairs are from the sources B and C over the partitioning subintervals $[1.00, 1.30]$ and $[1.31, 2.00]$, respectively. Analogous to the case of $k = 12$

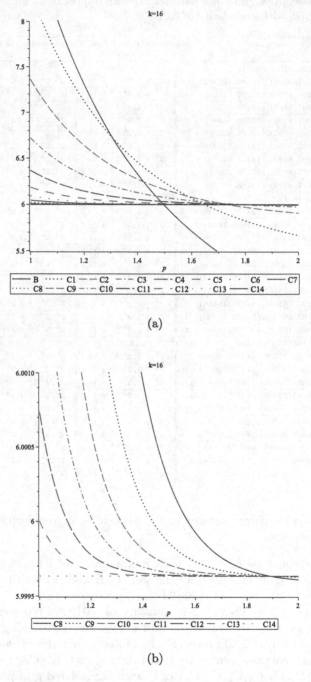

(a)

(b)

Fig. 6. Locality measures corresponding to the grid-point pairs in: (a) and (b) B and $C = \{C_t \mid 1 \leq t \leq k-2\}$ for $k = 16$ and p-granularity of 0.01.

subject to the underlying p-granularity and numerical approximation, the subsequence C' of all representative grid-point pairs (from the source $C = \{C_t \mid 1 \leq t \leq 14\}$) is the prefix $\{C_1, C_2, C_3, C_4, C_5, C_6, C_7, C_8\}$ of C with the isolated grid-point pairs C_{10} and C_{14}.

5 Conclusion

Our analytical study of the locality properties of the Hilbert curve family, $\{H_k^2 \mid k = 1, 2, \ldots\}$, is based on the locality measure L_p, which is the maximum ratio of $d_p(v, u)^m$ to $d_p(\tilde{v}, \tilde{u})$ over all corresponding grid-point pairs (v, u) and $(\tilde{v}, \tilde{u})$ in the m-dimensional grid space and index space, respectively. Our analytical results close the gaps between the current best lower and upper bounds with exact formulas for norm-parameter $p \in \{1, 2\}$, and extend to all reals $p \geq 2$. In addition, we identify all the representative grid-point pairs (which realize $L_p(H_k^2)$) for $p = 1$ and all reals $p \geq 2$. For all real norm-parameters $p \in [1, 2]$ with sufficiently small granularity and grid-orders $k \in \{2, 3, \ldots, 16\}$, our empirical study reveals the three major sources (A, B, and C) of representative grid-point pairs (v, u) that give $\mathcal{L}_{H_k^2, p}(v, u) = L_p(H_k^2)$. The empirical results also suggest that, subject to the underlying p-granularity and numerical approximation, all the representative grid-point pairs of B and C are from B and C', which is a prefix-subsequence of C together with some isolated grid-point pair(s) of C including C_{k-2} for some sufficiently large grid-orders $k \in \{5, 6, \ldots, 16\}$. The study will shed some light on an analytical study for determining the exact formulas for $L_p(H_k^2)$ for all reals $p \in (1, 2)$ and/or in arbitrary dimensions.

References

1. Alber, J.: Locality properties of discrete space-filling curves: results with relevance for computer science. Studienarbeit Universität Tübingen, Wilhelm-Schickard-Institut für Informatik (1997). (in German)
2. Alber, J., Niedermeier, R.: On multi-dimensional curves with Hilbert property. Theory Comput. Syst. **33**(4), 295–312 (2000)
3. Asano, T., Ranjan, D., Roos, T., Welzl, E., Widmayer, P.: Space-filling curves and their use in the design of geometric data structures. Theoret. Comput. Sci. **181**(1), 3–15 (1997)
4. Bader, M.: Space-Filling Curves - An Introduction with Applications in Scientific Computing. Texts in Computational Science and Engineering, vol. 9. Springer, Heidelberg (2013). https://doi.org/10.1007/978-3-642-31046-1
5. Ban, X., Goswami, M., Zeng, W., Gu, X., Gao, J.: Topology dependent space filling curves for sensor networks and applications. In: Proceedings of the IEEE INFOCOM 2013, Turin, Italy, 14–19 April 2013, pp. 2166–2174. IEEE (2013)
6. Bauman, K.E.: The dilation factor of the Peano-Hilbert curve. Math. Notes **80**(5), 609–620 (2006)
7. Böhm, C., Berchtold, S., Keim, D.A.: Searching in high-dimensional spaces – index structures for improving the performance of multimedia databases. ACM Comput. Surv. **33**(3), 322–373 (2001)

8. Chen, H.-L., Chang, Y.-I.: Neighbor-finding based on space-filling curves. Inf. Syst. **30**(3), 205–226 (2005)
9. Chochia, G., Cole, M., Heywood, T.: Implementing the hierarchical PRAM on the 2D mesh: analyses and experiments. In: Proceedings of the Seventh IEEE Symposium on Parallel and Distributed Processing, Washington, D.C., USA, pp. 587–595. IEEE Computer Society, October 1995
10. Dai, H.K., Su, H.C.: On the locality properties of space-filling curves. In: Ibaraki, T., Katoh, N., Ono, H. (eds.) ISAAC 2003. LNCS, vol. 2906, pp. 385–394. Springer, Heidelberg (2003). https://doi.org/10.1007/978-3-540-24587-2_40
11. Dai, H.K., Su, H.C.: Norm-based locality measures of two-dimensional Hilbert curves. In: Dondi, R., Fertin, G., Mauri, G. (eds.) AAIM 2016. LNCS, vol. 9778, pp. 14–25. Springer, Cham (2016). https://doi.org/10.1007/978-3-319-41168-2_2
12. Gaede, V., Günther, O.: Multidimensional access methods. ACM Comput. Surv. **30**(2), 170–231 (1998)
13. Gotsman, C., Lindenbaum, M.: On the metric properties of discrete space-filling curves. IEEE Trans. Image Process. **5**(5), 794–797 (1996)
14. Kaddoura, M., Ou, C.-W., Ranka, S.: Partitioning unstructured computational graphs for non-uniform and adaptive environments. IEEE Parallel Distrib. Technol. **3**(3), 63–69 (1995)
15. Lawder, J.K.: The application of space-filling curves to the storage and retrieval of multi-dimensional data. Ph.D. thesis, Birkbeck College, University of London, December 1999
16. Lempel, A., Ziv, J.: Compression of two-dimensional images. In: Apostolico, A., Galil, Z. (eds.) Combinatorial Algorithms on Words, SI Series, vol. F12, pp. 141–156. Springer, Heidelberg (1984.) https://doi.org/10.1007/978-3-642-82456-2_10
17. Mitchison, G., Durbin, R.: Optimal numberings of an $N \times N$ array. SIAM J. Algebraic Discrete Methods **7**(4), 571–582 (1986)
18. Moon, B., Jagadish, H.V., Faloutsos, C., Saltz, J.H.: Analysis of the clustering properties of the Hilbert space-filling curve. IEEE Trans. Knowl. Data Eng. **13**(1), 124–141 (2001)
19. Niedermeier, R., Reinhardt, K., Sanders, P.: Towards optimal locality in mesh-indexings. Discrete Appl. Math. **117**(1–3), 211–237 (2002)
20. Pérez, A., Kamata, S., Kawaguchi, E.: Peano scanning of arbitrary size images. In: Proceedings of the International Conference on Pattern Recognition, pp. 565–568. IEEE Computer Society (1992)
21. Platzman, L.K., Bartholdi III, J.J.: Spacefilling curves and the planar travelling salesman problem. J. ACM **36**(4), 719–737 (1989)
22. Sagan, H.: Space-Filling Curves. Springer, New York (1994). https://doi.org/10.1007/978-1-4612-0871-6
23. Voorhies, D.: Space-filling curves and a measure of coherence. In: Arvo, J. (ed.) Graphics Gems II, pp. 26–30. Academic Press (1991)
24. Wang, H., Jiang, C., Dong, Y.: Connectivity-based space filling curve construction algorithms in high genus 3D surface WSNs. ACM Trans. Sensor Netw. **12**(3), 22:1–22:29 (2016)
25. Xu, P., Tirthapura, S.: A lower bound on proximity preservation by space filling curves. In: IPDPS 2012 Proceedings of the 2012 IEEE 26th International Parallel and Distributed Processing Symposium, pp. 1295–1305, May 2012

A Comparative Study of Join Algorithms in Spark

Anh-Cang Phan[1(✉)], Thuong-Cang Phan[2], and Thanh-Ngoan Trieu[2]

[1] Vinh Long University of Technology Education, Vinh Long City, Vietnam
cangpa@vlute.edu.vn
[2] Can Tho University, Can Tho City, Vietnam
{ptcang,ttngoan}@cit.ctu.edu.vn

Abstract. In the era of information explosion, the amount of data generated is increasing day by day, reached the threshold of petabytes or even zettabytes. In order to extract useful information from a variety of huge data sources, we need effectively computational operations performed in parallel and distributed manner on a cluster of computers. These operations involve a lot of complex and expensive processing operations. One of the typical and frequently used operations in queries is a join operation to combine more than one dataset into one. Currently, although there are some studies on join operations in Spark, there has not been any study showing an adequate and systematic comparison of join algorithms in the Spark environment. Therefore, this study is dedicated to the join operation aspects in Spark. It describes important strategies of implementing the join operation in detail, and exposes the advantages and disadvantages of each one. In addition, the work provides a more thorough comparison of the joins by using a mathematical cost model and experimental verification.

Keywords: Join operation · Big data analytics · Spark · MapReduce · Bloom filter

1 Introduction

Analyzing and processing collected data is a very important requirement for applications in commerce, scientific research, health care, security, customer behavior, natural disasters, etc. In the case of Big Data, processing huge datasets requires compatible systems to work in parallel and distributed manner. The main model to handle the problem is MapReduce [10], which works with two main phases: Map and Reduce. The Map phase transforms and organizes data while the Reduce phase aggregates data. This model proposed by Google in 2004 has become the current standard and the most popular model for handling large datasets on parallel and distributed systems.

A join operation is one of commonly used operations in data analysis. This is a complex and costly operation when implemented in the MapReduce

© Springer Nature Switzerland AG 2020
T. K. Dang et al. (Eds.): FDSE 2020, LNCS 12466, pp. 185–198, 2020.
https://doi.org/10.1007/978-3-030-63924-2_11

environment. The join operation combines data from two or more different datasets with a key join and results a new dataset. The join operation in MapReduce goes through two phases, map and reduce, with expensive shuffling costs (moving data from mapper to reducer). Therefore, executing join queries on large datasets in MapReduce presents great challenges for researchers. One of the solutions for reducing costs of join computation is removing redundant elements that are not involved in join operation.

As a scientific basis, this study provides an overview of common join algorithms in MapReduce. We evaluate the join algorithms based on general cost model and experiments in Spark. We use some abbreviations described in Table 1.

The rest of this paper is organized as follows. Section 2 presents the theoretical background about Spark and Filters. Section 3 shows the current algorithms for two-way join in MapReduce. Section 4 provides the comparison of join algorithms through cost models and experiments. The conclusion of the paper is presented in Sect. 5.

Table 1. List of abbreviation

Abbreviation	Algorithm
MSJ	Map-side join
RSJ	Reduce-side join
BCJ	Broadcast join
BFJ	Bloom join
IBJ	Intersection bloom join

2   Background

With the continuous development of Big Data, it is believed that traditional database technologies are not enough to store and process data with high performance and flexibility requirements. In the new era of information and technology, data is stored in many different forms thus using join operation for data processing and analysis is one of the most useful activities.

Currently, there are a lot of researches on join operations in MapReduce with Apache Hadoop [3,6,12,18]. The join algorithms investigated mainly include Map-side join [6,12], Broadcast join [6] that is considered to be a Hash join [9,17], and Reduce-side join [12,21] that is similar to a Repartition join [6]. In addition, a number of algorithms is developed to improve the effectiveness of join operations. Most of these algorithms focus on solving the problem of removing redundant data before performing join operations such as Parallelize set-similarity joins [17], Bloom join [8,13,14,16,18], and Intersection filter-based Bloom join [18]. The study [2] has shown a survey on join algorithms in Spark. However, it does not provide a general cost model for join algorithms thus it is lack of mathematical arguments for comparing join algorithms.

Recently, with the popularity of Apache Spark [4], there have been a few studies on join activities but mainly done based on the support of database systems such as NoSQL [20], Hive [15], or queries made directly from Spark SQL [5]. Since Hadoop framework has slow processing speed than Apache Spark [22], our study conducts experiments on Spark for the commonly used join algorithms.

2.1 Apache Spark

Apache Spark [4,22] is an open source computing framework on a cluster, used for fast data analysis that satisfies two criteria, which are fast in execution and fast in read/write data. Spark solves memory management issues by using Resilient Distributed Datasets (RDDs) with two types of operations (Transformations and Actions).

An RDD will be re-initializes in each Action so that it will take a lot of time if we encounter a case that an RDD is reused many times. Therefore, Spark supports a mechanism called persist or cache. Persisting an RDD, the nodes containing the RDD partitions will store it in memory, and that node will only calculate once. Spark will recalculate the missing parts of RDD if necessary.

2.2 Bloom Filter and Intersection Bloom Filter

The Bloom Filter (BF) [7] was introduced in 1970 by Burton Bloom, is a probability data structure used to check whether an element is belong to a collection or not. A BF structure consists of an array of m bits and k independent hash functions with each function hashes elements to a position in the m bits array.

Intersection Bloom Filter (IBF) [18,19] is a probability data structure designed to represent the intersection of datasets. It is used to identify common elements of collections with a false positive probability. The false positive element is the element defined by IBF as belonging to the intersection two datasets but in fact it does not. There are three approaches to build up a IBF for two datasets S_1 and S_2.

- *Approach 1: Using two BFs*
  Use BF_{S1} for set S_2 to select the common elements of S_2; and use BF_{S2} for set S_1 to select the common elements of S_1. The combining of the above results are the common elements of both datasets.
- *Approach 2: Using the intersection of two BFs*
  This approach requires two BFs to have the same size m bits and k hash functions. To build the IBF, we calculate the intersection of the two filters BF_{S1} and BF_{S2} by and AND bit operation.
  $IBF_{S1,S2} = BF_{S1} \; AND \; BF_{S2}$
- *Approach 3: Using the intersection of two partitioned BFs*
  Partitioned Bloom filter [11] is a variant of the standard BF, defined by an array of m bits divided into k separated sub-arrays with size $mp = m/k$ bits. Similar to approach 2, the $IBF_{S1,S2}$ is generated by an AND operation of BF_{S1} and BF_{S2}.

3   Join Algorithms in MapReduce

3.1   Map-Side Join

Map-side join [6,12] is similar to sort-merge join in Relational Database Management Systems - RDBMS. The operation is done by joining two datasets at the map stage without shuffle and reduce stages. However, this algorithm requires that the input datasets must be arranged in the order of the join keys and all datasets with the same join key must be brought together in a partition. The flow diagram of the Map-side join algorithm is as follows (Fig. 1):

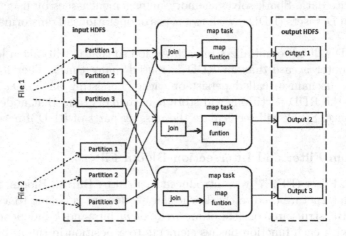

Fig. 1. Map-side join algorithm flowchart

The MSJ algorithm does not generate intermediate data and does not cost for the shuffle and reduce stages since it only runs through the input data and performs join operation in the map stage. However, this algorithm requires strict input data, which means that the datasets must have the same number of partitions arranged by the join key. In order words, this algorithm will cost for pre-processing the input data in accordance with the requirements. Furthermore, the algorithm needs to have two buffers containing all the same key sets of the input data, which can lead to memory overflow at computational nodes.

3.2   Reduce-Side Join

Reduce-side Join [12,21] is known as a "re-partition join", which will be performed at the reduce stage. The algorithm maps the input datasets to have intermediate data in form of key-value pairs and shuffles the data to the reducers for performing join operation. All key-value pairs with the same key join must be sent to the same reducers and sorted by the key join. The Reducers then perform a combination of values with the same key. The RSJ algorithm flowchart is as follows (Fig. 2):

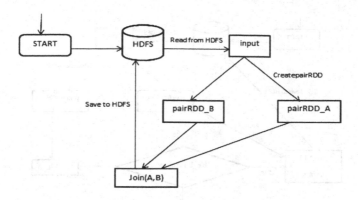

Fig. 2. Reduce-side join algorithm flowchart

RSJ algorithm has no requirements on input data. It limits the case of memory overflow like MSJ algorithm because the buffer only contains data that participate in join operation. However, this algorithm will cost more on I/O and shuffling data since it creates intermediate data at the map stage and transfer over the network.

3.3 Broadcast Join

Broadcast Join [6] is similar to the algorithm that uses hash join in RDBMS. It is a special case of the MSJ algorithm. The map stage does not produce intermediate data and does not cost for shuffle and reduce stages. However, in this algorithm, one of the two input datasets is very small to be able to broadcast to all computing nodes.

3.4 Bloom Join

Bloom Join [13,16,18] is a join algorithm improved from RSJ algorithm using Bloom filter, an effective space-efficient data structure. The algorithm is also derived from the BFJ approach in the RDBMS, which is an improvement of the semi-join method by using filters to contain the keys of a dataset. This algorithm has achieved certain efficiency for filtering unnecessary data from one of the two input datasets that is not involved in join operation. However, there is a need of pre-processing step to build up the filter by scanning one input dataset. In particular, this approach also accepts a false positive probability for filtering data in one dataset (Fig. 3).

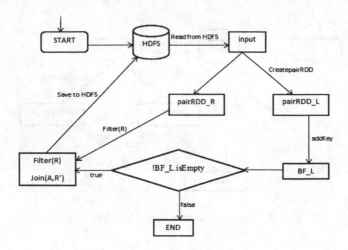

Fig. 3. Bloom join algorithm flowchart

3.5 Intersection Bloom Join

Intersection filter-based Bloom join [18] is an improved algorithm from BFJ algorithm with the use of Intersection Bloom Filter (IBF) instead of the standard Bloom filter. This algorithm uses the IBF to filter data on both input datasets to eliminate most of the tuples that are not participating in join operation. In consequence, it significantly reduces the costs of join operation. It has been shown to be more efficient than other join algorithms [19]. Therefore, the IBJ will be the most optimal algorithm compared to the current join algorithms (Fig. 4).

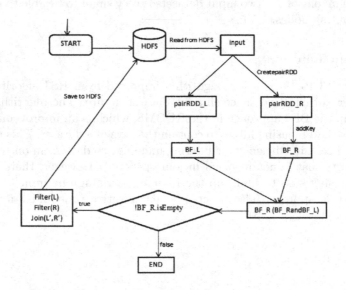

Fig. 4. Intersection bloom join algorithm flowchart

4   Evaluation

4.1   Cost Model

Join computation cost is the total cost of several stages including cost for pre-processing task (C_{pre}), cost for reading data (C_{read}), cost for transferring data (C_{tr}), and cost for writing data (C_{write}). The general cost model for join computation of two datasets can be described as in Eq. 1. The parameters of the cost model are clarified in Table 2.

- The cost for pre-processing task will be depended on the algorithms used for join operation.
- The cost for reading data includes cost of remotely reading two datasets R and L.
- The cost for writing data is cost of remotely writing the result dataset O.
- Them cost for transferring data between nodes is the cost of transferring intermediate dataset D. The intermediate dataset will be calculated depending on the type of two-way join algorithms.

Table 2. Parameters use in cost model

Parameters	Meaning
$|R|$	Size of dataset R
$|L|$	Size of dataset L
c_l	Cost for read/write data locally
c_r	Cost for read/write data remotely
c_t	Cost for transferring data from node to node
e_R	Number of executors for dataset R
e_L	Number of executors for dataset L
$e = e_R + e_L$	Total number of executors
$B + 1$	Size of sorting buffer on pages
m	Size of Bloom filter (bits)
f_L	False positive probability of BF
$f_{(R,L)}$	False positive probability of IBF
δ_L, δ_R	Join rate of two datasets R, L
$|D|$	Size of intermediate dataset for join task
$|O|$	Size of result dataset for join task
C_{pre}	Total number cost for pre-processing task
C_{read}	Total cost for read data
C_{tr}	Total cost for transferring data
C_{write}	Total cost for writing data

$$C = C_{pre} + C_{read} + C_{tr} + C_{write} \tag{1}$$

where:

- $C_{read} = c_r.|R| + c_r.|L|$
- $C_{tr} = c_t.|D|$
- $C_{write} = c_r.|O|$
- $|D|$: *depending on join algorithms*
- C_{pre}: *depending on join algorithms*

In comparing the effectiveness of the join algorithms, we will consider the cost of pre-processing task C_{pre} and the intermediate dataset D since the other costs stay the same.

4.1.1   Map-Side Join

MSJ splits two datasets into the same partitions and sort in order of the join keys before performing join operation. The pre-processing task needs to transfer tuples of the two datasets to the same partitions.

$$C(MSJ) = C_{pre} + C_{read} + C_{tr} + C_{write} \tag{2}$$

where:

- $C_{pre} = c_l.|D|.2.([log_B|D| - log_B(e)] + log_B(e))$
- $C_{tr} = c_t.|D|$
- $|D| = |R| + |L|$

4.1.2   Reduce-Side Join

RSJ implements join operation by joining data of the tuples with the same keys in reduce stage. There is no need for pre-processing task however the intermediate data (key-value pairs) of both dataset needs to be transferred to the reducers.

$$C(RSJ) = C_{pre} + C_{read} + C_{tr} + C_{write} \tag{3}$$

where:

- $C_{pre} = 0$
- $C_{tr} = c_t.|D|$
- $|D| = |R| + |L|$

4.1.3   Broadcast Join

BCJ join two datasets by broadcasting all the records of the small dataset to all reducers. This is a special case that having a dataset which is much smaller than the other dataset. We assume that $|R| >> |L|$. The whole dataset $|L|$ needs to be sent to all reducers.

$$C(BCJ) = C_{pre} + C_{read} + C_{tr} + C_{write} \tag{4}$$

where:

- $C_{pre} = 0$
- $C_{tr} = c_t.|L|$

4.1.4 Bloom Join

BFJ implements join operation by filtering redundant date in one of the two datasets using Bloom filter.

$$C(BFJ) = C_{pre} + C_{read} + C_{tr} + C_{write} \tag{5}$$

where:

- $C_{pre} = 2.c_t.m.e_L$
- $C_{tr} = c_t.|D|$
- $|D| = |L| + \delta_L.|R| + f_L.(1 - \delta_L).|R|$

The pre-processing task calculates the BF for a dataset, e.g. L. Each executors for dataset L adds keys to the m bits BF and send the BF to Spark driver. The driver performs OR operation to combine the BF from e_L executors and then broadcast the final BF to the executors. Since there is a BF of L, we use that BF for filtering dataset R. The intermediate data of BFJ is now the whole dataset L plus the tuples from dataset R that can be participated in join operation with a false positive probability of f_L.

4.1.5 Intersection Bloom Join

IBJ joins two datasets by filtering redundant data in both datasets with IBF.

$$C(IBJ) = C_{pre} + C_{read} + C_{tr} + C_{write} \tag{6}$$

where:

- $C_{pre} = 2.c_t.m.e$
- $C_{tr} = c_t.|D|$
- $|D| = \delta_L.|R| + f_{(R,L)}.(1 - \delta_L).|R| + \delta_R.|L| + f_{(R,L)}.(1 - \delta_R).|L|$

The pre-processing task calculates the IBF for both dataset L and R. The number of executors e adds keys to the m bits BF_L and BF_R. The IBF of the two dataset is a combination of the two BF with AND operation, $IBF = BF_L$ $AND\ BF_R$. The IBF will be sent to Spark driver. The driver broadcasts the final IBF to the executors. The intermediate data of BFJ includes the tuples from dataset L plus the tuples from dataset R. Those tuples can be participated in join operation with a false positive probability of $f_{(R,L)}$.

4.1.6 Analyze the Cost Model of Join Algorithms

The MSJ performs pre-processing task that sorts the join keys of all datasets in an order and all the same keys must be put on the same partitions. The RSJ does not have pre-processing cost however it costs for the shuffling data between nodes. From formula 2 and formula 3, the total costs of the two algorithms are almost the same except that the MSJ needs to have a cost for sorting data in pre-processing task. Thus, the total cost for computing MSJ is larger than that of RSJ, $C(MSJ) > C(RSJ)$.

The intermediate data ($|D|$) is an important parameter since the data transferring through the network will affect the cost of the algorithm. We have:

$|D|_{RSJ} = |L| + |R|$ (*)
$|D|_{BFJ} = |L| + \delta_L.|R| + f_L.(1 - \delta_L).|R|$ (**)
$|D|_{IBJ} = \delta_R.|L| + f_{(R,L)}.(1 - \delta_R).|L| + \delta_L.|R| + f_{(R,L)}.(1 - \delta_L).|R|$ (***)

In comparing between RSJ and BFJ, it is clearly seeing that the intermediate data generated by RSJ is greater than that of BFJ. The value of false positive probability of BF (f_L) is much smaller than 1 (0.001 in our experiments) and the join rate between two datasets is usually small so that $\delta_L.|R| + f_L.(1-\delta_L).|R| << |R|$. Thus, from (*) and (**) we can conduct that $C(RSJ) > C(BFJ)$.

Similarly, the intermediate data generated from IBJ is smaller than BFJ. The value of false positive probability of IBF is much smaller than 1 (0.001 in our experiments). The redundant data is filer out in both datasets L and R instead of one dataset as in BFJ ($\delta_R.|L| + f_{(R,L)}.(1 - \delta_R).|L| << |L|$). Thus, from (**) and (***) we can conclude $C(BFJ) > C(IBJ)$.

After analyzing the cost model between algorithms on general datasets, we can conclude that:

$$C(MSJ) > C(RSJ) > C(BFJ) > C(IBJ) \tag{7}$$

In special case, the dataset L is much smaller than the dataset R, we will use the BCJ algorithm and this will cost less than the other algorithms.

4.2   Experiments

4.2.1   Spark Cluster

The experiments are conducted on a cluster of 14 computing nodes (1 master and 13 slaves). Each computer is configured with 4 CPUs Intel Core i5 3.2 Ghz with 4 GB RAM, and 500 GB HDD. A node is installed Ubuntu 14.04 LTS 64 bits operating system. The installed applications are Java 1.8, Hadoop 2.7.1, and Spark 2.1. This cluster is provided by The Mobile Network and Big Data Laboratory of College of Information and Technology, Can Tho University.

The data used for the experiments is the standard data generated by PUMA: Purdue MapReduce Benchmarks Suite [1]. The datasets are stored in text file format with each line has a maximum of 39 fields separated by commas, each field with 19 characters. The key join used in the experiments are the 5th column (the first dataset) and the 4th column (the set second dataset).

Table 3. Datasets used in the experiments

Input	Dataset 1	Dataset 2	Total
Test 1	5 GB	10 GB	15 GB
Test 2	10 GB	10 GB	20 GB
Test 3	10 GB	20 GB	30 GB
Test 4	20 GB	20 GB	40 GB
Test 5	1 GB	10 GB	11 GB
Test 6	1 GB	20 GB	21 GB

4.2.2 Results

The experiments use five algorithms, which are Map-side join, Broadcast join, Reduce-side join, Bloom join, and Intersection Filter-based Bloom join. We have six test datasets that is described in Table 3. For each algorithm, we conduct experiments twice to have the average execution time and the number of intermediate data.

Figure 5a and Fig. 5b show the amount of intermediate data that needs to be transported across the network of the join algorithms. This results clearly show the effectiveness between algorithms when performing join computation in Spark. At the same time, IBJ significantly reduces the amount of redundant data that does not participate in the join operation due to the Intersection Bloom filter. The execution time of the algorithms are also different because of the amount of intermediate data transmitted through the network.

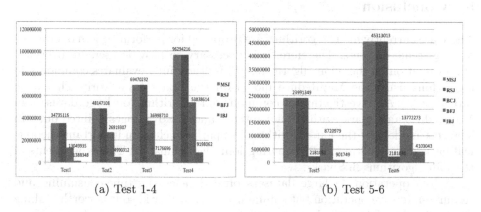

(a) Test 1-4   (b) Test 5-6

Fig. 5. Intermediate results in records

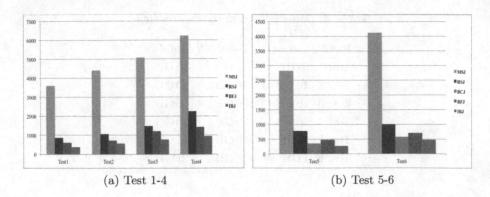

(a) Test 1-4   (b) Test 5-6

Fig. 6. Execution time in seconds

MSJ is the best option in case that we have datasets partitioned and sorted in advance. However, in Fig. 6a and Fig. 6b, MSJ has the longer execution time. It is because the datasets used in the experiments are the standard datasets without sorting and partitioning in advance. These two tasks degrade the overall performance of the algorithm. The IBJ is the one with the best performance. It is reasonable since this algorithm uses the intersection bloom filter to significantly reduce the redundant data. The experiment results are appropriate with the cost models presented above. The cost models can be used as a scientific basis for estimation and prediction before implementations.

5   Conclusion

There are currently many algorithms are proposed for performing join operations on large-scale datasets. Therefore, it is necessary to provide users an overview and evaluation on these join algorithms. This study fully evaluates common join algorithms using the MapReduce model on the Spark framework. This work provides: (1) An investigation of common join algorithms on large datasets in MapReduce and Spark, with the advantages and disadvantages pointed out; (2) The cost models for the join algorithms in Spark which is an important theoretical basis for evaluating and comparing join algorithms; (3) The experiments of the join algorithms in Spark.

A join operation on large datasets often is a costly, time-consuming and resource-intensive operation but commonly used in Spark, so it is worth making this evaluation. Through the cost model and the experiments, we have demonstrated the advantages and disadvantages of the current join algorithms. In general, joins based on Intersection Bloom Filters dominate over the other joins because they require no special input data and minimize non-joining data as well as communication costs.

References

1. Ahmad, F.: Puma benchmarks and dataset downloads (2011). https://engineering. purdue.edu/~puma/datasets.htm. Accessed: 05 Apr 2019
2. Al-Badarneh, A.: Join algorithms under apache spark: revisited. In: Proceedings of the 2019 5th International Conference on Computer and Technology Applications, ICCTA 2019, pp. 56–62. Association for Computing Machinery, New York (2019)
3. Apache: Apache Hadoop (2002). https://hadoop.apache.org. Accessed 03 Apr 2019
4. Apache: Apache spark (2009). https://spark.apache.org. Accessed 03 Apr 2019
5. Armbrust, M., et al.: Spark SQL: relational data processing in spark. In: Proceedings of the 2015 ACM SIGMOD International Conference on Management of Data, SIGMOD 2015, pp. 1383–1394. Association for Computing Machinery, New York (2015)
6. Blanas, S., Patel, J.M., Ercegovac, V., Rao, J., Shekita, E.J., Tian, Y.: A comparison of join algorithms for log processing in MapReduce. In: Proceedings of the 2010 ACM SIGMOD International Conference on Management of Data, SIGMOD 2010, pp. 975–986. Association for Computing Machinery, New York (2010)
7. Bloom, B.H.: Space/time trade-offs in hash coding with allowable errors. Commun. ACM **13**(7), 422–426 (1970)
8. Bratbergsengen, K.: Hashing methods and relational algebra operations. In: Proceedings of the 10th International Conference on Very Large Data Bases, VLDB 1984, pp. 323–333. Morgan Kaufmann Publishers Inc., San Francisco (1984)
9. Chen, S., Ailamaki, A., Gibbons, P.B., Mowry, T.C.: Improving hash join performance through prefetching. ACM Trans. Database Syst. **32**(3), 17 (2007)
10. Dean, J., Ghemawat, S.: MapReduce: simplified data processing on large clusters. Commun. ACM **51**(1), 107–113 (2008)
11. Kirsch, A., Mitzenmacher, M.: Less hashing, same performance: building a better bloom filter. Random Struct. Algorithms **33**(2), 187–218 (2008)
12. Lee, K.H., Lee, Y.J., Choi, H., Chung, Y.D., Moon, B.: Parallel data processing with MapReduce: a survey. SIGMOD Rec. **40**(4), 11–20 (2012)
13. Lee, T., Kim, K., Kim, H.J.: Join processing using bloom filter in MapReduce. In: Proceedings of the 2012 ACM Research in Applied Computation Symposium, RACS 2012, pp. 100–105. Association for Computing Machinery, New York (2012)
14. Mackert, L.F., Lohman, G.M.: R* optimizer validation and performance evaluation for distributed queries. In: Proceedings of the 12th International Conference on Very Large Data Bases, VLDB 1986, pp. 149–159. Morgan Kaufmann Publishers Inc., San Francisco (1986)
15. Mehta, T., Mangla, N., Guragon, G.: A survey paper on big data analytics using map reduce and hive on Hadoop framework a survey paper on big data analytics using map reduce and hive on Hadoop framework, February 2016
16. Michael, L., Nejdl, W., Papapetrou, O., Siberski, W.: Improving distributed join efficiency with extended bloom filter operations. In: Proceedings of the 21st International Conference on Advanced Networking and Applications, AINA 2007, pp. 187–194. IEEE Computer Society (2007)
17. Mishra, P., Eich, M.H.: Join processing in relational databases. ACM Comput. Surv. **24**(1), 63–113 (1992)
18. Phan, T.C., d'Orazio, L., Rigaux, P.: Toward intersection filter-based optimization for joins in mapreduce. In: Proceedings of the 2nd International Workshop on Cloud Intelligence, Cloud-I 2013. Association for Computing Machinery, New York (2013)

19. Phan, T.-C., d'Orazio, L., Rigaux, P.: A theoretical and experimental comparison of filter-based equijoins in MapReduce. In: Hameurlain, A., Küng, J., Wagner, R. (eds.) Transactions on Large-Scale Data- and Knowledge-Centered Systems XXV. LNCS, vol. 9620, pp. 33–70. Springer, Heidelberg (2016). https://doi.org/10.1007/978-3-662-49534-6_2
20. Van Hieu, D., Smanchat, S., Meesad, P.: Mapreduce join strategies for key-value storage. In: 11th International Joint Conference on Computer Science and Software Engineering (JCSSE), pp. 164–169, May 2014
21. White, T.: Hadoop: The Definitive Guide, 4th edn. O'Reilly Media Inc., Sebastopol (2015)
22. Zaharia, M., Chowdhury, M., Franklin, M.J., Shenker, S., Stoica, I.: Spark: cluster computing with working sets. In: Proceedings of the 2nd USENIX Conference on Hot Topics in Cloud Computing, HotCloud 2010, p. 10. USENIX Association, USA (2010)

Blockchain and Applications

Blockchain-Based Forward and Reverse Supply Chains for E-waste Management

Swagatika Sahoo$^{(\boxtimes)}$ and Raju Halder

Indian Institute of Technology Patna, Patna, India
{swagatika_1921cs03,halder}@iitp.ac.in

Abstract. In this paper, we propose a novel smart e-waste management system, by leveraging the power of blockchain technology and smart contract, that considers both forward and reverse supply chains. This allows the proposed system to capture whole life cycle of e-products, starting from their manufacturing (as new products) to their disposal (as e-wastes) and their recycling back to raw materials. In this context, we address various challenges and limitations which existing blockchain-based solutions are facing, especially incomplete coverage of e-products' life cycle, access control, payment mechanism, incentivization, scalability issue, missing experimental validation, etc. We present a prototype implementation of the system as a proof-of-concept using Solidity on Ethereum platform, and we perform an experimental evaluation to demonstrate its feasibility and performance in terms of execution gas cost.

Keywords: E-waste management · Blockchain · Smart contract · Traceability · Supply chain

1 Introduction

Due to the advancement in modern technology and change in consumer demands, the global market of Electrical and Electronic Equipment (EEE) has grown exponentially. Several factors, including built-in obsolescence, shorter lifespan, presence of more non-repairable parts, etc., have resulted into generation of e-waste at an unprecedented rate [28,31]. When e-waste products are placed in landfills or incinerated, they impose a severe threat to the environment and human health due to the presence of hazardous materials/substances such as lead, mercury, cadmium, etc. As reported in [27], this is observed that 50 million tonnes of e-waste are produced every year, and it will grow up to 25–50 billion by this year end. In reality, e-waste management and recycling market face major challenges due to lack of proper regulatory interface and supporting infrastructure. The Basel Action Network (BAN)[1] in its report stated that many developing and underdeveloped nations are used as dumping ground of e-waste products by the developed nations, where recycling is almost entirely left to the informal

---

[1] https://www.ban.org.

© Springer Nature Switzerland AG 2020
T. K. Dang et al. (Eds.): FDSE 2020, LNCS 12466, pp. 201–220, 2020.
https://doi.org/10.1007/978-3-030-63924-2_12

sector, which does not even have adequate means to handle this. In most of the cases, the whole process of e-waste products collection, segregation, dismantling, and recycling is done manually by untrained labours or they are thrown along with garbage. The current lack of interactiveness among different stakeholders, improper dissemination of information, unmonitored activities, etc., make the e-waste regulatory framework almost impossible to implement.

1.1   Motivation and Contributions

Blockchain technology [23] enables secure, transparent, and immutable record keeping in distributed systems, without the need of any trusted intermediary. A new addition to the power of blockchain technology comes with the support of smart contracts [21], an executable codes on blockchain written in high-level turing complete language. The role of smart contracts is to remove all intermediary untrusted third parties between the participating members and to automatically execute and enforce the terms of agreement between them. Research on blockchains has gained significant momentum with a wide range of applications spanning cryptocurrencies, supply chain, health care, IoT, and many others [8,32]. Interestingly, in recent times, we are also witnessing its footstep in e-waste management, as detailed in Sect. 2.

After an exhaustive search, we observed that few research proposals and few business products are available in the literature. While the research proposals [17,24,30] lack in many aspects such as incomplete coverage of e-products' life cycle, access control, payment channel (in few cases), incentive mechanism, scalability issue, missing experimental validation, etc., the other proposals [1–7,13] exist only in the form of business products without any publicly available research component. Moreover, many of them target different kinds of waste, and therefore they are not directly applicable to the case of e-waste due to the involvement of different stakeholders and the waste-flow specific to e-products. These give us a motivation to investigate various challenges and limitations as mentioned above and to propose a novel approach covering complete life cycle of e-products, starting from their manufacturing to e-waste conversion to recycling back to raw materials. To this aim, we leverage the power of blockchain technology in order to achieve the following desire goals:

- **Transparency and Traceability:** One of the most prominent capabilities of blockchain technology in this context is to enable transparency and traceability of e-products by storing the entire life cycle, starting from their origin through every point of contact on the journey. The form of a decentralized ledger that recorded all activities in a verifiable and permanent way and replicated among participants establishes a complete trust and transparency in the system.
- **Cost Savings:** In e-waste management system, use of blockchain and smart contract play a vital role in massive cost-cutting by removing all un-trusted intermediaries in the system. Moreover, the technology also eliminates fees associated with funds passing into and out of bank accounts and payment

processors. Such fees cuts turn into profit margins, so being able to take them out of the equation is significant.

- **Monitoring of e-waste Generation:** Blockchain technology helps to monitor the growing volume of e-waste by capturing the moment of e-products manufacturing to their expiry. Blockchain technology can be adapted for automated event generation when any e-product reaches its end-of-life as per the expiry date recorded during registration. This allows the system to easily track the generation of e-wastes and to start monitoring their afterward activities.
- **Optimized Sorting and Automated Segregation:** To maximize recycling efficiency and consequent raw material recovery, processing of e-wastes to sort and segregate into right bins is an important task. Blockchain technology can significantly facilitate to design a cost-effective automated means of e-waste segregator. It would be driven by the stored details of e-products along with their types and by the events to be generated as soon as they meet their expiry dates.
- **Elimination of error prone paper works:** The seamless collaboration between all parties through blockchain eliminates the need of manual paperworks and dramatically speeds up all validation and certification processes.
- **Fraud and Manipulation:** The current e-waste management system doesn't use any proper mechanism to examine e-waste disposal reports submitted by stakeholders. Since reports can be manipulated, one can easily perform payment frauds. Blockchain technology is found to be most suitable to prevent this kind of fraud and manipulation.
- **Black market and Counterfeit Products:** The blockchain-based immutable audit trail of complete life cycle of e-products to e-waste generation and the association of related documents in a tamper-proof manner make the approach powerful enough to prevent any kind of black marketing and the creation of counterfeit products in the market.

To summarize, this paper makes the following contributions:

1. We propose a novel approach which provides a smart e-waste management system by leveraging the power of blockchain technology and smart contracts. We show in detail how our approach overcomes the challenges and limitations in the existing solutions.
2. We consider both Forward Supply Chains (FSC) and Reverse Supply Chains (RSC) of e-waste management, enabling the proposed system to capture all activities happening throughout the life cycle of e-products, starting from their manufacturing (as new products) to their disposal (as e-wastes) and their recycling back to raw materials.
3. We come up with an access control mechanism which ensures that only authorized stakeholders can get access to the right documents associated with desire products.

4. We introduce a payment mechanism in the system to digitize fair trade among stakeholders on the product marketplace. In addition, an incentive mechanism is introduced to attract more participants and to motivate them to act honestly in the system.
5. Finally, we present a prototype implementation of the system as a proof-of-concept using Solidity language on Ethereum platform, and we perform an experimental evaluation to demonstrate its feasibility and performance in terms of execution gas cost.

The structure of the paper is organized as follows: The related works are discussed in Sect. 2. The detailed descriptions of our proposed approach are presented in Sect. 3. Section 4 presents a proof of concept and experimental results. We provide a detail discussions in Sect. 5. Finally, Sect. 6 concludes our work.

2   Related Works

Post the advent of the bitcoin by Satoshi Nakamoto in 2008 [23], blockchain technology has emerged as a ground-breaking disruptive technology showing its enormous potential to a wide range of applications, such as E-waste Management, Supply Chain Management, Land Registry, Insurance, E-Governance, Health Care, Smart Agriculture, and many more. A comprehensive survey of possible applications of blockchain technology can be found in [8,32]. The prime objectives of the use of blockchain technology is to increase accountability, transparency, and trust with regard to the storage, safeguarding and sharing of information among the stakeholders.

Supply Chain Management [10,15,18,19,22] is considered as one of the most significant and beneficial use cases of this technology. [18] proposed a blockchain-based logistics monitoring system aiming to achieve traceability, authenticity, and accountability of parcel. The authors in [10] adopted blockchain technology to enable customers to verify the composition of wines and to ensure accountability, protection and security from grape growers to retailers. The authors in [19] proposed the system to address the issue of drug safety using blockchain and encrypted QR code, allowing one to trace the drugs (including their pharmaceutical ingredients) from manufacturer to end consumer and to identify counterfeit-drug. The author in [15] proposed blockchain-based system for food agriculture, which helps to assure geographic and biological origin of the products and to trace them from farm to fork. In [22], the authors proposed a blockchain-based system for traceability of carbon fibre components used in aerospace and composite materials used in live seafood.

Let us now discuss the state-of-the-art on blockchain-based solution to waste management. Gupta and Beddi [17] proposed the flow of EEE products among five stakeholders through a number of smart contracts. The primary aim of the proposal is to validate the amount of e-waste to be exchanged between the stakeholders. In [30], the blockchain-based solution aims to provide effective management of various activities pertaining solid waste and trash bins. The microcontrollers and sensors associated with trash bins collect information about the status of trash bins and store them into a public blockchain. Gudio et al. [24] discussed the benefits and various design challenges involved in adopting blockchain technology in the case of waste management.

In addition to the above, few other solutions in the form of business products are also available, which are developed by various start-up companies [1–7,13]. Plastic Bank [4] is an app for global recycling ventures to reduce plastic waste in developing countries. People who bring plastic garbage to bank recycling centers are rewarded by issuing blockchain-secured digital tokens. The initiative in [6] offers users to earn coins from waste sorting. People can deposit aluminum, e-waste, and plastic bottles through vending machine and receive reward-coins in their account as an exchange. Swachhcoin [7] provides blockchain-based solution for existing waste management companies where the household waste contributors are rewarded for the waste they produce. Agora Tech Lab [1] offers digital tokens in return of recycled goods, which can be used for various public services later on. The Dutch Ministry for Infrastructure [2] plans to use blockchain technology to enhance accountability and visibility of waste in transit. HashCash [3], a Blockchain-based waste management platform, offers monitoring, analysis, and management related to waste disposal and recycle processes to help enterprises. Prismm Environmental company [5] facilities waste management by accepting information and paying Bitcoins for recycling. Goodr [13] is an app to solve problem of food waste in America using blockchain technology. It allows food service agencies to connect with local charities to facilitate the delivery of leftovers. A brief survey on the above products can be found in [16].

As e-waste management has a long research tradition, let us highlight briefly a number of non-blockchain-based proposals [9,11,12,20,26]. Ravi et al. [26] proposed an analytic network process model to analyze an alternative for the reverse logistics option for End-of-Life computers in a hierarchical form. The proposed Reverse Supply Chain (RSC) model in [12] is specifically designed for Taiwanese electronic companies, which adapts fuzzy analytic hierarchy process. Hung Lau and Wang [20] presented a model for RSC of electronic companies in China, taking into consideration the key factors such as financial issues, management skills, technical issues, public awareness, environmental regulations, etc. The effect of improper e-waste management and possible implementation barrier in India are reported in [9,11].

3   Proposed E-waste Management System

We are now in a position to describe in detail our proposed blockchain-based solution to e-waste management system.

As our objective is to enforce effective monitoring and regulatory activities throughout the whole life cycle of e-products, we consider a generic model of the e-waste supply chain depicted in Fig. 1. The model can be divided into two parts: Forward Supply Chain (FSC) and Reverse Supply Chain (RSC). The forward flow of the supply chain focuses on the trading of e-products that starts with raw material suppliers and ends with consumers/bulk consumers as end-users.

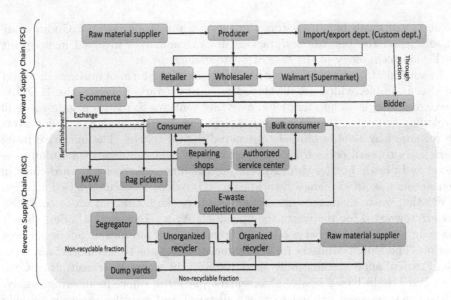

Fig. 1. Forward and reverse e-waste management supply chain

This involves a number of stakeholders (producer, importer/exporter, wholesaler, retailer, etc.) with necessary technologies for producing, importing/exporting, assembling, and delivering products to the end-users. In contrast, the reverse supply chain flow mainly deals with e-waste collection, segregation, refurbishment, and recycling back to raw materials. These are performed through specific channels, such as e-waste collection centers, repairing shops, Municipal Solid Waste (MSW), Ragpickers, etc. The primary reason to consider both FSC and RSC in our proposal is to capture all activities happening throughout the life cycle of e-products, starting from their manufacturing (as new products) to their disposal (as e-wastes) to their recycling back to raw materials.

Figure 2 depicts the overall components in our proposed system, where different stakeholders and a set of smart contracts serving various functionalities are involved. Since our proposed system is able to capture both forward and reverse supply chains, we consider all stakeholders right from the beginning of e-product manufacturing until the end of their lifetime. This includes producers, suppliers, wholesalers, customers, etc., in case of FSC, and recyclers, disposers, e-waste collectors, etc., in case of RSC. Observe that all stakeholders involved in both FSC and RSC use the services(such as registration, transfer ownership, access control, payment, incentive) provided by the smart contracts. The system comprises of the following phases:

1. Registration of Stakeholders
2. Collection and Channelization of E-waste Products
3. Access Control and Data Retrieval

Fig. 2. Proposed blockchain-based e-waste management system

4. Incentive Mechanism
5. Payment Channel

Let us now describe each phase in detail.

3.1 Stakeholders Registration

The first task of all stakeholders in the system is to register themselves through RegistrationSc smart contract. On successful registration, each stakeholder receives a unique digital identifier which needs to be used in future to associate relevant information with the corresponding stakeholder. To prevent counterfeit, any government certified national identity database could be interfaced to verify the correctness of the submitted details during registration process. This can be achieved either through a merkle-tree-based verification approach [25] or through a designated trusted miner node [29]. Figure 3 depicts the interactions among stakeholders, RegistrationSc smart contract and national identity database, where steps (1)-(3) perform the registration process.

3.2 Collection and Channelization of E-waste Products

This is the core phase in our approach to control the flow of e-products (under FSC) and e-wastes (under RSC) through proper channel in the system and to ensure their traceability and auditability. The following subphases assist to achieve these objectives:

Product Registration. To enable supply chain flow under both FSC and RSC, the producers are responsible for registering products at the early phase of their life cycle just after manufacturing. Now onwards, we use the term "product" to refer all products which are currently in use under FSC and to refer e-waste products in case of RSC. Observe that registration of e-products is done by only manufacturers, which requires product-specific details such as make, model, color, etc. Each product obtains a unique product ID through this registration process. Note that, recycling process under RSC may generate raw materials which may require to pass through this registration process again to acquire new unique identifies for them. The product registration phase is shown in steps ④ and ⑤ in Fig. 3.

Fig. 3. Interaction-diagram during registration phase

Product Transfer. Any product after manufacturing can be transferred to other stakeholders down the line. Under FSC, the transfer takes place among manufacturers, producers, wholesalers, retailers, etc., whereas in the same takes place among disposer, collector, and recycler under RSC. The smart contract TransferOwnershipSc is introduced to facilitate this transfer process by changing the ownership information in the corresponding state variables.

In order to improve scalability in case of transferring products in bulk amount, we introduce aggregate operation and adopt digital tokenization, which provides unique token value to group of products enabling their traceability as a whole. Moreover, given a group of products represented by a unique token value, we also introduce splitting mechanism as a way to allow transfer of only a part of it without disturbing their traceability property. The smart contract TokenSc is responsible for performing these aggregate and splitting tasks.

In the rest of the paper, we use the notations $'\langle\ \rangle'$ and $'\succ\{\ \}'$ to denote aggregate and splitting operations respectively. Figure 4 exemplifies these aggregation, splitting and transfer processes. On the left side, observe that the token value

'0 × 500' denotes a group of three products represented by product IDs '0 × 10', '0 × 20' and '0 × 30' respectively. In the same way, token value '0 × 600' supports nested tokenization consisting of products '0 × 45', '0 × 90' and the token value '0 × 500'. On the other hand, token value '0 × 800' is obtained by performing splitting operation, which consists of product '0 × 600' and a part {'0 × 10', '0 × 30'} of products represented by token value '0 × 500' which is a part of 0 × 600 token. The creation of token '0 × 500' (shown within dotted box on left side) and its transfer is shown on the right side in Fig. 4.

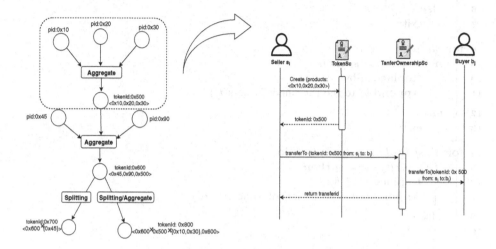

Fig. 4. Tokenization, splitting and transfer.

The overall algorithm to perform product-transfer and product-traceability is depicted in Algorithm 1. The algorithm takes seller identity s_i, buyer identity b_j, and the collection P of products for which ownership needs to be transferred. Observe that P may contain either a number of basic product p or previously generated tokens t_i or splitted tokens t_j. Steps 2, 8, and 14 identify a set of all basic products, tokens, and splitted tokens belonging to P. Steps 3, 9, and 15 verify whether the transfer request is issued by original owner of the product. After successful verification, it updates the ownership information in steps 4, 10 and 16. The algorithm not only transfers the product ownership but also maintains a trace by appending all new owners to the list in steps 5, 11 and 17. Finally, a transfer identifier is generated afterward.

Algorithm 1: TransferOwnership

Input : Seller s_i, Buyer b_j, Collection P
Output: Transfer ID h

1 **Create** a new token t to uniquely identify P;
2 **for** *all basic product unit $p \in P$* **do**
3   **if** Owner$(p) = s_i$ **then**
4   **Replace** s_i by b_j;
5   **Append** b_j to the list inheritOwners(p);
6   **else**
7   exit;

8 **for** *all token $t_i \in P$* **do**
9   **if** Owner$(t_i) = s_i$ **then**
10   **Replace** s_i by b_j;
11   **Append** b_j to the list inheritOwners(t_i);
12   **else**
13   exit;

14 **for** *all splitted token $t_j \rtimes \phi \in P$* **do**
15   **if** Owner$(t_j \rtimes \phi) = s_i$ **then**
16   **Replace** s_i by b_j;
17   **Append** b_j to the list inheritOwners$(t_j \rtimes \phi)$;
18   **else**
19   exit;

20 **Generate** and **Store** the transfer ID h;
21 **Return** h;

This is worthwhile to mention that e-wastes can be generated in two possible ways under reverse supply chain.

– When the e-product reaches expiry date or End-Of-Life (EOL), and
– When e-products get damaged or non-reparable before it expires.

In the first case, the status is converted from e-product to e-waste automatically, based on the expiry date of the product recorded during registration. As the e-waste management system has collection centers in strategic locations, in the second case, either owner or any collection center (after damaged products are deposited and transferred by the owners) can change the status of the product into e-waste. People who deposit e-wastes to a collection center will be entitled to receive incentives in the form of reward points depending on the quantity, quality, etc., of the e-wastes (discussed in Sect. 3.4). Observe that, on e-wastes deposition, events would be generated to notify legitimate collectors to collect e-wastes from the collection points. In the same way, when products are transferred down the line, events would be generated and notified to the next level stakeholders for further processing of the e-products.

InterPlanetary File System (IPFS) Storage. Any product in the system may have a number of supportive documents such as purchase-bill, warranty-card, transfer documents, e-waste disposal reports, etc. In order to associate these documents with the corresponding product during either registration or transfer process, we use the InterPlanetary File System (IPFS), which facilitates these documents to upload in its servers and returns their corresponding IPFS hash. This IPFS-hash is encrypted by owner's public key and stored it into the corresponding smart contract's state variable. The whole process is depicted pictorially in Fig. 5. Observe that, along with ownership transfer of any product, all documents associated with the product will also be transferred. To achieve this, proxy re-encryption [14] is applied, which converts the cipher-text of the IPFS-hash (originally intended for the previous owner) into another cipher-text (intended for new owner).

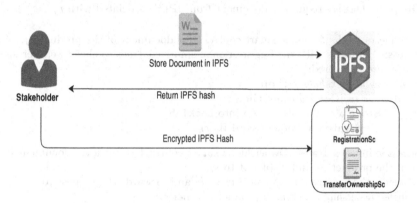

Fig. 5. Document storage in IPFS during registration and transfer

3.3 Access Control and Data Retrieval

At the time of buying or transferring products, if the recipient wants to check/download product-related documents (such as product bills, warranty cards, e-waste disposal reports, etc.), which are stored in IPFS, the recipient must pass through an access control mechanism. The access control policy is deployed through the smart contract AccessSc. When a stakeholder s_i requests for a document associated with product p_j, AccessSc first checks with RegistrationSc whether both s_i and p_j are already registered. If both are already registered, AccessSc creates an entry in the look-up table LookTab with record ID r_k for the issued request and then fetches the list of documents D from TransferOwnershipSc stored under p_j. Once $d \in D$ is selected by s_i, the access request $\langle r_k, p_j, d, s_i \rangle$ for d is issued to TransferOwnershipSc to search product's owner. After getting owner information, AccessSc smart contract asks for owner's permission. The permission by owner would be given in the form of interaction ID I which is being generated based on the interaction between owner and AccessSc meanwhile. When TransferOwnershipSc realizes that the interaction ID provided by the owner having owner ID o_l is same as the one notified by AccessSc through an event generation, the encrypted IPFS-hash is shared with AccessSc passing through a proxy re-encryption process. The proxy re-encryption converts the encrypted IPFS-hash (which is intended for o_l) into another form (which is intended for s_i). Finally, AccessSc forwards this to the requester s_i who decrypts it using her private key and gets access of the document from the IPFS. The algorithm is depicted in Algorithm 2.

Algorithm 2: AccessControl

Input   : Stakeholder s_i, Product p_j
Output: Display requested document from IPFS associated with p_j

1 s_i requests to the AccessSc smart contract for document of the product p_j;
2 AccessSc interacts with the RegistrationSc smart contract to check weather s_i and p_j are registered;
3 **if** s_i *is valid stakeholder* **then**
4   **if** p_j *is registered product* **then**
5   **Store** a new tuple $\langle p_j, s_i \rangle$ into LookTab;
6   **Generate** an unique record ID r_k;

7 AccessSc invokes TransferOwnershipSc smart contract to retrieves document-list D of the product p_j and display it to s_i;
8 s_i selects the required document d from D and forwards the request to TransferOwnershipSc to search product's owner o_l;
9 AccessSc asks o_l for the permission;
10 Owner o_l checks LookTab through AccessSc to grant permission for accessing document;
11 **if** $\exists (r_k, s_i, p_j) \in LookTab$ **then**
12   **Store** $\langle d, o_l \rangle$ into LookTab;
13   **Return** interaction ID I to the owner through AccessSc and simultaneously notify TransferOwnershipSc;
14 Owner gives permission to TransferOwnershipSc by sharing I and subsequently it shares re-encrypted IPFS-hash Y (intended for s_i) to AccessSc;
15 AccessSc forwards it to s_i;
16 s_i decrypts Y with her private key and download the document d from IPFS;

3.4   Incentive Mechanism

The primary goal of this phase is to encourage people to use the proposed blockchain-driven e-waste management system, and to promote more organized and unorganized sectors to participate for disposal, collection, processing, and recycling of e-waste products. This can be achieved by giving incentives to the stakeholders involved in RSC (disposer, collector, segregator, etc.) who are help-ing to channelize the e-waste products. The incentives are given in the form of some reward points and the amount of rewards depends on the quantity, qual-ity, etc., of e-wastes and the type of stakeholders. For example, more incentives should be given to the customers (i.e., disposer) who wish to dispose their EOL products, as this is the starting point of e-wastes channelization. Stakeholders can use these rewards points in future in many possible ways, such as availing discount on product's MRP, tax benefit from Government, etc.

3.5 Payment Channel

To enable payment in the system during the purchase or transfer of products, the smart contract PaymentSc is deployed. This payment channel is applicable for trading among stakeholders in both FSC and RSC.

Let s_i be the seller and b_j be the buyer of the requested product p_k. Once the orders are placed through PaymentSc, s_i shares the price information of p_k with b_j. When b_j deposits the required amount 'val' to PaymentSc, this triggers a notification to s_i to initiate the dispatch of the product. On successful product delivery, b_j sends an acknowledgment to PaymentSc which immediately releases the payment to the seller's account. The whole process is shown in Fig. 6.

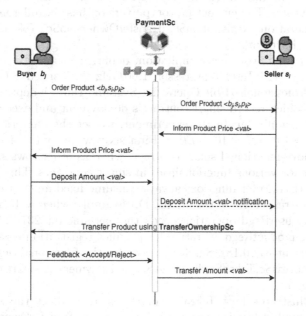

Fig. 6. Payment interaction-diagram between sender, receiver and PaymentSc

Table 1. Transaction gas costs for smart contract functionalities

Sl. No.	Functions	Task	Transaction gas	Execusion gas	Actual cost (*Ether*)	USD ($)
1	RegistrationSc	Deployment	3,441,178	2,549,599	0.006882356	2.13
2	TransferOwnershipSc	Deployment	4,656,882	3,606,784	0.009313764	2.88
3	TokenSc	Deployment	2,569,725	1,998,765	0.005139450	1.59
4	AccessSc	Deployment	6,878,071	5,624,807	0.013756142	4.26
5	PaymentSc	Deployment	3,952,163	2,452,798	0.007904326	2.45
6	IncentiveSc	Deployment	170,975	88,935	0.00034195	0.10
7	userRegd	Execution	237,614	206,563	0.000475228	0.14
8	productRegd	Execution	291,866	241,342	0.000583732	0.18
9	userLogin	Execution	27,902	2,581	0.000055804	0.017
10	tracing	Execution	23,752	2,288	0.000047504	0.014
11	conHash	Execution	29,509	9,352	0.000059018	0.018
12	verifyLookup	Execution	21,806	17,832	0.000051612	0.015
13	geneID	Execution	21,509	5,909	0.000043018	0.013
14	accPerm	Execution	16,764	7,668	0.000033528	0.010
15	makePayment	Execution	251543	201,987	0.000059086	0.018
16	reward	Execution	17,675	5,645	0.000035350	0.010

4   Proof of Concept and Experimental Results

In this section, we present a prototype to evaluate the practicality of our proposal. The programming language that we have used in the implementation is Solidity and Python. The current prototype version has six different smart contracts implementation: RegistrationSc, TransferOwnershipSc, TokenSc, AccessSc, IncentiveSc and PaymentSc.

We perform smart contract compilation, deployment and executions on the system configured with Intel i5 processor, 1.90 GHz clock speed, 8 GB RAM and Windows 10 Professional 64-bit Operating System. Table 1 depicts the experimental results which record smart contract's deployment and execution costs in terms of gas consumption. In the experiment, we set the gas price to 2 *Gwei*, where $1\ Gwei = 10^9\ wei = 10^{-9}\ Ether$. First six rows show the deployment gas cost for the above-mentioned smart contract, whereas other rows show the execution gas cost for various functionalities in smart contracts. This is to observe that these smart contract functions always consume fixed amount of gas during their execution irrespective of the inputs. For example, when a stakeholder joins the system, the userRegd operation needs the gas amount 237,614 (equivalent to $0.14) where productRegd operation for product registration uses gas amount 291,866 (equivalent to $0.18). Similarly, costs for the functionalities in TransferOwnershipSc, AccessSc, TokenSc, IncentiveSc, and PaymentSc smart contracts are depicted in Fig. 7.

Figure 8 illustrates how TokenSc smart contract affect the scalability in the system through recording the execution costs of TransferOwnershipSc with tokenization and without tokenization. Observe that the gas cost varies linearly w.r.t. input data collection size. Note that, in order to perform encryption of IPFS-hashes (during Registration) and their proxy re-encryption (during

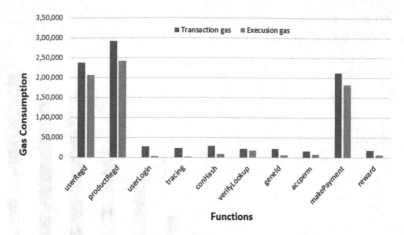

Fig. 7. Gas costs of different functions in smart contract

Product Transfer and Access Control), we used 'npre'[2] library which requires 'libssl-dev' and 'libgmp-dev' as its pre-requisites. This is a customized library written in Python and is a slightly refined version of the same algorithm in the charm crypto library. The interaction between proxy re-encryption off-chain computation and the smart contract is established using oraclize[3].

5 Discussion

In this section, we perform a comparative study among the existing research proposals and the software products (discussed in Sect. 2) with our proposal. Then we assess our proposed system in terms of blockchain-assisted goals mentioned in Sect. 1.1. We also highlight the scope of possible improvements in our system.

The system proposed in [17] aims to validate the amount of e-waste to be exchanged between five stakeholders. The waste-flow in the proposal is very restrictive in the sense that consumers send the e-wastes to collection centers via producers. The authors in [24] do not propose any new solution. Rather, they discuss only the benefits and design challenges involved in adapting blockchain technology to the case of waste management. The prime focus of [30] is to perform coordinated actions by a number of municipality workers using blockchain according to the states of the deployed trash bins (under cleaning, already cleaned, full, etc.). In case of the business products [1–7,13], we observed that the associated websites and few white-papers highlight only various features of the product, rather than their technical details.

Table 2 depicts a comparative summary of the proposals (including supply chain management of the products other than e-waste) in the literature, where BC, FSC, RSC, R, and BP stand for "Blockchain Technology",

---

[2] https://github.com/nucypher/nucypher-pre-python/tree/master/npre.
[3] https://provable.xyz/.

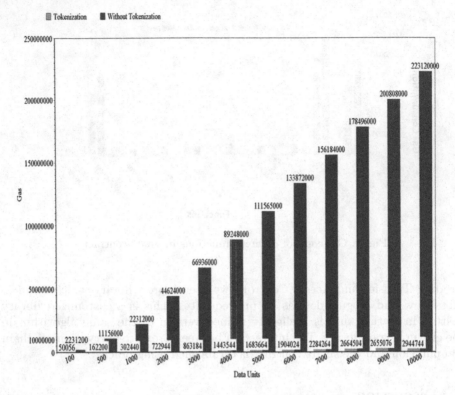

Fig. 8. Gas costs for TransferOwnershipSc with tokenization and without tokenization w.r.t. input size.

"Forward Supply Chain", "Reverse Supply Chain", "Research-based" and "Business Product" respectively. The notation "NM" indicates that the authors have not mentioned anything about the blockchain platform they used in their proposal, whereas "NA" stands for "Not Applicable". We have used the notations 'Y' and 'N' to indicate 'Yes' and 'No' respectively. This is to observe that the existing proposals [10,15,18,19,22] on supply chain management of products other than e-waste do not involve RSC and they do not consider any access control mechanism, payment channel, and incentive mechanism. Interestingly, all proposals on e-waste, except [17], are restricted to RSC only. Although [17] addresses both FSC and RSC, the solution does not consider any access control mechanism or payment system. As highlighted in the last row of the table, our proposal addresses all of them.

Let us now assess our proposed system in terms of blockchain-assisted goals mentioned in Sect. 1.1. Given unique identifier to every stakeholder and e-products in the system using RegistrationSc, one can easily trace the movement of products under FSC and RSC with the help of TransferOwnershipSc smart contract. It records ownership of the e-products during their transfer in FSC, their transition from e-products to e-wastes when EOL is reached, and their

Table 2. A comparative summary w.r.t. literature

Proposals	Is BC-based?	Blockchain platform	Product type	Support FSC/RSC/Both?	Support access control?	Use payment system?	Incentive?	Availability
Helo et al. [18]	Y	Ethereum	Parcel	FSC	N	N	N	R
Biswas et al. [10]	Y	Multichain	Wine	FSC	N	N	N	R
Kumar et al. [19]	Y	NM	Drugs	FSC	N	N	N	R
Galvez et al. [15]	Y	NM	Food	FSC	N	N	N	R
Mondragon et al. [22]	Y	NM	Aerospace sector and sea food	FSC	N	N	N	R
Agora Lab [1]	Y	Ethereum	Solid waste	RSC	N	N	Y	BP
Swachhcoin [7]	Y	Ethereum	Households and industries waste	RSC	N	N	Y	BP
Plastic Bank [4]	Y	Hyperledger fabric	Plastic waste	RSC	N	N	Y	BP
Dutch [2]	Y	Ethereum	Solid waste	RSC	N	N	Y	BP
Recereum [6]	Y	Ethereum	Household waste	RSC	N	Y	Y	BP
HashCash [3]	Y	NM	E-waste	RSC	N	Y	Y	BP
Prismm [5]	Y	NM	Paper and factory aste	RSC	N	Y	Y	BP
Goodr [13]	Y	NM	Food waste	RSC	N	N	Y	BP
Thada et al. [30]	Y	NM	Solid waste	RSC	N	N	N	R
Ongena et al. [24]	Y	NM	Dump waste	RSC	N	N	N	R
Chiou et al. [12]	N	NA	E-waste	RSC	N	N	N	R
Lau et al. [20]	N	NA	E-waste	RSC	N	N	N	R
Rani et al. [26]	N	NA	E-waste	RSC	N	N	N	R
Awasthi et al. [9]	N	NA	E-waste	RSC	N	N	N	R
Chaudhary et al. [11]	N	NA	E-waste	RSC	N	N	N	R
Gupta et al. [17]	Y	Ethereum	E-waste	Both	N	Y	Y	R
Our Proposal	Y	Ethereum	E-waste	Both	Y	Y	Y	R

journey as e-wastes under RSC. The ability to trace product's complete journey and to record of a complete audit trail of all changes using TransferOwnershipSc definitely help the regulatory bodies of the country to monitor e-waste generation, hence improves the transparency and trust in the system. Our system makes use of IPFS pinning service[4] to store all relevant documents (which are associated with stakeholders and e-waste products) permanently in the IPFS. Few alternatives to IPFS are Swarm, Sia, Stroj, etc.[5] Observe that the deployment of smart contracts TransferOwnershipSc and PaymentSc leads to a cost-cutting by eliminating fees involved in handling intermediaries, fulfilling common contractual conditions and legal obligations. As recyclables materials need to be sorted and segregated efficiently, TokenSc facilitates optimizing the sorting and to automatically segregate (based on their types recorded in RegistrationSc) by using the mechanism of tokenization and splitting. AccessSc, on the other hand, prevents the system from any fraud and manipulation by restricting the access to the documents and by establishing proper payment channels among legitimate stakeholders using PaymentSc. The registration of all e-products after their manufacturing and details of their journey in the blockchain removes any possibility of black market and counterfeit products.

This is to observe that a permissioned blockchain is best suited in our proposed system due to its access control feature for efficiently managing and protecting crucial data in the system. As the execution of smart contracts on Ethereum blockchain platform requires gas cost, Hyperledger Fabric can be considered as an alternative to this.

As possible future scopes, the proposed system can be integrated with AI techniques and IoT-enabled smart dustbins to facilitate various tasks under FSC and RSC, such as image analysis to identify e-waste type, automated sorting and segregation processes, etc.

6   Conclusion

This paper presents a novel blockchain-driven approach to e-waste management. In comparison to the related research [17,24,30] in the literature, our proposed system improves in many aspects: (i) by covering complete life cycle of e-products, starting from their manufacturing to e-waste conversion to recycling back to raw materials, and (ii) by addressing various challenges and limitations, including access control, scalability issue (in terms of the number of stakeholders and the flow of wastes), incentive mechanism and payment channel (in few cases), etc. To the best of our knowledge, none of the existing research proposals [17,24,30] demonstrates any experimental validation results. As our future aim, we are now exploring its possible extension to other kinds of waste products and their management.

---

[4] https://docs.ipfs.io/concepts/persistence/#pinning-in-context/.
[5] https://ethersphere.github.io/swarm-home/, https://sia.tech/, https://storj.io/.

Acknowledgement. We thank Dr. Subrata Hait and Mr. Amber Trivedi for their helpful suggestions on e-waste management.

References

1. Agora: Waste management fueled by blockchain. https://www.agoratechlab.com/. Accessed 2018
2. Dutch: Dutch govt to use blockchain for waste transportation automation with Belgium: Ministry of infrastructure and water management. https://sociable.co/technology/blockchain-waste-transportation/. Accessed 2010
3. Hashcash: Hashcash to help enterprises with blockchain based waste management platform. https://jotup.co/node/583249. Accessed 06 Dec 2019
4. Plastic bank: Winning the plastic war with blockchain. https://www.blockchain-council.org/blockchain/winning-the-plastic-war-with-blockchain. Accessed 15 Dec 2019
5. Prismm environmental. https://www.prismm.co.uk/. Accessed 01 May 2019
6. Recereum whitepaper. http://recereum.com/files/WhitePaper-Recereum.pdf
7. Swachh coin white paper. https://swachhcoin.com/whitepaper.pdf
8. Aggarwal, S., Chaudhary, R., Aujla, G.S., Kumar, N., Choo, K.K.R., Zomaya, A.Y.: Blockchain for smart communities: applications, challenges and opportunities. J. Netw. Comput. Appl. **144**, 13–48 (2019)
9. Awasthi, A., Wang, M., Wang, Z., Awasthi, M., Li, J.: E-waste management in India: a mini-review. Waste Manage. Res. **36**, 408–414 (2018)
10. Biswas, K., Muthukkumarasamy, V., Lum, W.: Blockchain based wine supply chain traceability system, November 2017
11. Chaudhary, K., Mathiyazhagan, K., Vrat, P.: Analysis of barriers hindering the implementation of reverse supply chain of electronic waste in India. Int. J. Adv. Oper. Manage. **9**, 143 (2017)
12. Chiou, C.Y., Chen, H.C., Yu, C.T., Yeh, C.Y.: Consideration factors of reverse logistics implementation -a case study of Taiwan's electronics industry. Procedia - Soc. Behav. Sci. **40**, 375–381 (2012)
13. Crowe, J.: Goodr: Solving food waste and food security with blockchain. https://www.foodabletv.com/blog/goodr-solving-food-waste-and-food-security-with-blockchain. Accessed Jan 2017
14. Egorov, M., Wilkison, M.: Nucypher KMS: decentralized key management system. CoRR (2017)
15. Galvez, J.F., Mejuto, J., Simal-Gandara, J.: Future challenges on the use of blockchain for food traceability analysis. TrAC Trends Anal. Chem. **107**, 222–232 (2018)
16. Gopalakrishnan, P., Radhakrishnan, R.: Blockchain based waste management. Int. J. Eng. Adv. Tech. (IJEAT), June 2019
17. Gupta, N., Bedi, P.: E-waste management using blockchain based smart contracts. In: International Conference on Advances in Computing, Communications and Informatics (ICACCI), pp. 915–921 (2018)
18. Helo, P., Hao, Y.: Blockchains in operations and supply chains: a model and reference implementation. Comput. Ind. Eng. **136**, 242–251 (2019)
19. Kumar, R., Tripathi, R.: Traceability of counterfeit medicine supply chain through blockchain. In: 11th International Conference on Communication Systems Networks (COMSNETS), pp. 568–570, January 2019

20. Lau, C., Wang, Y.: Reverse logistics in the electronic industry of china: a case study. Supply Chain Manage. Int. J. **14**, 447–465 (2009)
21. Liu, J., Liu, Z.: A survey on security verification of blockchain smart contracts. IEEE Access **7**, 77894–77904 (2019)
22. Mondragon, A.E.C., Coronado, C.E., Coronado, E.S.: Investigating the applicability of distributed ledger/blockchain technology in manufacturing and perishable goods supply chains. In: IEEE 6th International Conference on Industrial Engineering and Applications (ICIEA), pp. 728–732, April 2019
23. Nakamoto, S.: Bitcoin: a peer-to-peer electronic cash system. In: Cryptography Mailing list at https://metzdowd.com, March 2009
24. Ongena, G., Smit, K., Boksebeld, J., Adams, G., Roelofs, Y., Ravesteyn, P.: Blockchain-based smart contracts in waste management: a silver bullet? In: Bled eConference, pp. 345–356, June 2018
25. Qu, C., Tao, M., Zhang, J., Hong, X., Yuan, R.: Blockchain based credibility verification method for IoT entities. Secur. Commun. Netw. **2018**, 1–11 (2018)
26. Ravi, V., Tiwari, M.: Analyzing alternatives in reverse logistics for end-of-life computers: ANP and balanced scorecard approach. Comput. Ind. Eng. **48**, 327–356 (2005)
27. Ryder, G., Houlin, H.: The world's e-waste is a huge problem. it's also a golden opportunity. In: World Economic Forum, January 2019
28. Santhanam, N., Melvin, S., Ramalingam, C.: Electronic waste - an emerging threat to the environment of urban India. J. Environ. Health Sci. Eng. **12**, 36 (2014). https://doi.org/10.1186/2052-336X-12-36
29. Tariq, A., Haq, H., Ali, S.: Cerberus: a blockchain-based accreditation and degree verification system. ArXiv, December 2019
30. Thada, A., Kapur, U., Gazali, S., Sachdeva, N., Shridevi, S.: Custom block chain based cyber physical system for solid waste management. Procedia Comput. Sci. **165**, 41–49 (2019)
31. Victor, S., Kumar, S.: Planned obsolescence - roadway to increasing e-waste in Indian government sector. Int. J. Soft Comput. Eng. **2**, 554–559 (2012)
32. Xie, J., et al.: A survey of blockchain technology applied to smart cities: research issues and challenges. IEEE Commun. Surv. Tutor. **3**, 2794–2830 (2019)

A Pragmatic Blockchain Based Solution for Managing Provenance and Characteristics in the Open Data Context

Tran Khanh Dang[1,2](✉) and Thu Duong Anh[1,2]

[1] Ho Chi Minh City University of Technology (HCMUT), 268 Ly Thuong Kiet Street,
District 10, Ho Chi Minh City, Vietnam
khanh@hcmut.edu.vn, duonganhthu43@gmail.com
[2] Vietnam National University Ho Chi Minh City (VNU-HCM), Linh Trung Ward,
Thu Duc District, Ho Chi Minh City, Vietnam

Abstract. Nowadays, open data is a vital part of the most variety of resource input for many systems. Information originates from different sources and is reused by many various applications under different purposes, thereby exposing several problems about managing data provenance and characteristics. Meanwhile, blockchain is a new raising technology that gets much attention around the world. With its immutability, transparency, distributed mechanisms, and automation capabilities, using blockchain is a possible direction to solve these problems. This paper presents the model design of integrating blockchain into an open data platform to resolve this issue. The research involves some related studies, integration mechanisms, and operating procedures, showing the standard model of communication between two platforms and experimental real model with CKAN and Hyperledger Fabric. The result shows that this combination is logical and a feasible direction of high applicability. Also, the proposed solution is general and scalable for further requirements in the future.

Keywords: Open data · Blockchain · Data provenance · CKAN · Hyperledger fabric · W3C PROV

1 Introduction

This century is the era of data, and everything is data centric. Gathering, mining, analyzing, transforming, converting data becomes an essential process of many systems and services. Building a multi-application ecosystem like Smart Home or Smart City is the primary goal of many incorporation and government. To achieve that, we need to gather enormous volume input data from many various resources, in many different fields, domains [1–3]. Usually, finding data in Open Data Platform (ODP) is an efficient way to archive that. ODP allows and incentivizes user sharing data in different forms, formats, under different terms and conditions. These platforms are a potential resource and contain many trust issues related to the rightness, usefulness, and quality of information. Since open data means being shared freely, after a lot of process sharing,

© Springer Nature Switzerland AG 2020
T. K. Dang et al. (Eds.): FDSE 2020, LNCS 12466, pp. 221–242, 2020.
https://doi.org/10.1007/978-3-030-63924-2_13

converting, or transforming by different parties, no one can ensure that data is always correct, not be tampered or altered. That is why presenting a transparent view of how data is updated and finding the origin of data could be a challenge for many platforms. Besides that, shared data involves many characteristics, and some might carry sensitive data like medical profiles, personal information, and classified financial reports. Some data is only allowed to be shared under specific circumstances and only for the limited scope of related field or organization. These kinds of data need to be categorized, assessed, and identified using purpose to protect data privacy [4, 5]. Understanding and managing these data's characteristics is going to help us adjust system behavior appropriately for each kind of data. Also, updated data is going to change its characteristic, and systems need to find a flexible way to follow up on these changes and avoid violation of new rules.

Data provenance [6, 7] is proposed to address this problem. By presenting this metadata, users could better understand where data are coming from, who change the data, when the data is updated, and sharing in which conditions, using by which system, mean the full history of the dataset. However, again, how can we trust this metadata and make sure this content is reliable or correct? One of the challenges with the data provenance storage system is the collection process and assurance of the immutability, confidentiality, and privacy. Many data management systems were developed to store and process these kinds of data, such as the PReServ (Provenance Recording for Services [8], ORCHESTRA [9]. Most of them based on a centralized model. The weakness of this is when the central system is attacked, all stored provenance info will be stolen, replace, or counterfeited. Also, the availability of access is not guaranteed.

With all concerns above, this paper proposed an approach direction by using blockchain. Proven by mathematics, data inside blockchain cannot be changed or denied. This means when data provenance is saved inside blockchain, users could confidently trust this info. Moreover, additional blockchain security concepts like distributed ledger, traceability, transparency, integrity, and auto-execute smart contract are the missing pieces to fulfill open data picture. Our contributions could be summarized as followed:

- A mechanism to capture provenance metadata from Open data platform and protect these data from tampering by using Permissioned blockchain.
- A mechanism to manage user between open data platform and blockchain, also support solution for different kinds of user could interact directly with blockchain system.
- By using smart contract concept, we could automatically update, validate, standardize and store the provenance data.
- By using credential from blockchain, we could allow other authorized applications to consume data provenance to improve confident of shared dataset.

2   Background

In this section, we present some basic knowledge, definitions, and property of data provenance. At the same time, briefly introduce some popular open data platforms, specifically focusing on the CKAN platform - the main object in this paper. The content also includes some information about the blockchain platform structure, namely the Hyperledger Fabric and related work combine blockchain and open data.

2.1 Data Provenance

Data provenance is metadata about objects, activities, and individuals involved in the creation, interaction, and modifications. This metadata can be used for many different purposes, such as to evaluate the quality and reliability of a dataset, determine ownership, verify, examine, and reproduce the data.

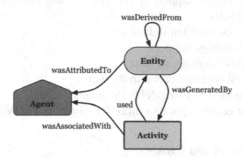

Fig. 1. W3C model primer [10]

Data provenance helps us answer these questions: When and how the data is changed? who changes data and the factors that influence data change? and what is the history forming data? The most recent standard related to data provenance is W3C PROV [10]. W3C PROV aims to build a standard model of data origin, allowing sharing and exchanging between systems, unifying regulations on the structures, components, and relationships. Figure 1 diagram shows us a high-level overview of the structure W3C model. This includes the concept of three main components and five relationships between them. The three main components are:

- *Entity*: Represents the object we are interested in, wanting to record the origin information. The entity can be a specific physical object around or an abstract concept.
- *Activity*: An activity that represents an action that occurs at one particular time, has an impact on the entity in any way.
- *Agent*: The person responsible for ongoing activity. An actor is not necessarily a person, and it could be an organization, a library, a process.

  Five basic relationships:

- *Generation*: Represents the relationship of a new entity created by an activity - wasGeneratedBy.
- *Usage*: Representing a relationship an activity that takes place using an entity - used.
- *Derivation*: Representing the relationship between two entities, this entity is a derivative of the other entity – wasDerivedFrom.
- *Attributed*: Represents the relationship between the entity and the agent, said the entity is related to the specific actor – wasAttributedTo.
- *Associated*: Represents the relationship between the action and the agent, indicating the activity taking place in connection with the specific actor - wasAssociatedWith.

Besides the concept present above, W3C PROV also allows some expansion definition to meet the requirements of changes different business domain. W3C PROV is widely used on many platforms today, so the tools to support the format conversion are also developed quite diverse in many languages.

- PROV Translator: an online web service that allows checking and converting between native information formats, supporting six types of data formats TTL, RDF, ProvN, Prov-XML, TRIG, JSON.
- PROV Toolbox: a toolkit written in Java.
- ProvJS: JavaScript language support.
- PROV Python: Python language support
- PROV Extract: PROV data embedded in the web.
- PROV-Vis: visualize the PROV model with images.
- PROV-N-Editor: the editor supports syntax definitions in PROV.

2.2 Open Data Platform and CKAN

Open data is defined as data that can be freely used, reused, and redistributed by anyone, subject only, at most, to the requirement to attribute and share alike. Existing open data platforms can be divided into two categories: Commercial products provided as cloud-based services (e.g., Socrata [11]) and open-source platform (e.g., CKAN [12]). Differences of platforms largely depend on the specific technology used, the organization model, the types of formats supported, community support capabilities, data interconnection between systems. However, they still have some common standard basic features, and we can summarize some of them as follows:

- Ability to store data.
- Ability to query, integrate with other applications inside the ecosystem.
- Ability to share data for the community.
- Ability to visualize data.

In this paper, we will choose CKAN [12], one of the most popular open data platforms, to integrate the proposed solution. CKAN was developed by the non-profit OKFN (Open Knowledge Foundation), an open-source platform for creating open data websites. The main goal of CKAN is to manage and share data for everyone in various forms and is now widely used by countries and research organizations around the world. In this platform, the data-sharing unit is called datasets. For example, the dataset can be crime statistics for an area, spending data for a part of the government, or temperature index from different weather stations. When users search, the search results they see will be individual datasets.

A dataset in CKAN will consist of 2 main components:

- Metadata: including name, description, license, file type, tags, upload time, author, update maintainer
- Content: Data in form of CSV or Excel, XML, PDF documents, image files, linked data.

The CKAN system includes a web interface and API that can be used for further searching, deleting, and editing data sets, authorization management, and user analysis. Also, users can preview data in the form of charts, graphs, and tables. For geospatial data (if the data includes latitude and longitude information), map view support is available. CKAN uses a VDM (Versioned Domain Model) model to store a user's entire operating history. Data sharing and communication features include the ability to integrate Google+, Twitter, and Facebook, RSS. There are over 60 extensions available for CKAN that can add independently. Currently, CKAN is an open data platform deployed in many countries such as OGPD in Germany [13], US government portal [14], general portal of the European Union [15], Australia government portal [16], Canada government portal [17], etc.

Plugins in CKAN: CKAN supports a mechanism to extend the platform through concept plugin. CKAN allows the plugin to interfere with the operation through the predefined interface. Each object in CKAN will have a life cycle with many different stages including different contexts, such as: the newly created stage, the edited stage, the tested stage, the pre-archive stage, the archive stage, and the post-archive stage. Many different contexts such as: which dataset is modified, by which user, at what time, the role and circumstances of the object being edited, indirectly edited by another action or directly edited by the user, what information is modified, what is the data before modification…. We could observe and collect changes to construct data provenance based on these life cycles through a plugin adapter.

Background Jobs: In CKAN, the system supports creating jobs that run in the background, synchronized or asynchronously with the primary system. Understandably, for every change that has just been observed, the plugin could create a job and put it in the queue. A process parallel with the primary system is responsible for executing this queue and does not affect the primary system's performance. Besides, CKAN also supports the ability to manage background tasks such as adjusting the start time, ending a task, the maximum timeout, error handling, recycling job.

Dataset Structure in CKAN: The relationship and properties of dataset in CKAN are stored in form of relational database. As described in Fig. 2, a single dataset is going to include many resources. We could consider dataset as a big document contains many files inside, which are the resources. Also, having metadata to describe profile about that big document like how many resources inside, display in which format, updated by with user, the checksum of each content file storage, and physical URL to access these resources, etc.

2.3 Blockchain and Hyperledger Fabric

Blockchain is a platform that includes many concepts of cryptographic, peer to peer networks, data security, and distributed storage. The main goal of blockchain is to provide a secure, immutable, and transparent platform for environments lacking trust between actors. The first and most widely recognized application of blockchain is the cryptocurrency Bitcoin [18]. Like Bitcoin, Ethereum [21] is also a cryptocurrency but has taken

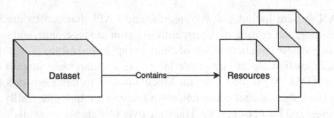

Fig. 2. CKAN dataset structure

a different approach by combining all the properties of Bitcoin with the new concept of smart contract to create the operating platform for distributed applications. Both bitcoin and Ethereum are considered as a public blockchain. Along with other technology, many businesses are starting to be interested in applying blockchain to systems outside the concept of monetary [20–23]. These systems have requirements that go against the previous public blockchain's definition:

- Ability to manage and identify users - Identity Management. In the B2B business, business owners have the right to decide who can view their information.
- Ability to ensure privacy and information confidentiality. In a real business context, not all nodes, all data are equal. There is a need that having some secret channel for sharing classified data and communication only for the participant node.
- Requires high-performance transaction speed, efficient processing.

The concept of Permissioned Blockchain was created, which is represented by Hyperledger Fabric. This new concept has brought blockchain beyond financial boundaries and applied to different domains. Hyperledger Fabric (HF) [24] is one of many permissioned blockchain platforms designed to serve the business context, supporting to meet completely different capabilities compared to others. HF was developed by the Linux Foundation, which has long development history and is very successful in building open source projects as well as developing sustainable communities and thriving ecosystems. Fabric's community has grown with the participation of more than 35 organizations and more than 200 developers around the world.

To adapt changes of frequent innovation, requiring flexible domain logic like banking, finance, or health insurance, HF using a modular architecture. By applying this design, HF allows freeway to configuration, plug in any kind of component. Another point needs to mention is that usually, other platform using DSL for writing smart-contract like solidity in Ethereum, Archetype in Tezos, Simplicity in bitcoins. However, HF's strategy is different by using popular programming languages (GPL) like Java, Go, Nodejs. This help developer could be more natural to approach and get used to with new technology. There are few primary concepts in HF we could summarize as below

Distributed Ledger: This is the general concept of blockchain systems. Ledger is a place to record all transactions in the system. Each participating node will store 1 version of the ledger. Data in ledger is append-only, cannot be changed or modified. This immutable property is well suited for concept data provenance verification. That is why blockchain system is described as a system of proof. In HF, data inside ledger divided into two parts:

the history of all transactions and the current state (the final state when all transactions are processed).

Peer Node: Blockchain is a network of many connected peer nodes, each peer stores a copied version of the ledger. In a public blockchain, all peers have the same role. However, in permissioned blockchain like HF, each peer has a different role and contributes to the system's different processes. Primarily, we have three main types:

- Endorser: In charge of authorizing the transaction. Only this node type having installed smart contract (aka chaincode in HF). Whenever having a request to append new data in blockchain, Endorser will be authorized request, ensure request is valid, and execute local chaincode in peer. The result after execution is then sent back to client for further process, not updated directly in ledger. Base on design and configuration rule, we could have many nodes are endorser node in system.
- Anchor: In charge of receive all updated ledger and broadcast this update to the remaining node in the same organization. Usually, an organization structure will contain many nodes and must have at least one anchor peer. Communications between different organizations can only make through these anchor peers.
- Orderer: The central contact point of the entire system, responsible for the consensus process, arrange, order transactions before generating a new block. After creating a new block, block data will be sent to anchor peer to update all replicate ledger.

Certificate Authority (CA): CA is one of the essential components of the system, responsible for managing and issuing certificates. In HF, all components and activities are identified by certificates, and a unique fingerprint represents each certificate. Only authorized components can participate and execute transactions within the system. This is where HF is guaranteed to be a Permissioned blockchain. Based on the certificate, we can quickly realize which fingerprint is a user or a node or organization, what role that node has, which organization to join, which channel participant organization or which user has what rights or attribute. All certificates in HF are in standard X509 format and apply the certificate chain concept.

Organizations: In HF, the Organization is a group of nodes running with their own rules and configuration. Internal node's communication could be separate with rules apply to channel. The same approach is applied for connection between organizations. Different organizations could communicate with each other by joining channels. After joining the channel, all interactions are accomplished between the organization's anchor node then broadcast back to internal nodes. The rules and policy of channels limit information's scope exchange, that is why we could have many channels between only two organizations or nodes.

Consensus: In any decentralized system, the consensus protocol is the process of synchronizing data so that only valid transactions are updated and in the same order. For any kind of blockchain, we can see consensus protocol is the heart, the rules of the system. Any process involved must obey and not violate the law. Public blockchains like Ethereum or Bitcoin, nodes have the same role, and can all participate in the consensus process. Nodes are encouraged to check the validity of the transaction through problem-solving such as Proof of Work in Bitcoin or through monetary power such as Proof of Stake in Ethereum to gain the right to close the block. However, in HF, each node has a different role, so the consensus process goes through many stages. We can divide into three main stages.

- Authentication phase – Endorsement.
- Stage of arrangement – Ordering.
- Confirmation and commitment phase - Validation and Commitment.

2.4 Related Work

There is already some research related to the combination of data provenance and blockchain. We could consider DataProv [25], the specific target platform is the data provenance for medical data, which is sensitive and needs to ensure privacy, the blockchain platform used is Ethereum, and all provenance is stored in the format of Open Provenance Model, an early model of W3C PROV. The strength of this approach allows automation of the entire process of monitoring changes, all data is encrypted, and only the data owner can know the content, ensuring data privacy. The consensus is performed by the monetary mechanism in the Ethereum network, rewards for valid action, and penalties for malicious behavior. However, the empirical results show that in certain situations, the cost of the solution is relatively high, and the issues of concurrent disputes on a dataset have not been resolved. Similarly, to DataProv, ProvChain [26] uses Tierion blockchain platform for protected data provenance in cloud storage applications. After data is stored inside blockchain, a receipt is returned with info of transaction and hash of Merkle tree. Cloud storage system going to use this info to validate the Merkle hash again, if the process is failed then notify abnormal behavior to cloud provider. To identify deepfake video, authors in [27] briefly present a solution using Ethereum blockchain to keep track of the changes of video and from that detect and combat the deepfake digital content. By using blockchain Hyperledger Fabric, authors in [28] design a system called ProvHL to manage provenance data when having a transition in storage of file and also using that for manage access control from the user. MedichanTM [29] apply Hyperledger Fabric for processing provenance data in the medical context.

As we can see with many researches above, the approach using blockchain to protect data provenance is a promise feasible direction. However, most results are only applicable to a single domain, specific to platform, and not generalized enough for further extension. Also, solutions related to open data still have not received adequate attention, mainly focus only on the commercial and service sectors. Therefore, this paper proposes a solution to protecting data provenance in the context of open data, specifically, CKAN. The goal of the solution is not only to adapt CKAN platform but also to expand the deployment to many others and building an ecosystem of provenance.

3 Proposed Solution

This section will present our approach to protecting data provenance extracted from CKAN platform by using blockchain Hyperledger Fabric. The main goal is to find an appropriate solution to capture, synchronize, and store provenance data inside blockchain and allow the authorized interaction from other applications to consume this information. Figure 3 illustrates the overview of the solution proposed. As we can see, the blockchain system plays a central role, and different kinds of ODP with various technology could connect to the blockchain through the portal. The concept of Portal will be present in the later section. Each ODP is operating separately, and while running, they are going to synchronize some metadata to the blockchain. Blockchain will be in charge of storing, protecting these metadata, and also manage to authorize access from different applications to consume these data. User on blockchain is not necessary from an ODP, they could directly interact and create their own data. We are going to walk through more detail of this through these sections below.

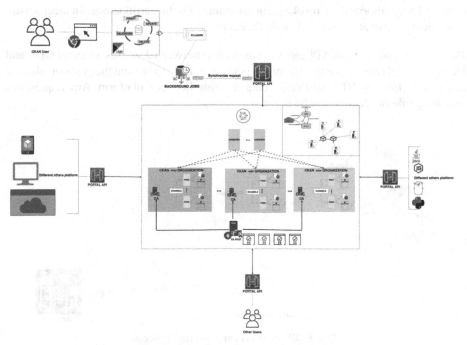

Fig. 3. Overview of proposed solution

3.1 Capture Provenance Data and Protected Data by Using Blockchain

As demonstrated in Fig. 4, we present the proposed solution by first introducing two generic concepts:

Platform Identity: In order to connect many different platforms, we identify them by issuing X509 certificates. It is unique for each platform and could be represented shortly by a generated fingerprint. Any ODP before integrating with blockchain system, would require administrator complete the registration step to get this certificate as shown in

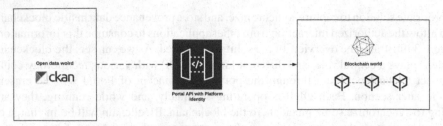

Fig. 4. Portal gateway to connect outside platform to blockchain system

Fig. 13. This certificate is the one inside HF's system issued by CA, as mentioned in Sect. 2.3. By presenting this certificate, we could easily manipulate the process of validation, update, authorized, or revoke permission through the certificate chain mechanism. User identity also applies based on this concept.

Portal: Each portal is an API gateway connection between 2 worlds, external ODP and HF system. All requests coming from this portal will have to present the platform identity as defined above so HF could verify data and rule between platform. Any request not matching rule or identity will be rejected.

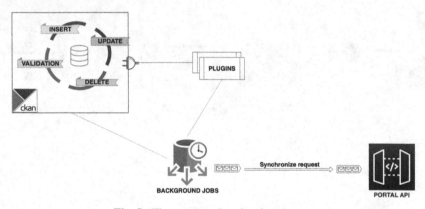

Fig. 5. Illustrate synchronize data process

Using these concepts, we could extend our scope to integrate with other platforms, not only in CKAN.

Synchronize Data Process

Regarding the specific platform like CKAN, there are four objects in the system that will be synchronized. First is platform data information. Any changes regarding platforms like platform name, administrator, contact, URL identified, version update, rules, or policies acquire … should be synchronized to blockchain to keep consistent context for other processes. Since the data sharing unit of CKAN is the dataset, the second and third targets need to focus will be metadata about the dataset and resources associated inside.

As datasets and resources are created and modified by users, changes in users should be captured and synchronized also. With the plugin and background jobs concept, the synchronize solution could be achieved, as shown in Fig. 5 by developing plugins that allow monitoring changes of these objects in CKAN. With any changes capture, create background jobs, and push to execution queue. Each job will invoke an HTTP request through the portal include platform identity and send data to blockchain system, similar to webhook mechanisms we often see in other systems. Since the background job queue is running parallel with the primary platform, combined with retry failure ability, the synchronized process will not affect the performance of the overall system. Moreover, after the synchronized process, data on blockchain cannot be modified and be accessible only by presenting an appropriate identity. Only platform administrator with platform identity or activated user owner of data could interact on blockchain.

3.2 Storage and Processing Data in Blockchain

When received synchronize requests from ODP, we could extract two kinds of information: First, information about objects from ODP. Second, context changes of the object's properties, which will be the data provenance.

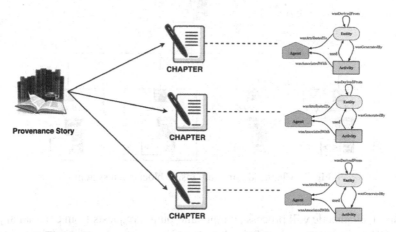

Fig. 6. Provenance structure as a story with chapters of changes

About objects from ODP, we are using the JSON format and involves three parts:

- The required information depends on the object's type
- Freestyle extra information to allows flexibility when integrating with various system's schema
- Attributes correlated to fingerprint in blockchain system - we could use this data to extend our system to adapt other solutions like role-based access control or granting permission to other platforms

Regarding the provenance info concept, the storage of provenance data is the process of recording the changes while identifying the relevant factors leading to the change.

As Fig. 6 we can consider all this data to be a story about the object, and each change will be a chapter about the object. A series of chapters will form a complete story, from the beginning to present. As mentioned above in Sect. 2.1, we will use the W3C PROV standard for data origin, so the characters in the story will correspond to the components of PROV like objects, actions, and relationships between them. With each change happening, a new version of the object is built, a new chapter is added. Based on the story we have; we can rely on this information to rebuild the object's structure.

The entire process collecting data is execute automated via chaincode inside HF. We consider five elements in our story: dataset, resources inside dataset, user interact with resource and dataset, the platform where user, dataset, and resource belong. The fifth ingredient will be the provenance info corresponding to four elements above. So, we will have five chaincode structures like Fig. **7** regarding five elements. While the provenance chaincode plays a central role, any update or changes execute by other chaincode will finally trigger the provenance chaincode to update the provenance story.

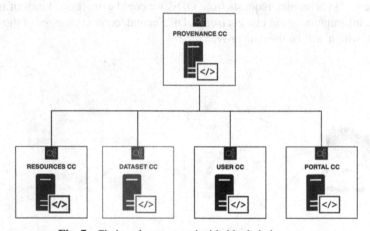

Fig. 7. Chaincode structure inside blockchain system

In short, chaincode will process all input and output requests from external applications to HF as illustrated in Fig. 8. Each request has to include a fingerprint to identify actors. Based on the fingerprint presented, with the help of CA inside HF, chaincode could find certificate related and review the validity of credentials. Some rules like:

- Fingerprints exist or not.
- Which object belongs to the fingerprint.
- Whether the fingerprint is still valid or has expired.
- Attributes related to fingerprints.
- Subjects identified by fingerprint are entitled to access or update data or not.

If the validation process is successful, the data will return or update upon request.

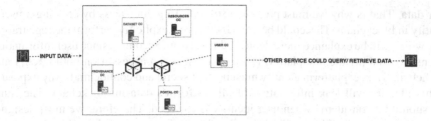

Fig. 8. Chaincode responsible for executing and query data request from external system

3.3   Mapping User from Open Data Platform and Blockchain System, Support the Capability to External Application Interact to Blockchain

The goal of protecting data provenance is to build user confidence and trust in shared datasets and allow external applications to consume this provenance info. To achieve that, we must concern the users related to these datasets. User is the key factor to allow interaction with the dataset. There are two strategies of users to concern in this solution as shown in Fig. 9

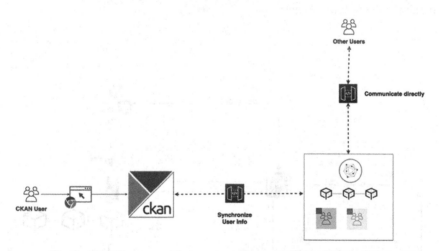

Fig. 9. CKAN's user and free user can interact with blockchain system

- Users from ODP like CKAN.
- Free users - Users do not belong to any platform.

User from ODP

Systems like CKAN will have a large number of user interactions. There are two issues we should consider in this strategy. Firstly, as presented in the section above, user's information is also included in the synchronize process of ODP. As the user's data is now on blockchain, they must have the ability to access blockchain to perform rights on their data. That is why we must provide a solution to grant access by creating a user's identity in blockchain. This could be done by the user explicitly perform the registration step, which will be explained more detail in this section. Secondly, since user information is sensitive and private, the platform's administrator can access it on both CKAN and blockchain. Hence, platform identity must be kept secret and confidential. Any exposure of this identity will leak information of all platform's data in blockchain. The same risk should be considered when user identity is exposed. Therefore, we must design a mechanism to handle this situation. Details of this process are explained in this section also. As certificates issued by CA manage both platform and user identity, we could easily revoke and renew the certificate.

- *Explicit registration process for users from CKAN or ODP:* In CKAN platform, each active user will have a unique API key and must be kept secret. The API key is intended to use for integration with other applications under this user's credentials. Additionally, any user can always revoke and create a new API key at any time. When synchronizing user data to blockchain, we already include this API key. However, at this point of time, only platform identity could access these data. Our proposed solution will use this API key as input, combined with platform identity to create a user certificate to access blockchain system. The detailed process is present in Fig. 10, containing the following steps:

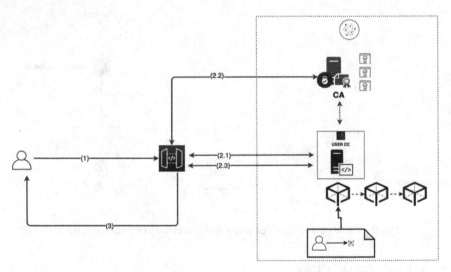

Fig. 10. Explicit registration process for user from CKAN

1. User issue a registration request to portal service include API key information. At this point of time, all user information is already synchronized to blockchain system

2. Portal service when received registration request will combine request data with platform identity and do subsequent steps:

2.1. Validate user information with API key, make sure API key is valid and exists from ODP system

2.2. Request CA (Certificate Authority) to issue a new certificate combine user information with the API key and ODP client identity

2.3. After getting issued certificate, extract unique fingerprint of new certificate and updated this fingerprint to user data inside blockchain ledger and mark this one as active fingerprint

3. Return newly issued certificate to user. From now on, user could directly interact with blockchain system with this certificate. Every request to blockchain system needs to present a certificate. Chaincode will always validate the request's fingerprint and only allow valid one to continue the process. In our scenario, the valid case will only be the fingerprint of admin platform certificate or active user certificate. Also, as we can see, every time user creates a new API key on CKAN, the access certificate with a combination of old one is going to be invalid at the same time

- *Revoking and issuing certificates to users when information is leaked*: Somehow, in the real-world scenario, there might be a chance user credential is leaked. Consider this issue, we provide a solution to overcome that. When leaking information, users will need to revoke the certificate and issue a new certificate. Illustrated in Fig. 11 The revoking process is to notify the CA to revoke the old certificate by putting the leaked certificate in the revoking list and issuing a new certificate. When a new certificate is issued, the fingerprint will also be changed, so it is necessary to update the new fingerprint information to the blockchain. However, this update does not have to remove old fingerprints altogether, but rather adds new one to the list of fingerprints. A user, a portal can contain many different fingerprints, but only one fingerprint be activated at a time. Preserve this list ensures that previous information of other objects mapping to old revoked fingerprints is maintained.

1. By using web interface, user could get a new API on CKAN system

2. When new API key in CKAN updated, plugins will trigger synchronize process, update new user's data include API key to blockchain system

3. User now could use new API Key, send request issue new certificate to blockchain through Portal service

4. When receive request generate new certificate, portal service will combine request data with platform identity and do subsequent steps:

4.1. Query and validate user data on blockchain with new API key provided, make sure new API key provided exist and is valid on ODP system. This step also allows us getting current active fingerprint (which is the invalid one now)

4.2. Request CA (Certificate Authority) process 2 things. First, issue a new certificate include information of the user and new API key. Second, revoke certificate related to current fingerprint

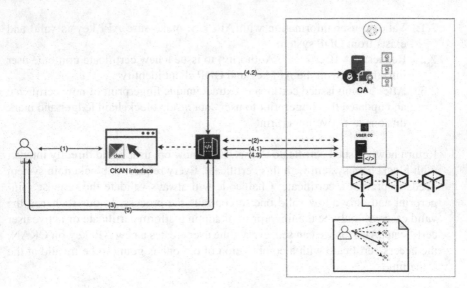

Fig. 11. Revoke and issue new certificate

4.3.   After getting issued certificate, extract unique fingerprint of new certificate and updated this fingerprint to user data inside blockchain ledger and mark this one as active fingerprint. Also mark all others fingerprint in list as inactive

5.   Return new issued certificate to user. From now on, user could continue to access blockchain system with new certificate. All access from old one will be invalid at this moment.

Free Users - Users Do Not Belong to Any Platform
Our solution does not restrict users to must go from an open data platform; any individual from the outside world can fully interact directly with the blockchain network and create their identifier with their own data. The process and concerning issues are quite similar to the previous strategy. The only difference is not having some data synchronized to blockchain beforehand. When performing the registration step, the API key will be replaced with a secret factor provided by the user. The validation step inside blockchain is not concerned about platform identity; only need to ensure there is no duplication in secret user provide, and all data is in a valid format. The same result is an X509 certificate is returned, user now could use this certificate to access blockchain or delegate other application to access data.

3.4   Blockchain Architect Design

We now could synchronize data from ODP to blockchain and allow consume data by different users and applications. The remaining issue is the architect of blockchain suitable

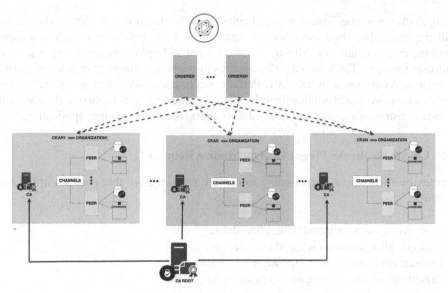

Fig. 12. Mapping organization concept in blockchain with an ODP system from outside

for ODP integration. As present in the section above, we using permissioned blockchain HF structured with some concepts in [24]. With the proposed solution, visualized in Fig. 12, an ODP connected to blockchain will be equivalent to an organization inside the HF network. Based on [24], an organization will need at least the following components:

- CA: Certificate authority.
- Peer: Each node is a workstation; at least two workstations in an organization, each machine can play multiple roles simultaneously. An unlimited number of workstations. Depending on the node's role, each node consists of two processing units: Database and smart contract.
- Orderer: The center is responsible for arranging and managing, it should be at least 1, the more Orderer, the less the risk of the system being attacked at a single point (single point of failure). Orderers can be used among multiple organizations.
- Channel: To be able to communicate between machines in the same organization, it is necessary to have at least one common channel, an organization can have many channels; each channel has a different purpose.

Similarly, the blockchain network will consist of many organizations, and each organization could be configured with different policies, different numbers of each component, based on the logic domain required. Organizations could choose to communicate and to share data with others through channels or to run solo separately.

4 Implementation

In this implementation, we set up a local instance of CKAN with full configuration for web interface, storage server, and plugin support. HF blockchain system is deployed by using docker-machine, installed five chaincode as described in the section above. We will implement both two scenarios of management: users belong to CKAN and users from the external platform. All dataset info is input and upload as regular operation of end-user through CKAN web interface and using webhook plugin to capture metadata in system. As proposed in Sect. 3.1, Portal concept is considered as server API using NodeJS framework and applicable to handle all request for synchronizing data as well as user registration strategy and query data request from the consumer application.

4.1 CKAN Webhooks Plugin for Synchronize Request

Written by Python, our plugin going to capture four objects table changes in CKAN system:

- User: After_insert, after_update, after_delete
- Package: after_create, after_update, after_delete
- Dataset: after_insert, after_update, after_delete
- Organization: after_insert, after_update, after_delete

To implement the synchronized process, inside the plugin, we will filter only changes related to 4 entities above. As present in previous section, dataset is a big container of multiple resource objects, any changes of resource inside going to be cascade as updated in dataset outside. When we upload a physical resource file to storage server, plugin going to extracted metadata of new file also calculates hash MD5 checksum. A JSON object is constructed to describe new changes, including the domain of website, types of changes (insert, update, delete). A new job is created and push in Redis queue waiting for execution. The execution could be successful or error. Due to the result received, we could decide to retry that task or terminate after maximum times. Using a queue, we could ensure that the order of changes in blockchain is always consistent as in CKAN.

4.2 Platform Registration Process for Getting Platform Identity

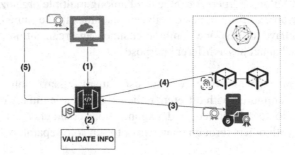

Fig. 13. Registration process for getting platform identity

Follow Fig. 13, we have five steps to process as shown below:

1. CKAN administrator issues register platform request with contents of platform name, domain, description, contacts, category, license-related and some secret value info for later retrieval or revoking this identity.
2. Portal received this request, validate content, and make sure all information is correct and valid then continue forward to the next step.
3. Portal forward request to blockchain system, CA going to receive this one and issue a new X509 certificate for platform identity.
4. Portal received certificate result, create a fingerprint represented of new certificate and combine with platform info, and secret value and send it back to HF again, at this time, a new record is created, and platform info is stored inside leger.
5. A pair of information client Id and client secret associated with new certificate is returned to administrator. From now, platform administrator could use these pair of value to manage their own identity.

4.3 User Registration Through Portal for Granted Access to Blockchain System

As discussed above, since the API key is unique and secret for each user, to get access to the blockchain system, the CKAN user will use their API key to activate the access. Request contains API key is sent to portal, portal going to combine this info with platform identity, and issue request to blockchain system. Like process present in 3.3 and Fig. 10, by validated user info already synchronized in system, CA will issue a new certificate for user and updated fingerprint related to user info inside ledge. A new certificate is returned, and from now, users could use these credentials to access their data in blockchain further.

Process for an outside user should be the same. The only difference is that the initial request also includes user profile, since it does not have any profile information in this case, and instead of the API key, users need to present a secret password along with their profile. Final result respond will be the same as CKAN user.

4.4 Chaincode Execution in HF

Our chaincode is like a mini program, installed in every validation node inside HF. Each request hitting blockchain system is going to be processed by these chain codes. All requests must include a fingerprint to present identity. If not, request will be rejected. First, chaincode will start extracting fingerprint identity from body content, invoking CA to validate this fingerprint, and getting context attributes from related certificates. Based on object domain logic, it will require some extra validation, role, and rule for further access. If access is valid, starting to execute or query data, except for query request, all modifications after success executed will trigger provenance chaincode to create a new chapter in the story. The consensus mechanism will be triggered after the result of chaincode is successfully returned, then a new block is closed, and data is protected forever inside the ledger.

4.5 Retrieving Provenance Data in W3C Format

Since our provenance data structure is oriented by the W3C PROV standard in JSON format. Thanks to this standard, we could display and visualize provenance results as

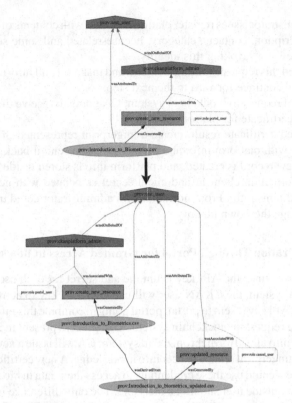

Fig. 14. An example of data provenance of changes presenting in W3C PROV visualize format

Fig. 14 supported by a lot of tools and applications. On the top part of diagram, the first version of a resource file created on CKAN. We could easily understand that this file is created by a user on the CKAN platform. Then behind the scene, CKAN using portal credentials with the role "portal_user" to synchronize this metadata to blockchain system. On the lower part, the same diagram having additional information about new changes in this resource file. User perform some update changes directly on blockchain system with the role "casual_user". A new version of data is created derived from previous data.

5 Conclusion

As the approach presented above, by using blockchain we could ensure the transparency of the system, data provenance cannot be changed or altered. The synchronize process is flexible and completely independent with regular operation. Not limited to the scope of CKAN, our proposed solution could be applied freely to any ODP integration. The structure of metadata in blockchain is stored in a dynamic structure, not depend on integrated ODP, and able to adapt changes. By using chaincode to manage logic update and query ledger, data in blockchain is handled automatically by W3C PROV standard format, the computer can read and convert between many forms, which is very suitable input for other provenance platforms. Thanks to the nature of blockchain, the entire history of an object can be recorded and recreated. Moreover, the identity and certificate management mechanism could adapt users from different scenarios, allow external applications to access and consume data but still ensure security perspective. It is possible to continue to research further aspects to adapt requirements from open data context like attribute/role-based access control with user and object attribute [30], management sharing license under GDPR compliance [31], or dynamic blockchain network configuration to update chaincode and policies. Besides, some other security-related characteristics of open data like those of outsourcing database services [32, 33] are also of our great interest in the future.

Acknowledgment. This work is supported by a project with the Department of Science and Technology, Ho Chi Minh City, Vietnam (contract with HCMUT No. 42/2019/HD-QPTKHCN, dated 11/7/2019). We also thank all members of AC Lab and D-STAR Lab for their great supports and comments during the preparation of this paper.

References

1. Espinosa, R., Garriga, L., Zubcoff, J.J., Mazón, J.: Linked open data mining for democratization of big data. In: Proceedings of IEEE International Conference on Big Data, pp. 17–19 (2014)
2. Schenk, T.: Building a government data strategy: aligning open data and advanced research with the public and open science principles. In: Proceedings of 2nd International Conference on eDemocracy & eGovernment, Quito, p. 18 (2015)
3. Chan, C.M.L.: From open data to open innovation strategies: creating e-services using open government data. In: Proceedings of the 46th Hawaii International Conference on System Sciences, pp. 1890–1899 (2013)
4. Vanezi, E., et al.: GDPR compliance in the design of the INFORM e-Learning platform: a case study. In: Proceedings of the 13th International Conference on Research Challenges in Information Science, Belgium, pp. 1–12 (2019)
5. Pape, S., Serna-Olvera, J., Tesfay, W.: Why open data may threaten your privacy. In: Workshop on Privacy and Inference, September 2015
6. Moreau, L., Groth, P.: Provenance: An Introduction to PROV. Synthesis Lectures on the Semantic Web: Theory and Technology, vol. 3(4), pp. 1–129 (2013)
7. Wang, J., Crawl, D., Purawat, S., Nguyen, M., Altintas, I.: Big data provenance: challenges, state of the art and opportunities. In: Proceedings of the IEEE International Conference on Big Data, pp. 2509–2516 (2015)
8. Groth, P., Miles, S., Moreau, L.: PReServ: provenance recording for services. In: Proceedings of the UK OST e-Science 2nd All Hands Meeting, Nottingham, UK, September 2005
9. Todd, G.J., Karvounarakis, G., Ives, Z.G., Tannen, V.: Provenance in ORCHESTRA. IEEE Data Eng. Bull. **33**, 9–16 (2010)
10. Graham, K., et al.: PROV-AQ: Provenance Access and Query (2012)
11. SOCRATA Open Data: https://dev.socrata.com
12. CKAN Documentation: https://docs.ckan.org
13. Open Government Data Germany: https://daten.berlin.de
14. US Government's Open Data: https://www.data.gov
15. General Portal of the European Union: https://www.europeandataportal.eu/

16. Australia Government Portal: https://data.gov.au
17. Canada Government Portal: http://open.canada.ca
18. Nakamoto, S.: Bitcoin: a peer-to-peer electronic cash system (2008)
19. Wood, G.:Ethereum: a secure decentralised generalised transaction ledger. Ethereum project yellow paper, vol. 151, pp. 1–32 (2014)
20. Salah, K., Rehman, M.H.U., Nizamuddin, N., Al-Fuqaha, A.: Blockchain for AI: review and open research challenges. IEEE Access **7**, 10127–10149 (2019)
21. Daraghmi, E., Daraghmi, Y., Yuan, S.: MedChain: a design of blockchain-based system for medical records access and permissions management. IEEE Access **7**, 164595–164613 (2019)
22. Sifah, E.B., Xia, H., Cobblah, C.N.A., Xia, Q., Gao, J., Du, X.: BEMPAS: a decentralized employee performance assessment system based on blockchain for smart city governance. IEEE Access **8**, 99528–99539 (2020)
23. Alladi, T., Chamola, V., Parizi, R.M., Choo, K.R.: Blockchain applications for industry 4.0 and industrial IoT: a review. IEEE Access **7**, 176935–176951 (2019)
24. Androulaki, E., et al.: Hyperledger fabric: a distributed operating system for permissioned blockchains. In: Proceedings of the 13th EuroSys Conference (2018)
25. Ramachandran, A., Kantarcioglu, M.: Using blockchain and smart contracts for secure data provenance management. arXiv:1709.10000 (2017)
26. Liang, X., Shetty, S., Tosh, D., Kamhoua, C., Kwiat, K., Njilla, L.: ProvChain: a blockchain-based data provenance architecture in cloud environment with enhanced privacy and availability. In: Proceedings of the 17th International Symposium on Cluster, Cloud and Grid Computing, pp. 468–477 (2017)
27. Hasan, H.R., Salah, K.: Combating deepfake videos using blockchain and smart contracts. IEEE Access **7**, 41596–41606 (2019)
28. Demichev, A., Kryukov, A., Prikhodko, N.: The approach to managing provenance metadata and data access rights in distributed storage using the hyperledger blockchain platform. In: ISPRAS, Russia (2018)
29. Rouhani, S., Butterworth, L., Simmons, A.D., Humphery, D.G., Deters, R.: MediChainTM: a secure decentralized medical data asset management system. In: Proceedings of the iThings, GreenCom, CPSCom, and SmartData, Canada, pp. 1533–1538 (2018)
30. Thi, Q.N.T., Si, T.T., Dang, T.K.: Fine grained attribute based access control model for privacy protection. In: Dang, T.K., Wagner, R., Küng, J., Thoai, N., Takizawa, M., Neuhold, E. (eds.) FDSE 2016. LNCS, vol. 10018, pp. 305–316. Springer, Cham (2016). https://doi.org/10.1007/978-3-319-48057-2_21
31. Ha, T., Dang, T.K., Dang, T.T., Truong, T.A., Tuan, N.M.: Differential privacy in deep learning: an overview. In: Proceedings of the 13th International Conference on Advanced Computing and Applications (ACOMP), IEEE CPS, November 2019, Vietnam, pp. 97–102
32. Dang, T.K.: Ensuring correctness, completeness and freshness for outsourced tree-indexed data. Inf. Resour. Manage. J. **21**(1), 59–76 (2008)
33. Dang, T.K.: Security protocols for outsourcing database services. Inf. Secur. Int. J. **18**, 85–108 (2006)

Industry 4.0 and Smart City: Data Analytics and Security

OAK: Ontology-Based Knowledge Map
Model for Digital Agriculture

Quoc Hung Ngo$^{(\boxtimes)}$, Tahar Kechadi, and Nhien-An Le-Khac

School of Computer Science, College of Science,
University College Dublin, Belfield, Dublin 4, Ireland
hung.ngo@ucdconnect.ie, {tahar.kechadi,an.lekhac}@ucd.ie

Abstract. Nowadays, a huge amount of knowledge has been amassed in digital agriculture. This knowledge and know-how information are collected from various sources, hence the question is how to organise this knowledge so that it can be efficiently exploited. Although this knowledge about agriculture practices can be represented using ontology, rule-based expert systems, or knowledge model built from data mining processes, the scalability still remains an open issue. In this study, we propose a knowledge representation model, called an ontology-based knowledge map, which can collect knowledge from different sources, store it, and exploit either directly by stakeholders or as an input to the knowledge discovery process (Data Mining). The proposed model consists of two stages, 1) build an ontology as a knowledge base for a specific domain and data mining concepts, and 2) build the ontology-based knowledge map model for representing and storing the knowledge mined on the crop datasets. A framework of the proposed model has been implemented in agriculture domain. It is an efficient and scalable model, and it can be used as knowledge repository a digital agriculture.

Keywords: Ontology · Knowledge map · Knowledge management · Digital agriculture

1 Introduction

The knowledge from crop studies is turned into profitable decisions in digital farming only when it is efficiently managed. Farming knowledge can be created by the experience of farmers, by research studies in agronomy, or by analyses of data that has been collected for a number of years. In particular, the knowledge discovery in agricultural data is one of the most diverse, large, and dynamic in digital farming.

Moreover, one of the key challenges of knowledge management is the representation of the mined results, which are not consistent among different sources of knowledge. For example, consider two results that were obtained from two data mining studies, with the overall goal of predicting farming conditions of high crop yield of winter wheat. The concept *high crop yield* used in the two

© Springer Nature Switzerland AG 2020
T. K. Dang et al. (Eds.): FDSE 2020, LNCS 12466, pp. 245–259, 2020.
https://doi.org/10.1007/978-3-030-63924-2_14

studies can be different, depending on the way authors define the range of *high crop yield*. Therefore, the overall insight may not be consistent to be used in the same system or to compare those results. This issue can also occur with input attributes used by different predictive models. In addition, the farming knowledge represented using an ontology is static and it is difficult to generalise to different regions, which have different farming conditions. The knowledge represented as rules in expert systems does not scale well and there is no way to refine the rules and it is also very difficult to check the coherence of all rules within a system. To summarise, while the knowledge mined from data mining processes is dynamic and flexible but its representation differs from one process to another. Some knowledge representation models are rules oriented while others are stored as vectors or trained models.

In this paper, we propose a scalable ontology-based knowledge map (OAK) model for representing, storing, managing and retrieving knowledge of any type. The main contribution of the model is to support data scientists and agronomists in managing and using mined knowledge for decision making with ease. The next section gives an overview of knowledge concepts and how to create knowledge in the agriculture domain. Section 3 describes in details the proposed OAK model, which includes definitions, architecture and its three main modules. Section 4 provides various experiments on the knowledge management system, which is based on OAK model. Finally, we conclude and give some future directions in Sect. 5.

2   Related Work

According to the Collins dictionary[1], *knowledge* is an information and understanding about a subject, which a person has, or which all people have, while the Cambridge dictionary defines the knowledge as an information and understanding that you have in your mind. *Knowledge Map* (KMap) is defined as a spacial representation of information [22]. Knowledge maps are used extensively in enterprises to describe how, what or where to find useful knowledge within the enterprise organisations [6]. *Knowledge graph* (KG) is a set of pairs of knowledge (V, E), where V is a set of nodes mapped to pieces of knowledge in the domain and E is a set of knowledge relations between two nodes. *Ontology* is a formal specification of the vocabulary to be used in specifying knowledge and the purpose of the ontology is to provide a uniform text-based knowledge representation, which is comprehensible by either human or machines [8]. The difference between these three concepts (KMap, KG, and ontology) is that ontology is used for formal and static knowledge, while KMaps and KG are used for handling more dynamic knowledge types, such as enterprise KMaps or Google Knowledge Graph[2].

---

[1] https://www.collinsdictionary.com/dictionary/english/knowledge.
[2] https://developers.google.com/knowledge-graph.

In the following, discuss some relevant knowledge discovery processes in agriculture, particularly data mining, and review the knowledge representation and management gaps as a consequence of proliferation of big data analytics.

2.1   Knowledge Discovery in Agriculture

There are many ways in creating knowledge in any specific domain. The first method is to acquire knowledge manually by experts. The result of this approach is knowledge-base (known as taxonomy or ontology), or rule-based system (known as expert systems). Another way is to acquire knowledge automatically via a knowledge discovery process from structured or unstructured data. However, knowledge graphs are normally built from Wikipedia, Freebase, DBpedia and agriculture websites, such as, the AgriKG [4] and Cn-MAKG [5] systems.

During the last decade, the advances in digital agriculture have led to numerous significant studies on the application of data mining process to agricultural datasets. These datasets include including soil, weather, crop yield, and disease prediction. Moreover, the scope of research for data mining in agriculture is also diverse, including data construction as well as forecasting models. In this context, there are several computational soil studies, such as building datasets of soil profiles [21], monitoring soil characteristics under effects of other factors and crop yield [3], or using soil characteristics to predict other soil characteristics [23]. Another common application of knowledge mining in agriculture is crop yield prediction (e.g., predicting yield or wheat yield based on soil attributes, weather factors, and management factors [1,12,18]). Finally, the third common application of knowledge mining is the disease prediction or the protection plan (e.g., detecting nitrogen stress in early crop growth stage of corn fields [14], or detecting and classifying sugar beet diseases [7], etc.).

Data mining has four main categories of techniques; clustering, classification, regression, and association rule. To date, only classification and regression are widely used in digital agriculture. Usually, classification approaches are used to detect the disease (mostly based on the images processing techniques [7]), or to classify crop yield (as low, medium or high yield). Regression techniques are mainly used to predict crop yields based on different input attributes [1,3]. Although the number of knowledge model types is not large, input and output attributes for forecasting models are totally different and diverse, and the number of agricultural attributes is very large. In addition, the idea of using KMaps for handling mined knowledge has been proposed in [9] and [10], however, it only proposed as a prototype for handling rules in data mining result. Therefore, the challenge of these knowledge types and KMaps approach for these knowledge types is that most of them are stored as pre-trained models or as computer software and their final results are mostly published as scientific papers or reports.

2.2   Methodology for Building Knowledge Map

There are many approaches for building knowledge maps (KMap). Most of these methodologies were dedicated to enterprise KMaps while several others are used to build specific domain of KMaps. For example, Bargent [2] proposed an 11-step methodology for building an enterprise KMap, which is a common strategy of software development life-cycle. Similarly, Kim et al. [8] proposed a 6-step methodology for capturing and representing organisational KMaps with knowledge profiles and business processes, while Pei et al. [19] introduced a 7-step methodology to build an enterprise KMap for matrix organisations, including setting up a development team, analysis knowledge resources, definition of the business knowledge domain boundaries, determination of the structure and relationship for the KMap, selection of the development tools, identification of locations of knowledge items and drawing the initial KMap, and finally evaluation and updates of KMap.

Moreover, several studies have used ontology for building their knowledge maps. Lecocq [11] developed a 4-phase methodology with planning, collecting, mapping and validating phases based on an ontology for visually representing knowledge assets. In another study, Mansingh et al. [15] introduced a 3-stage methodology for building KMaps of medical-care processes; including creation of an ontology from the medical cases, creation of the process map with flowcharts and petri nets, and extraction of KMaps from instances of different medical-care processes (represented as medical files) by using vocabulary and relationships in that ontology. The method was tested in a healthcare organisation and was found to be suitable to build a KMap, which combines conceptual and process maps for medical-care processes.

To summarise, existing methodologies for building KMaps can be divided into two typical types; methods for building enterprise KMaps [2,8,13,19] and methods for building conceptual KMaps [11,15]. For building enterprise KMaps, although methodologies have different number of steps, they use basic stages: (1) identify the scope, domain of KMap and the develop team, (2) identify knowledge resources or materials, (3) identify knowledge in each knowledge item, (4) extract and build KMap, (5) evaluate, use, and update the KMap. For building conceptual KMaps or hybrid with conceptual maps, existing methodologies also have the same basic stages, however, one step in identifying knowledge resources or materials is to use an ontology as a conceptual framework for building KMap in subsequent stages. This step aims to locate the knowledge items in the final KMaps.

3   Ontology-Based Knowledge Map Model

We propose an ontology-base knowledge map model for representing knowledge obtained from learning processes applied to agricultural data, from research articles, or from experts in the domain. Moreover, the model allows knowledge handling and exploitation in a flexible and scalable way. As illuminated in an example in Fig. 1, the knowledge representation shows the results of a clustering model with 5 input attributes (Soil pH, seed rate, nitrogen, wheat name, and mean yield).

To implement the model and validate it experimentally, the system is designed and developed in two major phases: during the first phase we build

an agriculture ontology and in the second phase we use the ontology vocabulary along with initial data schema (as in the data warehouse) to model the
knowledge. Before going into the details, we need to define the key concepts
behind this model, which are *knowledge representation, ontology, knowledge map
model, concept, transformation, instance, state, relation, lexicon* and *hierarchy*.

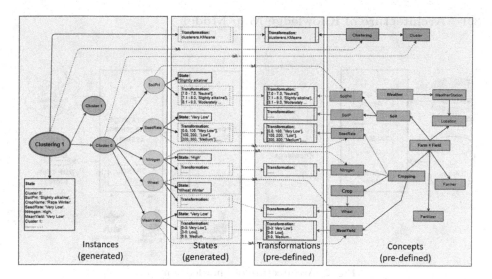

Fig. 1. Approach for knowledge map model for clustering.

Definition 1. *A Knowledge representation* $\mathbb{K}$ *is defined by a set of four ele-
ments, containing instances* $\mathbb{I}$, *transformations* $\mathbb{T}$, *states* $\mathbb{S}$, *and relations* $\mathbb{R}$:

$$\mathbb{K} = (\mathbb{I}, \mathbb{T}, \mathbb{S}, \mathbb{R}) \tag{1}$$

Definition 2. *An Ontology* $\mathbb{O}$ *is defined by a set of three elements, containing
concepts* $\mathbb{C}$, *transformations* $\mathbb{T}$, *and relations* $\mathbb{R}$:

$$\mathbb{O} = (\mathbb{C}, \mathbb{T}, \mathbb{R}) \tag{2}$$

Definition 3. *A Knowledge Map Model* $\mathbb{KM}$ *is defined by a set containing five
elements,* $\mathbb{C}$, $\mathbb{I}$, $\mathbb{T}$, $\mathbb{S}$, *and* $\mathbb{R}$, *which are corresponding sets of concept c, instance
i, transformation t, state t and relation r.*

$$\mathbb{KM} = (\mathbb{C}, \mathbb{I}, \mathbb{T}, \mathbb{S}, \mathbb{R}) \tag{3}$$

Where $\mathbb{C}$ is a set of concepts $\{c\}$, and represents a set of entities or attributes
of an entity within a domain and four data mining categories of results (clustering, classification, regression, and association rule).

$\mathbb{T}$ is a set of transformations $\{t\}$, and represents a set of functions $f(x)$ to
transform the value of entities x from value range $\mathbb{R}_x$ to value range $\mathbb{R}_y$.

$\mathbb{I}$ is a set of instances $\{i\}$, and represents a set of entities.

$\mathbb{S}$ is a set of states $\{s\}$, and represents a set of real attributes of instances $\{i\}$ when applying transformation $\{t\}$.

$\mathbb{R}$ is a set of relations r, and represents a set of relationships r between concept c_1 and concept c_2.

3.1   Architecture of Knowledge Map Model

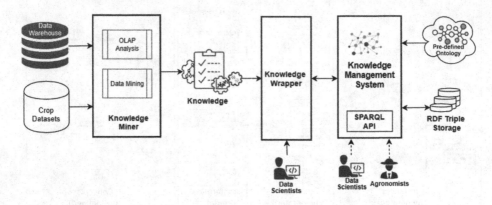

Fig. 2. Architecture of knowledge map

As illustrated in Fig. 2, the architecture of OAK consists of the following key components: (i) Knowledge Miner, (ii) Knowledge Wrapper and (iii) Knowledge Management System.

- **Knowledge Miner** is a key component, which is used to extract knowledge from data; this component can be a *Data Mining* or an *OLAP Analysis* module.
  - **Data Mining** refers to mining tools and techniques, which are used in analyzing datasets from various dimensions and perspectives, finding hidden knowledge and summarizing the identified relationships. These techniques are classification, clustering, regression, association rules.
  - **OLAP Analysis** refers to mining processes used in analyzing different dimensions of multidimensional data, which is collected from multiple data sources and stored in data warehouses.
- **Knowledge Wrapper** is the main module to transform the knowledge from the output of the *Knowledge Miner* module to the *Knowledge Management System* module to store them. This module collects the mining result, identify the type of the data mining task, data mining algorithms, list of agriculture concepts, correlative transformation functions, and states. Then, it generates the KMap representation before converting it into RDF turtles and import into the *Knowledge Management System*.

- **Knowledge Management System** is a graph database server, which supports RDF triple storage and SPARQL protocol for the queries. This module receives the domain knowledge from the pre-defined ontology, the mined knowledge representations from the *Knowledge Wrapper* module, and then store in the RDF Triple Storage as a set of RDF turtles.

In general, the proposed OAK model includes two knowledge layers. The first layer is the background knowledge about agriculture. This layer is defined as a core MKap and it is built from a pre-defined agricultural ontology (mainly cropping knowledge in this project). This layer defines most of concepts (agricultural entities related to crop) in the KMaps and common relations between them. The second layer includes knowledge representations of data mining results, which are mined from cropping datasets by data mining algorithms (included in the Knowledge Miner module). These knowledge representations are integrated into the Knowledge Management System by the Knowledge Wrapper module.

3.2 Agriculture Ontology

In general, most ontologies describe classes (concepts), instances, attributes, and relations. Moreover, some ontologies also include restrictions, rules, axioms, and function terms. In our case, as a formal presentation of KMaps, we propose an ontology with the following components:

- **Concepts**: Concepts in the ontology include concepts in agriculture and concepts for representing four main tasks of data mining. For example, agriculture concepts have field, farmer, crop, organization, location, product, while data mining concepts have clustering, classification, regression, and association rule.
- **Transformations**: They are pre-defined transformation functions of agriculture concepts and existing data mining techniques for four main tasks of data mining.
- **Relations**: ways in which concepts (and then instances) can be related to others. They are defined as the $\mathbb{R}$ set in definitions.

At this stage, we propose an agricultural ontology AgriOnt for the purpose of using it in the OAK model. The agricultural ontology contains 4 sub-domains: agriculture, Internet-of-Thing (IoT), geographical, and the business sub-domain (Fig. 3). In addition, the ontology is also added concepts in data mining domain as shown in Fig. 4. These concepts and relations will be knowledge frameworks to transform mined knowledge from data mining to knowledge representations and import them into the knowledge maps.

After building a knowledge hierarchy, the ontology not only provides an overview of the agriculture domain but also describes agricultural concepts, and life cycles between seeds, plants, harvesting, transportation, and consumption. It also gives the relationships between agricultural concepts and related concepts, such as weather, soil conditions, fertilizers, farm descriptions. In addition, this ontology also includes data mining concepts, such as classification, clustering,

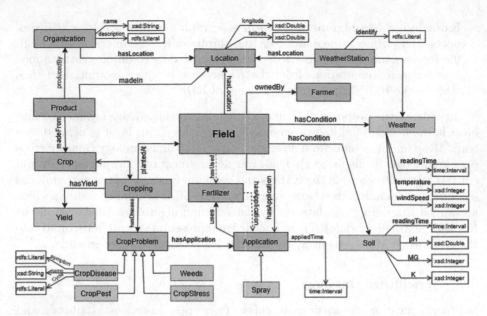

Fig. 3. An overview of agricultural ontology architecture

Table 1. AgriOnt's ontology metrics

Figure	Core	With transformations	With geo-data
Axiom	7,947	10,484	13,917
Logical axiom count	3,782	5,194	7,892
Declaration axioms	1,796	2,218	2,460
Class count	361	361	361
Object property count	90	90	90
Data property count	156	156	156
Individual count	1,183	1,605	1,847

regression, and association rule. These concepts combined with agricultural concepts that are used to represent mined knowledge. In fact, this ontology has 361 classes and over 7,947 axioms related to agriculture (as shown in Table 1, and partly presented in [16]). As result, the AgriOnt ontology can be used as the core ontology to build the knowledge maps for agriculture. Moreover, this ontology with agricultural hierarchy can help to integrate available resources to build larger and more precise knowledge maps in agriculture domain.

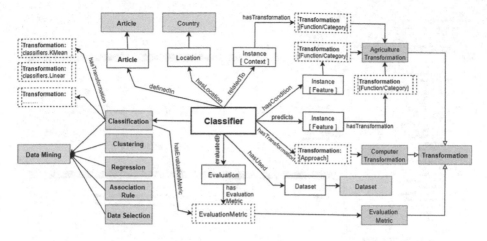

Fig. 4. Main data mining concepts in the ontology.

3.3 Knowledge Management System

The knowledge consumption is handled in the Knowledge Wrapper module. This wrapper transforms the mined knowledge to the Knowledge Maps layer. The Knowledge Maps layer stores and indexes RDF-based data. The Knowledge Maps layer provides the Data Access interfaces for query processing SPARQL engine. The SPARQL engine enables the application developers to query data via a SPARQL Endpoint or a SPARQL-based application in the Application layer respectively. The SPARQL Endpoint serves one-shot queries using an extension of SPARQL 1.1 query language.

In our approach, we use **Apache Jena**[3] for SPARQL Engine and **Fuseki**[4] for SPARQL Endpoint. Both Apache Jena and Fuseki are free and open source. Fuseki is an HTTP interface to RDF data and it supports SPARQL for querying and updating data.

3.4 Knowledge Wrapper

The procedure for mapping mined knowledge into a knowledge representation in the ontology-based knowledge map is defined in the *Knowledge Wrapper* module. The *Knowledge Wrapper* module is the main module to transform the mined knowledge into a knowledge representation k (as defined by $k = (\{i\}, \{t\}, \{s\}, \{r\})$ in *Definition* 1, Sect. 3) before converting into RDF tubles and import them in to the RDF Triple storage. This module has six steps (Fig. 6):

- **Step 1, Identify model:** Select data mining pattern based on the data mining algorithm and generate the data mining instances (such as classification, clustering, clustering, and association rule instances for the corresponding

---

[3] https://jena.apache.org/index.html.
[4] https://jena.apache.org/documentation/fuseki2/.

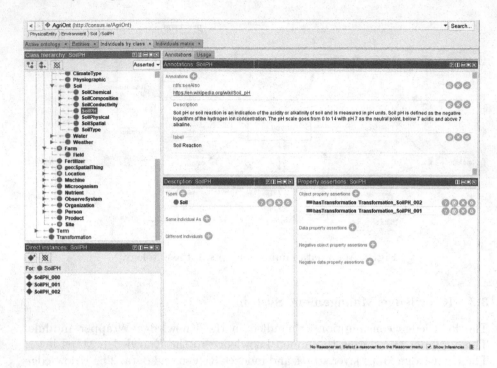

Fig. 5. A screenshot of agricultural ontology on protege

data mining tasks) and link to the data mining algorithm as the transformation objects of the data mining instances.

- **Step 2, Identify concepts**: Identify agricultural concepts in mining results and locate them in the ontology. Basically, these concepts occur in the mined results as input features and predicting features, for example, SoilPH, SeedRate, Nitrogen, Wheat, MeanYield.
- **Step 3, Generate instances**: Generate agricultural instances of each located concept and link them to data mining instances (in **Step 1**) based on the framework of data mining tasks.
- **Step 4, Identify transformations**: Identify transformations of each concept in the mining results, locate them in the ontology part of the KMap, then link them to the agricultural instances (in **Step 3**).
- **Step 5, Generate states**: Identify states of each concept in the mining results, generate states and link to instances (in **Step 3**) in the knowledge representation.
- **Step 6, Generate turtles**: Transform the knowledge representation into RDF turtles and import them into the RDF triple storage.

In fact, the set of instances $\{i\}$ is created in Step 1 and Step 3, while the set of transformations $\{i\}$ is created in Step 1 and Step 4. The set of states $\{s\}$ is generated in Step 5, however, not all knowledge representations have sets of states. For example, in the model to predict crop yield, the input values only occur when the model is executed. Therefore, the set of states for this knowledge representation is nearly none. Finally, set of relations $\{i\}$ is based on relation *isA, hasTransformation, hasState, hasCondition,* and *predicts.*

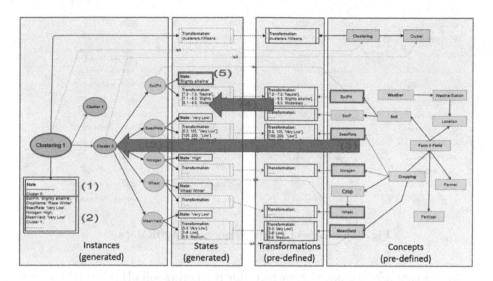

Fig. 6. Generating knowledge representation the ontology.

4 Experimental Results

Firstly, we have set up a SPARQL Server as a knowledge management system (cf. Sect. 3.3) with Apache Jena and Fuseki library. The system has also created a new knowledge map with a pre-defined ontology (as described in Sect. 3.2) and several samples of knowledge representations, which are created manually by Protege tool (as shown in Fig. 5). The SPARQL Endpoint can be accessed at http://localhost:3030/manage.html on local machine for query.

Basically, SPARQL queries can be run on the Endpoint with a web interface. Figure 7 shows the results for the query "What are conditions and the target attribute of the knowledge model *Regressor_004*?". The SPARQL query for this question is shown below:

```
PREFIX AgriOnt:  <http://www.ucd.ie/consus/AgriOnt#>
PREFIX AgriKMap: <http://www.ucd.ie/consus/AgriKMap#>
SELECT ?predicate1 ?object1 ?predicate2 ?object2
WHERE {
    AgriKMap:Regressor_004 ?predicate1 ?object1 .
    ?object1  ?predicate2 ?object2 .
}
```

QUERY RESULTS

Table | Raw Response

Showing 1 to 64 of 64 entries — Search: — Show 100 entries

	predicate1	object1	predicate2	object2
1	rdf:type	AgriOnt:Regressor	rdf:type	owl:Class
2	rdf:type	AgriOnt:Regressor	rdfs:subClassOf	AgriOnt:Regression
3	AgriOnt:definedIn	AgriKMap:Article_004	rdf:type	AgriOnt:Article
4	AgriOnt:definedIn	AgriKMap:Article_004	<http://purl.org/dc/elements/1.1/title>	"Predicting soil pH by using nearest fields."
5	AgriOnt:definedIn	AgriKMap:Article_004	rdfs:seeAlso	"https://link.springer.com/chapter/10.1007/978-3-030-34885-4_40"
6	AgriOnt:hasCondition	AgriKMap:Location_001	rdf:type	AgriOnt:Location
7	AgriOnt:hasCondition	AgriKMap:Location_001	rdf:type	owl:NamedIndividual
8	AgriOnt:hasCondition	AgriKMap:SoilPH_001	rdf:type	AgriOnt:SoilPH
9	AgriOnt:hasCondition	AgriKMap:SoilPH_001	rdf:type	owl:NamedIndividual
10	AgriOnt:hasCondition	AgriKMap:SoilPH_001	AgriOnt:isConditionOf	AgriKMap:Regressor_004
11	AgriOnt:hasCondition	AgriKMap:SoilPH_001	AgriOnt:hasTransformation	AgriOnt:Transformation_SoilPH_Min
12	AgriOnt:hasCondition	AgriKMap:SoilPH_002	rdf:type	AgriOnt:SoilPH
13	AgriOnt:hasCondition	AgriKMap:SoilPH_002	rdf:type	owl:NamedIndividual
14	AgriOnt:hasCondition	AgriKMap:SoilPH_002	AgriOnt:isConditionOf	AgriKMap:Regressor_004
15	AgriOnt:hasCondition	AgriKMap:SoilPH_002	AgriOnt:hasTransformation	AgriOnt:Transformation_SoilPH_Max

Fig. 7. Example of SPARQL query on AgriKMaps.

In this example, the mined knowledge for predicting soil pH [17] can be represented as a knowledge representation *Regressor*_004 in the system. Inputs of the model are pH information and the output of the model is also the pH value (concept *SoilPH*), however, they used different transformations. Specifically, input features are calculated as pH_{min}, pH_{max}, and pH_{avg} (three different transformations of SoilPH in the system) of nearest neighbour fields, while the output feature is predicted as the original pH value of the field (these conditions are defined as Soil_001, Soil_002, Soil_003 and Soil_000 instance, as shown in Fig. 7).

In addition, the knowledge management system based on the OAK model can be benefit for both data scientists and agronomists. Data scientists can have queries about potential transformations of agriculture attribute c_x (for example, *Soil pH* or *Temperature*), and these queries can be implemented by a SPARQL query as below:

```
PREFIX AgriOnt:  <http://www.ucd.ie/consus/AgriOnt#>
PREFIX AgriKMap: <http://www.ucd.ie/consus/AgriKMap#>
SELECT ?subject ?predicate ?object
WHERE {
    ?subject AgriOnt:transformationOf AgriOnt:SoilPH .
    ?subject ?predicate ?object
}
```

For agronomists and also farmers, they can have queries about potential knowledge models or attributes to predict an attribute, such as *crop yield*. The SPARQL query returns all potential knowledge models that are used to predict *CropYield* as below:

```
PREFIX rdf: <http://www.w3.org/1999/02/22-rdf-syntax-ns#>
PREFIX AgriOnt:  <http://www.ucd.ie/consus/AgriOnt#>
PREFIX AgriKMap: <http://www.ucd.ie/consus/AgriKMap#>
SELECT ?subject ?predicate ?object
WHERE {
    ?subject ?predicate ?object .
    ?subject AgriOnt:predicts ?object2 .
    ?object2  rdf:type AgriOnt:CropYield .
}
```

Similarly, agronomists also can have queries for a specific state during farming, such as how to get a *high crop yield* or how to identify the *Leaf brown spot disease*. For example, the below query returns a knowledge representation *Classifier_016*, which is study of Santanu Phadikar [20] for detecting 4 rices diseases, including Leaf brown spot, Rice blast, Sheath rot, and Bacterial blight. In which, Sheath rot is one of four predicting states of the model. The query also provides all information related to input attributes, prediction method and evaluation information (Fig. 8).

```
PREFIX rdf: <http://www.w3.org/1999/02/22-rdf-syntax-ns#>
PREFIX AgriOnt:  <http://www.ucd.ie/consus/AgriOnt#>
PREFIX AgriKMap: <http://www.ucd.ie/consus/AgriKMap#>
SELECT ?subject1 ?predicate2 ?object2
WHERE {
    ?subject1  ?predicate1 ?object1 .
    ?object1   AgriOnt:hasState   AgriOnt:SheathRot .
?subject1  ?predicate2 ?object2 .
}
LIMIT 100
```

QUERY RESULTS

Table | Raw Response

Showing 1 to 11 of 11 entries

Search: Show 100 entries

	subject1	predicate2	object2
1	AgriKMap:Classifier_016	rdf:type	AgriOnt:Classifier
2	AgriKMap:Classifier_016	rdf:type	owl:NamedIndividual
3	AgriKMap:Classifier_016	AgriOnt:definedIn	AgriKMap:Article_016
4	AgriKMap:Classifier_016	AgriOnt:evaluatedBy	AgriOnt:Evaluation_016
5	AgriKMap:Classifier_016	AgriOnt:hasCondition	AgriKMap:CropImagery_001
6	AgriKMap:Classifier_016	AgriOnt:hasCondition	AgriKMap:CropImagery_002
7	AgriKMap:Classifier_016	AgriOnt:hasCondition	AgriKMap:CropImagery_003
8	AgriKMap:Classifier_016	rdfs:isDefinedBy	"Phadikar, Santanu, Jaya Sil, and Asit Kumar Das. "Rice diseases classification using feature selection and rule generation techniques." Computers and electronics in agriculture 90 (2013): 76-85."
9	AgriKMap:Classifier_016	AgriOnt:hasTransformation	AgriOnt:Transformation_Classifier_RuleGeneration
10	AgriKMap:Classifier_016	AgriOnt:predicts	AgriKMap:RiceDisease_016
11	AgriKMap:Classifier_016	AgriOnt:relatedTo	AgriOnt:Rice

Showing 1 to 11 of 11 entries

Fig. 8. Returns of SPARQL query for Sheath rot disease

5   Conclusion

In this paper, we present an architecture for the OAK - an ontology-based knowledge map model to represent mined knowledge from data mining tasks in digital agriculture. The architecture includes Knowledge Miner, Knowledge Wrapper, Knowledge Management modules based on an pre-defined ontology. We have also built an agricultural ontology to provide the domain knowledge in agriculture and a knowledge management system to store knowledge representations and support the knowledge retrieval efficiently.

With the proposed ontology-based knowledge map model, the knowledge management system based on this model is a promised architecture for handling mined knowledge in agriculture as well as other domains. As result, we plan to import more knowledge items in the digital agriculture domain into the knowledge management system for retrieval. Moreover, the knowledge management system also supports a knowledge browser function as a further method to access knowledge for both data scientists and agronomists.

Acknowledgment. This work is part of CONSUS and is supported by the SFI Strategic Partnerships Programme (16/SPP/3296) and is co-funded by Origin Enterprises Plc.

References

1. Aggelopoulou, A.D., Bochtis, D., Fountas, S., Swain, K.C., Gemtos, T.A., Nanos, G.D.: Yield prediction in apple orchards based on image processing. Precis. Agric. **12**(3), 448–456 (2011)
2. Bargent, J.: 11 Steps to Building a Knowledge Map (2002). www.providersedge. com/docs/km_articles/11_Steps_to_Building_a_K_Map.pdf
3. Bishop, T.F.A., McBratney, A.B.: A comparison of prediction methods for the creation of field-extent soil property maps. Geoderma **103**(1–2), 149–160 (2001)
4. Chen, Y., Kuang, J., Cheng, D., Zheng, J., Gao, M., Zhou, A.: AgriKG: an agricultural knowledge graph and its applications. In: Li, G., Yang, J., Gama, J., Natwichai, J., Tong, Y. (eds.) DASFAA 2019. LNCS, vol. 11448, pp. 533–537. Springer, Cham (2019). https://doi.org/10.1007/978-3-030-18590-9_81
5. Chenglin, Q., Qing, S., Pengzhou, Z., Hui, Y.: Cn-MAKG: China meteorology and agriculture knowledge graph construction based on semi-structured data. In: 2018 IEEE/ACIS 17th International Conference on Computer and Information Science (ICIS), pp. 692–696. IEEE (2018)
6. Eppler, M.J.: A comparison between concept maps, mind maps, conceptual diagrams, and visual metaphors as complementary tools for knowledge construction and sharing. Inf. Vis. **5**(3), 202–210 (2006)
7. Karimi, Y., Prasher, S.O., Patel, R.M., Kim, S.H.: Application of support vector machine technology for weed and nitrogen stress detection in corn. Comput. Electron. Agric. **51**(1–2), 99–109 (2006)
8. Kim, S., Suh, E., Hwang, H.: Building the knowledge map: an industrial case study. J. Knowl. Manag. **7**(2), 34–45 (2003)

9. Le-Khac, N.-A., Aouad, L.M., Kechadi, M.-T.: Knowledge map: toward a new approach supporting the knowledge management in distributed data mining. In: Third International Conference on Autonomic and Autonomous Systems (ICAS 2007), p. 67. IEEE (2007)
10. Le-Khac, N.-A., Kechadi, M.T.: Admire framework: distributed data mining on data-grid platforms. In: International Conference on Software and Data Technologies (ICSOFT 2006), Setubal, Portugal (2006)
11. Lecocq, R., Valcartier, D.: Knowledge mapping: a conceptual model. Quebec: Defense Research and Development Canada-Valcartier. Acedido Dezembro, vol. 21, p. 2011 (2006)
12. Liu, J., Goering, C.E., Tian, L.: A neural network for setting target corn yields. Trans. ASAE **44**(3), 705 (2001)
13. Liu, L., Li, J., Lv, C.: A method for enterprise knowledge map construction based on social classification. Syst. Res. Behav. Sci. Off. J. Int. Fed. Syst. Res. **26**(2), 143–153 (2009)
14. Maltas, A., Charles, R., Jeangros, B., Sinaj, S.: Effect of organic fertilizers and reduced-tillage on soil properties, crop nitrogen response and crop yield: results of a 12-year experiment in Changins, Switzerland. Soil Tillage Res. **126**, 11–18 (2013)
15. Mansingh, G., Osei-Bryson, K.-M., Reichgelt, H.: Building ontology-based knowledge maps to assist knowledge process outsourcing decisions. Knowl. Manag. Res. Pract. **7**(1), 37–51 (2009)
16. Ngo, Q.H., Le-Khac, N.-A., Kechadi, T.: Ontology based approach for precision agriculture. In: Kaenampornpan, M., Malaka, R., Nguyen, D.D., Schwind, N. (eds.) MIWAI 2018. LNCS (LNAI), vol. 11248, pp. 175–186. Springer, Cham (2018). https://doi.org/10.1007/978-3-030-03014-8_15
17. Ngo, Q.H., Le-Khac, N.-A., Kechadi, T.: Predicting soil pH by using nearest fields. In: Bramer, M., Petridis, M. (eds.) SGAI 2019. LNCS (LNAI), vol. 11927, pp. 480–486. Springer, Cham (2019). https://doi.org/10.1007/978-3-030-34885-4_40
18. Pantazi, X.E., Moshou, D., Alexandridis, T., Whetton, R.L., Mouazen, A.M.: Wheat yield prediction using machine learning and advanced sensing techniques. Comput. Electron. Agric. **121**, 57–65 (2016)
19. Pei, X., Wang, C.: A study on the construction of knowledge map in matrix organizations. In: 2009 International Conference on Management and Service Science (2009)
20. Das, A.K., Phadikar, S., Sil, J.: Rice diseases classification using feature selection and rule generation techniques. Comput. Electron. Agric. **90**, 76–85 (2013)
21. Shangguan, W., et al.: A China data set of soil properties for land surface modeling. J. Adv. Model. Earth Syst. **5**(2), 212–224 (2013)
22. Vail, E.F.: Knowledge mapping: getting started with knowledge management. Inf. Syst. Manag. **16**, 10–23 (1999)
23. Wang, F., Yang, S., Yang, W., Yang, X., Jianli, D.: Comparison of machine learning algorithms for soil salinity predictions in three dryland oases located in Xinjiang Uyghur Autonomous Region (XJUAR) of China. Eur. J. Remote. Sens. **52**(1), 256–276 (2019)

A Novel Approach to Diagnose ADHD Using Virtual Reality

Seung Ho Ryu[1]($\boxtimes$) , Soohwan Oh[2], Sangah Lee[3],
and Tai-Myoung Chung[1]($\boxtimes$)

[1] Department of Computer Science and Engineering, Sungkyunkwan University,
Suwon, Gyeonggi-do, Korea
{shryu321,tmchung}@skku.edu

[2] Department of Psychiatry, Samsung Medical Center, Seoul, Korea
sooho19@gmail.com

[3] School of Art, Sungkyunkwan University, Seoul, Korea
sangahlee9797@gmail.com

Abstract. The main procedures of attention-deficit hyperactivity disorder (ADHD) assessment are interviews with the subject, his or her parents and teacher, observation of the subject, and self-screening questionnaires. However, these traditional medical assessments have serious problems. Interviews may be efficient to an adult subject; however, adolescent subjects are not familiar to express their emotion and mental status precisely. Observation and self-screening questionnaires require a long period of time to be finished, being easily forged by an observer or a subject. To resolve these obstacles, we propose a virtual reality (VR)-based ADHD diagnosis model, in which the VR contents close to reality (such as a school environment) diagnose whether a subject is suspected ADHD or not by various sensors in VR and responses in the VR contents based on the ADHD categorization. We implement the VR contents to diagnose ADHD by using the Unity, which finds major ADHD characteristics by the ADHD categorization based on the Diagnostic and Statistical Manual of mental disorders (DSM-5). We present the medical data engineering and security features in our diagnosis method to protect a patient's information.

Keywords: ADHD · Virtual reality · Digital therapeutics · Medical data · Categorization

1 Introduction

Attention-deficit hyperactivity disorder (ADHD) is an exceedingly wide-spread, combined, and intractable mental disease, interrupting a patient's daily and academic life, and work [10]. In recent years, ADHD prevalence rates have been increased; a 2014 the Centers for Diseases Control and prevention (CDC) report in the United States presented that there had been a steady increase in the

T. K. Dang et al. (Eds.): FDSE 2020, LNCS 12466, pp. 260–272, 2020.
https://doi.org/10.1007/978-3-030-63924-2_15

percent of children between the ages of 4 and 17 diagnosed with ADHD. The report was informed the ADHD prevalence rate was 7.8% in 2003, 9.5% in 2007, and 11% in 2012 [4]. In 2016, the National Survey of Children's Health (NSCH) found that 9.4% (6.1 million) of the children in the United States between the ages of 2 and 17 had ever received an ADHD diagnosis [3]. According to the reports from the CDC and NSCH, ADHD have become one of the major mental diseases, especially being adversely affected to children and adolescents. Children and adolescents who have ADHD symptoms have showed lower reading and math standardized scores, and poor academic results in long-term period [3, 12]. The researches clearly demonstrate that the association between ADHD and negative academic outcomes.

Diagnosis of ADHD relies on screening and evaluation [10]. Screening includes medical examination, intellectual ability test, and ADHD questionnaires that inattention and hyperactivity-impulsivity may cause interferes with functioning or development [10]. One of the evaluation method is an interview with a patient and his or her parents to examine with the symptoms of ADHD [10]. Most ADHD assessments (including questionnaires) consist of many questions that have to be answered, and take several hours to be completed [14].

This paper suggests the ADHD categorization for our model from the DSM-5. A psychiatrist diagnoses whether a patient is ADHD or not by the results of medical examination, ADHD questionnaires tests, and interviews with a patient and his or her parents [10, 14]. However, the distinct criteria are required to diagnose ADHD by VR to minimize observation by a physician, and interviews with a patient. The ADHD categorization analyzes the ADHD symptoms observed through VR contents. We also suggest the medical data engineering process to gather a patient's identified information, and enhanced security features to protect a subject's personal information, medical data analysis, and VR diagnosis results by observing Health Insurance Portability and Accountability Act (HIPAA) rules.

Usual diagnostic procedures including traditional medical examination and interviews are highly based on subjective assessments [7]. Gualtieri et al. indicates that the current ADHD diagnostic approaches are relied on an expert's subjective reports even though it is a clinical diagnosis. By the current diagnostic assessments, psychiatrists are not able to observe a patient's ADHD symptoms in home or school environment. To overcome the weaknesses, we implement a realistic 3D environment by VR. ADHD-VR diagnostic contents suggest close-to-reality environments, and a subject is tested whether he or she has ADHD symptoms by executing instructions and solving the suggested problems. The main contributions of this paper are as follows:

- We propose the ADHD categorization method based on the ADHD diagnosis criteria in the DSM-5.
- We suggest how to diagnose ADHD by the VR contents, which minimizes traditional medical examination and interviews.
- We present the medical data engineering process based on patients' data analysis, and its security features to protect a patient's privacy.

The rest of the paper is organized as follows. Section 2 describes related work. Section 3 introduces the model to construct the VR-based ADHD diagnosis model by the ADHD categorization based on the DSM-5, and its data engineering and security features. Section 4 discusses how to implement the proposed model by using the Unity with the VR contents for diagnosing ADHD. Section 5 justifies the ADHD-VR diagnosis method against attack protection and the diagnosis result scenarios. Section 6 provides the Discussion while Sect. 7 concludes the paper.

2   Related Work

The start of ADHD research was in 1798 by Sir Alexander Crichton, but the contemporary approach to ADHD as defined in the DSM-IV-TR in 2000 [9]. Compared to other psychiatric disorders, ADHD research is relatively new. Despite of the short period of the analysis of ADHD, the fundamental criteria are defined in the DSM-5 released in 2013 [1]. The DSM-5 specifies ADHD presentations in three major groups: both inattention and hyperactivity-impulsivity are happened, only inattention symptoms are happened, and only hyperactivity-impulsivity symptoms are happened [1].

Although extensive ADHD research has been conducted in recent decades, ADHD diagnosis have been concentrated on traditional ways using questionnaires, interviews, and medical examination. The ADHD-VR diagnosis method is the first VR-based diagnosis method for ADHD until the time writing this paper. The ADHD-VR diagnosis method is different from the traditional diagnostic techniques by minimizing a physician's observation and subjective reports.

Based on the guideline above, Akili Interactive Labs, Inc. introduced the game-based digital therapy for treating pediatric ADHD patients in 2016 which is called the "EVO", an ADHD therapeutic game [2]. After this research, EndeavorRx from Akili has become the first digital therapeutics software to relieve and treat ADHD, which are permitted by the U.S. Food and Drug Administration (FDA) in June 2020 [16]. Cognifit provides scientifically validated tasks to precisely measure and train cognitive skills like task-based games [15]. Cognifit is used for not only ADHD patients, but all psychiatric patients who need cognitive training, so it may be not suitable to diagnose ADHD symptoms. EndeavorRx and Cognifit have been operated on a flat display; they only contains 2D graphical effects. However, VR-based 3D graphical contents implemented in our diagnosis method provide more realistic experience and are less disturbed by exterior environmental factors. For this reason, Akili and Cognifit have implemented other approaches in ADHD and other mental diseases, but not become complete solutions for diagnosing ADHD.

Mbonihankuye et al. stated that healthcare data should adhere to HIPAA because it suggests a strict guideline to protect identified medical information from fraud and theft [13]. By respecting HIPAA rules, we protect a subject's sensitive information in our diagnosis method. Therefore, the ADHD-VR diagnosis system suggests not only a novel diagnostic method, but an improved medical data engineering and a security solution to protect a patient's sensitive information. Furthermore, by implementing more VR contents and integrating security features in all the system, the ADHD-VR diagnosis method can be evolved in the future to solve other medical data security issues.

3 Design Principle

3.1 Terminology

The crucial aspect of the ADHD-VR diagnosis method is to implement an authentic 3D environment. This research proposes not only realistic ambience (e.g.. sky, buildings, and a playing field), but a diagnostic plot that detects various ADHD symptoms. There are four key components in the ADHD-VR diagnosis method: **Background**, **Space**, **Content**, and **Scene**.

By implementing a VR environment, we need to designate a site that a patient shows signs of ADHD. A **background** is a large site or location (such as a school) where the diagnosis method is operated in a VR environment. A psychiatrist is not possible to observe a subject's usual reaction in home or a school. A **space** is a smaller place inside of a background: i.e. a classroom, playing field, storage, and gym.

We define a **content** as several diagnostic activities operated in a same space. A **content** is highly similar to a subject's school or daily life that one's ADHD symptoms are usually revealed [6]. Playing basketball in a gym, solving math problems in a classroom, and forming a line in a cafeteria during lunch time are examples of contents.

A **scene** is a specific plot including one or more contents to construct a scenario of the ADHD-VR diagnosis method. In a school, playing in a gym, studying in a classroom, and having lunch with classmates are continuous and time-based tasks in a school. To observe a patient's steady reaction in a background, we have matched several contents to construct one scene.

3.2 ADHD Categorization Criteria

Compared to the traditional ADHD diagnosis methods, the novel ADHD-VR diagnosis system have to detect a subject's ADHD symptoms when he or she works on the contents in VR without or minimizing a physician's observation and medical assessments including the questionnaires. In order to identify the manifestations by our model, we have employed the "ADHD Categorization" which is the guideline and integration of the ADHD symptoms happened in various backgrounds. This helps to recognize diverse ADHD symptoms by the contents and sensors in VR.

The ADHD categorization is mainly based on the ADHD diagnostics in the DSM-5. The DSM-5 suggests 18 detailed persistent patterns of ADHD in three major categories described in the diagnostic criteria part A: inattention, hyperactivity, and impulsivity [1].

The ADHD categorization and ADHD-VR diagnosis are especially based on the criteria A in the DSM-5 which focuses on a persistent pattern of inattention and/or hyperactivity-impulsivity. However, we need more concrete ADHD symptoms and distinct for the VR contents and scenes. For this reason, we have adopted the ADHD Rating Scale-IV (ADHD-RS-IV) and the Korean version of the Child Behavior Checklist for Ages 6–18 (K-CBCL) for supplement [5,11].

The ADHD categorization is composed of three parts: the major divisions, minor divisions, and observation by VR. The major divisions are classified into inattention, hyperactivity, and impulsivity. The minor division is the combination of the characteristics in the observation by VR. The precise categorizations are shown in below (Tables 1, 2 and 3).

Table 1. Inattention in the ADHD categorization.

Minor division	Observed data by VR
General inattention	Chooses a wrong answer to an easy problem
	Skips a suggested problem without an answer
	Exceeds time limit when performs complicated tasks
	Does not react to review requirement
	Turns a subject's eyes to unrelated things frequently
	Correct answer rate decreased by voice problem suggestion
	Turns a subject's eyes away from tasks
	Task performance status is increased by voice feedback
	Chooses "listen a problem again" more than two times.
	Task performance status is decreased when a task requires multiple steps
	Not perform a task for a designated period of time
	Answers randomly if difficult tasks are repeated
	Chooses the exit button if an instruction is long
	Measures the frequency of looking outside during the contents
	Measures a subject's eye movements and reaction velocity when a loud event is evoked outside
Executive function	Does not complete tasks in limited time
	Does not put objects back to the original positions
	Tries to leave a room or play other activities
	Does not complete scheduled tasks
	Does not plan or change an order of scheduled tasks
Working memory	Chooses "replay instructions" because of forgetfulness
	Task performance status is increased if continuous feedback is suggested
	Does not able to pack a subject's personal belongings

Table 2. Hyperactivity in the ADHD categorization.

Minor division	Observed data by VR
Behavioral characteristics	Measures the number of walking in the middle of the contents
	Runs in the hallway although it is forbidden
	Tries to climb trees or higher places when other classmates do the same thing
	Measures the voice volume during the contents
	Measures the time when a subject changes a viewpoint or chooses an exit button after tedious instructions are suggested
	Measures reaction velocity when a subject should be waited until a teacher comes into a classroom
Linguistic characteristics	Measures the frequency of yelling excessively loud voice during the contents

Table 3. Impulsivity in the ADHD categorization.

Minor division	Observed data by VR
Behavioral characteristics	Chooses an exit button when there is a waiting line
	Does not able to wait a subject's turn
	Does not look carefully when a subject crosses a road
	Takes others' belongings forcefully in the contents
Linguistic characteristics	Answers just after a problem is suggested
	Keeps talking when a subject should listen others
	Keep answering a wrong answer although feedback is suggested
	Interrupts a teacher's instruction during the contents

4 Implementation

According to the ADHD categorization, we have implemented the three major segments and their sub-elements in the ADHD-VR diagnosis method. We have constructed the VR contents to detect the ADHD symptoms described in the ADHD categorization using the Unity.

4.1 ADHD-VR Diagnosis Process

The ADHD-VR diagnosis method requires to obtain a subject's personal information to suggest personalized VR contents and difficulty levels. Personal information includes a subject's age, sex, intellectual level, education, and family background. We may not employ all the personal information in this implementation. Personal information is used for providing optimized VR contents for a subject because a patient may have different preferences depending on his or her age, sex, and so on.

After gathering the expected personal information, a subject starts to conduct the ADHD-VR diagnosis contents. A subject wears a Head Mounted

Display (HMD), and handles two controllers (one controller on the left hand and the other on right hand). A HMD shows an authentic 3D VR environment which is necessary for the VR contents, and a headset is integrated on the HMD for playing sound. Two controllers are also essential elements; a subject can move in the VR environment by clicking the buttons on the front, and hold an object by pulling the button on the back. A subject can swing his or her arms or hands by waving two controllers. To detect a HMD and controllers, at least two base stations are required. Base stations should be placed on the top of a room and recognizes the movements of a HMD and controllers. A patient should execute instructions to proceed next contents and scenes, but he or she may give up a current procedure and skip to next contents or scenes. Withdrawing the contents is an important criterion to detect a subject's concentration skill. After a subject completes or gives up the VR diagnosis, then the VR diagnosis draws the result whether a subject is ADHD suspected or not by the VR contents score and a subject's movement which identifies his or her ADHD symptoms based on the ADHD categorization.

Observation by a physician is an optional process to enhance the diagnosis quality of our method. It is not possible to observe all the symptoms of ADHD by VR in the current version, so a psychiatrist observes a subject's behaviors and talk to improve the diagnosis system. However, it does not mean a physician suggest a traditional medical assessment for ADHD; he or she just detects the specific ADHD symptoms not captured by VR.

4.2 ADHD-VR Diagnosis Contents

We set the Unity 2018.4.22f1 version in the PC, Mac & Standalone environment for VR development. We have implemented several VR contents including "Whack-A-Mole," "Baseball Game," and so on. One of the VR contents is "Car Repairing Game." In the car repairing game, a subject should assemble parts into a complete automobile as the suggested order as shown in Fig. 1. A subject must assemble each part in 10 s; the remaining time is shown on the top right side of the VR content. When a patient clicks the start button, then the content is started and the instruction, "Pick an automobile part and assemble at the designated place", is appeared. If a patient is finished to assemble a part (the green one) in the designated time, then he or she proceeds to the next step. If not, the content shows an pop-up window that gives a choice to a subject may re-try the same process or restart the car repairing game.

4.3 Acquiring VR Diagnosis Data

In our current VR diagnosis implementation, a subject's head, left hand, and right hand movement are measured in every one second. In addition, the total score of a VR content, the number of failure in each process, and the number of retry in each process are assessed. We match these sensor and content data with the ADHD categorization to diagnose ADHD. These measured values are in $X = \{X_1, X_2, X_3, ..., X_{n-1}, X_n\}$; for example, X_1 is order remembrance, X_2

Fig. 1. The suggested instruction of the car repairing game.

is the number of assembling correct parts, X_3 is the time of assembling parts, and so on. If the measured values in X matches the observation by VR in each major division, then we define a subject has an ADHD symptoms. The Type I, II, and III symbolizes the ADHD presentations in the DSM-5. The Type I is only inattention symptoms are happened, and the Type II represents only hyperactivity-impulsivity symptoms are happened. The Type III means both inattention and hyperactivity are happened (Fig. 2).

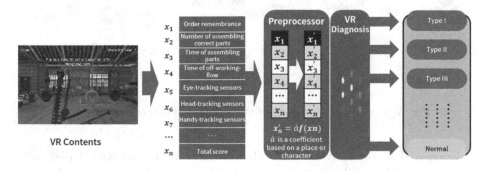

Fig. 2. ADHD diagnosis process by the VR contents.

The preprocessor step gathers the acquired raw data from the VR contents and converts them to analyzable results based on normal children's data.

$$X_{garage,p_1} = \{(x_1, 5), (x_2, 7), (x_3, 12), (x_4, 5)\} \tag{1}$$

$$\overline{X}_{garage,p_1} = \{(x'_1, 0.3), (x'_2, 0.5), (x'_3, 0.9), (x'_4, 0.3)\} \tag{2}$$

$$Y_{garage,p1} = f(\overline{X}) = \{\text{Type II}\} \tag{3}$$

The Eqs. 1, 2, and 3 are examples to show the preprocessing and classification process to get VR diagnosis result. From the VR contents, a physician gets only acquired raw data from VR devices and contents. These data should be compared to the normal data and changed to show the difference between the acquired data and normal standards. Equation 1 shows the original collected data from VR, and Eq. 2 provides the preprocessing result. By comparing preprocessed data with the ADHD categorization, a subject has the type II ADHD symptoms which represents hyperactivity-impulsivity symptoms are happened only.

5   Securing Personal Information

In this section, we describe how the ADHD-VR diagnosis method works and its security features to protect a subject's sensitive health information. Traditional diagnostic methods (such as ADHD questionnaires and interview results) are stored in paper records although a subject's final diagnostic result may be uploaded to electronic medical reports. However, HIPAA Security Rule only protects electronic medical records, not paper medical forms [8] (Fig. 3).

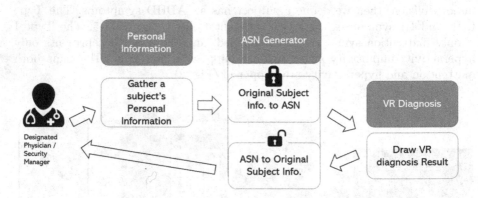

Fig. 3. The ASN architecture of the ADHD-VR diagnosis method.

Compared to the conventional techniques, the novel ADHD-VR diagnosis method assembles a subject's personal data, if required, by a designated physician or security manager. A subject may provide his or her personal information for personalized VR contents; however, this information has to become anonymous not to distinguish a subject. For this reason, we have introduced the Arbitrary Subject Number (ASN). The ASN generates an arbitrary number only used in the ADHD-VR diagnosis method, so a patient's information is unexposed. The ASN generator takes over a patient's personal information, generating an arbitrary number only used in the ADHD-VR diagnosis method.

After the ASN generation, it passes a subject's data to the VR diagnosis to draw a ADHD result. When the VR diagnosis draws out a conclusion, the ASN generator converts ASN to the original subject information, and passes to a designated physician or security manager.

In the VR diagnosis process, a subject's head, left hand, and right hand movement, and total VR contents score data are extracted in every one second. These data also encrypted by SHA-256 after the VR diagnosis step. The encrypted information is directly sent to the ASN after the diagnosis for data protection. The ASN generator decrypts the measured data to the notice that indicates whether a subject is ADHD suspected or not.

Figure 4 shows the prevention of a malicious attack to a patient's personal information by ASN. A designated physician or security manager is the permitted person to insert and modify a subject's personal information to protect a subject's privacy. Figure 4(a) describes the authority access page for a designated physician or security manager. The manager must type in the correct manager ID and password to access a patient's personal information. Figure 4(b) shows that the input page of a subject's personal information. Figure 4(c) shows the personal information gets into the ASN generator converting to randomized information not to distinguish a subject. The post-ASN personal information is not visible to any people because of enhancing security and protecting personal information, but Fig. 4(c) is a visualized example for suggesting the ASN concept.

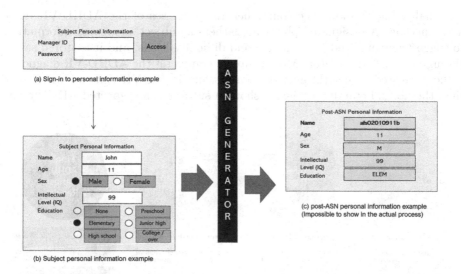

Fig. 4. A patient's personal information attack protection example by the ASN.

The final diagnosis attack prevention procedures are as follows: Fig. 5(a) describes the actual code of the car repairing game to compute the game score. The non-encrypted extracted data which are the results from the VR contents shows in Fig. 5(b). These data are vulnerable to external attacks, and a subject's diagnostic result may be leaked because of non-encryption. Figure 5(c) shows the encrypted extracted result data from a subject: it can be decrypted in the ASN, so a subject's diagnostic report are safe from external attacks.

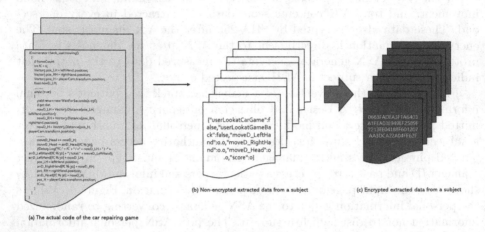

Fig. 5. An ADHD-VR diagnosis result attack protection example by the extracted data encryption.

Finally, Fig. 6 shows the comprehensive processes of the ADHD-VR diagnosis method. A designated physician gathers a subject's personal information to suggest personalized VR contents and difficulty levels, and it is stored safely through the ASN generator. After a subject completes the ADHD-VR diagnosis, if the measured values through the sensors and in the VR contents are higher than the normal standards, then it shows a subject is a suspected ADHD case.

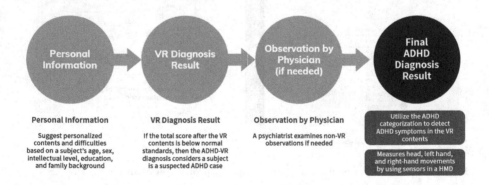

Fig. 6. The overall processes of the ADHD-VR diagnosis.

6   Discussion

Most of the traditional medical ADHD assessments requires several hours to be completed, because of its extensive amount of questionnaires and time for interviews. Although the diagnosis of many mental disorders still rely on the classic approaches, ADHD is widely and especially appeared to many children and adolescents. For this reason, our ADHD-VR diagnosis method is a better option to diagnose ADHD symptoms in a shorter period without subjective judgements. In the future, we will extend the VR-based diagnosis method to other mental disorders, and enhance the quality and accuracy of ADHD diagnosis.

7   Conclusion

In this paper, we present and implement the ADHD-VR diagnosis method with the ADHD categorization. Based on the HIPAA Security Rule, we also enhance the security of a patient's privacy to protect malicious attacks which expose a subject's sensitive health information. The ADHD-VR diagnosis method is a modern and developed diagnostic system as shown. We demonstrate that the ADHD-VR diagnosis method with the ASN generator successfully prevents a diagnosis result attack. At last, our ADHD-VR diagnosis method and the ADHD categorization will construct an objective diagnostic approach in ADHD.

Acknowledgements. This work was supported by Institute of Information & communications Technology Planning & Evaluation (IITP) grant funded by the Korea government (MSIT) (No. 2020-0-00990, Platform Development and Proof of High Trust & Low Latency Processing for Heterogeneous·Atypical·Large Scaled Data in 5G-IoT Environment).

References

1. American Psychiatric Association.: Diagnostic and Statistical Manual of Mental Disorders. 5th edn. American Psychiatric Association, Arlington (2013)
2. Akili Interactive Labs Inc: A randomized, controlled parallel-group, intervention study to assess at-home, game-based digital therapy for treating pediatric participants ages 8 to 12 years old with Attention Deficit Hyperactivity Disorder (ADHD). Akili-001R, Version 1.02 (2016)
3. Barbaresi, W., Katusic, S., Colligan, R., Weaver, A., Jacobsen, S.: Long-term school outcomes for children with attention-deficit/hyperactivity disorder: a population-based perspective. J. Dev. Behav. Pediatr. **28**, 265–273 (2007). https://doi.org/10.1097/DBP.0b013e31811ff87d
4. Danielson, M., Bitsko, R., Ghandour, J., Holbrook, M., Kogan, M., Blumberg, S.: Prevalence of parent-reported ADHD diagnosis and associated treatment among U.S. children and adolescents, 2016. J. Clin. Child Adolesc. Psychol. Official J. Soc. Clin. Child Adolesc.Psy chol. **47**, 199–212 (2018). https://doi.org/10.1080/15374416.2017.1417860
5. DuPaul, G., Power, T., Anastopoulos, A., Reid, R.: ADHD Rating Scale-IV: Checklists, Norms, and Clinical Interpretation. The Guilford Press, New York (1998)

6. DuPaul, G., Chronis-Tuscano, A., Danielson, M., Visser, S.: Predictors of receipt of school services in a national sample of youth with ADHD. J. Attention Disord. **23**, 1303–1319 (2019). https://doi.org/10.1177/1087054718816169
7. Gualtieri, C., Johnson, L.: ADHD: is objective diagnosis possible? Psychiatry (Edgmont) **2**, 44–53 (2005)
8. Institute of Medicine.: Beyond the HIPAA Privacy Rule: Enhancing Privacy, Improving Health Through Research. The National Academies Press, Washington, DC (2009). https://doi.org/10.17226/12458
9. Lange, K.W., Reichl, S., Lange, K.M., Tucha, L., Tucha, O.: The history of attention deficit hyperactivity disorder. Attention Defic. Hyperact. Disord. **2**, 241–255 (2010). https://doi.org/10.1007/s12402-010-0045-8
10. Lee, M., et al.: The revised Korean practice parameter for the treatment of attention-deficit hyperactivity disorder (II). J. Korean Acad. Child Adolesc. Psychiatry **28**, 58–69 (2017). https://doi.org/10.5765/jkacap.2017.28.2.58
11. Lee, S., et al.: Clinical utility of the Korean version of CBCL6-18 in the diagnosis of attention-deficit hyperactivity disorder. Korean J. Clin. Psychol. **34**, 829–850 (2015). https://doi.org/10.15842/kjcp.2015.34.4.001
12. Loe, I., Feldman, H.: Academic and educational outcomes of children with ADHD. Ambul. Pediatrics **32**, 82–90 (2007). https://doi.org/10.1016/j.ambp.2006.05.005
13. Mbonihankuye, S., Nkunzimana, A., Ndagijimana, A.: Healthcare data security technology: HIPAA compliance, internet of things for healthcare using wireless communications or mobile. Computing (2019). https://doi.org/10.1155/2019/1927495
14. Pliszka, S.: Practice parameter for the assessment and treatment of children and adolescents with attention-deficit/hyperactivity disorder. J. Am. Acad. Child Adolesc. Psychiatry **46**, 894–921 (2007). https://doi.org/10.1097/chi.0b013e318054e724
15. Siberski, J., et al.: Computer-based cognitive training for individuals with intellectual and developmental disabilities: pilot study. Am. J. Alzheimer's Dis. Dement. **30**, 41–48 (2015). https://doi.org/10.1177/1533317514539376
16. The U.S. Food and Drug Administration (FDA) Homepage. https://www.fda.gov/news-events/press-announcements/fda-permits-marketing-first-game-based-digital-therapeutic-improve-attention-function-children-adhd

A Three-Way Energy Efficient Authentication Protocol Using Bluetooth Low Energy

Thao L. P. Nguyen[1,2], Tran Khanh Dang[1,2(✉)], Tran Tri Dang[1,2], and Ai Thao Nguyen Thi[1,2]

[1] Ho Chi Minh City University of Technology (HCMUT),
268 Ly Thuong Kiet Street, District 10, Ho Chi Minh City, Vietnam
phuongthao.nguyenle@gmail.com, khanh@hcmut.edu.vn
[2] Vietnam National University Ho Chi Minh City (VNU-HCM), Linh Trung Ward,
Thu Duc District, Ho Chi Minh City, Vietnam

Abstract. Bluetooth Low Energy (BLE) is increasing in popularity. Many scientists are proposing it as a technique for contact tracing to combat COVID-19. Additionally, BLE is being used in applications involving transferring sensitive information such as home security systems. This paper provides a new authentication solution for BLE with enhanced privacy, but minimal impact on energy consumption. We also provided a framework to demonstrate our protocol can be implemented on real devices, which support BLE modules, and can withstand typical types of cyberattacks.

Keywords: Authentication · IoTs · BLE · Energy-efficient

1 Introduction

In 1999, the term "Internet of Things" (IoTs) first appeared in a presentation of Kevin Ashton [1]. Also within this year, Neil Gershenfeld was speaking about similar definition from the MIT Media Lab in his book "When Things Start to Think" [10]. 1999 can be considered as a big year for IoTs. Nearly twenty years have passed, now IoTs systems are so familiar in our daily life. The number of IoTs devices increases rapidly every year and is forecast to grow to almost 31 billion worldwide in 2020 [11]. The appearance of IoTs changes the ways in which individuals and organizations interact with the physical world and communicate among themselves. For example, the interaction with home equipment, automotive, mobile devices and industrial machines will be not the same as before. In all aspects of modern life, i.e. learning, traffic, health care, working ..., applying IoT technology helps to improve the quality of services and increase satisfaction of users. With this growth of IoTs, security becomes a survival problem. In fact, Gartner's 2016 IoT Backbone Survey showed that 32% of Information Technology leaders cited security as a top barrier to IoT success [9]. In order to

© Springer Nature Switzerland AG 2020
T. K. Dang et al. (Eds.): FDSE 2020, LNCS 12466, pp. 273–289, 2020.
https://doi.org/10.1007/978-3-030-63924-2_16

keep the IoT the system safe, the authentication process between IoT devices must be well-controlled. However, IoTs environment also has its own constraints which make it different from other systems: the uncontrolled environment, the heterogeneity, the need for scalability, as well as the constrained resource [19]. As a result, the authentication protocol in IoT must be lightweight and flexible. Device to Device (D2D) connection is very common in IoTs. One of the most popular standards for Device to Device connection is Bluetooth. To adapt with the expansion of IoTs, The Bluetooth Special Interest Group (SIG) introduced Bluetooth Low Energy (also called Bluetooth Smart or BLE). BLE started as part of the Bluetooth 4.0 Core Specification. IoT applications can rely on BLE for local connection between smart phones and resource constrained peripherals since this standard is designed to be low cost, robust and especially energy-efficient. In 2016, Bluetooth SIG releases Bluetooth 5.0 with 4x range, 2x speed and 8x broadcasting message capacity comparing with Bluetooth 4.0 [18]. The enhancements of Bluetooth 5.0 aim to increase the functionality of Bluetooth for the IoT, hence, it can be used in smart home automation, enterprise, and industrial markets.

In this paper, we propose a new authentication mechanism for IoTs devices which uses BLE as connection method due to its above advantages. We use party and meeting as research scenario, then explain how this protocol is applied in real life. We call our scheme to be "Friend-supported authentication scheme". We also perform security analysis to guarantee the security of our protocol. The main contribution of this article can be stated as below:

- We introduce a new authentication scheme for IoTs devices based on BLE framework and encounter history.
- We conduct experiment on real devices (Raspberry Pi 3 Model B) and perform evaluation with BLE.
- We prove that our proposed scheme can overcome many kinds of attacks that usually happen in IoT.
- Our proposed scheme can also preserve the privacy of participants thanks to BLE security features.

The remainder of the paper is organized as follows. Section 2 is for reviewing some related works recently proposed. In Sect. 3, we explain clearer about our motivation and scenarios for this protocol. Section 4 is where we thoroughly explain our proposed scheme when experiment explanation and performance evaluation are discussed in next section. In Sect. 6, we prove that our protocol is resilient to different kinds of common attacks before finally making a conclusion about our work in Sect. 7.

2   Related Works

Security in IoT is a popular research aspect of these recent years, especially when IoT is growing really fast and becoming an important part of our daily life. In the paper of M El-hajj et al. published in 2019 [13], they stated that the main IoT security concerns include: authentication, authorization, integrity, confidentiality, non-repudiation, availability, and privacy. In this paper, we focus on the authentication. About the taxonomy of IoT Authentication Schemes, we would have six main criteria:

1. Using token:
   (a) Token-based Authentication: Authenticates a user/device based on an identification token created by a server such as OAuth2 protocol [4,7] or open ID [3].
   (b) Non-Token based authentication: Involves the use of the credentials when there is a need to exchange data (e.g., TLS/DTLS [12,17]).
2. Using Authentication factors: Identity or/and Context.
   (a) Identity: An information kept by one devices and distinguishing it from another, is used to authenticate itself [15,16].
   (b) Context: can be behavioral (gait, voice...) or physical (fingerprint, iris...) [8].
3. Using Authentication procedure: One-way authentication, Two-way authentication and Three-way authentication.
   (a) One-way authentication: In scenario of two devices need to communicate with each other, only one party will authenticate itself to the other one, while the other one is still unauthenticated.
   (b) Two-way authentication: It is also called mutual authentication, in which both devices authenticate each other, this is the most common way.
   (c) Three-way authentication: When there is a central authority authenticates the two parties and support them mutually authenticating themselves.
4. Using Authentication architecture: Distributed or Centralized.
   (a) Distributed: Using a distributed straight authentication method between the communicating parties.
   (b) Centralized: Using a centralized server or a trusted third party to distribute and manage the credentials used for authentication. Whether centralized or distributed, the authentication scheme architecture can be:
   (c) Hierarchical: Using a multi-level architecture to deal with the authentication procedure.
   (d) Flat: No hierarchical architecture is used.
5. IoT layer: We have perception layer, network layer and application layer.
6. Hardware-based: The authentication process might require the use of physical characteristics of the hardware or the hardware itself, so we have Implicit hardware-based and Explicit hardware-based.
   (a) Implicit hardware-based: Using hardware features such as Physical Unclonable Function (PUF) [2] or True Random Number Generator (TRNG) [14].
   (b) Explicit hardware-based: Some authentication schemes are based on the use of a Trusted Platform Module (TPM) [6].

Our paper is an example of using multi-authentication criteria. We use identity such as Device Bluetooth MAC address, location, time and encounter history of participants as our factors. We also provide a distributed authentication scheme cause we do not need centralized server. Our framework is an application based on BLE framework to utilize the advantages of BLE technology, which is inspired by the research result of Dang in [5].

3   Scenario

To understand better about the protocol, we need to have the scenarios where we will apply it. We will use party as a specific context to begin with. Imagining you, as Party-Crasher, suddenly discover that there is an interesting party happening near your place, then you would like to join it. The party may last 6 h, you are late but you do not want to miss any excited events in the party. Since you are not invited, you suppose not to be able to join the party and watch its events in the party timeline. You are also not allowed to join party chat group, but you need to keep track with previous party activities to join the conversations. How can you get permission for these activities? You need to prove that you are able to join this party. You can be considered to join this party if you know most of participants of the party (more than 50%), and they give positive feedback about you or you received special permission of Party-Owner. If you have one of the requirements, you would be provided permission to see party timeline, join chat groups and communicate in the party.

The second scenario is supposing you are a member of the development team, so you are allowed to join team technical discussion meeting. However, by some mistake, you did not receive the invitation from meeting organizer. Since you are not invited, you suppose not to be able to join the meeting and follow its previous discussions and decisions. You are not allowed to discuss in the conference chat room. You need to prove that you are able to join this meeting. You can be considered to join this meeting if you are teammate of team members and you get permission from team leader. In that case, you would be provided permission to see previous discussion, join chat groups and express opinions during the meeting.

From the above scenarios, we assume that to apply this protocol, the event must have the below features:

1. There is a person in the event acting as Event owner, who know all event participants and be trusted by them.
2. Event participants can give their individual judgment for the uninvited guest. The judgment can be not the same in different party.
3. All information related to event is shared on the web pages, or server that only people who connect to the Local network can see and update, which can be referred as a transient secret.
4. All event members will have at least one device which supports Bluetooth low energy.

5. This event happens in a closed space, which only nearby devices can connect with each other. From the above assumption, to be able to implement this protocol we will use Bluetooth Low Energy (BLE) connection together with Wireless Local Area Network (Wi-Fi).

4 Proposed Protocol

4.1 Why We Choose BLE?

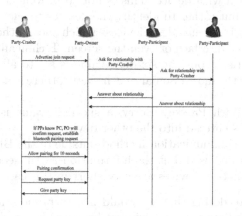

Fig. 1. Party-crasher protocol

After long time researching about possible connections for near distance object, we realize that Bluetooth low energy will be a good choice for our protocol. We decide to use BLE in our protocol because of these reasons:

1. Low cost.
2. Robust.
3. Effective in short range.
4. Popular.
5. Energy saving.

From Bluetooth 4.0, Bluetooth Low Energy (BLE) protocols are supported. Bluetooth 4.0 is also known as Bluetooth Smart, Bluetooth Smart Ready and Bluetooth Low Energy. Most wearable devices and smartphones are supporting Bluetooth 4.0 and 5.0. Bluetooth Smart devices are peripheral devices like speakers, headphones, fitness trackers, smart pens, medical devices and so on. These devices get resource constraints and limited amount of battery. They are suitable for simple calculation. They often have paired hosts and require periodic connection to it, like during data transfer. These peripheral are also able to maintain the pairing despite long sleep periods between active modes to prevent a second device from pairing. Our smart phones and laptop are considered as

Bluetooth Smart Ready devices. They have powerful processor and can control peripheral devices via Bluetooth connection. Bluetooth Smart Ready can also exchange data with old Bluetooth 2.0 or 3.0 device. With 4x range, 2x speed and 8x broadcasting message capacity comparing with Bluetooth 4.0, the enhancements of Bluetooth 5.0 aims to increase the functionality of Bluetooth for the IoT. In BLE, security-related tasks happened and are decided beforehand in pairing process. There are four different pairing methods:

1. Numeric Comparison: both devices display the same six digit value on their respective screens or LCD displays, then users have to check whether they match and confirm with device. This is not to prevent a man-in-the-middle (MITM) attack, but rather to identify the devices to each other.
2. Just Works: this is for headless devices, which means those devices do not have Graphic User Interface or even the screen. Technically, it is the same as Numeric Comparison, but the six-digit value is set to all zeros. Just Works method is clearly the most popular one, however, there is no MITM protection with Just Works.
3. Passkey Entry. With Passkey Entry, a six-digit value is displayed on one device, and this is entered into the other device.
4. Out Of Band: A communication method outside of the Bluetooth communication channel is not used, but the information is still secured. The distance between two connected devices are very short in this case.

In our protocol, considering that we would like to propose a general approach and many Bluetooth Smart devices will not have screen, we will use Just Works.

4.2   Detailed Proposed Protocol

Our work is an improvement of Just Works Bluetooth method. The procedure of our protocol can be describe as Fig. 1. Cause we use a party as our scenario, our proposed protocol can be called Party-Crasher protocol.

Here are the abbreviation Table 1 that will be used in our explanation:

Table 1. Abbreviation table.

Abbreviation	Explanation
BLE	Bluetooth low energy
PC	Party-Crasher
PO	Party-Owner
PP	Party-Participant
LTK	Long term key
IRK	Identity Resolving Key
CSRK	Connection Signature Resolving Key

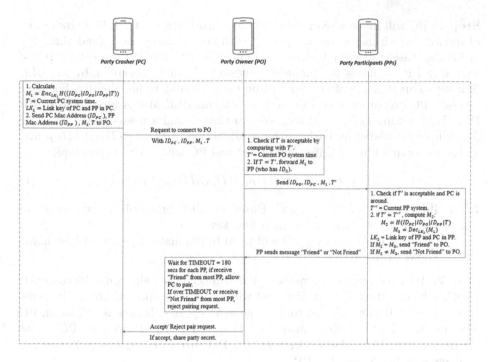

Fig. 2. Detailded proposed authentication protocol

PC will send request to PO that he would like to join the party, and he is a good friend with PPs. PO will need to verify this information before he can accept PC 's request. Hence, PO will forward the message from PC to the PPs that PC says he knows for verification. If most of PPs (more than 50%) replies to PO he knows and trusts PC, PO will request to pair with PP, in order to ensure the safety for communication channel between him and PC. After pairing, PO will share party secret to PC, which may be a Wi-Fi access key, so PC can truly join the party. We describe this procedure in Fig. 2. Detailed communication steps are explained as follow:

Fig. 3. Same link key in PC and PP

Step 1: PC will made a scan about devices inside the party. If he knows most of devices, which means he has paired with them before and stored their key in his database, PC will advertise his join request to PO. To prove he is friend with any PP, he needs to compute a message M and encrypt it by his BLE link key. This message afterward will be used to validate his identity. For each message PC exchanges with PO, he will send his BLE Mac Address ID_{PC}, PP BLE MAC address ID_{PP}, current system time T and a message M_1. Message M_1 will be calculated by hashing the combination of ID_{PC}, ID_{PO}, ID_{PP} and T, then encrypted by BLE link key of PP and PC with AES cryptography.

$$M_1 = Enc_{LK_1}(H(ID_{PC}|ID_{PO}|ID_{PP}|T))(1) \tag{1}$$

LK_1: BLE link key of PP and PC. Based on BLE protocol, as we can see in Fig. 3, paired devices share a common link key.

The number of M message PP will need to calculate depends on how many PP he knows in the party.

Step 2: After receiving PC 's request, PO will need the help from PPs to decide whether he can trust PC. At first, PO will check if he and PC are in the same time frame. A 10 min different time range is acceptable. If time is validated, PC will contact PPs to confirm about PC. For each PP, PO will send PC's Mac Address ID_{PC}, PO's Mac Address ID_{PO}, PO current system time T' and M_1 message sent by PC for that PP.

To not burden the network, PO will set TIMEOUT about 180 s until he receives response from PP. Over TIMEOUT, PO will reject connection request from PC and authentication process is terminated.

Step 3: Each PP also performs time check at the first step. After that, he will check whether PC is nearby by scanning all discoverable BLE devices at the area at that moment. If both conditions are satisfied, PP will verify the M_1 from PC by using his BLE Link key with PC. In order to verify the time, 10 min different is acceptable. The M_2 and M_3 will be computed afterward with below formulas:

$$M_2 = H(ID_{PC}|ID_{PO}|ID_{PP}|T'')(2) \tag{2}$$

Then message from PC will be decrypted by link key stored in PP.

$$M_3 = Dec_{LK_2}((ID_{PC}|ID_{PO}|ID_{PP}|T''))(3)$$

Since the Link key are the same between PP and PC if they are friends, M_2 is expected to be equal M_3. By this result PP will reply "Friend" or "Not Friend" to PO. This response will be encrypted by BLE connection and be considered as M_4 and M_5

$$M_4 = Dec_{LK_2}(H(Friend|T''))(4) \tag{3}$$

$$M_5 = Dec_{LK_2}(H(Friend|T''))(5) \tag{4}$$

Step 4: PO will set TIMEOUT about 180 s until he receives response from each PP. Over TIMEOUT, PO will act as he receive "Not Friend" message from PP. If most of PP confirms he is "Not Friend" with PC, PO will reject PC's request. On the other hand, PO will accept to pair with PC and they can exchange data securely. Hence, PO can give PC the party secret, which is now exchanged in a secure channel, i.e the Wi-Fi key. Cause we use BLE framework, the communication between PC and PP are supposed to be safe since they are protected by security methods apply in BLE.

5   System Implementation and Experiment

We have a set up of 3 Raspberry Pi 3 Model B and a Asus laptop. 3 Raspberry Pi boards are set up as Fig. 4 and we establish an secure shell connection from our Asus laptop to them to control.

Fig. 4. Raspberry Pi boards set up

Below is some description about hardware and software information regarding to our experiment.

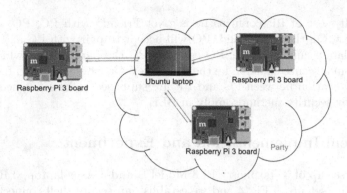

Fig. 5. Experiment model

5.1 Hardware

Raspberry Pi 3 Model B+ and Asus laptop (This can also be replaced with a Raspberry Pi 3 Model B+).

5.2 Library Information

Python version 2.7
Plugin for python 2.7:
 – https://pypi.org/project/PyBluez/
 – https://pypi.org/project/pycrypto/
Below buitlin libraries in python 2.7
 – base64
 – datetime
 – hashlib
 – os
 – sys
 – uuid

5.3 OS Information

Raspberry Pi boards are installed to boot up with fresh Raspbian Stretch Lite OS version 2018-06-27.
Asus laptop uses Ubuntu 14.04.

5.4 Description

All devices are configured to be able to use all features of BLE. We made a simple implementation for our proposed protocol using BLE RFCOMM protocol with 4 devices, representing 3 elements of this Protocol: PC, PP and PO. D1 is PC, D2 is PO and D3 is PP. We have 1 D1, 1 D2 and 2 D3. The assumptions here are:

1. D1 and D2 do not know each other.
2. Each D3 is a closed friend of both D1 and D2.
3. If the devices have been authenticated before, their BLE devices have been already paired and exchanged data, so the connection between them is considered as safe via BLE standard.
4. When 2 BLE devices have been paired, they will have the same link key in the database.

Function Interface

1. **Class NewDevice1:** #Support following functions for PC:
   (a) Send request to join to D2
       Input: ID of D2.
       Output: True/ False.
       Function interface:

$$\text{def DeviceRequestJoin(id2)}$$

   (b) Create Message, send to D2 so D2 can forward to D3 for help. This message is encrypted by D1 and D3 link key.
       If D3 knows D1, D2 will authenticate with D1.
       Input: ID of D3, message.
       Output: True/ False (result of D1 and D2 authentication).
       Function interface:

$$\text{def DeviceAuthenticate(id3, message)}$$

   (c) Running function:
       Running authentication process.
       Input: None
       Output: None
       Function interface:
$$\text{def Running()}$$

2. **Class NewDevice2:** #Support following functions for PO:
   (a) Receive Join request from D1:
       Input: ID1.
       Output: Message created by D1, ID D1, ID D3, time of authentication.
       Function interface:

$$\text{def ReceiveJoinRequest(id1)}$$

   (b) In case D2 does not know D1, and need support from D3, D2 need to forward D1 message to D3.
       Input: Message created by D1, ID D1, ID D3, time of authentication.
       Output: True/ False (depend on relationship between D1 and D3).
       Function interface:

$$\text{def ForwardJoinRequest(id3, id1, m, t)}$$

(c) Running function:
Running authentication process.
Input: None
Output: None
Function interface:

$$\text{def Running()}$$

3. **Class NewDevice3:** #Support following functions for PP:
(a) Accept connection from D2.
Input: D2 connection
Output: True/ False
Function interface:

$$\text{def DeviceConnect(id2)}$$

(b) Get D1 data from D2.
Input: D2 connection
Output: message created by D1, D1 ID
Function interface:

$$\text{def GetData(d2)}$$

(c) Help D2 authenticate with D1.
Input: message created by D1, D1 ID.
Output True/ False (depend on relationship between D1 and D3).
Function interface:

$$\text{def SupportAuthenticate(id1, m)}$$

(d) Running function:
Running authentication process.
Input: None
Output: None
Function interface:

$$\text{def Running()}$$

4. **Common functions**
We also have supporting functions which are shared between all devices:
(a) Hash message Input: Message.
Output: hash value.
Function interface:

$$\text{def hashMessage(message)}$$

(b) Encrypt message
Input: Message, key, padding character
Output: encrypted message.
Function interface:

$$\text{def encryptMessage(privateMsg, encodedSecretKey, paddingCharacter)}$$

(c) Decrypt message
Input: Encoded message, key, padding character.
Output: decryted message.
Function interface:

```
def decryptMessage(encodedEncryptedMsg, encodedSecretKey, paddingCharacter)
```

(d) Get Bluetooth link key. This key will exist if 2 devices paired with each other before.
Input: device self Bluetooth MAC address and partner Bluetooth MAC address.
Output: Key.
Function interface:

```
def getLinkKey(selfAddr, devAddr)
```

(e) Check if a device is nearby.
Input: MAC address of device which we need to check.
Output: True/ False.
Function interface:

```
def checkNearbyDev(devAddr)
```

(f) Verify time whether it is acceptable. (10 min should be fine.)
Input: sending time, receiving time.
Output: True/False.
Function interface:

```
def verifyTime(devTime, receivedTime)
```

5.5 Experiment

We set up our experiment to have 3 type of devices here:

1. Ubuntu laptop, work as PO (D2 device).
2. Raspberry Pi 3 Model B+, work as PC (D1 device).
3. Raspberry Pi 3 Model B+, work as PP (D3 device).

There are 3 stages:

1. Beginning stages: PC knows PP and PO knows PP. PC does not know PO but wants to authenticate with it.
2. Running stage: PC send request to authenticate with PO with support from PP.
3. Final stage: complete authentication process. PO is paired with PC and can see information of PC. Now we will see link key inside PO and PC. This link key will be used to generate key for each communication between PO and PC in the future.

6   Security Analysis

6.1   Security Analysis

Our protocol is implemented by using BLE connection, so we can utilize the BLE security features. BLE 4.2 devices are fully backwards compatible with BLE 4.0 and 4.1 devices, this means that 4.2 devices can perform the exact same pairing process as 4.0 and 4.1 devices. However, BLE 4.2 are also capable of creating what are known as LE Secure Connections. Instead of using a TK and STK, LE Secure Connections use a single Long Term Key (LTK) to encrypt the connection. This LTK is exchanged/generated using Elliptic Curve Diffie Hellman public key cryptography which offers significantly stronger security compared to the original BLE key exchange protocol. In LE Secure Connections, both phase one and phase three of the pairing process are exactly the same as they are in LE Legacy connections. Thus, the only differences occur during phase two of the pairing process. The way phase two works in LE Secure Connections is as follows. Both devices generate an ECDH public-private key pair. The two devices will then exchange their public keys and then start computing the Diffie-Hellman key. One of the pairing methods is then used to authenticate the connection. Once the connection is authenticated, the LTK is generated and the connection is encrypted.

AES-CCM is used in Bluetooth LE to provide confidentiality as well as per-packet authentication and integrity. Because the LTK is used as input for the encryption key, successful encryption setup provides implicit authentication. Similarly, data signing using Identity Resolving Key (IRK) provides implicit authentication that the remote device holds the correct Connection Signature Resolving Key (CSRK).

6.2   Key Generation

Key generation in Bluetooth with low energy is performed by the Host on each low energy device independent of any other. When using Bluetooth LE Secure Connections, the following keys are exchanged between master and slave:

- Connection Signature Resolving Key for Authentication of unencrypted data: CSRK is an 128-bit key used to sign data and verify signatures on the receiving device.
- Identity Resolving Key for Device Identity and Privacy: In LE Secure Connections, the public/private key pair is generated in the Host and a Secure Connection Key is generated by combining contributions from each device involved in pairing. IRK is a 128-bit key used to generate and resolve random address.

6.3   Encryption

Encryption in Bluetooth with low energy uses AES-CCM cryptography, which is also known as Counter with CBC-MAC, is a mode of operation for cryptographic block ciphers. This is an authenticated encryption algorithm that provides both confidentiality and authentication.

6.4   Signed Data

Bluetooth with its low energy features supports the ability to send authenticated data over an unencrypted transport between two devices with a trusted relationship. This means that in some circumstances where the communication channel is not encrypted, the device could still have a method to maintain and ensure the data authentication. This is accomplished by signing the data with a CSRK. The sending devices place a signature after the Protocol Data Unit (PDU). The receiving device verifies the signature and, if the signature is verified, the Data PDU is assumed to come from the trusted source. The signature is composed of a Message Authentication Code generated by the signing algorithm and a counter, which is used to protect against a replay attack. This counter is increased on each signed Data PDU sent.

6.5   Privacy Preserving

BLE provides feature that reduces the chance of an attacker to track a device over a long period by often changing an advertising device's address. Only the devices that have been authenticated before can resolve the real Bluetooth MAC address (or we can call ID here) of devices thanks to the IRK. If the advertising device was previously discovered and has returned to an advertising state, the device can only be identifiable by trusted devices in future connections without going through discovery procedure again. The IRK stored in the trusted device will solve the problem of maintaining privacy while saving discovery computational load and connection time. The advertising devices IRK together with other keys was sent to the master device during initial bonding. The a master device then can use the IRK to identify the advertiser as a trusted device.

7   Conclusion

In this paper, we provide a new authentication protocol which is safe to used with IoTs environment. Because we use BLE as the framework to test our protocol, we can utilize its low-energy feature. We also proved that our work can withstand different kinds of cyberattacks. The short range communication of BLE is also a good point to strengthen the proposed protocol. In this paper, we only use the Star model of BLE, however, in future works, we can have an improved protocol which uses Mesh model. It will not only help to widen the authentication area, but also allow more devices can join the party. We can also make the protocol better by doing experiments with around 100 devices as BLE mentioned in its specs and measure the exact energy we need. Another interesting topic is making a comparison between BLE and 5G, which is the top trend of current technologies for networking.

Acknowledgment. This research is funded by Vietnam National University Ho Chi Minh City(VNU-HCM) under grant number B2018-20-08. We also thank other members of the project, specially Chau D. M. Pham, for their meaningful help and comments during this paper preparation.

References

1. Ashton, K.: That "Internet of Things" thing. RFID J. **22**, 97–114 (2009)
2. Barbareschi, M., De Benedictis, A., Mazzocca, N.: A PUF-based hardware mutual authentication protocol. J. Parallel Distrib. Comput. **119** (2018). https://doi.org/10.1016/j.jpdc.2018.04.007
3. Blazquez, A., Tsiatsis, V., Vandikas, K.: Performance evaluation of OpenID connect for an IoT information marketplace, pp. 1–6 (2015). https://doi.org/10.1109/VTCSpring.2015.7146004
4. Chae, C.J., Choi, K.N., Choi, K., Yae, Y.H., Shin, Y.: The extended authentication protocol using e-mail authentication in OAuth 2.0 protocol for secure granting of user access. J. Internet Comput. Serv. **16**, 21–28 (2015). https://doi.org/10.7472/jksii.2015.16.1.21
5. Dang, T.K., Tran, K.T.K.: The meeting of acquaintances: a cost-efficient authentication scheme for light-weight objects with transient trust level and plurality approach. Secur. Commun. Netw. **2019**, 8123259:1–8123259:18 (2019). https://doi.org/10.1155/2019/8123259
6. Delaune, S., Kremer, S., Ryan, M.D., Steel, G.: A formal analysis of authentication in the TPM. In: Degano, P., Etalle, S., Guttman, J. (eds.) FAST 2010. LNCS, vol. 6561, pp. 111–125. Springer, Heidelberg (2011). https://doi.org/10.1007/978-3-642-19751-2_8
7. Emerson, S., Choi, Y.K., Hwang, D.Y., Kim, K.S., Kim, K.H.: An OAuth based authentication mechanism for IoT networks, pp. 1072–1074 (2015). https://doi.org/10.1109/ICTC.2015.7354740
8. Ferrag, M.A., Maglaras, L., Derhab, A.: Authentication and authorization for mobile IoT devices using biofeatures: recent advances and future trends. Secur. Commun. Netw. **2019** (2019). https://doi.org/10.1155/2019/5452870
9. Gartner: Leading the IoT (2018). https://www.gartner.com/imagesrv/books/iot/iotEbook_digital.pdf
10. Gershenfeld, N.: When Things Start to Think. Hodder & Stoughton, London (1999). https://books.google.it/books?id=y2SPPwAACAAJ
11. IHS: Internet of things (IoT) connected devices installed base worldwide from 2015 to 2025 (in billions) (2018). https://www.statista.com/statistics/471264/iot-number-of-connected-devices-worldwide/
12. Kothmayr, T., Schmitt, C., Hu, W., Bruenig, M., Carle, G.: DTLS based security and two-way authentication for the Internet of Things. Ad Hoc Netw. **11** (2013). https://doi.org/10.1016/j.adhoc.2013.05.003
13. El-hajj, M., Fadlallah, A., Chamoun, M., Serhrouchni, A.: A survey of Internet of Things (IoT) authentication schemes. https://www.mdpi.com/1424-8220/19/5/1141/htm
14. Thamrin, M.N., Ahmad, I., Khalil-Hani, M.: A true random number generator for crypto embedded systems (2006)
15. Mahalle, P., Anggorojati, B., Prasad, N., Rangistty, N.: Identity authentication and capability based access control (IACAC) for the internet of things. J. Cyber Secur. Mobility **1**, 309–348 (2012)

16. Salman, O., Abdallah, S., Elhajj, I., Chehab, A., Kayssi, A.: Identity-based authentication scheme for the Internet of Things, pp. 1109–1111 (2016). https://doi.org/10.1109/ISCC.2016.7543884
17. Santos, G., Guimaraes, V., Rodrigues, G., Granville, L., Tarouco, L.: A DTLS-based security architecture for the Internet of Things, pp. 809–815 (2015). https://doi.org/10.1109/ISCC.2015.7405613
18. Sig, B.: Bluetooth 5 (2018). https://www.bluetooth.com/~/media/files/marketing/bluetooth_5-final.ashxla=en
19. Vasilomanolakis, E., Daubert, J., Luthra, M., Gazis, V., Wiesmaier, A., Kikiras, P.: On the security and privacy of Internet of Things architectures and systems. In: 2015 International Workshop on Secure Internet of Things (SIoT), pp. 49–57 (2015). https://doi.org/10.1109/SIOT.2015.9

Clustering-Based Deep Autoencoders for Network Anomaly Detection

Van Quan Nguyen[1], Viet Hung Nguyen[1], Nhien-An Le-Khac[2],
and Van Loi Cao[1(✉)]

[1] Le Quy Don Technical University, Hanoi, Vietnam
nguyenvanquan87@mail.ru, {hungnv,loi.cao}@lqdtu.edu.vn
[2] University College Dublin, Dublin, Ireland
an.lekhac@ucd.ie

Abstract. A novel hybrid approach between clustering methods and autoencoders (AEs) is introduced for detecting network anomalies in a semi-supervised manner. A previous work has developed regularized AEs, namely Shrink AE (SAE) and Dirac Delta Variational AE (DVAE) that learn to represent normal data into a very small region being close to the origin in their middle hidden layers (latent representation). This work based on the assumption that normal data points may share some common characteristics, so they can be forced to distribute in a small single cluster. In some scenarios, however, normal network data may contain data from very different network services, which may result in a number of clusters in the normal data. Our proposed hybrid model attempts to automatically discover these clusters in the normal data in the latent representation of AEs. At each iteration, an AE learns to map normal data into the latent representation while a clustering method tries to discover clusters in the latent normal data and force them being close together. The co-training strategy can help to reveal true clusters in normal data. When a querying data point coming, it is first mapped into the latent representation of the AE, and its distance to the closest cluster center can be used as an anomaly score. The higher anomaly score a data point has, the more likely it is anomaly. The method is evaluated with four scenarios in the CTU13 dataset, and experiments illustrate that the proposed hybrid model often out-performs SAE on three out of four scenarios.

Keywords: Autoencoder · Deep learning · Anomaly detection · Clustering · Latent representation

1 Introduction

Anomaly detection is the task to identify patterns in data or events representing the operation of systems that vary so much from the expected behavior [1,6]. In network security, the network anomaly detection means the discrimination of illegal, malicious activities and other damaging forms of network use and abuse

© Springer Nature Switzerland AG 2020
T. K. Dang et al. (Eds.): FDSE 2020, LNCS 12466, pp. 290–303, 2020.
https://doi.org/10.1007/978-3-030-63924-2_17

from normal connections or expected behavior of network systems [13]. These actions are considered network anomalies. In many scenarios, data representing the normal behavior of network systems tend to be available and easy to obtain, while anomalies are scarce and sometimes impossible to collect [5]. Thus, the semi-supervised learning approach, such as one-class classification techniques, is a suitable learning scheme to construct models from only normal data for identifying network anomalies. In such approach, One-class Support Vector Machine (OCSVM), Local Outlier Factor (LoF), and Autoencoders (AEs) are well-known methods used for anomaly detection.

There has been a widespread use of AEs in anomaly detection domain [8,10, 12,14] in recent years. This AE method can be used to build anomaly detectors by itself, or used as representation blocks in hybrid anomaly detection models. In the latter approach, the bottleneck layer of the AE trained on normal data is used as the new feature representation (latent representation) for enhancing the performance of following anomaly detection methods. This is because the latent feature space can represent normal data in more meaningful features (lower dimension and reveal robust features) than the original feature space. The work in [5] is known as a typical study of using the latent representation. In [5], two regularized AEs, namely SAE and DVAE, were developed to construct a robust feature representation in which normal data is mapped into a very small region being close to the origin in the latent representation of SAE. The rest of latent feature space is reserved for possible anomalies appearing in the future. This work is based on the assumption that normal data points may share some common characteristics, and they can be forced to distribute in a small single cluster. In some scenarios, however, normal network data may contain data from very different network services, which may result in a number of clusters in the normal data. Therefore, representing such data into single cluster in the bottleneck layer of AE may damage valuable characteristics of normal data.

In this paper, we introduce a hybrid learning model that can inherited the strengthens from both autoencoders (AEs) and clustering methods for anomaly detection. In other words, AEs have the ability to map normal data in a lower feature space in which more robust features representing normal behavior can be revealed, whereas clustering methods can learn to discover sub-classes (i.e. clusters) in the normal data. When clustering methods working in a lower dimension with more robust features such the latent representation of AEs, they can perform more efficiently than those in the original input data. Therefore, this work aims to propose a novel learning scheme that combines the learning strategies of an AE and a clustering method at each iteration. This means that the AE learn to represent normal data into robust feature space in its middle hidden layer, while the clustering method automatically discovers a number of sub-classes and forces them being close together. This work is performed at each iteration until these training processes are stable. Our proposed model is novel to the exist hybrid between AEs and clustering techniques introduced in [15]. In [15], the authors aimed to discover a number of image clusters in the latent feature space of an AE in an unsupervised manner. The main difference is that the hybrid in [15] was trained to pull each image cluster far away from each others while CAE learns to force normal clusters being close together because these normal clusters share some common characteristics of the normal behaviors. The proposed model is evaluated on the four scenarios in the CTU13 dataset. Our experimental results show that CAE often out-performs SAE and DVAE on three of four scenarios where the normal data seems to have more than one classes.

The rest of this paper is organized as follows. We shortly introduce to AEs and a clustering method in Sect. 2. Section 3 briefly reviews some recent studies related to using latent representation for anomaly detection. This is followed by a section proposing the hybrid between AEs and clustering methods. Experiments, results and discussion are presented in Sects. 5 and 6 respectively. The paper concludes with highlights and future directions.

2   Background

2.1   Autoencoders

A classical autoencoder [2,11], often called autoencoder, is a neural network that consists of two parts: *encoder* and *decoder* as shown in Fig. 1. An autoencoder is trained to copy network's input to its output. The *encoder* is defined as a feature extractor that allows to explicitly represent an input x in a feature space. Let f_θ denote the encoder, and $X = \{x_1, x_2, ...x_n\}$ be a dataset. The *encoder* f_θ map the input $x_i \in X$ into a latent representation $z_i = f_\theta(x_i)$. The *decoder* g_ϕ attempts to map the *latent representation* z_i back into the input space, which forms a reconstruction $\hat{x}_i = g_\phi(z_i)$. The encoder and decoder are commonly represented as single-layer neural networks in the form of activation functions of affine mappings as follows:

$$f_\theta(x) = \psi_f(Wx + b) \tag{1}$$

$$g_\phi(z) = \psi_g\left(W'z + b'\right) \tag{2}$$

where $\theta = (W,b)$ and $\phi = (W',b')$ are parameters set for training encoder and decoder, respectively. ψ_f and ψ_g are the activation functions of the encoder and decoder, such as a *logistic sigmoid* or *hyperbolic tangent* non-linear function, or a linear *identity* function. The reconstruction loss function over training samples can be written as:

$$\mathcal{L}_{AE}(\theta; \phi; x) = \frac{1}{n}\sum_{i=0}^{n} l(x_i, \hat{x}_i) = \frac{1}{n}\sum_{i=0}^{n} l(x_i, g_\phi(f_\theta(x_i))) \tag{3}$$

Where $l(x_i, \hat{x}_i)$ is the discrepancy between the input x_i and its reconstruction $\hat{x}_i$; n is the number of data samples in the dataset. Autoencoders learn to optimize the objective function in (3) with respect to the parameters $\theta = (W,b)$ and $\phi = (W',b')$ by using a learning algorithm such as the stochastic gradient descent with back-propagation. The choice of the reconstruction loss depends

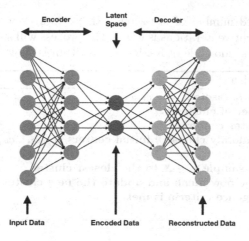

Fig. 1. Autoencoder

largely on the appropriate distributional assumptions on given data. The *mean squared error* (MSE) in Eq. 4 is commonly used for real-valued data, whereas a *cross-entropy* loss in Eq. 5 can be used for binary data.

$$\mathcal{L}_{\mathrm{AE}}(\theta; x) = \frac{1}{n} \sum_{i=1}^{n} \left(\parallel x_i - \hat{x}_i \parallel^2 \right) \tag{4}$$

$$\mathcal{L}_{\mathrm{AE}}(\theta; x) = -\frac{1}{n} \sum_{i=1}^{n} \left(x_i \log(\hat{x}_i) + (1 - x_i) \log(1 - \hat{x}_i) \right) \tag{5}$$

By compressing input data into a lower dimensional space, the classical autoencoder avoids simply learning the identity, and removes redundant information [12].

2.2 Clustering Techniques

Clustering techniques consider samples in datasets as objects. They classify these objects into different groups or clusters, so that objects within a cluster are similar to each others and distinguished with objects from other clusters. There are variety type of clustering algorithms and every methodology follows a different set of rules for defining the similarity among data points. One of the most popular clustering algorithms is K-means. It was originally proposed by MacQueen in 1967. K-mean is a unsupervised, interative method of clustering. The idea behind this technique is that the algorithm starts with a given dataset and initial clustering centers. Following this, two steps are operated iteratively: relocating each data point to its new closest center; updating the clustering centers by calculating the mean of all members. The process is repeated until a convergence criteria is met (a predefined number of iterations). If no changes in clustering centers between two consecutive iterations is found, the process will stop, and return the optimal solution. Pseudo-code of K-Means algorithm is showed in Algorithm 1.

Algorithm 1 K-Means

1: **Input: given a datasets $X = \{x_1, x_2, ...x_n\}$**
   and the number of cluster k.
2: **Output: k cluster centers.**
3: **Initialize: Randomly choose k initial centers $\{c_1, c_2, ...c_k\}$.**
4: **repeat**
5:     **Assign each sample $x_i \in X$ to the closest cluster.**
6:     **Calculate the new mean and update the new cluster center.**
7: **until a convergence criteria is met**
   =0

---

3   Related Work

Autoencoders (AEs) have been widely used for anomaly detection. The network architectures can be used by itself as a stand-alone classifier or a feature representation block in a hybrid between AEs and classification methods. In the latter approach, the bottleneck layer of AEs can be used as a new feature space for the following classifiers [3–5,7,10,15,16]. The latent feature representation can be constructed in supervised learning [16], semi-supervised learning [3–5] and unsupervised learning [7,10]. Once the training process of a AE finished, the encoder is used as a feature representation block enhancing the following anomaly detection method. The central idea is that the bottleneck layer can map original data into a lower dimension, and discover more robust features representing the normal behavior. The remain of this section, we will discuss some typical work for three latent representation approaches mentioned above.

In supervised manner, Vu et al. [16] introduced Multi-distribution VAE (MVAE) to represent normal data and anomalous data into two different areas in the middle hidden layer of VAE. Classical Variational autoencoders (VAEs) can learn to map input data into a standard Gaussian distribution $\mathcal{N}(0, 1)$ in its bottleneck layer. In [16], the class labels (normal and anomaly) are incorporated into the loss function of VAE to push the two data classes into two different regions. These regions have the same Gaussian distribution shape with $\sigma = 1$, but different mean values. The proposed model was evaluated on two publicly network security datasets, and it produces promising performance.

In semi-supervised manner, Cao et al. [5] proposed two regularized AEs, called Shrink AE (SAE) and Dirac Delta VAE (DVAE), to capture the behaviors of normal data. SAE and DVAE are aimed to put normal data towards a very small region being close to the origin of the latent feature space, and attempt to reserve the rest of the latent feature space for anomalies appearing in the future. The authors assumed that only normal samples are available for training, and no anomalous data can be used for estimating hyper-parameters. These regularized AEs are aimed to address the problem of identifying anomalies in high-dimensional network data. The latent representation of SAE and DVAE were then used for facilitating simple one-class classifiers. SAE and DVAE were then evaluated on eight well-known anomaly detection datasets. The experimental results confirmed that their models not only can produce a better performance, but also are less sensitive on a wide range of parameter settings in comparison to stand-alone OCCs, and those of other feature representation methods.

The study [7] is a typical unsupervised learning approach that employs the latent representation of an AE, namely a deep belief network (DBN). Erfani et al. [7] used a deep belief network (DBN) for constructing a robust feature representation for an one-class classifications (OCCs). The OCCs are One-class Support Vector Machine (OCSVM) and Support Vector Data Description (SVDD). The proposed model aimed to deal with the problem posed in high-dimensional anomaly detection data. The DBN was first pretrained in the greedy layer-wise fashion by stacking Restricted Boltzmann Machines (RBMs) trained in unsupervised manner. OCSVM and SVDD were then stacked on top of the DBN. The hybrid model were evaluated on eight high-dimensional UCI datasets, and the experimental results showed that the model often out-performs stand-alone the one-class classifiers.

In this work, we attempt to construct a latent representation for identifying network anomalies in semi-supervised manner. This means that we first train an AE on normal data to map the original data into several clusters in the latent feature space of the AE with a proposed regularized loss. It then performs the K-mean task: assigning data points to each clusters; relocating the cluster centers. These tasks are operated iteratively until a early-stopping criteria met. The trained CAE is then employed for classifying querying data points. The distance from the data point to the nearest cluster center is used as anomaly score. By imposing a classification threshold, the data point can be classified as an anomaly if its distance is greater than the threshold.

4   Proposed Approach

In this section, we explain our proposed model for anomaly detection that is called Clustering-based deep AutoEncoder (CAE). Our model is a combination of a variation of k-mean clustering algorithm and an AE. It is clear that the original version of AE, which forces normal input samples into a sole cluster may not produce expected results on datasets in which practically have several clusters. CAE aims to learn the latent representation of normal data and parallelly force data points in the bottleneck of AE into a number of clusters. During the training process, the centers of these clusters are also put toward to the origin of the latent representation. This is based on the assumption that normal data may have several sub-classes inside, but they still share some common characteristics in overall. Thus, normal data points should be appeared close each others.

In practice, we propose a new regularizer to the loss function of the AE in the hybrid CAE. Unlike classical K-mean methods, which try to minimize distances within a cluster and maximize the distances between clusters, we aim to design a variance K-mean that minimizes both distances within each cluster and between clusters. Therefore our regularizer consists of two terms: (1) minimizing the distances of data points to their corresponding centers; (2) minimizing the distances of the cluster centers to the origin of the latent representation. In the Eq. 3, the first term is the reconstruction error (RE) of the AE, and the second and the third terms are the two regularized terms (1) and (2) respectively. The CAE model trained on normal training data forces almost normal data into inner clusters and these cluster centers are also pulled closer to the origin of the CAE latent representation. In the querying stage, the model will be employed to distinguish whether a query data point belonging to normal class or anomalous class by evaluating its distance to the closest cluster center. This means that if the distance is greater than a predetermined threshold, the data point will be classified as an anomaly. The loss function in this case can be defined as in Eq. 6 below:

$$\zeta_{CAE}(\theta, x^i, z) = \frac{1}{n}\sum_1^n \left|\left|x^i - \hat{x}^i\right|\right|^2 + \lambda_1 \frac{1}{n}\sum_1^n \left|\left|f^{(t)}(x_i) - c_i^*\right|\right|^2 + \lambda_2 \frac{1}{k}\sum_1^k \left|\left|c_j^t\right|\right|^2$$

(6)

$$c_i^* = \underset{c_j^{t-1}}{argmin} \left|\left|f^{(t)}(x_i) - c_j^{t-1}\right|\right|^2$$

(7)

$$c_j^t = \frac{\sum_{x_i \in C_j^{t-1}} f^t(x_i)}{\left|C_j^{t-1}\right|}$$

(8)

where n is the number of samples in the normal training set; $\hat{x}^i$ is the reconstruction of the sample x^i; The first component in (6) is the reconstruction error (RE), and the second and the third terms are two regularized components (pulling data points closer to their cluster centers, pushing the centers of all clusters being close to the origin as well as possible). λ_1 and λ_2 are used to trade-off between these components. $f^t(x)$ is the mapping function (the encoder of CAE) at the tth iteration; c_i^* is the closest cluster of the ith observation; c_j^{t-1} is the jth cluster centroid, which is produced at the $(t-1)^{th}$ iteration.

Figure 2 is an example for representing noramal data in the latent feature space of CAE during the co-training process of CAE. We suppose that the normal training set consists of three clusters (illustrating in green, blue, and red). In the training phrase, observations in the same cluster are forced to be close to their corresponding cluster centers as showed in small purple arrows, meanwhile three cluster centers are also pushed towards the origin of the latent feature space as illustrated with red arrows.

We present our proposed method as in Algorithm 2. At the first iteration C^0, we randomly initialize K cluster centers. CAE is trained on the normal training set to optimize the loss function (6). This process will gradually force the normal training data in the latent feature space (called latent normal data) into several clusters. Following this, the latent normal data is assigned into K clusters via formula (7) and these cluster centers are updated using the Eq. (8). These training steps will be operated until an early-stopping criteria met or the

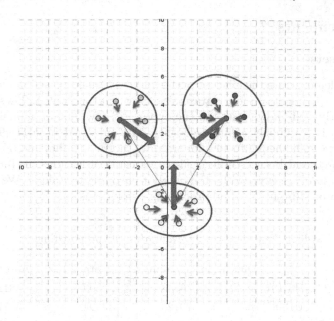

Fig. 2. An illustration of our proposed model (Color figure online)

iteration exceed a threshold T. In this work, we use a normal validation set for the early-stopping. The model trained on the normal training set is evaluated on the validation set once every few iterations. The training process will stop if the RE on the validation set does not improve for a certain threshold in a number of successive iterations. Finally, the output of the algorithm is the cluster centers in the latent feature space and CAE model.

Algorithm 2 Clustering-based deep AutoEncoder (CAE)

1: **Input: a given dataset X, the number of clusters K, a set of AE hyper-parameters θ and ϕ, the maximum number of iterations T.**
2: **randomly choose K cluster centers (C^o)**
3: $t = 1$
4: **repeat**
5:     **Train CAE on X to optimize the loss function (6).**
6:     **Classify X into K clusters**
7:     **Update all new K cluster centers (C^t) via formula (8).**
8:     $t = t + 1.$
9: **until an early-stopping criteria met or $t < T$.**
10: **Output: CAE model and cluster centers C.**
    =0

---

5   Experiments

5.1   Datasets

In order to demonstrate the efficient performance of the proposed model, we conducted the experiments on four datasets as shown in the Table 1. These datasets are the mostly well-known issues in the cyber security domain, namely CTU13. The CTU13 is a publicly available botnet data provided in 2011 [9]. In each experiment we split them into 40% for training (normal traffic) and 60% for evaluating (normal and botnet traffic). Three categorical features, including *dTos*, *sTos* and *protocol* are encoded by the one-hot encoding technique. We follow the processing procedure in [5] to preprocessing these datasets.

Table 1. Four datasets for evaluating the proposed models

No	Dataset	Dimension	Training set	Normal test	Anomaly test
1	Rbot (CTU13-10)	38	6338	9509	63812
2	Murlo (CTU13-8)	40	29128	43694	3677
3	Neris (CTU13-9)	41	11986	17981	110993
4	Virut (CTU13-13)	40	12775	19164	24002

5.2   Experimental Settings

In this work, our model will be constructed from the normal class only. The configuration of CAE is described as follows. The trade-off parameters of the loss function λ_1 and λ_2 are set equal to 300 and 1500 respectively. The number of hidden layer is 5, and the middle hidden layer size is calculated using the formula $h = [1 + \sqrt{n}]$, where n is the number of input features [4]. The learning rate is set at 10^{-1}, and the batch size is 100. The weights of CAE are initialized using the Xavier initialization method to speed up the convergence process. We use *Adadelta* optimization algorithm for training CAE. The activation function is the TANH function. For the variance K-mean, we manually choose the number clusters equal to 2. We realize that $k = 2$ is the best choice, but it is acceptable. How to automatically estimate the number of sub-classes (clusters) in normal network data is a question for our future work. We use validation sets to evaluate our proposed models at every 5 epochs for early-stopping. The normal training data, normal testing data and anomaly testing data in the latent representation are visualized for getting into the insight of the latent feature space.

We carry out two experiments for evaluating the proposed model. Firstly, the performance of CAE is compared with SAE and DVAE in the study [5]. Therefore, we reproduce the same experiments as in [5], and report the performance of SAE and DVAE on two cases: the following classifiers are CEN and MDIS as showed in Table 2. The reason for choosing CEN and MDIS is that CEN was reported as the best classifier when combining with SAE and DVAE in the study [5] while MDIS was considered as the worse case. In our model, we use the distance from a querying data point to its nearest cluster center as anomaly a score. To estimate the distance, our model first calculate the distance from that point to every cluster centers, and decide which one is the nearest cluster center. The process is very similar to CEN proposed in [5], but for multiple centroids. We call the method to estimate anomaly score in our proposed model as Multi Centroids (M-CEN). Secondly, the latent data of the training set and testing set are visualized to get into insight the behavior of the latent representation of CAE as visualizing in Figs. 3, 4, 5, and 6. We also visualize the Are Under the ROC curves when evaluating CAE on four scenarios as showed in Fig. 7.

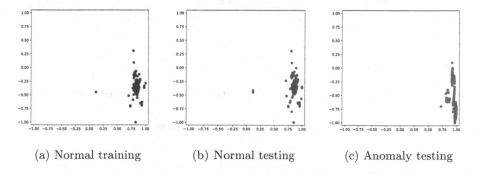

(a) Normal training   (b) Normal testing   (c) Anomaly testing

Fig. 3. Visualize the latent data of the CTU13-10 dataset (Color figure online)

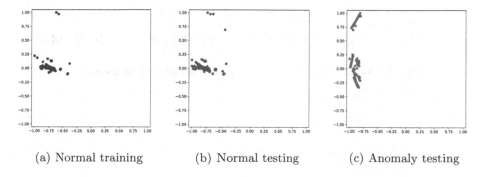

(a) Normal training   (b) Normal testing   (c) Anomaly testing

Fig. 4. Visualize the latent data of the CTU13-08 dataset (Color figure online)

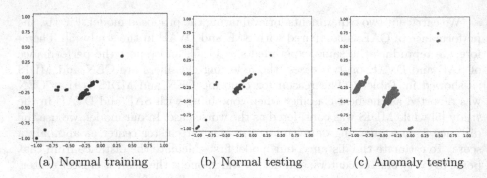

(a) Normal training   (b) Normal testing   (c) Anomaly testing

Fig. 5. Visualize the latent data of the CTU13-9 dataset (Color figure online)

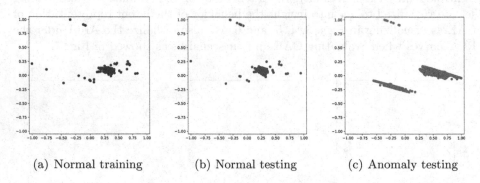

(a) Normal training   (b) Normal testing   (c) Anomaly testing

Fig. 6. Visualize the latent data of the CTU13-13 dataset (Color figure online)

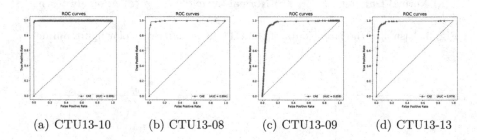

(a) CTU13-10   (b) CTU13-08   (c) CTU13-09   (d) CTU13-13

Fig. 7. The ROC curves of our proposed model on four datasets

Table 2. AUCs from the hybrid SAE-OCCs, DVAE-OCCs, and the CAE model.

Representation	One-class classifiers	Datasets			
		CTU13-10	CTU13-08	CTU13-09	CTU13-13
SAE $\lambda = 10$	CEN	0.999	0.991	0.950	0.969
	MDIS	0.999	0.990	0.950	0.968
DVAE $\lambda = 0.05,\ \alpha = 10^{-8}$	CEN	0.999	0.982	0.956	0.963
	MDIS	0.999	0.984	0.957	0.964
CAE	M-CEN	0.996	**0.994**	**0.959**	**0.979**

6   Results and Discussion

This section presents the experimental results of evaluating the proposed model, CAE, on the four scenarios in the CTU13 dataset. The performance of these classifiers is evaluated by using AUC as summarized in Table 2. The training data and testing data represented in the latent feature space of CAE are plotted to investigate the behavior of CAE. The ROC curves produced from the CAE classifier are also visualized to evaluate the performance of CAE on a number of classification thresholds as showed in Fig. 7.

It can be seen from Table 2 that the CAE classifier performs (in terms of classification accuracy) very well on all datasets, and the CAE performance is often better than those of SAE and DVAE with CEN and MDIS on the CTU13-08, CTU13-09 and CTU13-13 scenarios. This suggests that the normal data may originally distribute in two sub-classes. Thus, when CAE represents the normal data into two clusters, the AUC scores are improved in comparison to those produced from SAE-CEN and DVAE-CEN.

In order to support for our discussion above, we will investigate the latent data of both the normal training data, and the testing data consisting of normal data and anomalies. In the Figs. 3, 4, 5, and 6, we plot the first two features of the data in the latent feature space: the normal training data in blue; the normal testing data in green; and the anomaly testing data in red. Figure 3 shows that both the normal training data and the normal testing data seem to distribute in only one region in the latent feature space. This suggests that the normal data in CTU13-10 may contain only one cluster. Therefore, the AUC score on CTU13-10 decreases when the normal data is forced into two clusters (the AUC of CAE is slightly lower than those of SAE-CEN and DVAE-CEN). On the other hand, the Figs. 6, 4, and 5 show promising results. The latent data of the normal training, and the latent data of the normal testing distribute into two small areas in the latent feature space. These small areas tend to be close together. The latent data of the anomaly data appears in some regions not overlapping the normal data. This can imply that the normal data of CTU13-13, CTU13-08, and CTU13-09 may contain more than one sub-classes, which results in the increase in the AUC scores in comparison to those of SAE-CEN and DVAE-CEN as showed in the last row in Table 2.

The results in the Figs. 3, 6, 4, and 5 are very useful for the explanation why CAE can out-performs SAE and DVAE on the CTU13-13, CTU13-08, and CTU13-09 scenarios while on CTU13-10 it does not. Base on our experimental results and analysis, we can confirm that our proposed model, CAE, can perform well on anomaly detection datasets in which the normal data contains more than one sub-classes.

7   Conclusion and Future Work

A novel hybrid between clustering methods and AEs, namely CAE, is proposed for automatically revealing a number of clusters in normal data. This aims to overcome the drawback of a previous study [5] where normal data is considered as only one cluster. In CAE, a variation of K-mean and an AE co-train at each training iteration in which the AE maps normal data into the latent representation while the clustering-based method attempts to group the data into several clusters being close to the origin. In querying stage, the distance of a given data point to the closest cluster center can be used as an anomaly score. The higher anomaly score a data point has, the more likely it is anomaly. CAE is evaluated on four scenarios in the CTU13 dataset and experiments illustrate that CAE out-performs SAE and DVAE on three out of four scenarios.

In this work, we choose the number of clusters manually. The study of automatically estimating the true number of clusters in normal data will be postponed to the future work.

References

1. Aggarwal, C.C.: Outlier analysis. Data Mining, pp. 237–263. Springer, Cham (2015). https://doi.org/10.1007/978-3-319-14142-8_8
2. Bourlard, H., Kamp, Y.: Auto-association by multilayer perceptrons and singular value decomposition. Biol. Cybern. 291–294 (1988). https://doi.org/10.1007/BF00332918
3. Bui, T.C., Cao, V.L., Hoang, M., Nguyen, Q.U.: A clustering-based shrink autoencoder for detecting anomalies in intrusion detection systems. In: Proceedings of the KSE, pp. 1–5. IEEE (2019)
4. Cao, V.L., Nicolau, M., McDermott, J.: A hybrid autoencoder and density estimation model for anomaly detection. In: Handl, J., Hart, E., Lewis, P.R., López-Ibáñez, M., Ochoa, G., Paechter, B. (eds.) PPSN 2016. LNCS, vol. 9921, pp. 717–726. Springer, Cham (2016). https://doi.org/10.1007/978-3-319-45823-6_67
5. Cao, V.L., Nicolau, M., McDermott, J.: Learning neural representations for network anomaly detection. IEEE Trans. Cybern. 49(8), 3074–3087 (2018)
6. Chandola, V., Banerjee, A., Kumar, V.: Anomaly detection: a survey. ACM Comput. Surv. (CSUR) 41(3), 15 (2009)
7. Erfani, S.M., Rajasegarar, S., Karunasekera, S., Leckie, C.: High-dimensional and large-scale anomaly detection using a linear one-class SVM with deep learning. Pattern Recogn. 58, 121–134 (2016)
8. Fiore, U., Palmieri, F., Castiglione, A., De Santis, A.: Network anomaly detection with the restricted Boltzmann machine. Neurocomputing 122, 13–23 (2013)

9. Garcia, S., Grill, M., Stiborek, J., Zunino, A.: An empirical comparison of botnet detection methods. Comput. Secur. **45**, 100–123 (2014)
10. Hawkins, S., He, H., Williams, G., Baxter, R.: Outlier detection using replicator neural networks. In: Kambayashi, Y., Winiwarter, W., Arikawa, M. (eds.) DaWaK 2002. LNCS, vol. 2454, pp. 170–180. Springer, Heidelberg (2002). https://doi.org/10.1007/3-540-46145-0_17
11. Hinton, G.E., Zemel, R.S.: Autoencoders, minimum description length and Helmholtz free energy. In: Advances in Neural Information Processing Systems, pp. 3–10 (1994)
12. Japkowicz, N., Myers, C., Gluck, M.: A novelty detection approach to classification. In: IJCAI, pp. 518–523 (1995)
13. Phoha, V.V.: Internet Security Dictionary. Springer, Heidelberg (2007)
14. Sakurada, M., Yairi, T.: Anomaly detection using autoencoders with nonlinear dimensionality reduction. In: Proceedings of the MLSDA, p. 4. ACM (2014)
15. Song, C., Liu, F., Huang, Y., Wang, L., Tan, T.: Auto-encoder based data clustering. In: Ruiz-Shulcloper, J., Sanniti di Baja, G. (eds.) CIARP 2013. LNCS, vol. 8258, pp. 117–124. Springer, Heidelberg (2013). https://doi.org/10.1007/978-3-642-41822-8_15
16. Vu, L., Cao, V.L., Nguyen, Q.U., Nguyen, D.N., Hoang, D.T., Dutkiewicz, E.: Learning latent distribution for distinguishing network traffic in intrusion detection system. In: ICC 2019–2019 IEEE International Conference on Communications (ICC), pp. 1–6. IEEE (2019)

Flexible Platform for Integration, Collection, and Analysis of Social Media for Open Data Providers in Smart Cities

Thanh-Cong Le[1,3], Quoc-Vuong Nguyen[1,3], and Minh-Triet Tran[1,2,3]([✉])

[1] University of Science, Ho Chi Minh City, Vietnam
{ltcong,nqvuong}@selab.hcmus.edu.vn
tmtriet@fit.hcmus.edu.vn
[2] John von Neumann Institute, Ho Chi Minh City, Vietnam
[3] Vietnam National University, Ho Chi Minh City, Vietnam

Abstract. Developing infrastructure and intelligent utilities for smart cities is an important trend in the world as well as in Vietnam. Thus, it is important to assist developers in building services for open data and smart city utilities. This motivates our proposal to develop a flexible platform with useful components, which can be integrated to develop these solutions quickly, to listen and analyze data from different social media sources with the diversification of data types, to provide open data providers in smart cities. Our method focuses on the ability to flexibly integrate artificial intelligence applications into the system to be able to both analyze effectively social events and serve smart cities in creating open data providers. We do not develop a particular system, but we create a platform, including different components, which are easy to be extended and integrated to create specific applications. To evaluate our platform, we develop four systems, including a face recognition system for celebrity recognition in news videos, an object detection system for brand logo recognition, a video highlighting system for summarizing football matches, and a text analysis system serving for keyword occurrences and emotional text analysis for admissions of universities. In these systems, we have collected and analyzed nearly 1000 videos from CNN, CBSN, FIFATV channels on YouTube, thousands of posts from admission pages of universities on Facebook. Each system gives a unique meaning to each specific situation for open data providers in smart cities.

Keywords: Social listening · Open data provider · Software architecture · Object detection · Face recognition · Video highlights

1 Introduction

Smart cities are not only a trend but also a challenging topic in integrating intelligent technologies and applications into building smarter cities. To develop

---

T.-C. Le and Q.-V. Nguyen—Both authors contribute equally.

T. K. Dang et al. (Eds.): FDSE 2020, LNCS 12466, pp. 304–324, 2020.
https://doi.org/10.1007/978-3-030-63924-2_18

a smart city, the first thing is to have data providers in open form, one of the essential needs is the open data provider that can help us understand the information social media in society. This has led to a demand for applying to listen and analyze social media data for open data providers in smart cities.

The development of media, as well as devices to record information and data in everyday life, has created a rich and diverse data source in both genre and quantity. According to statistics in BBTEL, by 2020, there are 6 billion mobile phone users worldwide and 2.3 trillion GB of data generated daily. With the growth of the Internet, smartphones have been contributing to a massive amount of data, from photos and videos to status lines and comments posted on news sites—i.e., forum or social network. In addition to phones, information sources from security cameras, traffic cameras, cameras in everyday life, or other information recording devices such as cameras and voice recorders are also diverse and rich sources of information, providing more diverse and multidimensional perspectives on everyday life. The amount of data, as well as information, is created more and more, along with the development of the media, making the ability to share and receive information more quickly and diversified.

Information sources can come from anywhere, from news sites, social networks, forums, TV channels, etc., and the information is not only in text language format but also in many formats. Another special is multimedia format such as audio, image, video. Information presented in a variety of formats will give us insight into what it means and the message it delivers.

Which mentioned information is of great interest in the world as well as in Vietnam, typically through applications that enable people to analyze and listen from social media. These solutions usually rely on the periodic and regular collection of information to get information from a variety of sources such as websites, communities, forums, social networks as well as YouTube channels, comment sections where people mention a certain brand, an organization, or a person, especially a celebrity. Analysis of these factors will help people know which information is mentioned a lot or not, trends in society, discover problems or problems that are likely to occur related to a brand, certain individuals, organizations. Therefore, the applications that serve this are developed in many ways, at the same time, also have a variety of features and mainly focus on listening, gathering, analyzing, and making reports for individuals and organizations to have appropriate actions.

The features of social media analytics applications are increasingly being added and enhanced to help us analyze better, instead of initially including only functions such as statistics of exported keywords. Currently, and the number of times people share, mention, etc., and the newly added features are also being developed by researchers and businesses. A solution based only on text analysis will have the disadvantage of not having a general view and not making full use of the diversity of data sources.

To solve the above problem, using images and videos for data analysis is indispensable. With the prevalence and variety of image and video data on the Internet, we can make the most of the data they bring.

Through the analysis process, we see that the problem of listening and analyzing social media data is interesting and has the potential to be widely applied in life more and more. There are three issues to consider as follows:

1. The variety of data sources is not only in the form of text but also in the form of audio, images, and video, so the construction solution also needs to be flexible and suitable for many different formats.
2. The analytical features are not necessarily limited to the features related to statistics, comparison, etc., but can expand to integrate other analytical features such as analysis of the event, counting objects, abnormal phenomenon detection. These functions are so diverse that, depending on the context and the specific application, it is necessary to be able to integrate into this system easily.
3. The solution is not necessarily associated with the data collection process because, in addition to the data that we can collect, there is much data that has been collected with specific characteristics. Individuals or organizations also need analysis that the solution built can apply and integrate these easily.

After analyzing the general situation as well as the characteristics of interest and three issues above, we define the objectives to develop software tools and accompanying solutions to be able to build an application for collecting and analyzing recorded information from social media in everyday life.

Within this topic, we do not aim to develop a specific application but to create a set of mechanisms and solutions that are frequently used and can be integrated together to create specific applications for this problem.

Due to the wide variety of practical needs, when meeting a specific requirement in a specific application of a particular customer, our toolkit and solutions can be quickly used to create an application that serves that request. Because of the diverse and rich needs and new requirements that will arise later, the architecture must be flexible to be able to pair, integrate to serve different needs and, at the same time, expand in the future. Therefore, there is a need for a clear solution to guide the users of the tool, and this solution can integrate and add other features according to actual needs.

When doing this solution, it will help provide open data providers, based on it, not only the government but also organizations, and individuals have the ability to quickly develop intelligent services or applications to serve the smart city. For example, in the enrollment process, it can help the unions visualize their needs, or the news is more attractive to people when they can organize the news related to famous people in the news.

The structure of this paper is as follows. In Sect. 2, we briefly review existing methods and approaches for social listening, social media data analysis systems, and AI applications, which are used to provide intelligent suggestions or improvements. Section 3 presents our proposal for overview architecture with the ability to flexibly integrate artificial intelligence analysis applications into the system based on using multiple data source management. We also develop four systems for case studies with their practical meanings, which are described in Sect. 4. Finally, the conclusion is in Sect. 5.

2   Related Work

The establishment and application of social media data analysis systems are the issues that organizations and businesses have focused on developing in recent years.

YouNet Group is a leader in Marketing & Technology, developed on the Social Intelligence platform. In 2013, the subsidiary YouNet Media was established and market leader in the field of social media information analysis thanks to technology applications and multichannel data sources, namely SocialHeat. In 2015, by owning Buzzmetrics, YouNet Group has affirmed its leading position in Social Listening & Data Analytics market with over 70% market share. Besides, Viettel has also researched and built a Reputa platform to support the monitoring and analysis of social media information. Both SocialHeat's YouNet Group and Viettel's Reputa are quality products that bring positive signals that open up new trends of market analysis for businesses - the trend of analyzing social media information.

In general, SocialHeat is a product that supports YouNet Media's monitoring and analysis of social media information - a member of the YouNet Group ecosystem - a pioneer in the application of social intelligence and technology to operations and regulations on marketing process that brings comprehensive digital steps and boosts business efficiency for customers in Vietnam and international markets. This is an integrated platform with a Sentiment Rating Engine [6,12] with an accuracy of 80–85%. With SocialHeat, businesses can monitor brand status in the media, detect and warn brand crises, identify those who harm the brand, identify people used for branding, identifying brand attributes on social networks, what topics are of interest and brand-related trends, and analyzing trends over time.

Besides, Reputa is one of the pioneering platforms of Viettel to support social media information analysis. The Reputa system supports business organizations to collect and analyze information on social networks to help manage brands, capture needs, and take care of customers on the Internet and social networks. Reputa offers the main solutions: monitoring brand health every day through automatic nuances analysis, preventing communication crisis risk, understanding the market and competitors through tools support classification, and statistical market trends. Reputa also supports application of artificial intelligence technologies such as Natural Language Processing (NLP), Automatic Speech Recognition (ASR) [7], Optical Character Recognition (OCR).

One of the features of the social listening system is that it not only collects but also can analyze that information to provide intelligent suggestions or improvements. With object detection, many algorithms are introduced, but the most common ones are Faster R-CNN [4], Histogram of Oriented Gradients (HOG), Single Shot Detector (SSD) [15], YOLO [1], etc. With face recognition recently featured with FaceNet, Face detector using Dlib or OpenCV [3]. The algorithms have opened up many approaches that yield auspicious results.

3   Our Proposed System

To develop smart cities, the first thing is to have data providers in open form, one of the essential needs is open data providers that can help us understand what social media information is available in the community. To do these quickly, it is essential to use utilities and components that can be easily integrated and extended, which motivates us in proposing a platform with the appropriate components and utilities to help quickly create such systems.

3.1   Overview of Method

In this section, we present our proposed method to provide a flexible platform, components, and utilities to crawl and analyze data from social networks with the diversification of data types like text, image/video from multiple data sources such as Facebook, YouTube, E-news, etc. There are four main components in our method: gateway, crawler, statistics, and analysis (Fig. 1).

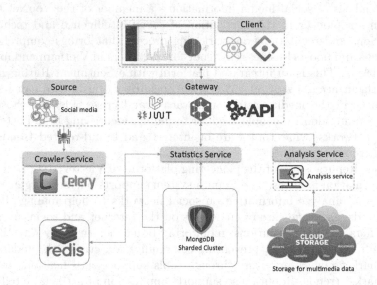

Fig. 1. Overview architecture

Gateway: We aim to build a support module that provides API services to communicate with clients with JWT authentication [2] and load balancing [5] ability to adjust traffic to the system.

Crawler: This module is provided to collect data from many social data sources such as Facebook, YouTube, or online newspapers like VnExpress. The details of the process of this module are described in Sect. 3.2.

Statistics: The analytical system always needs data for statistics and visualization. The data after being collected in the crawler module will be calculated and stored in the database like MongoDB so that it is reasonable. Additionally, data need to be cached, and we use Redis for caching. This module does that task, and the process content is covered in Sect. 3.3.

Analysis: The process of this module is illustrated in Sect. 3.4, which is focused on how we can integrate different components from Google Colab to create a smart API. Especially, it is described how we can break the gap between developing a regular distributed system with APIs and intelligent functions. In this one, we propose a simple, efficient architecture that can be used to convert a regular system, which can be deployed on Google Colab. Besides, we also suggest a mechanism to communicate between different modules and services.

The approach of our proposed method emphasizes the ability to integrate artificial intelligence analysis applications into the system flexibly. Moreover, the use of artificial intelligence applications as a replaceable module according to user needs will bring extremely high scalability.

3.2   Crawler

Collecting data from social media such as news sites, social networks, etc. helps to diversify sources of information, providing additional data to support analysis. However, data from social media is immense and varied. Therefore, a solution is needed to help gather data from many sources quickly and effectively. Moreover, the solution needs to be highly flexible to expand the collection of data from many other sources in the future.

Celery is a highly scalable, parallel task queue management system. Figure 2 shows the four steps of the Celery data collection process.

1. The task of collecting data from Facebook, YouTube, and VNExpress will be declared and sent to the Celery client.
2. The Celery client will distribute tasks into the RabbitMQ queues.
3. Depending on the status of the Celery worker, the tasks in the RabbitMQ queues will be transferred to a certain Celery worker for processing.
4. The collected data will be stored in MongoDB. Multimedia data such as images, videos, etc. will be stored as strings, which is a link to their direct storage source.

3.3   Statistics

This module is responsible for using collected data to calculate the metrics needed for visualization, and also expose the APIs for other services to use: information APIs supporting for details of sources and statistics APIs supporting for analysis metrics of sources.

The statistics module needs fast access efficiency and consistent storage capabilities so a combination of a database for storage and a database for caching is needed.

MongoDB not only stores, updates and retrieves information, but also supports calculating data thanks to the Aggregation Framework. Through API calls into MongoDB, it is easy to retrieve the data for comparison and statistics. However, when the number of requests to access information and data is increasing, the use of the cache to store the results of frequent queries in the database is a necessary solution. To avoid querying too much into the database as well as quickly responding to query results.

We use Redis as a cache server to store the results of queries into MongoDB. The strategy of updating the cache when having a query like this:

1. Find data in the cache. If the data exists (cache hit), go to step 4. Otherwise, if the data does not exist (cache miss), continue to step 2.
2. Retrieve data from the database.
3. Add newly retrieved data to the cache.
4. Return retrieved data.

Thus, with the above cache update strategy, it is possible to avoid caching unnecessary data, but the data in the cache may be inaccurate when the database is updated. We solve this problem by using TTL (Time to Live) for the data cached.

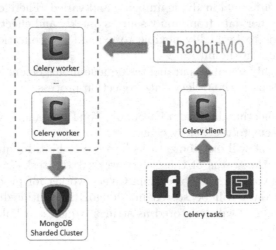

Fig. 2. Crawler

3.4 Analysis

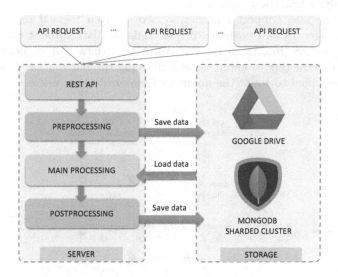

Fig. 3. Overall architecture of an analysis service

The overall architecture of a data analysis service is described in Fig. 3, which shows a general model for data analysis that includes both textual and multimedia data. Specifically, most API calls go through three stages: preprocessing, main processing, and postprocessing. The preprocessing stage has the main task of processing input inputs, saving necessary data into Storage. The main processing stage will depend on the needs and purpose of the processing, for example, object detection will use the CenterNet [17] library, face recognition will use the Face recognition of Dlib [13] library and then load the model from Storage to process, and return results. The postprocessing phase will save the results to Storage and finish the processing. Data of the same format will be converted to a common format and centrally stored in a Storage that can be easily saved and shared. We use MongoDB to store textual data, and Google Drive to store multimedia data such as images and videos because we found the fit.

We can have many different features for a social media data analysis system. However, through the analysis of common needs, we first recommend integrating system analysis with the following common we use component for the artificial intelligent process. We focus on two main data types: text and video/image. Therefore, we currently integrate the following API into our system.

Text Analysis. First, for text processing, we incorporate systems capable of doing parts involving sentimental analysis. For English, we use the model that has been trained with the English dataset to integrate into the Sentimental analysis model in Fig. 4. For Vietnamese, we first use the Vietnam sentiment analysis model and we also study to use PhoBERT [11] in the future.

This module is integrated and turned out to be a Sentiment analysis model of main processing in Fig. 4 to provide features to support positive or negative nuances analysis from user comments.

Besides, we also support counting keywords from textual data. Counting keyword occurrences is a basic feature to make statistics about the frequency of keywords we are interested in. The input text data will be normalized by returning all characters to lowercase and deleting the bar marks. Then, use the dictionary provided to count the number of keyword occurrences.

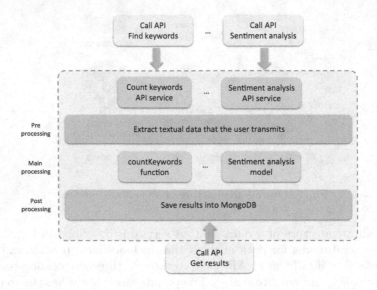

Fig. 4. Process of text analysis

Video/Image Analysis. For video/image data type, we focus on two common types of analysis: face recognition and object detection. We also consider features related to highlight videos [10]. To do this, we use the CenterNet algorithm for object detection, the Dlib library for face recognition, and the video volume solution for a video highlighting in Fig. 5. The procedure for each type of analysis will be presented in the succeeding part.

Object Detection. We use CenterNet for object detection because CenterNet is one of the leading new, fast, and accurate approaches to object detection in early 2020.

CenterNet's new approach is to bring the object detection problem to the keypoint estimation problem, thereby also deducing the size and calculating the bounding box for the object detection problem.

When using the CenterNet library, we can either use the pre-trained model or create a new personal model. To create a new model, the first thing is to

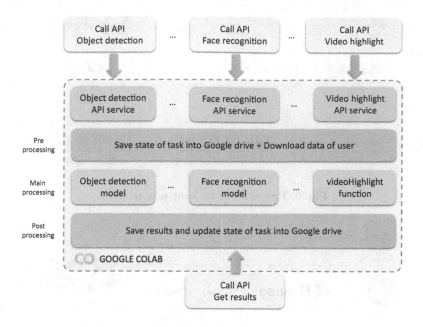

Fig. 5. Process of video/image analysis

prepare the labeled training set in the COCO format. We can store the label set data directly into the CenterNet folder on Cloud storage or compress it and upload it to a Google drive then pass the link to the API train new model shown in Fig. 6.

Figure 6 demonstrates the general process for adding new models that can be applied to both Object detection and Face recognition with a similar way of just changing the Training model step with their respective tools. The process is mainly divided into 2 phases corresponding to API train new model and API deploy model, which is to create a new model but the model has not been used, only when the model is deployed and creates a new URL for other services to access from. The new exterior is actually applied. Information about the link dataset, model name will be saved at Init model to mark the model being processed. Next, the Download dataset step will rely on the link dataset to download and save to the CenterNet folder on Cloud storage like Google drive. The Training model will use that data to train the new model. The training model will use the function of CenterNet library. So if we want to use another library or use Face recognition instead, we just need to change this part. After the training model is complete, the Finish model will save the model and its attached information to Cloud storage like Google drive.

As object detection and face recognition are both image-focused, images uploaded from Cloud storage will be analyzed directly. However, for video, we need preprocessing to convert it to an image by cutting out frame by frame. We use FFmpeg [16] tool to do this transformation. After the video is preprocessed,

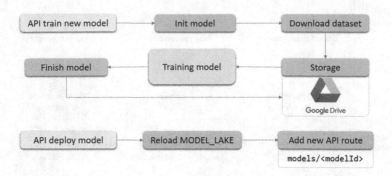

Fig. 6. Procedure of training new model

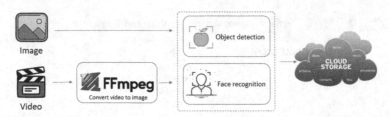

Fig. 7. Object detection and face recognition with video and image

object detection and face recognition input has been converted to a single image format in Fig. 7. The data is then processed through object detection models that are preloaded into the model lake on the server and stored in Cloud storage.

Face Recognition. We use the face_recognition [8] library, which was built using dlib's state-of-the-art face recognition built with deep learning, by Adam Geitgey. The model has an accuracy of 99.38% on the Labeled Faces in the Wild benchmark [14]. In this paper, we're not going into algorithm analysis but artificial intelligence uses and integrations into the system, here we explore how to use the face recognition library.

The face recognition training new model process is similar to object detection in Fig. 6. This library-based face training is divided into the following steps. First, prepare training data with a directory of subfolders that are the names of the characters to be recognized for, and within those folders are face images. Note, the images used for training must be images with only one face. Then, when we install, we go through the folders in turn and use the face_recognition library to upload each image, marking the position of the face and the corresponding label. Then, we will have an array of facial features in the form of vectors and labels respectively. This data is further processed by scikit-learn's Support Vector Machine [9] library, SVC, and saved as a model. Finally, the model is stored on Cloud storage and loaded up as needed.

Video Highlight. The approach of summarizing this video is not based on training of models, visual event tracking, but on the sound of the video. Most videos, not all, have climax in the big soundtrack that is suddenly compared to the rest. In football, every time a player scores, the commentator and the audience will cheer loudly. Thus, audio tracking from a video can be handled using the moviepy.editor library in Python [18].

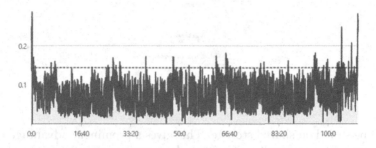

Fig. 8. Volume per second of a football video

For example, steps for highlighting video is as followed. First, calculate the average volume per second of the audio portion from the video in Fig. 8. However, to see the differences in sound, the volume should be calculated at 10-s intervals. Next, to take the standout scenarios, we can take the occurrences of the top 10%. After that, all you need to do is cluster the occurrences no more than 1 min apart into the same group. As a result, we have event groups that have the volume in the top 10% of the video, the rest is cutting the video according to those time groups.

New API Service Integration. At present, we follow these APIs, but in the future, based on the architecture we can easily integrate more components by wrapping. Therefore, in this part, we briefly introduce the basic process to wrap an API into the system. First, we deploy a template analysis service API on Google Colab that includes preprocessing, main processing, and postprocessing. Then, depending on the analysis needs, the developer can write custom wrapper functions to replace the contents of the above steps. Finally, the API is published and used by other services and modules.

3.5   Source Provider

Many data sources will be attributed to only two types of storage: database for text and cloud storage for video/image. The source provider we use is MongoDB and Google drive in Fig. 9.

Information sources are managed by converting it to a single common format. Specifically, data collected automatically from social networks and user-uploaded

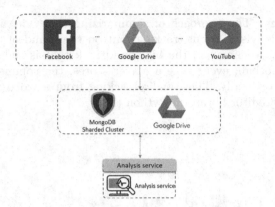

Fig. 9. Source provider

data will be stored on shared storage. This gives a prominent advantage to user-private data such as surveillance camera data, traffic cameras, personal photos, and videos.

When a user has a data set that does not allow direct access, we can only use the exact data that he or she provides. The idea is simple to solve by uploading data on a common cloud storage. At that time, we chose Google drive to turn into cloud storage for storage purposes. However, it can be used with another technology such as Amazon Drive, Dropbox, OneDrive, etc.

For textual data and accompanying statistics, a database will be suitable for storage. We use MongoDB and design a schema according to data source and username appropriately.

For multimedia data, the management of data sources of various origins is addressed according to the storage directory hierarchy. Data folder on Cloud storage contains folders by data format names such as Image, Video. The Video folder will contain subfolders according to the Username. Each Username folder will contain subfolders that are the names of data source sources like YouTube, Drive. These folders will again contain Source ID folders. Inside the Source ID are the user data files and associated analytics files.

4 Case Study

This section presents the system architecture and the main functions of four prospective systems in potential case studies we have constituted with modules and solutions mentioned in Sect. 3.

4.1 Face Recognition System

Using our proposed method to custom crawler services and integrate AI service as Face recognition on Google Colab into overview architecture, we have successfully developed a system for collecting, analyzing, and recognizing celebrities' faces in Fig. 10.

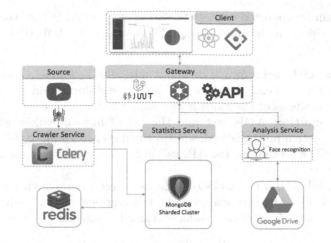

Fig. 10. Face recognition system

The system offers the ability to collect data from YouTube's huge video source, allowing users to choose the channels they want to follow. At the same time, the system helps users to track and statistic of channel parameters from likes, followers to feedback from videos on the channel. In particular, the system supports celebrity facial recognition according to the needs of users on videos from the channel they subscribe to. From there, the system will count the number of faces appearances of famous people, then display visually on the analysis charts to help users identify which celebrity appears more on videos in order to assess the popularity of that person's image on social media.

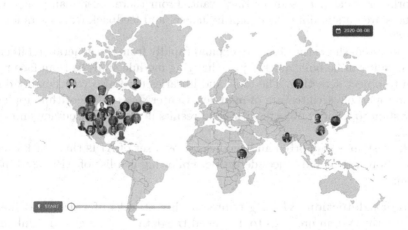

Fig. 11. Maps of celebrities in news videos

The system is supported and syndicated by a set of APIs that track channel information, video, and facial recognition. Following is a list of APIs used in this system:

- **Statistics APIs**: get information about subscribers, channel views over time, including start and end, are passed in. Moreover, information about the comments, likes, shares of the video is also supported.
- **Face recognition APIs**: get into the list of links of videos and images. Then, the system proceeds to download the data according to the link and is identified. The user makes the API call again to see job status or result after identification.
- **Face model APIs**: Get links of a dataset and accompanying information of a model. The API then executes the training new model according to the dataset submitted. After the model is trained, users can use it normally.

Users can choose to go to YouTube project to see the comparison statistics between channels. Select each channel to see statistics about the number of views and subscribers of that channel.

Besides, users can choose the tab Face analysis to see statistics and visualizations on the appearance of the celebrity's face they are tracking in Fig. 11. The image size represents the frequency of the celebrity's appearance on news videos. The location of such people is linked to predefined coordinates on the map depending on their nationality.

4.2 Object Detection System

The system offers similar capabilities to the facial recognition system but will focus on recognizing objects that the user wants to track its appearance on social networks or other data sources they want. From there, users can grasp which products are outstanding, have high influence, and feedback from users for that product.

The system shows the ability to expand rapidly from the general architectural model, so it can be built quickly just changing module analysis from face recognition to object detection. The tools and libraries used also vary flexibly due to the interoperable architecture of modules. CenterNet is an algorithm applied in this system to identify objects with good results in terms of accuracy and speed (Fig. 12).

The system is supported and syndicated by a set of APIs that track channel information, video, and object detection. Following is a list of APIs used in this system:

- **Object detection APIs**: get into the list of links of videos and images. Then, the system proceeds to download the data according to the link and is identified. The user makes the API call again to see job status or result after identification. We use CenterNet to implement the main processing of these APÍ and Object model APIs below.

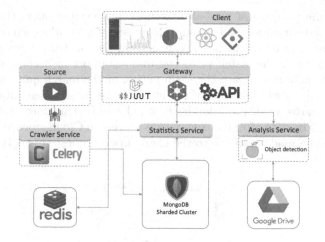

Fig. 12. Object detection system

– **Object model APIs**: Get links of a dataset and accompanying information of a model. The API then executes the training new model according to the dataset submitted. After the model is trained, users can use it normally.

Fig. 13. Object detection for the compact brand in a video

Similar statistical and visualization features to the Face recognition system. However, instead of focusing on celebrities' faces, we will focus on object detection, brand logos. Specifically, we tested the system to recognize the logo of the Compact drinking water brand in the TV show - The Brain Vietnam in Fig. 13.

4.3   Video Highlight System

Thanks to the combination of the overall architecture with the right tools and solutions, we have successfully built a system to collect, analyze, and summarize the outstanding progress of football matches. The system offers the ability to collect video data from football channels from social networks such as YouTube, and also supports statistics of match videos from the football channel. The most prominent feature is the match video summary support to become a short featured video to help users grasp the main action of the match quickly.

Module analysis will take care of receiving the required video data, then process and summarize video evolution based on the audio transformation throughout the video. The data after the summary is stored on Cloud storage like Google drive and will be made available to the client upon request (Fig. 14).

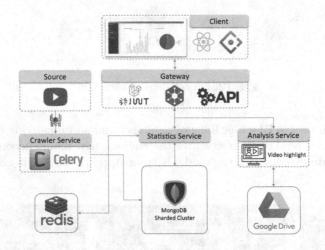

Fig. 14. Video highlight system

The system is supported and syndicated by a set of APIs that track channel information, video, and highlight video. Following is a list of APIs used in this system:

– **Video highlight APIs**: get into the list of links of videos. Then, the system proceeds to download the data according to the link and is identified. The user makes the API call again to see job status or result after identification. We use the technique of video splitting and clustering high volume clips to summarize the video, which is covered in the Sect. 3.4.

4.4   Text Analysis System

We have built a system of collecting, analyzing and statistics keywords appearing on posts on social networks. The system offers the ability to collect data from social networks, namely Facebook, from which to capture information of admission pages, then statistics and track shares, and likes to capture the situation of daily admission information.

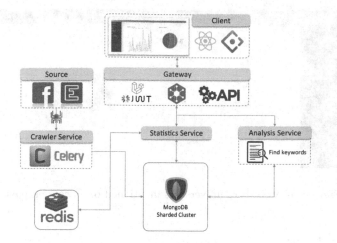

Fig. 15. Text analysis system

The change mainly lies in the crawler module when the system mainly collects text data from the world's most popular social network, Facebook. In addition, the system also supports electronic newspapers such as VnExpress - the most viewed Vietnamese newspaper.

The system is supported and syndicated by a set of APIs that track fan pages information from Facebook with their post, posts from VnExpress, and text analysis with counting keywords and sentimental analysis. Following is a list of APIs used in this system:

- **Counting keywords APIs**: the input text data will be standardized again by bringing all the characters to lowercase and removing the accent marks. Then, use the dictionary provided to count the number of keyword occurrences.
- **Sentimental analysis APIs**: we used pre-trained sentiment analysis models for English, after processing textual data, they will be classified into one of two categories: positive and negative. We also study to use PhoBERT for getting the highest speed and accuracy possible on Vietnamese.

Users can choose the news viewing function with articles from the VnExpress source summarized and can go to the original link to view details. In addition, there are statistical functions that compare the shares and likes of enrollment pages in a visual way. The function of tracking keyword appearance is statistically and visually displayed in the Text analysis tab in Fig. 16.

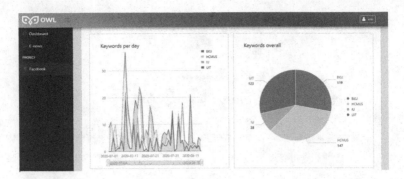

Fig. 16. Keywords of universities mentioned on Facebook pages

5   Conclusion

In this paper, we develop a flexible platform to support the creation of systems to collect and analyze social media data. We provide components and utilities that are used to quickly generate open data providers based on different social media sources. There are four main components in our architecture: gateway, crawler, statistics, and analysis. We link modules and services through APIs and centrally managed data storage. Diverse data sources are referred to as text data stored on the database and video/images stored on Cloud storage. Besides, our method focuses on the ability to flexibly integrate artificial intelligence analysis applications into the system to be able to both analyze intelligently social events and serve smart cities in creating open data providers. Moreover, the use of artificial intelligence applications as a replaceable module according to user needs will bring extremely high scalability.

In our method, we deploy services related to data analysis with artificial intelligence on Google Colab. Services can be deployed on other similar server services. Also, the centralized data stored on Cloud storage gives the advantage of handling private and user-provided data cases such as surveillance cameras, personal data, or data of organizations.

Smart cities need open data providers. Since open data providers need to be supported quickly, those input sources are social media, so we need to develop this flexible platform. We experimented with many sources: text, image, video including analysis by AI applications related to vision, sound, even NLP. Furthermore, it is especially important that we make several systems to demo specific cases for supporting open data providers in smart cities.

We develop four systems for illustrating our proposed solutions. The four systems include a face recognition system for celebrity recognition, an object detection system for brand logo recognition, a video highlight system for summarizing football match, and a text analysis system serves for keyword occurrences and emotional text analysis for admissions of universities. Each system gives a unique meaning to each specific situation in life.

Currently, we are studying other text analyses for Vietnamese with PhoBERT [11], researching for other artificial intelligence to integrate into our systems. We will also research new mechanisms and solutions to increase system performance, load balancing, data visualization, and security. We aim to quickly and flexibly integrate solutions to support open data providers in smart cities now and in the future.

Acknowledgment. This research is supported by research funding from Honors Program, University of Science, Vietnam National University - Ho Chi Minh City.

References

1. Adarsh, P., Rathi, P., Kumar, M.: YOLO v3-Tiny: object detection and recognition using one stage improved model. In: 2020 6th International Conference on Advanced Computing and Communication Systems (ICACCS), pp. 687–694 (2020)
2. Ahmed, S., Mahmood, Q.: An authentication based scheme for applications using JSON web token. In: 2019 22nd International Multitopic Conference (INMIC), pp. 1–6 (2019)
3. Boyko, N., Basystiuk, O., Shakhovska, N.: Performance evaluation and comparison of software for face recognition, based on dlib and opencv library. In: 2018 IEEE Second International Conference on Data Stream Mining Processing (DSMP), pp. 478–482 (2018)
4. Chen, X., Zhang, Q., Han, J., Han, X., Liu, Y., Fang, Y.: Object detection of optical remote sensing image based on improved faster RCNN. In: 2019 IEEE 5th International Conference on Computer and Communications (ICCC), pp. 1787–1791 (2019)
5. Chi, X., Liu, B., Niu, Q., Wu, Q.: Web load balance and cache optimization design based nginx under high-concurrency environment. In: 2012 Third International Conference on Digital Manufacturing Automation, pp. 1029–1032 (2012)
6. Hutto, C.J., Gilbert, E.: VADER: a parsimonious rule-based model for sentiment analysis of social media text. Behav. Res. **323**(6088), 1–8 (2014)
7. Dong Yu, L.D.: Automaic Speech Recognition. A Deep Learning Approach, pp. 1–7. Springer, New York (2015). https://doi.org/10.1007/978-1-4471-5779-3
8. Geitgey, A.: Modern face recognition with deep learning (2018). https://github.com/ageitgey/face_recognition
9. Hearst, M.A.: Support vector machines. IEEE Intell. Syst. **13**(4), 18–28 (1998)
10. Liu, H.: Highlight extraction in soccer videos by using multimodal analysis. In: 2017 13th International Conference on Natural Computation, Fuzzy Systems and Knowledge Discovery (ICNC-FSKD), pp. 2169–2173 (2017)
11. Nguyen, D.Q., Nguyen, A.T.: PhoBERT: pre-trained language models for Vietnamese (2020)
12. Crossley, S.A., Kyle, K., McNamara, D.S.: Sentiment analysis and social cognition engine (SEANCE): an automatic tool for sentiment, social cognition, and social-order analysis. Behav. Res. Methods **49**(3), 803–821 (2016). https://doi.org/10.3758/s13428-016-0743-z
13. Sharma, S., Shanmugasundaram, K., Ramasamy, S.K.: FAREC—CNN based efficient face recognition technique using Dlib. In: 2016 International Conference on Advanced Communication Control and Computing Technologies (ICACCCT), pp. 192–195 (2016)

14. In the Wild Home, L.F.: A public benchmark for face verification (2020). http://vis-www.cs.umass.edu/lfw

15. Womg, A., Shafiee, M.J., Li, F., Chwyl, B.: Tiny SSD: a tiny single-shot detection deep convolutional neural network for real-time embedded object detection. In: 2018 15th Conference on Computer and Robot Vision (CRV), pp. 95–101 (2018)

16. Zeng, H., Zhang, Z., Shi, L.: Research and implementation of video codec based on FFmpeg. In: 2016 International Conference on Network and Information Systems for Computers (ICNISC), pp. 184–188 (2016)

17. Zhou, X., Wang, D., Krähenbühl, P.: Objects as points. CoRR abs/1904.07850 (2019). http://arxiv.org/abs/1904.07850

18. Zulko: Automatic soccer highlights (2014). http://zulko.github.io/blog/2014/07/04/automatic-soccer-highlights-compilations-with-python

Post-quantum Digital-Signature Algorithms on Finite 6-Dimensional Non-commutative Algebras

Nikolay A. Moldovyan[1], Dmitriy N. Moldovyan[1], Alexander A. Moldovyan[1], Hieu Minh Nguyen[2(✉)], and Le Hoang Tuan Trinh[3]

[1] St. Petersburg Federal Research Center of the Russian Academy of Sciences (SPC RAS), St. Petersburg Institute for Informatics and Automation of the Russian Academy of Sciences, 39, 14th Line, 199178 St. Petersburg, Russia
[2] Institute of Cryptographic Science and Technology, 105 Nguyen Chi Thanh Street, Hanoi, Vietnam
hieuminhmta@ymail.com
[3] Kien Giang University, 320A Highway 61, Kiengiang, Vietnam

Abstract. There are introduced three methods for defining finite 6-dimensional associative algebras over the ground finite field $GF(p)$, every one of which contains a set of the global right-sided units. Formulas describing the set of the global units are presented for every of the considered three algebras that contain p^s global units, where $s = 2, 3, 4$. The algebras are used as carriers of the hidden discrete logarithm problem that is used as the base cryptographic primitive of the post-quantum digital signature algorithms.

Keywords: Finite associative algebra · Non-commutative algebra · Discrete logarithm problem · Non-commutative multiplication · Public-key cryptography · Post-quantum cryptography · Digital signature

1 Introduction

Currently, the most widely used public-key algorithms and protocols are based on the computational complexity of the discrete logarithm problem and the factorization problem. However, there are known polynomial algorithms for solving each of these two problems on a quantum computer [1–3]. Therefore, after appearance of such calculator in practice the mentioned algorithms and protocols will be insecure. Since a sudden appearance of the quantum computer is expected after 2025, NIST announced a competition for the development of post-quantum public-key cryptosystems as the first step of the process of introducing the post-quantum standards relating to the public-key cryptography [4,5]. The research community is also paying considerable attention to post-quantum public-key cryptography [6,7].

© Springer Nature Switzerland AG 2020
T. K. Dang et al. (Eds.): FDSE 2020, LNCS 12466, pp. 325–341, 2020.
https://doi.org/10.1007/978-3-030-63924-2_19

A promising approach to the development of post-quantum public-key cryptoschemes relates to the use of the discrete logarithm problem in a finite cyclic group hidden in a finite non-commutative associative algebra (FNAA), called also hidden logarithm problem (HLP) [8]. Initially [9,10], the HLP was formulated over a finite non-commutative group Γ containing the elements G and Q, having large prime order q and satisfying the condition $G \circ Q \neq Q \circ G$, as follows. Suppose somebody selects two random integers $x < q$ and $w < q$ as his private key and computes his public key in the form of the group element Y :

$$Y = Q^w \circ G^x \circ Q^{-w}. \qquad (1)$$

The HLP consists in finding the pair of the values Q^w and x, when the group elements Y, G, and Q are known. The exponentiation operation G^x is the base one, since it introduces the main contribution to the computational difficulty of the HLP. The left-sided multiplication by the element Q^w and the right-sided multiplication by the element Q^{-w} are used as mechanism of masking the value G^x. Therefore, the cyclic group generated by the element G can be called the base cyclic group. In the known form of the HLP there is masked the value G^x, the base cyclic group is not masked though.

Using the finite algebra of quaternions as the carrier of the HLP and the public key defined with the formula (1), the public encryption algorithm and public key-agreement protocols were introduced in [10]. The HLP defined in the form described by the formula (1) was also used to construct a commutative cipher [10], however no digital signature scheme based on the HLP had been proposed earlier. Some potential attacks on the HLP-based cryptoschemes [10] had been considered in [11,12]. The main practical result of the paper [12] consists in the conclusion that the HLP defined in the form (1) in the finite algebra of quaternions over the field $GF(p)$ can be reduced in polynomial time to the discrete logaritm problem in the field $GF(p^2)$, therefore for designing the post-quantum public-key crytoschemes on the base of the HLP one should try to use other types of the FNAAs as carriers of the HLP in the form (1).

In this paper, there are considered three methods for defining the 6-dimensional FNAAs over the ground finite field $GF(p)$, which contain no global two-sided unit, however every one of them contains p^s ($s = 2, 3, 4$) different global right-sided units. Using features of the proposed algebras two new forms of the HLP are introduced, which are characterized in masking both the generator of the base cyclic group and the output of the base exponentiation operation. The introduced versions of the HLP are used to design digital signature schemes that represent interest as candidates for post-quantum cryptoschemes.

2   Proposed 6-Dimensional FNAAs

Suppose e_0, e_1, ... e_5 are some formal basis vectors and $a_o, a_1, \ldots a_5 \in GF(p)$, where p is a sufficiently large prime number, are coordinates of the vector $A = (a_0, a_1, \ldots, a_5)$ that is also represented in the form of the following sum of the single component vectors: $A = a_0 e_0 + a_1 e_1 + \cdots + a_5 e_5$. Addition of two vectors $A = \sum_{i=0}^{5} a_i e_i$ and $B = \sum_{j=0}^{5} b_j e_j$ is defined as follows $A + B = \sum_{i=0}^{5} (a_i + b_i) e_i$. Note that $+$ denotes the addition operation in the 6-dimensional vector space and the addition operation in the field $GF(p)$.

The multiplication operation $\circ$ of two 6-dimensional vectors A and B, as elements of some finite associative algebra, is defined with the following formula

$$A \circ B = \sum_{j=0}^{5} \sum_{i=0}^{5} a_i b_j e_i \circ e_j, \tag{2}$$

where for all possible pairs of the values i and j the product $e_i \circ e_j$ is to be replaced by some one-component vector in accordance with so called basis vector multiplication table (BVMT). Tables 1, 2, and 3 illustrate examples of the BVMTs. We assume that the left basis vector e_i defines the row and the right one e_j defines the column of the BVMT. Thus, the single-component vector τe_k, where $\tau \in GF(p)$, contained in the cell at the intersection of the ith row and jth column gives the value of the product $e_i \circ e_j$. If $\tau \neq 1$, then the integer τ is called structural constant.

Using formula (2) for product of the vectors A, B, and $C = \sum_{k=0}^{5} c_k e_k$ one can get the following

$$(A \circ B) \circ C = \sum_{i=0}^{5} \sum_{j=0}^{5} \sum_{k=0}^{5} a_i b_j c_k (e_i \circ e_j) \circ e_k;$$

$$A \circ (B \circ C) = \sum_{i=0}^{5} \sum_{j=0}^{5} \sum_{k=0}^{5} a_i b_j c_k e_i \circ (e_j \circ e_k).$$

The last formula shows the operation of the multiplication of the vectors is associative, if the BVMT defines associative multiplication of the basis vectors.

2.1 The 6-Dimensional FNAA Containing p^3 Global Right-Sided Units

Proposition 1. The formula (2) together with the following formula

$$e_i \circ e_j = \begin{cases} e_{i+2+4j}, & \text{if } j \equiv 0 \bmod 2 \\ \tau e_{i+2+4j}, & \text{if } j \equiv 1 \bmod 2, \end{cases} \tag{3}$$

where addition and subtraction is performed modulo 6, $\tau \in GF(p)$ is a structural constant, and $i, j = 0, 1, \ldots 5$, defines associative multiplication operation of the 6-dimensional vectors.

Proof. Suppose j', k' are odd integers (i. e., $j' \equiv k' \equiv 1 \bmod 2$) and j'', k'' are even integers (i. e., $j'' \equiv k'' \equiv 0 \bmod 2$). Then one should consider the following cases:

$$i) \begin{cases} (\mathbf{e}_i \circ \mathbf{e}_{j'}) \circ \mathbf{e}_{k'} = \tau \mathbf{e}_{i+2+4j'} \circ \mathbf{e}_{k'} = \tau^2 \mathbf{e}_{i+4+4j'+4k'}; \\ \mathbf{e}_i \circ (\mathbf{e}_{j'} \circ \mathbf{e}_{k'}) = \mathbf{e}_i \circ (\tau \mathbf{e}_{j'+2+4k'}) = \tau^2 \mathbf{e}_{i+4+4j'+4k'}, \end{cases}$$

$$ii) \begin{cases} (\mathbf{e}_i \circ \mathbf{e}_{j'}) \circ \mathbf{e}_{k''} = \tau \mathbf{e}_{i+2+4j'} \circ \mathbf{e}_{k''} = \tau \mathbf{e}_{i+4+4j'+4k''}; \\ \mathbf{e}_i \circ (\mathbf{e}_{j'} \circ \mathbf{e}_{k''}) = \mathbf{e}_i \circ \mathbf{e}_{j'+2+4k''} = \tau \mathbf{e}_{i+4+4j'+4k''}, \end{cases}$$

$$iii) \begin{cases} (\mathbf{e}_i \circ \mathbf{e}_{j''}) \circ \mathbf{e}_{k'} = \mathbf{e}_{i+2+4j''} \circ \mathbf{e}_{k'} = \tau \mathbf{e}_{i+4+4j''+4k'}; \\ \mathbf{e}_i \circ (\mathbf{e}_{j''} \circ \mathbf{e}_{k'}) = \mathbf{e}_i \circ (\tau \mathbf{e}_{j''+2+4k'}) = \tau \mathbf{e}_{i+4+4j''+4k'}, \end{cases}$$

$$iv) \begin{cases} (\mathbf{e}_i \circ \mathbf{e}_{j''}) \circ \mathbf{e}_{k''} = \mathbf{e}_{i+2+4j''} \circ \mathbf{e}_{k''} = \mathbf{e}_{i+4+4j''+4k''}; \\ \mathbf{e}_i \circ (\mathbf{e}_{j''} \circ \mathbf{e}_{k''}) = \mathbf{e}_i \circ \mathbf{e}_{j''+2+4k''} = \mathbf{e}_{i+4+4j''+4k''}. \end{cases}$$

Thus, in all cases we have $(\mathbf{e}_i \circ \mathbf{e}_j) \circ \mathbf{e}_k = \mathbf{e}_i \circ (\mathbf{e}_j \circ \mathbf{e}_k)$ and therefore, Proposition 1 holds true.

The formula (3) defines the BVMT shown as Table 1 that can be directly used to solve vector equations, for example, the vector equation

$$A \circ X = A, \tag{4}$$

where $X = (x_0, x_1, \ldots, x_5)$, solutions of which are the right-sided units of the vector A. Using Table 1 one can represent the Eq. (4) in the form of the following system of six linear equations with the unknowns $x_0, x_1, x_2, x_3, x_4, x_5$:

$$\begin{cases} \tau a_0 x_1 + a_0 x_4 + a_2 x_2 + \tau a_2 x_5 + a_4 x_0 + \tau a_4 x_3 = a_0; \\ \tau a_1 x_1 + a_1 x_4 + a_3 x_2 + \tau a_3 x_5 + a_5 x_0 + \tau a_5 x_3 = a_1; \\ a_0 x_0 + \tau a_0 x_3 + \tau a_2 x_1 + a_2 x_4 + a_4 x_2 + \tau a_4 x_5 = a_2; \\ a_1 x_0 + \tau a_1 x_3 + \tau a_3 x_1 + a_3 x_4 + a_5 x_2 + \tau a_5 x_5 = a_3; \\ a_0 x_2 + \tau a_0 x_5 + a_2 x_0 + \tau a_2 x_3 + \tau a_4 x_1 + a_4 x_4 = a_4; \\ a_1 x_2 + \tau a_1 x_5 + a_3 x_0 + \tau a_3 x_3 + \tau a_5 x_1 + a_5 x_4 = a_5 \end{cases} \tag{5}$$

The system (5) can be represented in the form of the following two systems each of which contains three equations:

$$\begin{cases} (\tau x_1 + x_4) a_0 + (x_2 + \tau x_5) a_2 + (x_0 + \tau x_3) a_4 = a_0; \\ (\tau x_1 + x_4) a_2 + (x_2 + \tau x_5) a_4 + (x_0 + \tau x_3) a_0 = a_2; \\ (\tau x_1 + x_4) a_4 + (x_2 + \tau x_5) a_0 + (x_0 + \tau x_3) a_2 = a_4; \end{cases} \tag{6}$$

$$\begin{cases} (\tau x_1 + x_4) a_1 + (x_2 + \tau x_5) a_3 + (x_0 + \tau x_3) a_5 = a_1; \\ (\tau x_1 + x_4) a_3 + (x_2 + \tau x_5) a_5 + (x_0 + \tau x_3) a_1 = a_3; \\ (\tau x_1 + x_4) a_5 + (x_2 + \tau x_5) a_1 + (x_0 + \tau x_3) a_3 = a_5. \end{cases} \tag{7}$$

From the systems (6) and (7) one can see that every vector $(x_0, x_1, x_2, x_3, x_4, x_5)$ coordinates of which satisfy the following system of three linear equations

Table 1. The BVMT defining the FNAA containing p^3 global right-sided units

∘	e_0	e_1	e_2	e_3	e_4	e_5
e_0	e_2	τe_0	$e_4 \cdot$	τe_2	e_0	τe_4
e_1	e_3	τe_1	e_5	τe_3	e_1	τe_5
e_2	e_4	τe_2	e_0	τe_4	e_2	τe_0
e_3	e_5	τe_3	e_1	τe_5	e_3	τe_1
e_4	e_0	τe_4	e_2	τe_0	e_4	τe_2
e_5	e_1	τe_5	e_3	τe_1	e_5	τe_3

$$\begin{cases} \tau x_1 + x_4 = 1; \\ x_2 + \tau x_5 = 0; \\ x_0 + \tau x_3 = 0; \end{cases} \Rightarrow \begin{cases} x_4 = 1 - \tau x_1; \\ x_2 = -\tau x_5; \\ x_0 = -\tau x_3 \end{cases} \tag{8}$$

is simultaneously a solution of the system (5) for all possible values A. Since the solutions of the system (8) do not depend on the value of the vector A, one can conclude that every of these solutions defines some vector R acting on all vectors of the considered FNAA as the right-sided unit. The vector R can be called the global right-sided unit. From (8) one can write the following formula describing p^3 different global right-sided units R in the considered FNAA:

$$R = (-\tau x_3, \ x_1, \ -\tau x_5, \ x_3, \ 1 - \tau x_1, \ x_5), \tag{9}$$

where $x_1, x_3, x_5 = 0, 1, \ldots p - 1$.

2.2 The 6-Dimensional FNAA Containing p^4 Global Right-Sided Units

Proposition 2. The formula (2) together with the following formula

$$e_i \circ e_j = \begin{cases} e_{i+3+3j}, & \text{if } (j \bmod 3) = 0 \\ \lambda e_{i+3+3j}, & \text{if } (j \bmod 3) \neq 0, \end{cases} \tag{10}$$

where addition is performed modulo 6; $i, j = 0, 1, \ldots 5$; and $\lambda \in GF(p)$ is a structural constant, defines associative multiplication operation of the 6-dimensional vectors.

Proof. Suppose j', k' are integers such that $(j' \bmod 3) \neq 0$; $(k' \bmod 3) \neq 0$ and j'', k'' are integers such that $j'' \equiv k'' \equiv 0 \bmod 3$. Then one should consider the following cases:

i) $\begin{cases} (e_i \circ e_{j'}) \circ e_{k'} = \lambda e_{i+3+3j'} \circ e_{k'} = \lambda^2 e_{i+3j'+3k'}; \\ e_i \circ (e_{j'} \circ e_{k'}) = e_i \circ (\lambda e_{j'+3+3k'}) = \lambda^2 e_{i+3j'+3k'}, \end{cases}$

ii) $\begin{cases} (\mathbf{e}_i \circ \mathbf{e}_{j'}) \circ \mathbf{e}_{k''} = \lambda \mathbf{e}_{i+3+3j'} \circ \mathbf{e}_{k''} = \lambda \mathbf{e}_{i+3j'+3k''}; \\ \mathbf{e}_i \circ (\mathbf{e}_{j'} \circ \mathbf{e}_{k''}) = \mathbf{e}_i \circ \mathbf{e}_{j'+3+3k''} = \lambda \mathbf{e}_{i+3j'+3k''}, \end{cases}$

iii) $\begin{cases} (\mathbf{e}_i \circ \mathbf{e}_{j''}) \circ \mathbf{e}_{k'} = \mathbf{e}_{i+3+3j''} \circ \mathbf{e}_{k'} = \lambda \mathbf{e}_{i+3j''+3k'}; \\ \mathbf{e}_i \circ (\mathbf{e}_{j''} \circ \mathbf{e}_{k'}) = \mathbf{e}_i \circ (\lambda \mathbf{e}_{j''+3+3k'}) = \lambda \mathbf{e}_{i+3j''+3k'}, \end{cases}$

iv) $\begin{cases} (\mathbf{e}_i \circ \mathbf{e}_{j''}) \circ \mathbf{e}_{k''} = \mathbf{e}_{i+3+3j''} \circ \mathbf{e}_{k''} = \mathbf{e}_{i+3j''+3k''}; \\ \mathbf{e}_i \circ (\mathbf{e}_{j''} \circ \mathbf{e}_{k''}) = \mathbf{e}_i \circ \mathbf{e}_{j''+3+3k''} = \mathbf{e}_{i+3j''+3k''}. \end{cases}$

Thus, in all cases we have $(\mathbf{e}_i \circ \mathbf{e}_j) \circ \mathbf{e}_k = \mathbf{e}_i \circ (\mathbf{e}_j \circ \mathbf{e}_k)$ and therefore, Proposition 2 holds true.

The formula (10) defines the BVMT shown as Table 2. Using this BVMT one can represent the vector equation (4) in the form of the following system of equations:

$$\begin{cases} a_0 (x_1 + \lambda x_3 + x_5) + a_3 (\lambda x_0 + x_2 + x_4) = a_0; \\ a_1 (x_1 + \lambda x_3 + x_5) + a_4 (\lambda x_0 + x_2 + x_4) = a_1; \\ a_2 (x_1 + \lambda x_3 + x_5) + a_5 (\lambda x_0 + x_2 + x_4) = a_2; \\ a_0 (\lambda x_0 + x_2 + x_4) + a_3 (x_1 + \lambda x_3 + x_5) = a_3; \\ a_1 (\lambda x_0 + x_2 + x_4) + a_4 (x_1 + \lambda x_3 + x_5) = a_4; \\ a_2 (\lambda x_0 + x_2 + x_4) + a_5 (x_1 + \lambda x_3 + x_5) = a_5 \end{cases} \quad (11)$$

From the systems (11) one can see that every vector $(x_0, x_1, x_2, x_3, x_4, x_5)$ coordinates of which satisfy the following system of two linear equations:

$$\begin{cases} x_1 + \lambda x_3 + x_5 = 1; \\ \lambda x_0 + x_2 + x_4 = 0; \end{cases} \Rightarrow \begin{cases} x_0, x_1, x_2, x_3 = 0, 1, \ldots p - 1; \\ x_4 = -\lambda x_0 - x_2; \\ x_5 = 1 - x_1 - \lambda x_3. \end{cases} \quad (12)$$

is simultaneously a solution of the system (5) for all possible values A. The solutions of the system (12) do not depend on the value of the vector A, therefore every one of these solutions defines a global right-sided unit R of the considered

Table 2. The BVMT defining the FNAA containing p^4 global right-sided units

$\circ$	$\mathbf{e}_0$	$\mathbf{e}_1$	$\mathbf{e}_2$	$\mathbf{e}_3$	$\mathbf{e}_4$	$\mathbf{e}_5$
$\mathbf{e}_0$	$\lambda \mathbf{e}_3$	$\mathbf{e}_0$	$\mathbf{e}_3$	$\lambda \mathbf{e}_0$	$\mathbf{e}_3$	$\mathbf{e}_0$
$\mathbf{e}_1$	$\lambda \mathbf{e}_4$	$\mathbf{e}_1$	$\mathbf{e}_4$	$\lambda \mathbf{e}_1$	$\mathbf{e}_4$	$\mathbf{e}_1$
$\mathbf{e}_2$	$\lambda \mathbf{e}_5$	$\mathbf{e}_2$	$\mathbf{e}_5$	$\lambda \mathbf{e}_2$	$\mathbf{e}_5$	$\mathbf{e}_2$
$\mathbf{e}_3$	$\lambda \mathbf{e}_0$	$\mathbf{e}_3$	$\mathbf{e}_0$	$\lambda \mathbf{e}_3$	$\mathbf{e}_0$	$\mathbf{e}_3$
$\mathbf{e}_4$	$\lambda \mathbf{e}_1$	$\mathbf{e}_4$	$\mathbf{e}_1$	$\lambda \mathbf{e}_4$	$\mathbf{e}_1$	$\mathbf{e}_4$
$\mathbf{e}_5$	$\lambda \mathbf{e}_2$	$\mathbf{e}_5$	$\mathbf{e}_2$	$\lambda \mathbf{e}_5$	$\mathbf{e}_2$	$\mathbf{e}_5$

FNAA. From (12) one can write the following formula describing p^4 different global right-sided units in the FNAA connected with the Table 2:

$$R = (x_0, \ x_1, \ x_2, \ x_3, \ -\lambda x_0 - x_2, \ 1 - x_1 - \lambda x_3), \tag{13}$$

where $x_0, x_1, x_2, x_3 = 0, 1, \ldots p - 1$.

2.3   The 6-Dimensional FNAA Containing p^2 Global Right-Sided Units

Proposition 3. The formula (2) together with the following formula

$$\mathbf{e}_i \circ \mathbf{e}_j = \mathbf{e}_{3j+4i} \tag{14}$$

where subtraction is performed modulo 6 and $i, j = 0, 1, \ldots 5$, defines associative multiplication operation of the 6-dimensional vectors.

Proof.

$$(\mathbf{e}_i \circ \mathbf{e}_j) \circ \mathbf{e}_k = \mathbf{e}_{3j+4i} \circ \mathbf{e}_k = \mathbf{e}_{3k+4(3j+4i)} = \mathbf{e}_{3k+4i};$$
$$\mathbf{e}_i \circ (\mathbf{e}_j \circ \mathbf{e}_k) = \mathbf{e}_i \circ \mathbf{e}_{3k+4j} = \mathbf{e}_{3(3k+4j)+4i} = \mathbf{e}_{3k+4i}.$$

Thus, Proposition 3 holds true.

After construction of the BVMT defined with the formula (14) we have found distributions of the structural constants λ and τ, which conserves the property of the associativity of the multiplication operation. The resultant BVMT is presented as Table 3. Using this BVMT one can represent the vector equation (4) in the form of the following system of linear equations:

$$\begin{cases} a_0 \left(\lambda x_0 + x_2 + \tau x_4\right) + a_3 \left(x_0 + \tau x_2 + \lambda x_4\right) = a_0; \\ a_1 \left(\lambda x_1 + x_3 + \tau x_5\right) + a_4 \left(\tau x_1 + \lambda x_3 + x_5\right) = a_1; \\ a_2 \left(\lambda x_0 + x_2 + \tau x_4\right) + a_5 \left(x_0 + \tau x_2 + \lambda x_4\right) = a_2; \\ a_0 \left(\tau x_1 + \lambda x_3 + x_5\right) + a_3 \left(\lambda x_1 + x_3 + \tau x_5\right) = a_3; \\ a_1 \left(x_0 + \tau x_2 + \lambda x_4\right) + a_4 \left(\lambda x_0 + x_2 + \tau x_4\right) = a_4; \\ a_2 \left(\tau x_1 + \lambda x_3 + x_5\right) + a_5 \left(\lambda x_1 + x_3 + \tau x_5\right) = a_5 \end{cases} \tag{15}$$

From the system (15) one can see that every vector $(x_0, x_1, x_2, x_3, x_4, x_5)$ coordinates of which satisfy simultaneously the following two independent systems of two linear equations with three unknowns:

$$\begin{cases} \lambda x_0 + x_2 + \tau x_4 = 1; \\ x_0 + \tau x_2 + \lambda x_4 = 0; \end{cases} \tag{16}$$

$$\begin{cases} \tau x_1 + \lambda x_3 + x_5 = 0; \\ \lambda x_1 + x_3 + \tau x_5 = 1 \end{cases} \tag{17}$$

Table 3. The BVMT of the FNAA with p^2 global right-sided units $(\lambda \neq \tau^2;\ \tau \neq \lambda^2;\ \lambda\tau \neq 1)$

$\circ$	e_0	e_1	e_2	e_3	e_4	e_5
e_0	λe_0	τe_3	e_0	λe_3	τe_0	e_3
e_1	e_4	λe_1	τe_4	e_1	λe_4	τe_1
e_2	λe_2	τe_5	e_2	λe_5	τe_2	e_5
e_3	e_0	λe_3	τe_0	e_3	λe_0	τe_3
e_4	λe_4	τe_1	e_4	λe_1	τe_4	e_1
e_5	e_2	λe_5	τe_2	e_5	λe_2	τe_5

represents a solution of the system (15) for all possible values A, i. e., a global right-sided unit of the considered FNAA. In the case $\lambda \neq \tau^2$ and $\tau \neq \lambda^2$ the system (16) gives the following p solutions:

$$
\begin{cases}
x_0 = 0, 1, 2, \ldots, p - 1; \\[4pt]
x_2 = \dfrac{\lambda + \left(\tau - \lambda^2\right) x_0}{\lambda - \tau^2}; \\[4pt]
x_4 = \dfrac{(\lambda\tau - 1) x_0 - \tau}{\lambda - \tau^2};
\end{cases}
\tag{18}
$$

In the case $\lambda \neq \tau^2$ and $\lambda\tau \neq 1$, the system (17) gives the following p solutions:

$$
\begin{cases}
x_1 = 0, 1, 2, \ldots, p - 1; \\[4pt]
x_3 = \dfrac{\left(\lambda - \tau^2\right) x_1}{\lambda\tau - 1}; \\[4pt]
x_5 = \dfrac{\left(\tau - \lambda^2\right) x_1 + \lambda}{\lambda\tau - 1}.
\end{cases}
\tag{19}
$$

Thus, the 6-dimensional FNAA with the multiplication operation defined by Table 3 contains the set of p^2 different global right-sided units, which is described as follows:

$$
R = \left(x_0,\ x_1,\ \frac{\lambda + \left(\tau - \lambda^2\right) x_0}{\lambda - \tau^2},\ \frac{\left(\lambda - \tau^2\right) x_1}{\lambda\tau - 1}, \right.
$$
$$
\left. \frac{(\lambda\tau - 1) x_0 - \tau}{\lambda - \tau^2},\ \frac{\left(\tau - \lambda^2\right) x_1 + \lambda}{\lambda\tau - 1} \right).
\tag{20}
$$

2.4 Local Units

A common feature of the considered 6-dimensional FNAAs is the presence of a set of global right-sided units. Except the set of the global right-sided units $\{R\}$ every of the considered FNAAs contains the local right-sided units

$R' \notin \{R\}$ that acts in frame of some subsets of the "marginal" elements $A' = (a'_0, a'_1, a'_2, a'_3, a'_4, a'_5)$ of the algebra. For example, in the case of the FNAA considered in Subsect. 2.1 coordinates of the vectors A' satisfy simultaneously the following two conditions $\Delta' = 3a'_0 a'_2 a'_4 - a'^3_0 - a'^3_2 - a'^3_4 = 0$ and $\Delta'' = 3a'_1 a'_3 a'_5 - a'^3_1 - a'^3_3 - a'^3_5 = 0$, where Δ' and Δ'' are the main determinants of the systems of linear Eqs. (6) and (7) correspondingly. The "marginal" vectors and relating to them local units R' are not used in the proposed forms of the HLP and cryptoschemes. Therefore we do not derive formulas describing the set of the local right-sided unites relating to the some given vector A'.

It is obvious that the introduced three 6-dimensional FNAAs contain no global left-sided unit nor global two-sided unit. The algebras contain local left-sided units, i. e., the left-sided unit elements acting in frame of some subsets of the elements. The local left-sided unit corresponding to some 6-dimensional vector A can be computed as solution of the vector Eq. (21):

$$X \circ A = A. \tag{21}$$

Coordinates of the vector A defines the main determinant Δ_A of the system of linear equations connected with the vector equation (21). If $\Delta_A \neq 0$, then there exists the single solution $X = L_A$ that represents the local left-sided unit of the vector A. Suppose the set of the "marginal" elements is denoted as $\{A'\}$.

Proposition 4. Suppose $A \notin \{A'\}$ and $\Delta_A \neq 0$, then there exists some integer ω such that $A^\omega = L_A$ and the vector L_A is simultaneously one of the global right-sided units.

Proof. Let us consider the sequence of the vectors $A, A^2, \ldots A^h, \ldots A^k, \ldots$. For all integer values i one has $A^i \neq O$, where $O = (0, 0, 0, 0, 0, 0)$, since $\Delta_A \neq 0$. Due to finiteness of the considered algebras and condition $\Delta_A \neq 0$ the indicated sequence is periodic, i. e., for some integer h and minimum integer $k > h$ we have the following:

$$A^k = A^h \Rightarrow A^{k-h} \circ A^h = A^h \Rightarrow (A^{k-h} \circ A - A) \circ A^{h-1} = O \Rightarrow$$
$$A^{k-h} \circ A - A = O \Rightarrow A^{k-h} \circ A = A \Rightarrow A^{k-h} = L_A,$$
$$A^{k-h} \circ A = A \Rightarrow A \circ A^{k-h} = A \Rightarrow A^{k-h} = R_A = L_A = E_A,$$

where R_A, L_A, and E_A is the right-sided, local left-sided, and local two-sided unit of the vector A, correspondingly. Since $A \notin \{A'\}$, all right-sided units of the vector A are global, therefore R_A is an element of the set of the global right-sided units. Thus, Proposition 4 holds true.

The value $\omega = k - h$ such that $A^\omega = E_A$ can be called the local order of the vector A. Proposition 4 shows $A^{\omega-1} \circ A = A \circ A^{\omega-1} = E_A$, i. e., the vector $A^{\omega-1}$ is the two-sided inverse value of the vector A relatively the local two-sided unit E_A.

The number of different local units generated by all locally invertible vectors A (for which we have $\Delta_A \neq 0$) does not exceed the number of the global right-sided units. On average, the same local two-sided unit is generated by p^3,

p^2, and p^4 different vectors of the FNAAs from Sects. 2.1, 2.2, and 2.3, respectively. All locally invertible vectors A corresponding to some fixed local two-sided unit compose a finite group. Evidently, some fixed locally invertible vector A is included only in one of such groups.

3   The Proposed Forms of the HLP

The FNAAs containing many different global right-sided units can be used as carriers of the HLP of new types that are defined as follows. Suppose the FNAAs are defined over the field $GF(p)$, where the prime $p = eq + 1$; e is a 16-bit even integer; q is a 256-bit prime. Then one can generate the parameters of the first proposed form of the HLP as follows:

1. Select the following elements of some fixed FNAA:
   - some vector G having local order equal to q;
   - random locally invertible vectors D and N such that the conditions $D \circ G \neq G \circ D$ and $N \circ G \neq G \circ N$ hold true;
   - random global right-sided units R_1 and $R_2 \neq R_1$.
2. Compute the vector H such that

$$H \circ D = R_1. \tag{22}$$

3. Compute the vector Q such that

$$Q \circ N = R_2. \tag{23}$$

4. Generate a random integer $x < q$ and compute the first Y and the second Z elements of the public key:

$$Y = D \circ G^x \circ H; \quad Z = N \circ G \circ Q. \tag{24}$$

5. Compute the third T element of the public key from the following equation:

$$H \circ T \circ N = R_3, \tag{25}$$

where R_3 is a global right-sided unit computed simultaneously with the unknown T.

The computed triple (Y, Z, T) represents the public key. In the signature scheme based on the proposed forms of the HLP (see Sect. 4) one can use two versions of the signature generation procedure. In the source version of the signature generation procedure the private key (connected with the public key (Y, Z, T)) represents the set of the following four values: the integer x and three vectors G, D, and Q. Only the last four values are used to generate signatures associated with the public key (Y, Z, T). The vectors N, H, R_1, R_2, and R_3 are needed only for executing the procedure for computing the vectors D, Q, Y, Z, and T.

Actually, to compute a signature one can apply the alternative signature generation procedure in which it is sufficient to use the public key (Y, Z, T)

and only one element of the private key, namely, the value x. Therefore, in the practical case solving the HLP consists in finding only one value x that is to be computed from the public values (Y, Z, T).

The parameters of the second proposed form of the HLP are formed as follows:

1. Select at random the following elements:
   - the vector G having local order equal to q;
   - the locally invertible vector N such that the condition $N \circ G \neq G \circ N$ holds;
   - the global right-sided units R_1 and $R_2 \neq R_1$.
2. Compute the vector H such that

$$H \circ N = R_1. \tag{26}$$

3. Compute the vector Q such that

$$Q \circ N = R_2. \tag{27}$$

4. Compute the vector D from the following equation:

$$H \circ D = R_3, \tag{28}$$

   where R_3 is a global right-sided unit computed together with the unknown D.
5. Generate a random integer $x < q$ and compute the public key in the form of the pair of the vectors Y and Z :

$$Y = D \circ G^x \circ H; \quad Z = N \circ G \circ Q. \tag{29}$$

The computed pair of the vectors (Y, Z) represents the public key. One can easily prove that the vectors Y and Z generates cyclic groups with the units $E_Y = D \circ E_G \circ H$ and $E_Z = N \circ E_Z \circ Q$, correspondingly, each of which has order equal to q. Therefore, for arbitrary non-negative integer k the vectors Y^k and Z^k are locally invertible, i. e., $\Delta_{Y^k} \neq 0$ and $\Delta_{Z^k} \neq 0$ (see the formula (21)).

In the source version of the signature generation procedure the private key (connected with the public key (Y, Z)) represents the set of the following four values: the integer x and three vectors G, D, and Q. The vectors N, H, R_1, R_2, and R_3 are needed only for executing the procedure for computing the vectors D, Q, Y, and Z.

In the alternative signature generation procedure it is used the public key (Y, Z) and only one element of the private key, namely, the value x. Therefore, solving the HLP defined in the second proposed form also consists in finding only one value x connected with the public values (Y, Z).

Due to the used advanced masking mechanism (that hides both the generator G of the base cyclic group and the output value of the base exponentiation operation G^x) in the proposed versions of the HLP, the method proposed in [12] for reducing the known version of the HLP to the DLP in the finite field $GF(p^2)$ is not applicable for the introduced forms of the HLP.

4   Post-quantum Digital Signature Schemes

4.1   Using the GOST and DSA as Prototypes

In the signature schemes described in this section one supposes using a one-way 256-bit hash function F_h that satisfies the collision-resistance requirement. The first signature algorithm, which is based on computational difficulty of the HLP of the first form, is described as follows.

The signature generation algorithm uses the private key (that represents the non-negative integer x and three vectors G, D, and Q) and includes the following steps:

1. Select a random integer $k < q$ and compute the vector $V = D \circ G^k \circ Q$.
2. Compute the first signature element $v = F_h(V)$.
3. Compute the hash function value u from the signed document M and the second signature element $s : u = F_h(M)$ and $s = ku - xv \bmod q$.

This algorithm outputs the signature (v, s) each element in which has length equal to 256 bits.

Verification of the 512-bit signature (v, s) to the document M is to be performed, using the public key (Y, Z, T), as follows:

1. Compute the hash-function value u from the document $M : u = F_h(M)$.
2. Compute the integer $d = u^{-1} \bmod q$.
3. Compute the vector $V' : V' = Y^{vd} \circ T \circ Z^{sd}$.
4. Compute the hash-function value v' from the vector $V' : v' = F_h(V')$.
5. If $v' = v$, then the signature is accepted as genuine. Otherwise the signature is rejected as false one.

The correctness proof of of the first signature scheme is performed as follows:

$$V' = (D \circ G^x \circ H)^{vd} \circ T \circ (N \circ G \circ Q)^{sd}$$
$$= D \circ G^{xvd} \circ H \circ T \circ N \circ G^{sd} \circ Q$$
$$= D \circ G^{xvd} \circ R_3 \circ G^{(ku-xv)d} \circ Q$$
$$= D \circ G^{xvd+k-xvd} \circ Q = D \circ G^k \circ Q = V \Rightarrow v' = v.$$

To generate the signature to the document M the signer can also use the following *alternative signature generation procedure* in which only one element of the private key, namely, the value x is used:

1. Select two random integers $k_1 < q$ and $k_2 < q$ and compute the vector $V = Y^{k_1} \circ T \circ Z^{k_2}$.
2. Compute the first signature element $v = F_h(V)$ and the value $k = xk_1 + k_2 \bmod q$.
3. Compute the hash function value u from the signed document M and the second signature element $s : u = F_h(M)$ and $s = ku - xv \bmod q$.

The second signature algorithm uses the second form of the HLP and includes the following steps:

1. Generate a uniformly random integer $k < q$ and compute the vector $V = D \circ G^k \circ Q$.
2. Compute the first signature element $v = F_h(V)$.
3. Compute the hash-function value u from the signed document M and the second signature element $s : u = F_h(M)$ and $s = (xv + u)k^{-1} \bmod q$.

Verification of the 512-bit signature (v, s) to the document M is to be performed, using the public key (Y, Z), as follows:

1. Compute the hash-function value u from the document $M : u = F_h(M)$.
2. Compute the integer $d = s^{-1} \bmod q$.
3. Compute the vector $V' : V' = Y^{vd} \circ Z^{ud}$.
4. Compute the hash-function value v' from the vector $V' : v' = F_h(V')$.
5. The signature (v, s) is accepted as genuine, if $v' = v$. Otherwise the signature is rejected.

The proof of correctness of the second signature scheme is as follows:

$$V' = (D \circ G^x \circ H)^{vd} \circ (N \circ G \circ Q)^{sd}$$
$$= D \circ G^{xvd} \circ H \circ N \circ G^{ud} \circ Q = D \circ G^{xvd} \circ R_3 \circ G^{ud} \circ Q$$
$$= D \circ G^{(xv+u)d} \circ Q = D \circ G^{(xv+u)s^{-1}} \circ Q$$
$$= D \circ G^k \circ Q = V \Rightarrow v' = v.$$

In the frame of the second signature scheme the signer also can use only one element of the private key to generate a signature to the document M, namely, the value x. The *alternative signature generation procedure* is as follows:

1. Select two random integers $k_1 < q$ and $k_2 < q$ and compute the vector $V = Y^{k_1} \circ Z^{k_2}$.
2. Compute the first signature element $v = F_h(V)$ and the value $k = xk_1 + k_2 \bmod q$.
3. Compute the hash function value u from the signed document M and the second signature element $s : u = F_h(M)$ and $s = (xv + u)k^{-1} \bmod q$.

Each of the described signature algorithms generates the digital signature having size equal to 512 bits. One should note the cryptoschemes of the Russian signature standard GOST R 34.10−94 [13] (prototype of the first proposed signature scheme) and of the USA signature standard DSA [14] (prototype of the second proposed signature scheme) are based on computations in a finite cyclic group having sufficiently large prime order. In the signature standards the cyclic finite group is defined evidently, but in the proposed HLP-based signature algorithms the base cyclic group is hidden in the FNAA used as the algebraic support of the HLP. Due to this fundamental feature the proposed signature algorithms acquire their security against the attacks using quantum computers.

4.2   Using the Schorr Signature Scheme as Prototype

The method for formal security proof of the DLP-based signature schemes proposed in [16] is not applicable to the GOST and DSA signature schemes, since the hash function value is computed directly from the document M which is to be signed [17]. Therefore that method is not applicable also to the HLP-based signatures introduced in Subsect. 4.1. To design a provably secure signature scheme based on the HLP one can use as prototype the Schnorr signature scheme [15] in which during the signature generation process the base exponentiation operation G^k (where $k < q$ is a secrete non-negative integer selected at random) is always performed before computation of the hash value v, since the value v is computed as follows: $v = F_h(M, V)$, where $V = G^k$, i. e., to compute the hash value one should know the value G^k. In the formal security proof of the Schnorr-like signature schemes it is supposed that the hash function F_h is free of some properties that the potential attacker can take advantage of [17]. Such assumption is reasonable when the used one-way hash-function satisfies the collision-resistance requirement.

The Schnorr signature scheme had been initially defined in the finite cyclic subgroup of the multiplicative group of the finite field $GF(p)$ [15]. However it can be defined also over some other finite cyclic group, for example, over the group generated by the element G (having sufficiently large prime order q) of one of the FNAA considered in Sect. 2. In last case the public key represents the element $Y = G^x$, where the non-negative integer $x < q$ is the private key and G is the public parameter common for many different users.

The signature generation is performed, using the private key x, as follows:

1. Select a random integer $k < q$ and compute the value $V = G^k$.
2. Compute the first signature element $v = F_h(M, V)$, where M is the document to be signed.
3. Compute the second signature element $s : s = k + vx \bmod q$.

The signature verification procedure is performed, using the public key Y and the public parameter G, as follows:

1. Compute the value $V' = Y^{-v} \circ G^s$.
2. Compute the hash-function value $v' = F_h(M, V')$.
3. If $v' = v$, then the signature (v, s) is genuine.

A Schnorr-like signature scheme based on the HLP can be designed using each of the forms of the HLP considered in Sect. 3. When using the second form of the HLP in which the public key represents the pair (Y, Z) we have the following signature scheme. The signature generation algorithm uses the private key represented in the form (x, D, G, Q) and includes the following steps:

1. Generate a uniformly random integer $k < q$ and compute the vector $V = D \circ G^k \circ Q$.
2. Compute the first signature element $v = F_h(M, V)$, where M is the document to be signed.

3. Compute the second signature element s : $s = x^{-1}(k + v) \bmod q$.

This algorithm outputs the 512-bit signature (v, s).

The signature verification procedure is performed using the public key (Y, Z) as follows:

1. Compute the value $V' = Y^s \circ Z^{-v}$.
2. Compute the hash-function value v' from the document M to which the value V' is concatenated: $v' = F_h(M, V')$.
3. If $v' = v$, then the signature (v, s) is accepted as genuine. Otherwise the signature is rejected.

The proof of correctness of the proposed Schnorr-like signature scheme is as follows:

$$V' = (D \circ G^x \circ H)^{x^{-1}(k+v)} \circ (N \circ G \circ Q)^{-v}$$
$$= D \circ G^{k+v} \circ H \circ N \circ G^{-v} \circ Q = D \circ G^{k+v} \circ R_3 \circ G^{-v} \circ Q$$
$$= D \circ G^k \circ Q = D \circ G^k \circ Q = V \Rightarrow v' = v.$$

Like in the case of two signature schemes described in Subsect. 4.1, the signature can be also computed using only one element of the private key, namely, the value x and the following *alternative signature generation* algorithm:

1. Generate two uniformly random integers $k_1 < q$ and $k_2 < q$ and, using the public key (Y, Z), compute the vector $V = Y^{k_1} \circ Z^{k_2}$.
2. Compute the first signature element $v = F_h(M, V)$.
3. Compute the value $k = k_1 x + k_2 \bmod q$ and second signature element s : $s = x^{-1}(k + v) \bmod q$.

Thus, to forge a signature only the private value x is required. Actually, finding the value x from the known vectors Y and Z (that are elements of the known FNAA used as algebraic support of the signature scheme) represent the HLP of the second form introduced in Sect. 3.

In the method [16] providing formal security proof of the Schnorr signature scheme it is considered a forger that can compute the second signature element s equally well for different hash functions F_h and F'_h after the values $v = F_h(M, V)$ and $v' = F'_h(M, V)$ have been computed for the same value V. (Suppose the forger runs two computer programs that use the same input data, but different hash functions.) In the case of the Schnorr signature scheme for some fixed hash function value v there exists unique value of the second signature element s. Therefore, after computing the values $s = k + vx \bmod q$ and $s' = k + v'x \bmod q$ relating to the values v and v' the forger can easily compute the value of the private key $x = (s - s')(v - v')^{-1} \bmod q$ that represents the solution of the DLP in the cyclic group generated by the element G.

The method [16] can be used to provide security proof for the Schnorr-like signature scheme based on the HLP, since in the last signature scheme for the fixed values V and v the value of the second signature element is also unique (like in the Schnorr signature scheme) and therefore equal to $s = x^{-1}(k+v) \bmod q$. Computing the values $s = x^{-1}(k+v) \bmod q$ and $s' = x^{-1}(k+v') \bmod q$ for the same value k the forger gets the value $x = (v-v')(s-s')^{-1} \bmod q$ that represents the solution of the HLP, i. e., the value of the degree used to perform the base exponentiation operation G^x during the process of computing the public key, in which a random generator G represents a secret value.

Uniqueness of the value $s < q$ that satisfies the verification equation $V = Y^s \circ Z^{-v}$ for the fixed values V and v can be shown as follows. Suppose we have two values $s < q$ and $s' < q$ such that $V = Y^s \circ Z^{-v} = Y^{s'} \circ Z^{-v}$. Then we have $\left(Y^s - Y^{s'}\right) \circ Z^{-v} = O$. The vector $Z^{-v} = Z^{q-v}$ is locally invertible one for which the condition $\Delta_{Z^{q-v}} \neq 0$ holds true. Therefore, the vector equation $X \circ Z^{-v} = O$ has unique solution $X = O$ and $Y^s = Y^{s'} \Rightarrow s = s'$.

Relatively the first two signature schemes the advantage of the third HLP-based signature scheme is possibility to provide its formal reductionist-security proof. However, the main item for all three proposed candidates for post-quantum signature schemes is estimation of the computational difficulty of the proposed forms of the HLP when solving them on a hypothetic quantum computer. Like in the case of other candidates for post-quantum public-key cryptoschemes selected in frame of the NIST competition [4,5] decision about super-polynomial or polynomial security to quantum attacks is to be formulated at the expert level after several-year term of the analysis of the post-quantum cryptoschemes, which is to be performed by efforts of the wide cryptographic community [4,5].

5   Conclusion

Three new 6-dimensional FNAAs every one of which contains sufficiently large number of the global right-sided units have been introduced as carriers of the HLP defined in two novel forms. The proposed forms of the HLP suit well to design digital signature algorithms, based on computations in a finite cyclic group. Resistance to quantum attacks of the proposed signature algorithm is connected with hiding the used cyclic group in the 6-dimensional FNAAs. However, estimation of the computational difficulty of the proposed forms of the HLP in the case of solving this problem on a quantum computer represent an interesting problem for independent researchers. Since the proposed signature algorithms have many practical advantages (short signature size, no restrictions on number of the signed documents for one public key, possibility to use the standard architecture of the public-key infrastructure) in comparison with the signature schemes selected as candidates for post-quantum standards [5] one can suppose the task of estimating security of the proposed algorithms will attract attention from the part of the research community.

Using the 4-, 8-, and 10-dimensional FNAAs as carriers of the signature schemes, analogous to the proposed ones, also represents an interesting task for an independent study. The most interesting case relates to using the 4-dimensional FNAAs as algebraic supports of the proposed forms of the HLP and signature schemes. Research in this direction is to be started with developing methods for setting the 4-dimensional FNAA containing large sets of the single-sided global unites and investigating the properties of such algebras.

Acknowledgement. The reported study was partially funded by the Russian Foundation for Basic Research (project #18-07-00932-a); The Ministry of Science and Technology (MOST) under grant KC.01.22/16-20/.

References

1. Shor, P.W.: Polynomial-time algorithms for prime factorization and discrete logarithms on quantum computer. SIAM J. Comput. **26**, 1484–1509 (1997)
2. Yan, S.Y.: Quantum Attacks on Public-Key Cryptosystems, p. 207. Springer, Heidelberg (2014). https://doi.org/10.1007/978-1-4419-7722-9
3. Smolin, J.A., Smith, G., Vargo, A.: Oversimplifying quantum factoring. Nature **499**(7457), 163–165 (2013)
4. Submission Requirements and Evaluation Criteria for the Post-Quantum Cryptography Standardization Process. NIST PQCrypto project. https://csrc.nist.gov/CSRC/media/Projects/Post-Quantum-Cryptography/documents/call-for-proposals-final-dec-2016.pdf
5. First NIST standardization conference - 11–13 April 2018. http://prometheuscrypt.gforge.inria.fr/2018-04-18.pqc2018.html
6. Takagi, T. (ed.): PQCrypto 2016. LNCS, vol. 9606. Springer, Cham (2016). https://doi.org/10.1007/978-3-319-29360-8
7. Lange, T., Steinwandt, R. (eds.): PQCrypto 2018. LNCS, vol. 10786. Springer, Cham (2018). https://doi.org/10.1007/978-3-319-79063-3
8. Moldovyan, N.A.: Unified method for defining finite associative algebras of arbitrary even dimensions. Quasigroups Relat. Syst. **26**(2), 263–270 (2018)
9. Sakalauskas, E., Tvarijonas, P., Raulynaitis, A.: Key agreement protocol (KAP) using conjugacy and discrete logarithm problems in group representation level. Informatica **18**(1), 115–124 (2007)
10. Moldovyan, D.N.: Non-commutative finite groups as primitive of public-key cryptoschemes. Quasigroups Relat. Syst. **18**(2), 165–176 (2010)
11. Moldovyan, D.N., Moldovyan, N.A.: Cryptoschemes over hidden conjugacy search problem and attacks using homomorphisms. Quasigroups Relat. Syst. **18**(2), 177–186 (2010)
12. Kuzmin, A.S., Markov, V.T., Mikhalev, A.A., Mikhalev, A.V., Nechaev, A.A.: Cryptographic algorithms on groups and algebras. J. Math. Sci. **223**(5), 629–641 (2017). https://doi.org/10.1007/s10958-017-3371-y
13. Moldovyan, A.A., Moldovyan, N.A.: Blind signature protocols from digital signature standards. Int. J. Netw. Secur. **13**(1), 22–30 (2011)
14. International Standard ISO/IEC 14888–3:2006(E): Information technology - Security techniques - Digital Signatures with appendix - Part 3: Discrete logarithm based mechanisms (2006)
15. Schnorr, C.P.: Efficient signature generation by smart cards. J. Cryptol. **4**(3), 161–174 (1991). https://doi.org/10.1007/BF00196725
16. Pointcheval, D., Stern, J.: Security arguments for digital signatures and blind signatures. J. Cryptol. **13**, 361–396 (2000)
17. Koblitz, N., Menezes, A.J.: Another look at "provable security". J. Cryptol. **20**, 3–38 (2007). https://doi.org/10.1007/s00145-005-0432-z

Advanced Studies in Machine Learning for Security

Malicious-Traffic Classification Using Deep Learning with Packet Bytes and Arrival Time

Ingyom Kim[1]([✉])(iD) and Tai-Myoung Chung[2]([✉])(iD)

[1] Department of Electrical and Computer Engineering,
Sungkyunkwan University, Suwon, Korea
`igkim89@skku.edu`
[2] Department of Computer Science and Engineering,
Sungkyunkwan University, Suwon, Korea
`tmchung@skku.edu`

Abstract. Internet technology is rapidly developing through the development of computer technology. However, we haven been experiencing problems such as malware with these developments. Various methods of malware detection have been studied for years to respond to malicious codes. There are three main ways to classify traffic. They are port-based, payload-based and a machine learning method. We attempt to classify malicious traffic using CNN which is one of deep learning algorithms. The features we use for CNN are the packet's size and its arrival time. The packet's size and arrival time information are extracted and then converted into an image file. The converted image is then used for CNN to classify what type of attack the traffic is. The accuracy of the proposed technique was 95%, which showed very high performance, proving that classification was possible.

Keywords: Intrusion detection system · Malicious traffic ·
Convolutional Neural Network · Deep learning · Machine learning ·
ISCX-IDS-2012

1 Introduction

Various methods of malware detection have been studied for years to respond to malicious codes. These detections require an Intrusion Detection System (IDS) that protects and defends the system from attacks [1]. Although port-based or payload-based detection methods are mainly used in the detection method, there are problems that are difficult to apply to bypass or encrypted traffic, such as recent developments in hacking techniques and VPNs.

Thus, this paper attempts to classify traffic using packet bytes and time interval, instead of source and destination information, using deep learning without checking packet payloads.

© Springer Nature Switzerland AG 2020
T. K. Dang et al. (Eds.): FDSE 2020, LNCS 12466, pp. 345–356, 2020.
https://doi.org/10.1007/978-3-030-63924-2_20

In recent years, deep learning has been studied and used in a wide range of fields. Among deep learning techniques, Convolutional Neural Network (CNN) has been used frequently as a classification method using images. This paper first extracts packet size and interval time information through feature selection, and converts those information to images. Then, CNN is used to learn and classify the packets. The size of the packet is based on the maximum transmission unit (MTU) of Ethernet. The packet interval is measured based on the packet's arrival time. The learned modules detects malicious traffic by classifying traffic by type of malware (DDoS, Bruteforce-SSH, etc.).

2 Related Work

The purpose of this section is to introduce techniques and taxonomy of machine learning-based IDS on current studies.

2.1 Malicious-Traffic Classification

Traffic is becoming more diverse as well as malicious-traffic. Thus, classification systems for malicious-traffic have been studied. There are three main ways to classify traffic. They are a payload-based classification method [3], port-based classification method [2], and a classification method using machine learning [4].

The payload-based classification method is a method of checking the payload of packets directly and extracting application-specific features called signatures generated by a particular application, and classifying traffic through them. This is because you have to check the payload yourself, so the design is complicated, and you can't respond quickly to changes in applications. Therefore, you can't classify if the payload is encrypted.

The port-based classification method is to extract the header part of the packet and analyze it to analyze the 5 Tuple (port number or IP address, etc.) serviced by each application to analyze which application it is. This is relatively easy to design and fast to speed. But traffic is getting more and more complex these days. For example, if users change header information by using or bypassing any port number to avoid firewalls, they can't find any information that serves as an absolute criterion by analyzing only the header portion of the packet.

The third method is classification method using machine learning to be used in this paper. In this paper, we are trying to classify using CNN, one of the deep learning algorithms. When classifying with machine learning, it is easy to automatically extract characteristics and extract high-dimensional patterns that reflect the uniqueness of traffic through learning. We extract characteristics related to the size and arrival time of packets and classify them by learning patterns.

2.2 A Study on Machine Learning and Techniques Used in IDS

Machine learning techniques are divided into supervised and unsupervised learning. Supervised learning is suitable for labeled data and is mostly used for classification. Labeling data is a long and cumbersome task, and classification can be difficult if there is not enough labeled data. Unsupervised learning is easier to secure data by extracting characteristics from unlabeled data. However, supervised learning is mainly better when comparing detection performance alone [5].

New classification solutions of malicious traffic have also been studied as the use of machine learning increases. Support Vector Machine, Decision tree, Bayesian classification are applied with the previously introduced machine learning technology. There are also ways to detect malicious traffic by applying the K-means method. Shin et al. [6] applied the k-means algorithm. They proposed how to set up parameters that can detect DDoS attack and Witty worm attack and find data similarity through non-hierarchical clustering. Hatim et al. [7] proposed a system to detect attacks by applying Hybrid Machine Learning techniques that mixes the SVM method with k-means. However, while these existing detection techniques use separate machine learning methods for extracting patterns and learning in the past, new methods using improved DNNs are being introduced. Unlike rule-based or malicious attack patterns that are already known to be analyzed and detected, the algorithm model finds a direct relationship through a large amount of data related to the threat following anomalies. Ni Gao et al. [8] showed how to detect intrusions using Deep Belief Network (DBNs) and brought about a 6% improvement over the SVM model. in another study, Jo, Seongrae et al. [9] introduced studies comparing the results of Forward Adaptive Neural Network (FANN) with existing SVM models to detect intrusions. FANN is an algorithm created by supplementing the vulnerability of back-propagation. FANN shows better accuracy and detection rates than SVMs.

There are four typical studies in intrusion detection studies using deep learning models. First, Kim et al. [10] studied the intrusion detection system by the deep learning model. In this study, intrusion detection system using various deep learning models for supervisited, unsupervised, semi-supervised, weakly supervised, reforcement, etc. were analyzed. Secondly, Mathai et al. [11] showed that the State Preservation Extreme Learning Machine (SPELM) algorithm was used to improve performance more than the existing Deep Belief Network (DBN) algorithm. SPELM algorithms can be used for face recognition, pedestrian recognition, and network intrusion detection recognition. They used the SPELM method for NSL-KDD datasets to improve the detection rate by 93.2% over the detection rate of the existing DBN 52.85 performance. Third, Aggarwal et al. [12] studied intrusion detection methods using KDD CUP 99 data. In this study, KDD CUP 99 data were analyzed, and several class labels were analyzed. For these class labels, detection rates and false detection were analyzed for the Random forest, OneR, and Naive Bayes methods by simultaneously considering attribute classes from one to four. Such an analysis. Through this, they analyzed which attribute has the most important weight. Fourth, Gurung et al. [13] studied network intrusion detection using NSLKDD datasets. In this study, they suggested learning about patterns in the Sparse Autoencorders method and detecting behavioral patterns of users, learned through the Logistic classification. This method showed 87.2% detection rate.

2.3   Datasets Used by IDS

The main view of machine learning is to extract valuable information from data. The performance of machine learning depends largely on the quality of the input data. Accordingly, input data into IDS should be easy to acquire and incorporate characteristics of users or networks. Mainly used data formats include packets, flows, sessions, and logs. Creating your own datasets is complex and time-consuming. Thus, the published dataset is used for analysis by many researchers. Additional published datasets can be used to compare results from other studies with those from their own studies as credible data.

The most frequently used public dataset is DARPA1998, KDD99, NSL-KDD, UNSW-NB-15, and finally CICIDS to be used in this paper. DARPA1998 was produced at MIT's Lincoln Laboratory [14]. The traffic data were collected for nine weeks. The first seven weeks data are used for learning and the remaining two weeks for testing. The dataset consists of packets and labels, normal, denial of service (DOS), Probe, User to Root (U2R), and Remote to Local (R2L). KDD99 is a characteristic of DARPA1998 in 41 dimensions [15], including basic features, content features, host-based static features, and time-based static features. The dataset is not suitable for comparing results, because the number of data varies greatly by characteristic and there is a large number of duplicates. NSL-KDD is a dataset designed to overcome the shortcomings of KDD99 [16], which has a more uniform number of data and eliminated redundant data to revive individuality. UNSW-NB15 is a data set produced by South Wales University that captures traffic with three virtual servers [17]. Characteristically extracted in 49 dimensions and has more attack types than KDD99 and contains a total of 1 general data and 9 types of attack data. Finally, the CICIDS dataset to be used in this paper is produced by the Canadian Institute for Cybersecurity (CIC), and has the most representative dataset, ISCX-IDS 2012 [18]. The dataset consists of four types of attack data and one general data type. The attack type consists of Http flooding, DDoS, infiltrating, and bruteforce SSH.

3   Methodology

3.1   Pre-processing

The ISCX-IDS 2012 dataset is a seven-day traffic dataset that consists of infiltrating, HTTP flooding, DDoS and bruteforce SSH as general and malicious traffic data. The dataset was created with a tool called Argus, which is an open source network capture tool. Argus details real-time or stored packet data. Network analysis tools capture and store the traffic for future reference. The captured traffic are then put together into a pcap file. Pcap stands for "packet capture" and represents an API used to capture network traffic on Windows and UNIX systems [19]. Pcap files have a global header. A Global header contains capture information like timestamp accuracy, maximum length of a packet and data link information.

The dataset has six Pcap file. Those approximately 3 million flows. Table 1 shows how many flows are in each pcap file and the amount of each type which are normal, attack and unknown. Unknown packets are flows usually generated during server maintenance or monitoring.

Table 1. Number of flow in ISCX-IDS-2012.

Day	Flow records		
	Normal	Attack	Unknown
June 11 + June 12	224173	3221	34947
June 13	221148	12853	45179
June 14	220156	12761	46263
June 15	1033972	34702	66332
June 16	663642	0	347914
June 17	612089	3294	19973

An overview of the extraction process is shown in Fig. 1. We classify only the attack traffic. Therefore We need to extract only the attack flows. ISCX-IDS 2012 is a labeled dataset with a xml file provided to inform us which packet is either attack or normal for each pcap file and also the packets' source and destination information with timestamp. We used Splitcap to divide the pcap files into each flow. Splitcap is a free tool designed to split capture files into smaller files based on a criterion, such as IP address, 5-tuple or MAC address. We divided all the pcap files into a single flow and then combine only attack flows into a single pcap per each attack type. We extract two features which are a packet length and an arrival time from the packets. Then we create a block per a certain period of time. The extracted features within this period are converted into a single image file.

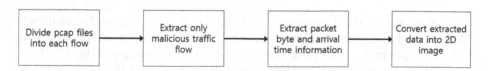

Fig. 1. Infiltrating, HTTP flood, DDoS and Bruteforce SSH

The packet length has the maximum transfer unit (MTU) of Ethernet is 1500, so only packets that are within 1500 are extracted. The extracted data resizes into an image of 150 * 150. If too few packets are extracted at a set time interval, at least 30 extraction processes per image are made to prevent the image from having a large amount of free space. The image form is png. The images are then used for CNN. The images created by type are shown below Fig. 2.

3.2   CNN Model

CNN has so far been widely used as a form of image classification. According to LeCun [20] that CNN is suitable for use with the following data - data in multiple array forms, correlated data, data with characteristics everywhere, data that does not change after distortion or translation. In particular, 1D-CNN is efficient for continuous data or language, 2D-CNN is suitable for image or audio form, and 3D-CNN is suitable for video or three-dimensional images.

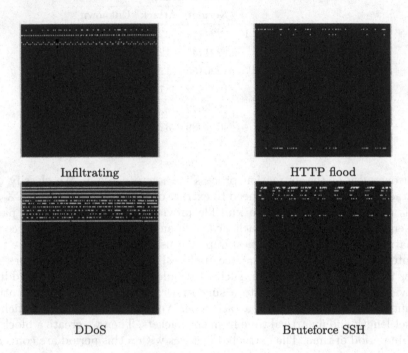

| Infiltrating | HTTP flood |

| DDoS | Bruteforce SSH |

Fig. 2. Overall pattern

CNN has been actively researched and used in analyzing traffic. Traffic data is a flow of one-dimensional bytes in a hierarchical structure as a series of data. This study attempts to analyze traffic and classify malicious packets using 2D-CNN. CNN's structure to be used in this study defines characteristics using multiple Convolution and Pooling layers and ultimately classifies the data entered in the Softmax layer into each class. The exact structure is shown Table 2.

3.3   Image Creation

To generate an image of a malicious packet, the packet's arrival time and byte size are used as coordinates, and each corresponds to x and y. In order to generate an image, the flow is separated by a specified amount of time and the corresponding section is used as a block and converted into an image. The format of the image

Table 2. CNN architecture.

Layer	Operation	Input	Filter	Stride	Pad	Output
1	Conv2D+ReLU	150 * 150 * 1	3 * 3	1	Same	150 * 150 * 64
2	Pooling	150 * 150 * 64	2 * 2	2	Same	75 * 75 * 64
3	Conv2D+ReLU	75 * 75 * 64	2 * 2	1	Valid	74 * 74 * 128
4	Pooling	74 * 74 * 128	2 * 2	2	Same	37 * 37 * 128
5	Conv2D+ReLU	37 * 37 * 128	2 * 2	1	Valid	36 * 36 * 256
6	Pooling	36 * 36 * 256	2 * 2	2	Same	18 * 18 * 256
7	Conv2D+ReLU	18 * 18 * 256	2 * 2	1	Valid	17 * 17 * 256
8	Full connect	17 * 17 * 256	–	–	–	73984
9	Full connect	73984	–	–	–	256
10	Softmax	256	–	–	–	4

being output used 8 bits. Each coordinate shall not exceed its value on the basis of 256 which is recognizable by the computer system for one color.

3.4 Interval Time and Grayscale

Because images need to be recognized using CNN, changes in accuracy were measured by changing the time and the value corresponding to the coordinates of the blocks in the process of image creation. We only use 2 features from a packet's header, the arrival time and byte. To create a block, we set a period of time using the packet's arrival time. If we set it 10 s, the packets arrived within that interval time are only used to create a image.

First, we divided the blocks into 10, 20, 30 and 60 s. The results are as shown in the Table 3.

Table 3. Different period of time simulation result

Time	Average precision	Average recall	Average f1-score
10 s	0.95	0.95	0.95
20 s	0.93	0.93	0.93
30 s	0.92	0.92	0.92
60 s	0.87	0.87	0.86

The values corresponding to the coordinates were then changed to 2, 5, 10 and 15 to measure whether the sharpness of the color affects accuracy. The results are shown in Table 4.

Table 4. Different grayscale simulation result

Grayscale	Average precision	Average recall	Average f1-score
2	0.90	0.91	0.90
5	0.92	0.92	0.92
10	0.90	0.90	0.90
15	0.89	0.90	0.89

According to the simulation result, we achieved a better result when we set the period to 10 s and grayscale to 5. Therefore, we created the block by breaking it every 10 s and then creating the image by setting the grayscale to 5. From this, we found that each image is clearly characterized and the clearer the image, the higher accuracy the result is. And if we set high grayscale for each value corresponding to the coordinates, more coordinates' values are beyond 255. That makes the images loose their identities and brings a lower result.

4   Experiments and Results

In this paper, 60% of dataset's flow was used as learning data, 20% as test data and the rest as verification data to test the detection algorithm of deep learning-based using CNN for malicious traffic detection. In this experiment, we classify and determine the accuracy of the four types of malicious codes that data sets have.

We ran 10 times of epoch to validate our model. An epoch indicates how many times the model has learnt a dataset. While the epochs, the training and validation data are used. The validation set is used as a test set during epochs. The difference between the validation set and test set are that the test set is used once after tuning the model with multiple runs of an epoch whereas the validation set is used during the epoch to tune the model. Training loss is the error on the training set of data. Validation loss is the error after running the validation set of data through the trained network. The accuracy is defined as the proportion for the amount of correct classifications divided by the total amount of classifications. If the train and validation loss are both increasing, this means the test is close to underfitting. If the train loss is decreasing but validation loss is increasing, this means the test is close to overfitting. When both the train accuracy and validation accuracy increase and the others decrease, that means the algorithm model works fine. Figure 3 shows the entire epoch. As a result, the loss values for both are decreasing and the accuracy values for both are increasing. This determines our model works effectively.

Table 5 and Fig. 4 show our experiment result. For accuracy determination, the detection rate (Recall) refers to the ratio of successful classification of input data, the rate of precision is the ratio of correct classification of four types. the 95% accuracy was clearly indicated to classify malicious code accurately.

Table 5. ISCX-IDS 2012 simulation result

Label	Precision	Recall	F1-score	Support
Infiltrating	0.93	0.96	0.95	120
HTTP flood	0.86	0.90	0.88	69
DDoS	0.97	0.96	0.97	204
Bruteforce SSH	0.98	0.95	0.97	60
Accuracy	–	–	0.95	453
Macro avg	0.94	0.94	0.94	453
Weighted avg	0.95	0.95	0.95	453

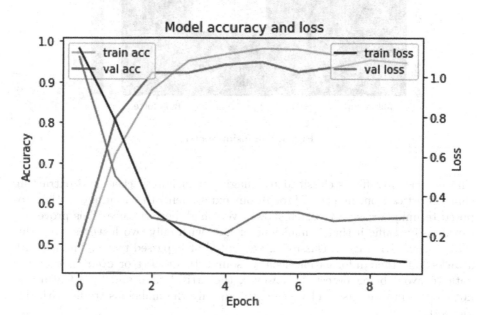

Fig. 3. Malware classification result

The advantage of this paper compared to previous studies is that the process of extracting and classifying characteristics for classifying malicious traffic is simple. This study produces images using only arrival time and packet size information without identifying source and destination information or patterns in the data in the header of packets. And this method uses the extracted image directly as an input to the classifier learning. Moreover, network attacks have been developed through the development of computer technology. However, with these developments, we are always experiencing problems such as malware. Various methods of malware detection have been studied for years to respond to malicious codes. In this paper, we tried to classify malicious packets using deep learning algorithm with only two features, a packet's arrival time and byte.

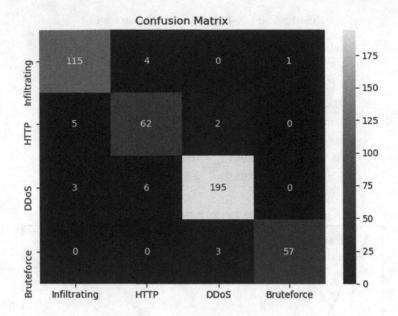

Fig. 4. Confusion matrix

The malicious traffic is classified by imaging malicious packets and extracting characteristics from images. Through our experiment, the accuracy of the proposed technique was 95%, which showed very high performance. This proves we can classify traffic if that is malicious or not, with only two features. And this shows huge advantage in classifying encrypted or bypassed traffic. The network attacks hide their information such as source IP or port or even encrypt the data to avoid being detected. However, the arrival time and byte feature do not change in that case and we can still identify the malicious traffic with this method.

It also has the advantage of being easy to preprocess even if IDS is run with machine learning later. And because the packet header generates images with only two features, this can be expected to reduce the computing power required rather than other image classification methods.

5 Conclusion

In this paper, the malicious traffic detection technique using deep learning based was conceived in order to respond to network attacks by applying the rapidly developing deep learning to the information security field by detecting or classifying malicious packets. In related studies, image-based malicious packet classification methods are also being studied, but the process for learning about new malicious packets or extracting features has been called for inference. In this paper, the characteristics of malicious packets are classified using CNN to image them and classify them automatically by type of attack. The pattern was confirmed to exist only by the size and arrival time of the packet, not by port or payload. Although port-based or payload-based detection methods are mainly used in the detection method, there are problems that are difficult to apply to bypass or encrypted traffic, such as recent developments in hacking techniques and VPNs. Those network attacks nowadays hide their information such as a source IP and port. Or they even encrypt the data to hide that they are malicious. Our experiment accuracy was 95%, showing very high performance. With this experiment, even if the packets are encrypted or bypassed, we are now able to identify if they are malicious. Because we only extract two features, arrival time and byte, and they are not affected when bypassed. Due to the characteristics of deep learning, if the learning continues using many malicious packets in the future, the accuracy and detection rate will evolve.

Acknowledgements. This work was supported by Institute of Information & communications Technology Planning & Evaluation (IITP) grant funded by the Korea government (MSIT) (No. 2020-0-00990, Platform Development and Proof of High Trust & Low Latency Processing for Heterogeneous·Atypical·Large Scaled Data in 5G-IoT Environment).

References

1. Tidjon, L.N., Frappier, M., Mammar, A.: Intrusion detection systems: a cross domain overview. IEEE Commun. Surv. Tutor. **21**, 3639–3681 (2019)
2. Auld, T., Moore, A.W., Gull, S.F.: Bayesian neural networks for internet traffic classification. IEEE Trans. Neural Netw. **18**(1), 223–239 (2007)
3. Crotti, M., et al.: Traffic classification through simple statistical fingerprinting. ACM SIGCOMM Comput. Commun. Rev. **37**(1), 5–16 (2007)
4. Wagh, S.K., Pachghare, V.K., Kolhe, S.R.: Survey on intrusion detection system using machine learning techniques. Int. J. Comput. Appl. **78**(16), 30–37 (2013)
5. Alhakami, W., et al.: Network anomaly intrusion detection using a nonparametric Bayesian approach and feature selection. IEEE Access **7**, 52181–52190 (2019)
6. Shin, D., Choi, K., Chune, S., Choi, H.: Malicious traffic detection using K-means. J. Korean Inst. Commun. Inf. Sci. **41**(2), 277–284 (2016)
7. Tahir, M., et al.: Hybrid machine learning technique for intrusion detection system. In: 5th International Conference on Computing and Informatics (ICOCI) (2015)
8. Gao, N., Gao, L., Gao, Q., Wang, H.: An intrusion detection model based on deep belief networks. In: 2014 2nd International Conference on Advanced Cloud and Big Data (CBD), pp. 247–252 (2014)
9. Jo, S., Sung, H., Ahn, B.: A comparative study on the performance of SVM and an artificial neural network in intrusion detection. J. Korea Acad. Ind. Coop. Soc. **17**(2), 703–711 (2016)
10. Kim, K., Aminanto, M.E., Tanuwidjaja, H.C.: Network Intrusion Detection using Deep Learning. A Feature Learning Approach. SCSSN. Springer, Singapore (2018). https://doi.org/10.1007/978-981-13-1444-5
11. Mathai, K.J.: Performance comparison of intrusion detection system between deep belief network (DBN) algorithm and state preserving extreme learning machine (SPELM) algorithm. In: 2019 IEEE International Conference on Electrical, Computer and Communication Technologies (ICECCT). IEEE (2019)

12. Aggarwal, P., Dahiya, D.: Contribution of four class labeled attributes of kdd dataset on detection and false alarm rate for intrusion detection system. Indian J. Sci. Technol. **9**(5), 1–8 (2016)
13. Gurung, S., Ghose, M.K., Subedi, A.: Deep learning approach on network intrusion detection system using NSL-KDD dataset. Int. J. Comput. Netw. Inf. Secur. (IJCNIS) **11**(3), 8–14 (2019)
14. Lippmann, R.P., et al.: Evaluating intrusion detection systems: the 1998 DARPA off-line intrusion detection evaluation. In: Proceedings DARPA Information Survivability Conference and Exposition, DISCEX 2000, vol. 2. IEEE (2000)
15. Kayacik, H.G., Zincir-Heywood, A.N., Heywood, M.I.: Selecting features for intrusion detection: a feature relevance analysis on KDD 99 intrusion detection datasets. In: Proceedings of the 3rd Annual Conference on Privacy, Security and Trust, vol. 94 (2005)
16. Dhanabal, L., Shantharajah, S.P.: A study on NSL-KDD dataset for intrusion detection system based on classification algorithms. Int. J. Adv. Res. Comput. Commun. Eng. **4**(6), 446–452 (2015)
17. Moustafa, N., Slay, J.: UNSW-NB15: a comprehensive data set for network intrusion detection systems (UNSW-NB15 network data set). In: 2015 Military Communications and Information Systems Conference (MilCIS). IEEE (2015)
18. Shiravi, A., Shiravi, H., Tavallaee, M., Ghorbani, A.A.: Toward developing a systematic approach to generate benchmark datasets for intrusion detection. Comput. Secur. **31**(3), 357–374 (2012). https://doi.org/10.1016/j.cose.2011.12.012. ISSN 0167-4048
19. Velea, R., Apostol, I., Patriciu, V.: LightPcapNg: implementing a library for general-purpose tracing based on PcapNg. In: 2016 IEEE 14th International Symposium on Intelligent Systems and Informatics (SISY). IEEE (2016)
20. LeCun, Y., Bengio, Y., Hinton, G.: Deep learning. Nature **521**, 436–444 (2015)

Detecting Malware Based on Dynamic Analysis Techniques Using Deep Graph Learning

Nguyen Minh Tu[1], Nguyen Viet Hung[1(✉)], Phan Viet Anh[1], Cao Van Loi[1], and Nathan Shone[2]

[1] Le Quy Don Technical University, Hanoi, Vietnam
hungnv@lqdtu.edu.vn
[2] Liverpool John-Moore University, Liverpool, UK

Abstract. Detecting malware using dynamic analysis techniques is an efficient method. Those familiar techniques such as signature-based detection perform poorly when attempting to identify zero-day malware, and it is also a challenging and time-consuming task to manually engineer malicious behaviors. Several studies have tried to detect unknown behaviors automatically. One of effective approaches introduced in recent years is to use graphs to represent the behavior of an executable, and learn from these graphs. However, current graph representations have ignored much important information such as parameters, variables changes… In this paper, we present a new method for malware detection by applying a graph attention network on multi-edge directional heterogeneous graphs constructed from Windows API calls collected after a file being executed in cuckoo sandbox… The experiments show that our model achieves better performance than other baseline models at both TPR and FAR scores.

Keywords: Malware detection · Dynamic analysis · Deep learning · Graph representation

1 Introduction

Malware is referred to "any software that does something that causes harm to a user, computer, or network" [11]. Detecting malware remains a significant security challenge, predominantly. Malware analysis techniques can be categorized into two types: static and dynamic. The former including signature-based is considered a simple and lightweight approach. However, malware samples that employ obfuscation techniques such as refactoring code, inserting nop-code, encryption etc. can easily bypass static analysis. The latter includes two types of behavioral data, static behavior data (or code analysis) and dynamic behavior data (or behavioral analysis). In code analysis data are collected by static methods such as reverse-engineering and can give us a sight on what the software does. However, it faces the same problem of being evaded by obstruction techniques such as binary packers, polymorphism, metamorphism and anti-debugging etc. Hence, behavioral analysis becomes attractive to analysts because it can tackle it from a black box perspective, whereby only the end result on the system can be observed.

T. K. Dang et al. (Eds.): FDSE 2020, LNCS 12466, pp. 357–378, 2020.
https://doi.org/10.1007/978-3-030-63924-2_21

This method requires emulating a safe virtual environment and executing the malware inside it to monitor its behavior. Although there are tactics to prevent behavioral analysis, this strategy is less vulnerable to obfuscation techniques.

Manually analyzing an executable file to identify malicious behavior is a highly laborious process, therefore recent research projects have focused on automating this process. Devised techniques range from extracting features using text-mining algorithms, to learning features from graphs that represent behaviors of executable files. These approaches are very inspiring and have proved their efficiency in existing literature [8, 14, 15]. However, behavioral obfuscation techniques (e.g. system call reordering or bogus call injection) pose a challenge to approaches that represent behavioral data in sequences. One major limitation of current graph methods [8, 14, 15] is that they an abstract view of system behavior and omit important information.

This paper introduces a new graph representation for a file that contains multiple types of information, including API calls, connection types, and key arguments of each API. After obtaining the graph, verifying whether a file is a malware is done by applying a neural network to learn the node-level embedding and semantic-level embedding. Our main contributions in this work are as follow:

- A new method to represent an executable file as a **M**ulti-edge **D**irectional **H**eterogeneous **G**raph (MDHG) that can retain the most important behavioral characteristics of malware.
- A new deep learning model to learn features from built graphs, introducing edge-weighing layer, along with data encoding techniques, to focus on the argument of each API to weigh the importance of that call.

The rest of the paper is organized as follows: Sect. 2 presents an overview of existing research focused on detecting malicious software automatically. Section 3 provides a detailed description of our proposed approach. In Sect. 4, experimental results are discussed. Finally, conclusions are drawn in Sect. 5.

2   Related Work

In response to the steadily increasing complexity of modern malware, much research has been conducted to find alternative malware detection strategies. One efficient way is to analyze the behavior of the software after executing it in a virtual safe environment. Many studies rely on system call traces to evaluate and identify the malicious behaviors of malware samples.

Almost all proposed methods need to depend upon behavioral data (e.g., for example API calls), which to maximize accuracy must be performed in a specific way. The difficulties of this task lie in how to represent this behavioral data efficiently, whilst reducing noise without losing any useful information. In terms of API calls being used to analyze and learn features from, there are two popular approaches used to represent such data: sequences of text, the other uses graph.

With text-based representation, features can be extracted by applying conventional algorithms, or using deep learning model such as Recurrent Neural Networks (RNN) or

Convolutional Neural Networks (CNN) to extract features automatically, and a classifier would then be applied to learn from features extracted. Yu eta al. [1] gave an overview of behavioral description methods including XML-based, semantic description methods, description languages and several text-based. Hongfa et al. [2] represented system call sequences with MIST instructions and used an n-gram algorithm to extract features. In [3] Zhao et al. proposed the use of a control flow graph to generate an execution tree and form an opcode stream. N-gram is also used to generate feature set afterwards. Sequence alignment algorithms was used in [4] for common call sequence extraction. However, the complexity of sequence alignment algorithms was too large and computing time was too high. Based on NLP techniques, Tran et al. in [5] enhanced the conventional ML algorithms for API calls analysis by doc2vec, N-gram and TF-IDF methods. The n-gram analysis method archived some good results, but it faced to the optimizing the values of n and L. The current pace of malware development requires models that can seek patterns and informative features autonomously. Pascanu et al. in [6] were the first to use a hybrid model of RNN and a machine learning classifier to predict the next API call. Kolosnjaji et al. in [7] proposed a method to detect and classify malware in series of opcodes representation, using a Convolutional Neural Network (CNN) and feed-forward layers. This model used static analysis of portable executable files so hard to detect malware with obfuscation and detection evasion techniques. RNN and LSTM are also experimented with in various existing works but largely face the same problems [8–10].

In recent years, graph neural network has been a trend in related literature that has proven to be an effective format for representing linked data and extracting features. Inspired by this approach, many studies have attempted to present behavioral data in graph form. Authors of [19] generated Markov chain graphs from dynamic trace data, and applied graph kernels to acquire similarity matrix, which was sent to a Support Vector Machine (SVM). Naval et al. [12] extracted system call traces by monitoring malware execution and transforming the traces into Ordered System-Call Graphs (OSCGs). Another common type of graph that is used frequently in visualizing malware behavior data is Quantitative Data Flow Graph (QDFG) as introduced by Wüchner et al. [14], however, this work only formalizes heuristics to identify malware. Work by Hung et al. [15] outline an extended version of the traditional QDFG by subsequently applying a graph neural network (GCN). Although this graph succeeded in expressing more informative data, it still lack some details, for example each entity is only identified by its type (i.e. process, file, registry, network) but does not contain any more data such as its name, path or arguments etc.

It can be inferred that behavioral data contains different types of information, including different API categories, different objects and resources that the software influences. Therefore, this signifies that heterogeneous graph would be a suitable format in which to illustrate behavioral data. Currently, there is very little existing work investigating the use of heterogeneous graphs, and we believe our work is the first to represent behavioral data as a heterogeneous graph. Further details are outlined in Sect. 3.

3   Proposed Method

In our paper, we use the dynamic behavioral data, or more precisely, the API calls collected from Cuckoo sandbox to construct multi-edge directional graphs. To generate graph embedding and identify malicious objects from benign samples, we apply an attention neural network, as inspired by the work of Wang et al. [16].

3.1   Graph Representation

Entities and Connections. Our graph contains six main types of entities or nodes: Process, File, Registry, and three for three types of API calls: ProcessAPI, FileAPI and RegistryAPI. There are five types of connection accordingly:

- Process-ProcessAPI performs connection between a process handle (process entity) to a Process API (an API that belongs to process category),
- File-FileAPI performs connection between a file handle (file entity) and a File-API,
- Registry-RegistryAPI performs connection between a registry handle (registry entity) and a RegistryAPI,
- Process-FileAPI performs connection between a process entity and a FileAPI,
- Process-RegistryAPI performs connection between a process entity and a RegistryAPI,
- Self-loop: for each node to have its own features taken into consideration.

Note that there would never be a connection between a file handle and a registry API or a registry handle and a file API. Details of how the graphs are constructed are presented below.

The entities and connections are built on API calls that belong to 3 categories respectively: process, file and registry. Inherited from the work of Wüchner et al. [14], processes, files, sockets, and registry keys are of much significance when identifying malicious actions. Notice that there is no restriction on the number of types of entities or nodes in our graph, but we limit the three types of nodes because of the limitation in data collection. Therefore, with more types of nodes and edges the graph needs to represent, feature space would become bigger, and the data would be inadequate for learning in such a huge feature space. The edge data would be important arguments of each call. For each API call node (entity), only the name of the API is used for encoding as features, and all arguments are placed in edge data. Therefore, there might be multiple connections to one single API call node. The graph is also directional. The principles to determine the direction of each connection is similar to the work done by Hung et al. [15]. In the work, all API calls that operate the task of opening, creating, writing, or any modifying actions towards a file or registry would be the source nodes, and the destination nodes would be the file or registry themselves. In other cases, this will be reversed (i.e. the file or registry are the source node and the API calls are destination node). The text below is an example of the behavior from a malware sample collected from a cuckoo report.

List 1. An example of a behavior generated by cuckoo

```
{
    "category": "process",
    "status": 1,
    "stacktrace": [],
    "api": "WriteProcessMemory",
    "return value": 1,
    "arguments": {
        "process identifier": 768,
        "buffer": "MZnu0090nu0000nu0003nu0000nu0000...",
        "process handle": "0x0000007c",
        "base address": "0x01000000"
    },
    "time": 1556629733.164881,
    "tid": 3812,
    "flags":{}
},
```

This small piece of behavior constructs 2 nodes: one is a process entity (id 768) and another is a ProcessAPI entity (WriteProcessMemory) (because this API belongs to category process). One edge from the API entity to the process entity, with features are generated by encoding some information. The data used for acquiring features of each node is either its API name (if it is an API entity) or the name of its type (if it is a process/file/registry entity). For each connection, its data is obtained from the flags fields of the API that the connection links to (or from). Flags fields are generated by Cuckoo giving an insight into important information about that call.

In our paper, we define meta-path differently from the original work of Wang et al [16]. We do not define connections between two nodes of the same type (for example movie-movie) through a middle node of different types (such as movie-actor-movie and movie-director-movie). We only define a type for the connection between two nodes directly. For example, Process-ProcessAPI through Process-ProcessAPI edge, or write Process-(Process-ProcessAPI)-ProcessAPI. After all, the importance of a heterogeneous graph is the heterogeneity of nodes and edges the graph can support.

Embedding Entities and Edges Argument. As mentioned earlier, insufficient data is a big problem and has a great effect on how graphs are constructed, or more precisely what text data should be used for encoding, and how it should be encoded. In this paper, we will test on both skip-gram and TF-IDF encoding for node names (API names) and edge arguments (flags fields of an API). Figure 1 shows a representation of a malware and a benign sample.

3.2 Malware Detection

Detecting malware from a constructed graph can be considered as a graph classification task. There are two main approaches for this task: graph embedding (try to find representations of graph nodes and edges) and graph feature extraction (e.g. using graph

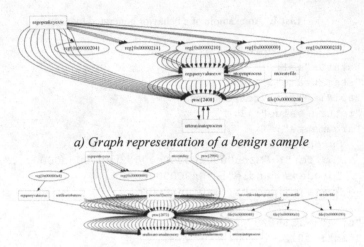

a) Graph representation of a benign sample

b) Graph representation of a malware sample

Fig. 1. Graph representation of a malware and benign sample.

convolutional neural network). A recent survey in [17] classified graph deep learning models into 5 categories: graph convolution, graph attention, graph generative, graph spatial-temporal networks and graph auto-encoders. Zhou et al. [18] examined graph models in terms of the main characteristics: graph types, training methods and propagation types; convolution and attention networks are both demonstrated to have contributed to the propagation step. Hung et al. [15] used GCN to extract features from graph but this spectral approach requires training and detection on a specific graph structure, since the learned filters depend on the Laplacian eigenbasis. Graph attention network, instead of statically normalizing the sum of the features using convolution operation like GCN, uses attention mechanism for weighting neighbors features with feature dependent and structure-free normalization.

For heterogeneous graph, the most distinctive feature is the heterogeneity, where each type of connection or each type of node would have a different importance in the overall consideration. Wang et al. [16] proposed the heterogeneous graph attention network (HAN) which utilizes node-level and semantic-level attentions and the model has the ability to consider node and meta-path importance simultaneously.

When analyzing the behavior of malware, many calls between two entities and related information may be very important and should take into account for detecting malware. Inspired by the idea of Wang [16], we propose a new approach with main contribution is the edge-weighing layers that can learn the importance of each connection among set of connections between two nodes, since our graphs is multi-edge. More concretely, the pipeline is presented as in Table 1:

The notations are inherited from the work of Wang [16], therefore the table above explains only new symbols.

Table 1. Notations and explanations.

Notation	Explanation
e_{ijp}	Importance of node j to node i through path p
$\alpha_{ijp}^{\emptyset}$	Weight of node pair (i, j) through path p
$\mathcal{P}_{ij}$	Set of connections between node pair (i, j) (from node j to node i)
u_p^{ij}	Importance of path p in the set of connections from node j to node i
U_{ij}	Edge-level attention vector from node j to node i
l_p	Initial edge features
l_p'	Weighted edge features
γ_p^{ij}	Weight of path p
τ_i	Weight of final node i
$\mathbf{Z}$	Graph embedding

Edge-Weighing. In [16], embedding $z_i^{\emptyset}$ of node i is computed by weighted-aggregation of the embedding of its meta-path based neighbors:

$$z_i^{\emptyset} = \sigma \left(\sum_{j \in \mathcal{N}_i^{\emptyset}} \alpha_{ij}^{\emptyset} . h_j \right) \tag{1}$$

$$\alpha_{ij}^{\emptyset} = \frac{\exp\left(\sigma\left(a_{\emptyset}^T . [h_i || h_j]\right)\right)}{\sum_{k \in \mathcal{N}_i^{\emptyset}} \exp\left(\sigma\left(a_{\emptyset}^T . [h_i || h_k]\right)\right)} \tag{2}$$

However, in our problem, each edge has features. Therefore, the importance of node j to node i should be deduced not only from the embedding of node j and node i, but also from the connection between these two nodes. Intuitively, we would concatenate the features of edge p (between node j and node i) and calculate e_{ijp} (the importance of node j to node i through path p). The Eq. (2) would then become:

$$\alpha_{ij}^{\emptyset} = \frac{\exp\left(\sigma\left(a_{\emptyset}^T . [h_i || l_{ij} || h_j]\right)\right)}{\sum_{k \in \mathcal{N}_i^{\emptyset}} \exp\left(\sigma\left(a_{\emptyset}^T . [h_i || l_{ik} || h_k]\right)\right)} \tag{3}$$

This is the case when there is only one connection between node j and node i, l_p therefore is l_{ij}. However, graphs in our problem are multi-edge, which means there could be multiple connections between two nodes. For example, Fig. 2 exemplifies multiple calls to `RegQueryValueExW` but with different arguments, therefore it should have different importance values.

Although we can still concatenate l_p and h_j as in Eq. (3), to acquire:

$$\alpha_{ijp}^{\emptyset} = \frac{\exp\left(\sigma\left(a_{\emptyset}^T . [h_i || l_p || h_j]\right)\right)}{\sum_{k \in \mathcal{N}_i^{\emptyset}} \sum_{m \in \mathcal{P}_{ik}} \exp\left(\sigma\left(a_{\emptyset}^T . [h_i || l_m || h_k]\right)\right)} \tag{4}$$

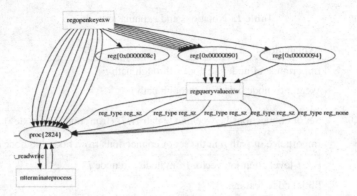

Fig. 2. Same API (RegQueryValueExW) is called from process id 2824 with different arguments.

This concatenation still enables the model to learn the importance of node j to node i through path p, but note that this concatenation makes the graph become a uni-edge graph where node i has m connections to m other nodes (having features $h_j||l_p$; $p \in m$) instead of m connections to one node (having features h_j). However the purpose of building a multi-edge graph is to expect that the model could learn the importance of each edge in the set of connections between two nodes In other words, we want to focus more on the edge arguments to learn the importance.

Inspired by the idea of the attention network, we use an additional attention layer to learn the importance of each edge in one set of connections:

$$u_p^{ij} = att_p(l_p) = \sigma\left(U_{ij}^T.l_p + b\right) \tag{5}$$

The weight coefficient of path p is the softmax of u.

$$\gamma_p^{ij} = \text{softmax}(u_p^{ij})$$
$$= \frac{\exp\left(\sigma\left(U_{ij}^T \cdot l_p + b\right)\right)}{\sum_{m \in \mathcal{P}_{ij}} \exp\left(U_{ij}^T \cdot l_m + b\right)} \tag{6}$$

And the weighted embedding of path p:

$$l_p' = \gamma_p^{ij}.l_p \tag{7}$$

Node-Level Embedding. By replacing l_p in Eq. (3) with l_p' in Eq. (7) we calculate the importance of node j to node i though path p:

$$\alpha_{ijp}^{\emptyset} = \text{softmax}\left(\sigma\left(a_{\emptyset}^T.\left[h_i\middle|\middle|l_p'\middle|\middle|h_j\right]\right)\right) \tag{8}$$

And the meta-path based embedding of node i (Fig. 3):

$$z_i^{\emptyset} = \sigma\left(Q^T. \sum_{k \in \mathcal{N}_i^{\emptyset}} \sum_{m \in \mathcal{P}_{ik}} \alpha_{ijp}^{\emptyset}.[h_i||l_p']\right) \tag{9}$$

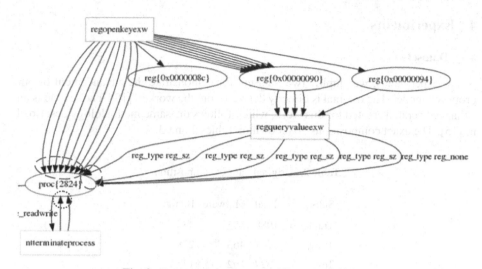

Fig. 3. Aggregation of meta-path based neighbors

Semantic-Level Embedding. Once we have the node-level embedding, an attention network is used for learning semantic meaning:

$$w_{\emptyset_i} = \frac{1}{|\mathcal{V}|} \sum_{i \in \mathcal{V}} q^T . \sigma \left(W . z_i^\emptyset + b \right)$$

$$\beta_{\emptyset_i} = \text{softmax} \left(w_{\emptyset_i} \right) \tag{10}$$

And the final embedding of node i:

$$Z_i = \sum_{k=1}^{\mathbb{P}} \beta_{\emptyset_k} . z_i^{\emptyset_k} \tag{11}$$

Graph Embedding. There are a variety of ways to obtain the graph embedding after computing the embedding for the nodes. In this work, the final graph embedding is obtained by accumulating the weighted final node embedding as in (12):

$$Z = \sum_{i \in \mathcal{V}} \tau_i . Z_i \tag{12}$$

4 Experiments

4.1 Datasets

In our experiments, we employ two datasets for demonstrate the advancement of our proposed model. The original is directly derived from the work in [15]. The second is an enhanced version created for this work, which follows the same methodology described in [15]. The exact compositions are shown in Tables 2 and 3.

Table 2. Original dataset composition

Subset	Total	Malware	Benign
Train/test	1088	655	433
Train	761	463	298
Test	327	192	135
Unknown	637	637	0

Table 3. Enhanced dataset composition

Subset	Total samples	No. malicious samples	No. benign samples	Purpose
Enhanced train/test	2379	1391	998	–
Train	1665	954	711	Training
Test	714	437	227	Testing
Unknown	637	637	0	Testing
pack1	4620	4620	0	Testing
benign_555	555	0	555	Testing

We use the *train/test subset* for training and testing, which is the same as in [15]. This dataset includes 1088 samples in total (655 malware and 433 benign samples). Training and testing files are exactly the same as in [15]. The same *unknown subset* is used for testing. The unknown subset includes 637 malware samples that ClamAV (an open source anti-virus engine used in a variety of situations) was unable to detect until 2/6/2019. These two subsets are also used to compare the effectiveness of our method and others. We also collect extra data using the same strategy as described in [15] for further experiments and enhancing training set. The *benign_555 subset* consists of 555 benign files, and the *pack1 subset* comprises 4620 malware samples. These two subsets, which do not contain any sample from the Original Dataset, are used for testing purpose only.

The Original Dataset composition is shown in Table 2, it is important to note, that none of the samples are duplicated in any subset.

The Enhanced Dataset composition is show in Table 3. It is larger than the Original Dataset but it is important to note that the same methodology and same 7:3 train:test ratio was observed.

The *enhanced train/test subset* consists of 2379 items, 987 of which are benign, the rest are malware. This enhanced subset is made up by combining the original *train/test subset* (described in Table 2), *benign_555 subset*, (555 benign samples), and additional 741 malware samples, which are not previously seen in any set (original *train/test*, *unknown* or *pack1 subset*). The train/test ratio is 7:3, the same as that of the *train/test subset* in the Original Dataset. The experiment schemes are as follow:

- Evaluate on Original Dataset. We train on train set of train/test subset and experiment on test set (of train/test subset) and unknown subset.
- Evaluate on Enhanced Dataset. We train on train set of enhanced train/test subset and experiment on test set (of enhanced train/test subset), unknown, pack1 and benign_555 subset.

4.2 Results

For the evaluation we utilized two types of encoding for node names and edges arguments: skip-gram and TF-IDF. For nodes names, since we only consider 3 types of API to construct nodes, the vocabulary size for node names is not relatively small. It contains 31 words, 28 of which are APIs (from the three considered categories), the 4 remain words are: proc (for process entities), file (for file entities), reg (for registry entities), and other (just in case a non-standard entry occurs in the dataset, though this would be rare). The vocabulary size for edge arguments is bigger, containing 138 words, one for each of the 137 cases covered, and a "null" entry for potentially unseen words.

When using TF-IDF encoding, we use three max elements and one second-min element to construct a 4-dimensional feature vector of each edge. For skip-gram encoding, input is the whole argument string sequence and the output is a 10-dimensional feature vector. Table 4 shows evaluation of different model (trained on *train/test subset* in Original Dataset) with different ways of encoding node and edge data on the Original Dataset. It can be seen that using edge-weighing gives the best performance on *train/test subset*. And using edge-weighing layers outperformed original GAT model for heterogeneous graph proposed by Wang et al.

Table 4. Results different text encoding and model on the Original Dataset

| | Train/test (1088 total) | | | | | | Unknown 637 malware |
| | Train (761 total) 298 benign 463 malware | | | Test (327 total) 135 benign 192 malware | | | |
	Acc	TPR	FAR	Acc	TPR	FAR	TPR
Skip-gram + TF-IDF	**96.19%**	**96.98%**	**5.03%**	**92.66%**	**92.19%**	**6.67%**	89.64%
Skip-gram	93.82%	95.90%	9.40%	88.69%	89.06%	11.85%	**96.55%**
TF-IDF	90.41%	92.44%	12.75%	91.74%	**92.19%**	8.89%	96.23%
Skip-gram (no edge-weighing)	88.04%	86.39%	10.07%	85.63%	83.33%	11.11%	85.22%
TF-IDF (no edge-weighing)	80.81%	79.05%	16.44%	84.40%	80.21%	9.63%	84.46%

The Original Dataset is the same as literature [15], therefore we conduct a comparison between our best model (using skip gram encoding for node names and TF-IDF encoding for edge arguments) and others on this dataset.

Tables 5 and 6 show comparison results on two subsets: test set from *train/test subset* and *unknown subset*. The results of other methods are inherited from literature [15]. Our first model outperformed in both cases.

Table 5. Evaluation result comparison of our model

	Acc	TPR	FAR
Our model (1st model)	**92.66%**	**92.19%**	**6.67%**
MalGCN	86.22%	88.02%	9.66%
QDFG-GCN	74.31%	87.05%	44.04%
QDFG-KNN	62.37%	49.59%	15.49%

We have implemented a simple classifier on embedding sequences using these two encoders to investigate the performance of each encoding method, the results from this are shown in Table 7. It is noticeable that the classification performance on the TF-IDF encoded data is quite poor on *benign_555*. Additionally, encoding node data using skip-gram for *benign_555* results in an even worse performance. This is because sequences of nodes names only, do not convey much meaning, in a sense that there is not much difference between the sequences of API called by benign and malware samples. As mentioned in Sect. 2, differences usually lie within the arguments of each call. Also, this is just to help us understand how the encoding method may affect our model, hence we just simply apply a classifier on encoded sequences of API called (ordered

Table 6. Comparison of our model and others on unknown subset

Engine	Accuracy	Engine	Accuracy	Engine	Accuracy
Our model (1ˢᵗ model)	**89.64%**	ESET-NOD32	77.75%	Sophos	70.29%
MalGCN	84.03%	K7GW	74.21%	AVG	69.63%
McAfee-GW631	82.59%	Endgame	74.08%	GData	69.24%
Fortinet	82.59%	K7AntiVirus	73.95%	Rising	68.06%
Microsoft	78.93%	Invincea	73.43%	Avira	67.54%
MccAfee	77.75%	CrowdStrike	72.38%	VBA32	67.28%

by the appearance of that call in the report generated by cuckoo). TF-IDF on the other hand considers the frequency of separate words, and the way words are chosen from each sequence is the same in every circumstance, (3 max and 1 second-min elements), therefore can detect from an early stage which calls seem to be abnormal.

Table 7. Classifying based on encoding edge arguments and nodes names only

	Train/test (1088)				Unknown (637 malware)		Pack1 (4620 malware)		Benign_555 (555 benign)	
	Train (761) 298 benign 463 malware		Test (327) 135 benign 192 malware							
	Edge	Node	Edge	Node	Edge	Node	Edge	Node	Edge	Node
Skip-gram	77.1%	82.3%	78.9%	75.8%	90.9%	97.5%	74.1%	59.3%	14.3%	0.0%
TF-IDF	98.2%	97.4%	87.3%	90.9%	81.3%	92.8%	64.2%	51.7%	26.4%	73.2%

When we conduct experiments to evaluate these models (trained on *train/test subset* from Original Dataset) on *pack1* and *benign_555* subsets, all models still give high True Positive Rate (TPR) on the *pack1 subset*. However, they achieve worse False Alarm Rate (FAR) on the *benign_555 subset*. The results are shown in Table 8. It can also be inferred from this table that combining skip-gram and TF-IDF encoder (using skip-gram for encoding the edge arguments and TF-IDF for encoding the nodes names) gives more promising results, and is superior in stability as well. Since *pack1* contains only malwares and *benign_555* contains only benigns, only TPR and FAR are considered in these two subsets respectively.

However, all experiments result in higher FAR on *benign_555* when compared with *train/test subset*. This might be due to the difference in DLL usage between the *benign_555* and *train/test* subsets. More specially, *benign_555* samples all require external DLLs loaded to be able to execute, whereas none of the samples in *train/test subset*

Table 8. Results on pack1 and benign_355 subset

	Acc	TPR	FAR	Acc	TPR	FAR
	Pack1 (4620 malware)			Benign_555 (555 benign)		
Skip-gram + TF-IDF (1st)	–	81.28%	–	–	–	21.29%
Skip-gram (2nd)	–	**95.30%**	–	–	–	29.53%
TF-IDF (3rd)	–	82.42%	–	–	–	21.77%
Skip-gram (no edge-weighing) (4th)	–	59.65%	–	–	–	26.24%
TF-IDF (no edge-weighing) (5th)	–	49.65%	–	–	–	**16.25%**

require any DLLs, because all benign samples in *train/test subset* are Windows system files. Therefore, we train and evaluate our model (the 1st model) on the Enhanced Dataset. The results are shown in Table 9.

Table 9. Evaluation when training with enhanced dataset

Dataset/testset		Acc	TPR	FAR
Enhanced train/test	Train	96.22%	96.02%	3.52%
	Test	93.00%	92.68%	6.45%
Unknown		–	88.23%	–
Pack1		–	90.77%	–

It can be seen from Tables 8 and 6 that our model (when trained on *enhanced train/test subset*) cause a slight decline in TPR (or accuracy) on *unknown subset*, however, it is still a better result than other models.

4.3 Discussions

Edge-Weighing. For a more intuitive evaluation and deeper understanding, we have visualized the weights of each edge produced by our model.

List 2 shows an example of a signature for malicious activity of a malware sample. The signature is generated along with cuckoo report by applying YARA rules which are contributed by the open community. The call to **NtAllocateVirtualMemory** API is indicated as malicious when it requires not only read, write but also execute permissions, and its allocation type is **MEM_COMMIT** and **MEM_RESERVE**. The graph of this malware after edge-weighing layers is illustrated in Fig. 4.

List 2. A signature for malicious activity according to yara rules

```
{
  "markcount": 2,
  "families": [],
  "description": "Allocates execute permission to another
process indicative of possible code injection",
  "severity": 3,
  "marks": [
    {
      "call": {
        "category": "process",
        "status": 1,
        "api": "NtAllocateVirtualMemory",
        "return_value": 0,
        "arguments": {
          "process_identifier": 2508,
          "region_size": 36864,
          [...]
        },
        "time": 1556598469.154953,
        "tid": 2468,
        "flags": {
          "protection": "PAGE_EXECUTE_READWRITE",
          "allocation_type": "MEM_COMMIT|MEM_RESERVE"
        }
      },
      [...]
    },
    ...
  ]
}
```

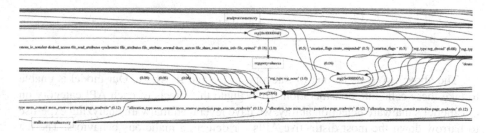

Fig. 4. Visualization of edge after weighted

As can be seen from Fig. 4, our model has been able to learn the importance of the API call using the parameters protection and allocation_type, similar to the signature from the cuckoo report. It can be inferred that distinctive behaviors that humans can manually analyze and label as malicious activities, could be learned automatically using this approach. However, we expect the model could learn not only behaviors that human can explicitly see but also those that are more abstract that prove difficult or impossible for humans to manually analyze.

Information Used for Embedding. For now, only three types of API are represented in our graph, therefore, some important information might be ignored. For example, the two behaviors shown in List 3 and 4 are considered malicious activities:

List 3. A query for the computer name

```
"call": {
  "category": "misc",
  "status": 1,
  "api": "GetComputerNameA",
  "return_value": 1,
  "arguments": {
    "computer_name": "WIN7X86-PC"
  },
  "flags": {}
}
```

List 4. Check for the Locally Unique Identifier on the system for a suspicious privilege

```
{
  "call": {
    "category": "system",
    "status": 1,
    "api": "LookupPrivilegeValueW",
    "return_value": 1,
    "arguments": {
      "system_name": "",
      "privilege_name": "SeDebugPrivilege"
    },
    "flags": {}
  }
}
```

The above two calls belong to category misc and system. Our model is unable to take these calls into consideration. To evaluate the effects of each API category on our model's malware detection ability, we have leveraged malware analyzing expertise to narrow down the most distinctive APIs for detecting malicious behaviors. The list of these APIs with their corresponding category is described in Table 10. The number of those APIs grouped by category is presented in Table 11. Note that these categories are organized by Cuckoo, of which there are 16 in total: certificate, crypto,

exception, file, iexplore, misc, netapi, network, ole, process, registry, resource, services, synchronization, system
and ui. Other sandboxes might have different methods to group APIs.

Table 10. The most distinctive API for detecting malicious behaviors

API	Category	API	Category	API	Category
NtDuplicateObject	System	ReadProcessMemory	Process	DeviceIoControl	File
URLDownloadToFileW	Network	CreateServiceW	Service	CryptGenKey	Crypto
MoveFileWithProgressTransactedW	File	ControlService	Service	NtDelayExecution	Synchronisation
NtCreateUserProcess	Process	NtCreateProcess	Process	NtClose	System
GetComputerNameW	Misc	ShellExecuteExW	Process	NtCreateKey	Registry
URLDownloadToFileW	Network	NtCreateProcessEx	Process	NtWriteFile	File
NtSetInformationFile	File	RegSetValueExW	Registry	OpenServiceW	Service
CreateProcessInternalW	Process	InternetSetOptionA	Network	CryptEncrypt	Crypto
NtProtectVirtualMemory	Process	LdrGetDllHandle	System	CreateServiceA	Service
RtlCreateUserProcess	Process	CryptExportKey	Crypto	NtOpenProcess	Process
MoveFileWithProgressW	File	RegOpenKeyExW	Registry	InternetOpenW	Network
NtAllocateVirtualMemory	Process	RegSetValueExA	Registry	Process32FirstW	Process
NtDeviceIoControlFile	File	RegOpenKeyExA	Registry	NtCreateFile	File
SetWindowsHookExW	System	SetFileAttributesW	File	InternetOpenA	Network
EnumServicesStatusW	Service	InternetReadFile	Network	Process32NextW	Process
SetWindowsHookExA	System	GetUserNameA	Misc	NtLoadDriver	System
LdrGetProcedureAddress	System	RegQueryValueExA	Registry	CryptHashData	Crypto
GetComputerNameA	Misc	RegQueryValueExW	Registry	NtOpenFile	File
GetAdaptersAddresses	Network	OpenServiceA	Service	LdrLoadDll	System
ObtainUserAgentString	Network	NtTerminateProcess	Process	NtSetValueKey	Registry
EnumServicesStatusA	Service				

Table 11. Number of interesting apis by category

Category	Total API	Category	Total API	Category	Total API
Crypto	4	Network	8	Service	7
File	8	Process	13	Synchronisation	1
Misc	3	Registry	8	System	8

Not only the API is the model missing out, but the flags field also conveys limited information. For example, the action demonstrated in List 5 would highly be a suspicious behavior since it is trying to register itself to execute whenever Windows starts, which is a common covert activity of malware:

List 5. An activity of a malware trying to install itself for auto-run at Windows startup

```
{
  "category": "registry",
  "status": 1,
  "stacktrace": [],
  "api": "RegSetValueExA",
  "return_value": 0,
  "arguments": {
    "key_handle": "0x00000078",
    "value": "c:\\windows\\system32\\mssrv32.exe",
    "regkey_r": "ImagePath",
    "reg_type": 1,
    "regkey":
"HKEY_LOCAL_MACHINE\\SYSTEM\\ControlSet001\\services\\msu
pdate\\ImagePath"
  },
  "time": 1556598470.626408,
  "tid": 2512,
  "flags": {
    "reg_type": "REG_SZ"
  }
},
```

Our graph only encodes the flag field, however, the importance does not lie within the flag field, but the `regkey` in the `arguments` section, which specifies the registry path this API is trying to modify. Similarly, when changing the content of a file, the distinctive information used to distinguish between malware and benign samples is often the path to which the API is referring, or the value the API is trying to set. With such information, we cannot simply use n-gram or similar encoding methods, since the path vary. One solution is to encode each part of the path and assign a corresponding severity level. For example, the path `HKEY_LOCAL_MACHINE\\SYSTEM` `\\ControlSet001\\services\\msupdate\\ImagePath`, would be divided into 4 parts as follow:

ePath, would be divided into 4 parts as follow:

1. `HKEY_LOCAL_MACHINE\\`
2. `SYSTEM\\`
3. `ControlSet001\\services\\msupdate\\`

4. ImagePath

Here, **1.** would be the root element separated by \\, which indicates the category of the registry, (i.e. HKEY_CLASSES_ROOT, HKEY_CURRENT_USER, HKEY_LOCAL_MACHINE, HKEY_USERS, HKEY_CURRENT_CONFIG). Each value would be assigned a corresponding severity, in this case HKEY_CURRENT_USER and HKEY_LOCAL_MACHINE would be 1 and the others 0. This is because these two root category contain paths to important registry entries that malware usually interferes with (e.g. the path to set auto-start applications). **2.** would be the child element of the root registry object. This element would be assigned a severity level according to its presence on a blacklist. Any elements contained within this list would be set to 1, otherwise they would be set to 0. **3.** Regular expressions would be used to detect the presence of certain words in another blacklist, or to compute the number of elements separated by \\. There is considerable diversity in the strategy to encode the path and this is just one example of a possible solution.

Graph Embedding. As mentioned in Sect. 3, there are multiple methods for generating the graph embedding. Our model now only uses the weighted-sum of all the nodes to represent the graph embedding. However, this approach would omit information about the time each API is executed, in other word, the order of each API being called. Now, intuitively, the solution might be to concatenate the nodes' embedding in the order of time they are executed. Yet, it is intricate to determine the exact execution sequence if multiple APIs having the same time field value, as manifested in Fig. 5. Another hurdle is to decide whether to order the nodes just by time of execution or also by the process calling them. The first option would ignore the relationship between the caller and the node being called, and considers the time the nodes are called only. The latter groups all nodes being called by the same process, and then orders each group of nodes by the time they are called.

In previous works, there are already some efforts to represent the graph as a sequence of nodes to apply an RNN on. However, these works mostly use walking algorithms such as RandomWalk or DeepWalk to choose the order of the nodes [20, 21]. He et al. proposed a modified random walk on heterogeneous graph in [22]. Yet, all these models are not either designed for, or evaluated on malware detection tasks, and the information of the nodes in these literatures does not contain time data. Nevertheless, these approaches do produce promising results and are inspiring, although in this specific task they would still overlook time data.

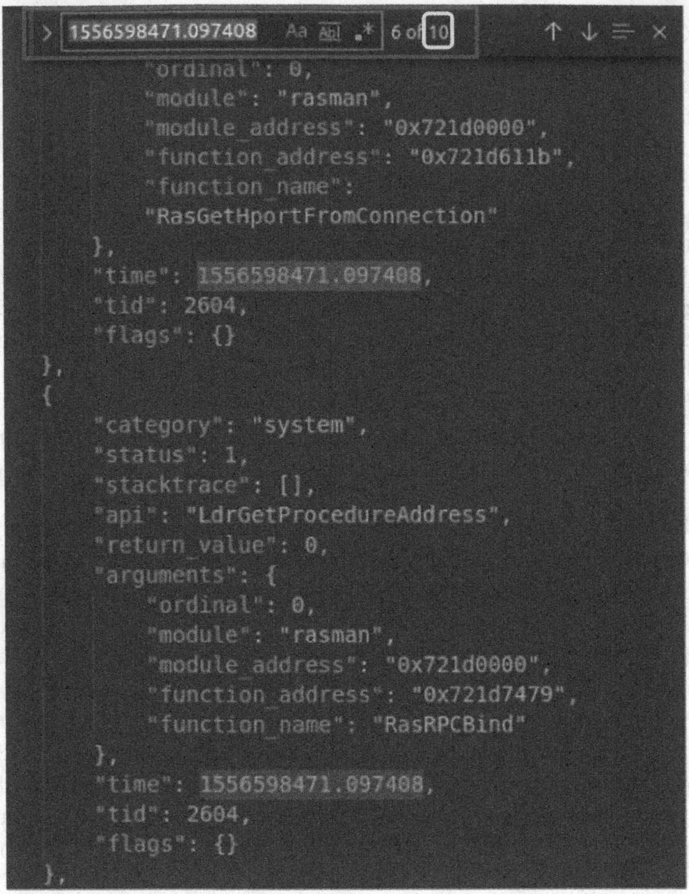

> 1556598471.097408   Aa ᴬᵇ| .*   6 of 10   ↑ ↓ ☰ ×

        "ordinal": 0,
        "module": "rasman",
        "module_address": "0x721d0000",
        "function_address": "0x721d611b",
        "function_name":
        "RasGetHportFromConnection"
      },
      "time": 1556598471.097408,
      "tid": 2604,
      "flags": {}
    },
    {
      "category": "system",
      "status": 1,
      "stacktrace": [],
      "api": "LdrGetProcedureAddress",
      "return_value": 0,
      "arguments": {
        "ordinal": 0,
        "module": "rasman",
        "module_address": "0x721d0000",
        "function_address": "0x721d7479",
        "function_name": "RasRPCBind"
      },
      "time": 1556598471.097408,
      "tid": 2604,
      "flags": {}
    },

Fig. 5. An example of 10 API containing the same value for time field

5   Conclusions and Future Work

In conclusion, this paper outlined several challenges faced in the field of malware detection. It has also proposed a novel approach in an effort to help address the challenges. Our method has achieved comparable results with other state-of-the-art techniques. However, there are still several limitations in our strategy of representing behaviors, which we have also discussed in Sect. 4 to aim for future research.

As with other deep learning approaches, this cannot simply be a replacement for existing time-served tactics for malware detection, such as signature-based, but it could be implemented as a module to analyze more complicated or unseen samples (it might be an additional validation after static analysis). However, this approach requires executing the sample in a virtual environment, hence it would take a while to first generate a report which contains behavioral data. Therefore, when implemented in a program, it would still be infeasible to process every file that static modules cannot detect as malware, but rather only execute suspicious files. Yet, knowing which files are suspicious might be another challenge.

Moreover, not every executable can be activated in a virtual environment due to anti-virtualization techniques, or the fact that some executable files require human interaction, especially those that are benign, which makes collecting benign samples a time-consuming task.

References

1. Yu, B., Fang, Y., Yang, Q., et al.: A survey of malware behavior description and analysis. Front. Inf. Technol. Electron. Eng. (2018)
2. Hongfa, X., Shaowen, S., Guru, V., Tian, L.: Machine learning-based analysis of program binaries - a comprehensive study. IEEE Access (2019)
3. Yuxin, D., Wei, D., Shengli, Y., Yume, Z.: Control flow-based opcode behavior analysis for malware detection (2014)
4. Ki, Y., Kim, E., Kim, H.K.: A novel approach to detect malware based on API call sequence analysis. Int. J. Distrib. Sens. Netw. 11, 659101 (2015)
5. Tran, T.K., Sato, H.: NLP-based approaches for malware classification from API sequences. In: 21st Asia Pacific Symposium on Intelligent and Evolutionary Systems (IES) (2017)
6. Pascanu, R., Stokes, J.W., Sanossian, H., et al.: Malware classification with recurrent networks. In: IEEE International Conference on Acoustics, Speech and Signal Processing (ICASSP) (2015)
7. Kolosnjaji, B., Zarras, A., Eraisha, G., et al.: Empowering convolutional networks for malware classification and analysis. In: International Joint Conference on Neural Networks (IJCNN) (2017)
8. Tobiyama, S., Yamaguchi, Y., Shimada, H., et al.: Malware detection with deep neural network using process behavior. In: 40th Annual Computer Software and Applications Conference (COMPSAC) (2016)
9. Wang, X,. Yiu, S.M.: A multi-task learning model for malware classification with useful file access pattern from API call sequence (2016). arXiv:1610.05945 [cs.SD], Cryptography and Security
10. Xiao, X., Zhang, S., Mercaldo, F., Hu, G., Sangaiah, A.K.: Android malware detection based on system call sequences and LSTM. Multimedia Tools Appl. 78(4), 3979–3999 (2017)
11. Sikorski, M., Honig, A.: Practical malware analysis: the hands-on guide to dissecting malicious software. xxviii
12. Naval, S., Rajarajan, M., Laxmi, V., Conti, M.: Employing program semantics for malware detection. IEEE Trans. Inf. Forensics Secur. (2015)
13. Mathew, J., Ajay Kumara, M.A.: API call based malware detection approach using recurrent neural network – LSTM. Intell. Syst. Des. Appl. (2018)
14. Wüchner, T., Ochoa, M., Pretschner, A.: Malware detection with quantitative data flow graphs. In: ASIA CCS 2014: Proceedings of the 9th ACM Symposium on Information, Computer and Communications Security (2014)
15. Hung, N., Dung, P., Ngoc, T., et al.: Malware detection based on directed multi-edge dataflow graph representation and convolutional neural network. In: 2019 11th International Conference on Knowledge and Systems Engineering (KSE) (2019)
16. Wang, X., Ji, H., Shi, C., et al.: Heterogeneous graph attention network (2019). arXiv:1903.07293
17. Wu, Z., Pan, S., Chen, F., et al.: A comprehensive survey on graph neural networks. Netw. Embed. Graph Neural Netw. (2019)

18. Zhou, J., Cui, G., Zhang, Z.: Graph neural networks. a review of methods and applications (2018). arXiv:1812.08434
19. Anderson, B., Quist, D., Neil, J., et al.: Graph-based malware detection using dynamic analysis. J. Comput. Virol. **7**, 247–258 (2011). https://doi.org/10.1007/s11416-011-0152-x
20. Jin, Y., Joseph, F.J.: Learning graph-level representations with recurrent neural networks (2018). arXiv:1805.07683
21. Perozzi, B., Al-Rfou, R., Skiena, S.: DeepWalk: online learning of social representations. In: Proceedings of the 20th ACM SIGKDD International Conference on Knowledge Discovery and Data Mining (KDD 2014), pp. 701–710. Association for Computing Machinery, New York (2014)
22. He, Y., Song, Y., Li, J., Ji, C.: HeteSpaceyWalk: a heterogeneous spacey random walk for heterogeneous information network embedding. In: 28th ACM International Conference (2019)

Understanding the Decision of Machine Learning Based Intrusion Detection Systems

Quang-Vinh Dang[✉] [ID]

Industrial University of Ho Chi Minh City, Ho Chi Minh City, Vietnam
dangquangvinh@iuh.edu.vn

Abstract. Intrusion Detection Systems (IDSs) is an important research topic in security engineering. The role of an IDS is to detect the malicious incoming network flows, hence it can protect a computer system from attack. Recent research studies in IDS focus in using different machine learning techniques to build an IDS. However, due to the black-box nature of the machine learning algorithms, it is difficult to understand and get insights of the system. In this work, we extend the recent studies by providing the explanation of the decisions of the IDSs built in the previous studies. Given a deeper understanding of the IDS, the users will have more trust to use the system while the engineers can rely on the explanation to tweet the system. The experimental results show that we can significantly reduce the computational power requirement of the IDS based on the explanation of the model.

Keywords: Intrusion detection system · Machine learning · Classification.

1 Introduction

According to the Forbes [11], the global cyber security market is worth $173B in 2020 and should raise up to $270B in 2026. Intrusion detection systems (IDSs) play an important role in cyber-security [24] as it continuously monitor computer networks and stop malicious incoming traffic.

In the early days of computer systems, the signature-based intrusion detection systems are widely used [44]. In order to using the signature-based IDSs, the researchers need to analyze the network traffic to understand the pattern then creating the signature to detect the benign and malicious traffic. Hence, the signature-based IDSs found difficult to deal with novelty attack, i.e. the attacks that appear for the first time [27]; and evolving attacks, i.e. the attacks that change themselves over-time [12].

Recently, the machine learning based IDSs attracted a lot of attention in both academia and industry [14]. The core idea of this approach is: i) collect a huge amount of network traffic data that we might or might not know which traffic

© Springer Nature Switzerland AG 2020
T. K. Dang et al. (Eds.): FDSE 2020, LNCS 12466, pp. 379–396, 2020.
https://doi.org/10.1007/978-3-030-63924-2_22

is benign and which is not; and ii) train one or many machine learning models that can automatically classify the network traffic. The approach utilizes the rapid development in machine learning community and does not require much human intervention. The model can evolved by itself to deal with the new forms of attack. The novelty or zero-day attacks can be handled by using anomaly detection methods [13].

The recent approaches, such as the work of [14] or [38] achieved very good predictive results. However, there is still a problem. The transparency and explainability of the machine learning algorithms has been questioned for years in both public media [48] and research studies [18]. The core issue is, machine learning algorithms usually are treated as a black box [46] despite many attempts to understand the decisions of these algorithms recently [47]. Several studies suggested that lacking understanding in how system works will lead to the lack of trust from users on the system [25]. Furthermore, if we don't understand why does the system make a particular decision, we will be limited in debugging the system, especially when the prediction is wrong. For instance, Fig. 1 shows a case when a benign email is marked as suspected spam. It is very difficult to fix the spam detecting system if we don't know what make the system give this decision.

[SUSPECTED SPAM] Payslip of 2020-07,

Fig. 1. A benign email is marked as suspected spam with no reason. If we don't understand how the spam detector makes this decision, we cannot fix the problem. The email turned out to be a benign one.

On the other hand, by understanding the system we can perform feature engineering [44] hence we can reduce the complexity of the model and improving the execution performance of the IDS. It is particularly important because a low-performance IDS will slow down the entire network.

In this paper, we study several state-of-the-art explainable machine learning techniques for IDSs. We analyze the performance of the system by understanding the feature influence and remove the unnecessary features. We evaluate our ideas using the CICIDS2017 - one of recent and comprehensive intrusion datasets. The experimental results show that we can maintain the predictive performance and reduce the running time significantly by performing feature engineering based on the explainability.

2   Related Works

There are two main approaches in using machine learning for an IDS [14]. The first approach is using the supervised learning approach. In general, the researchers will build a classifier that distinguish the benign and malicious traffic. This approach requires a dataset where the benign and malicious traffic have been labelled. The second approach is using the unsupervised learning method. In general, the researchers will build a model that detect any traffic that is *abnormal* compared to the normal benign traffic. This approach does not require labelled dataset, but require a *clean* dataset to learn the behavior pattern of *benign* traffic.

The researchers have evaluated different machine learning methods to build an IDS. Due to the nature of the classification problem, the most popular algorithms are decision tree [3,33,35,52], random forest [45] and SVM [4,43]. Most recently, the authors of [14] used *xgboost* [9] which belongs to the *boosting* algorithm family. They achieved the near-perfect predictive results. The authors claimed that with a careful feature engineering process, some simple learning algorithms such as Naive Bayes can do the classification task quite well.

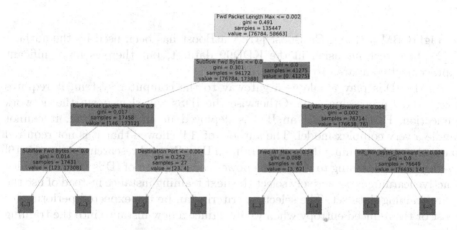

Fig. 2. A decision tree to classify the DDos attack trained on the CICIDS2017 dataset.

We visualized a single decision tree for the DDos classification task in Fig. 2. An advantage of decision tree is the explainability - most of the time the tree is self-explained. There are several efforts to perform reverse engineering in a particular machine learning model to convert the model into a decision tree [7]. However, the predictive performance of the decision tree algorithm is usually not comparable to other algorithms. The decision tree is often considered as a *weak learner* [44]. Two main approaches to improve the predictive performance of a decision tree is *boosting* and *bagging* as we visualized in Fig. 3.

In the bagging mechanism, we build multiple decision trees in parallel. Each single decision tree has access to a subset of training data and a subset of features. The final result is aggregated over all predictions of individual trees. On the other hand, in the boosting mechanism we build multiple trees in sequence. The following tree has to correct the errors made by the previous tree. The most popular instance of the bagging mechanism is the random forest algorithm [28]. There are several implementations of the boosting mechanisms such as xgboost

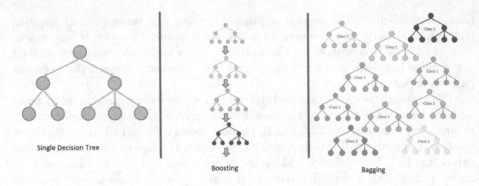

Fig. 3. Bagging and Boosting mechanisms to improve the predictive performance of decision tree.

[9], LightGBM [31] and CatBoost [41]. CatBoost has been used by the authors of [26] to detect intrusion in the KDD99 dataset, but there is no significant improvement compared to xgboost [14].

As the IDSs play a role as a gateway to the computer system, it requires a very short processing time. Otherwise the IDSs will slow down the network connection. Furthermore, if an IDS is deployed in an IoT system, it cannot handle a very complex model. The authors of [14] showed that it is not required to use the entire training dataset to train an IDS. Several research studies [15,16] leverage active learning to reduce the power consumption of IDSs. The main idea of active learning is we actively select the next training instance instead of use the entire training data set. The selection criteria can be the expected performance boost or the reduced entropy when we introduce a new instance into the training dataset.

One approach to reduce the power consumption of an IDS is to reduce the number of dimension of the dataset by dimensional reduction techniques such as Principal Component Analysis (PCA) [1]. The core idea of PCA is to projecting the existing data into a new data with fewer dimensions but keeping the most variance of the old data. The researchers such as the authors of [30,56] usually apply PCA before feeding the new data into a classifier, here is SVM. However, these approaches have some limitation: i) training PCA is time-consuming; ii) PCA cannot deal with null values that are very common in network intrusion datasets; and iii) eventually we still need to feed the new incoming data through a PCA model then a machine learning model, hence the power reduction is limited. More recently, the authors of [55] proposed to use the Deep Belief Networks [23] for the automatic feature learning, integrating with Particle Swarm Optimization (PSO).

In recent years, the researchers also use deep learning techniques to power the IDSs. For instance, in the work of [17], the authors use the multi-layer feedforward neural networks for the task of classification. The authors of [54] applied an embedding technique from the natural language processing (NLP) field to vectorizing the system log.

The deep learning techniques have been used extensively in the IoT settings [42]. The difference is, in the IoT environment the problem can be formulated as the multi-agent setting [41]. In [57], the researchers deploy a simulated test-bed and a deep learning model after a feature selection using random decision trees and Pearson correlation. Deep learning has been also utilized in other IoT environments, such as in-vehicle IoT [29] or IoT at home [6]. Most recently, the graph neural networks (GNN) are utilized for anomaly detection [8,42,58]. For instance, [58] proposed to use an attention-based temporal graph convolutional neural network [32] to detect the anomalous edges.

In some scenarios where the attack samples are hard to achieve or define, the researchers might use anomaly detection techniques [53]. The authors of [34] compared four anomaly detection at the time of writing, including LOF, k-nearest neighbors, Mahalanobis distance and unsupervised SVM. More recently, the authors of [13] included recent techniques such as Isolation Forest [36] into the comparison. The idea of the Isolation Forest is to classify a single instance in the dataset. More difficult it is to classify a particular instance, more outlier the instance is. The authors of [15] integrated the Isolation Forest into the active learning scheme to select the next training instance.

3 Our Methods

In recent years, the needs for an interpretable or explainable machine learning system is increased [40,48]. In many settings, it is required by law that a machine learning decision can be explained [5]. For instance, Facebook introduces a feature called "Why am I seeing this ads" as displayed in Fig. 4 to explain their recommender system to the users.

In this section, we describe the model we use, the techniques to explain the model, and the dataset for the evaluation.

3.1 The Predictive Model

We mainly use *xgboost* as the predictive model in our work. Here we give a brief description of the model.

The name *xgboost* stands for eXtreme Gradient Boosting [9] is a ensemble technique [22] that has been introduced as an extension of gradient boosting machine (GBM) model [19]. The gradient boosting models build sequential learners. The following learner will try to recover the errors made by the previous one, as we visualized in Fig. 3.

The formulation of xgboost prediction is:

$$F_m(x) = F_0(x) + \sum_{i=1}^{M} \rho_i h_i(x, a_i) \tag{1}$$

where:

Fig. 4. Facebook explained their recommender systems.

- $F_0(x)$ is the initial model: $F_0(x) = argmin_\rho \sum_{i=1}^N l(y_i, \rho)$.
- ρ_i is the weight value of the model number i.
- h_i is the base model (decision tree) at the ith iteration.

xgboost also introduced a new regularization term and define a new objective function as:

$$obj(\theta) = l(\theta) + \Omega(\theta) \tag{2}$$

where:

- l is the loss function (e.g.. squared-error $\sum (y_i - \hat{y}_i)^2$).
- Ω is regularization term.

Originally gbm does not introduce any regularization. In contrast, xgb explicitly added regularization term, and an author of xgb in fact called their model as "regularized gradient boosting" [14].

On the other hand, gbm introduced *shrinkage* as regularization techniques. This idea is reused by xgboost. To use shrinkage, while updating the model in each iteration:

$$F_m(X) = F_{m-1}(X) + \nu.\rho_m h(x; a_m), 0 < \nu \leq 1 \tag{3}$$

It means we do not take the *full* step toward the steepest-descent direction, but only a *part* of the step by the value of ν.

3.2   Partial Dependence Plot

The partial dependence plot (PDP) [22] described the marginal effect of a single feature or two features on the prediction of a machine learning model [19].

In short, a PDP shows us the relationship between a particular feature and the target, given all other features are fixed.

The definition of the partial dependence is as follows. Consider X_s is the feature set and X_c is the complement. The partial dependence of the response f at a point x_s is:

$$pd_{X_s}(x_s) = \mathbb{E}_{X_C}[f(x_s, X_C)] = \int f(x_s, x_C)p(x_C)dx_C \tag{4}$$

where:

- $f(x_S, x_C)$ is the output of model, here is the predictive probability of being malicious.

In practice, the partial dependence is calculated using Monte Carlo method [21].

$$pd_{X_S}x_S = \frac{1}{training\_data\_size} \sum_{i=1}^{n} f(x_S, z_C^i) \tag{5}$$

3.3 Shapley Value

Shapley value, named after the work of [49], is the concept the machine learning community borrowed from the game theory community [10]. Shapley value has been introduced in the work of [37] to explain a machine learning model. We can understand Shapley value as the distribution of payout in a game setting when the prediction is the outcome and the each feature is a player [40].

Consider a case when we predict an incoming network flow to be a benign or malicious flow. We consider only three features "Fwd Packet Length Max", "Fwd Packet Length Mean" and "Bwd Packet Length Min". The predictive probability of being malicious is 0.76. The question is how could we explain the decision of 0.76? The idea of using Shapley value is to explain the difference of a particular prediction to the average prediction by the contributions of all features. Assume that for all the network flows, the average prediction is 0.12, so the difference is $0.76 - 0.12 = 0.64$. We need to explain the contribution of the value of 0.64 by the value of each feature.

Shapley value is defined as "the average marginal contribution of a feature value across all possible coalitions" [40]. We calculate the Shapley values by permuting each features as randomly replacing its value by a value drawn from the training dataset.

SHAP, stands for *SHapley Additive exPlanations* is the model based on Shapley values to explain any machine learning model. SHAP is proposed in [37]. SHAP considered a contribution of a feature as a linear model, similar to the previous work of [46]. In SHAP, the explanation is specified as:

$$g(z') = \phi + 0 + \sum_{j=1}^{M} \phi_j z_j' \tag{6}$$

where:

– g is the explanation.
– $z' \in \{0, 1\}^M$ is the coalition vector. $z'_j = 1$ means the feature j is included in the coalition, when the value of 0 means the feature is absent. We note that, in the original paper [37] the coalition might contains *super* feature, such as a group of pixels, rather than individual features. However in our current work, the original features are considered.
– M is the maximum size of a coalition vector.
– ϕ_j is the feature attribution of the feature j.

SHAP can be considered as the extension of LIME [46] where LIME focuses on *local* explanation while SHAP can perform both local and global explanation.

We will use PDP to understand the global estimation on local prediction by each feature of a machine learning model, and SHAP to understand the global driven force of the model.

3.4   Dataset

For many years, KDD99 dataset [39] has been used to evaluate the intrusion detection systems [2]. However, the dataset has been criticised by many research studies by its unrealistic properties [14]. Furthermore, the dataset has been released more than 20 years ago. The Internet and the computer systems have changed a lot since then. Some more recent intrusion datasets have been introduced, for instance CICIDS'2012 [51] using in the work of [14].

In this work, we use the dataset CICIDS2017[1] released by the Canadian Institute for Cybersecurity. The dataset is introduced in [50]. The dataset is established by capturing the real-world network traffic from 3-July-2017 to 7-July-2017. CICIDS2017 is the first dataset that satisfies all eleven criteria of a reliable intrusion dataset defined by [20]. The criteria are:

– Complete Network configuration.
– Complete Traffic.
– Labelled Dataset.
– Complete Interaction.
– Complete Capture.
– Available Protocols.
– Attack Diversity.
– Heterogeneity.
– Feature Set.
– Meta Data.

The entire dataset contains more than 51 GB of the log data with $2,830,743$ network flows, labelling either BENIGN or one of following attack types. We also note the number of corresponding network flows.

---

[1] https://www.unb.ca/cic/datasets/ids-2017.html.

- BENIGN 2273097
- DoS Hulk 231073
- PortScan 158930
- DDoS 128027
- DoS GoldenEye 10293
- FTP-Patator 7938
- SSH-Patator 5897
- DoS slowloris 5796
- DoS Slowhttptest 5499
- Bot 1966
- Web Attack - Brute Force 1507
- Web Attack - XSS 652
- Infiltration 36
- Web Attack - Sql Injection 21
- Heartbleed 11

As the matter of fact, we will remove four least frequent attacks (Web Attack - XSS, Infiltration, Web Attack - Sql Injection and Heartbleed) as the number of them are too small to train a dataset.

The dataset include 78 features extracted by CICFlowMeter[2]. The list of first five features are:

- Flow Duration.
- Total Fwd Packets.
- Total Backward Packets.
- Total Length of Fwd Packets.
- Total Length of Bwd Packets.

4 Experimental Results

The experiments are done using xgboost version 1.2.0[3], sklearn 0.23.2[4] and SHAP 0.35.0[5]. The dataset is divided into train/val/test set with the ratio of 6:2:2.

All the experiments are done using Amazon EC2 server with the configuration of r5.4xlarge (128 GB memory, 16 CPU cores of 3.1 Ghz Xeon).

4.1 Baseline Model

We build a xgboost model on the full training dataset, similar to the work of [14]. We build two baseline models. The first model is a binary classifier, i.e. we only classify benign and malicious flows. The second model is a multi-class classifier, i.e. we want to classify to each individual attack types.

---

[2] https://github.com/ahlashkari/CICFlowMeter.
[3] https://xgboost.readthedocs.io/.
[4] https://scikit-learn.org/.
[5] https://github.com/slundberg/shap.

The confusion matrix of the model 1 is displayed in Fig. 5. Similar to the work of [14], we achieve a near-perfect predictive performance. We note that the evaluation is done using the out-of-sample dataset (testset). The ROC AUC score is 0.9999995, very close to the perfect score. The result is consistent with the previous works [14]. The training time is around 2.7 min and the prediction time is 2.7 s.

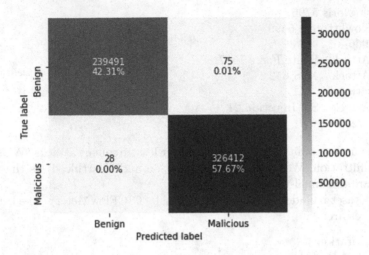

Fig. 5. Confusion matrix of the binary classifier when we do not consider individual attack types.

The multi-class classifier achieved the accuracy score of 99.993%. We display the confusion matrix in Fig. 6. The training time is about 9 min and the prediction time is about 3 s.

We can conclude that the predictive performance of xgboost on the full training dataset is mostly perfect and there is not much room for improvement. However, the required computational power is very high. In fact, the training process cannot be performed on the machine with 12 GB RAM and 2 CPU of 2.2 GHz - the process will soon consume all the memory then crashed. Hence, a lighter version of the model is required.

4.2 Lightweight Models

We perform feature understanding of the model by using PDP and SHAP value. We display two examples of PDP in Fig. 7 and 8.

The two PDPs show us very different views. Figure 7 stated a very strong and close relationship between the feature and the target (probability of being malicious), while Fig. 8 show almost the independence between the feature and the target. We can interpret Fig. 7 as higher the max value of forward packet length, the higher probability that this packet is malicious, but after the value

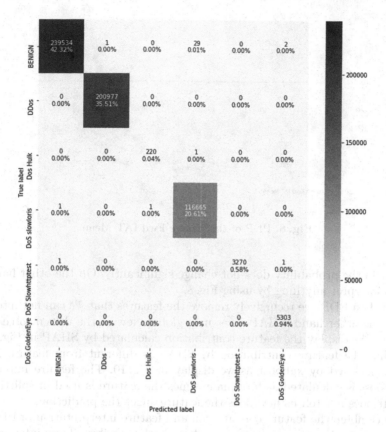

Fig. 6. Confusion matrix of the multi-class classifier.

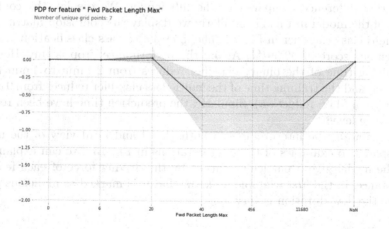

Fig. 7. PDP of the feature Fwd Packet Length Min

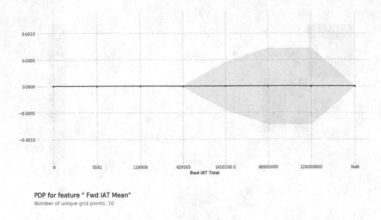

PDF for feature " Fwd IAT Mean"
Number of unique grid points: 10

Fig. 8. PDP of the feature Fwd IAT Mean

reaches 43 the probability does not change significantly. On the other hand, we cannot interpret anything by using Fig. 8.

Based on PDP, we recursively remove the features that we can not interpret.

On the other hand, SHAP gives us a global view of the driven force of the features. We display the feature contribution calculated by SHAP in Fig. 9. We note that the feature contribution by SHAP is different from feature importance calculated by xgboost as we display in Fig. 10. The feature importance by xgboost is calculated as how many times the feature is used in splitting the trees. It does not tell us how does the feature affect the prediction.

We combine the feature contribution and feature interpretation of PDP and xgboost, and select top ten features that are both contributed and interpretable. We build again two models: binary and multi-class classifiers.

The lightweight binary classifier achieved the ROC AUC score of 0.9999993, just a tiny difference compared to the full model. We display the confusion matrix of the model in Fig. 11. Similarly we display the confusion matrix of the light multi-class classifier in Fig. 12. The light multi-class classification achieved the accuracy score of 99.991%. Again, the performance drop is tiny. However, the training time of the binary classifier reduces from 2.7 min to 1 min (63% reduction) and the training time of the multi-class classifier reduces from 9 min to around 5 min (44% reduction). Similarly, the prediction time have been reduced at the same levels.

We maintain the interpretable in both global and local view of the model. We display two examples of the interpretations in Fig. 13. We can explain why does the model give a particular output by the driving force of each features. For instance, in the first example we know that it is marked as malicious partly because the flow duration is very long.

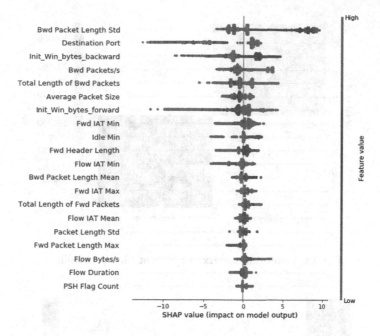

Fig. 9. SHAP of the binary model in the entire testing set. The plot shows the us the driven force of each feature in a global view.

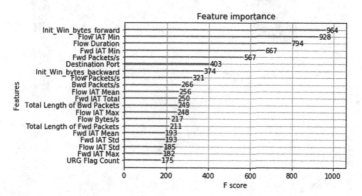

Fig. 10. Feature Importance calculated by xgboost using F-score. The feature importance plot shows us how big the influence of a feature is, but does not tell us how does the feature drives the model.

We conclude that, by understanding the decisions of a machine learning model using in IDSs, we can reduce significantly the training time of the model while maintaining the predictive performance. Furthermore, we can provide the explanation if we reject or accept a particular network flow, make it easier for engineers to debug the system.

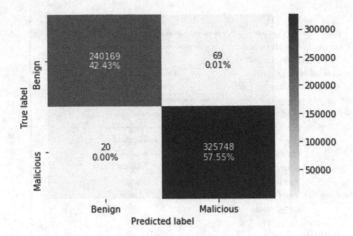

Fig. 11. Confusion matrix of the light binary classifier.

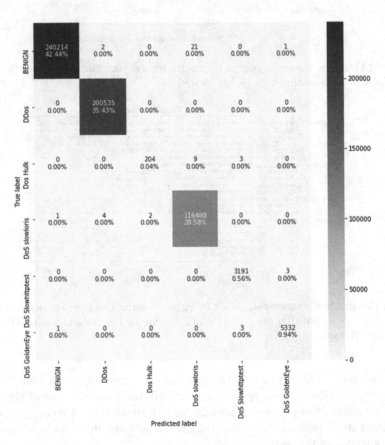

Fig. 12. Confusion matrix of the light multi-class classifier.

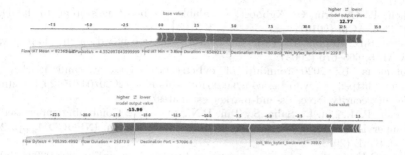

Fig. 13. Explanation of the prediction on two testing instances.

5 Conclusions

In this paper, we study the utilization of interpretable machine learning to understand the machine learning based IDSs, then remove the features that we cannot explain. By doing so, we maintain the predictive performance of the IDS but reduce significantly the required computational power, making IDSs be suitable for small devices or less important networks. As the predictive performance using the full training dataset is almost perfect, we believe that the future research studies related to IDSs should focus on the power and computational optimization. In the future works we will combine the feature reduction with training instance reduction to further optimize the training and predicting processes.

References

1. Abdi, H., Williams, L.J.: Principal component analysis. Wiley Interdisc. Rev. Comput. Stat. **2**(4), 433–459 (2010)
2. Ahmed, M., Mahmood, A.N., Hu, J.: A survey of network anomaly detection techniques. J. Netw. Comput. Appl. **60**, 19–31 (2016)
3. Amor, N.B., Benferhat, S., Elouedi, Z.: Naive bayes vs decision trees in intrusion detection systems. In: SAC, pp. 420–424. ACM (2004)
4. Bhamare, D., Salman, T., Samaka, M., Erbad, A., Jain, R.: Feasibility of supervised machine learning for cloud security. CoRR abs/1810.09878 (2018)
5. Bibal, A., Lognoul, M., de Streel, A., Frénay, B.: Impact of legal requirements on explainability in machine learning. arXiv:2007.05479 (2020)
6. Brun, O., Yin, Y., Gelenbe, E., Kadioglu, Y.M., Augusto-Gonzalez, J., Ramos, M.: Deep learning with dense random neural networks for detecting attacks against IoT-connected home environments. In: Gelenbe, E., Campegiani, P., Czachórski, T., Katsikas, S.K., Komnios, I., Romano, L., Tzovaras, D. (eds.) Euro-CYBERSEC 2018. CCIS, vol. 821, pp. 79–89. Springer, Cham (2018). https://doi.org/10.1007/978-3-319-95189-8_8
7. Buhrmester, V., Münch, D., Arens, M.: Analysis of explainers of black box deep neural networks for computer vision: a survey. arXiv:1911.12116 (2019)
8. Chaudhary, A., Mittal, H., Arora, A.: Anomaly detection using graph neural networks. In: 2019 International Conference on Machine Learning, Big Data, Cloud and Parallel Computing (COMITCon), pp. 346–350. IEEE (2019)

9. Chen, T., Guestrin, C.: Xgboost: a scalable tree boosting system. In: KDD, pp. 785–794. ACM (2016)
10. Cohen, S.B., Ruppin, E., Dror, G.: Feature selection based on the shapley value. IJCAI. **5**, 665–670 (2005)
11. Columbus, L.: 2020 roundup of cybersecurity forecasts and market estimates, https://www.forbes.com/sites/louiscolumbus/2020/04/05/2020-roundup-of-cybersecurity-forecasts-and-market-estimates/
12. Comar, P.M., Liu, L., Saha, S., Tan, P.N., Nucci, A.: Combining supervised and unsupervised learning for zero-day malware detection. In: INFOCOM, pp. 2022–2030. IEEE (2013)
13. Dang, Q.V.: Outlier detection in network flow analysis. arXiv:1808.02024 (2018)
14. Dang, Q.-V.: Studying machine learning techniques for intrusion detection systems. In: Dang, T.K., Küng, J., Takizawa, M., Bui, S.H. (eds.) FDSE 2019. LNCS, vol. 11814, pp. 411–426. Springer, Cham (2019). https://doi.org/10.1007/978-3-030-35653-8_28
15. Dang, Q.V.: Active learning for intrusion detection systems. In: IEEE Research, Innovation and Vision for the Future (2020)
16. Deka, R.K., Bhattacharyya, D.K., Kalita, J.K.: Active learning to detect DDoS attack using ranked features. Comput. Commun. **145**, 203–222 (2019)
17. Diro, A.A., Chilamkurti, N.: Distributed attack detection scheme using deep learning approach for internet of things. Future Gener. Comp. Syst. **82**, 761–768 (2018)
18. Dosilovic, F.K., Brcic, M., Hlupic, N.: Explainable artificial intelligence: a survey. In: MIPRO, pp. 210–215. IEEE (2018)
19. Friedman, J.H.: Greedy function approximation: a gradient boosting machine. Ann. stat. **29**(5), 1189–1232 (2001)
20. Gharib, A., Sharafaldin, I., Lashkari, A.H., Ghorbani, A.A.: An evaluation framework for intrusion detection dataset. In: 2016 International Conference on Information Science and Security (ICISS), pp. 1–6. IEEE (2016)
21. Greenwell, B.M., Boehmke, B.C., McCarthy, A.J.: A simple and effective model-based variable importance measure. arXiv:1805.04755 (2018)
22. Hastie, T., Tibshirani, R., Friedman, J.: The Elements of Statistical Learning: Data Mining, Inference, and Prediction. Springer Science & Business Media (2009)
23. Hinton, G.E.: Deep belief networks. Scholarpedia **4**(5), 5947 (2009)
24. Hodo, E., Bellekens, X., Hamilton, A., Tachtatzis, C., Atkinson, R.: Shallow and deep networks intrusion detection system: a taxonomy and survey. arXiv:1701.02145 (2017)
25. Ignat, C., Dang, Q., Shalin, V.L.: The influence of trust score on cooperative behavior. ACM Trans. Internet Techn. **19**(4), 46:1–46:22 (2019)
26. Jin, D., Lu, Y., Qin, J., Cheng, Z., Mao, Z.: KC-IDS: Multi-layer intrusion detection system. In: International Conference on High Performance Big Data and Intelligent Systems (HPBD&IS), pp. 1–5. IEEE (2020)
27. Jyothsna, V., Prasad, V.R., Prasad, K.M.: A review of anomaly based intrusion detection systems. Int. J. Comput. Appl. **28**(7), 26–35 (2011)
28. Kam, H.T., et al.: Random decision forest. In: Proceedings of the 3rd International Conference on Document Analysis and Recognition, vol. 1416, pp. 278–282 (1995)
29. Kang, M.J., Kang, J.W.: Intrusion detection system using deep neural network for in-vehicle network security. PloS one **11**(6), e0155781 (2016)
30. Kausar, N., Samir, B.B., Sulaiman, S.B., Ahmad, I., Hussain, M.: An approach towards intrusion detection using PCA feature subsets and SVM. In: 2012 International Conference on Computer & Information Science (ICCIS), vol. 2, pp. 569–574. IEEE (2012)

31. Ke, G., et al.: Lightgbm: a highly efficient gradient boosting decision tree. In: Advances in Neural Information Processing Systems, pp. 3146–3154 (2017)
32. Kipf, T.N., Welling, M.: Semi-supervised classification with graph convolutional networks. arXiv preprint arXiv:1609.02907 (2016)
33. Krügel, C., Toth, T.: Using decision trees to improve signature-based intrusion detection. In: Vigna, G., Kruegel, C., Jonsson, E. (eds.) RAID 2003. LNCS, vol. 2820, pp. 173–191. Springer, Heidelberg (2003). https://doi.org/10.1007/978-3-540-45248-5_10
34. Lazarevic, A., Ertoz, L., Kumar, V., Ozgur, A., Srivastava, J.: A comparative study of anomaly detection schemes in network intrusion detection. In: Proceedings of the 2003 SIAM international conference on data mining, pp. 25–36. SIAM (2003)
35. Li, X., Ye, N.: Decision tree classifiers for computer intrusion detection. J. Parallel Distrib. Comput. Practices 4(2), 179–190 (2001)
36. Liu, F.T., Ting, K.M., Zhou, Z.H.: Isolation forest. In: 2008 Eighth IEEE International Conference on Data Mining, pp. 413–422. IEEE (2008)
37. Lundberg, S.M., Lee, S.I.: A unified approach to interpreting model predictions. In: Guyon, I., Luxburg, U.V., Bengio, S., Wallach, H., Fergus, R., Vishwanathan, S., Garnett, R. (eds.) Advances in Neural Information Processing Systems 30, pp. 4765–4774. Curran Associates, Inc. (2017). http://papers.nips.cc/paper/7062-a-unified-approach-to-interpreting-model-predictions.pdf
38. Marín, G., Casas, P., Capdehourat, G.: Deepmal - deep learning models for malware traffic detection and classification. CoRR abs/2003.04079 (2020)
39. McHugh, J.: Testing intrusion detection systems: a critique of the 1998 and 1999 DARPA intrusion detection system evaluations as performed by lincoln laboratory. ACM Trans. Inf. Syst. Secur. (TISSEC) 3(4), 262–294 (2000)
40. Molnar, C.: Interpretable Machine Learning. Lulu (2020)
41. Prokhorenkova, L., Gusev, G., Vorobev, A., Dorogush, A.V., Gulin, A.: Catboost: unbiased boosting with categorical features. In: Advances in neural information processing systems, pp. 6638–6648 (2018)
42. Protogerou, A., Papadopoulos, S., Drosou, A., Tzovaras, D., Refanidis, I.: A graph neural network method for distributed anomaly detection in IoT. Evolving Systems. 1–18 (2020)
43. Reddy, R.R., Ramadevi, Y., Sunitha, K.V.N.: Effective discriminant function for intrusion detection using SVM. In: ICACCI, pp. 1148–1153. IEEE (2016)
44. Reis, B., Maia, E., Praça, I.: Selection and performance analysis of CICIDS2017 features importance. In: Benzekri, A., Barbeau, M., Gong, G., Laborde, R., Garcia-Alfaro, J. (eds.) FPS 2019. LNCS, vol. 12056, pp. 56–71. Springer, Cham (2020). https://doi.org/10.1007/978-3-030-45371-8_4
45. Resende, P.A.A., Drummond, A.C.: A survey of random forest based methods for intrusion detection systems. ACM Comput. Surv. 51(3), 48:1–48:36 (2018)
46. Ribeiro, M.T., Singh, S., Guestrin, C.: "why should I trust you?": explaining the predictions of any classifier. In: KDD, pp. 1135–1144. ACM (2016)
47. Roscher, R., Bohn, B., Duarte, M.F., Garcke, J.: Explainable machine learning for scientific insights and discoveries. IEEE Access 8, 42200–42216 (2020)
48. Sample, I.: Computer says no: why making AIs fair, accountable and transparent is crucial, https://www.theguardian.com/science/2017/nov/05/computer-says-no-why-making-ais-fair-accountable-and-transparent-is-crucial
49. Shapley, L.S.: A value for n-person games. Contrib. Theor. Games 2(28), 307–317 (1953)

50. Sharafaldin, I., Lashkari, A.H., Ghorbani, A.A.: Toward generating a new intrusion detection dataset and intrusion traffic characterization. In: ICISSP, pp. 108–116 (2018)

51. Shiravi, A., Shiravi, H., Tavallaee, M., Ghorbani, A.A.: Toward developing a systematic approach to generate benchmark datasets for intrusion detection. Comput. Secur. **31**(3), 357–374 (2012)

52. Stein, G., Chen, B., Wu, A.S., Hua, K.A.: Decision tree classifier for network intrusion detection with ga-based feature selection. In: ACM Southeast Regional Conference (2), pp. 136–141. ACM (2005)

53. Ranga Suri, N.N.R., Murty M, N., Athithan, G.: Outlier Detection: Techniques and Applications. ISRL, vol. 155. Springer, Cham (2019). https://doi.org/10.1007/978-3-030-05127-3

54. Vinayakumar, R., Alazab, M., Soman, K.P., Poornachandran, P., Al-Nemrat, A., Venkatraman, S.: Deep learning approach for intelligent intrusion detection system. IEEE Access **7**, 41525–41550 (2019)

55. Wu, Y., Lee, W.W., Xu, Z., Ni, M.: Large-scale and robust intrusion detection model combining improved deep belief network with feature-weighted SVM. IEEE Access **8**, 98600–98611 (2020)

56. Xu, X., Wang, X.: An adaptive network intrusion detection method based on PCA and support vector machines. In: Li, X., Wang, S., Dong, Z.Y. (eds.) ADMA 2005. LNCS (LNAI), vol. 3584, pp. 696–703. Springer, Heidelberg (2005). https://doi.org/10.1007/11527503_82

57. Yavuz, F.Y., Devrim, Ü., Ensar, G.: Deep learning for detection of routing attacks in the internet of things. Int. J. Comput. Intell. Syst. **12**(1), 39–58 (2018)

58. Zheng, L., Li, Z., Li, J., Li, Z., Gao, J.: Addgraph: anomaly detection in dynamic graph using attention-based temporal GCN. In: IJCAI, pp. 4419–4425 (2019)

Emerging Data Management Systems and Applications

Combining Support Vector Machines for Classifying Fingerprint Images

The-Phi Pham[1], Minh-Thu Tran-Nguyen[1], Minh-Tan Tran[1],
and Thanh-Nghi Do[1,2(✉)]

[1] College of Information Technology, Can Tho University, Cantho 92000, Vietnam
dtnghi@cit.ctu.edu.vn
[2] UMI UMMISCO 209 (IRD/UPMC), Sorbonne University, Pierre and Marie Curie
University - Paris 6, Paris, France

Abstract. We propose to combine support vector machine (SVM) models learned from different visual features for efficiently classifying fingerprint images. Real datasets of fingerprint images are collected from students at the Can Tho University. The SVM algorithm learns classification models from the handcrafted features such as the scale-invariant feature transform (SIFT) and the bag-of-words (BoW) model, the histogram of oriented gradients (HoG), the deep learning of invariant features Xception, extracted from fingerprint images. Followed which, we propose to train a neural network for combining SVM models trained on these different visual features, making improvements of the fingerprint image classification. The empirical test results show that combining SVM models is more accurate than SVM models trained on any single visual feature type. Combining SVM-SIFT-BoW, SVM-HoG, SVM-Xception improves 11.17%, 14.07%, 10.83% classification accuracy of SVM-SIFT-BoW, SVM-HoG and SVM-Xception, respectively.

Keywords: Fingerprint image classification · Visual features · Combining classifiers

1 Introduction

Fingerprint image recognition is studied since the 19th century. The task has great importance and use for the individual identification. It is successfully applied in both government and civilian applications such as suspect and victim identifications, the recovery of partial fingerprints from a crime scene in forensic science, border control, employment background checks, and secure facility access [16]. Fingerprint images are uniqueness and durable over time, making them suitable as long-term markers of individual identity.

The performance of fingerprint image classification largely depends on the feature extraction approach and the machine learning scheme. For a long time ago, the classical approaches commonly use minutiae (i.e. ridge ending, ridge bifurcation, etc.) as features and the matching method between fingerprints

© Springer Nature Switzerland AG 2020
T. K. Dang et al. (Eds.): FDSE 2020, LNCS 12466, pp. 399–410, 2020.
https://doi.org/10.1007/978-3-030-63924-2_23

[15,24]. More recent, the fingerprint image classification in [9] is performed by support vector machines (SVM [32]) models are learned from visual features such as the scale-invariant feature transform (SIFT [21,22]) and the bag-of-words model (BoW [2,19,30]). Some researches in [11,25,28] propose to train deep convolutional neural networks [18] to classify fingerprint images.

In this paper, we propose to train a neural network for combining SVM models learned from two popular handcrafted visual features, including SIFT-BoW, the histogram of oriented gradients (HoG [7]) and pre-trained deep learning network such as Xception [5], making improvements for the fingerprint image classification. The main idea is to combine advantages of classifiers and also to offer a full complement of visual feature types in the fingerprint image recognition. The empirical test results on real fingerprint image datasets show that combining SVM models learned from SIFT-BoW, HoG and Xception improve classification correctness compared to the ones on any single visual feature type. The triplet (SVM-SIFT-BoW, SVM-HoG, SVM-Xception) improves 11.17%, 14.07%, 10.83% classification accuracy of SVM-SIFT-BoW, SVM-HoG and SVM-Xception, respectively.

The paper is organized as follows. Section 2 illustrates our proposal for classifying fingerprint image datasets. Section 3 shows the experimental results before conclusions and future works presented in Sect. 4.

2 Combining SVM Models for Classifying Fingerprint Images

The classification system of fingerprint images in Fig. 1 follows the usual framework for the classification of images. It consists of three main steps:

1. collecting the dataset of fingerprint images,
2. extracting visual features from fingerprint images and representing them,
3. training SVM classifiers.

2.1 Datasets of Fingerprint Images

We start with the collection of fingerprint image datasets. Microsoft Fingerprint Reader (optical fingerprint scanner, resolution: 512 DPI, image size: 355×390, colors: 256 levels grayscale) is used to capture fingerprint images from our students and colleagues at the College of Information Technology, Can Tho University in 2016, 2017, and 2018. And then, we obtain three real fingerprint datasets called FP-235, FP-389, FP-559 which are fingerprint images of 235, 389, and 559 individuals respectively. There are from 15 to 20 fingerprint images captured for each individual (class label). Three datasets are described in Table 1.

2.2 Visual Approaches for Classifying Fingerprint Images

The classification task of fingerprint images is performed via two key steps of visual approaches. The first one is to extract visual features from images and

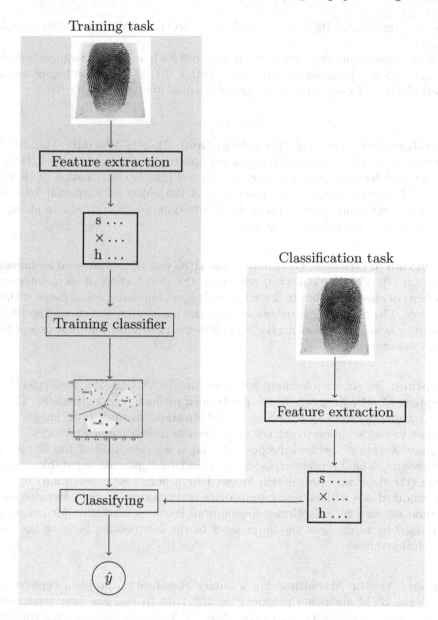

Fig. 1. Framework for classifying fingerprint images

Table 1. Description of fingerprint image datasets

ID	Dataset	#Datapoints	#Classes
1	FP-235	3485	235
2	FP-389	6306	389
3	FP-559	10270	559

represent them. And then, the second one is to train SVM models to classify images.

We propose to use two most popular methods for handcrafted features including the scale-invariant feature transform (SIFT [21,22]) and the bag-of-words model (BoW [2,19,30]), the histogram of oriented gradients (HOG [7]).

Scale-Invariant Feature Transform and Bag-of-Words: The SIFT descriptors [21,22]) extracted from images and the bag-of-words model (BoW) are the most habitual representation for tasks of images classification [2,19,30]. The SIFT method detects the appearance of the object at particular interest points in images, invariant to image scale, rotation, and also robust to changes in illumination, noise, and occlusion.

Histogram of Oriented Gradients: The HOG descriptors are used for human detection [7]. The HOG method computes the distribution of local intensity gradients or edge directions to describe local object appearance and shape within an image. The combined distributions form the image representation. The HOG descriptor is invariant to geometric and photometric transformations, except for object orientation.

Xception: Recent deep learning networks such as VGG19 [29], ResNet50 [13], Inception v3 [31], Xception [5] are pre-trained on ImageNet dataset [8]. These deep learning networks are used to extract invariant features from images. We propose to use Xception to extract deep features from fingerprint images.

The "Xception" network proposed by [4] is an extension of the Inception architecture. The Xception replaces the standard depthwise separable convolution (the depthwise convolution followed by a pointwise convolution) by the new modified one without any intermediate activation being the pointwise convolution followed by a depthwise convolution. Features extraction for images is performed by layers from the input layer to the last pooling layer or the last convolutional layer.

Support Vector Machines: For a binary classification problem depicted in Fig. 2, the SVM algorithm proposed by [32] tries to find the best separating plane furthest from both class +1 and class −1. To pursue this aim, the training SVM algorithm simultaneously maximize the margin (or the distance) between the supporting planes for each class and minimize errors.

The binary SVM solver can be extended for dealing with the multi-class problems (c classes, $c \geq 3$). The main idea is to decompose multi-class into a series of binary SVMs, including One-Versus-All [32], One-Versus-One [17]. The One-Versus-All strategy (as illustrated in Fig. 3) builds c different binary SVM models where the ith one separates the ith class from the rest. The One-Versus-One strategy (illustrated in Fig. 4) constructs $c(c-1)/2$ binary SVM

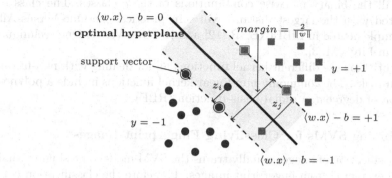

Fig. 2. Classification of the datapoints into two classes

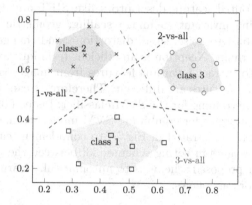

Fig. 3. Multi-class SVM (One-Versus-All)

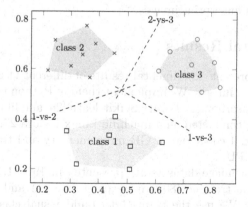

Fig. 4. Multi-class SVM (One-Versus-One)

models for all the binary pairwise combinations of the c classes. The class is then predicted with the largest distance vote. In practice, the One-Versus-All strategy is implemented in LIBLINEAR [12] and the One-Versus-One technique is also used in LibSVM [3].

SVM algorithms use different kernel functions [6] for dealing with non-linear classification tasks. The commonly non-linear kernel functions include a polynomial function of degree d, a radial basis function (RBF).

2.3 Combining SVMs for Classifying Fingerprint Images

Classical classification of images usually trains the SVM model on a single visual feature type extracted from fingerprint images. Therefore the classification correctness is restricted because any visual feature type has advantages and disadvantages. Our investigation aims to combine the strength of SVM models learned from different visual feature types for improving the classification of fingerprint images. The handcrafted feature descriptors like SIFT and HoG have several advantages, including invariant to image scaling, geometric and photometric transformations, robust to noise, small distortions, and changes in illumination [7,21,22,27]. Furthermore, Xception is an efficient technique among recent deep learning networks to extract invariant features from images [10]. However, the nature of these visual features are different. Therefore, it can not combine three visual features before training for the SVM classifier. Instead of this, we propose to train the neural network for combining SVM models trained on SIFT-BoW, HoG and Xception (as illustrated in Fig. 5) to complement each other. Instead of tuning by hand weights in voting scheme [33] between the prediction of each visual classifier, our proposed scheme is to automatically learn weights with the simple neural network as follows:

Input ⇒ **Full Connected** ⇒ **Sampling** ⇒ **Full Connected** ⇒ **Softmax**

And then, the network fuses SVM models trained on SIFT-BoW, HoG and Xception to classify fingerprint images.

3   Experimental Results

In this section, we present experimental results of different visual approaches for classifying fingerprint images. We implement them in Python using library Keras [4] with backend Tensorflow [1], library Scikit-learn [26] and library OpenCV [14]. All experiments are conducted on a machine Linux Fedora 27, Intel(R) Core i7-4790 CPU, 3.6 GHz, 4 cores and 32 GB main memory and the Nvidia GeForce GTX 960M 2 GB GPU.

Three fingerprint image datasets are presented in Table 1. Datasets are randomly split into the trainset (80% fingerprint images) and the testset (20% fingerprint images). We use the trainset to build visual classification models. Then, results are reported on the testset using the resulting visual classification models.

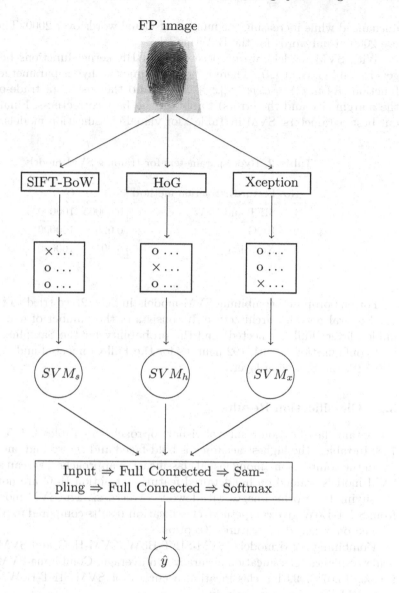

Fig. 5. Combining SVM models for classifying fingerprint images

3.1 Tuning Parameters

With methods for feature extractor and image representation, only handcrafted features SIFT and BoW model needs tuning the number of clusters (visual words) well-known as the parameter of $k$means algorithm [23]. The number of visual words are varied from 1000 to 3000. And then, experimental results are unchanged while increasing the number of visual words over 2000. Therefore, we use 2000 visual words for the BoW model.

With SVM models, we propose to use RBF kernel functions because it is general and efficient [20]. There is need to tune the hyper-parameter γ of RBF function $[K\langle x_i, x_j \rangle = exp(-\gamma ||x_i - x_j||^2)]$ and the cost C (a trade-off between the margin size and the errors) to obtain the best correctness. Finally, we find out best parameters' SVM in Table 2 for visual classification models.

Table 2. Hyper-parameters for training SVM models

No	Feature extraction method	γ	C
1	SIFT and BoW	0.00005	100000
2	HOG	0.025	100000
3	Xception	0.001	100000

For our proposed combining SVM models in Sect. 2, we tried to tune for the good neural network architecture. It consists of the number of neurons for the hidden layer (Full Connected) and the probability for the Sampling layer. The best configuration is with 192 neurons for the Full Connected and a probability of 0.5 for the Sampling layer.

3.2   Classification Results

We obtain classification results of visual approaches in Tables 3, 4, 5 and Figs. 6, 7, 8. In tables, the highest accuracy is bold-faced and the second one is in italic.

In the comparison among visual classification approaches, we can see that the SVM models trained on handcrafted feature extraction HoG are not suited for classifying fingerprint images with lowest correctness. The SVM models learned from SIFT-BoW give competitive classification results compared to SVM models trained on recent deep features Xception.

Combining SVM models (SVM-SIFT-BoW, SVM-HoG and SVM-Xception) achieves highest classification accuracy. On average, Combining-SVMs improves 9.87%, 13.07%, 9.51% classification accuracy of SVM-SIFT-BoW, SVM-HoG and SVM-Xception, respectively.

A typical example of the effectiveness of Combining-SVMs is given with classification results for FP-559 fingerprint dataset. The improvements of combining SVM-SIFT-BoW, SVM-HoG and SVM-Xception over each single visual classifier are 11.17%, 14.07%, 10.83%, respectively.

Table 3. Overall classification accuracy for FP-235

No	Visual approach	Accuracy (%)
1	SVM-SIFT-BoW	*89.38*
2	SVM-HoG	82.78
3	SVM-Xception	87.39
4	Combining SVMs	**96.70**

Table 4. Overall classification accuracy for FP-389

No	Visual approach	Accuracy (%)
1	SVM-SIFT-BoW	87.19
2	SVM-HoG	86.01
3	SVM-Xception	*87.75*
4	Combining SVMs	**97.22**

Table 5. Overall classification accuracy for FP-559

No	Visual approach	Accuracy (%)
1	SVM-SIFT-BoW	85.55
2	SVM-HoG	82.65
3	SVM-Xception	*85.89*
4	Combining SVMs	**96.72**

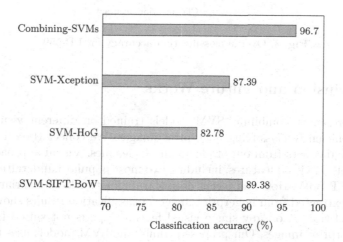

Fig. 6. Overall classification accuracy for FP-235

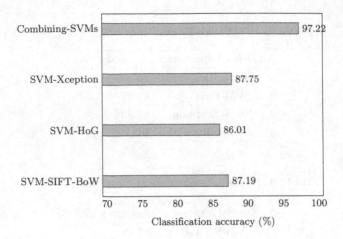

Fig. 7. Overall classification accuracy for FP-389

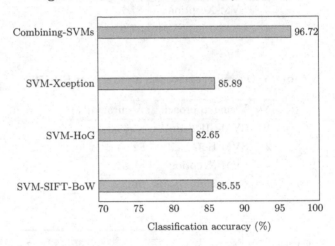

Fig. 8. Overall classification accuracy for FP-559

4   Conclusion and Future Works

We have presented combining SVM models trained on different visual feature types for efficiently classifying fingerprint images. We collect three real fingerprint image datasets from our students and colleagues. Visual approaches train SVM models on visual features, including two most popular handcrafted features such as SIFT-BoW, HoG and recent deep learning networks of invariant features Xception, extracted from fingerprint images. Classification results show that the SVM model trained on any single visual feature type is not suited for categorizing fingerprint images. Our proposed combining SVM models uses the neural network for fusing visual models (SVM-SIFT-BoW, SVM-HoG, SVM-Xception), making improvements of the classification correctness given by any single one.

In the near future, work will be to select efficient visual models learned from different feature types to improve fingerprint image classification results.

Acknowledgments. This work has received support from the College of Information Technology, Can Tho University. The authors would like to thank very much the Big Data and Mobile Computing Laboratory.

References

1. Abadi, M., et al.: TensorFlow: large-scale machine learning on heterogeneous systems (2015). Software available from tensorflow.org. https://www.tensorflow.org/
2. Bosch, A., Zisserman, A., Muñoz, X.: Scene classification via pLSA. In: Leonardis, A., Bischof, H., Pinz, A. (eds.) ECCV 2006. LNCS, vol. 3954, pp. 517–530. Springer, Heidelberg (2006). https://doi.org/10.1007/11744085_40
3. Chang, C.C., Lin, C.J.: LIBSVM: a library for support vector machines. ACM Trans. Intell. Syst. Technol. **2**(27), 1–27 (2011)
4. Chollet, F., et al.: Keras (2015). https://keras.io
5. Chollet, F.: Xception: deep learning with depthwise separable convolutions. CoRR abs/1610.02357 (2016)
6. Cristianini, N., Shawe-Taylor, J.: An Introduction to Support Vector Machines: And Other Kernel-based Learning Methods. Cambridge University Press, New York (2000)
7. Dalal, N., Triggs, B.: Histograms of oriented gradients for human detection. In: Proceedings of the 2005 IEEE Computer Society Conference on Computer Vision and Pattern Recognition, CVPR 2005, vol. 1, pp. 886–893. IEEE Computer Society (2005)
8. Deng, J., Berg, A.C., Li, K., Fei-Fei, L.: What does classifying more than 10,000 image categories tell us? In: Daniilidis, K., Maragos, P., Paragios, N. (eds.) ECCV 2010. LNCS, vol. 6315, pp. 71–84. Springer, Heidelberg (2010). https://doi.org/10.1007/978-3-642-15555-0_6
9. Do, T.-N., Lenca, P., Lallich, S.: Classifying many-class high-dimensional fingerprint datasets using random forest of oblique decision trees. Vietnam J. Comput. Sci. **2**(1), 3–12 (2014). https://doi.org/10.1007/s40595-014-0024-7
10. Do, T.-N., Pham, T.-P., Pham, N.-K., Nguyen, H.-H., Tabia, K., Benferhat, S.: Stacking of SVMs for classifying intangible cultural heritage images. In: Le Thi, H.A., Le, H.M., Pham Dinh, T., Nguyen, N.T. (eds.) ICCSAMA 2019. AISC, vol. 1121, pp. 186–196. Springer, Cham (2020). https://doi.org/10.1007/978-3-030-38364-0_17
11. Engelsma, J.J., Cao, K., Jain, A.K.: Fingerprints: Fixed length representation via deep networks and domain knowledge. CoRR abs/1904.01099 (2019)
12. Fan, R.E., Chang, K.W., Hsieh, C.J., Wang, X.R., Lin, C.J.: LIBLINEAR: a library for large linear classification. J. Mach. Learn. Res. **9**(4), 1871–1874 (2008)
13. He, K., Zhang, X., Ren, S., Sun, J.: Deep residual learning for image recognition. CoRR abs/1512.03385 (2015)
14. ItSeez: Open source computer vision library (2015). https://github.com/itseez/opencv
15. Jain, A.K., Feng, J., Nandakumar, K.: Fingerprint matching. IEEE Comput. **43**(2), 36–44 (2010)

16. Jain, A.K., Nandakumar, K., Ross, A.: 50 years of biometric research: accomplishments, challenges, and opportunities. Pattern Recogn. Lett. **79**, 80–105 (2016)

17. Kreßel, U.H.G.: Pairwise classification and support vector machines. In: Schölkopf, B., Burges, C.J.C., Smola, A.J. (eds.) Advances in Kernel Methods, pp. 255–268. MIT Press, Cambridge (1999)

18. LeCun, Y., Bottou, L., Bengio, Y., Haffner, P.: Gradient-based learning applied to document recognition. Proc. IEEE **86**, 2278–2324 (1998)

19. Li, F., Perona, P.: A Bayesian hierarchical model for learning natural scene categories. In: 2005 IEEE Computer Society Conference on Computer Vision and Pattern Recognition, CVPR 2005, 20–26 June 2005, San Diego, CA, USA, pp. 524–531 (2005)

20. Lin, C.: A practical guide to support vector classification (2003)

21. Lowe, D.: Object recognition from local scale invariant features. In: Proceedings of the 7th International Conference on Computer Vision, pp. 1150–1157 (1999)

22. Lowe, D.: Distinctive image features from scale invariant keypoints. Int. J. Comput. Vis. **60**, 91–110 (2004)

23. MacQueen, J.: Some methods for classification and analysis of multivariate observations. In: Berkeley Symposium on Mathematical Statistics and Probability, University of California Press, vol. 1, pp. 281–297 (1967)

24. Maltoni, D., Maio, D., Jain, A.K., Prabhakar, S.: Handbook of Fingerprint Recognition, 2nd edn. Springer, London (2009). https://doi.org/10.1007/978-1-84882-254-2

25. Minaee, S., Azimi, E., Abdolrashidi, A.: FingerNet: Pushing the limits of fingerprint recognition using convolutional neural network. CoRR abs/1907.12956 (2019)

26. Pedregosa, F., et al.: Scikit-learn: machine learning in Python. J. Mach. Learn. Res. **12**, 2825–2830 (2011)

27. Sharma, V., Gool, L.V.: Image-level classification in hyperspectral images using feature descriptors, with application to face recognition. CoRR abs/1605.03428 (2016)

28. Shrein, J.M.: Fingerprint classification using convolutional neural networks and ridge orientation images. In: 2017 IEEE Symposium Series on Computational Intelligence (SSCI), pp. 1–8 (November 2017)

29. Simonyan, K., Zisserman, A.: Very deep convolutional networks for large-scale image recognition. CoRR abs/1409.1556 (2014)

30. Sivic, J., Zisserman, A.: Video Google: a text retrieval approach to object matching in videos. In: 9th IEEE International Conference on Computer Vision, ICCV 2003, Nice, France, 14–17 October 2003, pp. 1470–1477 (2003)

31. Szegedy, C., Vanhoucke, V., Ioffe, S., Shlens, J., Wojna, Z.: Rethinking the inception architecture for computer vision. CoRR abs/1512.00567 (2015)

32. Vapnik, V.N.: The Nature of Statistical Learning Theory. Springer, New York (1995). https://doi.org/10.1007/978-1-4757-2440-0

33. Wolpert, D.: Stacked generalization. Neural Netw. **5**, 241–259 (1992)

Toward an Ontology for Improving Process Flexibility

Nguyen Hoang Thuan[1]([⊠]), Hoang Ai Phuong[1], Majo George[1], Mathews Nkhoma[1], and Pedro Antunes[2]

[1] RMIT University Vietnam, 702 Nguyen van Linh Blvd., Ho Chi Minh City, Vietnam
{Thuan.NguyenHoang,Phuong.HoangAi,Majo.George,
Mathews.Nkhoma}@rmit.edu.vn
[2] University of Lisbon, 1749-016 Lisbon, Portugal
pantunes@di.fc.ul.pt

Abstract. Process flexibility supports organisations to deal with changes, uncertainty, variations, and exceptions in business operations. Although several taxonomies of process flexibility have been proposed, the domain still lacks an ontological structure that clarifies and organises the domain. The current study fills this gap by building an ontology for improving process flexibility. Our results identify main business contexts, cases, dynamic modelling techniques, mechanisms to manage process flexibility, and their hierarchy relationships, which are structured into an ontology. The current study is significant as it provides a theoretical blueprint for improving the flexibility of organisational business processes.

Keywords: Business process flexibility · Design science · Ontology

1 Introduction

Process flexibility enables organizations to deal with change, uncertainty, variation, and evolution in their business operations. Given current disruptions to businesses, it is important for organizations to design business processes that are sufficiently flexible to cope with constantly increasing demands for change [1], including operational variations, foreseen and unforeseen events, unique cases, and exceptions [2, 3]. The demands for process flexibility are further highlighted by the Covid-19 disruption, where normal standard business processes have had to be adapted to support disrupted workflows, consisting of working from home, lack of suppliers, variations of work, and exceptional requests from customers.

From an organizational perspective, process flexibility enables organizations to manage standard operations and variant operations. This is particular true in cases where processes have to be dynamically adapted, for instance adapting "day to day" activities on-the-fly to carry on variant and unique cases [3]. Process flexibility further enables organizations to dynamically manage process-related information, including actors, information sources, and execution conditions, which support the relocation of skilled

T. K. Dang et al. (Eds.): FDSE 2020, LNCS 12466, pp. 411–428, 2020.
https://doi.org/10.1007/978-3-030-63924-2_24

workers, execution under incomplete information, changing external partners, and real-time decisions [4–6]. These cases suggest the important roles of process flexibility in organisations.

From an academic perspective, process flexibility has formed an important area of research within Business Process Management (BPM) for the last decades [1, 7]. Recently, the research area has received momentum due to increasing variations of business processes and uncertainty caused by disruptive innovations, disruptive technologies, and disruptive business environments [2, 3, 6]. Consequently, much research has been conducted on a variety of topics related to process flexibility, including modelling flexible processes [8, 9], managing process flexibility [10], and extending information systems to support process flexibility [11, 12].

With this variety, the research area of process flexibility is characterized by diverse viewpoints, heterogenous conceptualizations and diverse research approaches, including case studies, design studies, and development studies. This is logical as process flexibility "asks to take into account different aspects from several existing disciplines including organizational science, information science, computer science, and sociology" [3]. This diversity however leads to a lack of common understanding in the research area and can prevent organizations from fully utilizing the existing scientific knowledge on process flexibility.

While researchers agree that ontologies can improve understanding and knowledge structures in the research area [13–16], there are only a few ontologies supporting process flexibility in the related literature. Prior studies aiming to increase the understanding of process flexibility have focused on developing taxonomies [17–19], and representing its main concepts [1]. These studies highlight the need to structure knowledge in the research area, i.e. taxonomies structure knowledge by classifying main concepts in the area. Further, they suggest an avenue for ontology development, as a "taxonomy may be a step toward a future ontology" [20]. Furthermore, since ontologies explicitly define and integrate key concepts and the relationships [21], including agreements and contradictions, they contribute to build a holistic view over a research area.

Therefore, the current study aims to construct an ontology that can provide a foundation for improving process flexibility. The study sets up two objectives. First, we want to identify and analyse the main concepts and relationships concerning process flexibility. Second, based on the identified concepts and relationships, we structure an ontology to improve understanding and to support process flexibility. With these objectives, the current study conducts a scoping literature review [22] to identify and synthesize individual findings from the related literature, and then, following a design-based approach [23], constructs a preliminary ontology of process flexibility.

This study contributes to knowledge by consolidating an understanding on process flexibility, while addressing the diversity and heterogeneity of knowledge in the area. From an academic perspective, the ontology provides a theoretical foundation for understanding and managing process flexibility. From a practical perspective, our research is expected to enable organizations to understand, identify, and manage flexible processes. Using our proposed ontology, organizations will have more capability to deal with uncertainty, change, emergence, and evolution [2].

2   Literature Review

Process flexibility is regarded as the capability of organizational business processes to deal with expected and unexpected changes [2, 3]. With intensified unexpected changes coming from increasingly dynamic business environments, emerging technologies, and unforeseen exceptions, there is a strong need for organizational business processes to be flexible and adaptable. Consequently, the research area of process flexibility has attracted much attention. Researchers have widely studied different aspects of process flexibility from multiples disciplines like organizational science, business process management, and information systems in order to manage, conceptualize, support, and improve process flexibility [3, 10–12, 24, 25].

While such a wide range of studies highlights the importance of the research area, it brings a variety of multifaceted concepts and heterogenous views into the research area [2, 26]. This variety can be illustrated, for instance, through diverse mechanisms to manage process flexibility, including adaptive business rules and decision tables [5, 27], context-aware adaptions [28], changed patterns [29], and process families [30]. Such multifaceted concepts and heterogenous views can also be found in other process flexibility topics, including different conceptualizations of process flexibility, different modelling languages to facilitate process flexibility, and diverse drivers for process flexibility [1, 3]. Consequently, this variety makes difficult to classify, structure, and synthesize common understanding in the research area.

Given that, the research area still needs to be consolidated. With this need, we would expect to find commonly accepted ontologies of process flexibility, for three reasons. First, ontologies can provide holistic views on process flexibility by defining the main concepts of the research area. Second, as ontologies also clarify the relationships between these concepts, they help reduce semantic ambiguity [31–33]. Finally, ontologies provide a structured means for managing knowledge on process flexibility. Corcho et al. [21] and Wong et al. [34] refer to ontologies as not only research areas' conceptualizations, but also as knowledge that can be inferred from the research area.

However, to the best of our knowledge, ontologies of process flexibility seem to be absent. We could find only a few taxonomies and frameworks classifying concepts in the domain, which we will summarize in the next section.

2.1   Taxonomies and Frameworks for Process Flexibility

This section reviews the state of the art on how existing studies have structured knowledge in the research area of process flexibility. Given the heterogenous nature of the research area, a variety of taxonomies and frameworks have been proposed [6, 7, 17, 28]. However, most of them focus on particular aspects of process flexibility, considering in particular specific characteristics of process flexibility and factors motivating process flexibility.

A popular group of taxonomies have been proposed to characterize process flexibility. Schonenberg et al. [17] propose a taxonomy characterizing the nature of process flexibility under four categories: flexibility by design, flexibility by deviation, flexibility by under specification, and flexibility by change. In a more simple form, Kumar and Narasipuram [35] distinguish pre-designed flexibility from just-in-time, responsive flexibility. Soffer [36] differentiates between short-term and long-term flexibility. The former refers to temporary changes from a standard workflow, while the latter refers to permanent changes into a new workflow.

In this group of studies, the taxonomy proposed by Reichert and Weber [6] has been widely used to characterize process flexibility. Their taxonomy classifies flexibility into four categories: variability, adaptation, looseness, and evolution. Variability manages flexible processes by deriving variants from the same workflow. Adaptation manages flexible processes by handling occasional unforeseen changes at run-time without changing the standard workflow. Looseness manages flexible processes by handling run-time workflow without strict adherence to the standard workflow. Finally, evolution manages flexible processes by permanently modifying the workflow.

Moving to the next group of studies, several taxonomies analyze and classify factors motivating process flexibility. Cognini et al. [3] identify six common reasons for process flexibility, including exceptions, technology evolutions, new working methods, change in the laws, changes in the target goals, and cost savings. Snowdon et al. [37], focusing on the information support to process flexibility, classifies three factors influencing process flexibility: variety of information types, amount of information that has to be dealt with, and the need to operate in different ways.

We note that the above studies propose process flexibility taxonomies which consider specific facets, such as the nature of process and the information needs of process flexibility. Even though they define and structure elements in a specific domain, they are specific and thus do not provide an overall picture of the research area. This leads to the need for broader ontologies that structure the diversity of knowledge in the research area. However, our literature review found no such ontologies. The closest work we found is the semantic model for Software as a service (SaaS) proposed by Hidri et al. [28]. While the semantic model is derived from multiple concepts regarding three perspectives: business, service, and context, it is limited to SaaS processes. Consequently, there is a lack of ontologies supporting process flexibility as a whole. Fulfilling this gap, the current study aims to construct an ontology that can provide a holistic foundation for improving process flexibility.

3   Method

To build the ontology, the current study used a structured literature review [38] to gather concepts, which was then combined with a design-based method [23] to organize concepts. While the structured literature review enables us to identify key concepts and relationships and thus advances the breadth of understanding in the research area, the design-based method links and structures the identified concepts into the common frame of understanding offered by the ontology. This combination was adopted to achieve a holistic ontological coverage of meanings and relationships between the reviewed literature. To accomplish this strategy, we followed the five-stage process depicted in Fig. 1, which includes the search definition, literature search, refinement, analysis of selected papers, and presentation of findings. This process is elaborated below.

Literature Search Definition. To start, we set out criteria for inclusion and exclusion to ensure a quality holistic review. Aligning with Webster and Watson [39], we included peer reviewed sources (including academics journals, book chapters, and conference

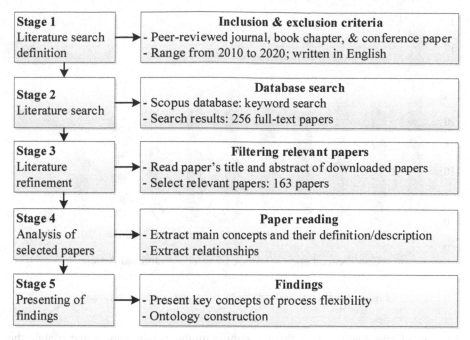

Stage 1 Literature search definition	Inclusion & exclusion criteria - Peer-reviewed journal, book chapter, & conference paper - Range from 2010 to 2020; written in English
Stage 2 Literature search	Database search - Scopus database: keyword search - Search results: 256 full-text papers
Stage 3 Literature refinement	Filtering relevant papers - Read paper's title and abstract of downloaded papers - Select relevant papers: 163 papers
Stage 4 Analysis of selected papers	Paper reading - Extract main concepts and their definition/description - Extract relationships
Stage 5 Presenting of findings	Findings - Present key concepts of process flexibility - Ontology construction

Fig. 1. Research method

papers), and excluded dissertations, editorials, and book reviews. We also defined a review period ranging from 2010 to 2020 to ensure the review and constructed ontology is up to date.

Literature Search. We used the Scopus database for the literature search to ensure a wide coverage, as Scopus indexes a wide range of academic sources. The searched keywords combined the notions of business process ("business process" OR "workflow management" OR "process concept" OR "organisational processes") and flexibility ("process flexibility" OR flexibility OR variability OR variant OR adapt OR adaptation OR adaptivity OR adaptive OR evolve OR evolution OR looseness OR dynamic OR context-ware). As a result, the search returned a total of 256 full-text sources.

The search results show some interesting statistics. Regarding the form of publications, the demographics show that 74% are conference papers, 4% are book chapters, and 22% are journal articles. The dominance of conference publications over journal publications confirms our assumption that the research area is still emerging and thus needs to be further established. Regarding the publication years, Fig. 2 shows the search results distributed per year from 2010 to 2020. Through this figure, we note an increase in the number of publications in the 2014–2016 period. Then, it seems that the number of publications decreases in 2017 and increases again in 2018 and 2019. We also note that our search was conducted in the middle of 2020, and thus publications for that year may not be updated and indexed yet.

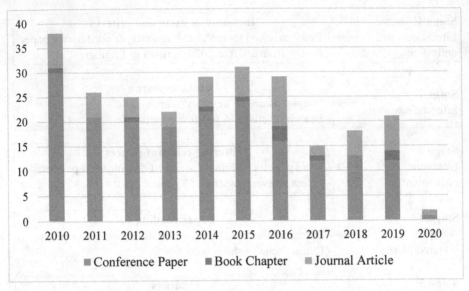

Fig. 2. Search results distribute by years and publication forms

Literature Refinement. Given that the sample might include papers that contain the search keywords yet indirectly link to process flexibility, we conducted further refinements. Using a screening technique suggested by Okoli [38], we performed the literature refinement by reading the sources' titles, keywords, and abstracts. We filtered out papers that only broadly refer to process flexibility, or that use process flexibility as a referencing example to discuss other concepts, e.g. process mining. In this process, there were some papers on the border line. Regarding these, we made the decision to include rather than to exclude them to ensure the review comprehensive. As a result of the refinement process, a total of 163 papers were selected for analysis.

Analysis of Selected Papers. At this stage, we analyzed the selected papers regarding their main concepts and relationships. The analysis consisted of three steps. First, we extracted concepts and relationships relevant to process flexibility. Second, we synthesized duplicated concepts, such as 'process variant', variability, and 'versioning variant'. Third, we extracted relationships among concepts, including relationships from existing taxonomies and sub-concept relationships by mapping the main concepts and their sub-concepts. The analysis results are presented in the next section.

4   Results

4.1   Main Concepts of Process Flexibility

We now report the results from the review analysis, starting with the most popular concepts of process flexibility. We identified concepts and sub-concepts recommended by multiple reviewed papers. We also note that the concept definitions and suggested relationships between concepts and sub-concepts may vary across the reviewed papers. In these cases, we chose the definitions and relationships adopted by the majority of sources. As a result, Table 1 presents 43 (sub) concepts identified in the reviewed papers.

At a high level, Table 1 reveals four main groups of concepts related to process flexibility: business contexts characterizing process flexibility, case management, dynamic BPM, and mechanisms to manage process flexibility. Within these groups, Table 1 presents main concepts, sub-concepts, their (simplified) definition, and selected papers supporting them.

Table 1 reveals a variety of concepts and sub-concepts suggested by the literature. It also provides descriptive textual definitions for these concepts, which contribute to the understanding of the research area. Here, we aligning with Mejri et al. [1] and suggest that the understanding can be further enhanced by structuring the concepts in a semantic way. This is the focus of the next section.

4.2 Preliminary Ontology of Process Flexibility

We structure the identified salient concepts as an ontology of process flexibility. We position our ontology as 'preliminary' as we understand that given the same group of concepts, different structures of the ontology could be proposed. Given that, we conducted a trial-and-error process in order to structure the identified concepts. We tried different structures (e.g. layer structure, tree structure, and radial structure) and found that the radial structure is suitable to represent the ontology. The radial structure enables us to center the concept of process flexibility around other related concepts, and thus it is suitable to provide a holistic view on the research area. Further, it demonstrates a logical connection to the four main groups of concepts (identified in Table 1), and thus reduces complexity by arranging sub-concepts into these groups. The results of the structuring process are presented in Fig. 3.

Figure 3 represents a preliminary ontology of process flexibility, which is structured into four groups of concepts. Overall, the ontology should be viewed from-inner-to-outer, which highlights four key concepts: business context, case management, mechanisms to manage flexibility, and dynamic BPM. Business context refers to the contextualization of business practice, where unexpected and unforeseeable changes in business contexts increase the needs for flexible processes. Analyzing business contexts enables us to understand aspects of flexibility, degree of flexibility, context changes, and event-driven changes in business processes (upper left-hand side of Fig. 3). We note that in analyzing business contexts, Reichert and Weber [6] highlight four flexibility aspects: variability, looseness, adaptation, and evolution (see Table 1 for definitions of these aspects).

Case management forms another important group of concepts in the ontology (upper right-hand side of Fig. 3). It represents different instances of adaptive and emergent cases that are executed for specific goals [57]. Adaptive cases are standard cases with certain features that enable them to be adapted by knowledge workers [43]. Emerging cases are new ad-hoc cases, which can be dynamically defined and re-defined by the knowledge

Table 1. Main concepts of process flexibility

Main concepts	Sub-concepts/dimensions	Definition from literature	Selected papers
Business context			
Aspects of flexibility		Different aspects that should be analyzed from a business context in order to manage flexibility. Four aspects are identified: variability, adaptation, looseness, and evolution	[1, 3, 6, 40]
	Variability	Manage flexible processes by deriving variants from the same workflow	[3, 6, 40]
	Adaptation	Manages flexible processes by handling occasional unforeseen changes at run-time without changing the standard workflow	[3, 6]
	Looseness	Manages flexible processes by handling run-time workflow without knowing the standard workflow	[3, 6]
	Evolution	Manage flexible processes by permanently modifying the workflow	[3, 6]
Degree of flexibility		Number of changes that have to be performed, which learns from a process model and a collection of its process variants	[11]
Context changes		Changes of context that are captured in the business environment	[28]
Event driven BPM		Events produced by the system are processed and eventually abstracted to generate high-level information about the situational status of the system	[41]

(*continued*)

Table 1. (*continued*)

Main concepts	Sub-concepts/dimensions	Definition from literature	Selected papers
	Real-time business events	Events originating from the real-time execution of a business process	[41]
	Real-time decision support	Real-time support that can be generated from high-level information about the situational status of the system	[42]
	Event driven process chains	Event-centric modelling language that treats events as fundamental elements of the business process	[6]
Case management			
Adaptive case management		Case management has features that allow processes to be adapted at run time by knowledge workers	[43]
	Flexibility knowledge intensive	The status and availability of knowledge that drives decision making and influences the flow of actions and events	[3]
	Collaboration oriented	Process creation, management and execution occurs in a collaborative multi-user environment	[3]
	Goal orientation	The process evolves through a series of intermediate goals or milestones to be achieved	[3]
	Business rules	Business rules control the behaviour of business processes regarding the adaptive cases	[3]
	High skills	Adaptive cases that require incorporating personal skills, experience, and collective judgment in the processes	[44]

(*continued*)

Table 1. (*continued*)

Main concepts	Sub-concepts/dimensions	Definition from literature	Selected papers
	Unpredictability	Case depends on situation and context-specific elements that may not be known a priori, may change during process execution, and may vary over different process cases	[44]
Emergent case management		An approach for the bottom-up managing of ad-hoc processes. The goal is to enable users to assign activities to a certain case, which can be dynamically defined by knowledge workers	[45]
	Collaborative tasks	A collaborative execution of certain process in whose execution at least two organizations/parties are involved	[45]
	Communicative tasks	Tasks that at least two organizations/parties need to communicate in order to operate the tasks	[45]
Dynamic BPM			
Collaborative modelling		A process where a number of people/users actively contribute to the creation of a process model	[46]
	Participate discover	Joint learning and mutual discovery are key for building consensus	[47]
End-user changes		Letting end users tailor business processes can result in business process management that may be better tuned to users' needs and organizational changes	[48]

(*continued*)

Table 1. (*continued*)

Main concepts	Sub-concepts/dimensions	Definition from literature	Selected papers
Model as you go		An approach to model a subject-oriented business process by enabling the process actors to record their subject communication and internal behaviour, just in time while they execute the process instance	[49]
	Structuredness	A state of a business process being structured, when the way to reach the output is well define	[49]
	Visibility	Process workers should collaborate with each other via discussions, wikis, documents, i.e. complete visibility of the collaboration	[49]
	Adaptation	The ability to create, store and edit model as it proceeds, enables adaptive approaches	[49]
Adaptive modelling languages		Multiple modelling languages that enable adaptive business processes	[3, 28]
Process stories		Process stories use a combination of textual and visual elements to model business processes	[2, 50]
Mechanisms to manage flexibility			
Design-time		Mechanisms to manage flexibility at design-time, which refers to the process design phase in the business process life cycle	[3, 6]
	Process-aware information systems	Information systems that provide dynamic and flexible support for business processes	[6, 51]

(*continued*)

Table 1. (*continued*)

Main concepts	Sub-concepts/dimensions	Definition from literature	Selected papers
	Pre-modelled	Define the expected flexibility requirements at build-time and apply them at run-time	[52]
	Well-defined adaptation - Rule-based - Case-based - Process-based	Well-defined adaptation allows self-adaptation of processes whose process model is completely known at design-time. Three main types of well-defined adaptations are rule-based, case-based, and process-based approaches	[53]
	Ill-defined adaptation - Late binding - Late modelling	Ill-defined adaptation allows adaptation of processes not known, or incompletely known, at design-time. Two main types of ill-defined adaptation are late binding and late modelling	[53]
Run-time		Mechanisms to manage flexibility at run-time, which consider the process implementation and enactment phases in the business process life cycle	[3, 6]
	Adaptive process modelling	Adaptive variant modelling enables the definition of a main process model with context-specific variants	[54]
	Ad hoc BPM (emergent process)	An unstructured process that is not predictable. It depends on external factors outside the control of the process	[54]
	Exception handling	Emerging exceptions hinder a predefined business process to be executed as expected	[54]

(continued)

Table 1. (*continued*)

Main concepts	Sub-concepts/dimensions	Definition from literature	Selected papers
	Fragments - Rules - Notation enhancements - Dynamic changes	A business process fragment is a connected, reusable sub-process that captures incomplete business rules and knowledge. Fragments relate to three sub-concepts: 1) Rules to avoid duplication of semantics of the patterns, 2) Notation enhance refers to BPM notation yet extended by exception handling on fragment-level, 3) Dynamic changes to insert new activities into a process instance.	[52, 55]
Flexible BPM		While the BPM objective stays the same, the BPM procedures change from time to time, and from one execution to another at run-time	[1, 54]
	Change execution paths	Alternative execution paths are defined at design time and the most appropriate execution path can be selected and operated at runtime for each process instance	[56]
	Declarative approaches	Describe activities that can be performed and use a set of constraints, like precedence or non-coexistence, to exclude undesired behaviours	[9]

workers [45]. Through the adaptive and emergent instances, case management captures process knowledge that may be subsequently reused.

The ontology also presents several mechanisms to manage flexibility (lower left-hand side of Fig. 3). By and large, the mechanisms to manage flexibility can be classified

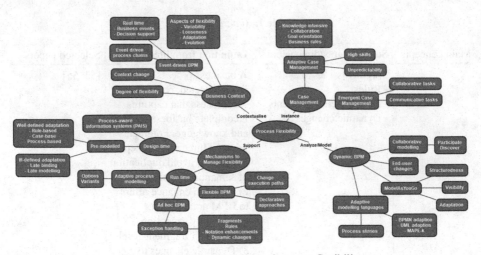

Fig. 3. Preliminary ontology of process flexibility

into two main categories: design-time and run-time [3, 6, 17]. Mechanisms to manage flexibility at design time aim to identify process deviations in the process model, which can then be applied at run-time. Examples include pre-modelled mechanisms like rule-based, case-based, and process-based approaches [52], which can be supported by process-aware information systems [51]. Mechanisms to manage flexibility at run time manage flexibility at implementation and operation times. Examples include exception handling, ad-hoc process management [54], and using business process fragments [52, 55].

Finally, the ontology presents concepts related to dynamic BPM (lower right-hand side of Fig. 3), which highlight modelling techniques used to analyze, model, and operate flexible processes. Common techniques include collaborative modelling, end-user ad hoc changes, model as you go, and adaptive modeling languages [48, 49]. Adaptive modelling languages can be further classified into two categories: prescriptive languages and process stories. Prescriptive languages define a structured set of essential process elements (e.g. events, activities, actors, and their interdependencies). Exemplars include BPMN adaptation, UML adaptation, and UML MAPE-k [3, 28]. Process stories combines textual and visual elements to model business processes [2, 50].

5   Discussion and Conclusion

There has been an ongoing research interest on process flexibility to deal with rapidly changing business contexts. Researchers have studied different aspects of process flexibility from a variety of viewpoints, which challenges common understanding on the research area [2, 26]. In this study, we review and structure knowledge reported in individual studies to identify the main concepts and relationships involved in process flexibility (Table 1). The identified concepts and relationships are then structured into a preliminary ontology (Fig. 3).

Considering the need to structure knowledge in the research area, several process flexibility taxonomies have already been proposed [3, 6, 7, 17, 28]. However, our ontology extends the scope of existing taxonomies. On the one hand, our ontology captures many concepts and relationships found in other taxonomies, in particular Reichert and Weber's [6] and Cognini's et al. [3]. This increases the confidence in our results and at the same time extends the existing works. On the other hand, our ontology reveals additional (sub) concepts and relationships, which enable a more systematic and comprehensive understanding of the research area.

Our study is also useful from a practical perspective. In particular, our ontology structures concepts in groups (Fig. 3). To some extent, these groups enable organizations to better understand and manage process flexibility considering four facets: why, where, what, and how. In particular, the business context group highlights aspects justifying why organizations should manage process flexibility. The case management group suggests instances where process flexibility can be applied. The group of mechanisms to approach process flexibility highlights how to manage process flexibility. And finally, the dynamic BPM highlights what mechanisms can be used to analyze, model, design, and manage process flexibility.

We believe that these four facets help organizations to better understand and thus improve process flexibility. For instance, organizations may realize that they can manage process flexibility through design-time and run-time mechanisms (lower left-hand side of Fig. 3). They can further identify and choose different BPM mechanisms to analyze, model, and manage process flexibility (lower right-hand side of Fig. 3). In short, the ontology can be used as a blueprint by organizations aiming to improve their process flexibility.

We note certain limitations of this study and suggest some directions for future research. First, we understand the risk of synthesizing ontological elements from different studies conducted in diverse contexts and using diverse viewpoints. To address this risk, future work should further explore multi and trans-disciplinary viewpoints on process flexibility. Second, we position our ontology as 'preliminary'. Future work is required to empirically evaluate the ontology. Third and finally, we also plan to apply the ontology in the field, e.g. in decision-making support, and case studies to assess its practical utility.

Acknowledgement. We would like to thank Nguyen Quoc Hung for his research assistance.

References

1. Mejri, A., Ghannouchi, S.A., Martinho, R.: Representing business process flexibility using concept maps. Procedia Comput. Sci. **100**, 1260–1268 (2016)
2. Antunes, P., Tate, M., Pino, J.A.: Business processes and flexibility: a theoretical perspective. In: Australasian Conference on Information Systems, Perth, Western Australia (2019)
3. Cognini, R., et al.: Business process flexibility-a systematic literature review with a software systems perspective. Inf. Syst. Front. **20**(2), 343–371 (2018)
4. Anastassiu, M., et al.: The quest for organizational flexibility: driving changes in business processes through the identification of relevant context. Bus. Process Manage. J. **22**, 763–790 (2016)

5. Hinkelmann, K.: Business process flexibility and decision-aware modeling—the knowledge work designer. In: Karagiannis, D., Mayr, H., Mylopoulos, J. (eds.) Domain-Specific Conceptual Modeling, pp. 397–414. Springer, Cham (2016). https://doi.org/10.1007/978-3-319-39417-6_18

6. Reichert, M., Weber, B.: Enabling Flexibility in Process-Aware Information Systems: Challenges, Methods, Technologies. Springer, Heidelberg (2012). https://doi.org/10.1007/978-3-642-30409-5

7. Schonenberg, H., Mans, R., Russell, N., Mulyar, N., van der Aalst, W.: Process flexibility: a survey of contemporary approaches. In: Dietz, Jan L.G., Albani, A., Barjis, J. (eds.) CIAO!/EOMAS - 2008. LNBIP, vol. 10, pp. 16–30. Springer, Heidelberg (2008). https://doi.org/10.1007/978-3-540-68644-6_2

8. Lukyanenko, R., Parsons, J., Samuel, B.M.: Representing instances: the case for reengineering conceptual modelling grammars. Eur. J. Inf. Syst. 28(1), 68–90 (2019)

9. Andaloussi, A.A., et al.: On the declarative paradigm in hybrid business process representations: a conceptual framework and a systematic literature study. Inf. Syst. 91, 101505 (2020)

10. Harmon, P.: Business Process Change: A Business Process Management Guide for Managers and Process Professionals. Morgan Kaufmann, Burlington (2019)

11. Mejri, A.: A quantitative approach for measuring the degree of flexibility of business process models. Bus. Process Manage. J. 24(4), 1023–1049 (2018)

12. Reichert, M.: Enabling flexible and robust business process automation for the agile enterprise. In: Gruhn, V., Striemer, R. (eds.) The Essence of Software Engineering, pp. 203–220. Springer, Cham (2018). https://doi.org/10.1007/978-3-319-73897-0_12

13. Gruber, T.R.: A translation approach to portable ontology specifications. Knowl. Acquis. 5(2), 199–220 (1993)

14. Osterwalder, A.: The business model ontology: A proposition in a design science approach. Institut d'Informatique et Organisation. Lausanne, Switzerland, University of Lausanne, Ecole des Hautes Etudes Commerciales HEC (2004)

15. Ostrowski, L., Helfert, M., Gama, N.: Ontology engineering step in design science research methodology: a technique to gather and reuse knowledge. Behav. Inf. Technol. 33(5), 443–451 (2014)

16. Thuan, N.H.: Business Process Crowdsourcing. PI. Springer, Cham (2019). https://doi.org/10.1007/978-3-319-91391-9

17. Schonenberg, H., et al.: Towards a taxonomy of process flexibility. In: CAiSE Forum (2008)

18. Regev, G., Soffer, P., Schmidt, R.: Taxonomy of flexibility in business processes. In: BPMDS 2006, vol. 236 (2006)

19. Nurdiani, I., Börstler, J., Fricker, S.A.: Literature review of flexibility attributes: a flexibility framework for software developing organization. J. Softw. Evol. Process 30(9), e1937 (2018)

20. Nickerson, R.C., Varshney, U., Muntermann, J.: A method for taxonomy development and its application in information systems. Eur. J. Inf. Syst. 22(3), 336–359 (2012)

21. Corcho, O., López, M.F., Gómez-Pérez, A.: Methodologies, tools and languages for building ontologies. Where is their meeting point? Data Knowl. Eng. 46(1), 41–64 (2003)

22. Paré, G., et al.: Synthesizing information systems knowledge: a typology of literature reviews. Inf. Manage. 52, 183–199 (2015)

23. Thuan, N.H., et al.: Building an enterprise ontology of business process crowdsourcing: a design science approach. In: PACIS 2015 Proceedings. AISeL (2015). **Paper 112**

24. Reichert, M., Hallerbach, A., Bauer, T.: Lifecycle management of business process variants. In: vom Brocke, J., Rosemann, M. (eds.) Handbook on Business Process Management 1. IHIS, pp. 251–278. Springer, Heidelberg (2015). https://doi.org/10.1007/978-3-642-45100-3_11

25. vom Brocke, J., Zelt, S., Schmiedel, T.: On the role of context in business process management. Int. J. Inf. Manage. **36**(3), 486–495 (2016)
26. Alter, M.J.: Science of Flexibility. Human Kinetics, Champaign (2004)
27. Boffoli, N., et al.: Driving flexibility and consistency of business processes by means of product-line engineering and decision tables. In: 2012 3rd International Workshop on Product LinE Approaches in Software Engineering (PLEASE). IEEE (2012)
28. Hidri, W., et al.: A Meta-model for context-aware adaptive business process as a service in collaborative cloud environment. Procedia Comput. Sci. **164**, 177–186 (2019)
29. Weber, B., Reichert, M., Rinderle, S.: Change patterns and change support features – enhancing flexibility in process-aware information systems. Data Knowl. Eng. **66**(3), 438–466 (2008)
30. Schnieders, A., Puhlmann, F.: Variability mechanisms in e-business process families. In: Business Information Systems–9th International Conference on Business Information Systems, BIS 2006. Gesellschaft für Informatik Ev (2006)
31. Fonseca, F., Martin, J.: Learning the differences between ontologies and conceptual schemas through ontology-driven information systems. J. Assoc. Inf. Syst. **8**(2) (2007). Article 2
32. Wand, Y., Weber, R.: On the deep structure of information systems. Inf. Syst. J. **5**(3), 203–223 (1995)
33. Guo, T., et al.: Codifying collaborative knowledge: using Wikipedia as a basis for automated ontology learning. Knowl. Manage. Res. Pract. **7**(3), 206–217 (2009)
34. Wong, W., Liu, W., Bennamoun, M.: Ontology learning from text: a look back and into the future. ACM Comput. Surv. (CSUR) **44**(4) (2012). Article 20
35. Kumar, K., Narasipuram, M.M.: Defining requirements for business process flexibility. BPMDS **6**, 137–148 (2006)
36. Soffer, P.: On the notion of flexibility in business processes. In: Proceedings of the CAiSE (2005)
37. Snowdon, R.A., et al.: On the architecture and form of flexible process support. Softw. Process Improv. Pract. **12**(1), 21–34 (2007)
38. Okoli, C.: A guide to conducting a standalone systematic literature review. Commun. Assoc. Inf. Syst. **37**(1) (2015). Article 43
39. Webster, J., Watson, R.T.: Analyzing the past to prepare for the future: writing a literature review. MIS Q. **26**(2), xiii–xxiii (2002)
40. Shishkov, B., Mendling, J.: Business process variability and public values. In: Shishkov, B. (ed.) BMSD 2018. LNBIP, vol. 319, pp. 401–411. Springer, Cham (2018). https://doi.org/10.1007/978-3-319-94214-8_31
41. Alexopoulou, N., Nikolaidou, M., Anagnostopoulos, D., Martakos, D.: An event-driven modeling approach for dynamic human-intensive business processes. In: Rinderle-Ma, S., Sadiq, S., Leymann, F. (eds.) BPM 2009. LNBIP, vol. 43, pp. 393–404. Springer, Heidelberg (2010). https://doi.org/10.1007/978-3-642-12186-9_37
42. Nunes, V.T., Werner, C.M.L., Santoro, F.M.: Dynamic process adaptation: a context-aware approach. In: Proceedings of the 2011 15th International Conference on Computer Supported Cooperative Work in Design (CSCWD). IEEE (2011)
43. Marcinkowski, B., Gawin, B.: A study on the adaptive approach to technology-driven enhancement of multi-scenario business processes. Inf. Technol. People **32**, 118–146 (2019)
44. Di Ciccio, C., Marrella, A., Russo, A.: Knowledge-intensive processes: characteristics, requirements and analysis of contemporary approaches. J. Data Seman. **4**(1), 29–57 (2015)
45. Böhringer, M.: Emergent case management for ad-hoc processes: a solution based on microblogging and activity streams. In: zur Muehlen, M., Su, J. (eds.) BPM 2010. LNBIP, vol. 66, pp. 384–395. Springer, Heidelberg (2011). https://doi.org/10.1007/978-3-642-20511-8_36

46. Rittgen, P.: IT support in collaborative modelling of business processes–a comparative experiment. Int. J. Organ. Des. Eng. 1(1–2), 98–108 (2010)
47. Cardwell, H.E., Langsdale, S.: Collaborative modeling for decision support—definitions and next steps. In: World Environmental and Water Resources Congress 2011: Bearing Knowledge for Sustainability (2011)
48. Schiffner, S., Rothschädl, T., Meyer, N.: Towards a subject-oriented evolutionary business information system. In: 2014 IEEE 18th International Enterprise Distributed Object Computing Conference Workshops and Demonstrations. IEEE (2014)
49. Gottanka, R., Meyer, N.: ModelAsYouGo: (re-) design of S-BPM process models during execution time. In: Stary, C. (ed.) S-BPM ONE 2012. LNBIP, vol. 104, pp. 91–105. Springer, Heidelberg (2012). https://doi.org/10.1007/978-3-642-29133-3_7
50. Antunes, P., Pino, J.A., Tate, M., Barros, A.: eliciting process knowledge through process stories. Inf. Syst. Front. 22(5), 1179–1201 (2019). https://doi.org/10.1007/s10796-019-099 22-0
51. Dumas, M., La Rosa, M., Mendling, J., Reijers, H.A.: Process-aware information systems. In: Fundamentals of Business Process Management, pp. 341–369. Springer, Heidelberg (2018). https://doi.org/10.1007/978-3-662-56509-4_9
52. Bauer, T.: Pre-modelled flexibility for business processes. In: ICEIS, vol. 2 (2019)
53. Oukharijane, J., et al.: A survey of self-adaptive business processes. In: International Business Information Management Association Conference, Seville, Spain (2018)
54. Geist, V., et al.: Towards functional safety and security for adaptive and flexible business processes. J. Softw. Evol. Process 30(5), e1952 (2018)
55. Andree, K., Ihde, S., Pufahl, L.: Exception handling in the context of fragment-based case management. In: Nurcan, S., Reinhartz-Berger, I., Soffer, P., Zdravkovic, J. (eds.) BPMDS/EMMSAD -2020. LNBIP, vol. 387, pp. 20–35. Springer, Cham (2020). https://doi. org/10.1007/978-3-030-49418-6_2
56. Martinho, R., Domingos, D., Varajão, J.: CF4BPMN: a BPMN extension for controlled flexibility in business processes. Procedia Comput. Sci. 64, 1232–1239 (2015)
57. Marin, M.A., Hauder, M., Matthes, F.: Case management: an evaluation of existing approaches for knowledge-intensive processes. In: Reichert, M., Reijers, Hajo A. (eds.) BPM 2015. LNBIP, vol. 256, pp. 5–16. Springer, Cham (2016). https://doi.org/10.1007/978-3-319-428 87-1_1

Sentential Semantic Dependency Parsing for Vietnamese

Tuyen Thi-Thanh Do[1(✉)] and Dang Tuan Nguyen[2(✉)]

[1] University of Information Technology, VNU-HCM, Ho Chi Minh City, Vietnam
tuyendtt@uit.edu.vn
[2] Saigon University, Ho Chi Minh City, Vietnam
dangnt@sgu.edu.vn

Abstract. Semantic dependency parse is the dependency graph of a sentence. This graph shows the grammatical dependencies between words in a sentence clearer than the dependency parse because it allows one word possibly be the dependant in two or more dependencies in a sentence. Therefore, it has been used to represent the meaning of a sentence. In order to represent the meaning of a sentence in Vietnamese, a method of parsing the sentence into semantic dependencies is proposed in this paper. This rule-based method transforms the result of Vietnamese dependency parser by using semantic constraints existing in a lexicon ontology called VLO. The test result shows that the proposed method can capture more dependencies than the state-of-the-art Vietnamese dependency parser with the precisions respectively being 0.5328 and 0.3113.

Keywords: Semantic dependency parsing · Rule-based dependency parsing · Semantic representation · Lexicon ontology

1 Introduction

Semantic dependency parse (SDP) is similar to dependency parse (DP) [1] except that it is a graph instead of a tree. It has been used to represent the semantic of the sentence [2–4] because it is able to represent more dependencies of a sentence than DP. Therefore, the semantic of a sentence can be identified by parsing the sentence into SDP. At this time, the state-of-the-art Vietnamese dependency parser [5] (D-Parser) can parse a Vietnamese sentence into DP. A research question is how to transform a DP into a SDP in order to identify the semantic of a Vietnamese sentence. Figure 1 shows the differences between the DP and the SDP of the same Vietnamese sentence *"Hayes và Lighthill đã đề xuất một mô hình vật lý"* (*"Hayes and Lighthill have proposed a physic model"*).

The sentential semantic dependency parsing method for Vietnamese is based-on constraints dependency parsing. In this method, transformation rules with semantic constraints are applied to adjust the DP. This paper presents the method in following sections. Section 2 presents backgrounds of semantic dependency parsing in rule-based approach. Section 3 proposes the sentential semantic dependency parsing method for Vietnamese. Section 4 presents the evaluation of the proposed method in comparison with the Vietnamese dependency parsing. Finally, some conclusions and future works are presented in Sect. 5.

© Springer Nature Switzerland AG 2020
T. K. Dang et al. (Eds.): FDSE 2020, LNCS 12466, pp. 429–447, 2020.
https://doi.org/10.1007/978-3-030-63924-2_25

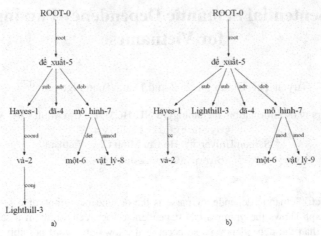

Fig. 1. a) The DP with [5] and b) the SDP of the same Vietnamese sentence

2 Backgrounds

2.1 Semantic Dependency Parsing

Semantic dependency parsing [2, 3] is the task of generating the semantic dependencies between words in a sentence. The types of semantic dependency are defined differently from each representation scheme such as Abstract Meaning Representation [6], Bilexical Semantic Dependency [7] and Universal Dependency [8, 9]. However, they should cover three types of dependency:

1. Predicate argument dependency presents the argument structure of verb in a sentence. There are three subtypes: subject type indicates the relation between a verb and its subject, direct object type indicates the relation between a verb and its object and indirect object type indicates the relation between verb and its indirect object.
2. Modifier dependency presents the relation between a word and its modifiers in a sentence. There are many subtypes of this type such as adjective modifier and adverb modifier [8, 9].
3. Complement dependency presents the relation between a word and its complement in a sentence. There are also many subtypes of this type such as object of preposition and adjective complement [8, 9].

The types of semantic dependency are very similar to types of dependency as in Universal Dependency [8, 9], therefore, semantic dependency parsing can be seen as the extension of dependency parsing which identifies all dependencies in a sentence [10] according to the meaning of the sentence. For example, the DP a) in Fig. 1 contains only one subject type dependency *sub(đề_xuất-5, Hayes-1)* while the SDP b) in Fig. 1 contains two subject type dependencies *sub(đề_xuất-5, Hayes-1)* and *sub(đề_xuất-5, Lighthill-3)* because Hayes and Lighthill are the author of the proposal according to the meaning of the sentence.

Although the semantic representation schemes are different, the semantic dependency parsers (SD-Parser) are very similar. Herschcovich et al. [10, 11] proposed parsers for UCCA scheme, Dozat [12] and Qi [13] proposed parsers for Universal Dependency scheme. These parsers are transition-based parsers trained on appropriate semantic dependency graphbanks. These graphbanks can be built on scratch or converted from dependency treebanks [4]. The converting task has to ensure that the converted dependencies satisfy the semantic constraints between words in the sentence in the way of Head-driven Phrase Structure Grammar [14, 15]. This is the problem that Schuster [4] has left to future works.

2.2 Semantic Constraints

Words of the same syntactic category may have different combinations in a phrase or in a sentence because of semantic constraints. In the example of Schuster [4], the sentence *"the store buys and sells cameras"* imply that *"cameras"* is the object of *"buys"* and *"sells"* while the sentence *"she was reading or watching a movie"* show that *"a movie"* is the object of *"watching"* only. The two example sentences show that two identical syntactic structure sentence may have different semantic dependency structures because the different words have different semantic constraints. In this case, *"buys cameras"*, *"sells cameras"* and *"watching a movies"* satisfy the semantic constraints while *"reading a movie"* is not.

Head-driven Phrase Structure Grammar (HPSG) [14, 15] is a framework to ensure the semantic constraints in sentence parse. In HPSG, every lexicon is represented in a syntactic and semantic combined structure, called Typed Feature Structure (TFS), in which syntactic and semantic constraints are explicitly showed. The parser uses respective TFSs to decide which words are able to combine together and the head (governor) among them. In order to define the TFS, an ontological category [15] containing semantic labels is needed to specify the sense of every word. These senses are the core of semantic constraints.

3 Semantic Dependency Parser

The approach of this paper is to define rules to transform the DPs of Vietnamese D-Parser [5] into SDPs because of these following reasons:

1. At present, there are not any large Vietnamese graphbanks to train a SD-Parser.
2. The SDP can be generated from DP [4] if there are semantic constraints to confirm the validity of semantic dependencies.
3. Utilizing the Vietnamese D-Parser [5] to reduce the cost of building a SD-Parser from scratch.
4. The transformation process can be apply to build large graphbanks from Vietnamese dependency treebanks [16] in order to train SD-Parser with deep learning models.

In SDP of Vietnamese sentence, there are five types of dependency *hasActor*, *has-DObj*, *hasIDObj*, *hasPComp* and *hasMod*. These dependency types has corresponding relations described in Vietnamese Lexicon Ontology (VLO) described below. All types of dependency of UD except conjunct dependency can be converted into these types with a mapping table. Similarly, all types of dependency used in Vietnamese D-Parser can be converted into five types of dependency by using Table 1.

Table 1. Mapping from types of dependency used in [5] to types of semantic dependency

Ord.	Types of dependency used in [5]	Types of semantic dependency
1	All types of dependency except the below types of dependency	*hasMod*
2	pob	*hasPComp*
3	sub	*hasActor*
4	dob	*hasDObj*
5	idob	*hasIDObj*

We use only the five types of dependency in SDP for two reasons. First, they can present all important relation between word senses in a sentence without losing the semantic of the dependencies. Second, a small number of dependency label is better for annotating graphbanks and parsing.

In order to parse Vietnamese sentence to SDP, we need an ontological category to define lexicon semantic of Vietnamese words and the semantic constraints to ensure the validity of every semantic dependency.

3.1 Vietnamese Lexicon Ontology

Vietnamese Lexicon Ontology (VLO) [17] is an ontology of word senses as demonstrated in Fig. 2. In VLO, individuals are word senses and similar senses are grouped into classes, called semantic classes. VLO is used as ontological category in HPSG [15] as following:

- Semantic classes are used to annotate the meaning of words instead of word senses in computation process because the number of word senses is noticeably larger than of the annotating semantic classes. In Fig. 2, the two words "*rượt*" (chase, dialect of South Vietnam) and "*đuổi*" (chase, dialect of North Vietnam) are annotated by semantic class "*Đuổi*" although their senses respectively are "*w_Rượt*" and "*w_Đuổi*".
- The relations between semantic classes, which are inferred from relations between respective word senses, are semantic constraints. In the latest version of VLO, there are eight important types of relation which cover the verb frame dependencies, conjunction dependency, modifier dependencies and complement dependencies:

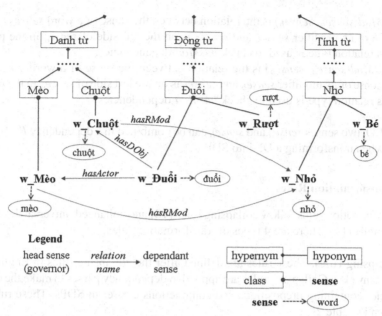

Fig. 2. The demonstration of VLO containing words, word senses, semantic classes and relations (semantic constraints) of the sentence *"mèo nhỏ đuổi chuột nhỏ"* (*"a small cat chases a small mouse"*)

- *hasActor(sense$_a$, sense$_b$)* is the relation between the sense of verb *sense$_a$* and the sense of its subject *sense$_b$*.
- *hasDObj(sense$_a$, sense$_b$)* is the relation between the sense of verb *sense$_a$* and the sense of its direct object *sense$_b$*.
- *hasIDObj(sense$_a$, sense$_b$)* is the relation between the sense of verb *sense$_a$* and the sense of its indirect object *sense$_b$*.
- *hasConj(sense$_a$, sense$_b$)* is the relation indicate that *sense$_a$* and *sense$_b$* have the same category. There are 6 categories are used to confirming *hasConj* relation: nominal (noun, proper noun, pronoun), verb, adjective, adverb, preposition and number.
- *hasPComp(sense$_a$, sense$_b$)* is the relation between the sense of a word *sense$_a$* and the sense of its complement *sense$_b$* and *sense$_b$* is on the left side of *sense$_a$* in the phrase. This type of relation can be seen as the super class of all types of complement dependency where the dependant word is on the left side of head (governor) word. This generalization will not lose the semantic of the dependency because the types of complement dependency are separated by the senses of words in the dependencies [8, 9] while *hasPComp* is established on two senses. This relation type is used to check *hasPComp* dependencies
- *hasRPComp(sense$_a$, sense$_b$)* is the relation between the sense of a word *sense$_a$* and the sense of its complement *sense$_b$* and *sense$_b$* is on the right side of *sense$_a$* in the phrase. This relation type is used to check *hasPComp* dependencies.

- *hasMod(sense_a, sense_b)* is the relation between the sense of a word *sense_a* and the sense of its modifier *sense_b* and *sense_b* is on the left side of *sense_a* in the phrase. This relation type is used to check *hasMod* dependencies.
- *hasRMod(sense_a, sense_b)* is the relation between the sense of a word *sense_a* and the sense of its modifier *sense_b* and *sense_b* is on the left side of *sense_a* in the phrase. This relation type is used to check *hasMod* dependencies.

In VLO, two senses *sense_a* and *sense_b* can be combined in a dependency *Rel(sense_a, sense_b)* when transforming a DP into SDP.

3.2 Transformation Rules

The transformation rules follow collapsing rules [18] and enhanced universal dependencies in English [4]. There are 4 types of transformation rules:

1. **Collapsing rules.** These rules are defined after the collapsing rules in English and Germany [18]. Collapsing rules are applied to dependency parses to make the dependencies containing prepositions and conjunctions clearer in SDPs. These rules are shown in Table 2.

   The results of applying collapsing rules in dependency parses are shown in Fig. 3 and Fig. 4.

2. **Adjusting dependency label and head.** There are dependencies with wrong dependency label or with wrong head word in DP because there is no the semantic constraints or the restrictions of tree structure in parsing. Rules of this type will correct these errors and they can be divided into three categories:

- **Adjusting modifier verb.** There are dependencies showing that verb is a modifier of a noun but the noun is actually the subject of the verb. In this case, these dependencies are adjusted with the rules in following Algorithm 1.

Table 2. Collapsing rules for Vietnamese DP

Ord.	Dependencies to be converted	Converted dependencies	Examples
Collapsing the object of preposition dependencies			
1	vmod(X,Y), pob(Y,Z)	vmod(X,Z), case(Z,Y)	vmod(*nghiên_cú u-1, về-2*), pob(*về-2, đặc_tính-4*) *collapsed to:* vmod(*nghiên_cú u-1, đặc_tính-4*), case(*đặc_tính-4, về-2*)
2	nmod(X,Y), pob(Y,Z)	nmod(X,Z), case(Z,Y)	nmod(*lý_thuyết-5, cúa-7*), pob(*cúa-7,newton-8*) *collapsed to:* nmod(*lý_thuyết-5, newton-8*) case(*newton-8, cúa-7*)
3	loc(X,Y), pob(Y,Z)	loc(X,Z), case(Z,Y)	loc(*góc-11, ó-12*), pob(*ó-12,đinh-13*) *collapsed to:* loc(*góc-11, đinh-13*) case(*đinh-13, ó-12*)
Collapsing the coord dependencies			
4	coord(X,Y), conj(Y,Z)	conj(X,Z), cc(Z,Y)	coord(*lụ c-16,và-19*), conj(*và-19,mômen-21*) *collapsed to:* conj(*lụ c-16,mômen-21*) cc(*mômen-21, và-19*)
Collapsing the dependencies of passive voice verb			
The word "*đuọc*" and "*bị*" ("*be*") are denoted by *wpass*			
5	R(U,wpass), R_i(wpass,X), vmod(wpass,Y)	R(U,Y), R_i(Y, X), vmod(Y, wpass)	root(*ROOT, đuọc-3*) sub(*đuọc-3, năng_luọng-1*), adv(*đuọc-3, có_thể-2*), vmod(*đuọc-3,giai_phóng-4*) *collapsed to:* root(*ROOT,giai_phóng-4*) sub(*giai_phóng-4, năng_luọng-1*), adv(*giai_phóng-4, có_thể-2*), vmod(*giai_phóng-4, đuọc-3*)

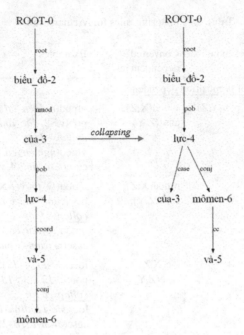

Fig. 3. Collapsing the object of preposition dependency and the coord dependency in DP of the phrase *"biểu đồ của lự c và mômen"* (*"the chart of force and moment"*)

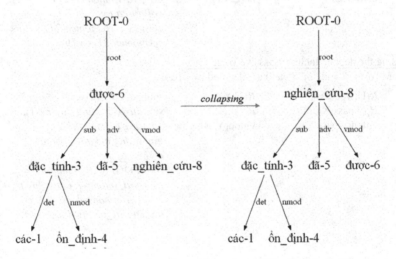

Fig. 4. Collapsing the dependency of passive voice verb (*nghiên_cứ u-8*) in DP of the sentence *"các đặc tính ổn định đã đượ c nghiên cứ u"* (*"the stable characteristics were studied"*)

Algorithm 1. Adjusting modifier verb
Input:

- dependency $R(w_i, w_j)$
- noun w_i, verb w_j,
- $sense_i$ and $sense_j$ are respectively word sense of w_i and w_j,
- i and j are word indices in the phrase or sentence.
- *VLO* containing semantic constraints

Output: dependency $Rs(A, B)$ is adjusted from $R(w_i, w_j)$

```
Rs ← R, A ← wᵢ, B ← wⱼ
if (i < j)
  if (wⱼ is passive)
  if (hasIDObj(senseⱼ, senseᵢ)∈VLO)
    Rs ← iob, A ← wⱼ, B ← wᵢ
  else
    if (hasDObj(senseⱼ, senseᵢ)∈VLO)
      Rs ← dob, A ← wⱼ, B ← wᵢ
  else
    if (hasDObj(senseⱼ, senseᵢ)∈VLO)
    Rs ← dob, A ← wⱼ, B ← wᵢ
  else
    if (hasIDObj(senseⱼ, senseᵢ)∈VLO)
      Rs ← iob, A ← wⱼ, B ← wᵢ
else
  if (wⱼ is passive)
  if (hasDObj(senseⱼ, senseᵢ)∈VLO)
    Rs ← dob, A ← wⱼ, B ← wᵢ
  else
    if (hasIDObj(senseⱼ, senseᵢ)∈VLO)
      Rs ← iob, A ← wⱼ, B ← wᵢ
  else
    if (hasActor(senseⱼ, senseᵢ)∈VLO)
    Rs ← sub, A ← wⱼ, B ← wᵢ
```

The result of applying adjusting modifier verb rules to a DP are shown in Fig. 5

- **Adjusting the predicate argument.** Subject dependencies, direct object dependencies and indirect object dependencies in passive voice may be wrong identified because the D-Parser does not have the semantic constraints. Therefore, rules of this type included in the following Algorithm 2 will correct the label of these dependencies.

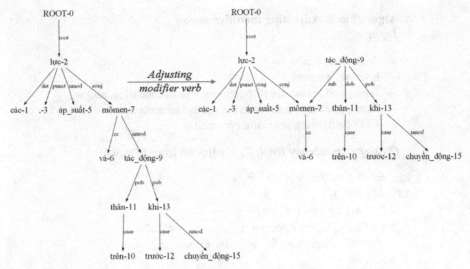

Fig. 5. Adjusting the dependency of modifier verb (*tác_động-9*) in the DP of the sentence "*các lự c, áp suất và mômen tác động trên thân trước khi chuyên động*" ("*the force, pressure and moment impact the body before the motion*")

Algorithm 2. Adjusting the predicate argument
Input:

- dependency $R(w_i, w_j)$,
- verb w_i is passive, nominal w_j,
- *sense_i* and *sense_j* are respectively word sense of w_i and w_j,
- i and j are word indices in the phrase or sentence,
- *VLO* containing semantic constraints.

Output: dependency $Rs(w_i, w_j)$ is adjusted from $R(w_i, w_j)$.

```
Rs ← R
if (i < j and R is dob)
if (hasIDObj(sense_i, sense_j) ∈VLO)
  Rs ← iob
else
  if (hasActor(sense_i, sense_j) ∈VLO)
    Rs ← iob
else
  if (i > j and R is sub)
  if (hasIDObj(sense_i, sense_j) ∈VLO)
    Rs ← iob
  else
    if (hasDObj(sense_i, sense_j) ∈VLO)
      Rs ← dob
```

The result of applying rules of adjusting the predicate argument to a DP are shown in Fig. 6.

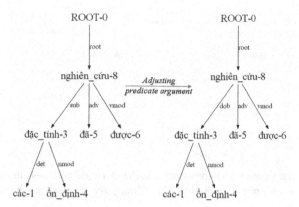

Fig. 6. Adjusting the predicate argument of passive verb (*nghiên_cứu-8*) in the DP of the sentence "*các đặc tính ổn định đã được nghiên cứ u*" ("*the stable characteristics were studied*")

- **Adjusting wrong head dependencies.** Because the D-Parser does not have semantic constraints, the modifier, complement and conjunction dependencies generated may have wrong head or wrong label. The rules of this type will correct these errors with the following Algorithm 3.

Algorithm 3. Adjusting wrong head dependencies
Input:

- dependency parse T,
- dependency $R(w_i, w_j) \notin \text{VLO}$,
- w_i and w_j are arbitrary words
- *sense_i* and *sense_j* are respectively word sense of w_i and w_j,
- i and j are word indices in the phrase or sentence,
- *VLO* containing semantic constraints.

The results of applying rules of adjusting wrong head to a DP are shown in Fig. 7 and Fig. 5. In Fig. 5, the dependency *nmod(lự c-2, áp_suất-5)* was adjusted to *conj(lự c-2, áp_suất-5)*

3. **Adjusting non-projectivity [19] graph.** After adjusting dependencies with the above transformation rules, the dependency graph may be non-projectivity. The rules of this type will correct the dependencies breaking the projectivity constraint with the following Algorithm 4.

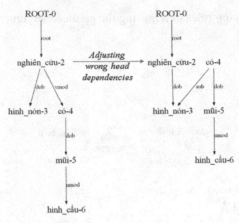

Fig. 7. Adjusting the wrong head dependency *vmod(nghiên_cứu-2, có-4)* in the DP of the sentence *"nghiên cứu hình nón có mũi hình cầu"* (*"study the cone having a modified spherical nose"*)

Output: dependency *Rs(A, B)* is adjusted from *R(w_i, w_j)*.

```
// DPLabel is a function converting semantic dependency
//         label to dependency label
// getSense is a function returning the sense of a word
Rs ← R, A ← w_i, B ← w_j
RSET ← {hasActor, hasDObj, hasIDObj, hasMod, hasRMod,
          hasPComp, hasRPComp, hasConj}
s ← min(i, j), e ← max(i,j)
CLIST ← {w_k|w_k is descendant of w_i in T, k ∈ (s,e)}
for t = i to j
  for Rt in RSET
    if (w_t∈CLIST and Rt(getSense(w_t), sense_j)∈VLO)

      Rs ← DPLabel(Rt), A=w_t, B=w_j
      return

PLIST ← {w_i}
while (PLIST[length(PLIST)] has parent w_k in T)
  PLIST ← append(PLIST, {w_k})
for t = 1 to length(PLIST)
  for Rt in RSET
    if (w_t∈CLIST and Rt(getSense(w_t), sense_j)∈VLO)
      Rs ← DPLabel(Rt), A=w_t, B=w_j
      return
```

The result of applying rules of adjusting non-projectivity graph to the dependency graph in Fig. 8 is shown in Fig. 9.

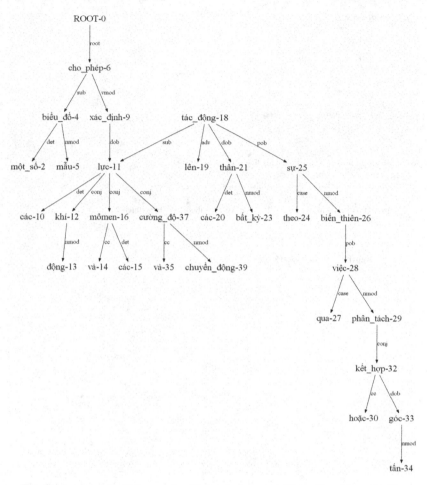

Fig. 8. A non-projectivity graph with dependency *conj(lực c-11, cường_độ-37)*

4. **Expanding dependencies.** The conjunction dependencies do not exist in SDP because they are syntactic dependencies to group words having similar semantic function. The rules of this type will replace the conjunction dependencies with appropriate dependencies with the following Algorithm 5.

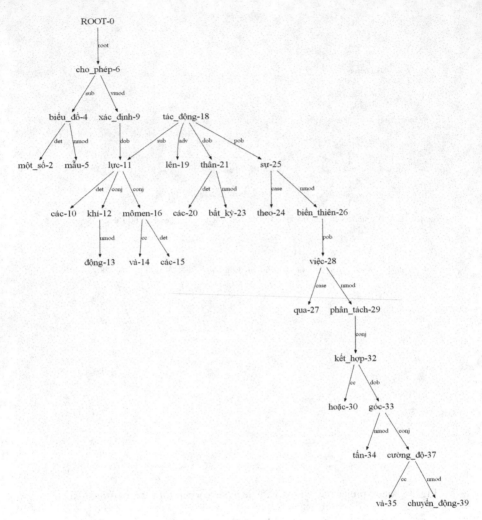

Fig. 9. A projective graph adjusted from the non-projectivity graph in Fig. 8

Algorithm 4. Adjusting non-projectivity graph
Input:

- non-projectivity dependency graph G,
- dependency $R(w_i, w_j)$ breaks the projectivity constraint,
- w_i and w_j are arbitrary words
- $sense_i$ and $sense_j$ are respectively word sense of w_i and w_j,
- i and j are word indices in the phrase or sentence,
- *VLO* containing semantic constraints.

Output: projectivity dependency graph G.

```
wₚ ← an ancestor of wᵢ that i<p<j or i>p>j
RSET ← {hasActor, hasDObj, hasIDObj, hasMod, hasRMod,
          hasPComp, hasRPComp, hasConj}
if (i < p and p < j)
  CLIST ← {wₖ|wₖ is descendant of wᵢ in T, k ∈ (p,j)}
  for t = j to p
    for Rt in RSET\{hasMod, hasPComp}
      if (wₜ∈CLIST and Rt(getSense(wₜ), senseⱼ)∈VLO)
        delete R(wᵢ, wⱼ) from G
        Rs = DPLabel(Rt)
        add Rs(wₜ, wⱼ) to G
        return
if (j < p and p < i)
  CLIST ← {wₖ|wₖ is descendant of wᵢ in T, k ∈ (j,p)}
  for t = j to p
    for Rt in RSET\{hasRMod, hasRPComp}
      if (wₜ∈CLIST and Rt(getSense(wₜ), senseⱼ)∈VLO)
        delete R(wᵢ, wⱼ) from G
        Rs = DPLabel(Rt)
        add Rs(wₜ, wⱼ) to G
        return
```

Algorithm 5. Expanding dependencies
Input:

- dependency graph G,
- *VLO* containing semantic constraints.

Output: expanded dependency graph G.

```
// SDPLabel is a function converting dependency label to
//          semantic dependency label
// getSense is a function returning the sense of a word
for R(wp,wi) in G
PLIST ← {wk|k=p or conj(wp,wk) ∈G}
CLIST ← {wk|k=i or conj(wi,wk) ∈G}
Rs ← SDPLabel(R)
for wk in PLIST
  for wl in CLIST
    if (k≠p and l≠i and (i-p)*(i-k)>0 and
          Rs(wk,wl) ∈VLO)
      add R(wk,wl) to G
```

The results of applying expanding dependencies rules are shown in Fig. 10 và Fig. 11.

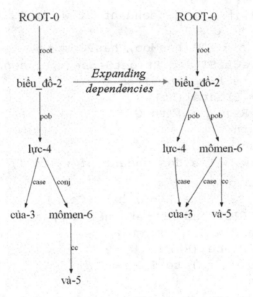

Fig. 10. The result of expanding dependency *conj(lự c-4, mômen-6)* in dependency graph of the phrase *"biểu đồ của lự c và mômen"* (*"the chart of force and moment"*)

3.3 Converting Dependency Label

After applying all transformation rules, the DP is transformed into semantic dependency graph with dependency labels therefore these dependendancy labels have to be replaced with semantic dependency labels by using Table 1.

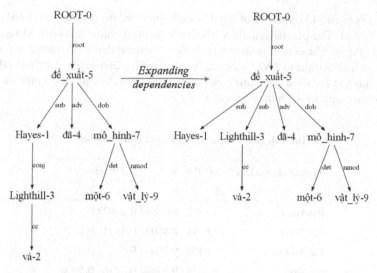

Fig. 11. The result of expanding dependency *conj(Hayes-1, Lighthill-3)* in dependency graph of the sentence *"Hayes và Lighthill đã đề xuất một mô hình vật lý"* (*"Hayes and Lighthill have proposed a physic model"*)

4 Evaluation

4.1 Test Dataset

The test dataset contains 343 sentences manually annotated in SDP. After converting dependency labels of all SDPs, the statistic of dependencies in the test dataset is in Table 3.

Table 3. The statistic of dependencies in test dataset

Type of dependency	Number	Ratio (%)
hasActor	407	5.7
hasDObj	841	11.7
hasIDObj	64	0.9
hasMod	4509	62.7
hasPComp	1363	19.0
Sum	**7184**	**100**

4.2 Evaluation

We implemented a SD-Parser follow Sect. 3 and used it to generate semantic dependency graphs from 343 sentences of the test dataset. Then we used Vietnamese D-Parser [5] to generate DPs from 343 sentences of test data and converted the dependency labels of DPs by using Table 1. The precision and recall of each result is calculated with 343 manually annotated graphs. These results shown in Table 4 indicate that the transformation rules with semantic constraints of VLO are really effective for converting DPs to SDPs with the precision and recall of generating predicate argument dependencies increased 10% to 24% when compare with the result of D-Parser.

Table 4. The results of SD-Parser and D-Parser

Type of dependency	SD-Parser		D-Parser	
	P	R	P	R
hasActor	0.3852	0.4619	0.2492	0.2015
hasDObj	0.6334	0.4602	0.5351	0.2176
hasIDObj	0.6400	0.2500	0	0
hasMod	0.4884	0.5962	0.3736	0.5006
hasPComp	0.4588	0.3925	0	0
Average	**0.5328**	**0.5681**	**0.3113**	**0.3512**

The overall precision and recall of the SD-Parser are only 0.5328 and 0.5681 because the F_1 score of the underlying D-Parser of the SD-Parser is 0.7353.

5   Conclusions and Future Works

The SD-Parser using transformation rules with semantic constraints shows that the semantic constraints are important in generating valid semantic dependencies. It also shows that we can build a SD-Parser by building a large set of semantic constraints and utilizing a D-Parser. This is a way to ensure the valid semantic dependencies and reduce the cost of building a SD-Parser from scratch. In addition, the transformation rules and semantic constraints are also used to convert dependency treebanks into semantic dependency graphbanks.

However, the proposed method depends greatly on VLO and Vietnamese D-Parser. If the DPs are not good, the generated SDPs will not be good also. Therefore, the Vietnamese D-Parser should be improved and VLO should include more word senses and relations.

References

1. Nivre, J.: Dependency grammar and dependency parsing. Technical report MSI report 05133 (2005)
2. Oepen, S., et al.: SemEval 2015 task 18: broad-coverage semantic dependency parsing. In: International Workshop on Semantic Evaluation, Denver, pp. 915–926. ACL (2015)

3. Oepen, S., et al.: Semeval 2014 task 8: broad-coverage semantic dependency parsing. In: International Workshop on Semantic Evaluation, Dublin, pp. 63–72. ACL (2014)
4. Schuster, S., Manning, C.D.: Enhanced english universal dependencies: an improved representation for natural language understanding tasks. In: International Conference on Language Resources and Evaluation, pp. 2371–2378 (2016)
5. Nguyen, D.Q., Dras, M., Johnson, M.: An empirical study for Vietnamese dependency parsing. In: Australasian Language Technology Association Workshop, Melbourne, Australia, pp. 143–149 (2016)
6. Banarescu, L., et al.: Abstract meaning representation for sembanking. In: 7th Linguistic Annotation Workshop and Interoperability with Discourse, pp. 178–186 (2013)
7. Oepen, S., et al.: Towards comparability of linguistic graph banks for semantic parsing. In: 10th International Conference on Language Resources and Evaluation, pp. 3991–3995 (2016)
8. De Marneffe, M.-C., Manning, C.D.: Stanford typed dependencies manual. Technical report, Stanford University (2016)
9. Nivre, J., et al.: Universal dependencies v1: a multilingual treebank collection. In: 10th International Conference on Language Resources and Evaluation, pp. 1659–1666. European Language Resources Association (ELRA) (2016)
10. Hershcovich, D., Abend, O., Rappoport, A.: Multitask parsing across semantic representations. In: 56th Annual Meeting of the Association for Computational Linguistics, Melbourne, Australia, vol. 1, pp. 373–385. ACL (2018)
11. Hershcovich, D., Abend, O., Rappoport, A.: A transition-based directed acyclic graph parser for UCCA. In: 55th Annual Meeting of the Association for Computational Linguistics, Vancouver, Canada, vol. 1, pp. 1127–1138. ACL (2017)
12. Dozat, T., Manning, C.D.: Deep biaffine attention for neural dependency parsing. In: International Conference on Learning Representations (2017)
13. Qi, P., Dozat, T., Zhang, Y., Manning, C.D.: Universal dependency parsing from scratch. In: The CoNLL 2018 Shared Task: Multilingual Parsing from Raw Text to Universal Dependencies, Brussels, Belgium, pp. 160–170. ACL (2018)
14. Levine, R.D., Meurers, W.D.: Head-driven phrase structure grammar: linguistic approach, formal foundations, and computational realization, 2nd edn. In: Encyclopedia of Language and Linguistics, pp. 237–252 (2006)
15. Pollard, C., Sag, I.A.: Head-Driven Phrase Structure Grammar. University of Chicago Press, Chicago (1994)
16. Nguyen, D.Q., Nguyen, D.Q., Pham, S.B., Nguyen, P.T., Le Nguyen, M.: From treebank conversion to automatic dependency parsing for Vietnamese. In: Métais, E., Roche, M., Teisseire, M. (eds.) Natural Language Processing and Information Systems, NLDB 2014. Lecture Notes in Computer Science, vol. 8455. Springer, Cham (2014). https://doi.org/10.1007/978-3-319-07983-7_26
17. Do, T.T.-T.: Building a Vietnamese lexicon ontology for syntactic parsing and document annotation. In: iiWAS, Vienna, Austria, pp. 619–623. ACM (2013)
18. Ruppert, E., Jonas, K., Martin, R., Chris, B.: Rule-based dependency parse collapsing and propagation for German and English. In: German society for Computational Linguistics and Language Technology, pp. 58–66. University of Duisburg-Essen (2015)
19. Covington, M.A.: A fundamental algorithm for dependency parsing. In: Proceedings of the 39th Annual ACM Southeast Conference, pp. 95–102 (2001)

An In-depth Analysis of OCR Errors for Unconstrained Vietnamese Handwriting

Quoc-Dung Nguyen[1,4]([✉]) [ID], Duc-Anh Le[2,5], Nguyet-Minh Phan[3],
and Ivan Zelinka[4]

[1] Van Lang University, 45 Nguyen Khac Nhu, Co Giang ward, District 1,
Ho Chi Minh City, Vietnam
dung.nguyen@vlu.edu.vn
[2] Center for Open Data in the Humanities, Tokyo, Japan
leducanh841988@gmail.com
[3] University of Information Technology, Quarter 6, Linh Trung Ward,
Thu Duc District, Ho Chi Minh City, Vietnam
minhpn@uit.edu.vn
[4] Technical University of Ostrava, 17. listopadu 15, 708 33 Ostrava-Poruba,
Czech Republic
ivan.zelinka@vsb.cz
[5] NTT Hi-Tech Institute, Nguyen Tat Thanh University, 300A Nguyen Tat Thanh,
District 4, Ho Chi Minh City, Vietnam

Abstract. OCR post-processing is an essential step to improve the accuracy of OCR-generated texts by detecting and correcting OCR errors. In this paper, the OCR texts are resulted from an OCR engine which is based on the attention-based encoder-decoder model for unconstrained Vietnamese handwriting. We identify various kinds of Vietnamese OCR errors and their possible causes. Detailed statistics of Vietnamese OCR errors are provided and analyzed at both character level and syllable level, using typical OCR error characteristics such as error rate, error mapping/edit, frequency and error length. Furthermore, the statistical analyses are done on training and test sets of a benchmark database to infer whether the test set is the appropriate representative of the training set regarding the OCR error characteristics. We also discuss the choice of designing OCR post-processing approaches at character level or at syllable level relying on provided statistics of studied datasets.

Keywords: OCR errors · OCR post-processing · Vietnamese handwriting · Encoder · Decoder · Attention model

1 Introduction

Optical Character Recognition (OCR) is the process of transforming scanned document images into digital texts. However, the output texts of this process often contain errors due to many reasons such as poor quality of scanned documents, unusual font sizes and layouts. The erroneous OCR texts make the texts

© Springer Nature Switzerland AG 2020
T. K. Dang et al. (Eds.): FDSE 2020, LNCS 12466, pp. 448–461, 2020.
https://doi.org/10.1007/978-3-030-63924-2_26

unreadable and limit the use of the texts in information retrieval and search applications. Therefore, OCR post-processing is an important step to detect and correct misspellings and linguistic errors in OCR outputs, which is the last activity in OCR pipeline.

Many approaches have been proposed and employed for OCR post-processing. They can be classified into three groups: manual, corpus-based and context-based approaches. In the first type, linguists manually review and edit OCR output texts. However, this approach is costly and time-consuming. The corpus-based type makes use of word and character n-gram information from external corpora and resources to detect erroneous words and replace them with correct ones automatically [1,2]. Although this type of approach is easy to implement, it has limitations in correcting grammatical and semantic context errors due to the fact that it only utilizes n-gram information without knowledge of OCR error characteristics as well as low coverage and quality of constructed n-gram dictionaries. The third type of context-based approach overcomes the drawbacks of the first two types. The strategies of this type are noisy channel and language models [3,4], machine learning methods [5,6], statistical and neural machine translation [7,8].

The characteristics of spelling errors including edit distance, word lengths, erroneous character positions, real word vs. non-word errors, and word boundaries are explored in the related works [9–11]. The statistics based on these characteristics of misspellings are also studied in [9,10,12,13], but they are at coarse level and by means of character edit operations. Recently, Nguyen *et al.* [11] have presented the detailed analysis on additional features like substitution mappings, erroneous character positions and OCR token lengths for English OCR text collections, which helps gain better insight into the design of effective OCR post-processing methods. However, these analyses are performed at character level only.

Regarding post-processing solutions for Vietnamese OCR texts, there are only a few published works [14,15]. In these works, the authors also learn the classes of Vietnamese OCR errors according to character edit operations. Nonetheless, statistical analysis of Vietnamese OCR errors and their specific causes are not given.

In this paper, we identify the different classes of Vietnamese OCR errors which are induced by the OCR engine using the attention-based encoder-decoder model for unconstrained Vietnamese handwritten text [16]. Then the statistics of Vietnamese OCR errors are analyzed in detail at both character level and syllable level, based on the typical OCR error characteristics including error rate, error mapping/edit, frequency and error length. In addition, the statistical analyses are completed on the training and test datasets to examine whether the test dataset is a suitable representative of the training dataset on each OCR error characteristic. Lastly, we provide suggestion for choosing character level or syllable level approaches to OCR post-processing of the studied datasets. The same analytical strategy can be conducted on other Vietnamese OCR text collections in order to have a better understanding of OCR errors when designing OCR post-processing methods.

The rest of the paper is structured as follows. Sect. 2 presents the dataset and OCR error classes. In Sect. 3, OCR error statistics are analyzed and discussed in detail at both character level and syllable level. Besides, we compare the statistics between training and test datasets. Finally, conclusions are drawn in Sect. 4.

2 Dataset and OCR Error Classification

In this section, we describe the dataset consisting of unconstrained Vietnamese handwritten texts that are the inputs to the OCR engine generating OCR output texts used in the experiments of this paper. Then we identify the different classes of Vietnamese OCR errors and their possible causes. In Vietnamese, each token is separated by space in monosyllabic form. Hence, we call a space-separated token as a syllable.

2.1 Dataset

OCR texts studied in this paper are the OCR output lines from the attention-based encoder-decoder (AED) model with the DenseNet encoder proposed by Le *et al.* [16]. The AED model comprises two components: a Convolutional Neural Network-based (CNN) encoder and a Long Short-Term Memory-based (LSTM) decoder. The encoder relies on DenseNet [17] for better feature extraction. The LSTM-based decoder with an attention mechanism generates output text. This AED model is an offline approach for unconstrained Vietnamese handwritten text recognition. The AED model recognizes Vietnamese handwritten text images converted from online handwritten texts of the VNOnDB database [18]. Only the VNOnDB-Line dataset is used to reduce the training time.

The HANDS-VNOnDB[1] (VNOnDB in short) database has been made public to encourage the studies of unconstrained Vietnamese handwriting recognition and used as a benchmark database for evaluating and comparing different proposed recognition methods in the Vietnamese online handwriting recognition competition[2] [19]. The database collected 200 unconstrained handwritten text from 200 Vietnamese in each writer's style without any restriction. It contains 1,146 Vietnamese paragraphs, 7,296 lines, more than 480,000 strokes and more than 380,000 characters. Three datasets (VNOnDB-Paragraph, VNOnDB-Line and VNOnDB-Word) with the ink data and ground truth are provided at paragraph, line and word levels respectively, where the ground truth information is originated from the VietTreeBank[3] corpus [20]. The statistics of VNOnDB-Line dataset for the training, validation and test sets are shown in Table 1.

---

[1] Source: http://tc11.cvc.uab.es/datasets/HANDS-VNOnDB2018_1.

[2] https://sites.google.com/view/icfhr2018-vohtr-vnondb/home.

[3] Source: https://vlsp.hpda.vn/demo/?page=resources.

Table 1. The statistics of VNOnDB-line dataset.

	Training	Validation	Test	Total
# Lines	4,433	1,229	1,634	7,296
# Strokes	284,642	86,079	110,013	480,734
# Characters	298,212	83,806	112,769	494,787*

* Including the space character

2.2   OCR Error Classification

Not like other Latin script languages such as English, German and French, Vietnamese consists of many diacritic marks (DM). They can be positioned above, under and through characters in order to transcribe sounds or indicate speech variations. Considering of different writing styles of writers, various shapes and sizes of characters and DMs are observed. Furthermore, DMs are not often placed right where they should be. These facts lead to difficulties in recognizing unconstrained Vietnamese handwritten text.

Depending on the OCR output texts of the AED-based OCR system, we encounter different kinds of OCR errors. The errors can be divided into two main groups: character-related errors and syllable-related errors. Table 2 shows the OCR error classes with examples. The "→" symbol means that the correct syllable on the left of "→" is recognized as the error (corruption) syllable on the right of "→".

In the character-related group, the errors are caused by wrong edit operations due to misrecognized characters or DMs, including non-syllable errors, real syllable errors, incorrect upper-/lower-case errors and split/merged syllable errors. A syllable is identified as a non-syllable error if it does not occur in any syllable n-gram dictionaries; while a real-syllable error is a valid syllable that occurs in wrong context. For split/merged syllable errors, they are related to wrong inter-syllable space detection.

On the other hand, the syllable-related errors such as inserted/deleted syllable errors and completely wrong recognition errors come from falsely identified text images. It is observed that the deleted syllable errors tend to happen more often than the inserted syllable errors. Interestingly, a new kind of errors induced by the neural network-based OCR system is the numeral conversion, particularly numeral syllables changed to numbers.

Moreover, many punctuations that come at the end of source text lines like full-stop (.), comma (,) or double quotes (") are removed or substituted by other punctuations in OCR text lines. It might be due to opaque or unclear end punctuations made by the writers. Additionally, the considerable number of punctuations like comma (,) or full-stop (.) is wrongly inserted in OCR text lines. This error type probably comes from the marks and punctuations alike, appeared in source text images unexpectedly. The punctuation-related errors are classified into the syllable-related group since punctuations are also separated by space like syllables in our pre-processing step.

Table 2. Vietnamese OCR error classification.

Error Group	Error Type	Example	Cause
Character-related	Non-syllable	Xuân → Xâân, trước → vước, Yên → Nghên, Tám → Tàm	Misrecognized characters or DMs
	Real syllable	lỗi → lâu, Trài → Trà, dày → dùng, bán → bàn, hãi → hài	
	Incorrect upper-/lower-case	có → Có, Tám → tám	
	Split/merged syllable	Indo → In do, Phước → A hước, To nhưng → Tonhưng	
Syllable-related	Inserted/deleted syllable	"Sau **bao** nỗ lực" → "Sau mỗ lực" (the "bao" syllable is deleted)	Falsely identified text images
		"kể từ ngày anh hi sinh" → "kể từ ngày anh **trai mình** hi sinh" (the "trai" and "mình" syllables are inserted)	
		"một người chủ **trang trại** ở khu vực Suối Cạn nói" → "một **trải** người chủ khu vực Suối Cạn nói" (both the inserted/deleted syllable errors occur)	
	Completely wrong recognition	"cặp, cẩn trọng như giấy tờ của chính mình..." → "cộc người nghèo nghiệp."	
		"là thanh niên 20 – 29 tuổi." → "trương bình."	
	Numeral conversion	hai → 2 (source text line "suốt hai năm qua") bốn → 4 (source text line "điểm danh bốn tiếng/lần")	Specific to neural network-based OCR system
	Inserted/deleted/ substituted punctuation	"in trong mắt mẹ." → "in trong mắt mẹ" (the full-stop mark at the end of the source text line is deleted in the OCR text line)	Unclear or unexpected punctuations in source text images
		"trùm đầu nậu. Trưa 28 - 10, chúng tôi ghé vào" → "tram đầu, nậu. Trưa 28 - 10, chúng tôi phé, vào" ("," wrongly inserted in OCR text line)	
		"Pháp Luật (TP.HCM)." → "Pháp Luật (TP.HCM?" (")" is substituted by "?" and "." is deleted in the OCR text line)	

The non-syllable and real syllable errors associated with wrong edit operations are further verified under different types of character edit operations including insertion, deletion, substitution and their combinations (see Table 3). The transposition operation is ignored as it can be considered a special case of the substitution operation.

Table 3. Non-syllable and real syllable OCR Errors in terms of Character Edit Operations.

Error type	Insertion	Deletion	Substitution	Combination
Non-syllable	Thuê → thuên ("n" inserted)	chim → chm ("i" deleted)	Ủy → Ởy ("Ủ" substituted by "Ở")	Oanh → Qnh ("a" deleted and "O" substituted by "Q")
Real syllable	Trưng → Trương ("ơ" inserted)	cheo → cho ("e" deleted)	Kiều → tiều ("K" substituted by "t")	việc → vực ("i" deleted and "ệ" substituted by "ự")

3   OCR Error Analysis and Discussions

In this section, we provide an in-depth statistical analysis of OCR errors using the OCR error characteristics including error rate, error mapping/edit, frequency and error length.

Based on the OCR error classification above, we will describe the statistics of the OCR errors from both syllable-level and character-level points of view to gain broad knowledge of the errors. This is the useful information because approaches to both OCR error detection and correction tasks can be implemented at character level or at syllable level.

In the AED model, the training and validation sets combine to train the model (5662 lines), and the test set (1634 lines) is used to evaluate the model performance. From now on, we call these two groups of data as the training dataset and the test dataset in the following statistics. In the two datasets, each source text line (ground truth - GT) is associated with a corresponding OCR output text line. Comparisons between the training and test datasets on the OCR error characteristics are made in the following statistics.

3.1   Syllable-Level Statistics

A syllable is considered as a string of contiguous characters between two white spaces. Table 4 shows the number of GT syllables in the training and test datasets. The number of syllables in the test dataset is approximately the one-fourth of that in total.

Table 4. Number of GT syllables in training and test datasets.

Dataset	# GT syllables	Percentage (%)
Training	88,522	77.4
Test	25,859	22.6

Error Rate. By aligning the source text lines (ground truth) and corresponding OCR text lines at syllable level, we count the pairs of unsimilar GT-OCR syllables. It is computed that 4.3% and 13.6% are the erroneous syllable rates in the training and test datasets respectively (see Table 5). The test dataset has much higher error rate than the training dataset. The higher error rate in the test dataset could make the post-OCR process more tough since new error patterns could occur in the test dataset. The characteristics of these error patterns might not be learnt by the OCR post-processing model when only the training dataset is used to build the model.

Table 5. Erroneous syllable rates in training and test datasets.

Dataset	# Erroneous syllable	Rate (%)
Training	3,809	4.3
Test	3,524	13.6

Erroneous Syllable Mapping. In Table 6 and Table 7, we depict the top-10 erroneous syllable mappings regarding punctuations and alphabet characters. In a "→" mapping, if the syllable on the left-hand side is missing, it means that the mapping is an insertion. In parallel, it is a deletion without the syllable on the right-hand side. The frequency is computed in proportion to the total number of syllable errors in the training and test datasets respectively.

According to the punctuation-related errors, most of the top-10 mappings are the insertion/deletion ones due to unclear or unexpected punctuations made by the writers in the source texts. The top-10 mappings in both the training and set datasets are quite similar. For the top-10 syllable mappings related to the alphabet, most of the errors come from incorrect upper-/lower-cases, substituted characters and DMs. The training and test datasets have several same mappings such as "Công → công", "cửa → của". In the syllable mapping tables, we do not consider the inserted/deleted syllable errors since they do not reveal any relation in the GT-OCR syllable mapping. Generally, the punctuation-related errors happen more frequently than the alphabet-related ones.

Error Length. Figure 1 shows that most of the erroneous syllables lie in the length of five characters or less, where the errors of three characters long have the highest occurrence. The erroneous syllables of three- and four-character lengths constitute about 65% of the total syllable errors (without taking account of the inserted/deleted syllable errors). Both the training and test datasets have the same trend; hence the test dataset well reflects the training dataset on this OCR error characteristic. Apparently, the longer the erroneous syllable is, the more probable it is to be corrected since it can have more correction candidates and more context to be involved. By having access to the information of error

Table 6. Top-10 erroneous syllable mappings regarding punctuations.

Training			Test		
GT → OCR	# Count	Frequency (%)	GT → OCR	# Count	Frequency (%)
. →	100	2.63	. →	65	1.84
→ ,	66	1.73	, →	62	1.76
, →	57	1.5	" →	36	1.02
" →	39	1.02	→ ,	25	0.71
→ .	23	0.6	, → .	20	0.57
: → .	18	0.47	→ .	15	0.43
- →	15	0.39	. → ,	14	0.4
, → .	14	0.37	) →	10	0.28
→ -	11	0.29	% →	10	0.28
→ "	11	0.29	- →	8	0.23

Table 7. Top-10 erroneous syllable mapping regarding Vietnamese alphabet characters.

Training			Test		
GT → OCR	# Count	Frequency (%)	GT → OCR	# Count	Frequency (%)
Cồng → công	10	0.26	Phương → phương	12	0.34
nậu → mậu	8	0.21	cưa → của	10	0.28
Chủ → chủ	8	0.21	Cồng → công	9	0.26
ký → lý	7	0.18	Hải → Hãi	7	0.2
thú → thủ	7	0.18	Tám → Tàm	6	0.17
rừng → lường	6	0.16	cưa → của	6	0.17
tôt → tốt	5	0.13	chim → chom	6	0.17
các → sác	5	0.13	Không → không	6	0.17
chỉ → chủ	5	0.13	sử → sở	6	0.17
cửa → của	5	0.13	không → thông	5	0.14

length, we can develop appropriate solutions to OCR post-processing to reduce the number of syllable errors.

From the syllable-level statistics above, the test dataset shows to be a proper representative of the training dataset on the OCR error characteristics like the erroneous syllable mapping and the error length, but they are disparate on the error rate feature.

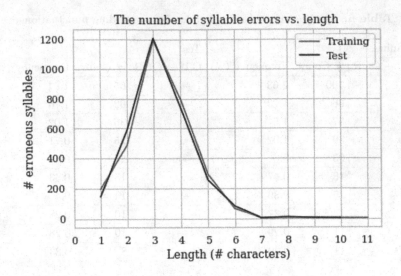

Fig. 1. The number of erroneous syllables versus the syllable length.

3.2   Character-Level Statistics

Table 8 shows the number of GT characters in the corresponding datasets. The number of characters in the training and test datasets have the similar percentages as those at the syllable level.

Table 8. Number of GT characters in training and test datasets.

Dataset	# GT characters	Percentage (%)
Training	382,018	77.2
Test	112,769	22.8

Error Rate. In order to count the character errors, we align each pair of the source text line and corresponding OCR text line at character level and look for pairs of unsimilar characters. It reveals that the erroneous character rates in the training and test datasets are 1.7% and 4.7% respectively (see Table 9). The higher error rate in the test dataset could make the evaluation performance of the OCR error detection and correction tasks worse.

Table 9. Erroneous character rates in training and test datasets.

Dataset	# Erroneous character	Rate (%)
Training	6,505	1.7
Test	5,245	4.7

Character Edit Operations. In Tables 10 and 11, we describe the top-10 edit operations of one- and two-character length. The frequency is determined in relation to the counted number of erroneous characters in the corresponding training and test datasets.

Regarding the top-10 one-character edit operations in the training dataset, two are the insertion operations (for "i" and "h" characters), the other two are the deletion operations (for "i" and "n" characters). Especially, there are the inserted and deleted while space operations ("space →" and "→ space") that are equivalent to the split/merged syllable errors. The remaining edit operations are substitution ones (e.g. "n → m", "m → n", "u → n") and case-sensitive error (e.g. "C → c") due to similarity of character glyph. For the test dataset, seven mappings of the top-10 appear same as those in the training dataset, except for three operations including "r" deletion, "t → T" and "K → k" case-sensitive errors.

Similarly, most of the two-character edit operations come from similar glyphs of characters due to free handwriting styles. It is interestingly seen that there are the variations of two-character mappings including 2:2, 2:1, 1:2, 0:2 and 2:0. In general, the two-character edit errors occur infrequent in both the training and test datasets (the frequency of most mappings equivalently 0.1% or less). Therefore, it is not necessary to investigate the edit operations with length higher than two characters.

Table 10. Top-10 edit operations of one-character length.

Training			Test		
GT → OCR	# Count	Frequency (%)	GT → OCR	# Count	Frequency (%)
→ i	72	1.11	i →	105	2
n → m	70	1.08	space →	77	1.47
→ h	66	1.01	n → m	65	1.24
m → n	63	0.97	C → c	51	0.97
i →	62	0.95	→ i	43	0.82
space →	59	0.91	r →	42	0.8
C → c	52	0.8	t → T	40	0.76
n →	51	0.78	m → n	36	0.69
→ space	48	0.74	→ h	35	0.67
u → n	40	0.61	K → k	29	0.55

Table 11. Top-10 edit operations of two-character length.

Training			Test		
GT → OCR	# Count	Frequency (%)	GT → OCR	# Count	Frequency (%)
ng → y	19	0.29	ng → y	13	0.25
ch → d	9	0.14	H → th	9	0.17
ừ → ườ	9	0.14	d → ch	6	0.11
→ hi	8	0.12	n, → m	5	0.1
y → ng	7	0.11	y → ng	5	0.1
gi → qu	7	0.11	gi → qu	5	0.1
ng → p	6	0.09	iê̄ → ừ	5	0.1
→ gh	6	0.09	ễm → ừn	5	0.1
r → lư	6	0.09	iê → â	5	0.1
ng →	6	0.09	u → hi	5	0.1

Character Edit Length. The relation between the number of character edit operations and the character edit length is depicted in Fig. 2. The edit length of an erroneous syllable is defined as the edit distance between the erroneous syllable and the corresponding GT syllable. It is shown that more than half of the syllable errors are single character edits in both the training and test datasets, about 61.11% and 69.03% respectively. For the errors with the higher edit distances, most of them are of two-character edit length. Obviously, the less edit operations a syllable includes, the more probability it is corrected. Relying on these statistics, OCR post-processing approaches can mainly focus on edit distances 1 and 2 (with totally 81.18% and 88.68% for the training and test datasets). Like the syllable level, the training and test datasets also have the same trend, thus the test dataset well characterizes the training dataset on the edit distance feature.

Same as the syllable-level point of view, the test dataset properly represents the training dataset on the character edit operation and error length features, but they show the dissimilarity on the character error rate.

Last but not least, by dividing this study into the syllable level and character level subsections, it is seen that most of the syllable errors have the length of four characters or less, and the errors with low edit distances 1 and 2 occupy more than 80% of the total errors where the ones of the edit distance 1 contribute over 60%. Furthermore, it is found that most of the top mappings at both syllable level and character level are related to the insertion, deletion and substitution operations of single characters (including space character and punctuation). Consequently, character level approaches for OCR error detection and correction would be the best fit with this case of Vietnamese OCR handwritten text.

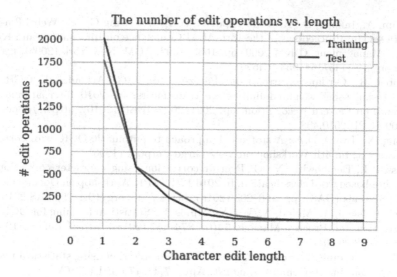

Fig. 2. The number of edit operations versus the character edit length.

4   Conclusions

In this paper, we present the various kinds of Vietnamese OCR errors with the examples derived from the OCR texts that are the outputs of the AED model. We observe several error kinds that are specific to Vietnamese handwriting and neural network-based OCR system. The statistics of the OCR errors are studied and analyzed in detail at both character level and syllable level, regarding the typical OCR characteristics such as error rate, error mapping/edit, frequency and error length. Following the studied datasets, we infer the right choice of OCR error detection and correction approaches is at character level. In addition, the statistical comparison between the training and test datasets shows that the test dataset is a suitable representative of the training dataset on the OCR features like error length and error mapping/edit. The similar analytical strategy can be employed as initial step of OCR post-processing approaches and applied for unconstrained Vietnamese handwritten text or Vietnamese text in general. In future work, we will conduct more statistical analyses on additional OCR error characteristics such as edit operation types, erroneous character positions and syllable error types to have a better understanding of OCR errors for designing more effective and robust OCR post-processing approaches.

References

1. Bassil, Y., Alwani, M.: OCR post-processing error correction algorithm using Google's Online spelling suggestion. J. Emerg. Trends Comput. Inf. Sci. **3**(1), 90–99 (2012)

2. Islam, A., Inkpen, D.: Real-word spelling correction using Google Web 1T n-gram data set. In: Proceedings of the 18th ACM Conference on Information and Knowledge Management, CIKM 2009, pp. 1689–1692. ACM, New York (2009). https://doi.org/10.1145/1645953.1646205

3. Llobet, R., Cerdan-Navarro, J.-R., Perez-Cortes, J.-C., Arlandis, J.: OCR post-processing using weighted finite-state transducers. In: 2010 International Conference on Pattern Recognition, pp. 2021–2024. IEEE (2010). https://doi.org/10.1109/ICPR.2010.498

4. Tong, X., Evans, D.A.: A statistical approach to automatic OCR error correction in context. In: 4th Workshop on Very Large Corpora (1996)

5. Kissos, I., Dershowitz, N.: OCR error correction using character correction and feature-based word classification. In 2016 12th IAPR Workshop on Document Analysis Systems (DAS), pp. 198–203 (2016). https://doi.org/10.1109/DAS.2016.44

6. Mei, J., Islam, A., Moh'd, A., Wu, Y., Milios, E.: Statistical learning for OCR error correction. Inf. Process. Manage. 54(6), 874–887 (2018). https://doi.org/10.1016/j.ipm.2018.06.001

7. Afli, H., Barrault, L., Schwenk, H.: OCR error correction using statistical machine translation. Int. J. Comput. Linguist. Appl. 7(1), 175–191 (2016)

8. Amrhein, C., Clematide, S.: Supervised OCR error detection and correction using statistical and neural machine translation methods. J. Lang. Technol. Comput. Linguist. (JLCL) 33(1), 49–76 (2018). https://doi.org/10.5167/uzh-162394

9. Kukich, K.: Techniques for automatically correcting words in text. ACM Comput. Surv. (CSUR) 24(4), 377–439 (1992)

10. Reynaert, M.: Text-induced spelling correction. Ph.D. Dissertation. Tilburg University (2005)

11. Nguyen, H.T.-T., Jatowt, A., Coustaty, M., Nguyen, V.N., Doucet, A.: Deep statistical analysis of OCR errors for effective post-OCR processing. In: 2019 ACM/IEEE Joint Conference on Digital Libraries (JCDL), Champaign, IL, USA, pp. 29–38 (2019). https://doi.org/10.1109/JCDL.2019.00015

12. Mitton, R.: Spelling checkers, spelling correctors and the misspellings of poor spellers. Inf. Process. Manage. 23(5), 495–505 (1987)

13. Young, C.W., Eastman, C.M., Oakman, R.L.: An analysis of ill-formed input in natural language queries to document retrieval systems. Inf. Process. Manage. 27(6), 615–622 (1991)

14. Vu Hoang, D.C., Aw, A.T.: An unsupervised and data-driven approach for spell checking in Vietnamese OCR-scanned texts. In: Proceedings of the Workshop on Innovative Hybrid Approaches to the Processing of Textual Data, HYBRID 2012, pp. 36–44. Association for Computational Linguistics, USA (2012)

15. Nguyen, D.Q., Le, A.D., Zelinka, I.: OCR error correction for unconstrained Vietnamese handwritten text. In: Proceedings of the 10th International Symposium on Information and Communication Technology, SoICT 2019, pp. 132–138. Association for Computing Machinery, New York (2019). https://doi.org/10.1145/3368926.3369686

16. Le, A.D., Nguyen, H.T., Nakagawa, M.: An end-to-end recognition system for unconstrained Vietnamese handwriting. SN Comput. Sci. 1(7) (2020). https://doi.org/10.1007/s42979-019-0001-4

17. Huang, G., Liu, Z., Maaten, L.V.-D., Weinberger, K.Q.: Densely connected convolutional networks. In: Proceedings of the 30th IEEE Conference on Computer Vision and Pattern Recognition, pp. 2261–2269 (2017). https://doi.org/10.1109/CVPR.2017.243

18. Nguyen, H.T., Nguyen, C.T., Pham, B.T., Nakagawa, M.: A database of unconstrained Vietnamese online handwriting and recognition experiments by recurrent neural networks. Pattern Recogn. **78**, 291–306 (2018). https://doi.org/10.1016/j.patcog.2018.01.013
19. Nguyen, H.T., Nguyen, C.T., Nakagawa, M.: ICFHR 2018 - competition on Vietnamese online handwritten text recognition using HANDS-VNOnDB (VOHTR2018). In: 16th International Conference on Frontiers in Handwriting Recognition (ICFHR), pp. 494–499 (2018). https://doi.org/10.1109/ICFHR-2018.2018.00092
20. Nguyen, T.P., Vu, L.X., Nguyen, H.T.-M., Nguyen, H.V., Le, P.H.: Building a large syntactically annotated corpus of Vietnamese. In: Proceedings of the 3rd Linguistic Annotation Workshop, ACL-IJCNLP 2009, pp. 182–185. Association for Computational Linguistics, Stroudsburg (2009)

Author Index

Printed in the United States
By Bookmasters